THE DIVINE ASPECT OF HISTORY

IN TWO VOLUMES

VOLUME II

CAMBRIDGE UNIVERSITY PRESS
C. F. CLAY, Manager
London: FETTER LANE, E.C.
Edinburgh: 100 PRINCES STREET

New York: G. P. PUTNAM'S SONS
Bombay, Calcutta and Madras: MACMILLAN AND CO., Ltd.
Toronto: J. M. DENT AND SONS, Ltd.
Tokyo: THE MARUZEN-KABUSHIKI-KAISHA

THE DIVINE ASPECT OF HISTORY

by

JOHN RICKARDS MOZLEY

Take better part, with manlier heart,
  Thine adult spirit can ;
No God, no Truth, receive it ne'er—
  Believe it ne'er—O Man !
But turn not then to seek again
  What first the ill began ;
No God, it saith ; ah, wait in faith
  God's selfcompleting plan ;
Receive it not, but leave it not,
  And wait it out, O Man !

ARTHUR HUGH CLOUGH

VOLUME II

Cambridge :
at the University Press
1916

CONTENTS OF VOLUME II

CHAPTER XVI

JESUS CHRIST: A GENERAL SURVEY

The possibility of error in the Christian creeds must not be denied. The question asked, whether there is an infinite difference, as to origin and character, between Jesus Christ and ourselves. The belief in this infinite difference is capable of being very attractively put, and has been attractively put, both in the New Testament and by Christian poets. But the question is, on what the belief rests? In the fourth gospel it is distinctly made to rest on miracles; and thus the question of the truth of miracles is brought to the front. The miracles of healing however must be put on one side, for it is clear in the gospels that these are not regarded as constituting an infinite difference between Jesus Christ and ourselves. The question of the resurrection is crucial in the matter. The numerous and important inconsistencies between the gospels in their accounts of the resurrection show that the evidence for it was really visionary (though the gospels of course do not admit this); and from the epistles of the New Testament it is very manifest that the resurrection was not a fact discerned by the senses; the accounts of the conversion of Paul given in the Acts corroborate this. Further, the inconsistencies between the synoptic gospels on the one hand, and the fourth gospel on the other hand, are so great as to show that our authorities are very liable to be misled; and all things being considered, the conclusion is that the resurrection was an event taking place in a supersensuous region. This is a belief really consolatory, but it is consolatory because we may hope to enter that region ourselves; and hence the essential character of the resurrection is one that assimilates us to Jesus Christ, not one that differentiates us from him. Other considerations confirm this . . .

APPENDIX I TO CHAPTER XVI

On the Relations of the Synoptic Gospels to each other.

The Synoptic Gospels are declared to be drawn from a great number of shorter documents (and some oral utterances) which were repeatedly transcribed and circulated through the Christian world; some truth thus became part of the general knowledge, but some error as well

36025

CHAPTER XXI

VICTORIOUS CHRISTIANITY AND A FALLING EMPIRE

APPENDIX TO CHAPTER XXI

CHAPTER XXII

CHRISTIANITY FINDS A RIVAL IN ISLAM

CHAPTER XXIII

THE WORLD-STRUGGLE IN EUROPE AND ASIA

This chapter describes the extraordinary struggles which took place between Christianity and Islam during the seven centuries which elapsed between the death of Charlemagne and the Reformation. The intervention of the great Mongol invasion, under the grandsons of Jingis Khan, is referred to, and the damage done by it, partly to Christendom, but still more to Islam, is described. During the seven centuries referred to, the gains of Islam in Asia Minor, Constantinople and the countries around that capital, and finally in India, have to be balanced against the recovery of Spain by Christendom and the conversion of northern Europe to Christianity (half of Russia having been lost to Christendom and recovered again during this period). The progress of Islam in the arts and sciences (preceding the progress of Christendom in these matters) is described; the weakness of Islam lies in its defect in determining the relations of man to man. Instances of this defect are given. In Christendom, the gradual but real progress of human relations, through the operation of the Church and also by the institution of chivalry, is described. Yet the Church did in many ways oppress the intellect. The breach between the eastern and the western churches was a calamity, and the crusades are not to be justified, though some good is ascribed to them. Hildebrand is carefully estimated; so also is Baber, the Mohammedan conqueror of India

CHAPTER XXIV

THE INWARD GROWTH OF MEDIÆVAL CHRISTENDOM

Islam is just touched upon at the beginning of this chapter, mainly in regard to its merits; but the chapter as a whole is devoted to describing the various forms of progress in Christendom (chiefly in the west) and the most notable persons connected with this progress. The Christian character of Magna Charta is referred to; also the growth of parliamentary government in England; also the work of Jeanne d'Arc in liberating France. The commercial towns of Germany owed much to the Church; so did the arts in Italy—painting, sculpture, architecture. Mediæval philosophers are referred to—Abelard, Albertus Magnus, Roger Bacon, Thomas Aquinas; also that heroic missionary and thinker, Raymund Lull. The force which Christianity gave to men is shown in literature, in great voyagers and travellers, and even in science (especially is Copernicus noted). Francis of Assisi did much to reform men on the moral and spiritual side. On the other hand, the persecuting spirit of the Church is to be regretted; especially when exemplified in that vigorous teacher, Dominic de Guzman. The various reformers (before the Reformation) are noted and characterised; Albigenses, Waldenses, Apostolicals, Wycliffe and the Lollards, and (most saintly of all) John Huss

CHAPTER XXV

THE REFORMATION ERA

The Reformation should rather be styled a just rebellion; it liberated men, but the constructive power in it was imperfect. The question discussed, whether the Roman church had an intrinsic sacredness which rendered any rebellion against it unlawful; the negative answer to this shown to be in accordance with the gospels and with the New Testament generally; and even the Fathers of the first two centuries do not hold the apostle Peter to have been sole head of the Church (which is the view on which the church of Rome bases itself). The further question is discussed, whether the church of Rome had on other grounds an authority which, at the beginning of the sixteenth century, ought to have been accepted without challenge. As against this, the rectitude of the protest of Luther against the sale of indulgences is strongly affirmed, and is shown to have been practically accepted as just, at the council of Trent, by the Roman church itself. The protest of Luther against indulgences, considered in themselves and apart from their sale, has of course never been accepted by the Roman church; but the argument is here advanced, that the protest was also just in this respect. A general account of Luther follows; it is said of him that he combined a singular prudence in action with a singular rashness in speech. His doctrine of Justification by Faith is held to be truly vital, though capable of being expounded, and sometimes even expounded by himself, wrongly. His faults are noted, but he is treated as a true hero. Other leaders of the Reformation, on the Continent or in Great Britain, are spoken of (Zwingli and Calvin especially—in the English church, Richard Hooker is said to embody its spirit most truly). On the other hand, the courage and discipline of Ignatius Loyola, and of the Jesuits, receive praise. On the whole, the effect of the Reformation is held to have been for good, even inside the Roman church, much more in the com-

APPENDIX TO CHAPTER XXV

CHAPTER XXVI

THE GATHERING FORCES OF SCEPTICISM

The subject of religious music, especially fostered by the German Reformation, is just touched upon. Then the whole sceptical movement of the eighteenth century is described, especially as exhibited in Voltaire and Rousseau. Voltaire is held to be the man who did more to restrain judicial and religious cruelty than any man else did; and Rousseau, the man who first pleaded successfully the rights of the poor: but both these great writers did harm by their wrong disposition in sexual questions.

CHAPTER XXVII

THE HOPE OF THE FUTURE

CORRIGENDA ET ADDENDA

Vol. II. p. 37, lines 22 and 23. Strike out the words "though I am not urging the use of the term" and insert "in theory; for in practice, it would be undesirable"

Vol. II. page 232. There is a letter, to be found on pages 105–107 of the *Historical Tracts of S. Athanasius* (Oxford, 1843), which though not said to be addressed to the Council of Tyre, may have been addressed to that Council, and is so set down in the *Acta Conciliorum*. It contains a mention of the retractation of Ischyras and may thus appear to contradict what is said in the note to the page above mentioned. But first, even if this letter were addressed to the Council of Tyre, it was not written till quite a late stage in the proceedings of the Council; nor is there any mention of its having been presented to that Council, or how they regarded it; secondly, Athanasius, who was in possession of the retractation of Ischyras, and who had had the opportunity (long before the letter here spoken of was written) of acquainting the Council of Tyre with that retractation, does not appear, from his own account, to have used that opportunity. All things considered, I think the statement stands, that the retractation of Ischyras was not voluntary.

CHAPTER XVI

JESUS CHRIST: A GENERAL SURVEY

To those who with me believe that Jesus Christ implanted in mankind the root of eternal life, I must begin by saying this: It cannot be my direct object to write this chapter so as to please you; and it may be my misfortune not to please you. For I must think that you, my fellow-Christians, have shared the lot of all men, even the best and wisest men, in all nations of the earth; and while attaining some truth, have mingled some error with it, even in your most formal utterances. From that error, you say, you were delivered not always, but in those choice moments, when your creeds were first accepted by the united Church, in its representative assemblies; and those creeds, being once true, are of course always true. That is your statement; I must think it overpresuming as a principle, though it might no doubt be correct as a fact; but the most ardent Christians propound it as a principle. Supposing, however, the unerringness of the Christian creeds not to be propounded as a principle, but the affirmation to be simply that the Christian creeds are entirely correct as facts, which is what more moderate Christians affirm; I am constrained to say that I cannot think that this affirmation holds. It is, however, a fair matter of argument whether the Christian creeds are entirely true or not; and I must try to show in the following pages the leading considerations which bear on this point.

The creed called the Nicene creed (though the appellation is not quite correct, but it may be adopted without serious mistake) is by far the most authoritative of the Christian creeds; it is true that the Eastern and Western Churches differ as to one expression in it; but that expression will not enter into the discussion of the present chapter. Putting the "Filioque" aside, the Nicene creed is the creed which commands the assent of all Christians in a degree in which no other creed does; it is the accepted Christianity of to-day. The disputed points which I am to discuss are contained in it much more clearly than in the simpler creed which is called the Apostles' creed.

If the Nicene creed be true in its entirety, Jesus Christ was infinitely different, as regards the principal part of his being, and as regards origin also, from every other man. That in his intercourse with men during his life on earth he wore the likeness of a man is no doubt affirmed; and the Nicene creed, while affirming divine operations on his part over the whole universe before he became incarnate, does not explicitly say that he continued to act on this vast scale after his birth as a man, while his earthly life continued. Yet Athanasius, the principal defender (if not the principal author) of the Nicene creed, clearly implies this[1]; and, in any case, the infinite difference between Jesus Christ and ourselves, even as regards his ordinary consciousness during his earthly life, is habitually affirmed by Christians, and must be understood to be a part of ordinary Christian belief. However often these statements, direct or implied, of the Nicene creed may have been made, however natural it may seem to Christians to make them, the ground for them does need to be carefully examined; nor is it without importance to inquire what their effect has been on the mind of Christians. If the divine government of the world is essentially bound up with the affirmations of the Nicene creed, the effects of that creed in promoting goodness and happiness among men ought to be clear.

Perhaps, at this point, I ought to give my own opinion, both on the negative and on the positive sides. I do not hold the clauses of the Nicene creed, which affirm the infinite difference between Jesus Christ and ourselves, to be founded on just grounds; nor do I believe them to have influenced human character for good. But the statement which is sometimes supposed to be the sole alternative to the statements of the Nicene creed, that Jesus Christ was merely an ordinary good man, does not appear to me to be true either. According to my reading of history, he was the man who first received, as his own proper inheritance, the Divine Spirit and Power in its fullness; and those who receive it after him have been helped by him either through his direct influence upon them, or by influences indirectly due to him; or, if they have stood altogether outside his influence (as is generally the case with Mohammedans), they have been unable

---

[1] See, as regards the opinions of Athanasius, the Appendix to chapter XXI of the present work.

to bring their goodness to permanent and ever-increasing fruitage. The progress of mankind is founded on him in a unique sense.

This makes him greater than his fellow-men; but it does not make him outside the range of comparison with them. An ancient Christian narrative still exists, which, though reference to the followers of Jesus was impossible in it, does involve a reference to his predecessors, and puts that reference under the most solemn possible sanction. The lost gospel of the Hebrews gave the account which I will now quote of what ensued after Jesus had been baptized:

It came to pass as the Lord ascended up out of the water, that the whole fountain of the Holy Spirit came down and rested upon him and said to him; "My son, in all the prophets I waited for thee till thou shouldst come and I might rest upon thee: for thou art my rest, thou art my firstborn son, who reignest for evermore." See Jerome on Isaiah xi. 1.

It must not be thought that the words here attributed to the Holy Spirit are inconsistent with the better known utterance which we read in the gospels of Matthew, Mark, and Luke. They are indeed more expanded; just as the words which the apostle Paul says that he heard at the moment of his conversion are more expanded in the twenty-sixth chapter of the Acts, than as given in the ninth and twenty-second chapters. Neither in this case, nor in the baptism of Jesus, must we think of the heavenly words as spoken to the outer ear. When this is understood, the relation of the prophets to their greater successor, as the gospel of the Hebrews puts it, is most touching and natural. The prophets had the divine inspiration, but not the divine rest; in Jesus rest was attained, a rest which all men might share. The prophets and Jesus are on the same plane; but Jesus has established that link which the prophets were in search of. I believe the gospel of the Hebrews to be perfectly correct in the whole narrative; but I say so in this place merely as defining my own position; I am not yet claiming my reader's assent to the view just stated.

It will, however, be a further explanation of the position here assigned to Jesus, if I add that he first of all men relied upon the divine method of government; which is government by attraction. Not by any compulsion did he seek to bind men to himself; nor, when his words are properly understood, by any terror (though I grant that this has often been thought— but an explanation will be given in the proper place); but by the mere exhibition of the beauty and strength inherent in goodness. He felt assured, and persistently taught, that the good man always wins and does not lose by his goodness. This assurance, by a singular reversal of natural thought, some persons in modern times have thought an indication of selfishness, on the ground that the good man ought to be good whether he wins or loses by it. But it cannot be indifferent to the good man whether the world is rightly directed or not; and what do we mean by right direction, if not that each man shall receive that which his deeds deserve? Jesus assumed and taught that this was the case; that each man would receive that which his deeds deserve. But to assume this, meant to assume that there was a life after this life in the flesh—a life after death; for it is perfectly manifest that each man does not receive his deserts in this life—that here, in the life which we know, many men suffer undeservedly, and without recompense. Jesus then assumed that there would be a future life for men; and what is more, that the time was come for this to be manifested; and as it had not hitherto been manifested, he declared that it would be made manifest in himself. By what combination of inner instinct, reliance on the authorities which had preceded him, and perception of the state of the world in his own day, he made this peculiarly personal assertion, I must not here detail; the subject belongs to the direct narrative. But that he did make this assertion is an essential thing in him; and it was intimately connected with his assumption that right government consists in selection by attraction; like goes to like, the good to the good, and in the eternal kingdom of God it would be felt that he, Jesus, worthily represented the divine motives, and carried the Divine Spirit in himself, around which men would naturally gather, and to which they would assimilate themselves. He taught also that his spirit and his power would reach to the world of men, visible in the flesh, whom he left behind him, and especially to his disciples and friends; though how, and with what concomitants, this was to happen, was naturally an obscure point; and it was not to be expected that the details of his prediction should be as clear as the general purport of it. His predictions of the future in detail are indeed sometimes apparently inconsistent; but this, under the conditions, was inevitable.

The above is, I think, a fairly complete account, in brief, of the general position of Jesus, as understood by myself, and as it will be put forward in the present treatise; but I must recur to the Nicene creed, which is the doctrine which holds the field at the present day. The Nicene creed, as I have said, places an infinite difference between Jesus and every other man; and the way in which it does so is by attributing to him a conscious eternal life before his life in the flesh; during which conscious eternal life he made all things which exist, animate or inanimate, expressing in this way the will of his Divine Father; and from this eternal pre-existent life he voluntarily came down, took a body in all respects like ours, being born of a human mother though not of a human father, and lived as a man among men; his difference from other men being completed (though this is a small thing compared to what has preceded) by the affirmation that on the third day after his violent death he rose again, that he ascended to heaven and sat on the right hand of God, and that he is about to return from thence as our judge. Looking at Christian belief with the eyes of the authors of the Nicene creed, we shall see that the points in the latter part of the above enumeration do not so absolutely differentiate Jesus from ourselves as the points in the former part of it; but his conscious divine pre-existence, his partnership from all eternity in the universal divine working, and his voluntary descent into a human body, do make him absolutely and infinitely different from ourselves.

It is now proper to remark that the scheme of belief presented to us in the Nicene creed has been received with real enthusiasm not only by Christian theologians, but by persons of singular ability and great freedom of thought, lay and not clerical, living in times which must be called modern, though of course not beyond the reach of ancient influences (as who would wish them to be?). The poet Milton in his later years did partly (by no means entirely) dissent from the Nicene creed; but his early poem *On the Morning of Christ's Nativity* does so precisely express the doctrine of that creed, and in so lofty a style, that it will be well to quote its two opening stanzas (they are from the Introduction, not from the Ode):

> This is the month, and this the happy morn,
> Wherein the Son of Heaven's Eternal King,
> Of wedded Maid and Virgin Mother born,
> Our great redemption from above did bring;
> For so the holy sages once did sing,
>   That he our deadly forfeit should release,
> And with his Father work us a perpetual peace.

> That glorious form, that light unsufferable,
> And that far-beaming blaze of majesty,
> Wherewith he wont at Heaven's high council-table
> To sit the midst of Trinal Unity,
> He laid aside; and here with us to be,
> Forsook the courts of everlasting day,
> And chose with us a darksome house of mortal clay.

After Milton, let me quote Tennyson. The stanzas which form the introduction to *In Memoriam* are not so precise in their detail as Milton's stanzas; but they are absolutely from the same point of view, and are specially notable as coming from a poet who was peculiarly interested in natural science. Here are his first five stanzas:

> Strong Son of God, immortal Love,
> Whom we, that have not seen thy face,
> By faith, and faith alone, embrace,
> Believing where we cannot prove;
> Thine are these orbs of light and shade;
> Thou madest Life in man and brute;
> Thou madest Death; and lo, thy foot
> Is on the skull which thou hast made.
> Thou wilt not leave us in the dust:
> Thou madest man, he knows not why;
> He thinks he was not made to die;
> And thou hast made him: thou art just.
> Thou seemest human and divine,
> The highest, holiest manhood, thou:
> Our wills are ours, we know not how;
> Our wills are ours, to make them thine.
> Our little systems have their day;
> They have their day and cease to be:
> They are but broken lights of thee,
> And thou, O Lord, art more than they.

With equal force and conviction does Browning, in his poem of *Christmas Eve* express the same doctrine, or at any rate imply it. Very wrong would it be to underrate the force of that against which one is arguing; and it is a serious fault to deny the sincerity of feelings which, nevertheless, one may think mistaken. I do recognise the sincerity of Milton, Tennyson, and Browning, and the sincerity of many Christians, who, without being able to express themselves with the force of those great poets, have felt the same. Where there is sincerity, there is generally underlying truth, though not always truth in the precise terms.

Far better known than even Milton and Tennyson and Browning are some sentences in the New Testament, generally

and justly interpreted as implying a doctrine closely akin to
that of the Nicene creed (even if not quite identical with it).
The following sentence from the fourth gospel appears there as
if spoken by Jesus himself; but it is doubtful if the author of
the gospel really meant this, and it is in any case a sentence
which a critical reader will attribute, with hardly a doubt, to
the evangelist himself.

God so loved the world, that he gave his only begotten Son, that
whosoever believeth on him should not perish, but have eternal life.
John iii. 16.

When the whole tenor of the fourth gospel is considered,
the words "only begotten Son" in this verse must be interpreted
as meaning one who lived consciously in heaven before his earthly
life; and the word "gave" implies the incarnation of that
"only begotten Son." The crucifixion could not have been out
of the mind of the evangelist in writing the verse, but it is not
prominent. It is more prominent in the following verse of the
apostle Paul:

If God is for us, who is against us? He that spared not his own Son,
but delivered him up for us all, how shall he not also with him freely
give us all things? Romans viii. 31, 32.

It cannot be doubted that the crucifixion is here in Paul's
mind; but if we consider the general tenor of his writings, we
must say that the incarnation is not absent, and with it the
divine pre-existence of Jesus. The most explicit affirmation of
the incarnation in Paul's writings is that in the epistle to the
Philippians (which I hold to be genuine) chapter ii. 5–8:

Have this mind in you, which was also in Christ Jesus: who, being
in the form of God, counted it not a prize to be on an equality with God,
but emptied himself, taking the form of a bondservant, being made in
the likeness of men; and being found in fashion as a man, he humbled
himself, becoming obedient even unto death, yea, the death of the cross.

This is definite in a way in which the passage from the
"Romans" is not so; but the same meaning can hardly be
absent from the passage in the "Romans," and it is felt to be
more forcible in the "Romans," because the feelings of the
Divine Father himself are also brought in there.

Now what am I to say to these passages? It is necessary
to remind the reader that the real crux of the argument has
not yet been reached; the contents of the gospels have to be
weighed before the end of the argument is reached. Still, at
the stage at which I now stand, what is to be said of affirmations

manifestly sincere, made by such great authorities as those
whom I have quoted, and which nevertheless I am opposing?

I answer, that all these great authorities—the apostles even
more than the poets—had the whole world before their eyes,
the whole infinite world, and were trying to interpret it in its
height and in its depth. We must not find fault with them
for doing so; we must not say, "It is a mistake for men to attempt
something so obviously beyond their powers." A full solution
of what this infinite world means may not be attainable by us;
none the less ought we to try to win the best solution which
our limited means allow. The eternal existence of Divine Love,
the assurance that that love had touched human nature, and
was leading human nature through many trials and sufferings
towards an immortal existence, this the apostles held, and this
we may hold. But when Paul and John tried to fit this large
belief into history as they knew it, and especially when they
tried to show how Jesus of Nazareth, by whom they had both
been so ineffaceably stirred and kindled, was related to the
divine purposes and to the eternal world-progress, it must not
be thought unnatural if in some respects they went wrong.
It may be said, "Yes, in their philosophy perhaps; but as
witnesses of plain facts they cannot be held to have gone wrong,
without grave imputation upon their honour." This reply at
once brings the whole New Testament before us, and especially
the question of miracles. The fourth gospel, generally accredited
to the apostle John, distinctly bases the belief in Jesus as the
Christ on his miracle-working power, even as the book of
Deuteronomy had based the Israelite belief in Jehovah on the
miracles of the Exodus and of Mount Sinai. What are we to
say to the fourth gospel? And what are we to say to the other
gospels, in which the belief in the importance of miracles, though
not so openly proclaimed as in the fourth gospel, is evidently
inherent?

In answer to these questions, I must begin by saying that
that caution which we invariably use when we meet with a
miraculous narrative in an ordinary history must certainly
not be laid aside when we are considering the Biblical miracles.
A historian may be accepted by us as trustworthy in ordinary
events; but when he relates a miracle, we generally simply
pass it by as not credible. We do not trouble ourselves to ask
why it should be disbelieved; we take the liberty of disbelieving
it without any hesitation. Thus, we give a general belief to

the narrative of the Persian wars by Herodotus; but when the historian tells us how Apollo defended[1] his temple at Delphi by rolling great crags on the assailing Persians, and by sending two supernatural heroes to pursue the enemy in their flight, we assume that that is not an exact account of what happened. When the ecclesiastical historian Socrates tells us what happened at the council of Nicæa, we believe him; but when he tells us[2] that the nation of the Iberi were converted to Christianity by a miracle wrought through the prayer of a female slave, a great pillar raising itself from the ground and standing upright in the air at some distance above its base, on which it finally settled down, we consider him credulous and mistaken. Similarly we accept Bede's account of the mission of Augustine and of the synod of Whitby; but when he tells us[3] how the stone sarcophagus, which had been prepared to contain the body of the pious king Sebbi, being found too small, miraculously enlarged itself to the necessary size, we do not think ourselves bound to regard that as true history. We exercise a natural discrimination; it does not seem necessary to argue so plain a matter.

Is there any reason why we should treat the gospels in any different way from that in which we treat the three eminent historians just quoted? In respect of one class of miracles, the miracles of healing, there is some reason. To deny that Jesus attempted to heal the sick, the blind, and the deaf, is so fundamentally destructive to the gospel records that it is very difficult to imagine what remains when this is gone; and again, to say that Jesus attempted to heal, but was entirely unsuccessful in doing so, is to attribute a blindness to his followers too great to be probable. The gospels may exaggerate; but a fair regard to probabilities compels us to say that Jesus did work remarkable cures. But it must be added that such cures are not unknown at the present day, though rare; the characteristic point being that they are cures worked through faith. Moreover it is very clear in the gospels that Jesus did not hold himself to be unique in performing works of healing; it is recorded that on one occasion he found fault with his disciples because they were unable to heal an epileptic boy, declaring[4] their inability to be due to their want of faith; and the spirit of his teaching invariably is that, not as any peculiar sign pertaining to himself alone, but as a general part of the divine beneficence, the healing of

[1] viii. 37–39.
[2] Socrates, *Hist. Eccles.* I. 20.
[3] Bede, *Hist. Eccles.* IV. 11.
[4] Matthew xvii. 14–20.

the natural defects and sicknesses of men shall follow the establishment of the kingdom of heaven upon earth. To this he looks forward; this he declares to have begun in his own day; but it is by no means his intention to say that this shall terminate in his own day. In saying this, it will be well for me to refer to the most remarkable assertion by Jesus of his own deeds which the three earlier gospels contain (the fourth gospel, which has more of the idealistic element in it, must be treated separately); this is his reply to the messengers whom John the Baptist had sent to make the inquiry of him whether he were the Christ (for this is the real meaning of the phrase "he that cometh"). His reply runs thus:

Go your way and tell John the things which ye do hear and see: the blind receive their sight, and the lame walk, the lepers are cleansed, and the deaf hear, and the dead are raised up, and the poor have good tidings preached to them. And blessed is he, whosoever shall not be offended in me. Matthew xi. 4–6.

This reply is likely to have been an abridged version of what was really said, but there is no reason to doubt its substantial truth. The principal points to remark on, for understanding its purport, are these: first, beneficence, and not wonder, is the main theme on which Jesus is laying stress; this is clear from the clause in which his affirmation of his deeds culminates: "the poor have good tidings preached to them"; and also he recognises that people may be offended in him, which shows that his deeds would not necessarily silence criticism at once. These points being taken into account, and the intrinsic improbability of a literal raising of the dead being also borne in mind, a metaphorical rather than a literal meaning may fairly be assigned to the words, "the dead are raised up." That Jesus did speak of "the dead" in a metaphorical sense, we see from his saying, "Let the dead bury their dead"; and also it is not easy to think that he gave his apostles a general instruction to "raise the dead" literally; and the instruction "raise the dead" is found in Matthew x. 8, as part of his address to the apostles when he sent them out on their first missionary journey. When all allowances are made, it is not to be denied that Jesus claimed to do some things which may well excite our wonder; but this, up to a certain point, should not be deemed incredible.

The case is quite altered when we come to such miracles as the creation of loaves and fishes, the walking on the sea, the turning of water into wine, or the raising of Lazarus. There has been a tendency of late years among the defenders of the truth of these miracles to say that, since to Jesus they were quite natural and ordinary acts, there was no deliberate intention on his part to appeal to them as credentials of his divine office and character. But in the fourth gospel (in which alone the raising of Lazarus is told) Jesus distinctly appeals to this miracle as a credential; the whole series of events connected with it happens, he tells his disciples, "for the glory of God" (John xi. 4), and "to the intent ye may believe" (verse 15); or again that the multitude may believe (verse 42). And how could Jesus possibly be ignorant that on the popular mind the miracle would act as a sign of his Messiahship? As a matter of fact, I do not believe that Jesus did appeal to works of wonder as signs or credentials at all, and there is strong evidence in the gospels that he did not; but no one who believes in the account of the raising of Lazarus given in the eleventh chapter of the fourth gospel can deny that he did so.

If we accept the gospel miracles as they stand, they must be held to have been worked as credentials of the divinity of Jesus; and by divinity we must mean that infinite difference from ordinary humanity which the Nicene creed affirms to be true of him. The miracles, as they stand in the gospels, are the true and proper support of the Nicene creed, and without them it would not be believed at all.

Now against believing the miracles here spoken of (those which really place an infinite distance between Jesus and other men) I have hitherto merely brought forward the fact that in other histories we always do reject, as a matter of course, miracles which are absolutely at variance with our experience. But by far the strongest defence of those gospel miracles of which I am now speaking, is the defence which accepts this fact that they are absolutely at variance with our experience, but alleges that this is exactly what proves their divine character, since God's power extends beyond man's experience.

This defence must be considered. Our attitude of caution must not be relaxed by it; we have still to remember that experience is against these miracles; but the allegation is that something superior to ordinary experience bids us accept them. Two questions now come to the front; first, how these miracles are related to the natural needs of our conscience; secondly, what is the weight of the testimony in favour of them.

With respect to the first question, the supreme need of our

conscience is this—to be strengthened when exposed to the trials of life. The career of Jesus reveals such strength; but how? By his absolute trust in God; by his seizing hold of eternal life as ordained for men by God's will; by his brave conduct, by his contempt for a plainly foreseen and cruel death. Herein lies strength and fire; men lift their hearts to Jesus and feel that he loves them now. But nothing like miracle enters in here. Yet it may be replied to me that the death of Jesus apart from his resurrection was a tragical failure, and that the resurrection was a miracle. On the question of the resurrection then I must now enter; it worthily occupies the chief place, when the miracles of the New Testament are spoken of; and the conclusions we may reach will be a guide to us in dealing with other miracles.

First, however, let me briefly indicate the value of the different parts of the New Testament, regarded as evidence. The gospels must occupy our first attention. If, in the gospels of Matthew, Mark, and Luke, we take that main narrative which begins with the preaching of John the Baptist and ends with the discovery by the women of the empty tomb, we have three documents which support one another not indeed in every detail, but very largely. It has been recently supposed that Mark was used as a model by Matthew and Luke; but the differences are too great to render that supposition really tenable; and it is plain that all three gospels, in that main part of their contents with which I am now dealing, were compiled from older documents, which must have been current in the Christian society for a considerable time, and which, as they were transcribed, were often altered—either from admixture with oral tradition or from other easily conceivable causes[1]. Generally speaking, and with a few exceptions, the contents of this part of the gospels are either true, or founded on some true fact. Next in authority comes the fourth gospel, taken down to the same point, the discovery of the empty tomb. The idealistic tone of this gospel is obvious; everything, from first to last, is made to serve as direct evidence, or direct affirmation, of the divinity of Jesus; the detailed precepts of morality, and the questions and controversies relating to ordinary life, are quite in the background. With all this, there is something historical in this gospel. As I read the evidence, it is a gospel which had an author, and which had an editor; but the editor played a much more important

[1] See Appendix I to this chapter, on the relations of the synoptic gospels to each other.

part than editors generally do. The author was the apostle
John, the son of Zebedee; he supplied the discourses, and the
substance of the narrative, even the miraculous narrative;
but the miraculous narrative was not, as delivered by him,
quite what it is now. Perhaps it may be thought that to attribute
the miraculous narrative, in any form, to him, and yet to disbelieve it, is to accuse him of falsehood. But those who urge
this do not remember what an extraordinary life the apostle
John had had, and how very likely such a man was, without
any insincerity, to mingle imaginations with his memories.
A man, evidently, in the highest degree sensitive and imaginative;
the author of the book of the Revelation, in which the first
three chapters approach to the historical tone, but in which
a visionary imagination is the overflowing and unremitting
characteristic[1]; filled with one single thought, devotion to his
great Master, and resolved not to let anything drop which could
stimulate devotion in others; conscious of suffering that he
had undergone himself, and of greater suffering which his most
intimate friends had undergone; yet, in his old age, surrounded
by attached disciples, who drank in his words implicitly; what
more likely character, and what more likely situation, can be
conceived, for the seed-ground of a history in which imagination
was a large accompaniment of memory? Yet I do not suppose
that the fourth gospel issued from the lips of the apostle John
exactly as we have it now. It was comparatively crude, and
without arrangement, as he delivered it. Then, after his death,
came his attached followers, and one in particular among them,
to arrange it, and to point the moral of it. (The attached
followers are the "we" of the penultimate verse of the gospel;
the one pre-eminent follower is the "I" of the last verse.) These
followers were Greek by race; and the one who took the office
of editor gave to the gospel that Greek beauty of form, and
carefulness of argument, which we see in it now. But the editor,
attending to these points, was very careless of historical
probability; only I must not dilate on this in this place. With
all its defects, the fourth gospel contains some true history,
taken down to the narrative of the discovery of the empty tomb,
which is told in the first ten verses of the twentieth chapter
of this gospel.

The resurrection narratives in all four gospels (taken after

[1] On the questions of the authorship of the Revelation and of the fourth gospel
see Appendix II to this chapter.

the discovery just mentioned) are inferior in mutual consistency to every other part of the gospel narratives; unless possibly the narratives of the infancy in the early chapters of Matthew and Luke should be deemed to stand on a yet lower level. The inconsistency between the resurrection narratives is then the point which I must now demonstrate; and it is only necessary to add that my object in doing so is not to deny the truth or the importance of the belief expressed in the words, "Christ is risen," but to show that the event thus indicated belonged to the spiritual world and not to the world discerned by our ordinary senses; from which it will follow that the resurrection, when rightly understood, was not a miracle, but that it implies a new kind of perception on our part, the perception of a world higher than the world of sense.

I begin then with the narrative of the resurrection as given in the first gospel. If that gospel were in its entirety written by the apostle Matthew, and if the accounts of the visit of the risen Jesus to his eleven faithful apostles, given in Luke xxiv. 36–49 and John xx. 19–23, and also of the visit a week later related in John xx. 26–29, be literally true, the omission of all mention of those visits in Matthew's gospel (seeing that he himself is said to have been present on both occasions) is most extraordinary. But suppose, as I believe to be the case, the first gospel as we have it not to be due to Matthew; even so, the inconsistency between the first gospel and the third and fourth gospels is of the most important character. According to the first gospel, the risen Jesus, appearing to the women who had just visited the tomb and found it empty, bade them instruct his disciples (i.e. his apostles) to meet him at a certain mountain in Galilee (this is over and above a command to the same effect which had previously been given to the women by an angel at the tomb); the women give the message to the apostles, and the apostles accordingly go to Galilee, and there receive from the risen Jesus a solemn commission to preach the gospel. But in the third and fourth gospels, the risen Jesus appears to the apostles in Jerusalem, on the evening of the very day on which, according to the first gospel, he had sent them a message that they were to meet him in Galilee; he discourses to them on the most important matters, and gives them a commission to preach the gospel ("as the Father hath sent me, even so send I you"); but never says a word in reference to the appointment for the meeting in Galilee. Is it not plain that the meeting in Galilee, and the meeting in Jerusalem, had absolutely the same intention and purport? That the one renders the other superfluous? Is it not plain that we have here two rival and inconsistent accounts of that solemn commission which, according to the belief of every Christian, the risen Jesus gave to his apostles? For the solemn commission given in Galilee is as absolutely ignored in the third and fourth gospels[1], as the solemn commission given in Jerusalem is ignored in the first gospel. Moreover, it is the evident meaning of the third gospel that Jesus ascended into heaven on the very day of his resurrection; this is none the less clear, although the same evangelist afterwards, in the Acts, interposed forty days between the resurrection and the ascension. Luke believed one thing at one time, another thing at another time; the inconsistency is plain to see in his own narratives.

As to the second gospel, Mark in his original resurrection-narrative agreed with the first gospel (except that he says the women through fear did *not* give the message to the apostles); but then, for lack of information it is to be supposed, stopped short. The last twelve verses of the second gospel are an appendix, in the main agreeing with the third gospel, though not entirely so; it is not probable that these verses came from Mark himself. On minor inconsistencies between the resurrection narratives, which are numerous, I must not enlarge; the reader may see them for himself. So devoid of the historical sense were the early Christian writers, and so devoid of the historical sense are Christians of the present day, when they think themselves confronted with the danger of losing the whole of their religion, that the most obvious inconsistencies between the gospel narratives on the subject of the resurrection were and are ignored or denied; or if not denied, are minimised, as if they did not matter. But how is it possible to think that God on the one hand performed the most wonderful miracles in order to convince men of the truth of the resurrection of Jesus, and on the other hand allowed the narratives which relate that resurrection to be left in the confusion in which we find them?

What are we to conclude? The only possible conclusion is this; that the resurrection was felt by the first disciples of Jesus to

---

[1] The appearance of the risen Jesus in Galilee narrated in John xxi. cannot possibly be the same as that narrated in Matthew xxviii. 16–20. The persons present are different; the incidents are different; the place is different.

be a point so full of delicacy that they did not for a long time describe it historically at all; it was their sheet anchor, no doubt, on which they relied for their preservation; nothing could equal it in the whole sphere of God's doings; but to describe precisely what happened was a delicate and difficult task and they preferred not to attempt it. When at last the attempt was made to describe what had happened it was impossible to obtain agreement except on this single fact, that the tomb had certainly been found empty.

All this points to the appearances of the risen Jesus to his disciples having been visionary. It would, however, be felt by the disciples that a vision, acknowledged to be a mere vision, would not have any constraining force on the belief of outsiders. There had been a constraining force on the apostles; they could not help believing in the risen Jesus; and they could express their conviction in the simple words, "Jesus Christ has risen; he has appeared to us." But they would shrink, for a long time, from greater particularity in describing appearances which were so very different from ordinary sensuous vision; their testimony would be given in general terms, not in detail. The need of detail was felt later, and was supplied imaginatively, in the way we see.

If we must infer this from the gospels, much more must we infer it from the rest of the New Testament. Look at the conversion of Paul as described in the Acts: in not one of the three accounts is it said, in the direct narrative, that Paul saw the risen Jesus. In all three accounts, in the ninth chapter, in the twenty-second chapter, and in the twenty-sixth chapter, it is said that he saw a bright light, and that he heard a voice. It is true that afterwards in the twenty-second chapter Ananias is represented as saying to Paul that God had appointed him "to see" the Righteous One, and in the twenty-sixth chapter Paul at first sight seems to imply the same thing (verse 16); but when we look at the latter passage more closely, we see that the appearance of Jesus to Paul at the time of his conversion is made parallel with the appearances at later times, which certainly were of a visionary character. Nor can it be said, that when Paul "heard" the risen Jesus, sensuous hearing is implied; otherwise the account of the words of the risen Jesus, as reported in Acts xxvi. would be entirely inconsistent with the words as reported in Acts ix. and Acts xxii.; it is only if we understand that Paul is reporting an effect on his mind, and not literal words, that the inconsistency, though still existing, becomes of little importance. Look again at the phrase in which Paul, in the first chapter of "Galatians," describes his conversion:

When it was the good pleasure of God, who separated me, even from my mother's womb, and called me through his grace, to reveal his Son in me, that I might preach him among the Gentiles.

Why does Paul say "to reveal his Son in me," rather than "to reveal his Son to me," unless because he felt the revelation to be internal, not external? There are two other references to the vision at his conversion in Paul's epistles, both in the first epistle to the Corinthians; one in chapter ix. 1, "Am I not free? am I not an apostle? have I not seen Jesus our Lord?" where it is true that the word "seen" is used without any qualification, so that the claim is made that it means ordinary ocular vision. But I may refer to the reasons already given for the proof that this ocular vision did not take place on the occasion of Paul's conversion; and especially to the consideration that if Jesus had then appeared to him in bodily form, he could not have said simply that he saw a great light, without mention of a person seen. But Paul would have weakened his appeal to the Corinthians if he had added the qualification, "have I not *spiritually* seen Jesus our Lord?" and he instinctively felt this, and therefore says simply, "have I not seen?" The other passage is chapter xv. 8, where the reference comes at the end of a list of appearances of the risen Jesus, as to none of which is any detail of time, place, or manner given. This absence of detail was just and right, if the appearances were what we call visionary, that is to say non-sensuous; for the details would then add little to the credibility; but if the appearances were of the ordinary physical kind, details were important, and should have been added.

It is worth referring to the expression in the first epistle of Peter, iii. 18, where it is said that Christ was "put to death indeed in flesh, but made alive in the spirit," where the latter expression must, I think, refer to the resurrection; though the traditional explanation is that it refers to an intermediate state of spiritual life between the death of Jesus and his resurrection; an explanation which allows the resurrection to be thought of as a physical event, witnessed by the senses. But the antithesis between flesh and spirit in the passage is much more fundamental than this traditional explanation assumes it to be; if this were not clear otherwise, we should be convinced of it by referring to the sixth verse of the fourth chapter, where the same train of

ideas is before the apostle's mind as in the third chapter. In
both the preaching of Christ to the dead is mentioned; the passage
in the fourth chapter running thus:

> For unto this end was the gospel preached to the dead, that they might
> be judged according to men in the flesh, but live according to God in
> the spirit.

In the third chapter, "the dead" are said to have been those
who sinned in the days of Noah; they had been judged for their
sins in the flesh; but now Christ delivers them, and they "live
according to God in the spirit." Is not this life, according to
God in the spirit, the eternal life; is it not exactly parallel to
the life which, after his death, Christ himself is said to have
resumed "in the spirit"; is not then the "life in the spirit,"
which is said to have belonged to Christ, the true eternal life,
and is it not placed in antithesis to the life in the flesh? If so,
the apostle Peter held the resurrection to be a spiritual, not
a physical, fact.

This is not indeed equivalent to saying that Peter, or Paul
either, held the resurrection to be wholly non-miraculous. To
affirm this would be incorrect; they did, if I understand their
minds rightly, think the disappearance of the body from the
tomb miraculous. But it would be premature for me to enter
upon that point now. It is the visionary appearances of the
risen Jesus to his followers of which I am now speaking; these,
whatever degree of importance we may assign to them, were
not miraculous.

Were these visionary appearances important in that age,
and are they important to us in this age? Are they a firm ground
for believing that Jesus did truly arise from the life of the flesh
into a new and higher spiritual life? Not, I think, in themselves;
but they were the natural accompaniments of other and deeper
experiences, which were real ground to the apostles for such
a belief. And as it is on this ground that our own experience
may coincide with the experience of the apostles, it will be well
for me to explain carefully the nature of those moral grounds
for belief to which I refer.

The true compulsion which forced the apostles to believe
that Jesus had risen from death was of a moral nature; it is
described for us most clearly in the case of Paul, but we may,
and indeed must, believe it to have been true for the earlier
apostles as well. But it is the conversion of Paul which I must
begin by explaining.

The deepest characteristic of the religion of Israel first, and of the Christian religion afterwards, was the search after righteousness. That is to say, the holy men of Israel first, and of the Christian Church afterwards, desired to find for themselves and for others that line of conduct which was most life-giving, most conducive to a permanent and pure happiness, not selfish but universal. This, the teachers of Israel, from the time of Ezra onwards (and indeed even earlier than Ezra) had affirmed to be the faithful following of the law which they read in their ancient scriptures, and which they believed to have been given by God to Moses on Mount Sinai, for the permanent instruction of Israel, nay in the end for the permanent instruction of all mankind. This deep-seated moral conviction of the teachers of Israel we may still read most emphatically expressed in the 119th psalm; in which psalm it is possible (though not certain, in view of the terms used) that the prophets also meet with some recognition; at any rate the teachers of Israel in the time of Jesus did generally regard the prophets as divinely instructive, though hardly as equal to the five books of the Pentateuch, in which the law is contained. Now Paul in all his early life embraced this conviction fervently; and he never, in all his life, said that it was a wrong thing for him to have embraced it, even after he had abandoned it as an active practical principle. God, he told the Galatians, had separated him, even from his mother's womb, and called him through his grace: and in these words he referred to the period while he was still a Pharisee in the most literal sense. In these early days, moreover, Paul read the law in such a sense, as to hold that the disciples of Jesus should be punished for their disparagement of it; for the disciples of the crucified Jesus, though they had not yet abandoned the practice of the law, did regard it as transitory, and held that it would pass away before the divine action of their Master, Jesus. This opinion Paul regarded as rebellious, and with all the fervour of his nature set himself to uproot and destroy it. The right and life-giving action, he held, consisted in upholding, by force if necessary, the honour of the Divine law, which had been committed to Israel to guard. Hence he took an important, though not absolutely a leading, part in the condemnation and death of Stephen, and became still more conspicuous afterwards. But while he persecuted the disciples of Jesus, something of their spirit slowly penetrated into him; we see this from the words which he afterwards reported the risen Jesus to have spoken to him at the moment of his utter prostration[1]—"it is hard for thee to kick against the goad." He had then been resisting some secret influence, for how long we do not know; the true meaning of the divine message to Israel, which Jesus had disentangled from the formal bonds which had at one time been a shelter to it, but now were a hindrance—this was now becoming visible to Paul; and in his heart the old and the new met in violent collision. It was this collision by which he was prostrated when on the road to Damascus; prostrated with such force that he fell to the ground, and after seeing a sudden blaze of light, his sense of sight failed him. In this desperate strait he sought for a guide; the new conviction forced itself upon him that his present action was wrong; and surely if wrong, it was personal wrong-doing of which he was guilty. But if personal wrong-doing, wrong-doing against whom? Beyond all the wrong-doing towards the disciples of Jesus, of which his conscience now accused him, wrong-doing towards their Master became revealed to him; it was Jesus whom, in the real root of the matter, he was injuring; the will of God was then revealed to him that he should listen to Jesus. He did listen, and though it is not believable that he did at that moment receive all that detailed message which he related afterwards to Festus and to Agrippa, he certainly received a new spirit, a new direction of the heart, which contained implicitly much more than he could immediately understand. What was more than a command, he received rest in his heart; and this rest centred in his acceptance of Jesus as his teacher, as the guide worthy to be followed, whose spirit had a natural vital quality which was lacking to the precepts of the law. It was then not merely a new set of principles which Paul received into his heart at that moment, but also a new personal attachment; new personal attachments, we may truly say, for with Jesus the disciples of Jesus could not but be associated; but the centre of his new feeling was inevitably directed towards Jesus as the Divine messenger, whom henceforth he must accept as revealing the true will of God.

It will be seen that, in giving this account of the conversion of Paul, I have adhered to the substance of the three narratives which relate that conversion in the book of the Acts, but have avoided the literal terms of those narratives; and for this reason, that I wished to show that the spiritual substance of those narratives remains, when the terms which imply sensuous experience

---

[1] Acts xxvi. 14.

are taken away. The reasons which compel us to discard the terms in which sensuous experience seems to be implied, have already been given; but it may be asked, what guarantee have we that the spiritual substance of Paul's experience was sound and not an illusion? This challenge can only be answered by a consideration of the consequences of Paul's conversion in his own time and in after times. The whole meaning of the Christian faith lies in the links between man and man that have been established by it, and in the evidence that these links have their origin in a sphere which is invisible to the senses, and divine; links of love and reverence. Have these links really been established, and was Paul's conversion one of the chief agencies in establishing them? The answer to this question has to be sought in the after history; and from the after history I answer it in the affirmative, as I shall endeavour to show; though I must also endeavour to show that Paul mingled with his genuine experiences something of the speculative temperament, in the use of which he was not always so successful.

But having said this, I must no longer separate Paul from his brother apostles, who were disciples of Jesus before he became so. It was impossible that Simon Peter and his companions should be subjected to that severe internal conflict of soul which Paul had to undergo in his conversion; but yet their restoration from their despondency into which the crucifixion of Jesus had thrown them demanded something more than mere reasoning to effect it. They were restored, they were strengthened, and their conduct showed no symptoms of fanaticism. It was through Jesus, as they held, that they were restored, through Jesus that they were strengthened. In rejecting the material representations of the resurrection which we find in the gospels, we do not reject the spiritual conviction which breathes so ardently in all the epistles of the New Testament, and in the book of the Revelation.

If, then, we understand by the resurrection the continued personal intercourse of Jesus with his disciples and followers in all ages, with all who feel in him the supporter of their souls, divinely present to them—such an understanding I hold to be true. But visions of the risen Jesus, such as the apostles had (and some persons in later ages also), though I am not despising them, cannot be brought forward as primary evidence. The difficulty of distinguishing between visions which are mere illusions, and visions which may perhaps mean something real, is so great, that no defender of Christian belief ought to appeal to such visions without very great caution. When everything is taken into account, there may be something really significant in them; but our spiritual life and belief ought not to be based upon them[1].

That on which our spiritual life ought to be based, the invisible powers which promote goodness, whether of that Divine Universal Parent on whom we all ultimately rest, or of Jesus Christ who has been such an example to us of the divine methods and such an institutor of divine faith and spiritual intelligence, these powers are not without evidence in the pages of history. The mutual affection of Christians was noted even by the heathen in the early ages of the Christian Church, and has never been absent from Christian society even up to the present day; it has not indeed been able to prevent bitter quarrels, but it would be incorrect to suppose that bitter quarrels are in themselves a proof of the absence of affection; an ardent temperament may be driven to hatred by causes not altogether dissimilar from those which lead to love. A regard and affection for one's fellow-men has been operative, however mixed with adverse influences, through Christendom in every century of the existence of the Christian society; the growth of humane sentiments, the growth of freedom, and the increased trustworthiness of workers, have all been fostered by it. When we take into account all those religious emotions, expressed in word and in act, which have aided in bringing about this result, we shall believe in something more than the example of Jesus as operating in his followers; we shall believe in his absolute presence, spiritual and invisible, but real. This, as I have explained it, is the true meaning of the resurrection; and not only the true meaning in itself, but the very heart of the meaning as held by the original disciples—by Peter and the Jewish Christians no less than by Paul and the Gentile Christians.

Yet, if I am allowed to appeal to the good fruit which has

[1] There is a difference, which will be at once perceived, between those moral experiences, those solutions of moral problems, through which I am affirming that the invisible spiritual world is made known to us, and the methods which are perhaps best described as those of the modern Psychical Society. Still there may be some common ground. I really am uncertain whether that Society would consider the following experience of my own too vague for their purposes. I had a dream, once in my life and only once, which did enlighten me as to my conduct in the past and my purposes in the future. In certain respects it was a religious dream, but not in its main purport. At first, I thought it accidental; my inclination now is to think t a true message from a higher world.

ensued in Christian society, and in the countries which have
been deeply affected by Christianity, through belief in the risen
Jesus, it is none the less necessary to take the faults of Christendom
into consideration, and to ask whether there is anything in the
primary belief in the resurrection, as held by the first disciples,
which may have furnished a seed of error? It is impossible
to look at the history of Christendom, and not to be sensible
that some error has been present in the working of the religion,
and error of no slight or negligible kind. Those who maintain
most stoutly the perfect truth of the Christian creeds cannot
deny that the upholders of those creeds in past times defended
them, for many long centuries, by the fire and sword of persecution; they dared not let those whom they called heretics have
equal rights of free speech with themselves. Was not this a
false timidity, not to be content with the Spirit of God, but to
compel acceptance of doctrine by earthly weapons? The time
of the most serious prevalence of this error was during the six
centuries from 1000 A.D. to 1600 A.D.; but the whole history of
it is not comprised in less time than that between the council
of Nicæa in 325 A.D. and the French Revolution in 1789 A.D.
Perhaps it may be said that before the council of Nicæa the
Church was perfectly pure. If, however, we look at the spirit
of the Church in those first centuries, we shall be sensible of an
error which, though one rather of omission than of commission,
was serious in its degree, and diverted the minds of men from
beneficent work to subtle problems, which, though not in themselves illegitimate, ought not to have been allowed to take
precedence over necessary duties.

The early Church reckoned the well-being of men in this
present life as a matter hardly deserving consideration; it is
a subject on which the Fathers never seriously enter; and though
natural good feeling could not but make the early Christians
sympathetic with suffering, and anxious to relieve it when it
came visibly before them, yet attempts to remove the causes
of suffering, and especially to remove the causes of disease and
of war, to increase the security of life, to make industry pleasurable
and to provide innocent pleasures for all men, these were topics
which they thought unworthy of beings who had eternity before
their eyes, and who stood in awe of the judgments of God. As
to Greek science, they positively despised it. They regarded
the present life, not as a seed out of which a future life might
naturally develop, but as a merely temporary arrangement,

serving indeed as a test of men's piety and obedience, but in itself
soon to be brought to an end by the direct action of God. How
much did they lose by this attitude of mind! how far more forcibly
could they have appealed to their heathen neighbours, if they
had shown themselves in all honest ways willing to work with
them, to exchange thoughts with them, to plan with them for
the benefit of mankind, and to receive from them those enlarged
methods of thinking and of acting in which both Greeks and
Romans had made such progress! It is true that the Christians
had more to give than they had to receive; but they had something both in intellectual and moral matters to receive; and from
the heathen they were very unwilling to receive it. The Christian
religion was very slow in expanding so as to place temporal
welfare among the things that should deliberately and largely
be aimed at; and in early days, if Christians aimed at it at
all, they did so in the scantiest fashion.

A sin of omission it was; not to be thought lightly of; and
how did it come? Very plainly, from the belief that this visible
state of things, with which all our practical action is concerned
(though not all our thoughts and feelings) was shortly about to
come to a violent end. And whence did they draw that belief?
Plainly again, from the belief that Jesus Christ was shortly
about to return to judge all mankind, to take some to heaven,
to send others to hell, both heaven and hell being separate from
this earth. They laid stress on the thought of his returning,
because Jesus himself had spoken of it (and in him it was not
an unnatural mode of speaking); but ought they not to have
thought that the return of Jesus might mean, not his descent
into the sphere of material things, but the elevation of his
followers into a clear apprehension of the spiritual world?
Whether such a meaning were consciously present to Jesus
himself or not, it satisfies the force of his words. The disciples,
too, were familiar with the thought that they could be raised
into a sphere beyond sense; ought it not to have occurred to
them that the kingdom of heaven progressed and increased
by testing and purifying this kind of experience? If this were
true, the reward of virtue would come, not by any destructive
catastrophe, but by the raising of the soul so as to be fit for
eternal life. This is a solution of the Christian problem which
interprets it as the raising of our ordinary experience to a higher
level; but by no means as abolishing our ordinary experience.
Is not this a solution which is consonant with all we know of

divine things and of the progress of the human character, of the human soul? Is not the view that God is about to put an end, suddenly and violently, to the present order of things, very much against all we know of the divine methods, and of the motives which operate fruitfully and beneficently on human character? Why then did the early Christians confidently adopt the latter version of Christian belief, and put the former version aside without a glance at it?

There can be no doubt that the general belief in miracles predisposed the early Christians to expect a sudden and violent catastrophe as the way in which the final destinies of mankind would be ushered in; but also the belief that the physical body of Jesus, which had been truly slain, was revivified after death and had gone up to heaven, had an effect on the minds of Christians peculiarly favourable to material conceptions of eternal life. Must we not then hold that true spirituality is very much against the belief, not only in the termination of the present order of things by a sudden catastrophe, but also against the belief in the resurrection, after death, of the physical body of Jesus?

This last is what the gospels relate. I have endeavoured to show that neither Paul nor Peter held it; but I have also said that Peter and Paul held that there was something miraculous in the resurrection. Was it not very natural that when Simon Peter found that the women had really told truth, and that the tomb was empty, he should leap to the inference that this happened by the direct will of God[1]? This, he thought, was the divine answer to the condemnation of Jesus by the Jews. It was a blameless, though as I hold a mistaken, thought. But he did not think that the body had risen from the tomb as a body of flesh and blood; he thought it had been changed into a spiritual body. This, at all events, we must infer from the fifteenth chapter of the first epistle to the Corinthians (verses 42–53) is what Paul thought; and it was what Peter would naturally think, when the vision of the risen Jesus stood before him. In saying this, indeed, it would not be right to leave unnoticed the single piece of evidence that Peter did hold the resurrection of Jesus to be a physical fact. This occurs

[1] The empty tomb is often, even in modern times, pressed as a proof that a miracle had occurred. But though we do not know by whom, or for what reason, the body of Jesus was removed, no one would now say that the removal was miraculous unless it were thought that the miracle was confirmed on other grounds; which, I have tried to show, it is not.

in the speech attributed to him in Acts x. 34–43, from which two verses ought now to be quoted:

Him God raised up the third day, and gave him to be made manifest, not to all the people, but unto witnesses that were chosen before of God, even to us, who did eat and drink with him after he rose from the dead.

The natural, and I suppose, the true interpretation of these words is that Jesus himself ate and drank after he rose from the dead. But if we remember that Luke, who reports this speech, is the only evangelist who says that Jesus after his resurrection ate or drank; and if we bear in mind that in reporting a speech it is very easy for any reporter to add a point, even involuntarily; and that Luke in particular does add points in his narratives, as for instance when he speaks of the "tongues" on the day of Pentecost as a miraculous speaking of foreign languages, while Paul in 1 Corinthians xiv. makes it clear that the "tongues" were entirely different from this; if we remember all these things, we shall feel that the evidence which this verse supplies as to Peter's belief is not strong evidence. Peter's words in his own epistle, which I have quoted above, lead to a very different inference as to the nature of Peter's belief.

To conclude what I have to say about the resurrection of Jesus; it can never be out of my recollection that I am liable to be attacked from both sides; for there will be many who will say that the evidence of spiritual experience is shadowy and unreal. But is there any one who will say that it is unimportant to note what things have made him a better man? Nothing is so important as real experience on that point; it is a question on which we are bound to exercise a judgment, even though we know that our judgment is fallible. Those who note the history of Christendom carefully will, I think, see that the belief in the risen Jesus has made men better and stronger; but they will also observe that belief in the physical resurrection of the body that was laid in the tomb has disordered men's anticipations of the future, has made men hope and fear unreal things, and diverted their minds from the true and sane ordering of life. The real evidence that Jesus, after death, rose into a higher life, where, though unseen, he has true connexion with ourselves, centres in this, that in this belief alone there lies organising power, capable of gathering men together in the pursuit of kindred purposes, not identical but harmonious, whereby life and energy continually increase in this earthly abode of ours.

If then the resurrection of Jesus, or in other words his rising out of death into new life, a life in which our own organised unity has its centre, be not a miracle but a fact of a non-sensuous order, apprehensible in our own experience to-day, we have weighty ground for thinking that those extraordinary miracles of which we read in the gospels (it will be remembered that I am not including the healings attributed to Jesus in my present argument) are mistakes and not true history. This judgment will be confirmed if we consider the general contents of the New Testament. The gospels teem with miracles; and it is evident that the first Christians did, for certain purposes, very much desire to have the support of miracles. But putting aside the resurrection (which, as I have explained, has its own natural meaning and value apart from miracle), the first Christians did not depend for their personal religious life on the gospel miracles. In the epistles of Paul; in the epistle to the Hebrews; in the epistle of James; in the first (and probably only genuine) epistle of Peter; in the epistles of John; in the epistle of Jude; and in the book of the Revelation; in all these works not one single gospel miracle, apart from the resurrection, is once mentioned. Is not this omission a very remarkable fact? There are plenty of references to the Old Testament miracles in these books; for instance, the Divine power as shown against Pharaoh in Romans ix. 17; the miracles of the Exodus in 1 Corinthians x. 1–9: the shining of the face of Moses in 2 Corinthians iii. 7; the miracles of the Exodus again in Hebrews xi. 28, 29, and a variety of other miracles in the verses that follow; the miraculous giving of the law on Mount Sinai in Hebrews xii. 18–21; the withholding of rain, and the giving of rain, through the prayer of Elijah, in James v. 17, 18; the flood, and the ark of Noah, in 1 Peter iii. 20. As against this collection of Old Testament miracles, the only reference to the gospel miracles in all the epistles of the New Testament is the reference to the transfiguration in the second epistle attributed to Peter, an epistle of very doubtful genuineness; and the transfiguration, as I shall endeavour to show in the proper place, is capable of a very simple natural interpretation. Must we not conclude that the ordinary religious life of the first Christians was not supported by the thought of the gospel miracles?

It is true that the word "powers," which is translated "miracles" in our English versions, is found in several passages of the epistles of Paul, as indicative of the divine working shown

in the action of faithful men; and "signs and wonders" are also
mentioned in a general manner by Paul, as worked by himself,
in Romans xv. 19, and 2 Corinthians xii. 12; but no example is
given, to show what kind of powers, what kind of wonders, are
meant. It would be an obvious method of illustrating Paul's
meaning, to refer to the Acts, written by Paul's disciple, Luke;
but Luke (like many other historians on whom we place a general
reliance) cannot be trusted in his narration of miracles. For
instance, Luke tells us, in the sixteenth chapter of the Acts,
how Paul and Silas were scourged and imprisoned at Philippi;
but were miraculously set free from their bonds, the prison being
at the same time shaken by an earthquake, and the doors thrown
open; all which had such an effect, that not only was the jailor
converted, but Paul was able next day to demand that the
magistrates of the city should themselves come and conduct
Paul and Silas out of the prison, a demand with which the magistrates complied. After reading this, we turn to Paul's first
epistle to the Thessalonians (ii. 2), and find that Paul mentions
the shameful treatment which he had suffered at Philippi, but
says not a word about the miracle, or the subsequent repentance
of the magistrates. If these latter points had been true, would
not Paul have given some brief indication of them in writing
about the incident?

We cannot tell precisely what Paul meant in speaking of
"powers" and "wonders" shown by himself or by other
Christians; they are mentioned as distinct from gifts of healing,
and spiritual power is of course a real thing; but we have not
the slightest reason for thinking that Paul ever did anything
analogous to the walking on the sea (to mention one of the best-
known gospel miracles); and though the narrative in Acts xx.
9–12, if taken literally, represents him as having restored life to
a boy who had been killed, the real death of the boy is by no
means assured to us; in other respects the incident is probably
true.

But how comes it that the gospels teem with miracles, when
the epistles are so silent about them? The adequate, and as I
hold true, reason is that the gospel narratives were needed for
the defence of the Christian faith against non-Christian assailants,
and especially against Jewish assailants. It was a matter of
course that Jews and Christians should meet in the conflict of
argument; and it was a matter of course that the Jewish
antagonist should ask what Jesus had done that he should be

regarded as the superior of Moses and Elijah. The Christian would not be able to deny the miracles attributed to Moses and Elijah in the Old Testament; he would then be obliged to maintain that Jesus had performed greater works than those two heroes of ancient Israel. Is it not plain that the tendency of those who maintained the Christian cause would be to give to the deeds of Jesus as much of the miraculous aspect as was possible?

It would be doing an injustice to the gospels to describe them simply as collections of miraculous narratives; they are much more that that; but still they fall short of what true biographies should be. The three earlier gospels bear the impress of the motives which had been dominant during their long and gradual compilation. As against outside assailants, the wonderful deeds of Jesus had been collected; for the instruction of Christians themselves, the sayings and parables of Jesus had been collected. Something there was over and above these two motives; so memorable, so deep-reaching a fact as the crucifixion had inevitably to be recorded; and some incidents of an ordinary kind entered in, though generally with a saying of Jesus attached to them, which had caused them to be remembered; and the order of events was more or less known, though in this important point the gospels greatly differ among themselves. The first gospel is by far the most instructive in its arrangement of events, and thereby gives us true insight into the motives of Jesus (is this point possibly due to the apostle Matthew, who cannot, however, have composed the whole gospel?); Mark also is not very wrong, despite the opinion of the presbyter whom Papias quotes; but Luke did not know how to manage his superabundant material, for which, in itself, we are greatly indebted to him; and the fourth gospel is yet more strangely wrong, betraying in this way the existence of an editor, over and above the apostle whose name it bears.

Without minimising the value of the gospels, it remains true that there is a great deal which a real biographer would have recorded, but which the gospels entirely omit. For instance, how long did the ministry, that is the active career, of Jesus last? It is wonderful how much we are in the dark as to this point, which really is an important one; and we are likewise ignorant as to the exact year in which the crucifixion took place. Again, what was it which led the brethren of Jesus, who at first were adverse to him, to join his cause? How little do we know of the actions of Jesus before his baptism! What amount of intercourse had he with John the Baptist? Where did the apostles go when sent out on their apostolic mission; what treatment did they receive at that time; what interval was there between their first selection as apostles and their being actually sent out? If biography, in the true and proper sense, had been the object of the evangelists, the points just mentioned could not but have attracted their attention. But they were defective in this way; and with all our regard for their industry (and for the industry of other Christians on whom the evangelists depended) we cannot but draw an inference unfavourable to their historical judgment. The leading motives which led to the construction of the gospels were those which I have mentioned above; and the collection of wonders took too high a place in the minds of our authorities.

However, I have said that the facts mentioned in the main part of the synoptic gospels, beginning with the preaching of John the Baptist and ending with the discovery of the empty tomb, are generally either true or founded on some true fact. It may be as well to show clearly what I think as to two of the most salient miracles recorded in this part of the history—the raising of the daughter of Jairus from death, and the feeding of the five thousand. As to the raising of the daughter of Jairus, the fact of the death of the girl is not properly assured to us. The signs of death are not stated; and from the terms of the narrative it does not seem that Jesus believed her to be dead; if his words are to be taken literally, he certainly said the contrary. It is, of course, a remarkable narrative in any case; but the point which would make it abnormal is not properly verified. As to the feeding of the five thousand, the explanation (due, I believe, to H. E. G. Paulus—but it was in Tolstoi that I read it) is that when the apostles said to Jesus, "We have but five loaves and two fishes," they had not gone round the whole five thousand or more persons to find out whether there were any provisions at all among them. There were hungry persons no doubt, who had made their hunger known; but when all were quietly seated, enough was provided to prevent serious distress. There never, it would seem, had been risk of real starvation, even on the showing of the gospels. No doubt, such an incident would not have been turned into a miracle had there not been a motive for so representing it; but it is very obvious that there would be such a motive, and a strong one.

I come to the fourth gospel; and I am compelled to use more

brevity than I could wish. Let me be allowed to assume that combination of author and editor in the composition of it which I have already affirmed; the Hebrew author, supplying the substance; the Greek editor, arranging it, supplying the chronology, adding details, pointing the arguments, correcting grammatical errors, if there were any such. The main question is: Do author and editor, in this combination, tell truth? In some respects, I think they do; in others, I am sure they do not; and it is the latter point that I am now concerned to prove.

Those who read the synoptic gospels, and especially the gospel of Matthew, will remember how critical the moment is when Jesus is first saluted as the Christ by one of his disciples; how ardent were the praises with which Jesus responded to that salutation; how he declared that Simon Peter, by whom the great acknowledgment was made, had had the truth revealed to him by God and not by man; how from that period onwards a new start is made, a new design entered upon, the design of a journey to Jerusalem, where Jesus knew full well that he would be slain. This crisis, so great, so fruitful, had for its dominant feature this—that then for the first time Jesus felt it needful to the success of his cause that his apostles should vitally bind themselves to him, heart and soul; that then for the first time they did so bind themselves; and the solemn bond was made sure by the fervour with which Simon Peter gave him the great title of Christ, the King Anointed of God, and the Son of God. Having received that acknowledgment, Jesus could not stand still, he must go forward.

Now in the fourth gospel, this great crisis does not exist at all; nor is this an accident; there is no room for it; the whole scheme of the gospel makes it an impossibility that it should exist. From the beginning to the end of the fourth gospel, Jesus is being designated either as the Christ, or by some term of equal honour and significance, continually and by all manner of persons; in the first chapter by John the Baptist, who points him out as "the Lamb of God, who taketh away the sin of the world"; by Andrew in plain terms as the Messiah (and Andrew informs Simon Peter, who thus, contrary to the first gospel, *does* receive the tidings that Jesus is the Christ from the lips of man); by Philip as "him of whom Moses in the law, and the prophets, did write"; by Nathanael as "the Son of God, and King of Israel." I need not dwell upon the second and third chapters, but the same tone is preserved in each; in the fourth chapter the Samaritan woman says, "Can this be the Christ?" (Jesus had told her that he was so;) and the Samaritan men say to the woman,

Now we believe, not because of thy speaking: for we have heard for ourselves, and know that this is indeed the Saviour of the world.

In the fifth chapter Jesus himself tells the Jews of Jerusalem,

Verily, verily, I say unto you, He that heareth my word, and believeth him that sent me, hath eternal life;

in the sixth chapter he tells the Jews of Galilee,

I am the bread of life: he that cometh to me shall not hunger, and he that believeth on me shall never thirst.

All these sayings, some uttered by Jesus himself, others by his disciples or associates, but all alike accumulating on Jesus the most honourable, the most splendid titles to our regard, were spoken, if the fourth gospel be true, before that acknowledgment by Simon Peter, which in the first gospel is spoken of as meriting and receiving from Jesus the most exalted praise which Jesus ever bestowed on any man.

There is one point, which makes the discordance between the first and fourth gospels keener yet. All three synoptic gospels tell us that, after Jesus had received from his apostles the acknowledgment that he was the Christ, he forbade them to tell any one that he was so. There were good reasons for this prohibition of his, but I must not stop to explain them here. But can anything be more remote from this reticence than the sayings of the fourth gospel throughout?

Have we not good reason for saying (even though I have not yet described the events of the life of Jesus in order) that, in the contrast noted, the first gospel is giving us deep and pregnant historical truth, whereas the fourth gospel is idealising?

I come to another point. The whole record of the life of Jesus during the six months preceding his crucifixion, is radically different in the synoptic gospels from what it is in the fourth gospel. In the synoptic gospels, it is only a few days before his crucifixion that Jesus spends in Jerusalem; but those few days are momentous. They are preceded by a triumphal entry into Jerusalem, during which Jesus is proclaimed by his followers as "the son of David," as "the King who cometh in the name of the Lord"; he then takes possession, if not of the whole temple, at all events of the large outer court which was called the court of the Gentiles, where those who sold doves for the

sacrifices were accustomed to sit, and those who supplied change
of money when needed by purchasers of the doves; Jesus drives
these commercial persons out of the court.   There then for several
days he takes up his position, his numerous followers being near;
he teaches, argues with the arguers, answers the questioners, from
morning till evening.   But his discourses are largely directed
against the Jewish authorities, who at last apprehend him,
try him, and procure his crucifixion.   It is evident that these
few days are the culmination of a great design; he knew that they
would end in his death, but with his death his heavenly career
would begin; thus would prophecy be fulfilled, and the will of
God be done.   All his utterances, during his journey from Galilee,
had been fashioned with a foresight of this issue.   His triumphal
entry into Jerusalem is the beginning of those actions and sayings
which, in the eyes of the Jewish authorities, constituted his chief
offence, the final point of which is his declaration, in reply to the
direct challenge of Caiaphas the high priest, that he is the Christ.

Now in the fourth gospel, the triumphal entry of Jesus into
Jerusalem is not the beginning, but the end, of those acts and
sayings by which he excited the hostility of the Jews of Jerusalem
against him.   His taking possession of the temple after this
triumphal entry, his discourses in the temple after it, are wholly
unmentioned; it is not even said that he set foot in the temple.
His public action, after his triumphal entry, is almost nothing;
his declaration before Caiaphas is unmentioned.   His expulsion
of the dove-sellers and money-changers from the court of the temple
had been, with singular improbability, transferred to the beginning
of his career, before he was known at all in any public manner.

On the other hand, the fourth gospel tells us that for the six
months before his triumphal entry into Jerusalem, Jesus had
been either in Jerusalem or in its neighbourhood (not its close
neighbourhood, but not very distant either); he had been in
the temple, during the earlier part of these six months, frequently,
but not after December[1] was over, it would seem, at all; his
discourses in the temple in the earlier days were entirely about
himself.   There is much in these discourses as reported that
would naturally have offended the Jews, but it is not these,
according to the fourth gospel, which determined the chief
priests and Pharisees to procure his crucifixion; it was an act
which would hardly have been supposed likely to prejudice
people against him (unless it were thought a mere false trick,

---

[1] Marked by the feast of the dedication, John x. 22.

but that is by no means the meaning of the fourth gospel)—
his raising of Lazarus from death to life. After this, no fresh
determination of the authorities against Jesus was necessary, or
was made. This, be it remembered, was considerably before
his triumphal entry into Jerusalem.

Is it not plain that the accounts in the synoptic gospels and
in the fourth gospel are wholly different—must it not be added,
wholly inconsistent with one another—and can we hesitate to
prefer the synoptic account?

But I must say something more about the raising of Lazarus.
Generally speaking, the omission of any event from a historical
record is not an argument against that event having taken
place. But the raising of Lazarus, if true, was not an ordinary
event. The most public, by far, of all the miracles attributed
to Jesus; reported and known all over Jerusalem; performed,
we cannot but suppose, in presence of all the apostles ("the disciples" are mentioned all through, and it is plain that casual
disciples are not intended); a miracle appealed to by Jesus,
and not once only, as furnishing a just reason for men believing
in him—how could such an event be forgotten by those who had
witnessed it, even apart from its effect in causing his death?
Yet neither Matthew, nor Mark, nor Luke, mention it. How
can we account for their silence?

But there is something more, still, to be said. All three
synoptic gospels tell us that after Jesus had taken possession
of the outer court of the temple, having driven out the dove-
sellers and money-changers, the chief priests and the elders of the
people came to him and said, "By what authority doest thou
these things? and who gave thee this authority?" Was not
that the very occasion when a reply reminding them of the
raising of Lazarus was required? An act, if true, certainly
showing superhuman power; an act previously appealed to by
Jesus himself, as proving his claim to come from God; an act
well known to these chief priests and elders; what could have
been urged against Jesus, if he had replied that that was the sign
of his divine authority? Yet, according to all three synoptic
gospels, he makes no reply of this kind at all. He shelters himself beneath the authority of his great predecessor, John the
Baptist. When all these things are considered, is it possible
to believe that the raising of Lazarus was a true fact?

Finally, in relation to the gospel miracles generally, it is
pertinent to remember that Jesus not only always refused to

show a sign (that is to work a miracle) when asked by the
Pharisees to do so, but reproved the request as intrinsically a
wrong one; whereas if he worked his miracles as signs, which
is a conclusion we cannot help drawing even from the synoptic
gospels, when we bear in mind the extraordinary miracles which
they relate, but which is more explicitly stated in the fourth
gospel—the Pharisees ought not to have been altogether reproved,
even though their immediate demand were not complied with.

It is not out of place, again, to refer to that notable sentence
of the apostle Paul; "Jews ask for signs, and Greeks seek after
wisdom; but we preach Christ crucified." (1 Cor. i. 22, 23.)
The "asking for signs" was a natural temptation; we cannot
be surprised if Christians, as well as Jews, fell into it.

I have been obliged in this chapter to dwell on the weaknesses
of the fourth gospel. It has a stronger side; but the exhibition
of this must be reserved for a future occasion.

Let me recur to a sentence which I wrote earlier in this chapter,
before entering on the detailed examination of what is meant,
or should be meant, by the resurrection of Jesus. I said that
the miracles (that is, the really abnormal miracles—and in these
must be included the resurrection from the grave of the dead
body of Jesus) did not satisfy the needs of our conscience.
Having given reasons for disbelieving these miracles as facts,
I may now add that they appear to me to detract from, and
not to add to, the love and reverence we owe to Jesus. That
he died for us is true; but if death to him was quite different
from what death is to us—if the sting of personal apprehension
did not touch him—is our love and reverence equally due to him?
I think not. If the miracles are true as they are related, if he
had knowledge of a pre-natal glorious state to which he would
return without possibility of failure; the true meaning of death
—what death is for us—was not for him. It may be said that
we have the evidence of his agony in the garden of Gethsemane
that he suffered. Yes; but if he had the means, unshared by
any other man, of knowing that he would emerge out of the
tragedy of the crucifixion alive and victorious, that suffering
should not be called the suffering of death. Pain it may have
been; but that is different. It does him more honour to say
that, though he trusted in his own ultimate victory, he did not
absolutely know it; but to say this, is not consistent with a belief
in the knowledge and power attributed to him in certain parts
of the gospels, nor is it consistent with a belief in the Nicene creed.

It will be seen that in the foregoing paragraph I have brought together, as closely allied, the belief in those miracles of the New Testament which are really abnormal, and the belief in the pre-natal glory and dominion of Jesus Christ. In truth these two beliefs will stand or fall together; but yet the connexion between them is not absolute or without possibility of exception. It was the apostle Paul who (as we must judge by the evidence before us) first attributed to Jesus pre-existent dominion and glory; and Paul, though a believer in miracles, was yet in his true spirit adverse to them (as will be seen by the last quotation which I made from him); and he had very little consciousness of any connexion between miracles and the pre-natal glory of Jesus. His belief in the pre-natal dominion of Jesus was founded, first, on his feeling that Jesus was now exercising a power truly divine, and that he, Paul, was himself a witness to this; and, secondly, on his interpretation of the Old Testament prophecies which claimed divinity for the future King of Israel, and Paul, in interpreting the meaning of this divinity, was imaginative rather than critical. I will not deny that Paul was also influenced in some degree by what he regarded as the miracle of the empty tomb, but the other reasons came first with him.

Few Christians, however, were so spiritually minded as Paul; and the desire to represent Jesus as a wonderful person in all the circumstances of his life and in all his actions was too natural for us to be able to ignore it. The questions, "Did Jesus exercise power? does he exercise power?" were not only inevitable, but right; for in the exercise of power the ultimate proof of goodness lies. But those delicate and slow methods in which the greatest powers have their manifestation are but little appreciated by the mass of men; more obvious evidences were required; and this feeling had its natural result in that exaggeration of wonder which the gospel narratives show in all things which related to Jesus.

As regards the Gentile converts, who ultimately formed the whole Christian society, two other motives entered in, which tended to make them think of Jesus as quite separate, in his true original essence, from ordinary men, and as a glorious heavenly being. For first, such a belief took away from the Gentile Christians that uncomfortable sense of being indebted to the Jewish nation, which, if Jesus were regarded as a Jew, it was incumbent on them to feel. But the obligation ought to have been acknowledged; and we, if we think of the Old

Testament as what it truly is, the literature of the ancient Jewish nation, shall be sensible how much we owe to that nation. But next, the contemplation of Jesus as a divine being in his original nature, in a sense not true of other men, made prayer easy; whereas to pray to an invisible God is felt by most men to be difficult. Now far must it be from me to say that any one who can conscientiously declare that Jesus Christ "sitteth at the right hand of God the Father Almighty" (to use a phrase now regarded as metaphorical) may not also pray to him; the belief and the act go together. But the belief is not one that ought easily to be embraced; I believe it true, but it is not written on the surface of history as an obvious fact; and it is not the first beginning of practical religion. Prayer to the invisible God is the proper first beginning of practical religion; and in hours of real need, men do not find it difficult so to pray. Prayer to Jesus Christ enters in afterwards, as part, and an important part, of the interpretation of religion; and after that again, prayer to the holy and blessed departed is natural and right; not because they are necessarily superior to ourselves, but because we are united to them by the tie of love. If any one chose to use the word Trinity to express this threefold heavenly existence, there appears no reason why he should not do so, though I am not urging the use of the term.

It has been by no means my intention, in what I have said in criticism of, and in dissent from, the Nicene creed, to deny that Jesus Christ had a mysterious pre-existence before his human birth. But that this was peculiar to him, is another matter; and in regard to this point, there is one of his sayings that should be considered. It is this:

Call no man your father upon the earth; for one is your Father, which is in heaven. Matthew xxiii. 9.

Jesus of course did not mean to deny the obvious fact of human fatherhood; but he affirmed that the Divine Father, not a human father, was the original author of our being; and therefore the origin of each one of us is mysterious, and not necessarily (nor, I think, reasonably) to be regarded as taking place in time at all. The subject is one in which sensuous experience gives us no help (at least as far as we can discern at the present day) and even spiritual experience appears unavailable; but the mystery which hangs over the origin of our personal being is not to be denied.

The narratives of the virgin birth in the first and third gospels ought not to be left quite without comment. The belief in their truth has had, and has, a great support in their imaginative beauty. But such imaginative beauty, though it is a reason for dealing tenderly with them, is not a reason for accepting them. Nor am I able to think that the state of virginity has any moral superiority over faithful and loving marriage. The beauty of the stories, then, does not really constitute a reason for our believing them. And the New Testament evidence, taken as a whole, is singularly adverse to their being regarded as part of the basis of Christian belief. Perhaps, however, I ought not to argue this point; I have argued enough in this chapter.

This consideration may also dispense me from writing on the subject of the Ascension, when regarded in the physical way in which it is regarded at the close of the third gospel, and in the first chapter of the Acts.

Two Appendices to this chapter will be necessary to clear up certain points as to the origin of the synoptic gospels, and of the fourth gospel, respectively; and the narrative of the life of Jesus, when these critical considerations have been completed, will naturally and in due course follow.

APPENDIX I TO CHAPTER XVI

ON THE RELATIONS OF THE SYNOPTIC GOSPELS TO EACH OTHER

BEFORE entering in detail on the subject of this Appendix, it will be well to consider the natural probabilities as to the way in which literature relating to Jesus Christ would grow up in a community such as we know the first disciples of Jesus to have been. There was more than one reason why such literature should be slow in its growth. In the first place, the disciples of Jesus were not by habit and station literary persons. Many of them, it is true, would be well acquainted with the Scriptures of the Old Testament; and there would be a continual tendency towards the increase of their knowledge on this particular subject, which was so important for the maintenance of their own belief; and the reading of the Old Testament, more especially of the psalms and the prophets, could not but have as its natural effect on the disciples, a desire to write something on their own

account, such as might assist the cause in which they were so
deeply concerned. Moreover, there would no doubt be differences
between them as to the capacity for writing; Matthew, the
tax-gatherer, might be expected to have more practice in this
direction than the apostles who had been fishermen. But
writing for the mere interest in what was written would be
absolutely unknown among them; their primary attention was
needed for their own organisation as a society, on terms of mutual
goodwill and help; the precepts of Jesus which impressed on
them this duty would at first be too vividly remembered to need
to be written down, and the prospect of his imminent return
as their ruler and their judge would seem to render it superfluous
to give sedulous care for the preservation of his maxims in the
past.

Yet in spite of such hindrances as these, the real need of
knowing what Jesus had done and said would make itself felt
more and more as time went on, and as the Christian community
spread beyond those places where its original cradle had lain.
Two pressing needs would be felt; first, as regards the relations
of the disciples to each other, the maxims of Jesus would be
needed for the determination of their conduct; next, as regards
the relation of the disciples to outsiders, it would be necessary
so to describe the deeds of Jesus that he should be felt to have
been endued with the Divine power, and to be worthily the
Divine leader of his own people, Israel. Out of the former need
would arise collections of the sayings of Jesus; out of the latter
need, narratives of his miraculous deeds, of his crucifixion as
a solemnly significant event, and affirmations of his resurrection,
and of his future return, as predicted by himself. As respects
the writings which arose out of this latter need, we have to
remember that the disciples had hardly any historical knowledge
outside the Old Testament, and that that use of the imagination,
which no historian can quite dispense with, and which in all
primitive and simple-minded historians is exercised in an undue
degree, would inevitably lead them to emphasise the wonder in
all the things which Jesus did.

Thus the sayings and the deeds of Jesus would begin to be
written down, and on the whole the record of the sayings would
be separate from the record of the deeds. When once these
records began to be committed to writing, many Christians
would desire to have them; and this desire would be felt long
before anything so elaborate as our present gospels came into

existence. Hence, all over the Christian world, manuscripts would begin to exist, brief or long as the case might be, in which the deeds or the sayings of Jesus, or both deeds and sayings, were related; and in some of these manuscripts a regard would be paid to the true chronological order. As time went on, these fragmentary records would be joined to each other by more or less skilful compilers, until at last an account of the ministry of Jesus during the whole period between his baptism and his death became possible, and entire gospels were built up, of which the gospels of Matthew, Mark, Luke, now familiar to us, have survived. The beginning and the end of Matthew and Luke, and the last twelve verses of Mark, were added at a later date; with these I am not here concerned.

The process which I have been describing as a natural probability has left clear traces of itself as an actual fact in our synoptic gospels. In tracing it, which I will now proceed to do, it must be borne in mind that the process does not imply identity in the exact terms of each narrative, as the narratives finally took shape in each gospel respectively. All manner of causes would enter in to prevent this identity of detail. There would be continual transcription of important documents; and the transcriber would not feel himself under any obligation to transcribe literally. He might be acquainted with another version of a parable or a miracle, which was more agreeable to him than the version which lay before his eyes; he would have no scruple in writing down the version which most commended itself to him, rather than that which he actually saw. Or he might lack time, or he might be insufficiently provided with parchment, for a full transcription; he would then abbreviate his transcription. Or he might rely on memory for details, and write down a rough abstract of the document before him; when he came to expand this abstract afterwards, what he wrote down was sure not to be precisely the same as what he had originally seen.

From these causes would naturally ensue that combination of identity in the general order of narration, with diversity in the several details, of which I will now proceed to give instances. Let anyone take the gospel of Matthew, and begin with the fourteenth chapter, and mark the subjects, whether narrative or discourse, down to the end of the first verse of the twenty-eighth chapter, omitting the following sections: the miracle in chapter xvii. 24–27; the greater part of chapter xviii., from verse 10 to verse 35; the parables in chapter xx. 1–16, chapter xxi. 28–32, chapter xxii. 1–14; the greater part of the discourse in chapter xxiii., from verse 8 to verse 39; the whole of chapter xxv.; and a few incidents in chapter xxvii., viz., verses 3–10, 19, 24, 25, 62–66. (These sections, which are about one-fourth part of the chapters indicated above, have no counterpart in Mark.) Next, let the gospel of Mark be taken, from the 14th verse of the sixth chapter to the end of the second verse of the sixteenth chapter; omitting the miracle in chapter viii. 22–26, and in chapter ix., verses 38–41 and verses 48–50, and in chapter xi., verses 24, 25; also the incident mentioned in chapter xii. 41–44, and the incident mentioned in chapter xiv. 51, 52. The exclusions here do not amount to five per cent. of the whole passage with which I am dealing. The gospels of Matthew and Mark, in that large portion of each which I have selected for comparison, contain, after these exclusions have been made, precisely the same incidents in precisely the same order. To exemplify this identity by detailed references to the entire series of passages of which I am speaking is hardly necessary; but a reference to four successive chapters in each gospel may be made, and will enforce my meaning. Here then are the subjects dealt with, and the exact references, in the gospel of Matthew between chapter xiv. 1, and chapter xvii. 23, in the gospel of Mark between chapter vi. 14 and chapter ix. 32:

Martyrdom of John the Baptist: Mark gives the fuller account.	Matthew xiv. 1–12.
	Mark vi. 14–29.
Feeding of the five thousand: Mark gives the fuller account.	Matthew xiv. 13–21.
	Mark vi. 30–44.
Jesus walking on the sea: Matthew gives the fuller account.	Matthew xiv. 22–33.
	Mark vi. 45–52.
Healing of the sick generally.	Matthew xiv. 34–36.
	Mark vi. 53–56.
Jesus rebukes formalism in religion, and quotes Isaiah.	Matthew xv. 1–20.
	Mark vii. 1–23.
Healing the daughter of the woman of Canaan: Matthew gives the fuller account.	Matthew xv. 21–28.
	Mark vii. 24–30.
General statement of healings in Matthew; a single healing described in Mark.	Matthew xv. 29–31.
	Mark vii. 31–37.
Feeding of the four thousand.	Matthew xv. 32–39.
	Mark viii. 1–10.
The answer of Jesus to the demand for a sign: Matthew gives the fuller account.	Matthew xvi. 1–4.
	Mark viii. 11–13.
The Pharisaic leaven disapproved.	Matthew xvi. 5–12.
	Mark viii. 14–21.
Jesus saluted as the Christ by Simon Peter: Matthew gives the fuller account.	Matthew xvi. 13–20.
	Mark viii. 27–30.

Jesus predicts his own violent death, and rebukes Simon Peter for disbelieving it.	Matthew xvi. 21–23. Mark viii. 31–33.
Jesus bids his followers take up the cross, and predicts the speedy advent of his own kingdom.	Matthew xvi. 24–28. Mark viii. 34–ix. 1.
The transfiguration.	Matthew xvii. 1–8. Mark ix. 2–8.
The questioning concerning Elijah.	Matthew xvii. 9–13 Mark ix. 9–13.
Healing of the epileptic boy: Mark gives the fuller account.	Matthew xvii. 14–21. Mark ix. 14–29.
Prediction of his own death by Jesus.	Matthew xvii. 22–23. Mark ix. 30–32.

The subjects in Matthew and Mark are here identical, and in identical order; and each gospel is continuous, except that five verses of Mark (viii. 22–26) have to be excluded. Looking at this resemblance, recent critics have frequently formed the opinion that our first evangelist had the gospel of Mark before him in writing his own gospel—Mark being in point of date certainly earlier than Matthew. But this opinion, that Matthew directly copied Mark, is not really tenable. For it is plainly not from Mark, but from some other quarter, that Matthew (or the author of the first gospel, whoever he was) got what is narrated in the following extracts: Matthew xiv. 28–31, xv. 24, 25, xvi. 17–19, xix. 10–12, xxi. 14–16, xxvi. 52–54. Yet all these extracts are important parts of narratives told alike by Mark and by Matthew; it is evident therefore that Matthew got his narrative from some other quarter, and not from Mark. Moreover, why should the writer of the first gospel, if he had Mark before him, have omitted so many things which Mark tells? Let me instance the selection of the apostles (Mark iii. 13, 14), the details of the apostolic journey (Mark vi. 12, 13), and the story of the widow's mite (Mark xii. 41–44). But these are merely specimens; many more instances might be given. And why, in all the earlier part of Matthew, from the third to the thirteenth chapter inclusive, should the order of the events narrated differ so much from the order in which the same events are narrated by Mark?

The just inference is that the two gospels, Mark as well as Matthew, were alike compilations; both were copied from earlier sources; and these earlier sources had continually suffered alteration during a series of previous transcriptions.

The parts of the two gospels which I have just put side by side extend, it will be borne in mind, from the fourteenth chapter of Matthew to the beginning of the twenty-eighth chapter, from the sixth chapter of Mark (verse 14) to the beginning of the sixteenth chapter. Now it is an inevitable question, whether our third evangelist, Luke, was in possession of this same source. On looking into his gospel, we see that he was in possession of a part of it, but not of the whole. The whole of the seventh chapter of Mark, and the greater part of the eighth chapter; the narratives of the death of John the Baptist, of the walking on the sea, and of the request made by the apostles James and John; all these, in which Matthew and Mark concur, have nothing correspondent to them in Luke. There are other omissions; on the other hand Luke has a great deal of new matter of high interest and importance. On the whole, if we except his eighteenth chapter from the 15th verse onwards, and the whole of his twentieth chapter, Luke has no minute correspondence with Matthew and Mark after the 50th verse of his ninth chapter.

But if we take Luke from the 31st verse of his fourth chapter down to the 19th verse of his sixth chapter, and again from the 4th verse of his eighth chapter down to the 50th verse of his ninth chapter, we shall find a correspondence between him and Mark in the earlier part of these gospels almost equal to that which we find between Matthew and Mark in the later half of those gospels. The correspondence between Mark and Luke just indicated begins, in Mark, with the 21st verse of the first chapter and goes (with three interposed passages) down to the 44th verse of the sixth chapter; it is resumed in the 27th verse of the eighth chapter and goes down to the 40th verse of the ninth chapter. But it will be best to set down the subjects thus treated by Mark and Luke in the same order in their respective gospels.

Cure of a demoniac, cure of Simon's wife's mother, cure of many persons, sick or possessed, prayer in the desert and preaching in the synagogues of Galilee.	Mark i. 21–39. Luke iv. 31–44.
Cure of a leper, cure of a paralytic, calling of Levi, feast at Levi's house, some notable sayings.	Mark i. 40–ii. 22. Luke v. 12–39.
Plucking ears of corn on the Sabbath, healing of the man with the withered hand, selection of the apostles.	Mark ii. 23–iii. 19. Luke vi. 1–19.
His mother and brethren seek him, parable and sayings (these two parts occur in Luke in reversed order).	Mark iii. 31–iv. 25. Luke viii. 4–21.
Stilling of the tempest, healing of the Gerasene demoniac, raising of Jairus' daughter.	Mark iv. 35–v. 43. Luke viii. 22–56.

Mission of the apostles, mention of the death of John the Baptist (in Mark, a full account of this), feeding of the five thousand.	Mark vi. 7–44. Luke ix. 1–17.
Acknowledgment by Simon Peter that Jesus is the Christ, declaration of the doctrine of the cross and of the speedy coming of the kingdom of heaven.	Mark viii. 27–29; viii. 34–ix. 1. Luke ix. 18–27.
Transfiguration, and cure of the epileptic boy.	Mark ix. 2–9; 14–29. Luke ix. 28–43.
Prediction by Jesus of his own sufferings, the questioning of the apostles as to who was the greater, a story respecting the apostle John.	Mark ix. 30–40. Luke ix. 44–50.

It will be seen that, though there are interposed passages both in Mark and Luke, yet the order of the incidents which they narrate in common is almost precisely the same, as far as the earlier part of these gospels is concerned. But this parallelism is not sufficient, when the differences as well as the likenesses between the two gospels are borne in mind, to warrant us in saying that Luke, in writing his gospel, had Mark's gospel in its entirety before him. A document cognate to a particular part of Mark he had before him no doubt.

As regards Matthew and Luke, they have in their respective gospels as much in common as Matthew and Mark have; but in their arrangement of these common parts they are remarkably at variance; and this to my mind renders it impossible to say (what has of late been supposed) that our first and third evangelists drew the parts of their gospels which they have in common from a single source which they both possessed. It is really simpler to say that their common matter came to them from many sources, and that they naturally arranged their materials differently. Not one of the synoptic evangelists is quite free from challenge in this matter of arrangement; and in Luke especially there are obvious misplacements. But it must be said on behalf of Matthew, that in the important chapters from the tenth to the twenty-fifth inclusive, the first gospel marks the cardinal points in the active career of Jesus with a clearness and force unknown elsewhere. (This striking fact will be brought out more fully in the chapters which follow.)

When all the circumstances mentioned in this Appendix are taken into consideration, we must come to the conclusion that a great many more persons than we now know, or could possibly have known, were concerned in the construction of our synoptic gospels. They are, each and all of them, examples of gradual growth; events and sayings recorded in the first instance separately were slowly put together; the documents relating the deeds and sayings of Jesus became fuller and longer as time went on, and as intercourse between Christians in different parts of the world increased. Yet it was not impossible that a manuscript might be broken up, and some of the differences in our present gospels may have taken rise from this cause. But the separation of a manuscript into two or more portions would be accidental; the design must always have been to build up, so that in the end a full picture of the life of Jesus might be laid before the Christian community. Such a purpose, latent at first, would be more and more definitely conceived as time went on, until our first, second, and third gospels were the result of it; but it is obvious even in these how very little was known of the early life of Jesus.

It will be seen that, from this kind of origin, genuine memory would have a considerable share in the formation of our synoptic gospels. They were, essentially, the popular account among Christians of what Jesus was believed to have said and to have done; and the conscientious character of the first Christians was a security that much truth would be found in them. But though conscientious, the first Christians were very ignorant of natural probabilities; and the pressure of many influences, some internal to the Christian body and some external, would continually enhance the amount of wonder which the written records contained. These motives are sufficient to account for everything which we find in the gospel of Mark, down to the beginning of the sixteenth (i.e. the last) chapter, and for the corresponding parts of the other two gospels. The resurrection narratives were added later, and show us the effect of strong internal impressions (some of them involving true contact with divine powers) on the minds of the disciples, plus a certain amount of visionary experience, the validity of which is still a theme of legitimate inquiry. In the beginning of our first and third gospels, poetic invention is found; this part of our synoptic gospels is, there can be little doubt, the latest of all in its composition.

Additional note on a point mentioned on page 42.

That the gospel of Mark is earlier than our present gospel of Matthew we may infer from the fact that in Mark there is no legend or late accretion, whereas Matthew has these. Yet within our present Matthew a stratum older than Mark does appear.

APPENDIX II TO CHAPTER XVI

ON THE AUTHORSHIP OF THE REVELATION AND OF
THE FOURTH GOSPEL

THE external evidence which connects the fourth gospel with the apostle John, the son of Zebedee, is by no means weak; but it must be remembered that a gospel to which he contributed the principal part of the substance was sure to be named after him, even though the form and arrangement were not his, and though the language had been cleared of grammatical errors or roughnesses (such as those which we find in the book of the Revelation) by the assiduous care of his Ephesian followers.

The nature of the external evidence is this. Up to about the year 170 A.D., it is confined to passages from the early Fathers in which the teaching appears to be drawn from the teaching of this gospel, which (as every reader is aware) is very marked in its character, differing from the earlier gospels and from every other writing in the New Testament except the three epistles which, like the fourth gospel, are attributed to the apostle John. Thus Ignatius of Antioch (*before* 117 A.D.) uses the expression "living water" in the spiritual sense in which that expression is used in the fourth gospel; and he[1] speaks of Jesus Christ as the "bread of God," "heavenly bread," "the bread of life," three expressions which are found in these identical terms (except that in place of "heavenly bread" we have "the bread from heaven") in verses 32–35 of the sixth chapter of the fourth gospel, and are there also applied to Jesus Christ. Does it not seem probable that Ignatius was acquainted with the sixth chapter of the fourth gospel? If not, it would seem that the writer of the fourth gospel was acquainted with the writings of Ignatius; but no one, as far as I am aware, has ever suggested this. Polycarp, again, in the seventh chapter of his letter to the Philippians, begins with a sentence which is a rough quotation from the first epistle of the apostle John (iv. 3). I cannot myself doubt that Justin Martyr was acquainted with the fourth gospel; his scheme of thought is full of the doctrine of the "Logos," the "Word"; and though literal quotations from the fourth gospel are not found in him, yet in his first *Apology* (c. LXI. ed. Otto) there is a passage so remarkable in its resemblance to a passage

---

[1] The letter of Ignatius to the Romans, c. VII.

in the third chapter of the fourth gospel, that it is difficult not to think that Justin had that chapter in his mind; and there are other passages in Justin, which are explicable as references to this gospel, and not easily otherwise. If Justin does not name the author of the fourth gospel, neither does he name any of the other evangelists; and though we can hardly doubt that our four gospels were beginning in his day to have that exclusive authority which they had in the time of Irenæus, thirty or forty years later, it was not so natural to name their authors as it became afterwards.

After the year 170 A.D. the testimony to the fourth gospel is not disputable. It was but little after that time that Tatian compiled his *Diatessaron*, a life of Jesus framed by fitting our four gospels into one narrative; and that Heracleon the Gnostic wrote a commentary on the fourth gospel, known to us through Origen; and that Theophilus of Antioch explicitly recognised the apostle John as the author of it. Irenæus, bishop of Lyons, was an important person in the Christian Church during the last thirty years of the second century; he mentions, in a letter preserved by Eusebius (*Eccl. Hist.* v. 20) that in his early years he had been accustomed to see and hear Polycarp, bishop of Smyrna, who himself had had familiar intercourse with John; and it is difficult to doubt that by "John" Irenæus means the apostle. It is true that there was another John at Ephesus, called by Papias and Eusebius "the presbyter"; but we know nothing of this presbyter John except from Papias (whom Eusebius quotes, *Eccl. Hist.* III. 39), whereas if he had been recognisable simply by his name we could hardly have helped hearing of him in some other quarter. If then Irenæus stood in so near connexion with the apostle John as this letter of his implies, is not his evidence as to the authorship of the gospel a strong point?

These are, I think, the most important, though they are not the only witnesses, to the authority of the fourth gospel in the second century, and either directly or by inference to the apostle John as the author of it. Against them may be set certain Christians of Byzantium, whom their enemies called "Alogi," who denied the genuineness, and indeed attributed the fourth gospel as well as the Revelation to Cerinthus. These "Alogi" are not quite to be forgotten; but still the great preponderance of external testimony is in favour of the authorship of the apostle John.

I come now to the internal evidence. In the first place, was not the author of the fourth gospel (and let me again remind the reader that I am using the word author in a sense which does not exclude a very important editor)—was not the author of the fourth gospel a Jew? Who but a Jew could have written the 22nd verse of the fourth chapter, in which Jesus is represented as addressing the Samaritan woman in these terms:

Ye (i.e. the Samaritans) worship that which ye know not; we worship that which we know; for salvation is from the Jews.

Or look again at the way in which the word "Israelite" is naturally used as a word of praise in the description of Nathanael (i. 47), "Behold an Israelite indeed, in whom is no guile!" Look at the continual references to the Old Testament (i. 23, 45, ii. 17, iii. 14, iv. 5, v. 45–47, vi. 31, vii. 19–23, 42, viii. 52, 53, ix. 28, 29, x. 34, xii. 14, 15, 34, 38–40, xiii. 18, xv. 25, xix. 24, 36, 37, xx. 9), most of them quite separate from the quotations in the other gospels. Look at the thoroughly Hebraic style of the discourses, and of the opening verses of the gospel. I grant the Greek element in the gospel too; but the conditions favoured *both* the Hebrew and the Greek element, and we must no more exclude the one than we must exclude the other.

Consider next this, that the twenty-first chapter of this gospel, which from its style cannot well have been written long after the other chapters, ascribes the authorship of the gospel to "the disciple whom Jesus loved"; and this practically limits the authorship to six of the seven persons mentioned in that chapter, unless we suppose the ascription a deliberate and baseless invention; but if this had been the case, the ascription would surely have been made more precise. The apostle John is one of these six persons; and it is hard to doubt that he is the person at all events *intended* in the penultimate verse of the gospel:

This is the disciple which beareth witness of these things, and wrote these things; and we know that his witness is true.

For could any other disciple have been thought of as "the disciple whom Jesus loved," except one of those three whom we know from the synoptic gospels to have been specially favoured by Jesus—Simon Peter, James, and John? Now Simon Peter is evidently excluded from the possibility of being *intended* by this title, and James from his early death nearly as obviously (for no one could have conceived the gospel to have been *written* by him); who then can be intended but John? This is the natural supposition, at all events.

It must be borne in mind that, according to my view, in the formation of this gospel, the utterances of the apostle John were arranged (in many respects very wrongly arranged), and corrected in point of grammatical style, by his Ephesian followers—by one follower in particular: this is I think a very natural supposition and one supported by the evidence of the last two verses of the gospel; and it takes away the greatest part of the improbability in identifying the author of the Revelation with the main author of the fourth gospel.

But the identification to which I have just referred is very important to my whole argument, and I may be allowed to emphasise in this Appendix what I have said in the foregoing chapter.

The important bearing of such an identification lies in this, that the main author of the gospel is thereby shown to have been a person of extraordinary imaginative power, and imaginative habit of mind; for this quality is seen in the Revelation; we must then be prepared to find it showing itself when he came to write history.

Can any one who reads the discourses in the fourth gospel doubt that the style of the author of the gospel, as well as that of the alleged speaker, is shown in those discourses? Most eminently is the third chapter of the gospel a proof of this; and most remarkable, too, is the parallel between the third chapter of the gospel and the twenty-second chapter of the Revelation, in this respect. Let me point out this parallelism in detail. In the third chapter of the fourth gospel, there are, nominally, two main speakers; Jesus, whose discourse occupies the main part of the chapter down to the end of the 21st verse; and John the Baptist, whose discourse occupies the verses from the 27th to the 36th. Jesus and John the Baptist speak in precisely the same style—and that style is a most peculiar one. But further; though the six verses from the 16th to the 21st are attributed to Jesus, it is impossible from their contents not to think that the author of the gospel has forgotten who the speaker is, and that he has insensibly glided into his own thoughts; for in these verses, Jesus never speaks in the first person, but is constantly referred to in the third person.

Now look at the twenty-second chapter of the Revelation. It begins with the words, "And he showed me a river of water of life," &c., where by "he" is meant an angel (who had come on the scene in chapter xxi. 9). This angel begins the speech in the sixth verse of chapter xxii.: he says, "These words are

faithful and true." But in the remainder of the verse, though
there is no intimation that the speaker has changed, the angel
is referred to in the third person; and in the next verse (again
without any intimation of a change of speaker) we find Jesus
himself speaking—for the words "behold, I come quickly" are
certainly meant to be words spoken by Jesus. Precisely the
same phenomenon—the change of speaker without any change
of subject, and without any notice that the speaker is changed,
is found in the verses of this twenty-second chapter from the
10th to the end (which is the end of the book). In the 10th verse
the angel begins; the words "the time is at hand" are the keynote of what he says; and he continues till the end of the 11th
verse. Then suddenly, without any notice that the speaker is
changed, we find Jesus taking up the same theme, and speaking
in his own person, and continuing, certainly till the end of the
16th verse, possibly till the end of the 17th. But from the
18th verse onwards it is difficult or impossible to think Jesus the
speaker (except of course in the few words "Yea, I come quickly"
inserted in verse 20); but there is no mention of a change of
speaker throughout.

Surely the peculiar practice shown in the third chapter of
the fourth gospel, and the same practice shown in the twenty-
second chapter of the Revelation, came from the same author;
and is it not a practice that belongs, essentially, to an imaginative
mind, to a mind which forgets everything except the main
central theme, and allows other matters to shape themselves
as they will? Can we be surprised if a mind which thought
so imaginatively allowed its imaginative faculty to overflow
beyond the region of discourses into the region of narrated
incidents? And looking at the extraordinary improbability,
which I think I have demonstrated, of the miracle of the raising
of Lazarus (see pages 33 to 35 above), is not the narrative of
that miracle to be explained as the intrusion of the imagination
into the domain of history? It must be remembered that while
I attribute the main part of that imagination to the apostle
John, the style of the narrative was, I think, perfected by the
editor of the gospel, and something in the contents was probably
due to him. Still, the core of this narrative, the conception
of this miracle, came, if I rightly understand the matter, from
the apostle John. And now I ask the question: Was the person
who imagined the interview between himself and the risen Jesus
in the first three chapters of the Revelation, who imagined the

heaven of heavens in the chapters from the fourth to the seventh, who imagined the things that should happen in the sensuous world in the chapters from the eighth to the eighteenth, who imagined the final day of judgment in the nineteenth and twentieth chapters, and the new heavens and the new earth in the twenty-first and the twenty-second chapters—was this person, so compact of imagination as he shows himself in the book of the Revelation, a person unlikely to imagine the miracle of the raising of Lazarus?

But it may be said, Look how the apostle John dwells on the necessity of truthfulness, the iniquity of lying; must he not have been particularly careful always to speak the exact truth? I answer, first, that the extraordinary stress which he lays on the iniquity of lying shows that he was far from realising the difficulty which there is in always speaking the truth; for always to speak the truth is a difficult, not an easy, duty. But next, the apostle John uses the words "truth" and "lying" with a peculiar and special meaning; "Who is the liar," he cries out in his first epistle, "but he that denieth that Jesus is the Christ?" 1 John ii. 22.

Lying, in the literal sense, has not been confined to the persons who have denied that Jesus is the Christ. But what John means is, of course, that the person who denies that Jesus is the Christ is denying the most important of all truths. His exclusive insistence on this point was not unnaturally combined with a certain carelessness as to points which he regarded as of minor importance; and this is precisely the imaginative or poetic turn of mind of which, I am contending, he was an example. I am not thinking or speaking of him with any dishonour; he was by nature half prophet, half poet; and, rightly understood, he was an apostle whom we may love for his ardour, and for his pure response to what he felt to be an inexhaustible fountain of goodness and of love.

However, the task on which I am now engaged is the demonstration of great and important resemblances between the fourth gospel and the Revelation, as indicating a common author of the two books (with limitations and exceptions already stated). One of these resemblances has been shown on a comparison of the third chapter of the gospel with the twenty-second of the Revelation. Let me mention another, from another part of these books respectively.

In the fifth chapter of the Revelation the seer is described as standing in the courts of heaven, in the very presence of God, and in the hand of God is a sealed book. Then a strong angel cries out, "Who is worthy to open the book, and to loose the seals thereof?" But no one in heaven or earth is found worthy to open the book; and the seer weeps much. But now one of the elders who stand before the throne of God intervenes with words of comfort; and this is what he says:

Weep not; behold, the Lion that is of the tribe of Judah, the Root of David, hath overcome, to open the book, and the seven seals thereof.

The seer looks as he is bidden, and continues thus:

And I saw in the midst of the throne and of the four living creatures, and in the midst of the elders...

(What is it that he sees? the Lion of the tribe of Judah, as had been promised him? but no—)

a Lamb standing, as though it had been slain....

Can the reader, with the literature of the world before him, find another instance of so startling a change of metaphor, performed with such ease that the reader hardly feels surprised, and does not smile at the incongruity? Parallel instances to it must, I think, be rare; but the fourth gospel supplies one. It is from the beginning of the tenth chapter, where Jesus is speaking to the unbelieving Jews:

Verily, verily, I say unto you, He that entereth not by the door into the fold of the sheep, but climbeth up some other way, the same is a thief and a robber. But he that entereth in by the door is the shepherd of the sheep. To him the porter openeth; and the sheep hear his voice.... This parable spake Jesus unto them: but they understood not what things they were which he spake unto them. Jesus therefore said unto them again, Verily, verily, I say unto you, I am the door of the sheep.

Jesus here explains his metaphor that he is the shepherd, by saying that he is the door of the sheepfold. The metaphor is changed, exactly as the metaphor in the fifth chapter of the Revelation was changed. Was it not a very remarkable mind which conceived such a change; a change totally illogical, a change which actually destroys the explanation which the words profess to give, and which yet is not felt to be either obscure or unnatural? Can we avoid seeing the probability that it was the same mind which conceived the passage in the Revelation, and the passage in the fourth gospel? Can we also avoid seeing that the writer of both passages was a person who scorned literal exactitude, and cared for nothing but the spirit? And this temper may easily have carried him into descriptions which were of a poetic rather than of a historical character.

But the list of striking resemblances between the fourth gospel and the Revelation does not end here. The tone of authority in the opening of both books is most marked; the writer has no doubt whatever that he will be listened to, and that his utterances will be received with extraordinary respect. He never condescends to argument; his assured confidence makes this needless. Alike in the gospel, and in the first epistle attributed to John, the writer claims to have seen Jesus in the flesh; in the epistle, even to have touched him. If in the Revelation the same is not said in so many words, the tone is what we should naturally expect from one to whom Jesus in the flesh had been personally known. Nor is there less likeness in the way in which Jesus is regarded spiritually. His eternity, in time past as well as in time future, is affirmed in the Revelation, in the epistle, and in the gospel alike. This is expressed in the Revelation by the words, "I am the Alpha and the Omega, the first and the last, the beginning and the end" (xxii. 13); in the epistle, by the words, "That which was from the beginning...the eternal life, which was with the Father, and was manifested unto us" (1 John i. 1, 2); in the gospel, by the opening phrase, "In the beginning was the Word," the Word being afterwards identified with Jesus Christ.

Again, all through the Revelation Jesus Christ is habitually designated "the Lamb"; and the meaning of the metaphor is shown by such expressions as "the Lamb that hath been slain"— "the blood of the Lamb"—the idea being that Jesus Christ was the true paschal lamb, the consummation of the ancient religion of Israel. Now this idea dominates the fourth gospel all through; Jesus Christ is "the Lamb of God, which taketh away the sin of the world" (i. 29); his death on the cross takes place at the exact time when the paschal lamb by the ancient law was slain and eaten (a parallelism that cannot be drawn from the account in the synoptic gospels); and the likeness of Jesus Christ to the paschal lamb is further emphasised by the fact that his bones were not broken, as the bones of the robbers who were crucified on either side of him were. This very remarkable resemblance between the Revelation and the fourth gospel is hardly diminished at all by the fact that the Greek word for "lamb" is different in the two books.

In no part of the New Testament, except the fourth gospel and the Revelation, is Jesus Christ called "the Lamb" or the "Lamb of God"; though there is a passage in the first

epistle of Peter in which the word is used by way of simile—
"the precious blood of Christ, as of a lamb without blemish
and without spot"; and when Paul says (1 Corinthians v. 7),
"Christ our passover hath been sacrificed," the same simile,
though not expressed, is implied. But the conversion of the
simile into a direct appellation belongs to the author of the
Revelation, and the author of the fourth gospel, alone; were
not these two authors one and the same person?

It must not be forgotten, again, that as in the opening verses
of the fourth gospel Jesus is called "the Word," so in Revelation xix. 13 he is called "the Word of God"; and in no other
book of the New Testament is Jesus indicated by this term.

Of minor resemblances between the fourth gospel and the
Revelation, there may be mentioned the "living water" of the
gospel, as compared with the "water of life" of the Revelation;
the frequent mention in both books (and in the epistles attributed
to John) of the idea of "witness" or "testimony"; the frequent
antithesis of "truth" and "lying"; the acknowledgment of some
faithful Jews, and yet the opening of the kingdom of heaven
without reserve to all the nations (John i. 47, iv. 22, x. 14–16;
Revelation vii. 4–10); the declaration that the unbelieving Jews
are children of the devil (John viii. 44), or "a synagogue of Satan"
(Revelation ii. 9, iii. 9).

What is to be said on the other side, against these great
and varied similarities? There is the difference in the language,
rough Greek and inaccurate in the Revelation, smoothly grammatical Greek in the fourth gospel; but still more, there is the
fierce and vehement style of the Revelation, as contrasted with
the gentle and tender style (as it is reputed to be) of the fourth
gospel. But the Greek editor of the gospel might be depended
on to make the language accurate; and as to the style, the
difference between the two books is mitigated by many points
of likeness, and so far as it is real, it is accounted for by the
difference in the circumstances under which the two books were
written. As to the points of likeness; the fourth gospel can be
severe and harsh, the Revelation has passages of exceeding
tenderness. But the circumstances under which either book
was written have still more to be considered. The Revelation,
on its own showing, was written under the sixth Roman emperor
(Rev. xvii. 10), who is either Nero or Galba, according as the
series is considered to begin with Julius or with Augustus. But
Galba is evidently intended; for of Nero it is said, in the next

verse, that he was, and is not—Nero being the "beast." Nero is not named; but we know that he is the "beast," because his number is given in chapter xiii. 18 as six hundred and sixty-six; and the Hebrew letters of Neron Cæsar, when reckoned as numbers and added together make six hundred and sixty-six. (I ought to say that this interpretation of the number is subject to one difficulty, which will be found stated in Renan's *L'Anté-christ*, p. 416; but the difficulty is not sufficiently serious to prevent the acceptance of the interpretation.) Nero then was dead when the book of the Revelation was written; and therefore Galba was then the reigning emperor. But though Nero was dead, the terrible persecution of the Christians which Nero had set on foot was an event not to be forgotten. It could not be forgotten even by the heathen, for Tacitus, who many years afterwards gives an account of it in his *Annals* (xv. 44), tells us that the extreme sufferings of the Christians aroused pity for them even in the hostile population of Rome; and Tacitus himself was hostile to them. Much less could the Christians forget it. Over and above the severity of their sufferings, the two most commanding apostles, Peter and Paul, had been slain in this persecution; and the memory of it is felt as a fount of tremendous indignation all through the book of the Revelation. Rome, says the writer, was "drunken with the blood of the saints, and with the blood of the martyrs of Jesus." (Rev. xvii. 6.) How exactly that corresponds with the description of the sufferings of the Christians under Nero, as related by Tacitus! Every point of the evidence converges to this conclusion, except only the assertion of Irenæus, that the banishment of the apostle John to Patmos, and the writing of the Revelation, took place in the reign of Domitian. Were we to believe Irenæus, it would still be more reasonable to hold that the banishment of John to Patmos took place quite early in Domitian's reign, and was a belated consequence of the persecution instituted by Nero. But this supposition would contradict the evidence of the Revelation itself; for Domitian could not possibly have been described as the sixth of the Roman emperors. Irenæus may very well have formed a casual and erroneous opinion, and so we must believe.

If then the Revelation was written in the year 68 A.D. at a time of terrible tragedy and attempted overthrow of the Christian faith; if on the other hand the fourth gospel, in its first immature sketch by the apostle, was dictated a quarter of a century later,

in the midst of a circle of reverent and admiring friends, at
Ephesus; can we be surprised at a difference in the tone of the
two books? We may be sure that so sensitive a soul as the apostle
John would exhibit the effects of such a difference very plainly.
Thus it appears to me that the difference of tone between the
two books is no more a reason for affirming a difference of authorship, than is the difference in grammatical accuracy. On the
other hand, the likenesses between the two books are numerous,
great, and all-pervading, as I think I have shown. It will be
remembered that Justin Martyr assigns the Revelation to the
apostle John as its author.

The result of the argument in this Appendix is then that
the apostle John, the son of Zebedee, is on the one hand the
author of the Revelation, and on the other hand the main author
of the fourth gospel, though it was a follower of his who arranged
that gospel, corrected it, and finally produced it in its present
form.

CHAPTER XVII

THE LIFE OF JESUS CHRIST

In my last chapter I endeavoured to clear the ground; or in other words, to show what those elements are in the New Testament which do not deserve our trust, and why they do not deserve our trust. I now come to the task of positive narration; which implies that there are some elements in the New Testament which do deserve our trust. The nature and consistency of the narrative which I shall try to unfold must be the real evidence of the trustworthiness, within certain limits, of our authorities, and of the belief based upon their testimony.

Yet, before coming to the actual career of Jesus of Nazareth, let me ask my readers to cast a look backwards. Many systems of noble thought and feeling had arisen among men, and were living and operative, at the epoch when Jesus of Nazareth was born; many yearnings after unity, breathings of the soul upwards; and by these systems men had actually been united, and had been helped to work together. It is true that the manner of this co-operation had been imperfect. While Buddhism attracts us by its inculcation of love and self-denial, it disparages unduly the positive elements of desire and outward energy. So likewise does Brahminism, and with even more serious disparagement of human happiness than Buddhism had shown, though also bringing into play a peculiar refinement of intellect. The Chinese habit of mind had been to make political unity, or in other words the ordinary laws of the state, the framework to which the thoughts and practices of men should cling with attachment; the correctives of this temperament which Lâo-tsze and Confucius introduced were inadequate to produce reform where reform was needed; and though the worship of ancestors was a consecration of tender feelings, it tended to obscure the real root of religion in individual minds. In religion as taught by Zoroaster, far more fervent honour and love was paid to God (under the name of Ahura Mazda) than in the Indian and Chinese systems; the duty of work was taught, and a life after death; but mercy, kindness, and self-denial were left in the background, and corruptions invaded the religion with unusual speed, owing to the ambition of the Magi. The Greek religion attracts our attention, in spite of its great original defects, by reason of the extraordinary efforts made to reform it, and to elicit what was good in it, on the part of the poets and philosophers of that country, among whom Socrates takes the central place; and Greek philosophy was really a unifying influence, and a source of good, though not commanding enough to subdue all the passions of men, especially of the powerful. The Roman republic was characterised from the first by a spirit of command, which naturally united itself to faithfulness in religion; and together with these instincts, and in natural alliance with them, the internal harmony of the Roman state grew up. But when empire had been attained, there was no further ideal for the Roman people to aim at; for their religion did not supply them with one; among the common people it still received a traditional honour, but it had no longer power to sustain the soul. There was something in the Roman spirit which had still vigorous life; but the old Roman religion had for all practical purposes vanished, at the time of which this chapter treats.

Much deeper, much more inspired by eternal truth than any of the foregoing religions, was the religion of Israel; though this too had its weaknesses. The culmination of the religion of Israel, in its pre-Christian form, was attained by the great prophet whose utterances are found in the last twenty-seven chapters of our book of Isaiah. In him we feel the intermingling of present suffering with exalted hope; and in that intermixture lies creative power. He is a patriot, and yet is not limited by patriotism; the universal religion of all mankind appears to be springing up under his hands. But the formation of such a religion demanded action of no ordinary kind; and the practical action of the prophet of whom I am speaking was greatly absorbed in bringing about the return of the exiled Jews to their ancient city of Jerusalem. Hence, though his visions were for eternity, his action was not of equal seminal force; and those who came after him regarded his visions as realisable only in the vague future, while they devoted all their strength to building up the temporal Zion, and to performing the ceremonies of religion

with immaculate perfectness. Ezra and Nehemiah put the seal
on this disposition, and the expansive, the universal element
in the religion of Israel went to sleep for a while. The book
of Daniel, written when the Maccabean wars had just passed
their crisis, reminded the Jews of lofty heights which lay before
them; but how to reach those heights they knew not.

It was in "the fifteenth year of the reign of Tiberius Cæsar"
(as Luke tells us) that the prophetic cry resounded again;
according to our ordinary reckoning, this would be either in the
latter part of 28 A.D., or in 29 A.D.; and the prophetic cry had
now an urgency which it never had had before.   John the Baptist
it was, on the banks of the Jordan, who warned men of their
danger; who warned his own nation emphatically; and yet
the significance of his warning lay in this, that he was addressing
individuals, rather than the nation. "Repent!" he cried; but
it was to individuals, rather than to the nation, that he spoke.
He told his Jewish hearers no longer to rely on their nationality;
if they boasted that they were children of Abraham, he answered
that God was able to raise children unto Abraham even out
of the stones of the wilderness. To each man severally he spoke
of the danger to which each was exposed:

"Even now," he said, "is the axe laid unto the root of the trees; every
tree therefore that bringeth not forth good fruit is hewn down, and cast
into the fire."

Yet we cannot think that he forgot his nation: that emphatic
challenge,

Who hath warned you to flee from the wrath to come?

was addressed, Matthew tells us, to those in whose eyes the nation
was all-important, and ceremonialism the highest command of
God, to the Pharisees and Sadducees; and these were they of
whom he spoke most severely, calling them the "offspring
of vipers." Plainly his condemnation, his threatenings, had
more than individuals for their mark; that very phrase, "the
wrath to come," implied a wide-sweeping terror. His voice was
as a trumpet to rouse all men from slumber; but when they were
roused, he no longer addressed them collectively; his advice,
his counsel, was given to them as individuals. His promises,
too, were not to the nation, but to individuals; each man
separately must present that fruit which would render him
worthy of the kingdom of God. Of such a tone there had been
a premonition in that great prophet of whom I have so often

spoken, the prophet of the captivity; as for example when he said:

I will bring forth a seed out of Jacob, and out of Judah an inheritor of my mountains; and my chosen shall inherit it, and my servants shall dwell there;

it is not the nation, but individuals, to whom the promise is made. The insistence on individual virtue has reached a higher pitch in John the Baptist; he appears as a continuator of the great prophet who lived nearly six centuries before him, but his words have a keener edge. How did he think that the vengeance of which he spoke would fall; in what guise did he think that the kingdom of the heavens would appear? It is very difficult to make precise to one's own thought the large forecasts of the future which animated one living so long ago, particularly when the nation of Israel was ceasing to be the central theme of prophecy, and when something unknown was taking its place. But we cannot doubt that John the Baptist discerned the danger which lay in the temper of the Jewish people; and yet he must have felt also that an upward aspiration characterised many humble souls, who were waiting for the kingdom of God. That a decisive hour was at hand, he held for certain; and both the ancient prophecies and his own temperament led him to say that a Divine presence, or in other words one bearing the Divine power, would be the agency whereby the souls worthy of God would be gathered up into the future kingdom. That office he did not claim for himself, but it would be a reality:

"I indeed baptize you with water unto repentance," he said; "but he that cometh after me is mightier than I, whose shoes I am not worthy to bear: he shall baptize you with the holy spirit and with fire: whose fan is in his hand, and he will throughly cleanse his threshingfloor; and he will gather his wheat into the garner, but the chaff he will burn up with unquenchable fire." Matthew iii. 11, 12.

(The reader will observe a slight alteration from our Revised Version in the above translation; the verbal difference is insignificant, the difference in effect is something.)

All the Messianic prophecies of the ancient Scriptures, John the Baptist felt, were now nearing their fulfilment. I have explained the substance of his preaching, but there are still a few things to add about him. His life of self-chosen privation, and for a considerable time (as we must believe) of solitude, was enforced on him by the terrible nature of the prophetic burden which he bore. As to that repentance, the need of which he emphasised as a necessary preliminary to future rectitude

and happiness, he demanded from those who acknowledged
this need that they should declare their acknowledgment by
a symbolic and visible act; by sitting or standing in the waters
of the river Jordan, while he poured water upon their heads.
This was Baptism; and it expressed, not only the repentance
of those who submitted to it, but also their faith in the cleansing
power of God's spirit. All who were his disciples accepted
baptism; and he had many disciples. He produced great
fruits in the way of amended and purified hearts; and lastly
he was slain, in a manner too well known to be related here,
for his steadfast courage in reproving a crime of the monarch
under whom he lived. One thing only remains to be told about
him; his connexion with Jesus.

To Jesus, then, I now come. If I say that the earliest thing
which we genuinely know about Jesus is his residence at Nazareth
with his parents and his brethren and his sisters, let me be
permitted to refer to the preceding chapter for the justification
of that remark. From a very early age he undoubtedly felt
himself peculiarly near to God, the Almighty Parent of spirits.
The anecdote in the second chapter of Luke, which tells how,
when he was twelve years of age, he accompanied his parents
to the feast of the passover held at Jerusalem, is entirely
probable, and we may accept it as true. He lingered behind
them at Jerusalem, it is said, when they started on their return
to Nazareth. During the first day of their homeward journey
they assumed that he was with some other members of the party
(which was evidently large); but not finding him, they became
alarmed, and hastened back to Jerusalem. There, after three
days, they found him in the temple, sitting in the midst of the
religious teachers, hearing their discourses, and putting questions
to them. His mother remonstrated with him:

Son, why hast thou thus dealt with us? behold, thy father and I
have sought thee sorrowing.

He answered:

How is it that ye sought me? wist ye not that I must be in my
Father's house? (Literally, "in the things of my Father.")

We need not suppose that this answer implied that clear and
absolute perception of the Divine Fatherhood which came to
him after his baptism; but it shows that his habitual thought
was in this direction. His parents, not unnaturally, were
perplexed by the answer; "they understood not," Luke says,
"the saying which he spake unto them." It was however some

eighteen years (taking the marks of time as given by Luke) before he did anything else which could cause them surprise; during all this time he lived at home, the eldest-born of a large family, his brethren and his sisters, as the gospels plainly tell us; and he worked as a carpenter. It is evident, from the surprise of his family and his neighbours when he began a public career, that the deep thoughts of his heart were thus far kept unexpressed, and steadily under control.

Did he pass any of this time in the company of John the Baptist? The chief reason for asking this question lies in the blood-relationship which the third gospel tells us existed between them; but though the relationship is possible, the particular part of the third gospel in which it is affirmed is not of great authority. When, however, Jesus went to be baptized by John in the river Jordan, it is impossible not to think that conversation took place between the two; and in the following most tantalising passage, the first gospel professes to give us that conversation:

> Then cometh Jesus from Galilee to the Jordan unto John, to be baptized of him. But John would have hindered him, saying, I have need to be baptized of thee, and comest thou to me? But Jesus answering said unto him, Suffer it now; for thus it becometh us to fulfil all righteousness. Then he suffereth him. Matthew iii. 13–15.

Supposing that to be a true account (it is unsupported by any other gospel, and though I incline to accept it, we cannot have certainty on the point)—how came John the Baptist to say to Jesus, "I have need to be baptized of thee"? There is an appearance, in view of the context, as if the Baptist were hereby acknowledging Jesus as the Christ: but if this really be the meaning, we must beyond doubt adjudge the words to be an invention and not a fact; for other parts of the gospels make it clear that the Baptist could not at that time have acknowledged Jesus as the Christ. (See Matthew xi. 2; Luke vii. 18, 19; and note also that in John i. 31–34 the words "I knew him not" refer to the whole time up to and including the baptism of Jesus.) Apart however from the context, the words "I have need to be baptized of thee, and comest thou to me," are a simple expression of the feeling of one holy man towards another still holier, deprecating an act that might seem to imply his own superiority. I incline to hold that this is their true meaning, and that they were really spoken; but if they were spoken, what was the ground on which John the Baptist acknowledged Jesus as holier than himself? Some intimate intercourse between the Baptist and Jesus while Jesus was working as a carpenter in Galilee is not quite an impossibility. But a far more probable ground would lie in some conversation (which has not been reported to us, and which we can well understand was not likely to be reported to us) between John the Baptist and Jesus immediately before the brief interchange of words which has been quoted above. It is almost certain that there would be some such conversation. We must not look upon John the Baptist as performing a mere external official function towards the persons whom he baptized; he spoke to their consciences; and how was this possible without conversation with them? Or if we look at it from the side of Jesus, how was it possible for him to offer himself for baptism without setting before the Baptist his reason for so offering himself? There must have been some conversation between the two; is there anything, in the nature of the case, that will guide us as to the purport of it?

Yes, there is something that will guide us; an expression found in both Matthew and Mark, and implied also in Luke; we are told that they who came to hear the Baptist "were baptized of him in the river Jordan, confessing their sins." To confess their sins was an essential preliminary to baptism; it was no accidental addition to the ceremony; it was an intrinsic part of its inward meaning. So it was in John the Baptist's time, and so it is to-day. It is true that, when infants are baptized, the confession on their behalf is generally understood to mean a confession of sinfulness, of the tendency to sin, rather than of positive sinful acts. But if this confession of sinfulness, of a tendency to sin, were taken away, it would be universally admitted that the ceremony of baptism had no spiritual meaning at all. How are we to escape saying that baptism had this meaning for Jesus, as well as for all others who were baptized? and that it involved this confession of sinfulness?

The Christian theologian generally debars this question from the first, on the ground that Jesus, who had voluntarily descended to earth from a glorious divine state in heaven, cannot be conceived to have had any speck of sinfulness at all. Now in the previous chapter I have given reasons for holding that the belief in this voluntary descent is a mistaken belief; and I might therefore simply go on to say that we have no reason for holding that the baptism of Jesus differed from the baptism of any other person in its spiritual meaning, and that therefore it involved the confession, at least, of a sinful nature. But

I will not treat the question on so narrow a ground. The Christian theologian, even on his own showing, cannot ignore the question, what Jesus did positively mean by undergoing baptism. He meant it to be an example to us, some would say. But is it a sincere act to go through the outward form of a ceremony as an example to others, when the ceremony has no meaning for oneself personally? That is surely exactly what one means by hypocrisy; the acting a part, when the inward motive, which the part naturally implies, is absent. Or will it be said that Jesus by his baptism was confessing, not his own sins, but the sins of mankind at large—that he was representing mankind, while decisively separating himself from them? I cannot say that, even on this showing, his submission to baptism appears to me a right act; it involves, as far as Jesus himself is concerned, an absolute reversal of the meaning which baptism is intended to convey; for whereas baptism was designed to imply the sinfulness of the person baptized, it was intended, on this view, to imply the sinlessness of Jesus. I cannot think it right so to reverse the natural meaning of an action. If Jesus desired to confess the sins of all mankind (though there is no evidence that on this occasion he did so desire) he could have done so in explicit terms; and is there any reason why he should not have declared such a motive plainly? Why should he distort the natural meaning of the baptismal ceremony?

Certainly I think we must hold that Jesus did intend to confess his own sinfulness. It is true that, if the first gospel be correct here, John the Baptist must have regarded him as a very holy person. But John the Baptist was not the final judge as to what the spiritual needs of Jesus himself were. It was to God that Jesus addressed himself, when he presented himself for baptism; John the Baptist was but the agent of the Divine Power. When John the Baptist remonstrated with him, he could but say, "Suffer it now; for thus it is befitting for us to carry every righteous act to its completion." (The phrase in our English versions here, "to fulfil all righteousness," has a large sound, as if the baptism of Jesus was the culmination of all the righteous acts in his career; which certainly cannot be the meaning.) Jesus assumes, that in submitting to be baptized, he is performing a righteous act; that this is what God requires of him; he does not argue the matter, but he is sure that John the Baptist will accept what he says. John the Baptist did accept it, and baptized him.

The baptism of Jesus, carried out as I have described, was an act of vital importance for the world, as well as for himself. Let me explain why it was so. It is impossible that he should not have felt, before his public ministry began, that keen sense of ruling power which he exhibited afterwards in dealing with his disciples, and which culminated in his declaration before the high priest, on the last day of his earthly life, that he was the Christ, the Divine King whom Israel was expecting. What was there more necessary, more important for him to acknowledge, at the commencement of such a career, than that he did not regard the station which he assumed as exempting him from that blame to which every human being is at some time or other liable—that he did not regard himself as immune from criticism? Such an acknowledgment was true humility; the humility of a King, a Ruler, a Saviour; but humility still. Can any one think of the history of the Christian Church, and not be sensible that Christian divines have shown a subservience to the literal words of Jesus which has hindered the freedom of their own spiritual perceptions? Is not this precisely the evil which the true meaning of his baptism counteracts and renders impossible? Ought not Christians to be sensible that the Divine Spirit is leading them upwards to truths which were indeed latent in the seed of truth cast into the world by Jesus, but which he himself, with the imperfect means and short time at his disposal, was unable clearly to discern in the course of his earthly career?

The humility of Jesus is often commended; but if by humility we merely mean a poor and suffering life, uncomplainingly accepted, we are underrating the force of the word. Spiritual humility means the consciousness that we may be faulty; and this, as I understand, is what Jesus meant by his baptism. That was true humility, and it received the reward of true humility. Let me quote the account of what happened next from Mark:

And straightway coming up out of the water, he saw the heavens rent asunder, and the Spirit as a dove descending upon him; and a voice came out of the heavens, Thou art my beloved Son, in thee I am well pleased. Mark i. 10, 11.

It is plain, from what followed, that with the hearing of these words a new experience had come to Jesus. When I speak of his hearing the words, I must not be understood to mean physical hearing; it was the interpretation into ordinary language of something which affected his whole spiritual and bodily nature. But what is the meaning of "my beloved Son"? A physical relation cannot be intended; but the reception of living power is intended; and the reception of living power from a Being to whom one bears a certain similarity. As Jesus had acknowledged his own imperfection before God, so the counterbalancing truth now flowed into him from God, that God acknowledged the purpose, the will, the action of Jesus as on the same lines with the Divine purpose and will and action, and that thus from the Divine source new life would always flow into Jesus himself, and new perceptions of God's love to him. That was the meaning of this new experience which took place in Jesus after his baptism. It was an experience which had been dimly felt by prophets[1] and psalmists in the ancient days of Israel, but which now came into clear light; and which was an experience not of Jesus alone, but of all who should recognise the Divine way and follow in the steps of Jesus in the after time. It is true that we cannot create this experience at will; we cannot summon it, as a thing absolutely due to us; but we can depend upon it in hours of spiritual danger. It is the beginning of our true attachment to the kingdom of God; which has indeed begun upon earth independently of ourselves, but which we may aid in all its future development.

Now to meditate on the duties which this new experience entailed upon him, Jesus departed into the wilderness. It was needful for him to be in solitude, and not at present to seek any guidance from man; but solitude had its inevitable dangers, which he had to meet before a true path could be opened before him. The tempter, we read, came to him. Who was the tempter? A personal evil spirit, is the ordinary belief; invisible perhaps, but still personal. Indeed Christians in former days (and many Christians I suppose, even to-day) have believed that the tempter was not merely a personal evil spirit, but a spirit who was the primary author of all evil, whom they call the devil, or Satan. Is there any ground for belief in such a being? I know none in the least adequate. To be tempted to do evil is a very common experience, and there are visible tempters enough in the world; we might even conceive that there are invisible spirits tempting us, though I know of no experience that justifies such a belief. The erring desires and natural ignorances which lie in the hearts of all of us, ready to spring up when circumstances foster them, are a sufficient cause of all the moral evil which I have ever known or read of. Yet even if there were invisible tempters, are we

---

[1] The most remarkable expression of it is in the book of Isaiah, lxiii. 16.

to look for the source of all evil in one invisible tempter? I know of no ground for such a belief, either in natural probability or in positive experience.

To personify an abstraction is, however, in certain cases very natural, and is not unexampled even at the present day, though to personify the spirit of evil is not so common at the present day as it was formerly. But men still personify their native country; an Englishman personifies England, a Frenchman France, a German Germany, very much as if England, France, Germany were actual persons. So likewise, even persons who disbelieve in a personal evil spirit will occasionally speak of the devil as of a person, from old habit. That Jesus himself employed personification in his thoughts when thinking of the tempter, I do not doubt; but it is not easy for us, nor do I think it necessary, to determine with perfect precision what his thoughts were on such a subject[1].

Let us consider the temptations in themselves, as they are recorded for us in the gospels. The two temptations which, in the gospel of Matthew, are the two earlier of the three, have a likeness to each other; they are suggestions that Jesus should, for the purpose of proving to himself that he is the Son of God, work a miracle. The miracle is in the one case to convert stones into bread for the relief of his own hunger, and it will be seen that this has a secondary purpose of bodily relief besides the main purpose that I have named. (He had fasted forty days, the gospels tell us; and we may believe that his food had been very sparing.) The second temptation was that he should throw himself down from a high part of the temple, in confidence that the angels of God would bear him up and preserve him from harm. The immediate ground for this latter temptation lay in two verses of the Psalms:

He shall give his angels charge over thee, to keep thee in all thy ways. They shall bear thee up in their hands, lest thou dash thy foot against a stone. Psalm xci. 11, 12.

Over and above this particular passage, it is evident that the whole tenor of the Old Testament encouraged the expectation that the power of God would be miraculously employed to save his faithful servants from dangers. It might seem then that trust in God would be eminently shown by appealing to him

[1] If one were to try to give a general account of what is meant by moral evil, I think one would say it was a deeply wrong bias, hard to describe explicitly, to which the human heart is by its own nature subject: which, however, the power of God can correct and set right.

to work the two miracles just mentioned; and trust in God was the primary element in the teaching of Jesus. Can we be surprised that these temptations assailed him? Though he had the natural instinct of a sane man against complying with these temptations, yet they seemed to come to him with a certain authority; and his conscience demanded a reason on the side of religion, to show why he should not comply with them. Happily the Old Testament was not devoid of maxims of a sane piety, and the air of duty which had arrayed the temptation was dispelled.

The third temptation was on a wholly different line from the other two, and it is impossible to think it can have rested on the mind of Jesus for more than a moment; yet let me quote the passage of the first gospel which records it:

Again, the devil taketh him unto an exceeding high mountain, and showeth him all the kingdoms of the world, and the glory of them; and he said unto him, All these things will I give thee, if thou wilt fall down and worship me. Then saith Jesus unto him, Get thee hence, Satan: for it is written, Thou shalt worship the Lord thy God, and him only shalt thou serve. Matthew iv. 8–10.

To imagine such a temptation as possible, even for a moment, we have to suppose a reaction in the mind of Jesus from the effort which he had been making to discern in the world of sense a counterpart to his inner conviction that he was God's beloved Son. The world of sense gave no counterpart to it; and we may understand that in this opposition between what he felt and what he saw, the thought might arise that what he felt was wrong, and what he saw was the only true guide; the consequence of which would be that he would worship the spirit of this world, and take the things of sense as the object toward which all his efforts would tend. So might he attain the victory which crowns the conquerors of men in this visible order of things. But such a thought, although entertained for a moment, was too alien from the spirit of Jesus to effect a lodgment there; and he dismissed it, as the gospel records. "Then," to quote the concluding words of the narrative, "the devil leaveth him; and behold, angels came and ministered unto him." In other words, he rested content with the divine influences, not seeking to snatch hastily the fruit which in due course of time was to ripen from the seed which lay in his own breast.

It is a natural question, in regard to the whole incident of which I have been speaking, whether Jesus did actually stand on the lofty wing of the temple and entertain in his mind the question as to the rectitude of throwing himself down, trusting in God to deliver him; whether he did actually climb the lofty mountain and survey cities and provinces lying beneath him; or whether these things only passed before his mind as a kind of vision, as thoughts rather than sensations. There is no reason why they should not have been actual facts; yet the possibility that he beheld and heard all these things in a kind of vision should not quite be forgotten. The nature of the temptations remains the same, whichever view be adopted.

The synoptic gospels do not tell us to what quarter Jesus directed his steps after the time of this temptation was over, nor do they mention any deed done by him or any speech spoken by him until after the imprisonment of John the Baptist by order of Herod Antipas. They do however imply, without directly stating, that he was in the south of Palestine, and probably not very far from the Baptist's place of sojourn. He would be known as belonging to the movement of which John the Baptist was the recognised leader; and the terms are noticeable in which the first gospel relates his return to Galilee:

Now when he heard that John was delivered up, he withdrew into Galilee. *Ibid.* iv. 12.

To withdraw into Galilee was not of course to withdraw from the region where Herod Antipas ruled. But when John the Baptist was imprisoned, his disciples would disperse; was not then the withdrawal of Jesus into Galilee one effect of this dispersal? Those who consider how invariably in the book of the Acts "the baptism of John" is regarded as the starting-point of the movement which Jesus afterwards led (Acts i. 22, x. 37, xiii. 24) will see that the first disciples of Jesus were in all likelihood taken simply from among the disciples of John the Baptist; and if so, the probability is that Jesus had been associating with them for some time before he went back from the south into Galilee. This too is the representation of the fourth gospel, though the fourth gospel adorns the simple fact; but upon this I have written in the foregoing chapter.

With the withdrawal into Galilee the public career of Jesus began: his life-work. Before entering upon it, let me remind the reader of that single verse in the gospels which briefly summarises the years of his boyhood:

And Jesus increased in wisdom and stature, and in favour with God and men. Luke ii. 52.

At the time of which I am speaking Jesus had advanced far beyond the years at which he "increased in stature"; but is it not evident, even from the slight records which we possess, that he had been increasing in wisdom all the time till now— and may he not have increased in wisdom even afterwards? Surely there is no age at which that process ceases, or ought to cease. But who had been his guides and assistants; what was his apparatus of knowledge? A Christian poet of the nine- teenth century, far indeed from wishing to be reckoned among the unorthodox (among whom I must reckon myself), wrote about the childhood of Jesus this touching stanza:

> Was not our Lord a little child
> Taught by degrees to pray,
> By father dear and mother mild
> Instructed day by day?

Surely that, or something like it, was true. But it does not look as if his neighbours in Nazareth were very competent instructors, at any rate in the ethical region; and the probability is that the main part of his acquirements resulted either from his own keen observation of men and things, or from his study of the ancient Scriptures, of which he was clearly a diligent student; or it may be, from some intercourse with John the Baptist. The tremors and aspirations (often wild and dangerous) of his own nation cannot have passed him unnoticed; but the only person who, as far as we know, can have in any degree acted as a guide to him, was the Baptist. That Jesus transcended his guide, is true; but it does not follow that he did not owe something in that quarter. It was a phase of the matter on which the evangelists were not likely to lay stress; but those who attend to the circumstances as they are told us will, I think, be of opinion that this was the case.

The first public preaching of Jesus took place, it would seem, immediately after his return to Galilee; and while renewing the proclamation of John the Baptist, "Repent!" he added to it the inspiration of hope. We may gather this from the form of his preaching given by Mark; let me translate it literally:

The time is fulfilled, and the kingdom of God has drawn nigh; repent ye, and believe (or trust) in the good tidings. Mark i. 15.

"Trust in the good tidings"; in those words there is hope; and with all his might Jesus strove to engraft this temper in those who listened to him. Luke tells us how, when he first

returned to Nazareth, and the volume of Scripture was given
to him to read in the synagogue, he selected the passage:

> The Spirit of the Lord is upon me,
> Because he anointed me to preach good tidings to the poor:
> He hath sent me to proclaim release to the captives,
> And recovering of sight to the blind,
> To set at liberty them that are bruised,
> To proclaim the acceptable year of the Lord.
>
> Luke iv. 18, 19.

That Scripture, he told them, was at that moment fulfilled;
and it was his air and manner, quite as much as his actual words,
whereby they understood that he meant that he was the fulfiller
of it. He had been well received in other places, it would seem,
when speaking in this way; but the people of Nazareth took
offence at it; they thought that they knew Jesus quite well,
and that for him to present himself as a deliverer was both
ludicrous and blasphemous. According to Luke, his life would
have been taken by them, had he not escaped miraculously:
we may believe that he ran some risk. He left Nazareth, and
settled in Capernaum.

The tone which he had adopted at Nazareth was in reality
essential to the message which he proclaimed, and he never
swerved from it. He offered men hope; but what was the ground
of hope? Wealth or power, in the ordinary sense, he had not
to offer. But the inflowing divine strength, which was to him
the perpetual proof and reminder that God had owned him
as his Son, was capable of being communicated to others, if they
would trust him. This it was which prevented the hope which
he offered being a mere abstraction. The favour and love of
Jesus might seem a small and insignificant matter in the eyes
of those who looked at externals only; but to those who felt
that it was of the same nature as the love of God for man, that
it was animated by the same impartiality, the same zeal, and
by a penetrating judgment, the favour of Jesus was precious
indeed. It had the eternal quality in it; and this was a thing,
once apprehended, not lightly to be resigned. The kingdom of
God was indeed the thing to be first sought; the love of God,
the helping power of God, were supreme; but this having been
acknowledged, as every Israelite did acknowledge it, then Jesus
pronounced his own judgments as truly consentient with God's
judgments, offered his own love as a possession never to be
dissolved or diminished, and instructed men with all the fervour

of his spirit to look for those consolations which, as being rooted
in the nature of God, could never be fruitless, never miss victory
in the end.

There were two classes of men towards whom the pity of
Jesus chiefly overflowed, and to whom he chiefly brought his
fervent help and consolation; those who suffered from poverty,
and those who suffered from sickness or bodily defect. To each
he brought hope, but it was hope not exactly of the same order.
The sick he strove to heal; the evidence is strong that he did
heal some of them. But the evidence, when we consider the
bias of the gospels, does not reach to this, that he healed all
who came to be healed; and we can only say (the gospels deserve
this amount of trust) that the healings which he did effect produced
a strong impression. We could wish to know more than the
gospels tell us of his actual words to the sick, and of his air and
manner towards them. The gospels give the note of command,
but not equally that of sympathy. There is a beautiful saying
ascribed to Jesus by one of the early Fathers (from internal
evidence one would say it was genuine): "With those that are
hungry I hungered, with those that are sick I was sick," and so
on in other terms expressive of sympathy with the afflicted. One
would be glad to read more of this in the gospels, and especially
in particular cases of healing; and one would be glad also to
know more of the persons healed. The only one of these who
appears in any other capacity than that of a person healed is
Mary Magdalene, who is important at a particular point of the
history; unless we are to add, as perhaps we should, "Joanna the
wife of Chuza, Herod's steward, and Susanna" (Luke viii. 2, 3);
who were also among those that helped by their pecuniary means
to maintain both Jesus himself and his apostles. It may be
observed in connexion with this point, that though Jesus underwent great privations in the early days of his preaching (as we
should naturally expect, and as the evidence shows), yet this
condition ceased afterwards; and in a general way he was not,
as regards ordinary living, an ascetic.

It is almost unavoidable that we should ask how far we
may regard these healings and restorations of infirmity, carried
out by Jesus so long ago, as examples for ourselves to-day.
They are examples up to a certain point; but as on the one hand
we must not discard the art of healing as a branch of purely
physical science, so on the other hand we must not forget that
the whole method of spiritual healing carried out by Jesus rested

on the principle of trust—of trust, that is, first in God and next
in himself; and trust is not a feeling that we can obtain for
ourselves or command in others at will, but has to be won by
worthy and consistent conduct. Moreover, there is a great deal
of very noble conduct which has perforce to act in a frail body
(the apostle Paul is an instance of this); and apparent difficulties
are not to be escaped in this subject, as in everything which relates
to so profound a thing as life.

As sickness is the most obvious evil which affects the
individual, so poverty is the most obvious evil which affects
society; the evil which, in proportion as it spreads over society,
debilitates it. Nothing was nearer to the heart of Jesus than
to correct this evil by inducing the rich to share their wealth
with the poor. He did not enter minutely into the precise
method which should be adopted in this sharing of wealth; but
there was nothing on which he was more emphatic than that
this should be done. "Give to him that asketh thee," was one
of his primary principles; and though it is a principle which
ought not to be applied with a bare literalness, yet when applied
with judgment nothing can be more important. One does not,
unfortunately, in naming sickness and poverty, exhaust the whole
catalogue of human ills; and having made this remark I now
come to the general early teaching of Jesus, as that is shown
in the Sermon on the Mount.

It is not at all probable that this discourse was ever delivered
as a whole, in the form in which we have it; in fact, though
Matthew collects it into one discourse, Luke disperses it over
many chapters, from the sixth to the sixteenth. Yet Matthew
is the more correct in the position which he assigns to it; for it
no doubt represents the early Galilean teaching of Jesus, at a
time when multitudes were crowding to hear him, and more
intimate disciples were beginning to join him; and certainly
later than the call of those eminent disciples, Simon Peter and
Andrew and James and John, who, while they were fishing in
the lake of Galilee, were summoned with the famous words,
"Follow me, and I will make you fishers of men." At the same
time, the choice of twelve special apostles must be reckoned
to be still in the future.

Before coming to the substance of the teaching of which
the Sermon on the Mount is a summary, let me say something
as to the form of it. At this early date, Jesus utters commands
as a ruler; he is not a mere adviser; he is an adviser who intends

that his advice shall be followed, at the peril of those who disregard it. How different from that noble Greek teacher, Socrates! Socrates said, "I do not know the truth, but I am in search of it." Jesus, with equal plainness, said, "I do know the truth, and woe be to you if you do not obey it!" Now this conviction of Jesus, that he did know the truth, was in itself an individual conviction; but the tone of command in which he uttered it, though in part belonging to his individual character, had yet a support beyond his individual character, which it is very important to observe. All the ancient Scriptures of Israel were full of the thought that a ruler was needed for Israel, and that that ruler would come; and further, that that ruler would come with Divine sanction, with the spirit of God in his heart and with power to make not only Israel but all the nations listen to him and obey him. Real force lay in these prophecies, confirming Jesus in that ruling authority which he felt himself capable of wielding; it was the voice of his own people, calling him; more than that, it was the Divine will calling him, through other channels than that of his own consciousness. He spoke therefore as a ruler, free from doubt; and if any questioned his authority, he did not argue; the future would decide the truth:

"Many will say to me in that day"—so runs one of the latest sayings in the Sermon on the Mount—"Lord, Lord, did we not prophesy by thy name, and by thy name cast out demons, and by thy name do many mighty works? And then will I profess unto them, I never knew you: depart from me, ye that work iniquity."

What is meant by the words "in that day" is not explicitly declared; but the imagination of the hearers would supply the defect.

Such then being the spirit in which Jesus teaches, what is the substance of his teaching, as far as the Sermon on the Mount can give it us? All through that discourse, one uniform feeling reigns; the conviction that an infinite store of power belongs to man through man's infinite parent, God. If we do but act in that spirit of love and faith which is the nearest approximation to the divine character attainable by us, God's inexhaustible energies will be dispensed to ourselves. Those who feel this cannot but esteem it unworthy to grasp inordinately at the good things of this world, or to quarrel about wealth or rank or fame; they will give to others, because by so doing they become partakers of the larger divine life, which is our proper heritage for eternity.

All through the Sermon on the Mount this feeling, that the true believer in God has illimitable riches at his command, is dominant. Thus:

Blessed in the spirit are the poor [such, as I believe, is the true though not the customary translation of the Greek words]; for theirs is the kingdom of heaven.

Blessed are the meek; for they shall inherit the earth.

I say unto you, Love your enemies, and pray for them that persecute you; that ye may be sons of your Father which is in heaven; for he maketh his sun to rise on the evil and the good, and sendeth rain on the just and the unjust.

Lay not up for yourselves treasures upon the earth, where moth and rust doth consume, and where thieves break through and steal: but lay up for yourselves treasures in heaven, where neither moth nor rust doth consume, and where thieves do not break through nor steal.

Be not anxious for your life, what ye shall eat, or what ye shall drink: nor yet for your body, what ye shall put on. Is not the life more than the food, and the body than the raiment?

Ask, and it shall be given you; seek, and ye shall find; knock, and it shall be opened unto you; for every one that asketh receiveth; and he that seeketh findeth; and to him that knocketh it shall be opened.

Such is the primary teaching of Jesus; such, according to him, is the nature of the kingdom of heaven. Let me not be thought to disparage such teaching, if I say that it is not fitted to be an entire rule of conduct for men. What it does furnish us with, is a spiritual atmosphere; these are the sentiments which we ought to aim to translate into action; the powers to which these sentiments appeal are powers which always lie in the background, and we can rely on them to bring a new creation into birth when the wealth, the forces, the gains of this material world vanish and escape from our grasp. Yet still earthly things have their value, and the Sermon on the Mount does not teach us by any direct exposition how earthly things ought to be divided among men or utilised. That question is not meaningless or unimportant; the right division, the right use, of this world's wealth is a problem which is always before our eyes, and which sometimes presses very keenly indeed. Is it possible that a starving man should not feel anxious for his life? Is it possible to see those dear to us perishing for want of food, clothing, and shelter, and not to seek with all our power to supply those needs? Would it be right, even apart from the duty of relieving positive suffering, to abstain from forethought as to the best way in which material wealth can be employed, or from inquiry as to the respective rights of men in the use of

it ? Certainly such problems, such questions, claim imperatively
our attention. The Sermon on the Mount does not explicitly
recognise them at all; and looking at the whole tenor of the
gospels, we cannot say that the early teaching of Jesus gave these
topics any real recognition. His latest sayings and parables,
especially the parable of the talents, show a higher estimate of
forethought and care in the management of earthly things than
the Sermon on the Mount shows; it is possible we may even
conjecture the incident which caused this expansion of his
teaching; it will be mentioned in its proper place.

Yet while affirming this distinction, it must also be remembered
that the Sermon on the Mount assumes a great deal which is not
stated therein in so many words. Though the duty of industry
in the ordinary occupations of life, sowing and reaping, spinning
and weaving, planting and building, is not named, yet the
assumption all through is that all the ordinary works of men
are going on, and such a saying as "Whatsoever ye would that
men should do to you, do ye even so to them," implies a good
deal in the way of positive fruitful action. What is most markedly
omitted, is the way in which self-regarding impulses stimulate
action; but if this theme had been entered on, the strong exhortations towards love might have been weakened; all things cannot
be expressed at once. The great new thing which the Sermon on
the Mount gives us is not direct instruction in the affairs of
this life, but a spirit which elevates us above this life, and which,
indefinite though it may appear to be, is yet of the highest
importance in setting us free from narrowness of outlook and
from the burden of excessive anxiety and sorrow. From such
a spirit a power flows into us which, though originally quite
separate from material things, is an indispensable help in our
use of material things.

Something similar may be said of the exhortations, which
so much strike the reader of the Sermon on the Mount, towards
abstinence from revenge, towards recompensing evil with good.
"Whosoever smiteth thee on thy right cheek, turn to him the
other also," is the maxim in which this kind of exhortation
reaches its height; and certainly one would say that such a maxim
ignores the need of checking violence in itself. It does not follow,
however, that Jesus meant to ignore it; it is the personal desire
for revenge against which he is contending; this, at any rate,
is wrong; compensation for undeserved suffering, punishment
for wrongful violence, are matters which stand on a different

footing, and there is no reason to suppose that Jesus ignored these as rightful motives. I do not know any instance in history in which the maxim just quoted was literally followed, but there have been approximations to it; and even in pre-Christian times, the famous reply of the Athenian Themistocles to the Spartan Eurybiades, "Strike me but hear me," is in the same direction; the importance of the occasion drowned the sense of personal wrong.

In all these maxims, it does not appear that Jesus was influenced by the feeling which so much influenced his followers afterwards, that the world was drawing to a close, and that therefore the distant results of action might be disregarded. All through his teaching he contemplated the world as it is, as being in a state of gradual growth; his affirmation of a future day of judgment was never meant by him to destroy our natural desire to make things better here in this life.

Nor did Jesus ever despise labour. It is true that the labour which he was chiefly practising and inculcating was not that of external duties. It was not the labour of the hands, nor the labour of the intellect, that he chiefly endeavoured to bring under his rule; it was the heart of man, with its desires and passions; that every man shall love and trust God, and love his neighbour as himself, is the final aim of Jesus. Out of this, if it be accomplished, all good will spring. With that accomplishment the sufferings of poverty will be no more, and the dissensions of men will cease.

Another topic necessarily entered into the teaching of Jesus (even into his earliest teaching), and that was the relation which he assumed towards the religion of Israel in the past. He declared his own faithfulness to it; and yet he made it appear that that religion might come to a natural end in the kingdom of God.

"Think not," he said, "that I am come to destroy the law or the prophets; I came not to destroy, but to fulfil. For verily I say unto you, Till heaven and earth pass away, one jot or one tittle shall in no wise pass away from the law, till all things be accomplished."

Such words assume that there is a fulfilment, which shall in itself be an end; a fulfilment and an end, like that of the flower when it passes into the fruit; an end, which is altogether honourable. Honouring in this manner the religion of Israel, he is yet far from being in harmony with its then living interpreters. They are making the law rigid, and neglecting its most fruitful parts:

"Except your righteousness," he says, "shall exceed the righteousness of the scribes and Pharisees, ye shall in no wise enter into the kingdom of heaven."

Is not the position so taken up both conservative and progressive; not breaking with the past, and yet tending to make the future better than the past?

Of the most important of the remaining topics of the Sermon on the Mount, that which concerns marriage, into which some difficult questions enter, it will be best to speak later.

When all is said about the Sermon on the Mount, the most important feature of it is that which I mentioned first, the assumption of an infinite store of spiritual power, accessible to man through God, and creative of a divine order, a divine life, a divine world. This it is upon which Jesus relies in all that he says or does, and on which he bids others to rely, which he bids them appropriate for themselves.

Such was the primary Galilean teaching of Jesus, and it is plain that it had large acceptance and won for him many followers. This does not mean that there was no opposition to his teaching; his very success rendered it probable that there would be such; his censure of the scribes and Pharisees made it certain. He denounced both the literalness of the Pharisaic adherence to the law (as for instance in regard of the Sabbath) and also their additions by tradition to the written law; most of all, their practical preference (so natural to all formal upholders of religion) of ceremonial ordinances to merciful and kindly acts. His own effort was, without representing religious ceremonial as worthless, to make it subordinate to right feeling. Similarly, while not disallowing the practice of fasting, he strove to make it natural and not formal, an impulse of the man himself, known to the man himself and to God, but to none other. Even as respects sacrifices he quoted the disparaging words of the prophet Hosea, who had represented God as saying: "I desire mercy and not sacrifice"; and he had bidden the Pharisees go and learn what this meant. All such teaching could not but arouse the suspicions, and to a certain extent the hostility, of the constituted authorities among the Jews; and Jesus was aware that a conflict was impending. Still the extreme acuteness of that conflict does not seem as yet to have been anticipated by him; and when he addressed his disciples with the words "Ye are the salt of the earth" and "Ye are the light of the world," he could hardly have foreseen the singular loneliness in which he would stand later on, when his decisive action would have to be taken without one follower at his side who understood the meaning or the necessity of it.

For conflict, however, Jesus did prepare himself; and what is more, he had to take the initiative in it; and he did so by selecting twelve out of the total number of his followers to be his special messengers or "apostles"; whose duty it became to spread the teaching and the practice of the kingdom of God, just as he himself was spreading it. Up to this time we have had in the synoptic gospels only five disciples specially named; the four already mentioned, Simon and Andrew, James and John; and a fifth, Matthew the tax-gatherer. It would not seem that any of these five had so far abandoned their homes or their ordinary way of living. (Matthew the tax-gatherer is called Levi by Mark and Luke, in the passage where his call to be a disciple is mentioned; the two must be identical unless our first gospel be under a mistake, which is hardly likely.) The twelve apostles consisted of the five just named, and also Philip, Bartholomew, Thomas, James the son of Alphæus, Thaddæus (or according to our third gospel, Jude), Simon the Zealot, and Judas Iscariot.

From our first gospel it would appear, and it is very credible, that it was a feeling of compassion in Jesus for the erring multitudes of his countrymen, which led to the appointment of the twelve apostles.

"Then saith he unto his disciples," we read, "The harvest truly is plenteous, but the labourers are few: pray ye therefore the Lord of the harvest, that he send forth labourers into his harvest."

Luke also tells us that before appointing them he continued all night on the mountain praying to God. The step was immediately recognised as significant: the twelve apostles were symbolic of the twelve tribes of Israel: Jesus stood out as a national leader far more clearly than before, and yet he had made no direct claim. It is probable also that he had already begun to speak of himself as "the Son of man"; a phrase which has various connotations. It may mean simply "man," and something of this most general sense attaches to it in the verse:

The Sabbath was made for man, and not man for the Sabbath; so that the Son of man is lord even of the Sabbath.

But even in this verse there is the implication that Jesus himself has an intimate relation with all the sons of men, and this is the

most general sense of the phrase; but beyond this there is also
a reminiscence in it of ancient prophecy. Ezekiel writes of
himself as so addressed by the divine voice; and still more we
may be sure that Jesus had in his mind that passage of Daniel,
in which it is told how "one like unto a son of man" was brought
before "the Ancient of days," and received "dominion, and
glory, and a kingdom, that all the peoples, nations, and languages
should serve him." (Daniel vii. 13, 14.) It was beginning to be
evident that, though Jesus was not exalting himself above the
message that he was delivering, he was yet exalting himself;
he proclaimed the kingdom of God, but his actions intimated
that if men wanted to learn what the kingdom of God was,
he alone could teach them. Such a conviction, if untrue, was
arrogant; but if true, was unavoidable and not arrogant.

However this might be, it was certainly dangerous to be
thought to aim at leadership; and the relations of Jesus (living,
as far as we know, still in Nazareth) became afraid for him, and
perhaps for themselves too; they declared that he was out of
his mind, and went to try to apprehend him (Mark iii. 21). But
Jesus was much too strong for such coercion, and nothing came
of the attempt. At the very same time, as Mark tells us, some
scribes came down from Jerusalem, seemingly for the purpose
of reporting on his doings; their conclusion was unfriendly:
"He hath Beelzebub, and by the prince of the devils casteth he
out the devils." It would seem that this was said in his presence;
his answer was strong and effective; but when he added, "Whosoever shall blaspheme against the Holy Spirit hath never forgiveness, but is guilty of an eternal sin," we cannot but trust that
the mercies of God may prevail in the end even over that sin,
whatever the letter of the passage may seem to imply. These
last words, according to both Matthew and Luke, were preceded
by others intended to show that the offence committed was not
against himself personally:

"Whosoever," he had said, "shall speak a word against the Son of
man, it shall be forgiven him." Matthew xii. 32.

Immediately after this, according to Mark, an incident
occurred, which Matthew and Luke place considerably later;
but Mark appears to be right; and in fact, the greater part of
the twelfth chapter of Matthew, where this narrative occurs,
rather belongs to the ninth chapter, in which a few verses of it,
with slight alterations, do actually occur. If this transposition

were made, Matthew and Mark would be fairly in agreement. I will now quote the account in Mark:

And there come his mother and his brethren; and, standing without, they sent unto him, calling him. And a multitude was sitting about him; and they say unto him, Behold, thy mother and thy brethren without seek for thee. And he answereth them, and saith, Who is my mother and my brethren? And looking round on them which sat round about him, he saith, Behold, my mother and my brethren! For whosoever shall do the will of God, the same is my brother, and sister, and mother. Mark iii. 31–35.

Is not that a very plain intimation that his mother and his brethren were not doing the will of God? If they had been, then "brother and sister and mother" would have been terms truly applicable to them, and Jesus would have hastened to meet and acknowledge them. What, then, were his mother and his brethren doing which was not according to the will of God? Is it not plain that they came on an errand similar to, though not the same as, that on which his "relations" or "friends" had come previously? The previous attempt had been forcibly to prevent his preaching; this was to persuade him to desist from it. On this ground, and on this ground only, can we understand Jesus refusing an interview to her who, of all others, stood in the nearest natural relationship to him. For the present, though not finally, his own family were standing aloof from him.

The twelve apostles, and some women, were now his nearest companions. It would not seem that he sent the apostles out on a mission immediately after their appointment; but at last he did send them, and gave them instructions. They were to preach as he had preached, to heal as he had healed, to secure, if possible, that thorough renovation of men's minds and hearts which Jesus accounted the most needful of all tasks. The danger against which he most guarded them was the danger of timidity. That they were in the position of command, that the new order of things was to issue out of their preaching, he did not suffer them to forget. There must be no hesitation in them, and no fear. They were to ask for the needful bodily maintenance from those friendly to them; they were to tell the unfriendly, that in the day of judgment, Sodom and Gomorrah would be visited with lighter sentence than they. That such bold procedure would subject his apostles to danger, Jesus knew well; he told them that they would be as lambs among wolves; but their safety would lie in their fearlessness. God would protect his own; and even if they were slain, their souls would live.

Matthew gives a whole chapter (his tenth) to these instructions to the apostles; but he certainly includes among them some sayings which really belong to a much later date. Thus the verses from the 17th to the 22nd of that chapter are placed by Mark (and more correctly) among the sayings uttered during the last days at Jerusalem; the 23rd verse is also conspicuously antedated; so also, I cannot but think, are the verses from the 34th to the 37th, and above all the mention of the cross in verse 38. It was the habit of the first evangelist to collect the sayings of Jesus into great groups, and on this occasion his habit has misled him in the matter of chronology. On the other hand, Mark and Luke are rather too brief at this particular point.

The apostles were sent out to preach and to heal; they performed their mission, and returned from it; but it is evident that the results of it fell far short of what Jesus had hoped. Mark and Luke try to intimate success, though with great reserve; and it may at first be thought that Matthew says nothing at all on the subject; but the eleventh chapter of Matthew, though hardly professing to treat of the mission of the apostles at all, is really, from what it implies, very eloquent as to the failure of that mission. Let me quote from that chapter, which is one of the most remarkable in the gospels. It begins thus:

And it came to pass, when Jesus had made an end of commanding his twelve disciples, he departed thence to teach and preach in their cities.

That can only mean that Jesus followed after his apostles, to assist and correct them, as each had need. However, at last the mission was over; the apostles had returned; and we may take for granted that some if not all of them were with Jesus during the scene which is next described. For now it is told how John the Baptist, who from his prison had heard of the deeds of Jesus, sent disciples to ask of Jesus the direct question, whether he were "he that cometh," or in other words the Messiah or the Christ. Jesus, without directly answering the question, bade the messengers observe what he did; and certainly, if the account is at all correct, he did some things that may well excite our wonder. However, as I said in the preceding chapter of the present work, where I treated of this incident rather fully, it was not the wonder of his doings, but the degree in which they contributed to the happiness and well-being of mankind, on which he desired to lay stress; nor (I may add) was it his own personality that was primary with him, but what he could effect for the amelioration of mankind. The messengers of the Baptist departed; and now Jesus was stirred to review the whole situation. What is the burden of his discourse? What is the feeling which is uppermost in his mind? It is dissatisfaction, most energetically expressed. The results of his preaching, and of the preaching of his apostles, had so far been of very small importance indeed.

Not, indeed, that Jesus had not had successes with individuals, and his apostles also may have had such; and even at this moment he had a remarkable measure of fame in his own country. But the solid framework of society had not yielded to his preaching one jot; the rich had abated nothing of their riches, the needy were still in need, hatreds were rife, contempt and scorn were common even between members of the same family. If Jesus did no more than he had done up to that time, his whole work would be swept away, as the work of countless reformers has been swept away, and no memory of it would be left in the thoughts of the generations who came after him. History, if it named his name at all, would speak of him but as an agitator who had failed; the citadels of the world would continue their serene defiance of his animadversions, and nothing would check the tendency, which an evil selfishness must create, towards universal decay.

That, Jesus determined within himself, should not be the end! His first words however, after the messengers had departed, were tranquil. He praised John the Baptist; none greater than he had been born among the children of men; yet when the kingdom of heaven should appear, even one of small consideration in that kingdom would excel the Baptist. But as to the children of the generation that then was, they were deaf, alike to the preaching of the Baptist, and to his own. They would neither listen to the teacher who reproved them from his severe ascetic solitude, nor to the teacher who mingled with them in their ordinary hours of cheerful converse.

We note that it was to "the multitudes" that Jesus was discoursing in this way; it was not any want of hearers of which he could complain; but the deeds of men exhibited no corresponding change. In Bethsaida and Chorazin and Capernaum the same unseemly appendages of civilised life were going on as had always gone on; thefts, murders, adulteries, fornications, imprisonments, executions, judicial floggings, divorces of wife from husband; and those in the high places of society cared not. Against the complacent tolerators of iniquity Jesus launched the divine malediction:

Woe unto thee, Chorazin! woe unto thee, Bethsaida! for if the mighty works which were done in you had been done in Tyre and Sidon, they would have repented long ago in sackcloth and ashes. Verily I say unto you, It shall be more tolerable for Tyre and Sidon in the day of judgment, than for you. And thou, Capernaum, shalt thou be exalted unto heaven? thou shalt be brought down to the place of death; for if the mighty works had been done in Sodom, which were done in thee, it would have remained until this day. Verily I say unto thee, it shall be more tolerable for the land of Sodom in the day of judgment, than for thee.

(It is worth observing, that the literal translation of the word rendered "mighty works" in the above passage, is "powers"; "the powers that were in thee.")

With the cities of the world Jesus was now at war; for it is not to be supposed that Bethsaida and Chorazin and Capernaum were worse than other cities of the time. And here, in this denunciation of the cities of Galilee, we have the turning-point in the whole career of Jesus. Direct victory, direct attainment of his aims, he saw, was not to be his. He had, it would seem, hoped for it before; he did not hope for it now. He was thrown back upon himself; partly upon the consideration of that measure of success which he had really won, small in comparison with the conversion of the world, but not to be despised as an earnest of future attainment; and even more profoundly he was thrown back on the reasons which he had for belief in his own divine mission. The reversion of his temperament to thankfulness, hope, and peace after the outburst of indignation just quoted is most memorable, and I must quote his words in their entirety:

I thank thee, O Father, Lord of heaven and earth, that thou didst hide these things from the wise and understanding, and didst reveal them unto babes: yea, Father, for so it was well-pleasing in thy sight. All things have been delivered unto me of my Father; and no one knoweth the Son, save the Father; neither doth any know the Father, save the Son, and he to whomsoever the Son willeth to reveal him. Come unto me, all ye that labour and are heavy laden, and I will give you rest. Take my yoke upon you, and learn of me; for I am meek and lowly in heart; and ye shall find rest unto your souls. For my yoke is easy, and my burden is light.

Such words show the profoundest trust in God, and the conviction that Jesus himself stood alone among men in his knowledge of the counsels of God. That conviction was a just one; yet none the less we must apply our own judgment, when we read his words, to the matters treated of. Let me take the above passage in detail:

I thank thee, O Father, Lord of heaven and earth, that thou didst hide these things from the wise and understanding, and didst reveal them unto babes.

What things? The necessity of a pure and good life, with trust in God; and over and above this, trust in Jesus himself, as carrying out the will of God.

All things have been delivered unto me of my Father.

True; and we have only to remember that in the kingdom of heaven, what is given to one is not taken away from another. Partnership in consciousness of the Divine Spirit is better than the solitary possession of it; the happiness which comes from God is not diminished when it is shared. As all things were delivered to Jesus Christ by his Father in heaven, so are all things delivered to us; but this is not the same thing as saying that we are the equals of Jesus; there is an order in the kingdom of heaven, which we cannot rightly disregard.

No one knoweth the Son, save the Father.

Such had been the experience of Jesus in his intercourse with men; and when we consider how far his most trusted disciple, Simon Peter, fell short of understanding the doctrine of the cross, when first presented to him, we cannot be surprised at Jesus feeling that no one knew him save his Divine Father alone:

Neither doth any know the Father, save the Son, and he to whomsoever the Son willeth to reveal him.

We must not suppose that Jesus meant to deny that a true and deep knowledge of the Divine nature had been attained by the ancient prophets on whose writings he did himself so largely rely, and to whom he so often referred. He held indeed that their knowledge was in itself incomplete, and was preparatory to his own; but it was not this that he intended to express in the verse just quoted. He was rather thinking of the men of his own day, who were going wrong in their conceptions of God's will; and against their mistaken thoughts he affirmed that he himself knew God's will truly, and could teach it to others.

Come unto me, all ye that labour and are heavy laden, and I will give you rest. Take my yoke upon you, and learn of me; for I am meek and lowly in heart, and ye shall find rest unto your souls. For my yoke is easy, and my burden is light.

Though the vision of crucifixion was almost dawning on the soul of Jesus, it could scarcely have been clearly before his mind when he uttered these last words; for the cross was no light burden. But his meaning was not directed to that kind of suffering which arises from the sins and follies of men, and which the bravest and best may have to undergo without any fault of their own; he did not mean to say that he was delivering men from all suffering of that sort. But what he meant to say was that the duty which God himself of his own nature and will imposed upon men was not a duty that involved extra-ordinary suffering; that the natural duties of man, which belong to him simply because he is man, are such that the heart of man leaps up spontaneously to meet them; and while certainly they cannot be accomplished without trouble, they receive such assistance both from God and from the higher nature of man himself that no one would complain of such a burden. And towards the real nature of these duties he affirmed that he could direct men, setting them free from artificial laws and customs of the world.

I have explained the above passage from the eleventh chapter of Matthew at some length, because it is often interpreted simply as a passage of transcendental doctrine about Jesus himself; whereas in reality it overflows with natural human feeling; the feeling, it is true, of a man who is heart to heart with God; but a feeling, none the less, caused by the circumstances and the experience of the moment, and not to be understood without reference to those circumstances. There is, of course, something transcendental in the passage, as there was in all the thoughts of Jesus; but the heavenly is mixed with the earthly, the con-templative with the practical. And while the passage does to a certain extent vindicate the authenticity of well-known expres-sions of Jesus respecting himself and his participation in the divine nature, which the fourth gospel reports, there are yet distinctions to be drawn; it is not every saying in the fourth gospel which can be thus vindicated. But the question of the discourses in the fourth gospel must be put off till I come to a later period in the life of Jesus.

I have been depicting occurrences which led to a change,

a remodelling, of the purposes of Jesus. He no longer hoped to convert the whole body of his fellow-countrymen. His work henceforth was selective; it was no longer an attempt to convert the Israel which he saw; it was an attempt to form out of the Israel which he saw the elements of a new and spiritual Israel. When, in his earlier teaching, he had said to his hearers, "Ye are the light of the world," he had meant it to apply not only to those who were sitting before him; the words applied to all who had received the law and the prophets, the great centres of true religion. But now it was plain that they who had received the true religion in form had not received it in spirit; "the children of the kingdom" were, as a body, unfaithful. Jesus accepted the fact, and emphasised it by instituting a new method of teaching, the teaching by parables. The parables separated those who cared to hear and understand from those who did not; if the negligent and scornful people wanted to cavil at his teaching, they should at least have some difficulty before their cavils began.

In fixing this as the time of the commencement of the teaching by parables, I follow the first gospel against the second, which puts the commencement of the parables considerably earlier, and before the mission of the apostles. That Matthew is right appears from the whole bearing of the narrative (I may be permitted to call our first evangelist by the familiar name, though it may not be exactly correct). The first of the parables, the parable of the sower, shows clearly that a large part of the nation were rejecting the teaching of Jesus, and is a natural sequence to the eleventh chapter of Matthew, which states the fact of this rejection. Is it necessary for me to quote the well-known parable? The division of men into those who hear the word and dismiss it without a thought, those who hear the word and are frightened by the persecution which the practice of it entails, those who hear and are seduced from it by pleasures, and lastly the good souls who hear and obey it, is clear proof that many had resisted the teaching of Jesus; but even more decisive is the colloquy with his disciples which intervened between his telling the parable and his explanation of it. Let me quote the colloquy in full:

And the disciples came, and said unto him, Why speakest thou unto them in parables? And he answered and said unto them, Unto you it is given to know the mysteries of the kingdom of heaven, but to them it is not given. For whosoever hath, to him shall be given, and he

shall have abundance; but whosoever hath not, from him shall be taken
away even that which he hath.   Therefore speak I to them in parables;
because seeing they see not, and hearing they hear not, neither do they
understand.   And unto them is fulfilled the prophecy of Isaiah, which
saith,

> By hearing ye shall hear, and shall in no wise understand;
> And seeing ye shall see, and shall in no wise perceive;
> For this people's heart is waxed gross,
> And their ears are dull of hearing,
> And their eyes they have closed;
> Lest haply they should perceive with their eyes,
> And hear with their ears,
> And understand with their heart,
> And should turn again,
> And I should heal them.

But blessed are your eyes, for they see; and your ears, for they hear.
For verily I say unto you, that many prophets and righteous men desired
to see the things which ye see, and saw them not; and to hear the things
which ye hear, and heard them not.   Hear ye therefore the parable of
the sower.   Matthew xiii. 10–18.

I need not pursue the passage into the actual explanation of
the parable.   But it is evident that the state of things thus
described is precisely the same as that described two chapters
earlier in the same gospel, where the obstinate impenitence of
the Galilean cities is contrasted with the faithfulness of the
followers of Jesus.   We may conclude, then, that the teaching
by parables dates from, and was a consequence of, the discovery
which Jesus had made, that his fellow-countrymen as a whole
were not with him; and this discovery was the result of the
mission of the twelve apostles.   The situation had had precedents
in the earlier history of Israel, as of course the passage of Isaiah
shows.

But it was very clear that however many parables Jesus
might utter as problems for his unbelieving fellow-countrymen
and as instruction for his attached disciples, the society which
he was calling into existence had as yet a frail basis.   Out of
it might come the regeneration of the world, if it could be made
to endure; but what would make it endure?   The gospels tell
us nothing about thoughts of Jesus in their incipient stage;
they tell us only his thoughts in their mature and final expression;
but the question, how to give permanence to the society of
disciples which he was establishing, was one that deserved,
and no doubt created in him, deep pondering and much prayer.
The wanton murder (for it was no less) of John the Baptist
by Herod Antipas, could not lighten the problem for Jesus.

If the first gospel is correct, the disciples of the Baptist came and themselves[1] told Jesus the sad news; and Jesus withdrew into the desert on hearing it. After this, in consequence of the crowds that followed him, there took place that incident which is known as the "feeding of the five thousand," an incident remarkable doubtless, but one from which the miraculous element is withdrawn, if we suppose (as I have argued in the foregoing chapter) that the inquiries of the apostles, respecting the amount of food which the multitude had brought with them, were not so perfectly conducted but that a good deal escaped notice, and was not produced until there was real need for it.

From the desert country Jesus returned to the populous parts of Galilee; and controversies which he held with the Pharisees are now recorded. Into the details of these it is not necessary to enter. But the demand that he should show a sign appears to have been recurrent; and one of the answers which he gave to this demand (at an earlier date, perhaps, than that at which I have arrived) is worth a moment's notice. He said:

An evil and adulterous generation seeketh after a sign; and there shall no sign be given to it but the sign of Jonah the prophet.

What was the sign of Jonah the prophet? I do not doubt that the late R. H. Hutton was right (in his *Theological Essays*, p. 266) when he said that the sign intended was the proclamation of Jonah when he entered Nineveh:

Yet forty days, and Nineveh shall be overthrown.

This is a meaning entirely natural and one which carries us back to the stern warning of John the Baptist and forwards to sayings of Jesus himself shortly before his crucifixion; it also suits the whole context in Luke (xi. 29–32). It is true that the first gospel interprets the "sign" as being the three days and three nights which Jonah spent in the whale's belly (Matthew xii. 40); but this is a far less forcible interpretation; it is liable to obvious objections; and we may easily believe it an afterthought, either of the evangelist himself or of some one whom the evangelist followed.

---

[1] Here there is a curious example of our first and second evangelists interpreting differently the brief statement of the authority which each evangelist had before him. In each gospel, somebody tells Jesus something; in Matthew it is as above; in Mark, it is the apostles who tell Jesus of their own doings. Though Luke supports Mark, I incline to the version in Matthew; it is more natural where it stands.

Just about the period with which I am dealing, there is a verse of Mark which may attract our attention (Mark vii. 24):

And from thence he arose, and went away into the borders of Tyre and Sidon. And he entered into a house, and would have no man know it; and he could not be hid.

Why should Jesus seek retirement? Surely that he might think over the problem before him. He had in his possession (to quote his own parabolic language) a pearl of great price, a hidden treasure; or, to use another of his similes, he had sown a seed, and was now watching the tender blades of the crop emerge out of the soil. Yet the pearl of great price, the hidden treasure, might even now be stolen from him; the tender crop was not yet safe from the accidents of storm and drought. How was he to secure that which he was guarding; how was he to make the crop one that would multiply unto eternity? It was to meditate on this problem, as we may reasonably believe, that he retired from the land of Israel into heathen parts. But "he could not be hid," says Mark; and the work of healing which succeeds is too touching to be omitted. I will quote it from Matthew, whose narrative here excels Mark's:

And behold, a Canaanitish woman came out from those borders, and cried, saying, Have mercy on me, O Lord, thou son of David; my daughter is grievously vexed with a devil. But he answered her not a word. And his disciples came and besought him, saying, Send her away, for she crieth after us. But he answered and said, I was not sent but unto the lost sheep of the house of Israel. But she came and worshipped him, saying, Lord, help me. And he answered and said, It is not meet to take the children's bread and cast it to the dogs. But she said, Yea, Lord; for even the dogs eat of the crumbs which fall from their master's table. Then Jesus answered and said unto her, O woman, great is thy faith: be it done unto thee even as thou wilt. And her daughter was healed from that hour. Matthew xv. 22–28.

The narrative has an undercurrent, and the manner of Jesus must have been from the first more relenting than his words; and in the end his yielding to the pathos of the woman's entreaty takes away all that may have seemed hard in his previous answers. But we can hardly avoid thinking that there was something which was turning the mind of Jesus away from that practice of healing with which he was so conversant. Some purpose must have been before him other than that involved in the immediate scene; the fact of the woman being a Canaanite was not the real cause of his tardiness in listening to her. If this is so, what was that purpose? Surely it was the momentous question, by what course of action he could make the planting of the kingdom of heaven upon earth a planting for eternity. That was the supreme question for him.

It ought not to be impossible, and it cannot be without deep instruction for us, to endeavour to follow those thoughts which led Jesus to the conclusion that in his own death lay the vital root, out of which the kingdom of God would eternally grow upon earth.

Chief among these thoughts must have been the obligation to preach the kingdom of heaven in that place, at that time, and in that manner, which would leave an impression never to be forgotten. That place must be Jerusalem; the time must be the feast of the passover, when Jerusalem would be, more than at any other time, crowded with faithful Israelites from all parts of the world; but what must be the manner? Here the ancient Scriptures came to his aid: they told how Israel was to expect a king, a deliverer; and was not he himself a deliverer? Must not he present himself as such? And was not he himself, who knew the counsels of God as none else did, the true king of Israel? That conviction had been long in him; it had inspired his words, his actions; but if he went up to Jerusalem it would lead him, he foresaw, into actions that would bring him into direct collision with the Jewish hierarchy; for the Jewish hierarchy were blind, and it was necessary to point out their blindness in unmistakable terms. What would be the immediate result of this collision? That he himself would be slain; for he would naturally appear as a disturber of public order, and the deep reasons which justified that disturbance were outside the vision alike of the Jewish hierarchy and of the Roman authorities. Moreover, he neither could nor would defend himself by physical force.

Was it then in accordance with the counsels of God that he should die; that he should be crucified, according to the habitual Roman manner of punishing criminals? Would this be the appointed path for him who was to lead mankind into the kingdom of God? Surely this question must have presented itself to Jesus as a question, before he gave it the affirmative answer which he did give. It must have been about the time of which I am speaking that he first gave it the definitely affirmative answer; but the possibility of it must have been before him earlier; and who shall say how long? The dawn of memorable thoughts is seldom accurately determinable. When he told his apostles,

"Fear not them who kill the body," the possibility of his own
violent death cannot have been out of his view; but this is not
the same as a definite prevision that it would happen. The
definite prevision had come to him now; the natural causes
were manifest, and the ancient Scriptures confirmed the prevision.
That he was acquainted with the chapter which is numbered
as the fifty-third of Isaiah we could not doubt, even had we
not been told (Luke xxii. 37) that he quoted one of its clauses;
and in that chapter the death of the suffering servant of God
is the immediate cause whereby he enters upon his heavenly
rule and his saving office towards his fellow-men.

"Therefore," writes the prophet, "will I divide him a portion with
the great, and he shall divide the spoil with the strong, because he poured
out his soul unto death, and was numbered with the transgressors; yet
he bare the sin of many, and made intercession for the transgressors."

How clear an indication this must have been to Jesus of the
path which he must follow, every one can see. So too, the
passage in Daniel (vii. 13) which gives a mysterious dominion
and glory to "one like unto a son of man," who was brought
before the Ancient of days "with the clouds of heaven," would tend
to fix the mind of Jesus on something beyond the present life,
and would divest a violent death, regarded as the close of his
earthly life, of any improbability. The Psalms, from the tenor
of many of them, would convey the sequence of suffering and
glory as natural to him who is favoured by God, and passages
in other prophets, especially in Zechariah, would have a like
bearing. The expression in Malachi (iii. 1), "The Lord, whom
ye seek, shall suddenly come to his temple," though not containing any mention of suffering, would make the proclamation
of the kingdom of God in the temple at Jerusalem appear specially
appropriate.

But having brought the career of Jesus down to the epoch
of this momentous resolution, it will be best to show the consequences of it in a new chapter.

CHAPTER XVIII

THE LIFE OF JESUS CHRIST—CONCLUDED

It is of the bravest act that ever was done by man that this chapter must tell; the bravest, because the keen suffering involved in it was not doubtful but certain, and because the anticipation of that suffering was vivid in Jesus for months before it took place; and, also, because ordinary human experience gave no prospect of a recompense, since with that suffering the life of Jesus in the flesh would terminate.

It would indeed be the reverse of truth to say that Jesus had no prospect of a recompense at all for those sufferings which he foresaw that he would endure. But the prospect was of a kind which to most men would have seemed too doubtful for any trust to be placed in it. Really and ultimately, it was God's justice on which he relied; this was the root of his confidence, without which all other grounds would have been illusory; if he, Jesus, were doing God's work, he felt sure that, even though he died, God would not abandon him. The justice of God was the basis of the action of Jesus all through the crisis which I am about to narrate; and his confidence in the justice of God was derived from his experience of God's love, of God's loving intercourse with him; for, as I remarked when treating of the Socratic philosophy, love is the sole root out of which justice can spring. By many signs within himself, by much experience drawn from his dealings with others, Jesus was well assured that the love of his heavenly Father was truly extended to him.

While, however, the personal experience of Jesus was the central ground of the assured confidence with which he acted, it would be wrong not to add that the prophets and psalmists of ancient Israel gave him an additional and much needed support. Prophet and psalmist had known that suffering, and even death, must precede victory; and their teaching had penetrated into the soul of Jesus. The mysteriousness of the whole subject did indeed create difficulties which it was impossible for Jesus fully to clear away, and the form of his predictions of the future was far from exact, if we judge it by the standard of modern science. But in all his predictions, nothing was said wantonly; there is guidance in them, even when, as is frequently the case, the first literal material meaning of the sayings has to be discarded.

Prescience of the future we may justly claim for Jesus, though exactitude of prescience was impossible for him; but that which binds us to him is the love, faith, and courage which enabled him to transcend this visible sphere, and not only to grasp eternity as his own heritage, but to give all mankind the same heritage as their own. This was his task, most ardently carried out in the closing period of his earthly life; and it is now necessary to show the details of his action, as the gospels record them for us.

Though he knew that he was to die, it would be very incorrect to say that to die was his primary purpose. His primary purpose was to preach this truth, that loving and merciful actions can never cease to be obligatory on us, can never cease to be the essence of a good character, whereas ceremonies cannot help changing and external bonds of union are liable to be shattered; and he was compelled to give a point to this teaching by taking the instance of his own nation, the Jews, and telling them that they were relying on bonds that were external and transitory, and were neglecting that universal love to which God was calling them as their true part, and that this error of theirs would bring them to ruin. Such preaching was his purpose; but his death was the seal which ratified the purpose as eternal.

To win his disciples to this cause; to make them understand that a new procedure was necessary, different from any that they had seen in him before, or had undertaken themselves; that the apparent scandal and shame of what would happen to him was in reality the reverse of shame, and the entrance into a divine career; this was now imperative on him. If his disciples shrank back, his purpose could not be carried out; but he trusted and believed that they would not shrink back.

However, the trial had to be made. It cannot have been long after his return from the heathen country, where, as I have said, he seems to have gone to meditate on the course which he should take, that he went with his disciples (by which we must understand his twelve apostles, though it does not follow that others were not present) into the region of Cæsarea Philippi, quite in the north of Palestine; and there the following scene took place, which I will quote from the fullest description that we have of it, that in the sixteenth chapter of Matthew (verses 13–20):

Now when Jesus came into the parts of Cæsarea Philippi, he asked his disciples, saying, Who do men say that the Son of man is [or, that I am, according to Mark and Luke]? And they said, Some say, John the Baptist; some, Elijah; and others, Jeremiah, or one of the prophets. He saith unto them, But who say ye that I am? And Simon Peter answered and said, Thou art the Christ, the Son of the living God. And Jesus answered and said unto him, Blessed art thou, Simon Bar-Jonah; for flesh and blood hath not revealed it unto thee, but my Father which is in heaven. And I also say unto thee, that thou art Peter, and upon this rock I will build my church; and the gates of Hades [or, "destruction"] shall not prevail against it. I will give unto thee the keys of the kingdom of heaven; and whatsoever thou shalt bind on earth shall be bound in heaven; and whatsoever thou shalt loose on earth shall be loosed in heaven. Then charged he the disciples that they should tell no man that he was the Christ.

There was a fervour in Simon Peter's answer that went beyond mere assent; it was rapturous assent; and Jesus felt that here was solid ground on which he might build. His doubt, whatever doubt he had had, as to the ability of his followers to continue his work, was dispelled. Here was one through whom, even though he himself were slain, he would continue to work; the kingdom of God would continue to grow upon earth. And was it to grow quite separately from Jesus himself? Was Jesus not to be a witness of the fruit of his own labour and suffering? Assuredly he believed that he should not only be a witness, but the chief in this exalted state, coming in the glory of his Father. But how this was to happen, cannot be said here; and before proceeding further, the last clause of the passage just quoted must attract our attention.

Why should Jesus bid his disciples keep silence on so important a matter as their conviction that he was the Christ? (It is clear that Simon Peter's declaration had been accepted by all the apostles as their own.) There was first this reason; the assumption of the title of Christ involved real danger; and though that danger could not be avoided, it ought not to be unduly hastened; Jesus alone, and not his apostles, could properly judge when that danger ought to be accepted; or in other words, at what moment the danger to Jesus personally ceased to be commingled with danger to the cause of which Jesus was the champion.

But there was a greater reason still for this injunction of silence. Irrespectively of all question of danger, the cause of the kingdom of God came first, the honour of Jesus himself came second, in his own estimation; it was only when the teaching of the kingdom of God had been thoroughly understood, . of what nature it was and what it involved, that the position of Jesus, as the leader of mankind into that kingdom, could properly be understood and proclaimed. Now then, after Jesus had ascertained the faithfulness of his disciples to himself, their acknowledgment, not only of the kingdom of God (for this had been implied from the very beginning of their discipleship), but also of Jesus as the supreme instructor and guide into that kingdom —now does he pursue that instruction, give that guidance, by communicating to them what his own action was henceforth to be, and what their action must be in sequence to his own, and modelled upon his own. Never before had he told them what he was now about to tell, and indeed it was not very long that the pressing duty before him had dawned on his own consciousness. Here is that duty plainly declared; I continue the quotation from Matthew (chapter xvi. 21–23):

From that time began Jesus to show unto his disciples, how that he must go unto Jerusalem, and suffer many things of the elders and chief priests and scribes, and be killed, and the third day be raised up. And Peter took him, and began to rebuke him, saying, Be it far from thee, Lord; this shall never be unto thee. But he turned and said unto Peter, Get thee behind me, Satan: thou art a stumblingblock unto me: for thou mindest not the things of God, but the things of men.

The first remark which may naturally be made on this passage concerns its authenticity, as a record of facts. Would any Christian, at the time when narratives respecting the career of Jesus were being gathered together (which must certainly have been during the life-time of Simon Peter), have ventured to invent the story that Jesus addressed that great and vigorous apostle with the words "Get thee behind me, Satan"? I feel sure that this was impossible to invent, especially when it is contrasted with the fervent commendation that had been bestowed by Jesus immediately before. No thought of man could have conceived that contrast, had it not been true; and yet the whole is perfectly in accordance with the character of Jesus.

Moreover, though the reproof to Simon Peter looks severe (and it is this prima facie strangeness which proves that it could not have been invented), there is no deep blame intended by it.

If Peter had taken the part of a tempter, it was from loyalty, not from wantonness or conceit, that he had done so. He desired to protect the honour of his Master; but he had no desire to dispute that Master's right to judge. No doubt the thought had occurred to him that the heroism of Jesus was passing the bounds of sanity; this is rather implied in his first words, of which "God have mercy on thee, Sir[1]!" would be the truest translation (and this appears, excepting the last word, in the margin of our Revised Version). But the decisive words of Jesus overbore that thought in him; and we may be sure that no offence was either intended or taken on either side.

But the culmination of the passage last quoted lies in the prediction of Jesus that "on the third day" he should be raised up. The same prediction occurs twice after this in the gospel of Matthew (xvii. 22, 23; xx. 17–19) as part of a general prediction of his sufferings and death; three times in Mark (who writes "after three days" instead of "on the third day"); and twice in Luke. What was the ground of this prediction? The general thought of living again, and ruling men after being put to death, was no doubt drawn by Jesus (in so far as it had any external sources) from the great prophet of the captivity, whose words I quoted towards the end of my last chapter. But why "on the third day"? It is possible that the turn of the phrase was suggested by some words of the prophet Hosea, at the beginning of his sixth chapter:

Come, and let us return unto Jehovah; for he hath torn, and he will heal us; he hath smitten, and he will bind us up. After two days will he revive us; on the third day he will raise us up, and we shall live before him.

It is probable in any case that the words "on the third day" mean an unknown, but not very distant time; for there is another passage in which this meaning appears to be the only admissible one. The passage to which I refer occurs in the gospel of Luke (xiii. 32, 33), and is the reply of Jesus to those Pharisees who, whether with friendly intentions or not, gave him a warning to depart from the dominions of Herod Antipas, as that monarch was minded to kill him. (This incident must have taken place

---

[1] The word "Kyrie" is translated "Sir" in our versions when anyone else but Jesus is thus addressed: see Matthew xxvii. 63, John xii. 21; and also under special circumstances when Jesus is addressed, as John iv. 11, xx. 15. I admit that variation could not entirely be helped: but "Sir" should in my opinion be used in some cases where it does not now appear.

during the last journey of Jesus to Jerusalem.) The reply of Jesus ran thus:

> Go and say to that fox, Behold, I cast out demons and perform cures to-day and to-morrow, and the third day I am perfected. Howbeit I must go on my way to-day and to-morrow and the day following: for it cannot be that a prophet perish out of Jerusalem.

It is clear that exactitude in time is not here intended; nor is it probable that it was intended in the phrase which I am now considering, that Jesus should "be raised up on the third day." At the same time this being "raised up" is clearly regarded as a not very distant event. But the full thought of Jesus is shown in the words which follow, down to the end of the chapter, which I must now quote:

> Then said Jesus unto his disciples, If any man would come after me, let him deny himself, and take up his cross, and follow me. For whoso-ever would save his life shall lose it; and whosoever shall lose his life for my sake shall find it. For what shall a man be profited, if he shall gain the whole world, and forfeit his life? or what shall a man give in exchange for his life? For the Son of man shall come in the glory of his Father with his angels; and then shall he render unto every man according to his deeds. Verily I say unto you, There be some of them that stand here, which shall in no wise taste of death, till they see the Son of man coming in his kingdom. Matthew xvi. 24–28.

Nothing can be clearer than the kind of anticipation which these words imply. After the violent death of Jesus himself, voluntarily undergone; after the violent death, also, of many of those who follow him, the pure and brave souls who had trusted God and loved man; then, and after no long time, but within the natural lifetime of some of those whom he addressed, the kingdom of God should come. Jesus, the Son of man, raised up from death, shall in that new state of things administer perfect justice, and shall assign to every man the lot which he has deserved. It is not necessarily implied that the resurrection of Jesus "on the third day" is coincident with the coming of the kingdom of God, or in other words with the coming of "the Son of man in the glory of his Father with his angels"; but the two events are not supposed to be very far apart; they are part of the same series of occurrences. What is to be the form and character of the kingdom of God, when it is once established Jesus nowhere says; his teachings are entirely concerned, with the preparation for that event. The whole object of the teaching which I have just been explaining is to prepare his disciples for present suffering, and at the same time to fill them with a transcendental hope, a hope of glory at no remote time.

Thus did Jesus impart to his favoured disciples (to the twelve apostles, I suppose, especially, but we are not told precisely who were present) his first sketch of what he believed on that great subject, the future of the world. It will be better for me to reserve my comments; for he spoke again on the same subject, and in more detail, a day or two before his crucifixion; and what we are to think on the subject, and on the foresight of Jesus respecting it, will better be determined when the whole of his sayings are before us.

The next event recorded in the synoptic gospels is proof how great a strain of high imaginative feeling possessed the mind of Jesus at this time, and in a considerable degree also the minds of his chief apostles. It was six days after the conversations just recounted that he took the three most favoured by him, Simon Peter, James, and John, "up into a high mountain apart." He was transfigured (we are told) before them; "his face did shine as the sun, and his garments became white as the light." And then, Moses and Elijah appeared and talked with him: but Luke makes an addition which must not be forgotten. "Peter and they that were with him," says Luke, "were heavy with sleep: but when they were fully awake, they saw his glory, and the two men that stood with him." The novelty of the situation, the solitude of the mountain, together with the state of sleep out of which the apostles had just awaked, all combined to deepen the impression made on them; and when we learn that they told no man till long afterwards what they had seen (Luke ix. 36: and compare Matthew xvii. 9, Mark ix. 9) we see that imagination in the matter had large opportunity to expand itself. At the same time, the presence of Moses and Elijah cannot have been primarily due to the imagination of the apostles. It was Jesus himself, we cannot doubt, who called upon these two, the ancient lawgiver and the ancient prophet, to converse with him; and did they truly come? We cannot penetrate so far into the secrets of the invisible world as to say that they did; all we can say is that there are possibilities which lie beyond our experience. But we can well understand that Jesus wished to lay his cause before the ancient representatives of Israel, and to be assured that the spirit in which he was acting was not unfaithful to the true spirit of those who had received guidance from God in the past: and it was doubtless he himself who called upon those great souls to be with him, who, as Luke says, "spake of his decease which he was about to accomplish at Jerusalem." We must not complain of these lofty imaginations, or be surprised that the apostles accepted them as unquestionable truths; and the naïve materialising of the whole conception by Peter cannot surprise us either. "Master," so we are told he said, "it is good for us to be here; and let us make three tabernacles; one for thee, and one for Moses, and one for Elijah"; not knowing what he said, Luke adds. It certainly is not an easy task to determine how far external reality can belong to such apprehensions of the supersensuous world; but it is important to remember that it is not a record of sensuous impressions, nor do I think that Peter in his true mind held it to be so.

It was on the descent from this mount of the transfiguration that one of the most naturally told of the healings accomplished by Jesus took place—the cure of the epileptic boy—and I think we should believe it to be a true narrative, with but little adornment, if any. It may be that about this time Jesus carried out that secret journey to Jerusalem at the time of the feast of tabernacles of which the fourth gospel tells us: we cannot accept all the adornments which the fourth gospel attaches to that journey, or believe that Jesus remained long in Jerusalem at that time; but in the journey itself there is nothing improbable.

When did the last great journey to Jerusalem, which terminated in the triumphal entry just before the feast of the passover, begin? We cannot say for certain. The gospel of Matthew gives two chapters to this journey, Mark gives one chapter, Luke apparently ten; but it is certain that much in these ten chapters is misplaced, and ought to come earlier or later. The three accounts must be more or less interwoven by us, if we wish to obtain the best understanding of the history possible; the fourth gospel is not available here, for reasons explained in my sixteenth chapter.

My own feeling is that a month is not at all too long a time to assign to this last journey, and it may have been longer; for though the journey from Galilee to Jerusalem could be accomplished in much shorter time, still it was not only in Jerusalem that Jesus was desirous of producing an effect; he could not treat the other parts of the country as of no account. It would appear that his first intention was to go the direct way through Samaria. Everything would lead us to believe that the disposition of Jesus towards the Samaritans was friendly; and there may be truth in the famous narrative of his conversation with the Samaritan woman, recorded in the fourth chapter of the fourth gospel, though it is impossible to fix the exact time of that conversation. Still it was no doubt his own people, the Jews, to whom he primarily appealed, nor did he ever swerve from this preference; and his followers are likely to have had more feeling against the Samaritans than we can attribute to himself. Hence, when he began the journey through Samaria, we find that he was stopped at the first village, "because his face was as though he were going to Jerusalem." So Luke tells us (ix. 53); and it is implied in such a phrase that the party which accompanied him was a large one. Had he been alone, or accompanied only by his twelve apostles, it is not likely that he would have found any difficulty in traversing Samaria; but a large number of followers would make a difference in the matter. If he had only a few hundreds following him, we can understand that the Samaritans might refuse a passage through their country to so large a number of enthusiastic Jews, bent (as might be supposed) on exalting the honour and glory of Jerusalem. In reality, it is not at all unlikely that he had at that moment a following of more than a thousand. The gospels represent him as being followed by thousands in Galilee; and it is difficult not to think that he was followed by several thousands on the occasion of his triumphal entry into Jerusalem; for the number of his followers certainly produced an impression. If we say that Jesus had, at the moment of which I speak, considerably more than a thousand followers in attendance upon him, we shall not be overrating their probable number; and it is a confirmation of this that Luke tells us very shortly afterwards of his sending out seventy disciples "to every city and place, whither he himself was about to come." This implies that they went to prepare the way for him; but had he not had a large number of followers, seventy would have been a needless number of messengers to prepare the way for him. It is almost impossible not to think that Luke exaggerates the apostolic office of these seventy disciples, of whom we have no account elsewhere. That they preached, is probable, in view of the fervour of all the disciples of Jesus at that time; but their principal office, it seems certain from Luke's own words, was to prepare the way in that last journey of Jesus which then was beginning. And this implies that the number of his followers was great.

It is to be observed that Matthew and Mark give an undesigned confirmation to this narrative of Luke about the Samaritans, when they represent Jesus as making his way to Jerusalem not by the direct route through Samaria, but by crossing to the east of Jordan and descending the river on that side.

Among those who accompanied Jesus on this last journey were, as we see from what is told us afterwards, his mother and his brethren. When was it that he had brought them over to the cause? We cannot tell with certainty; but a probable time is that visit of his to Nazareth which is told by Matthew and Mark considerably before the scene at Cæsarea Philippi. (Matthew xiii. 54–57; Mark vi. 1–5.) Their presence during all this period is buried in an obscurity which contrasts strongly with the importance of James, one of the brethren, in the after history, and with the still more transcendental glory assigned by later generations of Christians to the mother of Jesus.

It was after the crossing of the Jordan by Jesus that the Pharisees asked him a critical question: "Is it lawful for a man to put away his wife for every cause?" On the side of an affirmative answer they invoked the authority of Moses; and though the passage of Deuteronomy to which they doubtless referred (xxiv. 1, 2) hardly sanctions divorce absolutely without cause, it gives the husband great power of divorcing his wife. But Jesus, while allowing that for the hardness of men's hearts it might be proper for the legislator to give such permission, will not allow that it is intrinsically right; a man and his wife are one, and the union must not be rescinded. To this general prohibition Jesus, according to Matthew, admits one exception; a man may divorce his wife if she commits fornication. But Mark and Luke make no mention of this exception, and it cannot be held certain that Jesus ever uttered it. It is not indeed quite in his manner to balance a maxim by an explicit exception. We must remember however that Jesus is speaking of what is right in God's sight, and not of what human law, in all the complex circumstances of life, should ordain. Human law, though it must not forget what is absolutely right, cannot always enforce this on men, and must not always withdraw its protection from those who act on lower standards; and it hardly seems possible to deny that human law ought in certain cases to recognise divorce as legitimate, as indeed nearly every country does at present.

No reflecting person will deny the great difficulty of this

whole subject, and also its exceedingly great importance; but when we ask what help Jesus has given mankind towards solving the difficulties of it, there is a particular part of his sayings which has not received sufficient notice; moreover there is a saying of his, not reported in the New Testament, but vouched for on good authority, which will give us some light.

We read that, when Jesus had affirmed his prohibition of divorce at the mere will of the husband (for this he certainly did affirm), the disciples answered:

If the case of the man is so with his wife, it is not expedient to marry.

This reply does not in form controvert what Jesus had been saying, but it certainly does so in spirit: it means, "Then we are in a bad case indeed! how are men to get on?" What is more, Jesus admits the difficulty:

"All men," he says, "cannot receive this saying, but they to whom it is given. For there are eunuchs, which were so born from their mother's womb; and there are eunuchs, which were made eunuchs by men; and there are eunuchs, which made themselves eunuchs for the kingdom of heaven's sake. He that is able to receive it, let him receive it." Matthew xix. 11, 12.

To understand this answer, we must bear in mind that it is being applied to the case of a husband who dislikes his wife, and would gladly divorce her. That divorce Jesus declares to be wrong in God's sight; whereupon the husband asks, "How shall I obtain that happiness which is the natural result of wedded life, seeing that it is now debarred to me by the uncomely aspect or the ill deserts of my wife?" The answer of Jesus then is, "Seek not that alliance which lies in earthly union; seek that alliance which lies in heavenly union; the fountain of love will arise out of that source, and with love will come happiness." It is with reason that he adds, "All men cannot receive this saying"; but it does not follow that it is not the true solution, for those who can receive it. Some allowance must always be made for the weakness of men, and this precludes our visiting with too severe censure those who fall short of ideal conduct in their relations with others; and similarly, human law cannot always demand that a justly offended husband or wife shall forgive wrongs, though to forgive may be a diviner course than to exact a penalty. It is another question, whether divorce may sometimes be, not merely a course allowable by human law or pardoned by public opinion, but the absolutely true and right course. This must be, I think, at any rate rare; for it is at any rate the frustration of a divine hope; but a hasty answer ought not to be given to a question of this sort in the abstract. The most important practical question is, whether adultery or serious cruelty ought to be pardoned or not; and it is hard to deny that there are cases beyond pardon.

Illustrative of this whole subject is that answer of Jesus to which I referred above, which is not found in the New Testament, but the genuineness of which rests on very fair authority. He was asked, it is said, when the kingdom of God would come; and his answer (quoted in the epistle called the second epistle of Clement—really a sermon dating from the early part of the second century) ran thus:

> When the two shall be one, and when that which is without shall be as that which is within, and when the male with the female shall be neither male nor female.

For what this answer affirms is that the ordinary sexual union between husband and wife is based on a deeper spiritual union, in which sex is forgotten; when that deeper spiritual union is attained by husband and wife, and animates the actions of both, then the kingdom of God will have begun on earth; then desires will produce their natural fruit of a blameless happiness. There is not implied herein a suspension of the ordinary laws of generation upon earth; but the union of spirit with spirit is greater than the union of body with body, and has a command which the other lacks.

There are, of course, possible misinterpretations of the maxims of Jesus on which I have been commenting, but I need not linger on these. In all his own dealings with women, it is manifest that he regarded them as, in God's sight, the equals of men.

The conversation on which I have just been commenting took place in Peræa, the province east of the Jordan. It would no doubt be in this region that Jesus received a warning from certain Pharisees as to the hostile intentions of Herod Antipas, and answered them in the terms which I quoted above, towards the beginning of the present chapter.

It could not have been long after this that an incident took place, which shows us, on the one hand, that that divine spirit which Jesus bore was not the same thing as an absolute perfection of judgment under all conceivable circumstances; and also that Jesus himself was capable, as we all ought to be capable, of learning by experience. The occasion was one on which a difficult question was put to him, which had to be answered on the spur of the moment; and both the question, and the whole incident, deserve our careful consideration.

In all the earlier teaching of Jesus, and notably in the Sermon on the Mount, the doctrine taught respecting property is hardly distinguishable from what in modern times is called communism. It is inculcated on men that whatever riches they possess they hold for their neighbour's benefit as well as for their own, and that they must give freely to those in need. This is in many respects a very salutary doctrine, greatly needing to be impressed on any organised society; for the working of an organised society is generally, through obvious causes, unduly favourable to its wealthier members; added to which, those who have failed to obtain a place in the organisation are apt to suffer severely. Still the doctrine in question must not be pressed without consideration of its consequences. If money is given to a worthless idle fellow, he will squander it on worthless purposes; and still more must it be borne in mind that those engaged in important work generally need funds to carry on that work, and to divert those funds to other purposes may mean serious loss to the whole of society. It is one of the hardest tasks before mankind at the present day to strike a balance between the duty of seeing that none should starve, and the duty of directing work into its most profitable channels. In a perfect society, all would work, none would starve; but society never has been perfect and is not so to-day. In the earlier teaching of Jesus the principle that "none ought to starve" takes a decided precedence over the principle that "all ought to work"; and this preference culminates in the event to which I referred above, and which I will now quote as narrated by Mark (x. 17–27):

And as he was going forth into the way, there ran one to him, and kneeled to him, and asked him, Good Master, what shall I do that I may inherit eternal life ? And Jesus said unto him, Why callest thou me good ? none is good save one, even God. Thou knowest the commandments, Do not kill, Do not commit adultery, Do not steal, Do not bear false witness, Do not defraud, Honour thy father and mother. And he said unto him, Master, all these things have I observed from my youth. And Jesus looking upon him loved him, and said unto him, One thing thou lackest: go, sell whatsoever thou hast, and give to the poor, and thou shalt have treasure in heaven: and come, follow me. But his countenance fell at the saying, and he went away sorrowful: for he was one that had great possessions. And Jesus looked round about, and saith unto his disciples, How hardly shall they that have riches enter into the kingdom of God! And the disciples were amazed at his words. But Jesus answereth again, and saith unto them, Children, how hard is it for them that trust in riches to enter into the kingdom of God! It is easier for a camel to go through a needle's eye, than for a rich man to enter into the kingdom of God. And they were astonished exceedingly, saying unto him, Then who can be saved? Jesus looking upon them saith, With men it is impossible, but not with God: for all things are possible with God.

Could this young ruler (for such he was, as we learn elsewhere) have great possessions, and not have duties connected with those possessions? It is impossible. Could it be right for him to throw those duties all away? Surely not. He might have been required to discharge them more for the benefit of the poor, less for his own personal pleasure; but the extreme course of selling the possessions would have exhausted in one moment all his habitual means of working for others. It is very difficult to believe that this could have been a right course, even if all possible reflection had been bestowed on it, and on what it involved; could it be right to adopt it without reflection?

When we look at all the circumstances, the young man was certainly not blameless. He had not been content with the advice, comparatively commonplace, which Jesus gave him at first; having refused this, he ought to have expected that advice, or a command, not commonplace, would follow. He ought not therefore to have been repelled by such a command, though he need not have accepted it in the absolute form in which it was given. Still, when this is admitted, must we not also add that the command of Jesus had better have been put in a milder form? We may say this without any great surprise that it assumed the form which it did; for it was the practice of Jesus to reply swiftly; a practice adopted with good reason, and yet which had some dangers.

We have reason to think that this incident, and the loss of one who promised to be a disciple, did affect the teaching of Jesus afterwards. At all events, in two very important parables, almost his last legacy of counsel to his disciples, the parable of the ten virgins and the parable of the talents, principles are introduced which had never been put forward by him before. In the parable of the ten virgins, the five wise virgins refuse to part with their oil for the benefit of the five foolish virgins, on the reasonable ground that it was needed by them for their own duties. The ground for such a refusal, reasonable though it was, is nowhere recognised in the early discourses of Jesus. In the parable of the talents it is explicitly recognised that property is a trust given us, which we must use therefore for

God's purposes, not for our own pleasure; and that means that we must use it with a regard to the welfare of the entire community. This, while it implies that we are servants of mankind, implies also that we must not surrender property merely on the appeal of one who asks us for it, without good reason. It is worth noticing too, that the parable of the talents recognises the justice of accepting interest for money that we have lent. If any one should think that the principles implied in these parables tend to selfishness, that thought must be dispelled by the discourse which follows, the prophecy of what is called "the last judgment," in which the obligation of ministering to the wants of others is laid down in the most absolute terms (Matthew xxv.). The chapter here referred to is the fullest and most reasoned account of the duties of man in regard to material property which the gospels contain; and certainly it is an advance on the earlier teaching of Jesus.

The next place at which we find Jesus and the accompanying multitude is Jericho (to reach which he must have crossed again to the west bank of the Jordan); and here he was the guest of the rich tax-gatherer Zacchæus. There were some who disapproved, for the tax-gatherers (or "publicans") were unpopular, as being in the employ of the Roman government; and their gain was reckoned sinful. It is evident that Jesus did not disapprove of their employment in itself, though a "publican" who disregarded the poor would have been condemned by him equally with any other careless rich man. But the colloquy with Zacchæus is important for a special reason, and I will transcribe it:

And Zacchæus stood, and said unto the Lord, Behold, Lord, the half of my goods I give to the poor; and if I have wrongfully exacted aught of any man, I restore fourfold. And Jesus said unto him, To-day is salvation come to this house, forasmuch as he also is a son of Abraham. For the Son of man came to seek and to save that which was lost. Luke xix. 8–10.

The salvation of Zacchæus is clearly not thought of as dependent on any baptismal rite; the first gospel message, as delivered by Jesus, was free from all formal requirements. Indeed the whole requirements of Jesus were much more in the region of the spirit than in the region of material fact: it was only a short time since he had said to the rich young ruler, "Sell whatsoever thou hast"; but from Zacchæus he is quite contented with the voluntary offer of half his goods, to be given to the poor.

On the restoration of sight to the blind Bartimæus, an event not absolutely to be discarded as outside the bounds of possibility, but yet doubtful, I need not linger; it is recorded to have happened near Jericho.

To the closing scenes of the earthly life of Jesus I now come. Is it necessary for me to recount in detail how he, with the multitude attendant on him, journeyed from Jericho to the Mount of Olives; how, mindful of the prophecy of Zechariah, he sent for a young ass, mounted it, and descended the hill towards Jerusalem (weeping, Luke tells us, at the sight of that disobedient city); how his followers with acclamation declared him to be "the son of David," the "King of Israel," and cried out:

Blessed is he that cometh in the name of the Lord;

how they strewed their garments on the road before him, and threw down on the road branches cut from the trees? Few could doubt that he was claiming to be the Messiah; and when the scandalised Pharisees said:

Master, rebuke thy disciples, he answered, I tell you that, if these shall hold their peace, the stones will cry out.

Yet to be hailed as the Messiah was but a small thing in his eyes; to do that which the Messiah must do was far more important; and with this end in view he took possession of the temple. With the civil government of Jerusalem, or of Judæa, he had no concern; he was no rebel against the Romans; but the temple was sacred to him in whom he trusted, even God, and with the temple he had concern. It is true, that if technical rights were in question, the chief priests were the administrators of the temple, and he was an outsider; but Jesus penetrated beyond technical rights into the true meaning and spirit of the religion of Israel; he knew that he himself, and he alone, was the inheritor of the spirit of Abraham, of Moses, of Isaiah. That the holders of technical authority would slay him for what he meant to do and say, he knew well; it had been foretold that "he was numbered with the transgressors"; he was content to be so numbered, provided he gave life to mankind.

Meanwhile, the people of Jerusalem remained expectant. Jesus was known to them by repute, but (if the gospel of Matthew be right) not in person, save by a few; for we there read that as he entered "all the city was stirred, saying, Who is this?" which they would not have asked, had he been known to them. However, they would have been glad to accept him as a deliverer, if a deliverer he proved to be; and even the Jewish authorities, though no doubt not favourable to him, ventured on no open opposition to him at first. The general peacefulness of his followers prevented offence being taken on the ground of obvious material disorder.

Hence, when (on the day after his arrival at Jerusalem, as we learn from Mark) he proceeded to drive the money-changers and dove-sellers out of the large outer court of the temple, where they had been accustomed to ply their trade for the convenience of persons intending to offer sacrifice, no resistance was made. It is the only forcible act recorded of Jesus in his whole career; and his followers were numerous enough to secure that it should be carried out. But what did he mean by it? His words were:

Is it not written, My house shall be called a house of prayer for all the nations? but ye have made it a den of robbers. Mark xi. 17.

The words given in the fourth gospel (which misplaces the incident) are somewhat milder; on the whole, though not quite certainly, we ought to accept the version given in the three synoptic gospels. The critical reader may indeed remark that the money-changers and dove-sellers were probably as honest as other tradesmen; but we are not bound to literalness. There can be no doubt that Jesus felt the money-changers and dove-sellers to be adverse to the spirit in which the faithful soul should approach God; and he acted as one initiating a new spirit, a mode of religious conduct purer than that which had been customary in the past. It was the same kind of feeling with which he said (as the fourth gospel tells us, and it is herein credible):

Destroy this temple, and in three days I will raise it up (John ii. 19);

words which his accusers afterwards brought against him, though not without some change in the form of them. Yet we cannot be sure of the precise form which such words would assume; all that we can be sure of is that Jesus was predicting, and (as far as was then possible) originating, a method of religious worship free from the materialisms of the past. His action had a bearing against sacrifices, and this must have been intentional in him; it is even possible that sacrifices were suspended in the temple during the short time while he held authority there; we should infer this if we were to take literally the words in our second gospel:

He would not suffer that any man should carry a vessel through the temple. Mark xi. 16.

We cannot be certain of this; but if anyone should try to prove the contrary, and ask, Why have not the gospels plainly said that the sacrifices were suspended, supposing such to have been the case? the answer is that the disciples of Jesus for many years afterwards held the sacrifices appointed by the law to be sacred and obligatory, and the memory of any action of Jesus against them would tend to die away. In any case, his driving out the money-changers and dove-sellers was a parabolic act, and intimated disparagement of sacrifices as means of approaching the Most High, even as his appointment of twelve apostles intimated something more than lay in the primary purpose of such an act. To act by parables was as much a weapon in his hands as to speak by parables.

But what was it positively his design, his mission, to say to his own people, now that he was in the most central spot, where, according to both his and their judgment, it was most fitting for the Divine word to be promulgated? Here, I cannot but think, the synoptic gospels somewhat fail us. They give indeed with force and truth the collisions of Jesus with his opponents; the parables through which he made known to them (and they could not misunderstand his meaning) that they, although the inheritors of the divine law, had misinterpreted it to their own destruction; the intimation also, in the course of those parables, that they were seeking to slay him, and would slay him; his trenchant answers to the subtle questions which they put to him; and lastly, the question which he put to them, whereby he made clear his own conviction that it was not as the son of David that he came forward to be their leader, but as the son of God. The genuineness of almost all these sayings of his is transparent; though the parable of the king's marriage feast in the twenty-second chapter of Matthew has some doubtful verses (it should be compared with the similar parable in the fourteenth chapter of Luke). Further, though Jesus did not, any more than the Hebrew prophets before him, exhibit that careful minute reasoning which was characteristic of the Greek mind, there is penetrating force in all his answers, and in all his sayings. But the synoptic gospels represent him as more exclusively a combatant than we can quite think was the case. There is only one tender saying attributed to him in this part of the synoptic gospels; that in which he says to the scribe who had answered him "discreetly" (as the phrase is in the gospel of Mark), "Thou art not far from the kingdom of God." But it is probable that the parable of the good Samaritan really belongs to this point of the history. Luke, the only evangelist who tells that beautiful parable, puts it much earlier; but Luke's arrangement is one of his weak points; and those who look at the context of that parable will not be indisposed to assign it to the period of which I am speaking. (That other most beautiful parable, "the prodigal son," seems rightly placed by Luke.)

Even these touches of tenderness do not take away the impression which the synoptic gospels leave on us, that the temper of Jesus at this time was far more militant than consolatory or directly instructive. But the fourth gospel, if duly corrected as to its chronology, does modify this impression. The reader will bear in mind that the fourth gospel does not mention at all that Jesus entered the temple during the days between his triumphal entry into Jerusalem and his crucifixion; a strange omission, which we have to explain, and may explain in the following way. Seeing that it cannot easily be denied that the fourth gospel (through erroneous editing, as I have supposed) is altogether wrong in its transference of the "cleansing of the temple" from the end to the beginning of the career of Jesus, it is a natural sequence that the fourth gospel should also have transferred the discourses of Jesus to periods earlier than that at which they were actually spoken. (For further justification of this belief, let me refer to the sixteenth chapter of the present work.)

If we suppose that the public discourses of Jesus recorded in the fourth gospel, most of which are stated to have been spoken in Jerusalem and some even in the temple, were really spoken (in so far as they are authentic) during the few days between his entry into Jerusalem and his crucifixion, we shall see a real naturalness in many of the expressions which they contain, which is wanting in the ordinary view of them. To suppose that Jesus all through his career was talking about himself to the extent, and in the terms, which the fourth gospel seems to represent, is not pleasing to any one who preserves a sane judgment as to human conduct. But it is another thing if we suppose these discourses spoken in conscious anticipation of imminent death. We cannot disapprove of Jesus speaking about himself at such a time. He had delivered his moral precepts during his whole career; to his disciples little more remained for him to say; while his opponents had not the

disposition to listen to him on that subject. But of himself—
there was something that remained to be said about himself,
to those who would listen to it. What was the meaning of his
presence there, in Jerusalem? It was understood that he was
claiming to be the Messiah; but what did that mean? With
what spiritual disposition had he come? What was to be the
issue of his action? It was not unnecessary for him to say
something on these topics; and the fourth gospel, though I
am not representing it as in any part verbally correct, does
supply us with sayings of Jesus pertinent to so solemn an
occasion. To those who believed in Jesus, such a discourse as
the following would have an elevating and steadying effect
amid the perils of the hour:

Verily, verily, I say unto you, He that heareth my word, and believeth
him that sent me, hath eternal life, and cometh not into judgment, but
hath passed out of death into life. Verily, verily, I say unto you, The
hour cometh, and now is, when the dead shall hear the voice of the Son
of God; and they that hear shall live. For as the Father hath life in
himself, even so gave he to the Son also to have life in himself: and he
gave him authority to execute judgment, because he is the Son of man.
Marvel not at this: for the hour cometh, in which all that are in the
tombs shall hear his voice, and shall come forth; they that have done
good, unto the resurrection of life: and they that have done ill, unto
the resurrection of judgment. I can of myself do nothing: as I hear,
I judge; and my judgment is righteous, because I seek not mine own
will, but the will of him that sent me. John v. 24–30.

Take again the following passages:

My teaching is not mine, but his that sent me. If any man willeth to
do his will, he shall know of the teaching, whether it be of God, or whether
I speak from myself. *Ibid.* vii. 16, 17.

(How clearly in this passage, while the intimate connexion
between Jesus and God is affirmed, yet Jesus is Jesus, and God
is God! They are cognate, yet not identified.)

If any man thirst, let him come unto me and drink. He that believeth
on me, as the scripture hath said, out of his belly shall flow rivers of living
water. *Ibid.* vii. 37, 38.

I am the light of the world: he that followeth me shall not walk in
the darkness, but shall have the light of life. *Ibid.* viii. 12.

(In his early teaching, Jesus had said to his disciples, "Ye
are the light of the world"; but just before his death he might
well feel that he stood in a solitary position, in which none other
could share.)

If ye abide in my word, then are ye truly my disciples; and ye shall
know the truth, and the truth shall make you free. *Ibid.* viii. 31, 32.

My sheep hear my voice, and I know them, and they follow me; and I give unto them eternal life, and they shall never perish, and no one shall snatch them out of my hand. My Father, which hath given them unto me, is greater than all; and no one is able to snatch them out of the Father's hand. *Ibid.* x. 27–29.

There is a sublime self-consciousness, a sublime tranquillity, in such words as these; out of them his disciples might, if they believed him at all, well draw the assurance that they would hear his voice even after he had passed away. The Spirit was creating a new world; in that new world he would still be the supporter and the guide of those whom he had left behind. Such a promise was a worthy legacy, and we must not charge it with egotism; but it was distinctly a legacy; it could not have been spoken amidst the stress and strain of ordinary life.

I am not by any means saying that all the public discourses of Jesus recorded in the fourth gospel are genuine, even if we were to try to place them at the time of which I am treating, the last days before his crucifixion: for instance, it is surely quite impossible that Jesus should ever have said to Jews who had begun to believe in him, and who had committed no great offence in speech or action, "Ye are of your father the devil" (see the whole passage in John viii. 30–44). Incoherence of mind in author or editor is the only explanation of such a colligation; and there are other passages in which characteristics of the apostle John himself plainly appear. We must expect a mixture; the apostle himself was too remarkable a character not to infuse something of his own mind into that which he recorded. But for all that, I believe that these discourses, if assigned to the time to which I am assigning them, do supply a want, and do tell us something which the synoptic gospels do not tell us, of the way in which Jesus strengthened the hearts and the consciences of those who trusted him, during these last memorable days of his earthly life.

I must, however, now revert to the synoptic gospels for certain purposes. The answer of Jesus to the Pharisees, when they asked him whether it were lawful to give tribute to Cæsar, or not:

Render unto Cæsar the things that are Cæsar's, and unto God the things that are God's,

was in all probability a very crucial answer as revealing his intentions. It was apparent from it that it was no part of his intention to liberate the Jews from the temporal government of Rome. Is it not clear that the Pharisees, knowing this, would impart their knowledge to the people of Jerusalem generally? Is it not clear that the people of Jerusalem, knowing this, would lose all interest in Jesus, and would think that he had stimulated their hopes on false pretences? The spiritual government of the world was a subject beyond the range of their thoughts: it was the exaltation of Israel, of the Jewish nation, openly in the eyes of men, which they had hoped that Jesus might effect. When it was clear that he was not going to effect this, it was not doubtful what would follow. It is true that his Galilean followers would be unwilling to desert him; but even they would be discouraged.

The first result of this general conviction was probably one which is not stated in so many words in the gospel narratives, but which is implied in the closing words of the twenty-third chapter of Matthew. That chapter is the most vehement invective against the scribes and Pharisees which the gospels contain; we may regret some phrases in it, but on the whole it is a just censure of one of the most persistent of human errors, the over-valuing of ceremonial observances in religion. In the close of it there is a return to tenderness on behalf of the famous city of his own nation, and this is the passage to which I have just referred:

O Jerusalem, Jerusalem, which killeth the prophets, and stoneth them that are sent unto her! how often would I have gathered thy children together, even as a hen gathereth her chickens under her wings, and ye would not! Behold, your house is left unto you desolate. For I say unto you, Ye shall not see me henceforth, till ye shall say, Blessed is he that cometh in the name of the Lord.

The expression "your house is left unto you desolate," and the verse which follows, have no meaning, unless Jesus was leaving the temple, never to return to it. Yet why should he not return, unless he was being forcibly excluded? Surely it was involved in his whole claim, that he should go on preaching in the temple, as long as it was possible for him to do so. We must infer that he was being excluded by force; and the prediction of the utter destruction of the temple, which he made immediately afterwards (and in much more decided terms than he had used before) entirely suits this view.

From that moment the position of Jesus was that of one waiting to be seized, judged, and slain. No other issue was possible; yet the time which intervened before that took place was precious, for it had to be used in instructing his disciples. Those disciples had not been without understanding of the whole purpose of Jesus; for now four of them, Peter and James and John and Andrew, came to him as he sat on the Mount of Olives, and asked him a question of great importance, with a view to understanding that purpose better. That question is put in the gospel of Matthew in the following terms:

Tell us, when shall these things be? and what shall be the sign of thy presence, and of the consummation of the age?

If the question was really put in this form, there can be no doubt that these disciples had accepted the fact that Jesus was about to die; for his "presence" (or his "coming," as it is more frequently translated) certainly did not mean a bodily presence like that which he had as he sat with them that day on the Mount of Olives. The word implies a previous absence, which could only mean his death. Mark and Luke, however, put this question in another form; let me quote Mark:

Tell us, when shall these things be? and what shall be the sign when these things are all about to be accomplished?

These words do not in themselves imply that Jesus was about to die; but yet "the things" which were to be "accomplished" certainly include his coming in glory, which he had definitely predicted to them; and it is incredible that they should not have understood that this would be preceded by his death. Jesus, both in his immediate answer, and in everything which he says afterwards, assumes this knowledge in them. No doubt the whole subject was mysterious to them, and his death was not the part of it to which their minds would most readily turn; but they were not ignorant that that was about to happen. The important question was, What was to happen afterwards? and that was what they now asked.

The answer of Jesus could not be confined to the mere fact that he was about to return "in the glory of his Father with his angels." That he had already said to them: but the apostles felt that they must have some guide as to their future conduct after he had left them, and before that consummation took place. And now I must draw attention to a notable point; namely, that neither in the question of the apostles, nor in the answer of Jesus, is there any reference at all to the prediction which Jesus had made to them more than once, that after his death he was to be "raised up on the third day." This confirms

what I said in my comments on the scene at Cæsarea Philippi,
that the being "raised up on the third day" was not, when the
prediction was originally made, thought of as belonging to a
totally different epoch of time from the coming of the Son of
man "in the glory of his Father with his angels." The "third
day" meant simply, "within a brief space of time," as in that
other instance to which I referred, in Luke xiii. 32: and the Son
of man was to come "in the glory of his Father with his angels"
within the lifetime of some who then heard those words, which
was at any rate a time not very far distant. It is not said that
the two events are coincident in time; but they belong to the
same kind of epoch. Hence, when the apostles inquire concerning
that great series of events in which the whole action of Jesus
and the whole history of mankind are to culminate, they have
no sort of expectation or idea that he is to return to them twice
after his death, on the third day for the first time, at some
unknown epoch for the second time. That belief, which the
after course of events tended to produce, and which is the belief
of Christians even at the present day, was not in the thoughts
of the apostles at all when they asked the question which I
have quoted above, sitting on the slopes of Olivet, over against
Jerusalem. As it was a single departure of their Master through
death that they expected, so also it was a single return in glory
after death; and they asked the pertinent and necessary questions,
when that return was to happen, and with what preceding signs.
As the apostles in their question, so Jesus in his reply, assumes
that he is to return but once; once, and for ever; but not twice.
The being "raised up on the third day" is not mentioned at
all; it is, in truth, swallowed up in the general conception of
the return, which *is* mentioned. So it is in the parables which
follow, very notably in the parable of the talents; in that parable,
the lord of the servants departs once, and returns once. But
to speak more fully of this reply of Jesus (which occupies the
whole of the twenty-fourth and twenty-fifth chapters of Matthew,
and is told rather more briefly in Mark and Luke)—it is evident
that Jesus felt, as his apostles had felt, that the mere prediction
of his return in glory was not sufficient for their practical needs.
And now it is proper to remark that in the mind of Jesus himself
there was a double train of thought; two quite different considerations were before him, and the reconciliation of the two was not
easy. On the one hand, there was the justly founded belief
that the gospel influence was a natural seed sown in the heart

of man, which grew slowly and imperceptibly, and which had all the nations of the world for the field in which it must ripen and bear fruit. The ripening of such a fruit over so large a field might be expected to be a long process, and if the kingdom of God was only to appear when this process was completed, this train of thought tended to remove the coming of the kingdom of God to a distant period. On the other hand, it appeared to Jesus quite alien from the counsels of God, and unendurable in view of God's righteousness and of the tenor of the ancient prophecies, that he himself after his death should be very long removed from his faithful followers who were struggling on earth; he must be revealed and known to them ere long; and if he were revealed in his true Divine action, what could that be but the coming of the kingdom of heaven upon earth? So this train of thought tended to make the kingdom of God appear as an event near at hand.

We may see these contending trains of thought all through those chapters of the gospels of which I am now speaking. He tells his disciples that, after he has departed from them, they will not live in ease and quiet; the world will be a troubled world:

Nation shall rise against nation, and kingdom against kingdom; and there shall be famines and earthquakes in divers places.

And he adds:

All these things are the beginning of travail.

Of travail: not merely of sorrow; these are the birth-pangs out of which the kingdom of heaven is to issue. Compress this time of travail as much as he might, the issue of it could not be an immediate event; and while the travail continued, his disciples were not to be dismayed. They would be ill-treated, persecuted; but this must not dismay them; "he that endureth to the end, the same shall be saved." Nor must they follow anyone reported to be the Christ; they must wait till he himself should come; and his coming would be mysterious.

As the lightning cometh forth from the east, and is seen even unto the west; so shall be the coming of the Son of man.

That coming would be after special tribulation in the land in which they dwelt, in the land of Judæa; and the end would be a transformation of all things.

We cannot tell how far Jesus intended his words to be taken literally, how far metaphorically; there is, I think, an admixture of conscious metaphor in them; but we have also to remember that the courses of nature and the history of the world did necessarily represent themselves very differently to him from the way in which we view them; so that what he says may in part be intended literally. Here at all events are his words:

Immediately after the tribulation of those days, the sun shall be darkened, and the moon shall not give her light, and the stars shall fall from heaven, and the powers of the heavens shall be shaken: and then shall appear the sign of the Son of man in heaven: and then shall all the tribes of the earth mourn, and they shall see the Son of man coming on the clouds of heaven with power and great glory. And he shall send forth his angels with a great sound of a trumpet, and they shall gather together his elect from the four winds, from the one end of heaven to the other. Matthew xxiv. 29–31.

Nothing can well sound more miraculous; and yet even here, as in all the sayings of Jesus, the conception of natural law intervenes, and the most extraordinary events are made parallel with types in ordinary experience. For immediately, in the very next sentence, he declares that all these future events which are recounted in the above paragraph are parallel and similar to one of the most ordinary natural processes, the sprouting of the leaves of a fig-tree just before summer begins. Moreover, he evidently implies that his apostles will themselves see these things; and he adds:

Verily I say unto you, This generation shall not pass away, till all these things be accomplished. Heaven and earth shall pass away, but my words shall not pass away.

It is not surprising that Biblical commentators have been puzzled by a prophecy which declares that things so wonderful were so near at hand at the time when Jesus spoke. The assumption that Jesus spoke metaphorically carries us but a very little way. No metaphorical explanation can make it in the least true that Jesus did, within the lifetime of the generation to whom he spoke, send his angels and gather together his elect "from the one end of heaven to the other." And we may fairly say that Jesus was conscious of some ignorance on his own part; for in the very next sentence to the last above quoted, he says:

But of that day and hour knoweth no one, not even the angels of heaven, neither the Son, but the Father only.

In truth, those two trains of thought which filled the mind of Jesus at this time, the thought of the kingdom of heaven as a natural growth in the heart of man, and the thought of the kingdom of heaven as an external event near at hand, in which he himself should be the directing agent, were intrinsically difficult to accept in their combination: especially when the supreme importance of both views was to be insisted on. It is no arrogance on our part, nor any disloyalty to Jesus as the greatest Teacher whom the world has seen or ever will see, to say that we are capable of tracing the developments of his thought, and the way in which one part of his thought fits into another part of it, better than he himself could do; we have nineteen centuries more experience than he had, and it would be strange if mankind had not learned something new in those nineteen centuries.

We must accept his prophecies not in the letter, but in the spirit. What he prophesied as an extraordinary convulsion in the physical world (following the kind of representation made by the book of Daniel, and also feeling the necessity of infusing a force into his own words which might be lacking to a merely spiritual delineation of the future), had truth in the spiritual world; and small though such things may at first sight appear, they have a mighty effect in the future. It was true that a change was then being wrought in the hearts of men which would in the process of time remodel all the institutions of society and even the face of the earth and the whole bearing and direction of the physical forces with which we are surrounded, making them the servants of the spirit. This great change, infinitely to be carried on in the future, Jesus compressed into a few words; not indeed with absolute consciousness that he was so compressing the infinite future into a span, but because by instinct he seized those points which would have the greatest effect on those whom he addressed, and an effect leading them on to just and fruitful action. Those moral instructions which he crowded into the discourse of which I am now speaking, the exhortations to watchfulness in conduct, to watchfulness especially as knowing that their departed Master might at any moment reappear and demand an account of their conduct, the exhortations to soberness and industry, to mercy and pity and fellow-feeling—these may stand wholly unaltered, whatever changes may be required, through our added experience, in that direct vision of the future which Jesus imparted to his faithful disciples.

I believe in the genuineness of the discourse of which I have been speaking, as rendered by Matthew or Mark, almost in its entirety; hardly so completely as rendered by Luke. It is difficult not to believe that Luke added some points from his knowledge of what actually happened in the siege of Jerusalem, and after its capture. (See Luke xix. 43, 44; xxi. 24.) That siege is not mentioned in the reports by Matthew and Mark, though the terms used imply a dim forecast of some such event; it appears from both Matthew and Mark, that Jesus anticipated extraordinary troubles for Jerusalem and for all Judæa. That is to be believed; but the details added by Luke sound as if they proceeded not from prophetic forecast, but from knowledge.

One thing more I ought to add. The brevity which Jesus was compelled to use in his description of the future destinies of man, from which it has resulted that we must accept that description in the spirit but not in the letter, has in one respect had unhappy consequences. In the gospel of Matthew, the end of the discourse to which I have been referring contains a prediction of eternal punishment for the wicked. Had Jesus been asked, "Is there then no hope for these accursed ones?" I cannot but believe that he would have answered, as he did on another occasion to a similar question, "With God all things are possible." Must we not regret that, even without any specific question being addressed to him, some such word was not spoken by him in relation to the prediction of eternal punishment for the wicked? I find it impossible not to regret this. We have no doubt to bear in mind the risk which he might have run of weakening the effect of his warnings against iniquity; he desired, and rightly, to produce a strong effect in that direction. But the counter truth, the almighty power of God for recovery, was disastrously forgotten in the ages that followed; and the thought is not easily to be laid aside, though we may not too much insist upon it, that Jesus might have prevented this. We shall at all events best honour him by believing that he did not shut out hope. And so I truly believe.

That discourse, in many parts most tender and beautiful, which the fourth gospel assigns to Jesus as spoken by him on the last night before his crucifixion, has no doubt some measure of authenticity; though the personal beliefs and personal style of the apostle John mingle with the whole of it, as was to be expected; and not everything in it can be accepted as genuine. But it is unnecessary to go into detail here. It is not easy to place a discourse so long as this precisely where the fourth gospel places it, in view of what the other gospels tell us; it is more easy to think of it as dispersed, and that a good deal of the substance of what was said on several evenings of that week, is contained in it. That Jesus washed the feet of his disciples on the evening of his last supper is far from incredible, and is probably true.

Another incident which happened on one of the evenings of the last week of the life of Jesus is too striking and affecting not to be mentioned. As he was reclining at supper in the house of Simon the leper, at Bethany, a woman came bearing an alabaster cruse of ointment, very costly, and poured the ointment on his head. No doubt she meant it as symbolic of his royal office; but he (though he would not have refused this signification) turned the meaning into one more appropriate to the immediate position:

She hath wrought a good work on me.... She hath done what she could; she hath anointed my body aforehand for the burying. And verily I say unto you, Wheresoever the gospel shall be preached throughout the whole world, that also which this woman hath done shall be spoken of for a memorial of her.

The anticipation of death is combined in these words with the anticipation of a victorious progress for the gospel. This combination was absolutely permanent in the thoughts of Jesus. Nor was the habit of using symbols to express a truth which in its fullness was unimaginable less permanent with him. The most famous of all his symbolic acts was that which took the central place in his last supper, on the night before his crucifixion. That supper was, the synoptic gospels say, the true paschal meal. The fourth gospel puts the passover on the day following, so as to make it synchronise with the death of Jesus himself; this was in accordance with the striking idea which we find in Paul, and which was deeply rooted in the author of the Revelation and of the fourth gospel, that Jesus Christ himself was the true paschal lamb. There is something to be said in favour of the historical accuracy of the fourth gospel here; but on the whole, I feel sure that the synoptic gospels are right; there was no ideal motive to mislead them. Let me now quote from Matthew (xxvi. 26–29) the passage describing the symbolic act to which I have referred:

And as they were eating, Jesus took bread, and blessed, and brake it; and he gave to the disciples, and said, Take, eat; this is my body. And he took a cup, and gave thanks, and gave to them, saying, Drink ye all of it; for this is my blood of the covenant, which is shed for many unto remission of sins. But I say unto you, I will not drink henceforth of the fruit of the vine, until that day when I drink it new with you in my Father's kingdom.

That is what Jesus said in order to take away from his own death, what naturally would be felt to lie in it, the aspect of mere tragic sorrow and loss. Far other was the truth of the matter. Out of his death would spring life; his own exalted life first, and, sustained by that, the life of his followers and of all mankind. That was what he wished those who were then with him to understand. The bread and wine were the symbols by which they might image to themselves the true nature and power of Jesus after he had departed from them; and in order that they might image this to themselves more constantly, Paul and Luke tell us (what Matthew and Mark do not) that he added, "Do this in remembrance of me." On the whole, though not quite without doubt, we may accept it, that he did give this injunction; though to be remembered was, in his estimate, merely preparatory to being perceived and known. But what did he mean by saying that his blood was the blood "of the covenant," and that it was shed "unto remission of sins"? This: that he was forming with them a new and solemn compact and alliance; and that by adherence to it all the evils and wrongs which had accompanied the progress of mankind thus far would gradually fade away, with all that pain and distress which had been their consequences. Nor need we doubt that that remission of sins included the remission of the sins of those who were then, outwardly speaking, his enemies; of poor feeble Judas, who was betraying him; of scribes and Pharisees and chief priests, who, not recognising the new birth of time, thought they were vindicating the divine law; of Pilate, who yielded his better judgment to the desires of those whom Jesus had offended. The sins of those sinners were not worthy of being mentioned in the light of God's kingdom, which even then was dawning. If they are mentioned by us, it should be in forgiveness.

The glory of God's kingdom was even then dawning in the soul of Jesus, when he declared that he gave his body and blood to be food and drink for those who should come after him. But this heavenly vision, though it was eternal, had yet to struggle for possession with the earthly foresight which claimed its due, and which it was vain to disregard. Jesus and his disciples went out (we read), after singing a hymn, to the Mount of Olives,

to a place called Gethsemane, where was a garden. It ought
to be mentioned that before going there he had (according to
Luke xxii. 35–38) withdrawn any prohibition that he might
seem to have laid upon them against following the ordinary
customs of the world; he had even bidden each of them buy
a sword; though he made it clear that he was not speaking
with any view to his own protection.

Then, in the garden of Gethsemane, quite suddenly, the plain
meaning of what was about to happen, in its bare earthly reality,
struck upon the intellect and the heart of Jesus. The nearness
of it made it insistent. Up to that moment, the duty of
strengthening others had weakened the force of the imminence
of death, although he had foreseen its reality. Now, the terror,
the ignominy, stood menacing and unconcealed before him;
physical pain of unknown magnitude, the exulting scorn of
enemies, the sorrowful conviction of friends that they had trusted
in him vainly. Against all this he had, it was true, his trust
in God to support him; but the danger was lest this should
give way; and the struggle to retain it began in him. That
struggle was unescapable, and became an agony; he prayed
more earnestly; his sweat, Luke tells us, "was as it were great
drops of blood falling down upon the ground." Such was the
price he paid for retaining in his soul the Divine Spirit, the
earnest of the redemption of mankind.

Meanwhile he had taken with him, apart from the rest, his
three most favoured disciples, Simon Peter, James, and John.
He would gladly have had them stay awake with him; but sleep
overpowered them. They also felt sorrow, though it was not
like the sorrow of Jesus. "Simon, sleepest thou? couldest thou
not watch one hour?" was the gentle reproach he made to that
disciple whom he most trusted. Yet these disciples heard
some of his words:

My soul is exceeding sorrowful, even unto death.

O my Father, if it be possible, let this cup pass away from me: nevertheless, not as I will, but as thou wilt.

Then again, with absolute resignation:

O my Father, if this cannot pass away, except I drink it, thy will
be done.

The disciples could not realise the events that were about to
happen; a dark perplexity encompassed them; they trusted
in Jesus, and yet they were in a maze of doubt. But when the
rudely armed troop, sent by the chief priests, drew near to seize

him, the spirit of Jesus recovered its natural energy, and he addressed his disciples with irony:

Sleep on now, and take your rest: it is enough: the hour is come; behold, the Son of man is betrayed into the hands of sinners. Arise, let us be going: behold, he that betrayeth me is at hand.

And Judas Iscariot, whose treachery Jesus had perceived beforehand (though it is most unlikely that the perception can have been of long standing) drew near and kissed him. The troop of assailants recognised the sign, and encompassed Jesus. One of his followers (the fourth gospel says it was Simon Peter himself) drew a sword to defend him, but only succeeded in cutting off the ear of one of the servants of the high priest. The words of Jesus in reference to this, as reported by Matthew, are too characteristic to be omitted:

Put up again thy sword into its place: for all they that take the sword shall perish with the sword. Or thinkest thou that I cannot beseech my Father, and he shall even now send me more than twelve legions of angels? How then should the scriptures be fulfilled, that thus it must be?

The air of dominance, of infinite power, is resumed by Jesus at once, as soon as he finds himself in actual conflict: he would allow his friends, but not his enemies, to see his hour of weakness.

It can hardly have been much after midnight, and evidently the design of the chief priests was that Jesus should be condemned with the utmost possible speed. Though the fourth gospel is strangely fragmentary here (not describing in any way that most important event, the trial of Jesus before Caiaphas), we should probably accept its statement that Jesus was taken first before Annas; for Annas, the father-in-law of Caiaphas, had himself been high priest, and was a person of power in Jerusalem. The noble answer of Jesus, as told in the fourth gospel, when he was struck by an officer of the court before Annas (John xviii. 23) should probably be accepted as genuine:

If I have spoken evil, bear witness of the evil; but if well, why smitest thou me?

There was no didactic intention in such words; and yet it was right that the blow should be reproved as an outrage on propriety in a court of law. But it was in the trial before Caiaphas that the controversy of Jesus with his fellow-countrymen culminated. The chief priests could no doubt have easily procured his conviction on the minor charge of disorder; but they estimated his power more accurately than to suppose that he could be restrained by any punishment inflicted on such a charge; hence they endeavoured to prove him to be a blasphemer, and therefore liable to death by the Mosaic law. After efforts had been vainly made to procure proof of this (and not a mere probable appearance of it) the high priest Caiaphas resolved to win the admission of blasphemy (or what would be considered such) from the lips of Jesus himself; and therefore he put the direct question:

I adjure thee by the living God, that thou tell us whether thou be the Christ, the Son of God.

Before minor accusations Jesus had been silent. He could not be silent now: his work on earth was done, and this question gave him the opportunity of summing it up in the briefest and most trenchant way. Therefore he replied thus:

It is thou who hast spoken it. Yet I say unto you, Henceforth ye shall see the Son of man sitting at the right hand of power, and coming on the clouds of heaven.

These words, as he knew full well, sealed his death. Is it necessary to describe in detail the trial before Pilate? The plain truth as to that trial is written, as I believe, in the gospel of Mark: that Pilate asked Jesus whether he were the king of the Jews, and received an affirmative answer; and that then numerous accusations were made against Jesus, but without eliciting any answer from him—to Pilate's exceeding wonder. Matthew fully supports Mark in this most important point, and so on the whole does Luke. But the first gospel, both here and all through its close, has many unbelievable additions to the plain fact (the most notable is the allegation that Pilate placed a guard round the tomb of Jesus—which, had it been true fact, could not have been left unmentioned by the other evangelists). Whether Luke is right in saying that Jesus was sent before Herod, must be doubtful. The fourth gospel is entirely opposed to Matthew and Mark as to the silence of Jesus before Pilate; admitting it just for one moment; but essentially, Jesus defends himself, and is not silent, in the fourth gospel. We might believe this, and believe worthily of Jesus; but the silence attributed to him by Matthew and Mark is also worthy, and is on the whole to be credited.

In one extraneous matter we may probably believe the first gospel, and that is as to the suicide of Judas. He was likely to feel remorse; and it must lighten our condemnation of him.   Like all the apostles, he had been placed in a position of severe trial; he was the only one who gave way under the trial.

The sufferings of Jesus on the cross may be forgotten by us in comparison with the patience with which he endured them; in every utterance ascribed to him, in every record relating to him, this shines out.   We cannot be certain of the authenticity of all the sayings ascribed to him; but there is none which is unworthy of him.   The most strongly attested is his quotation of the beginning of the twenty-second psalm:

My God, my God, why hast thou forsaken me ?

Both Matthew and Mark record this; and the quotation is no sign of despair.   It must have been a comfort to him to think that the saints of old suffered as he was suffering; that they were his companions; and let us remember that this psalm, beginning in anguish, ends in triumph.

There is likewise a peculiar reason for believing that the saying addressed to the penitent robber, crucified by his side, is genuine.   Here is the passage:

And one of the malefactors which were hanged railed on him, saying, Art not thou the Christ? save thyself and us.   But the other answered, and rebuking him said, Dost thou not even fear God, seeing thou art in the same condemnation?   And we indeed justly; for we receive the due reward of our deeds; but this man hath done nothing amiss.   And he said, Jesus, remember me when thou comest in thy kingdom.   And he said unto him, Verily I say unto thee, To-day shalt thou be with me in Paradise.   Luke xxiii. 39–43.

I rely on the reading of our Revised Version here: it is certainly in favour of the authenticity of the incident that the penitent robber addresses Jesus simply by his name, without adornment; there is no parallel to this elsewhere in the gospels.   The robbers were probably Galileans, followers of Jesus, however erring.

The fourth gospel, all through its account of the crucifixion, shows great sobriety and probability (though the piercing of the side of Jesus with the spear probably took place before the death; see the margin of our Revised Version on Matthew xxvii. 49). We may believe that the apostle John was there, and that the sayings recorded by him are genuine.   From the first epistle of Peter (v. 1) we may infer that that apostle also was at some time present by the cross of Jesus; and so may other disciples have been, though it would be natural for them, for safety's sake, to come singly.   The women would be under no such restriction.

That Jesus died on the cross that evening, and was buried by Joseph of Arimathæa in a new tomb, hewn out of the rock, adjoining the place of crucifixion, we may believe on the authority of the gospels. That that tomb was found empty, thirty-six hours later, we may believe on the same authority; though that there was anything supernatural in that occurrence the state of the evidence does not authorise us to believe. But will any Christian of the present day, looking to the great and continuous changes through which the human body passes in the present life, say that it is important that the physical body of Jesus should have been rescued from that dissolution which is the natural end of all bodies? Is it not his personal being in which we are interested, his soul, his will, his emotional and intellectual part? With our present faculties we cannot frame a conception of the new state in which these may be preserved after death; but it is quite impossible to argue from this that they cannot be preserved. The positive reasons for believing in the permanent preservation of personal life must lie in the personal experience of each one of us: if, following upon trust in God, we find that trust in the risen Jesus is a natural condition of right and strong development of character, this will be a just reason for believing it. Amid all the complexities of history, experience does, I believe, point to this conclusion.

With the death of Jesus our earthly life for the first time struck root in the fields of eternity; and it is this that we mean when we say that we are saved; saved for new hopes, new work, and continually growing affections; for a retrieval of things done wrong in the past, and for worthy fruit in the future; saved with a salvation never hereafter to be reversed or frustrated.

If a further explanation be asked of the phrase that I have used, that with the death of Jesus our earthly life for the first time struck root in the fields of eternity, I answer, that in Jesus, in spite of the violent character of his death, no touch of turbulence or disquietude or doubt or hatred is traceable in his demeanour on his cross, or in his last utterances; such as he was then, such he might have wished to be, in all moral ways, through all eternity; the expansion of soul, which (if we believe in immortal life) must accompany the growing years of eternity, did not affect or alter this fact, that a permanent feeling of faith, hope, and love belonged to him, whereby the Divine power flowed into him and through him for ever. Herein lies the reconciliation of God and man; and we who come after Jesus, while, like him, we trust in the Eternal and Almighty and Invisible God, have this additional source of strength, that we have historical testimony of the Divine power so confirming, so filling the person of Jesus, as to enable us to lift our hearts to Jesus in the heavens, and to recognise him in the effect upon ourselves. For by lifting our hearts to him, as well as to the Divine Father, we obtain a stability of soul, and a confidence, which is more precious than any other possession; by means of which we forget the ills of the past and present, or look upon them as mere transient shadows, beyond which the light of an eternal future, growing in compass and in power, shines to us.

CHAPTER XIX

THE BIRTH OF THE CHRISTIAN CHURCH

THAT the life of Jesus Christ was not a tragedy and a failure, but the turning point in the history of this earth on which we live, and that through it all terrestrial life began to partake of the immortal quality, if not instantaneously and obviously, yet essentially and in the promise of the ages that shall be—this, the reader will have already perceived, is the doctrine of the present work. The Spirit of God is in the children of men, and with it has come strength; and it is the narrative of that increasing strength upon which I must now enter. Not always through nominal acceptance of Jesus Christ as the Saviour of mankind has the progressive power of the human race manifested itself; there have been, and are, disbelievers in the authority of Jesus Christ, who in spite of that disbelief have been wise and good men, sources of progress; nevertheless the belief in Jesus Christ as the Saviour of mankind has been a penetrating power, and to perceive the seminal character of his life and death is indispensable, if all mankind are to be united on the lines of true progress.

The duty of regenerating the world, after Jesus had died, fell upon his disciples; and I must now speak of that disciple who first took the lead in this duty—Simon Peter. It would not be just, in speaking of him thus, to forget that certain women preceded him in the declaration that Jesus had risen from death (or "from the dead," as the customary phrase then was); who these women were must be considered later on. But Simon Peter had a command over others which the women were unable to exercise, and he had also been the first to acknowledge Jesus as the Christ; it is to him (without denying the precedence of the women in the important point noticed) that our chief attention is due.

There is a particular point in the antecedent history, not yet noticed, but impossible to pass over without notice, since his character is intimately involved in it; I mean his denial in the court of the high priest, at the very moment when Jesus was being tried, that he was a disciple of Jesus, or that he knew Jesus at all. We shall think very differently of this act according to the account of it which we accept. If we take as a fair account what the synoptic gospels tell us (they are in practical accordance with each other, though not in every detail), we shall find it hard to blame him for any want of courage or fidelity; he may, perhaps, have erred; but it is incumbent on any one who positively affirms this to show what the probable consequences would have been if Peter, at that moment, had acknowledged himself a disciple. The narrative in the fourth gospel stands on different ground, and is much more adverse to him. It is necessary to consider the two accounts separately.

According to the synoptic gospels, Simon Peter was the only disciple who ventured into the close neighbourhood of the foes of Jesus; and his object in doing so, according to the first gospel, was "to see the end"; he wanted to know, with the utmost certainty possible, what was happening to Jesus in that terrible hour. It was an object of great importance, and one which would probably be frustrated if his identity were discovered. When, therefore, his identity was suspected by the servants of the high priest, he took the readiest means of dispelling this suspicion by denying that he knew Jesus at all. A faint denial would have been no good, and therefore he reinforced it by oaths; and it is evident that he did dispel the suspicion. But the natural reaction came; how dreadful an act, he could not but think, to deny his true, his adored Master! and he went out and wept bitterly. But it is clear that he did not see any way of amending what he had done; nor is it easy for us, who are in possession of plenty of leisure to consider the matter, to see the exact moral bearings of the case as it lay before him. Let me try, however, to show the leading points of it.

Was it, in the first place, his duty, at the first moment when Jesus was taken captive—and irrespectively of any question that he might be called on to answer—to enter the court of the high priest as an avowed witness in favour of Jesus? There was only one thing he could have said: "This is the Christ, the Divine King of Israel"; was it his duty to say it? I think not. Such an advocacy would have fallen on deaf ears; a man is not bound to essay the impossible. His duty might indeed lie in the direction of converting those who could be converted; but Caiaphas and the chief priests were not to be reckoned among

these. Thus, when Peter followed the captors of Jesus a short
distance behind them, and entered the court of the high priest
with the view of hearing what he could of the trial that must
ensue, he had not so far swerved from the lines of duty. But
now the direct charge is made against him: "Thou also wast
with Jesus the Galilean." Did it at once become his duty to
say, what before it was not his duty to say, "It is true: I was
with Jesus the Galilean; yes, and he is the Christ"? The
common opinion of Christians is that, when he was questioned,
this at once became his duty. If the contrary is affirmed, the
challenge is made: "What would have become of Christianity
if the martyrs had denied their faith? why should Peter be
privileged to deny his?" Despite the apparent justice of this
challenge, we must still remember that the same rule does not
always fit all cases. There was something so immature at this
time, in the thoughts of all the apostles, respecting the beliefs
which Jesus had been implanting in them, that reticence at this
moment was a necessity for them. It is true that Jesus had sent
them out as preachers, and this implied that they were not wholly
ignorant of the gospel message to men; but that was before
submission to the cross had become a recognised part of his
teaching[1]; they were staggered, now, at the thought of his
coming death. Simon Peter was in as much perplexity as any
other of the apostles; if he were required to say a word on behalf
of his Master, he could not say it. It was not that his faith was
destroyed; but he could give it no intelligible expression. Under
these circumstances did loyalty to Jesus really require him to
confess his discipleship to the accusing voices who assailed him
in the court of the high priest's house? If he had been able
to produce an impression on the judges—to kindle a flame of
true conviction in some part of that priestly and Pharisaic
audience—there might have been sufficient cause for him to lay
down his life, even though Jesus were not rescued thereby. But
this was precisely what he felt himself unable to do. If any ray
of light shone through the disorder of his thoughts, it was not
enough to enable him to reflect it to outsiders. As an advocate,
he was, for the present, useless. Meanwhile he was doing real
service to Jesus in a narrower sphere, by hearing what actually
happened at his trial, so as to be able to report it to others afterwards. As far as loyalty to Jesus is concerned, he did more

---

[1] Matthew x. 38 is a misplaced verse, as I have already remarked.

service to Jesus in this way than by the feeble avowal of a discipleship which he was unable to justify.

But it may be said that Peter owed it to his questioners to tell them the truth. I question whether he did owe it to them. They would certainly have made no good use of the knowledge; and though it would not be right to say that enemies have never a right to a true reply, I question whether they had such a right in this case. There was no malice against them in Peter's mind, as his subsequent conduct proved; but there would have been malice in their minds against him, if they had known who he was.

So far as to the synoptic gospels; but if the account in the fourth gospel is true, the case against Peter has real strength. My defence of him, when judged on the basis of the synoptic account, is essentially this, that he was doing an act of necessary duty when questioned in the high priest's house, and that to have answered the question truly would have been a bar to his carrying out that duty. But this ground of defence is cut away if we accept the account in the fourth gospel; for Peter, according to that gospel, had a companion, who was both a disciple of Jesus and also an acquaintance of the high priest; so well known, in fact, to the high priest's household, that the maid who kept the door of the court leading to the street outside let him in without hesitation. If this is true, then this other disciple was in a much better position than Peter to find out what was happening at the trial of Jesus; the presence of Peter was a superfluity; indeed worse than a superfluity, if it is true (as the fourth gospel alone tells us) that it was he who had just cut off the ear of the high priest's servant. If, in spite of these objections to his entering the court, he chose to enter it, the fact of his presence there was of interest only to himself; there was no very close connexion between his presence there and the promotion of the cause for which Jesus was contending. Hence, when he denied that he was a disciple of Jesus, he saved his own life, but not his honour; heroism and true discipleship have alike dropped off from him. Moreover there is something really mean in the character of his denial, if the fourth gospel be true in this part. The maid who kept the door would not let him in, not knowing him; it needed the request of the other disciple to persuade her to let Peter in; and she, with no hostile intent, but knowing that the other disciple *was* a disciple of Jesus, turns to Peter with the natural question, "Art thou also one of this man's disciples?" It is to this question according to the fourth gospel, that Peter returns the answer, "I am not." Yet, looking to the fact that the other disciple was known to be a disciple of Jesus, Peter could not have run any immediate risk by owning himself also to be such; or if he thought there was risk, there was time for him to retreat. Moreover, he denied the truth in presence of a friend, who, himself calm, knew that Peter was stricken with fear; for what motive but fear can on this view of the facts account for his denial?

Is there not improbability, and no slight improbability, in this account of the behaviour of an apostle who, some six or seven weeks afterwards, assumed naturally the headship of the whole body of the disciples, and who certainly showed no want of courage in facing the Jewish authorities?

Moreover, let me note one defect in the narrative of the fourth gospel here, which shows that the spirit of the whole incident has not been truly seized; this is the only gospel which does not mention that Peter, after his denial, wept at the thought of what he had done; wept bitterly, Matthew and Luke say. He wept, as I believe, from the consciousness not of sin, but of weakness; but weep he did, and bitterly. Was not the mention of this fact essential for the understanding of the true nature of the deed which he had done? Must not our confidence in the gospel which omits so essential a part of the matter be lessened?

Let it be remembered further with what extraordinary inaccuracies the fourth gospel is chargeable, even in parts where no miracle is being recorded, as I think I have shown in the sixteenth chapter of the present work. Many of those inaccuracies, as I there tried to show, were due to the Ephesian Christians; one of whom (with the aid of others, no doubt) acted as editor of the reminiscences of the apostle John. It was very natural for these Ephesian Christians to exalt their own apostle; they called him "the disciple whom Jesus loved"; and when they bring him into connexion with Simon Peter, it is always with some indication that John is at any rate not the inferior of the two. It is not that they wish to disparage Peter; they know that Peter was a great apostle, and had received a special commission from Jesus, unshared by the others; this, which both Matthew and Luke tell us, the fourth gospel does in its own imaginative way confirm (xxi. 15–17); and in the same passage reference is made to the martyrdom of Peter. The Ephesian Christians wished to honour Peter, and not to dishonour him; but they also wished to intimate that their own apostle, John, was at least the equal of Peter; and this wish of theirs has resulted, in the passage which describes Peter's denial, in what is practically a calumny on Peter. It is true that in this passage the disciple who is known to the high priest and who introduces Peter into the high priest's court is not said to be "the disciple whom Jesus loved"; but it is hard to think that "the disciple whom Jesus loved," or in other words the apostle John, is not intended, and this has been the common opinion.

Looking to all these points—looking also to the perfect simplicity and naturalness of the synoptic account here, and the absence of any desire in it to shield or excuse Peter—I accept that account, and reject the account in the fourth gospel. The inference from this is that Peter was the bravest of the twelve apostles; that his weakness under the circumstances was unavoidable; and while we acknowledge this weakness, his denial that he was a disciple of Jesus ought not to be reckoned against him as if it were cowardice.

Having done something, I trust, to dispel the most serious charge ever made against this great apostle, I now revert to the point of time with which the present chapter began, the early morning of the first day of the week after the crucifixion, when the women went down to the tomb in which the body of Jesus had been laid. They found the tomb empty: the body was not there.

When once the non-miraculous view of this occurrence has been adopted, as I do without doubt adopt it, the question by whom the body was moved, and why, though of great interest, becomes of minor importance. The most probable supposition is, perhaps, that it was moved by disciples, who desired to know whether Jesus were really dead, and who were afterwards afraid to say what they had done; the next most probable, that it was moved by the servants of Joseph of Arimathæa twenty-four hours after the first burial—which was not in itself an improbable act, but it entails the supposition that that member of the Sanhedrim was not definitely a disciple (Matthew and John call him a disciple, Mark and Luke do not). I do not perceive that either explanation is beyond the pale of reasonable possibility; nor is the supposition of a fraudulent motive, considering the number of the disciples, impossible in some of the less worthy of them; deeply as we should have to regret such an act, if it were true. But we cannot determine the question with certainty.

Who were the women who found the tomb empty? Matthew says, "Mary Magdalene and the other Mary"; this "other Mary" having been previously said to be "the mother of James and

Joses." Mark says, "Mary Magdalene, Mary the mother of James, and Salome"; and as Mark had previously described the second Mary as "the mother of James the little and of Joses," it will be seen that he entirely agrees with Matthew, except that he adds Salome to the two Marys. The appendix to Mark agrees with John in representing Mary Magdalene as the single witness, at the first, of the risen Jesus (the fourth gospel describes her proceedings in detail, making clear the meaning that she arrived alone at the empty tomb). Luke names Mary Magdalene, Mary the mother of James, and Joanna (who was the wife of the steward of Herod Antipas); but he seems to add other women as companions to those he names.

It is probable that the exact truth is given us either by Matthew or by Mark (who differ very little); and at any rate we can hardly refuse to believe that "Mary the mother of James the little and of Joses" did accompany Mary Magdalene to the tomb. But who was this second Mary? It is a question of some importance, and I must not pass it over unnoticed.

It will be seen that Luke calls this Mary, "Mary the mother of James"; and I am unable to doubt that Luke meant by "James," thus named without any explanation of his identity being thought necessary, the well-known James, spoken of as "the Lord's brother." This also agrees with Matthew and Mark; for James and Joses are spoken of together as brethren of Jesus elsewhere in the gospels; and though there is no intrinsic improbability in there being another pair of brothers named James and Joses, still the evident confidence of our first and second evangelists that their readers will know who are meant by "James and Joses" makes it improbable that any pair of brothers other than the brethren of Jesus is, as a matter of fact, meant. If then, as we must infer from the combined testimony of Matthew, Mark, and Luke, the mother of the brethren of Jesus visited the tomb on the Sunday morning after his crucifixion and death, is not this equivalent to saying that the mother of Jesus himself did so?

So, indeed, I believe; but there is a view which, admitting the identity of "James and Joses" with the "brethren of Jesus," yet says that their mother was not his mother; and this view I must now explain. It is based on the following passage of the fourth gospel (xix. 25):

But there were standing by the cross of Jesus his mother, and his mother's sister, Mary the wife of Clopas, and Mary Magdalene.

It would at first sight appear from this verse that Mary the wife of Clopas was sister of Mary the mother of Jesus. It may then have been Mary the wife of Clopas who was the mother of James and Joses. In that case, supposing the two families to have lived together, James and Joses might not unnaturally be called brethren of Jesus, being in constant and familiar intercourse with him, though really his first cousins. According to this view, it was Mary the wife of Clopas, and not Mary the mother of Jesus, who watched the entombment of Jesus on the Friday evening, and came to the tomb on the Sunday morning following. It is held to be a support to this view that (if we identify Clopas with Alphæus) it enables us to say that James "the Lord's brother" was also one of the twelve apostles. But it can hardly be denied to be an objection to this last identification that, at the time when the twelve apostles were chosen, the brethren of Jesus do not appear as yet to have become his followers. (See John vii. 5; and compare Matthew xii. 46–50, and the parallel passages in Mark and Luke.)

Still, the view which I do not myself hold, but have just been explaining, is not necessarily bound up with the identification of James the Lord's brother with James the son of Alphæus. We may reject that identification, and still hold that Mary the wife of Clopas was sister of Mary the mother of Jesus, and was herself the mother of James and Joses; and that the two Marys lived together, and that thus Jesus habitually lived with James and Joses, and treated them as brethren, and was treated by them as a brother. That is not an impossibility; but it must be confessed to be improbable; and in all the gospels there is not a shred of evidence that it was the case. Nor is there a shred of evidence that James, who is called "the Lord's brother," was really the Lord's cousin. Moreover it is certainly improbable that two sisters should each be called Mary; and the fourth gospel is not beyond suspicion of error, here as elsewhere. Or even supposing the fourth gospel to be accurate, we may fall back on the suggestion (made by Professor Joseph Mayor in his work on the epistle of James) that an "and," though not expressed, is to be understood between the words "his mother's sister" and "Mary the wife of Clopas." The same omission is found in the list of the apostles as given in Matthew and in the first chapter of the Acts. If this be the case here, "his mother's sister" would probably be Salome (see Mark xv. 40, and compare Matthew xxvii. 56).

Let me pause a moment. It is an intricate argument that

I have been pursuing; but is not the conclusion to which I have been guiding the reader a conclusion worth some intricacy of argument? Is it not a thought that must touch us, that the mother of Jesus was herself one of the visitants to the tomb on that early morning when the tomb was found empty; nay, as the evidence on the whole leads us to think, that she and Mary Magdalene were, in that first dawn of the morning, the only two visitants? And we may naturally suppose her more reticent than Mary Magdalene, which would in some degree reconcile the differing statements of Matthew and Mark as to the behaviour of the women.

Let me give a further point in the evidence which lies before us, tending strongly to confirm the view here put forward. The fourth gospel tells us that the mother of Jesus stood by his cross; we must recognise the probability that she would stand there, and the fourth gospel in this part, even if not absolutely accurate, has more than usual claims on our belief. That the mother of Jesus stood by his cross, must be held true. But if so, must we not suppose that Matthew, Mark, and Luke would mention it? Though the mother of Jesus had not in those days the transcendental glory which was assigned to her afterwards, she was not an unknown person, and her presence was not likely to be entirely overlooked. Now if she is the person intended by "the mother of James and Joses" or "the mother of James" then Matthew, Mark, and Luke do mention her presence near the cross; if she is not the person so intended, then Matthew, Mark, and Luke do not mention her presence. Is it not then probable that Matthew, Mark, and Luke, when they mention "Mary the mother of James and Joses" (or "of James" simply) are mentioning Mary the mother of Jesus?

I will admit that the writers of these three gospels, the writers that is of these gospels in the form in which we possess them, did not probably quite realise who it was that they described as "Mary the mother of James." Though it is allowable to speak of them as writers, they were in most respects more truly compilers; they inserted in their gospels the evidence which reached them, as it reached them. In the earliest days of the infant Christian society, Mary the mother of Jesus would be seen associating with her other sons (so we must infer from Acts i. 14—and the last clause of John xix. 27 is hardly to be accepted in the contrary sense): she would be described as the mother of James by those who saw her, and this description of her would be handed down at first orally, afterwards in writing, to others who had no means of knowing that the person so described was also the mother of Jesus.

It will be observed that I am hardly supposing any mistake in the evidence before us, except that the variation in the names of the women who visited the tomb implies a certain amount of pardonable error, and I cannot accept as it stands the isolated statement at the end of John xix. 27[1]. But I am taking the evidence as in its main points trustworthy; and though we should not have expected the mother of Jesus to have been called "Mary the mother of James," yet when we consider the way in which the evidence was gathered in and handed down, our surprise at such a designation will be very much lessened.

Let me now bring forward one more argument, drawn from the nature of the case. Was not the mother of Jesus, just as she had stood by his cross in the last hour before he died, so also certain to have joined in preparing the spices and visiting the tomb? Could she have left the last tender offices to other women to perform? "A sword pierced through her soul," we may well believe; but so much the more would she fulfil all offices of affection which it was in her power to fulfil. It is only positive illness of her own that would prevent her; but we have absolutely no ground for saying that any such illness happened to her; she was quite well, we know, on the Friday evening, and it is a gratuitous assumption to suppose that she fell ill before the Sunday morning. The evidence before us, taken as a whole, joins with this natural probability in leading us to believe that the mother of Jesus, just as she had stood by the cross, so also was one of the first to visit his tomb, prepared to do there all that was needful.

These acts to which I have just referred are the most deeply interesting things that we know about Mary the mother of Jesus. If she was not, as on the evidence of the gospels (duly weighed) we must hold she was not, a believer in the exalted mission of her son when he first began to preach in Galilee, she and all her sons believed in him afterwards, and formed an element in the Christian society by no means to be neglected. James is the member of the family of whom we hear most, and who was most influential, being the equal of the apostles themselves in the general management of affairs and in the respect paid to him;

---

[1] It is permissible to think, that though the sayings of Jesus to which this statement is appended were probably reported by the apostle John, this statement was appended by the editor of the gospel.

but the mother of Jesus had also her own peculiar station in the company of believers. So we must infer from the idealism of which she was the subject in after times; we can hardly think that it arose without something that really drew attention to her. If, as I incline to think, the first step in the idealisation of her lay in the vision which we read in the twelfth chapter of the Revelation, where the seer beholds "a woman arrayed with the sun, and the moon under her feet, and upon her head a crown of twelve stars," this woman being also the mother of him "who is to rule all the nations with a rod of iron," by which ungentle symbol the Christ is intended, then we have a certain link between history and legend; for the apostle John, who wrote down the vision, must have been intimately acquainted with the mother of Jesus, even if the last clause in John xix. 27 be not precisely true[1].

Whether Mary the mother of Jesus saw visions of her son in glory we do not know, but we may believe that Mary Magdalene did so, and we know that Simon Peter and the other apostles and many other believers afterwards did so. I have already said, in my sixteenth chapter, that these visions are not in themselves a proof of the true continued existence and power of Jesus Christ in the spiritual world, but that they were the natural accompaniments of what was proof, namely the sustaining power which flowed in upon believers when they lifted their hearts to Jesus Christ in the heavens, without which sustaining power they sank into inanition and feebleness.

If the fact were doubted, that the first believers had visions between the time of the crucifixion of Jesus and the day of Pentecost, fifty days afterwards, some evidence would be found in the speech of Peter to the throng of Jews who came together and heard him on the day of Pentecost; for he and the other disciples had been thought drunken; and he defends himself and his companions by saying that it was quite another spirit than drunkenness that had animated them; and to explain what that spirit was, he adds:

This is that which hath been spoken by the prophet Joel:
And it shall be in the last days, saith God,
I will pour forth of my Spirit upon all flesh:
And your sons and your daughters shall prophesy,
And your young men shall see visions;
And your old men shall dream dreams——.

[1] It is right to add that the woman in Revelation xii. 1 might conceivably be the city of Jerusalem; this metaphor is found in the apocalyptic second book of Esdras x. 40–58 (which is contained in our Apocrypha). But if this had been the meaning in the Revelation, the interpretation would probably have been given.

I need not finish the quotation. Had not then the apostles, and the other disciples at that early date, been dreaming dreams and seeing visions; if so, did not the risen Jesus enter into those dreams and those visions; and as it cannot be denied that Peter and Paul and John saw dreams and visions afterwards (for these are recorded in the pages of the New Testament), and that the risen Jesus entered into these dreams and visions, does not the whole evidence point to the conclusion that this was the case from the first, and that no broad distinction ought to be drawn between the "forty days[1]" which began with the Sunday after the crucifixion, and the subsequent history?

Taking this as the principle which is to guide our narrative, it is possible now to show the sequence of events after the discovery of the empty tomb, and after the first visions had been experienced, with refreshing effects on the souls of the disciples, and with gradual exaltation of their whole way of viewing things. We must not suppose that either the apostles on the one side, or the chief priests and leaders of the Jews on the other side, were at all concerned to make any inquiries as to what had, or had not, happened to the physical body of Jesus, which had been nailed to the cross and buried in the tomb of Joseph of Arimathæa. The Jewish leaders had no reason to think that their victory was not complete and final; the small company of believers appeared below contempt, now that their leader was gone. On the other hand, the believers in Jesus had things to think of, quite different from any judicial inquiry into physical facts (a kind of inquiry not at all habitual with them). The effect of what had happened had been to exalt them religiously; yet there was something tentative in this exaltation; and that which they felt to be tentative and needing further exploration was not the physical aspect of things. It was the will of God of which they were in search; and the will of God was revealed to them in the ancient Scriptures. So they looked through the Scriptures with care; even if they had not in their possession copies of the whole of them, they would have copies of the most important books; and as on the one hand the psalms and the prophets would make it clear that for the servant of God suffering must precede glory, so also, when they came to consider the ancient law, the sacrifice of the lamb at the most remarkable of all the

---

[1] These "forty days," be it observed, are not mentioned in any of the gospels, and are even opposed to Luke's gospel, as I remarked in chapter xvi (p. 15 above). The first chapter of the Acts is the only authority for them.

festivals of Israel, the passover, would appear to them eminently significative of that death of Jesus of which they had just been witnesses. Thus the conclusion which they arrived at (and a just conclusion, whatever exception might be taken to some of the details of their reasoning) was that a foreshadowing of the kingdom of God was now present with them, in a way in which it had not been before the crucifixion of Jesus. As to the full arrival of that kingdom, their thoughts were not without some admixture of error; they thought of it as happening in a more spectacular, more obviously visible way, than in the nature of things could be; they thought of Jesus appearing in majesty not only to his friends, but to his adversaries. From the words of Jesus it would seem that he himself thought this, though the possibility of a metaphorical meaning must not be forgotten in his case; I interpret his words before Caiaphas as having a mingling of metaphor in them, but not so much as to take away the sense that he, returning, should be visible to those who crucified him as much as to his devoted followers. Absolute accuracy must not be demanded in these deep conceptions at their first beginnings; but when the disciples met together during the weeks after the crucifixion, no harm would come from such an inaccuracy as this. They felt that they had Jesus for their teacher; Jesus, not indeed in the full splendour of that return to which they looked forward, but still truly present, not as a mere memory; whether by vision or by inward feeling, it was he who was with them and taught them. They felt what the evangelist Luke records in the words: "Then opened he their understandings, that they might understand the scriptures." With this divine presence about them, they read the Scriptures in a new light; their spirits were formed and trained for action. An interspace of such training was needed; but the hour for action approached; the hour, when with a deliberation, an openness, more than even Jesus himself had used in the course of his earthly ministry, it should be proclaimed to the world that Jesus was the Christ, the Son of God, the King of Israel, the Saviour of mankind.

Yet before this contact with the outside world could take place, before the disciples could let the multitudes of Israel into the secret of their souls, some things had to be transacted inside the company of the believers. One thing is recorded; two other things are not recorded, but must be presumed from what we know of the after history.

The thing which is recorded is the election of a twelfth apostle in place of the unhappy Judas. This was duly carried out, care being taken to show that the apostles did not arrogate the election to their own sole decision; they chose two competitors, but cast lots as to which of the two should be numbered with the twelve. (It must be remembered that the title "apostle" was not confined to the twelve.)

Such was the first act that we know the apostles to have performed during the interspace between the Passover of the crucifixion and the Pentecost which followed. But also it is told us in the last chapter of the first gospel, and in the appendix to Mark, that the risen Jesus bade his apostles baptize all mankind throughout the world. Inconsistent though these two accounts are as to the circumstances under which this command is said to have been given—unsupported though the statement is by the resurrection-narratives in Luke, John, and the Acts— we yet perceive the tradition to be real and ancient, that the determination of the apostles to make baptism the initial rite whereby any person might enter the Christian society and become permanently a member of it, was arrived at through intercourse with their Master, risen into the heavenly state of being after his death upon the cross. Such intercourse is a true and sublime possibility, not a breach of the order of nature but the addition of a new faculty to those which we have by nature; nor have we any reason to distrust the wisdom of the practice which the apostles thus adopted. It is true that the connexion of baptism with those fervent hopes, spiritual apprehensions, and self-denying resolutions in which the apostolic faith consisted, could not be guaranteed as an invariable, inevitable fact; but it was presumed that there would be this connexion; it was the intention of the apostles that the two should be united, i.e. the outward sign and the inward spirit, and the use of the sign was to signify to all men that the acceptance of this spirit had begun in the person baptized. Every religious rite is liable to be misused, and baptism is misused when it is considered as causative of a change which it only marks and signalises, or (in the case of infant baptism) anticipates; but we have no reason to say that this error had begun at the time of which I am speaking. A solemn change of mind and soul was expressed by a solemn act; we can find no fault with such an expression, and it emphatically made Christians known to one another. Had the example of Zacchæus been sufficiently remembered (whom Jesus admitted into his intimate companionship without baptism) the proper qualifications of the thoughts and feelings attendant on the rite would have been borne in mind, and all danger would have been averted.

Again, those who attend carefully to the words significative of religious practice in the 42nd verse of the second chapter of the Acts, will not have much doubt that what is generally considered by Christians their greatest sacrament, the breaking of bread in remembrance of Jesus as their Saviour, had been familiarly practised before the time indicated in that verse, or in other words before the day of Pentecost. The verse runs thus, and it applies to the whole body of disciples:

And they continued stedfastly in the apostles' teaching and fellowship, in the breaking of bread and the prayers.

The drinking of wine is not mentioned; and it need not be supposed that the heavenly meal was clearly determined in all its particulars at first as it was afterwards; but a religious ceremony must be meant. We can hardly doubt too that the apostles understood that in performing this ceremony they were doing the will of Jesus and having inward communication with him, whether the words reported by Luke and Paul, but omitted by Matthew and Mark, were actually said by Jesus or not: "Do this in remembrance of me." Love, and identity of purpose between Christians and their Master, and the reception of strength in their souls, were always understood when they broke bread as thus described; and this act, as a habitual one, must have been determined by the apostles during the time of which I am speaking, the interval between the Passover of the crucifixion and the feast of Pentecost.

In all essentials, the disciples of Jesus were now constituted as a society; a society that took its directions from heaven, but over which the apostles presided on earth. It was a society of great simplicity in its internal constitution; but what was its aim and purpose? Undoubtedly, to gather other members to itself; above all, to gather the Jewish nation to itself, to make the whole people of Israel believers in Jesus as the Christ, partners in the society of which mutual love was the distinguishing feature. It would not be correct to say that the practice of mutual love was the purpose of the Christian society; it was assumed to be of the essence of the society; the society was unthinkable without it. The purpose of the society was to extend itself; to gather to itself new life so as to replenish and amplify continually the kingdom of essential life. The nations outside Israel were not forgotten by the apostles; but their thought was that Israel must be converted first; the time of the Gentiles would come afterwards. But then also they expected, at some hour to them unknown, the return of Jesus Christ in the glory of his Divine Father, to consummate all things. Such was the first programme of the Christian society.

A programme, surely, full of fidelity and courage! Yet it must be confessed that some imperfections attached to it, such as cannot surprise us, the immense difficulty of the whole subject being considered; but these unfortunately became in the process of time a nucleus round which inferior and more selfish thoughts might cluster, the purity of the society being marred, and the worthiest members of heathen nations being sometimes repelled from it.

The finding of the empty tomb, and the consequent belief of the apostles in the miraculous translation of the body of Jesus into the heavenly sphere, and its spiritual revivification (according to the conception which is expressed in 1 Corinthians xv. 42–50) had been a great consolation to them and a source of hope; a justifiable consolation and hope, but partly mistaken in its grounds. The conception which they held, as explained by Paul, implies an appearance of the risen Jesus to his apostles, not indeed fleshly, but still with something miraculous about it. Hence it was natural for them to think of that return of which Jesus had spoken, his return after death "in the glory of his Father," as miraculous also. They did in their daily lives hold intercourse with him, the intercourse through visions or simply by spiritual trust; but they thought that a more striking and clearer intercourse would be granted to them, when he returned obviously to the apprehension of the whole world, believing or non-believing; and thinking thus, they assumed that some difficult problems must wait for their solution till that future time.

I cannot but think that this is part of the explanation why the original twelve apostles did not take a stronger line in liberating the new society from the ceremonial of the ancient law than they actually did. Another reason doubtless lay in their tenderness for their fellow-countrymen, and this, within certain limits, was a reason of legitimate force; but the attentive reader of the second chapter of the epistle to the Galatians will be of opinion that the apostles felt some personal scruple in affirming the cessation, in principle, of the ancient ceremonial law. They waited for a higher authority, an authority sanctioned by manifest miracle, to justify them in doing this; whereas Paul afterwards more correctly saw that the authority to do so was already present with them. Yet we must not therefore think that Peter, who founded the Christian church in its actual form, was inferior to Paul, who extended the base of it so immensely. Both apostles were entangled by difficulties not of their own making, difficulties which had come down to them from remote antiquity, difficulties which they had not in their own day the means of completely solving. Our perception of the points in which they respectively fell short ought to be drowned in our sense of the greatness of what they did.

But to return to the original apostles, and to the infant community of the disciples, as that existed during the interval between the Passover of the crucifixion and the day of Pentecost following. They were full of ardour in their new perceptions, in their new beliefs; the duty of converting their fellow-countrymen gathered force in them; and on the day of Pentecost this ardour overflowed into the outer world. It would seem that on that day the community were assembled in a house (probably the upper chamber where Jesus had celebrated his last passover); when the Divine Spirit suddenly impelled them to the revelation of what was in them. They must have issued forth into the street (though this is not definitely said); their utterances, the fervour of their gestures, attracted a crowd, who saw and heard with wonder and with curiosity. It does not need the miracles with which the book of the Acts surrounds this event to make it one of the most remarkable moments of history. It was the first collision of the disciples of Jesus, after their Master had departed from them, with the outer world. It was not surprising that some mocked at them; what precisely they had been saying is not recorded; it would seem to have attracted some sympathy, and yet it was incoherent, so as to give some colour to the suspicion that the apostles were drunk. But as soon as this was openly said by some among the crowd, Peter spoke with deliberation and firmness. Not in vain had Jesus trusted him. He declared to the crowd that the prophecies of old were fulfilled; that Jesus of Nazareth (whom, he said, "ye by the hand of lawless men did crucify and slay") was risen from the dead; that they, the apostles, were witnesses of this fact; and he ended, if the report in the Acts be correct, with these words:

Let all the house of Israel therefore know assuredly, that God hath made him both Lord and Christ, this Jesus whom ye crucified.

And now that I have got to this point, I perceive that, as I have defended the apostle Simon Peter against the representations of the fourth gospel, so I must now defend him against the equally formidable attack which modern men of science will make against him. For they will say: "What right had Peter to say that he and the other apostles were witnesses of the fact that Jesus had risen from the dead, without explaining to them that this witness consisted in the evidence of visions, and not in the evidence of outward physical eyesight?"

I answer, that Peter felt far more certain of the fact that Jesus Christ had risen from death, than of his own ability to explain the reasons which made him certain. He felt sure, also, that those who embraced the belief would find it confirmed by their own experience; though they also might feel the inability to put the grounds of their conviction into the form of exact reasoning. In truth, the whole Hebrew genius lay far more in perception than in argument.

Peter therefore was right in not venturing to state the precise grounds of his belief; they were grounds which convinced himself, and he felt it most important that other people should embrace the belief with the utmost speed, for the sake of the practical duties which the belief would bring along with it, the duties involved in the whole order of heavenly life; he did not preclude argument, but it was important that the practice should not be allowed to wait until the argument had been argued out. Such is the condition of us men; we are practical agents as well as theoretical reasoners; and very often indeed we cannot afford to wait for the proof of a fact before we begin to act upon it. Such was the case now. If Peter's instinct as to the truth was right, his conduct was right.

It is necessary, next, to observe how conciliatory his tone was towards those whom he addressed, towards his own nation, the Jews. It is unfortunate that a mistranslation in our Authorised Version has tended to hide this fact from ordinary readers of the Bible; for Peter is there represented as saying to the Jews that they had crucified and slain Jesus of Nazareth "by wicked hands"; the real meaning of the original being that they had slain Jesus of Nazareth "by lawless hands," or (according to what is probably the right reading) "by the hand of lawless men." These "lawless hands" or "lawless men" signify simply the Romans, who did not obey the law, as the Jews understood that word. There is no suggestion of wickedness at all in the passage; and the speech of Peter recorded in the third chapter of the Acts makes this non-aggressive meaning still more clear:

Ye denied the Holy and Righteous One, and asked for a murderer to be granted unto you, and killed the Prince of life; whom God raised from the dead; whereof we are witnesses....And now, brethren, I wot that in ignorance ye did it, as did also your rulers. But the things which God foreshowed by the mouth of all the prophets, that his Christ should suffer, he thus fulfilled.

Very faithful, and yet conciliatory, are these sentences. Ignorance, but nothing further, has been the true fault of the Jews and their rulers, as far as Jesus Christ is concerned; let them repent, and their ignorance will have passed away, their sins of the past will in God's sight be as nothing. That the Christ must suffer, had been foretold, and that could not be avoided; God had vindicated his Servant and his Son, whose dominion was assured; it was the iniquities of daily life from which the Jews must turn away, and belief in the crucified one will accomplish that deliverance for them. There is true magnanimity in such a speech. While nothing was further from the thoughts of Jesus than to give Peter any technical claim to preeminence among the apostles (for he had expressly told Peter that "many shall be last that are first, and first that are last," Matthew xix. 30), it still was true that Peter was the ruling spirit among the first disciples, and the line of conduct which he prescribed was for the time the only sound line. It had to be modified, no doubt, afterwards; but of that modification I must not speak now.

Before going further, let me say something of our only history of this period, the Acts of the Apostles. Though the speeches in the Acts have not the inimitable and forcible style which belongs to the sayings of Jesus in the synoptic gospels, and which is so great a guarantee to us of the genuineness of those sayings, they have yet no inconsiderable distinctiveness and verisimilitude; and in a great degree we may believe in their authenticity. No doubt they are generally abridgments of what was actually said; and something in them is no doubt due to the historian; but not so much as in the discourses of the fourth gospel. The historical narrative of the Acts has also fair trustworthiness; at the same time the delight of the writer in miracles is evident, and our trust must be limited in this direction. Nor is this the only bias which misleads this amiable writer (that he was really Luke, I do not doubt). It is certainly true (as Baur first noticed) that he ignores all important differences between the original apostles on the one hand, and Paul on the other hand; thus he makes no mention of the collision between Paul and Peter at Antioch.   Again, he has an unwillingness to represent Paul as in positions which might be thought humiliating; of the five Jewish scourgings and three Roman scourgings which Paul himself tells us that he suffered (2 Cor. xi. 24, 25) Luke only mentions one, and in that one case redeems Paul's honour by a miracle and by the practical acknowledgment on the part of the Roman authorities that they had erred.   But Paul's honour was beyond stain in any case; and with respect to the miracle, and the repentance of the magistrates, I have already observed (see page 28 above) that Paul himself says nothing about this part of the matter, though he does refer to the shameful treatment which he received at Philippi (where the incident in question took place); which surely is an argument that he had not received any satisfaction for the shameful treatment.

It is impossible not to criticise the Acts, just as it is impossible not to criticise the gospels; yet the great debt which we owe to Luke must not be ignored.   How infinitely poorer should we be if the Acts had not been written!   We have to exercise our judgment indeed, as to what to receive, and what to reject; this is more or less necessary in all histories, and especially where the historian is characterised by a certain simplicity of mind (as were all the early Christians); but a fair criticism will recognise how much remains to us that is of great value, after everything adverse has been said.   It is in the details, naturally, that weakness lies; and this is much more observable in the early part of the Acts, where the deeds of Peter are told us (for of him Luke had but a distant knowledge) than in the later chapters, where the deeds of Paul are described—many of which, though not all, had come under Luke's personal cognisance.

It is Peter, not Paul, who is my present theme; and that Peter was a true minister of Jesus Christ, and that his spiritual energy was worthily exercised (as also was that of the other disciples) we have every reason to say.   But not everything told of him is to be believed; and there is one miraculous story in the early part of the Acts which cannot be left without comment, for it has a tone apparently edifying but not really so; I mean the death of Ananias and Sapphira.

How can any one, who looks at the abundance of untruthfulness in the world, the greater part of which gets off without any punishment at all of an external description, say that the death of these two persons was justly deserved? A little shabby untruthfulness committed while doing an act of positive bene- volence, is surely a sin that might be treated with a gentle corrective. What would happen in our modern world if offenders against truth were treated with this severity? The ordinary Christian view is that the punishment of death was needed in this case as an indication of the abhorrence with which God regards the sin of lying; which having once been made known to us, subsequent offences of the kind are left to be dealt with according as men are perspicacious enough to find them out, or not so. But is it just that a single pair of offenders should be stigmatised for ever, while others, equally offenders in the same way, get off scot-free? Is this divine justice? It is much more likely to be what imperfect men have imagined to be divine justice, which is by no means the same thing.

I am not saying that the narrative of the death of Ananias and Sapphira is wholly without foundation. The consciences of the disciples of Jesus, in those early days, were at so great a strain that a severe reproof might act fatally on the person reproved; and this may have been the case with Ananias. But if Ananias did really die in anything like the manner narrated, it is to be hoped that the disciples then present were affected with more sorrow than the book of the Acts gives them credit for. "Great fear" came upon all who heard it, we are told; but sorrow, not fear, ought to have been predominant; and of sorrow there is no trace in the narrative. Moreover the absence of sorrow is accentuated by the behaviour attributed to Peter, which at any rate ought to be rejected as incredible. Can we believe that an apostle whom we have every reason to regard as merciful and tenderhearted was so oblivious of consideration for others as deliberately to tempt the wife of Ananias to tell a lie? That is what Peter, according to the book of the Acts, did. Three hours after the death of Ananias, we are told, Sapphira, his wife, came in, not knowing anything of what had happened. It was of course probable that she had been privy to her husband's deceit. This being so, what was Peter's duty? Surely, to preserve the wife from all danger of committing the sin which her husband had committed. Of her husband's death he might speak to her with commiseration; of her husband's sin he would speak truly, but yet with remembrance of God's mercy towards sinners; but, above all, he would try to direct the conscience of the wife, who yet survived, into truer channels. Precisely the reverse, if we are to believe the Acts, was Peter's conduct; he is said to have put to Sapphira the very question which was most likely to lead her to tell a lie; and a lie she tells, and dies for it, by what is supposed to be God's judgment. But surely neither God's judgment, nor Peter's character, is credibly represented to us here. The story is too famous to be forgotten; but it ought never to be read without an inward protest, and considerable incredulity.

It is apparent that Luke was under strong temptation to give a miraculous turn to his narrative, and that he yielded to this temptation. Yet this is not surprising, nor, under all the conditions, very censurable; and everything points to the general correctness of his account of the conduct of the first disciples, in the difficult circumstances in which they were placed. They tried to conciliate and convert their own nation first; it was not that they ignored the surrounding nations, but even for the conversion of the surrounding nations it seemed the best way to convert the Jews first. Nor were their efforts at converting their fellow-countrymen without considerable success. The petty persecution to which they were at first subjected ceased after a while; the converts numbered thousands; and Luke tells us that "a great company of the priests were obedient to the faith." The hopeful prospect for the future implied in such a fact might be illusory, but could not be altogether resigned. It might be that the Jewish hierarchy, and with them the whole Jewish nation, would accept Jesus of Nazareth as their divinely appointed leader. That gulf of severance which had been caused by the crucifixion of Jesus was spanned by the apostles through the ancient prophetic word. It had been divinely foretold that the chosen servant of God would die for the sake of his fellows, and that his death would be their salvation. The past could not be forgotten; but the message from it was a message not of vengeance, but of mercy.

Such was the olive-branch which these first apostles of Jesus held out to their fellow-countrymen; and we ought to take note of it, for along this same path must lie the true appeal of the Christian to the Jew, even at the present day. Not, indeed, that we can do quite what the apostles did; they might sincerely practise all the ceremonies of the Pentateuchal law, partly for the sake of ancient reverence, partly for the sake of peace with their fellow-countrymen; but we cannot do this. To us, the

Jewish prophets are more sacred than the Jewish ceremonial law; and, what is still more important, there is to us no intrinsic sacredness in Jewish nationality, though the virtues of the ancient Jews, of ancient Israel, are much to be remembered by us.   These are such commonplaces now that it would be quite vain for us to deny or to ignore them.   Moreover, these commonplaces were as true for the apostles as for us; but not all the first disciples, not all even of the apostles, discerned them to be true; and even those who did discern them to be true (among whom we may probably reckon Peter and the two sons of Zebedee) were up to a certain point right in not pressing them, for the sake of peace with their fellow-countrymen.

Up to a certain point; but up to what point? That was a question on which legitimate difference of opinion might exist; and among the disciples of Jesus there were some who thought that conciliation of the Jewish hierarchy might be carried too far.   There was a burning in the hearts of these disciples to vindicate the honour of their Master more vehemently, with more reproof of his enemies, than had yet been done.   Nor could they forget that one of the primary purposes of Jesus Christ had been to reprove his own nation for grievous errors of conduct which still existed, which had in no respect been abandoned—for a hard technicality in their interpretation of religion, for a want of mercy and tenderness towards the sinful, for a neglect of the miserable poor who were among them.   Were these reproofs never to be resumed? Were the threatenings with which Jesus had accompanied them to be regarded as a dead letter? Such were the thoughts which many of the disciples now entertained; and the growing power of the Christian society made it seem more incumbent to utter them plainly.   That feeling at last found expression through Stephen, the leader (it would seem) of those Jews whose original home was not in Palestine but in some Greek city; he had been recently appointed one of those afterwards called deacons, whose office it was to see that the contributions of the richer members of the Christian society in aid of the poorer members were justly apportioned, and especially that the Greek-speaking members of the society were not neglected.   But he now took upon himself a new and far greater task, from which immense results flowed.

His own career was brief.   What precisely he said to draw down the first attack on him, we do not know, but it was in the way of reproof and threatening.   The Jews flamed up at his words. In the relations between Christian and Jew, the Jews were then the persecutors, Christians the persecuted; and Stephen was accused, tried, and swiftly slain. For some reason, probably because he was regarded as an insignificant person, the Roman governor exacted no penalty from the Jewish authorities for an act which, strictly speaking, was beyond their rightful power.

The speech recorded in the seventh chapter of the Acts as delivered by Stephen at his trial is probably in substance genuine. The early part of it is calm, and is intended to point out what errors the chosen people had committed in earlier stages of their history. But at last he spoke with disparagement of the temple; and then his audience must have shown signs of anger; for suddenly he throws moderation to the winds, and inveighs against them with bitterness. He felt that the time had come to be outspoken; he was inspired to meet his death, and he embraced it with zeal; and before he died, he sealed his faithfulness by declaring that he saw the heavens opened, and the Son of man standing at the right hand of God. It is the only recorded instance in which any of the disciples names Jesus by the phrase, so common in his own discourse, "the Son of man." The vision was surely the work of imagination; but that imagination rested, as I believe, on eternal fact, the true presence of Jesus with his faithful disciples. I must quote the exact words in which the death of Stephen is described; the opening words refer to the vision which he had just announced.

But they cried out with a loud voice, and stopped their ears, and rushed upon him with one accord; and they cast him out of the city, and stoned him: and the witnesses laid down their garments at the feet of a young man named Saul. And they stoned Stephen, calling upon the Lord, and saying, Lord Jesus, receive my spirit. And he kneeled down, and cried with a loud voice, Lord, lay not this sin to their charge. And when he had said this, he fell asleep. And Saul was consenting unto his death.

It is seldom that we can be sure of the accuracy of the details in any remarkable scene of history; and I will not deny that I waver as to accepting the last words attributed to Stephen. If we were sure that they rested on the evidence of the "young man named Saul," we might no doubt rightly accept them; but they have not that characteristic ring which belongs to Stephen's declaration of his sublime vision, and they may be a later addition. On the whole, the general sanity of the narrative ought perhaps to incline us to accept them.

Was Stephen right in this sudden defiance of the Jewish

authorities? Such a question is not to be answered with absolute certainty, but conciliation was probably impossible. The hindrances which prevented the main body of the Jews from accepting Jesus as the Christ had a deeper root than the apostles realised, and could not have been speedily overcome. The belief in miracles, which at a later date, and in the Gentile world, acted on the side of conversions to Christianity, acted against such conversions with ordinary Jews; because these ordinary Jews believed in the miracles of the Exodus and of Mount Sinai, and did not believe that any equal miracles had been worked by Jesus. They judged by comparison of the material power displayed; Moses had delivered the Israelites from the Egyptian monarch, Jesus had not delivered the Jews from the Roman power. This was obvious; and though higher, tenderer, and more spiritual views were not wanting in the Jewish nation, and did make many Jews believers in Jesus as the deliverer of mankind from sin and wickedness, it was not to be expected, considering the general nature of men, that the predominating view among the Jews should be of this exalted cast. In short, there were historical reasons which set the ordinary Jew, and more particularly the Jewish hierarchy, against Jesus in a degree which did not exist in the case of the ordinary Greek or Roman.

Reasons such as these, which we in the comparative quiet of the twentieth century may discern, looking back upon past history, were not of course visible to Stephen in the first century. Stephen acted from instinct, not from reasoning; but his instinct was a right one; and with his death began that slow conversion of the Christian church, from being a Jewish society into being a Gentile society, which it took nearly two centuries to accomplish fully.

With his death, too, began that retrocession of the original apostles, even of Peter and of James and John, the sons of Zebedee, and of that other distinguished James, not one of the twelve but "the Lord's brother," into the background as propagators of the Christian faith; and towards the front comes marvellously "the young man named Saul," who began as a persecutor of Christians. Of him the next chapter must speak.

But meanwhile, let us not despise or think lightly of the first preachers of Jesus as the Christ; especially let us not think lightly of Simon Peter. If, in dealing with that difficult and memorable question, "Are Gentiles to be the equals of Jews in the church of Jesus Christ?" he vacillated as we read he did in Paul's epistle to the Galatians, it was not unnatural or unpardonable in him.   We should have liked to hear his account of the matter; he was probably not faultless; but he would have had something to say for himself.

It is curious that the frequent impression among many of this modern age, that Simon Peter was a commonplace person, is due entirely to the belief in miracles. Modern Christians think it was the simplest thing in the world for him and his companions to see the risen Jesus: why not, when the risen Jesus was before their eyes? These modern Christians could have seen him themselves if they had been there. But those who agree with the arguments in this book will agree that the risen Jesus was discernible, not by the senses, but by the pure spirit and benevolent heart; and this kind of discernment is not commonplace.

Let me not, before closing this chapter, fail to do honour to that brave spirit, James the son of Zebedee, the first martyr among the apostles.

CHAPTER XX

THE CONFLICT AND THE VICTORY OF THE CHRISTIAN CHURCH

In the foregoing chapter it has been told how the newborn Christian society failed, after steady and patient efforts, to win to its cause the main body of the Jewish nation, out of which it had sprung. The present chapter must tell how this same Christian society, growing with the years, did win to its cause, did convert and spiritually subjugate the great heathen empire of Rome, with its multitudinous and multiform population; and though it will be impossible in the present chapter to show either the full character or the full results of that victory, the victory itself is a worthy theme of narrative, a ground of much wonder and of many questionings.

The contrast just noted cannot but surprise us. If Christianity failed with the Jews, should we not much more expect that it would fail with the races outside Judaism? The Jews were expecting a Messiah, or Divine King; the outside races (whom we generally call the Gentiles) were not expecting one; if the Jews had determined that the pretensions of Jesus of Nazareth, their own fellow-countryman, to be such a Divine King, were baseless, would not one say that it was hopeless to think that the outside races would accept him? That certainly is the first natural view that we should take on the subject; but as it is proved by actual historical fact not to be the true view, we have to inquire what it was that caused a result so different from what we should have expected.

In the first place, then, we must not forget that a very large number of Jews did accept Jesus of Nazareth as their Divine King. The ruling authorities among the Jews did not then accept him, and never have accepted him; and the Jewish nation as a whole has followed these authorities, as was to be expected. But an immense multitude of Jews did accept Jesus as the Christ; and not only was this the case at the time of the first preaching of Christian belief on the day of Pentecost,

but all through the first century of our era, and through the
second century likewise, and even later, there were many Jews
who were also Christians.   Over and above all this, we know very
well that if there had not been most sincere and ardent believers
in Jesus as the Christ among the Jews, there would have been
no believers among the Gentiles either. Jewish discipleship
was a necessary preliminary to Gentile discipleship; the Jews
were the medium through which Christianity had to reach the
Gentiles, and without this medium it would not have reached
them.   In view of these facts, the question may perhaps be
asked, whether it is right to call the attempt of the apostles to
convert their own nation, the Jews, a failure.

Yes, we must call it so; but we must add that it was an
honourable failure, a failure full of promise for the future, a failure
that might some day be retrieved.   Again, we must not (up to
a certain point at any rate) blame those Jewish believers in Jesus
Christ who, from love of their own nation, and from regard for
ancient traditions, held strictly by the Pentateuchal law.   An
admixture of error there was in their position, doubtless; they
ought to have recognised what they did not recognise, that the
keeping of the ancient ceremonial law was no longer an obligation
on them; it had been wiped out in the new covenant, that direct
covenant with God which the death of Jesus Christ had created,
by virtue of which the eternal invisible world was laid open to
them.   Still up to a certain time it was not wrong in them to
keep up the fellow-feeling with their own nation through the
ancient rites, circumcision and the sacrifices of the law; and if
the Jewish priesthood, even at a late hour, had accepted Jesus
as the Christ, then the new spirit might have entered into the
nation, Jerusalem and the temple might have stood unharmed,
and the prophecies of glory which had rested upon Israel from
ancient times might have been literally fulfilled.   Such was the
kind of anticipation which, it is reasonable to suppose, actuated
that James[1] who is called "the Lord's brother" (an appellation
which I have taken literally and not as implying cousinhood
merely), the author of the noble epistle which finds a place in
our New Testament to-day.   In his conduct towards Gentile
believers there may have been some narrowness; so at least we
should conclude from what is told us in the second chapter of

[1] The explanation here given of the kind of thought which animated this
distinguished Christian leader was suggested to me by my uncle F. W. Newman,
in whose works, I think, it occurs somewhere.

Paul's epistle to the Galatians; but we must not expect perfection in any man; and when he was slain, a martyr to his belief in Jesus, through the fanatic zeal of the Sadducean high priest, even the Jews themselves considered that a sin had been committed. The last hope of conversion of the Jewish nation as a whole to Christianity was wiped out in his death; and the fall of Jerusalem happened not long afterwards.

Let me now repeat what I said in my last chapter, that the profoundest reason for the non-conversion of the Jewish nation, as a whole, to Christianity, lay in their belief in miracles. The Jewish priesthood felt, and truly felt, that Jesus was assuming a position higher than the ancient law; and it was incredible to them that a law which had been ushered in by the divine thunders and lightnings on Mount Sinai, and which in its leading tenets had been promulgated by the voice of God himself to the assembled nation of Israel, could ever be superseded in any of its provisions without miraculous signs as clear as those amidst which it had been first promulgated. That Jesus had ever worked signs equivalent to the Sinaitic miracles, they did not believe; and hence they rejected him.

But the Jewish believers in Jesus, by virtue of a true, deep, and imperative instinct, refused to accept the conclusion in which the Jewish priesthood rested, and without at all denying the Sinaitic revelation, said that the revelation by Jesus was greater; and now some among these believers, by their intense ardour, broke through the fence which separated the Jews from the outside world, and laid the foundation of that Gentile Christianity which is the Christianity of to-day. In preaching Christianity among the Gentiles, they had to meet with external opposition far more severe and bitter than that which they had experienced from the Jews; but no argument which heathen philosophers advanced against them equalled in plain directness that which the Jewish priesthood had advanced against them; and hence the result was that these Jewish believers in Jesus as the Christ converted the multiform races which constituted the Roman empire, though they had not been able to convert their own nation.

Such is a brief description of that drama, the most stupendous in the world's history, which I must now narrate in detail. And as, on the one hand, I have said with respect to the Jewish Christians, who continued to practise the Pentateuchal law, that a certain want of recognition of the magnitude and freedom of true religion, as that had been embraced and taught by their great instructor, Jesus, is imputable to them; so, on the other hand, we must not expect that those Jewish Christians, who broke through the letter of their law, claiming in this the sanction of the Divine Spirit, should be absolutely faultless in working out so great a transition. They did not, as I read the matter, wholly escape error; but still they did an immense work.

He who was the central and most active agent in that drama of which I have been speaking, the dissemination of Christian belief and Christian principles among the nations of the world, was no other than that persecutor who sat approving of the slaughter of Stephen, and who afterwards himself instituted a fierce persecution (doubtless not singly, but yet as a leader, not a mere subordinate) against those who held the faith for which Stephen had died. Saul was his Hebrew name; Paul was doubtless the name by which he was known in the Roman world generally, and Paul it is better to call him after his conversion.

That conversion, by which Saul the persecutor became Paul the apostle, was certainly one of the most marvellous events in history. Marvellous, and yet no miracle—at least if by miracle be meant an event wholly unparalleled in our ordinary experience. It was the reversal in direction of a great spiritual force; the change, from a direction in which that force was fruitless, into a direction in which it was fruitful; the change, from obedience to commands which symbolised the divine will, into an intelligent carrying out of that divine will itself. A change, not to be accomplished without some danger of error in the process; but in its total result memorably beneficent.

I see no reason to doubt that the three narratives, in which the conversion of Paul is told in the Acts, are essentially a true statement of what happened. They are indeed not entirely consistent with one another; but the inconsistencies do not go beyond what Paul himself might have committed, in repeating the story at different times, and with slightly different motives. That it was the true Jesus who touched the spirit of Paul, when the persecuting zeal of Paul had suffered collapse through its own fierceness and through the remonstrances of his conscience; this is not exactly the way in which the conversion is related, but this is the explanation of all the narratives, and on a really spiritual view of the universe it is a satisfactory and just explanation. In speaking of the remonstrances of Paul's conscience to the course which he was pursuing, I am in agreement with the

narrative which gives, as among the words of Jesus which he
heard, "It is hard for thee to kick against the goad"; words which
in their exact form were suggested to Paul by his Greek learning,
but of which the substance had a diviner source. That Paul
had remembered the death of Stephen we might be sure; it
was not a thing to be forgotten; of the earthly things which he
had known this approached nearest to heavenly things. But
the true heavenly touch lay in that which came with restorative
influence in the midst of his prostration, and which bade him
attach himself to that divine love which flowed from the gentle
ministrations of Jesus, and which, if he had patience, would
guide him right through the tangled courses of this world. We
can hardly suppose that Paul did immediately, as he lay on the
ground in his blindness and feebleness, form any direct purpose
of preaching Christ among the Gentiles, though this might perhaps
be inferred from what he says in the first chapter of his epistle
to the Galatians, and is more clearly implied in the twenty-sixth
chapter of the Acts; if any idea of this kind flashed through his
mind at that moment, it can have been only in rudimentary
form. But the purpose must have matured during that solitary
time which, as he tells us himself, he spent in Arabia immediately
afterwards; and it is likely that he preached not only to the
Jews, but to the Gentiles, when he returned to Damascus after
this Arabian sojourn. If he did this, we can understand why
the Jews were so bitter against him, and induced Aretas the
king of that country to try to seize him; he escaped (as we learn
both from the Acts and from his own testimony in the second
epistle to the Corinthians) by being let down from the city wall
in a basket. How long it was after this that he made that
journey to Jerusalem of which he tells us in the first chapter
of his epistle to the Galatians we do not precisely know, but it
is likely to have been very soon, and this we should infer from
the Acts; in any case, it was three years after his conversion.
At this visit he saw Peter, and also James "the Lord's brother";
doubtless he found from them that they would offer no hindrance
to his preaching to the Gentiles; and it must have been at this
visit also that he had that vision in the temple, of which he
afterwards gave an account in that speech which is recorded in
the twenty-second chapter of the Acts. It is fairly clear that,
whereas before this he had formed no large plan as to his evan-
gelising mission, he now deliberately resolved to convert the
whole Roman empire to the faith of Christ.

But having arrived at this point, it is necessary to look back a little.

We are now at that part of Paul's life of which the author of the Acts had no personal knowledge; and it is quite clear, when we compare the account in the Acts with the epistle to the Galatians, that Luke has too large an idea of the amount of intercourse which Paul had with the Christians of Jerusalem and Judæa, and especially his intercourse with the original apostles; the historian lays emphasis on lines which ought to have been much more lightly drawn. Still, we must not exaggerate in our minds the degree of Luke's divergence from the real fact; and the whole position of Peter and of the disciples who acted with him must be examined with some care.

The circumstances attending on the death of Stephen had startled both the Jewish hierarchy and the disciples of Jesus into the vivid apprehension of a hostility which had for some time been concealed. The keen censure which Stephen had expressed (in his recorded speech, if not earlier), and the growing number of the disciples, combined to make the disciples appear more formidable to the Jewish authorities than they had previously seemed to be; hence the attempt to put them down summarily. On the other hand, all the disciples (and the apostles among the rest) felt the need, not so much of taking thought for their own personal safety, as of meeting the hostile attack with new energy on their own side. The conversion of the Samaritans was immediately attempted, and with some success; the Samaritans, being a circumcised nation, stood on a different level from the heathen, and the extension of the gospel preaching into this region was not met with any remonstrance, even by the most ardent adherents of the ancient law who had ranged themselves under the banner of Jesus Christ. But when the heathen centurion Cornelius, known so far merely as an attached friend of the Jewish nation, but not enrolled among them by the rite of circumcision, sought for an interview with Peter, and was accepted as a disciple, and received baptism, then some murmurs did arise among those Christians who thought obedience to the ancient law obligatory; and some of the apostles joined in remonstrating with Peter. Peter however had an authority not easily to be set aside; and to conciliate those who remonstrated with him, he told them the quaint but expressive vision through which he had gathered that it was God's will that the Gentiles should not be refused admission into the Christian society.

Not then in Paul's mind alone, but through the whole society of believers in Jesus Christ a thrill passed after Stephen's martyrdom, awakening them to wider enterprises than any which they had hitherto undertaken for the extension of the faith. And we may be sure that through many channels the gospel now began to reach the Gentiles. If there were no other reason for saying so[1], the fact that an important Christian church existed in Rome, long before Paul went there, and a church containing many Gentiles, would be proof of this: the epistle of Paul to the Romans shows that such a church did exist. It would indeed be unreasonable to think, if any one ever entertained the thought, that to one person alone, this Paul of Tarsus, the whole conversion of the Gentile world was due; that without him the believers in Jesus Christ would have remained an absolutely Jewish society, except for some sprinkling of Samaritans, and a solitary Gentile here and there, originally well disposed to the Jewish race. That would be unduly to exaggerate the work of Paul; and yet the work which he did was immense.

Not only was a very large part of the conversion of the Gentile world to Christianity due to Paul's active initiative, but also—and this was peculiarly his work—to him was due the real equality of Gentiles with Jews in the Christian society. Whether Gentiles, uncircumcised and free from all obligation to practise the ceremonial of the Jewish law, should be reckoned equal to Jews in the Church of Christ, was the burning question among Christians at this early date. Jewish Christians had conceded the point, that uncircumcised Gentiles might join the Church; but they still held that, as long as these Gentiles were uncircumcised, their status was inferior and imperfect; they had not fulfilled the whole counsel of God; they must reckon themselves on the way to the perfect life, but not as having attained it.

Against this contention of the Jewish Christians Paul directed his full energy, both in preaching and in working. Not that he was incapable of making concessions on occasions; it was no sin, in itself, to perform the rites of the Jewish law; it might be well, now and again, to join in doing so. But against the obligation of doing so he set himself steadily and unremittingly. The obligations which a disciple of Christ must take upon himself

---

[1] I must consider it certain that Acts xi. 20 affirms that disciples belonging to Cyprus and Cyrene preached to (and converted) some of the Greeks; who were, of course, not Jews. Some of the MSS, indeed, read "Grecian Jews" instead of "Greeks"; but this, as Alford has remarked, gives no rational meaning, in view of the previous history.

were, according to Paul, not founded on a historical covenant, but on something very deep in the nature of man. Sinfulness, he said, was inherent in mankind; the transgression of the first man had caused it, and no external act was capable of eliminating it, or of drawing the erring impulses out of our veins; no sacrifice, no deed of man could do so. But over against the sinfulness of man stood, to the apprehension of Paul, one great restorative fact; one fact, in which the Divine Spirit was manifested—the crucifixion and death of Jesus Christ. By the Spirit the spirit could be cleansed; the erring impulses were washed away in those who put their trust in Jesus Christ crucified.

Now it must not be thought that Paul's teaching, in those deep aspects which I have just been explaining, came as altogether new or strange to the ears of the elder apostles. In many respects it was identical with what they themselves had proclaimed all through. From the first, the apostles had seized upon that chapter which we read as the fifty-third of Isaiah, and had believed it to contain the prediction of the death of Jesus, and to evince what that death spiritually meant. Now in that chapter it had been said of the future inheritor of God's power, "For the transgression of my people was he stricken," and that his soul should be "an offering for sin," and that "he bare the sin of many, and made intercession for the transgressors." The significance of the crucifixion and death of Jesus in cleansing the consciences of men from sin was part of the apostolic doctrine from the very first, and was by no means new in Paul's teaching. But Peter and the original apostles had not drawn the inference that the Jewish ceremonial law had now lost its *raison d'être*. That was Paul's inference; that was the new doctrine which Paul brought into the forefront; and it involved a far more decisive abandonment of the Jewish religious ceremonial than any which the original apostles had deemed possible. To Paul's mind, the redemption of Israel had sunk into the background as compared with the redemption of mankind. This indeed was the true sequence both of the teaching of John the Baptist and of the teaching of Jesus himself; for the Baptist had preached to individuals rather than to the nation, and had said that "God out of these stones can raise up children unto Abraham," and Jesus had said that "Many shall come from the east and the west, and shall sit down with Abraham and Isaac and Jacob in the kingdom of heaven; but the sons of the kingdom shall be cast out into the outer darkness." What Paul preached and did was the first practical attempt to carry out these maxims of John the Baptist and of Jesus himself; it was the transference of the main purport and highest promises of the Christian religion from Israel to mankind at large. Israel was dethroned; and it could not but be expected that the Jews should be stirred to extraordinary animosity by such a procedure.

But the original apostles, Peter and the rest, were, it is evident, not unmoved by Paul. We see this by Peter's conduct at Antioch, vacillating as it was; and, at a much later date, John the son of Zebedee, though in some respects taking a peculiar line of his own, was in practical agreement with Paul. It was of course much more easy to adopt Paul's trenchant deposition of Judaism when away from Jerusalem, than when living in Jerusalem; and hence we must not be surprised at finding James "the Lord's brother," whose permanent residence was in Jerusalem, the most Judaistic of the apostles.

The career of Peter, however, little as we know the details of Peter's later life, is particularly noticeable as showing the Pauline influence. It is probable that when Peter left Jerusalem (as we see from the epistle to the Galatians that he did) he went not only with the object of converting the scattered communities of Jews throughout the Roman empire to faith in Jesus Christ, but also with the object of inculcating on them the continuance in their own religious ceremonial, as enjoined in the Pentateuch. We should infer this from the Clementine Homilies; and though that spurious and imaginative work is no great authority, we may perhaps trust it so far as this, considering the natural probabilities of the case. If Peter urged his Jewish converts to adhere to the practice of circumcision, he would have been inculcating nothing to which Paul could take exception; and yet there would be real danger of collision between Jewish and Gentile Christians, as either side pressed their own practice to what appeared to be its legitimate development. Jewish Christians would naturally think circumcision a more perfect state than uncircumcision; Gentile Christians would hold the reverse opinion; the more tolerant members of either party would confine this difference of opinion within peaceable limits, but others would not do so; and the epistle to the Galatians, and the second epistle to the Corinthians (chapters x. and xi.) show clearly that peace was not always preserved in these controversies. But the tendency was for Peter gradually to come over to the side of Paul, not absolutely but still for practical purposes. This would happen partly because, in teaching the non-necessity of circumcision, Paul was really right, and Peter could not but in his own heart acknowledge this. But a more practical reason also would operate; for travelling in countries where the Jews were in a small minority compared with the heathen population, Peter would often find himself in the dilemma of having to choose between Jews who rejected the name of Jesus, and Gentiles who accepted it as the token of their faith; it would be very difficult for him, under the circumstances, not to prefer the latter. He would associate with Gentiles, he would make Gentile converts, and these converts would not accept circumcision. How could Peter reject them? He would not reject them; and he would thus come to occupy that neutral position which we find implied in his first (and probably only genuine) epistle It was an epistle no doubt written late in his life, and from Rome (for by "Babylon" towards the close Rome is preferably to be understood); and in its avowed purpose it is written to Jews; for the "Dispersion" in the first verse means naturally the Jews scattered over foreign countries. But there is not a single phrase in the epistle which would not be quite as naturally addressed to Gentiles as to Jews (and one verse, chapter iv. 3, would be more naturally addressed to Gentiles); and what is still more notable, there is not a single reference in the whole epistle to the controversy between Jewish and Gentile Christians; in which last point the epistle contrasts singularly with the epistles of Paul. All this implies that Peter felt the advocacy of circumcision among Christians to be a weak cause; and the martyrdom of James at Jerusalem must have increased this feeling.

Assuming, as from these probabilities and from these indications we may assume, that Peter during all the latter part of his life was gradually coming over to the side of Paul, and gradually (though in part unconsciously) separating the Christian society from the Jewish nation, among whom Christianity had had its birth; and remembering that the epistles of these two apostles testify that both of them were in Rome, a testimony which is confirmed by several of the early Fathers, notably by Ignatius of Antioch; are we to suppose that the two apostles met in Rome? It is uncertain; but in view of the fact that four of the epistles of Paul (those to the Ephesians, Philippians, Colossians and the second to Timothy) were written in Rome, and that Peter's epistle (the first) appears also to have been written in Rome—while yet neither Paul nor Peter mentions the presence of his brother apostle in Rome, still less any meeting between the two—it seems the more probable opinion that their presence in Rome was not simultaneous, but successive. Even so, the non-mention of Paul by Peter is singular; but perhaps it was difficult, without entering on undesirable controversy, to mention Paul to the Jewish Christians of Asia Minor. If the second epistle of Peter be genuine, he did mention Paul, and evidently after Paul's death; and it is the easiest supposition that the first epistle of Peter was written after Paul's death; but we cannot quite say. Of all the gaps in the early Christian history, none is so much to be regretted as the absence of any trustworthy account of the last days of Peter and Paul. The book of the Acts comes to an abrupt end; it would almost seem that some accident prevented its completion; for Luke must certainly have known more of the two years of Paul's first imprisonment in Rome than he tells us in the last verse of that book.

That both Paul and Peter were slain in the Neronian persecution has been the general belief of Christians, and may be accepted as probably true. All through the years up to that persecution the flood tide of success had been with the Gentile Christians, rather than with the Jewish Christians; though Jewish Christianity had not by any means ceased to exist. But if I am right in thinking that Peter arrived in Rome only after Paul's death (and the mention of Paul's two followers, Silvanus and Mark, by Peter, without the mention of Paul himself, must incline us to think this), then it would not be likely that Peter would find much to change in the way of life that he found established among the Christians of Rome, or in the Christian festivals as there held. His confirmation of what Paul had instituted in this way would no doubt be eagerly desired by the Roman Christians, and would be given with no reluctance; and thenceforth the Roman church claimed the title of the "apostolic church" in a peculiar degree, as having had the sanction of the two most famous and most laborious apostles to the scheme of Christianity there held, and in particular to the way in which the Easter festival was celebrated there. With this sanction, Gentile Christianity won its final victory in the Christian church; and this was before any of the four gospels that are now received by Christians had been written in its entirety.

I have been relating the victory of Paul; a victory which Peter at one time might have desired to modify, though hardly to reverse; but which in the end Peter accepted in its main points cordially, though not perhaps assenting to everything which Paul had taught and written. The victory of Paul, the victory of Gentile Christianity over Jewish Christianity, was in the main well deserved; Christianity was now established as a religion springing out of the deep necessities of human nature, and answering to those necessities; not as dependent for its intrinsic validity on Jewish history, or on its acceptance of Jewish rites. That was a just decision, and has been final in Christian belief. But still, Christianity had sprung, historically, out of Judaism; and the relation of the new religion to the old had to be correctly discerned, if possible. It was impossible that Paul should wish his original Pharisaic belief, to which he had adhered so long, to be dishonoured; he had resigned Judaism, but he never denied that Judaism had in a true sense come from God; and hence the problem was before him, By what train of reasoning, by what considerations of duty, was it right to declare a religion which had come from God to be antiquated and no longer to command the obedience of faithful men?

To the answer which Paul gave to this question we cannot, I think, give that absolute agreement which we may give to his practical decision as to the non-necessity of the Jewish law for human salvation. His conduct, and the conduct which he prescribed for mankind at large, was right; but the reasons which he gave for his practical decision were not entirely right. They were partly right; the position taken up by him in his epistles (and in the epistle to the Hebrews, which if not his, is by a follower of his) contains much just feeling and just reasoning; but there were errors in it, very difficult to avoid in that day, which we now, with the clearer knowledge of history which time has brought us, see to be errors.

To say, as Paul said in his epistle to the Galatians, that the law was the schoolmaster to bring men to Christ—or in other words, that the law taught men what was right and wrong in outward acts, whereas Christ taught men the spirit, by which right-doing would spontaneously be practised and wrong-doing be shunned—this was perfectly just by way of general contrast, if moral teaching like that of the ten commandments be set side by side with the moral teaching of the gospel. This, too, is in the main the contrast which is brought forward in the epistle to the Romans, as for instance when Paul says (iii. 31):

Do we then make the law of none effect through faith? God forbid: nay, we establish the law;

for here also rectitude in external acts is regarded as incumbent on men, but such rectitude is declared to be the natural outflow of faith in Jesus Christ, and not a matter of compulsory obedience. We can find no fault with Paul here; nor again in that other declaration, of the inferiority of ritual to inward faith, which he puts forward in the epistle to the Romans. In that epistle he describes circumcision as the seal of faith; and by this he evidently means to say that faith (as shown in Abraham) was the effective virtue, circumcision merely the stamp by which it was recorded for men's knowledge. This last contrast, between the symbol and the thing symbolised, is worked out very fully in the epistle to the Hebrews, in respect of the sacrifices of the ancient law, which are represented as merely types of that great sacrifice of himself which Jesus Christ offered up for the service of mankind and in obedience to the will of God.

In both respects just noticed, in the declaration of the superiority of the righteous and just spirit over any external act, and in the declaration of the cessation of any value in the ceremonies ordained by the ancient law, now that the self-sacrifice of Jesus Christ was eternally present to our thoughts, we must agree with the teaching of Paul. The reform of mankind had through the gospel penetrated to the depths of the human spirit, and divine goodness had shown itself in Jesus Christ, annulling the necessity of symbols of that goodness. But there still remained the question: What are we to think of the Jews themselves? Out of the Jewish nation Jesus Christ had come; was not that a title of honour for them? But then the Jewish nation crucified Jesus Christ and still rejected him; was not the honour which otherwise would have accrued to them wiped out, nay turned to dishonour, by this contumely, by this rejection? Here was the question to which Paul, with all his real tenderness for his own nation, did not, as I think must be acknowledged, give the right answer.

He did not put the question exactly as I have put it; but he put it in the terms which seemed natural to him, at the beginning of the third chapter of his epistle to the Romans. Here are his question and answer—and let it be premised that in the two preceding chapters he has been doing his best to show that Jews and Gentiles are equally sinners:

What advantage then hath the Jew; or what is the profit of circumcision? Much every way: first of all, that they were entrusted with the oracles of God.

It is obvious that for the Jews to have any advantage over the Gentiles, they must not only have been entrusted with the oracles of God, but also have profited by the possession of those oracles. Now this is precisely what Paul denies of the Jews; he will not allow them any superiority at all over the Gentiles, as far as the real substance of goodness is concerned. To prove that the Jews are no better than the Gentiles, he thinks it enough to quote a psalm in which it is said,

> There is none righteous, no, not one;
> There is none that understandeth,
> There is none that seeketh after God;
> They have all turned aside, they are together become unprofitable;
> There is none that doeth good, no, not so much as one, etc.,

without reflecting that the psalmist describes these egregious sinners as "eating up my people as they eat bread," so that "my people" are not, here at all events, included among the sinners. But not to dwell on this point; is it not clear that Paul is really wanting, first to make a concession to the Jews, and then to nullify that concession—which is not a reasonable thing to do? He is not fair to the Jews; who, whatever their faults, had made a most serious and earnest effort after righteousness; and many of whom, by their self-denial and holiness, had really prepared the way for the gospel. The prophets and psalmists of the Old Testament ought, even had there been no other reason, to have rescued the ancient people of God from such imputations as those which are contained in the psalm quoted by Paul. But the prophets and psalmists did not stand alone; and no doubt Paul, when not arguing for a special purpose, would have admitted that there were many Israelites in the olden times "of whom the world was not worthy," the salt of the earth; which was the very truth.

Why, then, did Paul not make this admission in his epistle to the Romans? He had a theological interest in disparaging the Jews; this is plain; had it not been so, his real tenderness towards his own people would have been effectively shown, and he would have admitted that many of them had been worthy of remembrance and of honour. What was the theological interest which, in the epistle to the Romans, makes him put this out of sight? What was the theological interest which made him disparage the Jews?

No one who takes note of the difficulties which lay in Paul's way will doubt what that interest was. His own conversion had been brought about by an experience which made him exalt Jesus of Nazareth into an unique position, a divine status, not to be paralleled in the case of any other man; this it was before which the Sinaitic covenant and the ceremonial law of the ancient Scriptures vanished, as the temporary vanishes before the eternal; and Paul naturally desired that what he felt, every Christian should feel. His conclusion as to the temporary nature of the Sinaitic covenant was right; but he was not able to support it by the argument which we can now see to be just, that the Sinaitic covenant had itself been placed in too high a position by Jewish tradition. Paul was unable to say that the narratives of Exodus and Deuteronomy were exaggerated narratives; he knew no reason for saying so; the thought that God had spoken with audible human voice amid thunders and lightnings to the whole people of Israel, and afterwards in mysterious solitude to Moses on the mountain, created in him no incredulity at all. Hence, to counterbalance this miraculous event, he had to place Jesus of Nazareth at an elevation before which every other man shrank into nothingness; and the human virtues of the ancient Israelites absolutely disappeared, when Paul was enunciating his creed in its purest form. So also did the virtues of all other men, past, present, or future; no man, according to Paul, ever had been, or ever would be, entitled to boast of his own doings.

Such a position was really paradoxical, and it was impossible for Paul himself to adhere to it absolutely; he does, in the eleventh and twelfth chapters of his second epistle to the Corinthians, celebrate his own sufferings, labours, and religious experiences, not in any way ungracefully or wrongly, but still he does celebrate them. But his theory has tended to produce in Christians an unreal and excessive humility; and in his own day, in that critical epoch of the deliverance of Christianity from ceremonial Judaism, it produced the effect, even more to be regretted, of taking away the one legitimate ground on which Christians and Jews might have cordially met. Though the Jewish ceremonial law was being abrogated, it might still have been owned by Christians what heroic and faithful and tender natures, even though they were not faultless, the old Judaism had fostered. The writer of the epistle to the Hebrews did say something in this way; but not enough to make the Jewish nation feel it was exalted in the exaltation of its children, as every other nation has felt itself exalted by the noble characters which have issued out of it. The Jewish nation has had the unparalleled misfortune of not being reckoned honourable through the virtues of the great men which it has produced ; and the reconciling balm which should have been administered to that nation by the Gentile Christians was sternly withheld. To say that this was entirely Paul's fault would not be just ; the causes of this unjust disparagement were deeply laid in the Jewish history ; but it was the success of Paul as a missionary in the Christian field through which these causes became largely operative. The natural tendency of events was to tear away Christianity from Judaism ; the Jewish Christians had no power to counteract this process ; the theory of Christianity which Paul upheld accelerated it. After the fall of Jerusalem, it is Gentile Christianity alone that can detain us ; and on the mighty success of Paul in laying the foundations of the Gentile Church we must now cast a glance.

We read the history of his spiritual campaigns, imperfectly, in the Acts. There was much that Luke did not know, and a good deal that he did not care to say ; any one who compares the first and eleventh chapters of the second epistle to the Corinthians, and the second chapter of the epistle to the Galatians, with the narrative in the Acts, will see how great the gaps are in our knowledge of Paul's missionary career. Many roughnesses, many calamities in that career, are omitted by Luke over and above the omission (which is probably accidental) of the closing years of Paul's life. Let us be thankful to Luke for what he has given us ; in those parts of the narrative where he himself was an eyewitness he is always picturesque, there is little exaggeration and a good deal of pathos ; we should be much poorer if we did not possess the book of the Acts. Still it is to Paul's own epistles that we must turn if we wish to understand his extraordinary genius and heroism. I do not think him more heroic or more loving than Peter ; and we have to remember that Peter preceded Paul in founding the Christian society on its historical basis, in giving the first laws to that society. But Paul was a greater genius than Peter ; he was a far greater master than Peter in that controversy which made Christianity a world-wide human religion ; if I have criticised some part of the belief which he promulgated as the issue of that controversy, I do not forget that a great part of the solution of it which he offered was purely just and true. The way in which his personal feelings mingle with his belief in all his epistles is most striking ; and equally so is his steady assumption of the eternal invisible world

as the true world, with which he always held converse, where
God and Christ reigned, and in which the spirits of the just
should be manifested in due time.　I confess that I believe in
the genuineness of all the epistles ascribed to him, except the
epistle to the Hebrews (which is entirely in the Pauline spirit,
but the authorship of which is a still unsolved problem).　The
genuineness of what are called the pastoral epistles, that is those
to Timothy and Titus, has been much impugned; and if there
were real improbability in Paul having made extensive journeys
after the last of those recorded in the Acts, it would be necessary
to give them up.　But the most recent views of the date of the
governorship of Festus take away this chronological difficulty;
and there is not, to my feeling, any other.　As to the internal
evidence, they appear to me sane and worthy epistles; we would
like indeed to know what the heretics who are reproved by name
in them had to say for themselves; but there is no improbability
in the existence of such heretics.　The critics have read ecclesiasti-
cism into these epistles; but it was a matter of course that every
church would have overseers and deacons; there is nothing
which would lead us to think that Paul would have had these
overseers and deacons exercise their office with technical rigidity.
I am not saying that Paul, or any early Christian teacher, knew
quite how to treat philosophy, whether of the Jewish or of the
Greek description; but the problem was a difficult one; and the
popular philosophy of Asiatic countries in that day was very inferior
to the best Greek or Roman philosophy as known to ourselves.

However, the epistles to Timothy and Titus are no doubt
carelessly written, compared to those great and admirable epistles
to the Romans and to the Corinthians; and though in this very
carelessness there are some Pauline features (notably in the first
chapter of the first epistle to Timothy) still they do not reach
the height of his highest inspiration. Perhaps the noblest
passages in his writings are the eighth chapter of the epistle to
the Romans, the thirteenth and fifteenth chapters of the first
epistle to the Corinthians, and the end of the fourth and beginning
of the fifth chapters of the second epistle to the Corinthians.
Let me quote two passages from these chapters.　Here is one
from the epistle to the Romans (viii. 18–22):

I reckon that the sufferings of this present time are not worthy to be
compared with the glory which shall be revealed to us-ward.　For the
earnest expectation of the creation waiteth for the revealing of the sons of
God.　For the creation was subjected to vanity, not of its own will, but by

reason of him who subjected it, in hope that the creation itself also shall
be delivered from the bondage of corruption into the liberty of the glory
of the children of God.   For we know that the whole creation groaneth
and travaileth in pain together until now.

How immense is the range of thought in these few brief words,
how penetrating the insight into the most honourable elements
of human nature! Of like character is the following passage
from the second epistle to the Corinthians (iv. 16–v. 2):

Wherefore we faint not; but though our outward man is decaying,
yet our inward man is renewed day by day.   For our light affliction,
which is for the moment, worketh for us more and more exceedingly an
eternal weight of glory; while we look not at the things which are seen,
but at the things which are not seen: for the things which are seen are
temporal; but the things which are not seen are eternal.   For we know
that if the earthly house of our tabernacle be dissolved, we have a building
from God, a house not made with hands, eternal, in the heavens.   For
verily in this we groan, longing to be clothed upon with our habitation
which is from heaven.

Could the ideal glory, which is the goal of each man and all
men, be more vividly expressed?

I am not saying that, even in relation to his Gentile converts,
Paul was absolutely perfect.   We may regret that he said (hastily,
we may hope) that men were predestined to work evil (Romans
ix. 17–21).   It is possible that he restricted too much the intercourse, and especially the marriages, between Christian and
heathen; at least it is natural to think that something of this
kind is implied in 2 Corinthians vi. 11–18; but it is not easy to
see the limitations of Paul's meaning.   Great souls are not to be
held free from criticism; therefore let us note these points.   Yet,
taking the whole career of Paul, his deeds, speeches, and writings,
must we not be filled with wonder at such complex activity,
such purity and self-denial, such practical good sense, such power
of love, such reliance on heavenly things, such noble grasp of the
way in which these heavenly things interpenetrate our earthly
experience?   Few men stand before us with such vividness.

And now let me note that on one question, in regard to which
the Christian mind was tending to a disastrous severity, the
question of the eternal destiny of the wicked, Paul, like Peter,
was merciful.   I have already referred to that notable passage
in which Peter writes

For unto this end was the gospel preached even to the dead, that they
might be judged according to men in the flesh, but live according to God
in the spirit,

as evidence that that apostle admitted hope after death for those who had sinned here; and Paul was of similar mind. For though it is true that in his epistle to the Thessalonians (2 Thess. i. 9) he speaks of those "who shall suffer punishment, even eternal destruction from the face of the Lord and from the glory of his might," yet in his later and better considered epistle to the Corinthians (1 Cor. iii. 15) he says, "If any man's work be burned" (i.e. as unworthy) "he shall suffer loss: but he himself shall be saved; yet so as through fire." The unworthiness of a man's doings, he says, entails suffering upon him, and yet he may be saved in spite of it. And if any one should ask whether Paul meant to include in this judgment those who had not embraced the faith in Christ, an answer is supplied in his epistle to the Romans (ii. 14, 15), where he writes thus:

When Gentiles who have no law do by nature the things of the law, these, having no law, are a law unto themselves; in that they show the work of the law written in their hearts, their conscience bearing witness therewith, and their thoughts one with another accusing or else excusing them; in the day when God shall judge the secrets of men, according to my gospel, by Jesus Christ.

That passage clearly abrogates formal external grounds of salvation, and makes the inner witness of a man's own conscience supreme (which is a different thing from a man's opinion about himself, as in his superficial imaginations he might present it to himself); and those who consider how emphatically Paul says that the heathen conscience shall have true power in the day of the divine judgment, will not think that Paul intends to exclude the heathen when he speaks of a man being saved even though his works have perished. For such sayings we must be grateful.

Let this be enough to say, in the present place, about this illustrious teacher, reformer, and converter of men, and his writings; I resume the sequences of history.

The early Christian society had been progressing, not with entire inward peacefulness, nor with many gifts of the intellect, but with extraordinary love and self-denial as its most distinguishing feature, when that collision took place, which was bound to happen sooner or later, the collision with the Roman empire; and it took place in a grievous tragic manner which entailed ill consequences on the whole after course of Christian history. To understand at all what happened, we have to remember that the Christians were unpopular, not only with the Jews, but with the heathen also; and we must understand why

they were unpopular. Had they merely preached and practised
mutual love, there would have been nothing in this to arouse
dislike; but they were also prophets of what they called "the
anger," that is to say the anger of God, which they conceived
as about to fall on an evil world. In truth, there were many
things in the world, as it then was, which deserved, and could
not but meet with, destruction. Even had these early Christians
put their prophecy in the most careful and just manner, they
could not but have incurred some unpopularity. But the manner
in which they conceived of the wrath of God as about to fall on
the world, was in the way of a sudden catastrophe; and they
no doubt often put their threatening prophecy in a form which
failed to discriminate between the good and the evil of the world
in which they were placed; and thus they came to be thought
of as "enemies of the human race," "hostes humani generis."
Hence it came about that the emperor Nero, finding himself
exposed (probably unjustly) to suspicion as being the author
of that terrible conflagration which devastated Rome in the
summer of A.D. 64, caught at a defence for himself, by charging
the Christians with having kindled the flames; and his procedure
against them was not altogether unwelcome to the Roman
populace. Moreover, though his extreme cruelty caused some
reaction in their favour, it did not take away all the prejudice
against them. It was thought an intrinsically wicked thing to
be a Christian; it was the same thing as being a rebel and a
disturber of the public safety. In short, however desirous the
Christians might be of peace, it was real war that now began
between the Christian society and the Roman empire. There
was no such war between the Roman empire and any other
religion; but then no other religion made its determination so
unflinchingly known to put all other religions down. Christians
did indeed acknowledge Cæsar as their ruler; but their obedience
to Cæsar ceased when matters of religion came into the field;
and both in religion, and in many matters of ordinary life, they
were of necessity opposed to all the subjects of Cæsar outside
their own ranks. So much as this was plain fact; but in addition
to this, scandalous tales were told, such as are always apt to
arise in vulgar minds against a much-hated religious body, of
gross wickedness secretly practised by Christians.

Thus then the Roman empire began a war in which (contrary
to all which might have seemed probable) it was to be finally
and absolutely defeated. The war, perhaps, could not have

been averted; but it was a lamentable thing that the worst of the Roman emperors should have been reigning at that particular time. Everything in the conflict which ensued was made worse by that accidental fact. Moreover, deeply as the Christians were to be honoured for their fidelity and courage, the violent and cruel attack which was made on them rendered it extremely difficult for them to accept any heathen critics as honourable opponents. Their whole duty seemed to be to consolidate their ranks, not to flinch, not to play the traitor or the coward, to abide by what they had been taught; there must, at any rate, be no disintegration from within. The faith must, at all costs, be maintained uncorrupted.

This is the temper, ardent, tender, and dutiful, yet exposed to those dangers which the zeal of mortal conflict brings with it, which we find exemplified in the last of the apostles whose written words have come down to us, John the son of Zebedee. His love for his Master, Jesus, his intense realisation of the sublime teaching of Jesus, carried him into the realms of imagination; this we see plainly in the book of the Revelation; but also I do not think we can resist the conclusion, for which I have given reasons in a previous chapter, that his memories of the life and deeds of Jesus became mingled with imagination, and that this mixture of memory and imagination, arranged and pointed by his Ephesian followers, was the source of our fourth gospel. There is something in this that we must regret; but we must always remember the very great difference of that time from our own, the immaturity of secular knowledge in the apostles, their unacquaintance with that caution which should characterise the historian. On his own ground, when he has to render flashes of spiritual truth, there is no writer in the Bible who excels the apostle John; and this is the same in all his works. Take two instances from the Revelation:

Be thou faithful unto death, and I will give thee the crown of life. ii. 10.

I heard a voice from heaven, saying, Write, Blessed are the dead which die in the Lord from henceforth: yea, saith the Spirit, that they may rest from their labours; for their works follow with them. xiv. 13.

And here are two instances from his first epistle:

The world passeth away, and the lust thereof; but he that doeth the will of God abideth for ever. ii. 17.

He that loveth not his brother whom he hath seen, cannot love God whom he hath not seen. iv. 20.

And here are two specimens from the gospel:

Jesus answered and said unto her, Every one that drinketh of this water shall thirst again: but whosoever drinketh of the water that I shall give him shall never thirst; but the water that I shall give him shall become in him a well of water springing up unto eternal life. iv. 13, 14.

Greater love hath no man than this, that a man lay down his life for his friends. xv. 13.

It was no ordinary man who could write thoughts so profoundly touching with such perfect simplicity. Yet that vehemence, which we can see from the gospels was a natural characteristic of his, and which found ample fuel to kindle it in his later life— first in his breach with the Jews, next with his experience of the cruel persecutions by the Roman empire, including his own exile in Patmos, and lastly in his conflict with heresies the moving source of which was unintelligible to him, and which really were wild and baseless—his vehemence under these provocations led him sometimes into expressions and acts which we must regret. Some are to be found in his Biblical writings; outside the Bible we may refer to his abhorrence of the heretic Cerinthus: he fled out of the public bath, it is said, finding that Cerinthus was there, and cried out, "Let us flee, lest the roof fall in, while Cerinthus, the enemy of the truth, is within." The Christian Father Polycarp, who had himself been a hearer of John, imitated this conduct but too faithfully when he met with the heretic Marcion.

The quarrel of the apostle John with the Jews never hindered him from recognising the sacredness of the ancient Jewish law; and this he showed in two remarkable ways. First, he wore the sacerdotal plate or coronet, made of gold, which in the book of Exodus (xxviii. 36–38) the high priest is commanded to wear. We learn this from Polycrates, who was bishop of Ephesus about A.D. 190 and who is quoted by Eusebius in his *Ecclesiastical History* (v. 24). It is to be supposed that John wore this plate when exercising his office in religious meetings of the faithful; and certainly he must have meant by it that the true fulfillers of the ancient law were not the Jews who had rejected Jesus Christ, but they who had accepted him.

The other instance of the apostle John's adherence to the ancient law is a more famous one. He always celebrated the passover; not indeed as the Jews celebrated it, with the slaying of a lamb; that mode of celebration, according to him, had come to an end when Jesus Christ died upon the cross. Jesus Christ was the true paschal lamb; this (as I have already said in a previous part of this work) is the informing idea both of the Revelation and of the fourth gospel. It was the "Saviour's passover" that he celebrated (to use the phrase of the Christian historian Eusebius); and we must understand by this phrase "the passover, with a particular reference to the death of Jesus Christ, as the true Lamb of God." This thought is really a striking one, and we can well understand why the Christians of Asia Minor clung in after times to the celebration of the passover, interpreted in this lofty ideal sense; but the rest of the Christian world (and especially the Roman church) had taken a different line. They celebrated the resurrection, rather than the death, of Jesus Christ; and hence the great Christian festival was not, over the Christian world generally, coincident with the Jewish passover, but always took place on the first day of the week. This general Christian practice was said to be derived from "apostolical tradition," a phrase which would naturally originate in the Roman church, and would mean the practice which Paul originated, and Peter sanctioned—the two chief apostles, who had both been at Rome, and had received there the crown of martyrdom. But Eusebius tells us that the Asiatic practice, sanctioned by the apostle John, was the more ancient of the two; and this would naturally be so; for there can be little doubt that the first disciples celebrated the passover exactly as the Jews did. Yet even according to the Jewish law, the sacrifice of a lamb would never take place at a distance from Jerusalem (see Deuteronomy xvi. 5, 6); unleavened bread would be the sole mark of the paschal festival for those who were in foreign lands. And this would continue in the festival as celebrated by Jewish Christians, who would eat unleavened bread at the time of the passover. But the apostle John is not to be counted among these Jewish Christians; and we must infer both from natural probability and from the expressions in the letter of Polycrates (quoted by Eusebius, *Eccl. Hist.* v. 24) that he and the Asiatic Christians after him simply terminated their fast at the day and hour when the ancient law ordained the sacrifice of the paschal lamb; they terminated their fast as celebrating the new life which had been given to the world by the death of Jesus Christ. The procedure was one worthy of this great though not faultless apostle. There is but one thing more that I need refer to in connexion with him; and that is the touching story told by Clement of Alexandria, how he reconverted to the ways of honesty and piety a robber who had once been a Christian but had taken to wicked ways.

If it be true, John must have possessed great courage; which in any case we have no reason to doubt; though he was not so forward in outward action as Peter and Paul were, or some of the other disciples; his nature was meditative.

Let me retrace my steps for a short time, and revert to a historical event deeply connected with Christianity, though not belonging to Christianity; I mean that fall of Jerusalem and of the Jewish power which took place a very few years after the Neronian persecution of the Christians. The conduct of the Roman governors in Judæa towards the Jews, though not equalling in wickedness that of Nero towards the Christians, was arbitrary and despotic; and great sympathy must be given to the Jews in their revolt against such tyranny as that exercised by Florus, under whom the rebellion of the Jews against the Romans broke out. Still it is manifest, when we compare Christians with Jews in their respective conflicts against the same arrogant imperial power, that the Christians had a knowledge, which the Jews lacked, of where their true strength lay. The Christians relied on spiritual weapons; the Jews relied on material weapons. At least the Jews did so, until they had been defeated in two most serious revolts; the revolt which ended in the capture of Jerusalem and the destruction of the temple, by Titus, in A.D. 70; and the revolt of Bar-Cochba in the reign of Hadrian. Then, a conquered and dispersed people, they did reconsider their ways. From the time of Hadrian to the present day, the Jews have been men of peace, and in these latter days have not been without influence among the nations of the world. Yet, putting that influence as high as they may choose to put it, is it not worth their while to consider, even now, whether their fellow-countryman, Jesus of Nazareth, was not in possession of a secret to which they themselves have had no access? I say this, not as being forgetful of the sins of Christians against Jews during many centuries of the past, nor doubting that some of the lines of true life which intermingle in our modern world belong to the Jewish people. But it is not among the Jews, as I read history, that the most seminative, the most vigorous, the most expanding and developing life of modern times exists. Of that life Christianity has been the main nurturer; though, as a Christian, I have to ask pardon of the Jews for many things done in the past. I have endeavoured, in a previous chapter of this work, to show how very much more noble the ancient Jews were than they are generally conceived to have been, above all during that century (or more than a century indeed) which succeeded to their first return from Baby-lon. Then, indeed, the greatest hope of the world was concentred in the Jewish people. But such times do not recur; and it is as vain for the Jews of to-day to think that they stand single in the religious impulse, as it would be for the Greeks of to-day to think that they stand single in exactitude of thought and precision of artistic feeling, or for the Italians of to-day to think that they stand single in their practice of equal law between man and man. It is an honour and glory to a people to have such memories as have the Jews, the Greeks, and the Italians; but the memories of ancient superiority must not be confounded with the possession of present superiority.

To the Christian Church then, and its conflict with the Roman empire, I now return. Splendid as was the courage and devotion of Christians in those days, we must not think that the conflict which they underwent and victoriously carried through was a conflict of pure light against simple darkness. That was very far from being the case. The military character which the Christian Church assumed, in some degree even before the Neronian persecution, and very decidedly indeed after that persecution, was a character that operated injuriously in two ways. It made Christian teachers convert their doctrines into weapons of attack, so that the doctrines were hardened in the process, and deprived of that flexibility which belongs in some degree even to the principles of material science, much more to spiritual knowledge; and, also, it practically prevented any acknowledgment of error in those records, discourses, and letters which lay at the foundation of Christian belief, and which gradually became formed into that volume which we call the New Testament. Hence it was that around that nucleus of pure light which the Christian Church possessed, and which was indeed a precious treasure, there grew films of darkness, which prevented clear determination of what religion truly is, alike in its first essence and in its historical character. Criticism was regarded as rebellion; literal accepta-tion of doctrines was a matter of course, and the severest form was preferred; and it would be difficult to say that heartfelt honour was ever given to any heathen institution, any definite historical act of the heathen world, any heathen philosophy. Two heathen philosophers indeed, Socrates and Plato, did receive honour from some of the early Christians, but their philosophy was not understood; and two famous Christian teachers, Clement of Alexandria and Origen, had a freedom of thought and an interest in heathen literature which might have led the way to better things; but the general Christian antagonism to the heathen world proved in the end too strong for this better spirit to take root in early times; and narrowness triumphed. Is it very surprising? A society which was outlawed, despised, and hated, the members of which were continually liable to torture and death, and were reduced to take refuge in catacombs for mere self-preservation, was a society not likely to honour the world which so treated it. Yet the restriction of thought which was the natural result of such sufferings was none the less unfortunate.

Two of the most famous of the Fathers of the early Church are evidences to us of the overpowering degree in which the military aspect of religious duty impressed itself on the minds of Christians after the collision with the Roman empire began. Clement of Rome is one; he wrote, it is generally supposed, not long after 90 A.D.; an earlier date, which is not impossible, is less probable. At whatever time his long and elaborate epistle was written, the cause of its composition lay in certain disturbances which had taken place in the church of Corinth; in which church the ruling presbyters had been deprived of their office through the action of some of the laity. It may be remarked in passing, that the church of Corinth had evidently at that time no bishop in the modern sense of that word; this is especially clear from the forty-fourth chapter of the epistle, in which bishop and presbyter are used as convertible terms. But the more important point to remark is this: that never, throughout the whole epistle, does Clement consider the case as it might be presented by the dissatisfied laity of the church of Corinth. He no more considers their case than a general in the midst of active warfare would consider the case of soldiers disputing the authority of their commanding officer; they are condemned as having originated a mutiny, and as having shown pride and self-will. Under the circumstances of those times, we cannot altogether blame Clement for this tone; yet his epistle would have tended more to the enlargement of the Christian spirit if it had contained any clause to the effect that the complaints of the laity, whether ultimately sanctioned or not, did deserve recognition. But his epistle contains no such statement.

I have accepted the general title of this epistle as the epistle of Clement, nor do I doubt the traditional authorship; but it is right to observe that the epistle itself does not give us this information. The epistle professes to be addressed by "the church of God sojourning at Rome to the church of God sojourning at Corinth," nor is there any word in the whole epistle to show that a single bishop was the author of it. It is probable that such an epistle would have a single author, and external evidence is to the effect that the author was Clement; but we must conclude that Clement did not perform public acts of this kind as a single individual, but as head of a board of presbyters, who associated themselves with him in his acts, and were recognised as representing the Roman church.

It is remarkable that the same inference is to be drawn from the epistles of Ignatius, written about twenty years later than that of Clement. Six of these epistles are addressed to churches; and it is quite manifest that the churches of Ephesus, of Magnesia, of Tralles, of Philadelphia and of Smyrna had each of them a bishop quite distinct from their presbyters. But when Ignatius addresses the church of Rome, he makes no mention either of bishop or of presbyters; it is the whole church "which sits pre-eminent in the place of the country of the Romans" to which he addresses himself; in this case, and in this case alone, does Ignatius make no mention of differences of rank in a community of Christians. It would be an error to infer from this that there was no board of presbyters at Rome, or that there was no president of that board, who in after times was named a bishop; we cannot but believe that there were such officers at Rome, as generally elsewhere; but it is plain that this difference of status did not imply at Rome such a difference of authority, at the beginning of the second century, as it did in the Asiatic churches. The church at Corinth must have been quite exceptionally democratic; but the democratic spirit, rebuked there by Clement, never found expression elsewhere in the ancient Christian Church. Before the second century had ended, the Roman bishop Victor had learned quite to dissociate himself from his presbyters, and to claim despotic authority; he was not successful in his personal claim, it is true; but the tendency towards despotism in the early Christian Church is none the less exemplified by his action.

To return to Ignatius, the martyred bishop of Antioch; he, like Clement, is witness to the fact that despotism did not exist in the Christian Church of those early times; but he, like Clement, is witness to that stringency of discipline which was beginning to exist in the Christian Church, and which was the natural forerunner of despotism. When Ignatius writes to the churches of Asia Minor, nothing can exceed the vigour of his injunctions to the laity, that they are to hold themselves in obedience to the authorities of their church, and especially to the bishop. I do not think that we can entirely approve of these injunctions, or of the vehemence of Ignatius against heretics, any more than we can entirely approve of the silence of Clement respecting the rights of the Corinthian laity; but there were ample reasons to account for the disposition shown by these two Fathers; for the dangers which threatened the Christian Church were then exceedingly great, and if internal discord had been added to external peril, the Church could not have survived. It should be added that, as the tenderness of Clement is very noteworthy amid all the stringency of his disciplinary action, so also the impassioned emotion of Ignatius in view of his impending martyrdom is evidence of a most noble temper; and this is especially shown in his letter to the church of Rome.

I have been dwelling on that characteristic of the early Christian Church which was peculiarly derived from the persecution to which it was subject, namely, its severe and often excessive discipline; but the most admirable characteristic of the Christians of those days, and that for which we owe them the greatest reverence, was undoubtedly their strenuous effort to implant the principles of love and duty into all the actions and thoughts of men. The conviction that men ought to repent of all those injurious and selfish actions to which mankind are naturally prone and into which every man has more or less fallen; moreover that a new life must begin in every soul of man, a life of unselfish devotion, and that the name of Christian implies this profound repentance, this ardent devotion—such a conviction breathes in every one of the early Fathers without exception. It was a conviction that had practical results; the Christians of those ages not only felt that they ought to be better than the heathen, but they actually were better than the heathen; this was the primary ground of their influence; through the perception that this was the case, converts did actually flow into the Christian Church.

Yet while we acknowledge this altogether true and right ground of the growing dominance of the Christian Church within the bounds of the Roman empire, it must be added that another motive, not so honourable, mingled with the forces which operated in favour of the Church; I mean the fear of hell, which was held before the eyes of unbelievers as a menace. It is as immoral to be influenced against one's conscience by the fear of hell as it is to be influenced against one's conscience by the fear of death;

this is a consideration which ought never to be forgotten by the Christian preacher, but has too often been forgotten. Certainly the early Church did not adequately remember it. The consideration of rewards and penalties after death is indeed, for those who believe in such results, a perfectly legitimate ground of action, and a right theme for preachers; but it must not be turned into a tyranny; and the withdrawal of hope from those subjected to penalties after death does turn it into a tyranny. In a previous chapter I have remarked that that hope which Jesus himself offered when the difficulty of converting rich men to the gospel was vividly present to him, "With God all things are possible," was equally applicable to the case of those whose earthly life had been altogether sinful, when we ask what will happen to them after death—to the case of the unrepentant murderer, robber, corrupt dealer, corrupter of others. Respecting these too we may well believe that Jesus would have said, "Though they have died in their sins, yet with God all things are possible, and even these may revive to the heavenly life." But the greater number of the Fathers of the early Church (I do not say every one of them) assumed that he never would have said such words as these; and the tendency to identify "the saved" with the visible Christian society was so strong, that to any one who was favourably inclined to Christianity, the fear of hell became a strong additional motive for becoming a Christian, and was almost sure to press unduly, and to the restriction of proper criticism. That this did happen, cannot be doubted. The eloquent author of the "Epistle to Diognetus" puts the case as he conceives it very clearly to his correspondent, whom he hopes to convert. After setting forth the unhappiness and blindness of men before the coming of Jesus Christ, and the new heavenly life which had thenceforth belonged to those who accepted the gospel, he proceeds to dwell on the mercy of God. God had sent his Son to men.

"Was it," he asks, "with a view to tyranny, to inflict fear and consternation, as a man might conjecture? No, but in clemency, in meekness. As a king sending his royal son, so he sent him; he sent him who was himself God; he sent him to men; in sending his Son he acted as a Saviour; he persuaded men, he did not compel them; for compulsion does not belong to God. He invited men, he did not persecute them; he loved men, he did not judge them. For he will send his Son as a judge; and who shall endure his appearing?" "Epistle to Diognetus," c. 7.

The last sentence of the above extract does in effect reverse all that has preceded it. For it appears in the next chapter that the heathen philosophers who deified fire are themselves to go into the fire; and while in the ninth chapter the goodness of God is again enlarged upon, the tenth chapter ends thus:

> Then wilt thou despise the deceit and error of the world, when thou shalt know the true life which is in heaven, when thou shalt despise that which here seems to be death, when thou shalt fear that which really is death, which is kept for those who shall be condemned to the eternal fire, which shall punish those committed to it until the end. Then shalt thou admire and bless those who endure on behalf of righteousness the earthly fire, when thou shalt know that other fire.

Is not that a very plain appeal to fear? I do not mean that an appeal to fear was altogether illegitimate; but, in the first place, the writer had said that God did not appeal to the fears of men; and, in the next place, what is much more important, he does not admit any hope in connexion with those who are condemned to the eternal fire. It may be thought, in view of the phrase "until the end," that he does not absolutely think such hope impossible; for it is possible that after "the end" some fresh development might take place. I am afraid the writer did not mean this; we see from Augustine's *De Civitate Dei* (book XXI) that the question was discussed among the early Christians; but evidently the preponderance of opinion was to exclude hope.

We see then, that as there were good and valid reasons for men becoming Christians in those days, so there were reasons which appealed to men's cowardly fears, and which ought not to have been accepted. I cannot but think that the spirit of imperial Rome, so dominant in many ways, was one of the causes that inspired this less worthy motive; Christianity, in contending against imperial Rome, caught the spirit of its great adversary sometimes in a righteous, sometimes in an unrighteous, manner; and this abnegation of the pardoning power of God was not the fruit of righteousness. The letter was embraced, the spirit was abandoned.

The signs are that if the true spirit of the Socratic philosophy, the spirit of the pious questioner, had been understood and accepted in the early Church, ecclesiastical decisions would have been characterised by less hardness, and quarrels between orthodox and heretic would have been less bitter than they were. It has indeed often been thought that the Christian Church was too philosophical after the manner of the Greeks, and that the Nicene creed is an instance of this. But the vein of subtlety, which is the single Greek element in the Nicene creed, is not nearly so important as the strong affirmative bias in it, which is Hebrew, or the determination with which it was pressed on dissentients, which was Roman. The spirit of Greek philosophy did try to effect an entrance into the Christian Church, but after many efforts it was rejected out of the primitive Church, and only entered into Christian thought very gradually at a far later date, coming in at last like a flood in that movement which we call the Renaissance, the beginning of which may be dated in the fifteenth century.

The real conflict during all the centuries between Nero and Constantine, was between the Christian Church and the heathen empire, and was too downright and too bitter to be softened, until at last it was ended by the overthrow of heathenism. But it will be well to show the efforts which Greek philosophy made to supply a medium between the principal antagonists, a medium in which a true peace might lie; the attempt was praiseworthy, though the end was not attained.

The first attempt was through those writers who collectively were termed Gnostics. It is true that this so-called Gnosticism was very far from being pure Greek philosophy; many Eastern elements contributed to the formation of it, and also certain veins of thought and feeling which had nothing to do with philosophy at all, but which arose out of the accepted Christian belief, and were intended (however ignorantly) to defend it against heathen objections. Still the deepest characteristic of the Gnostics[1] was one which had hardly existed in the Christian Church in its earlier stages, and which was certainly Greek; the delight, namely, in the intellectual aspect of Christianity, as it was surveyed and accepted. Such intellectual pleasure cannot be the primary characteristic of true religion; but it should not be altogether absent from true religion.

It would rather seem, however, that Gnosticism began in a quarter which was neither Eastern nor Greek nor Christian, nor even Jewish; namely, among the Samaritans. A large imaginative theorising in a religious sense, accompanied with a claim to supernatural powers, would seem to have marked the teaching of two Samaritans, Simon of Gitta and Menander; of whom the former is identified by Justin Martyr with the Simon Magus of the Acts. But this part of the subject is wrapped in deep

---

[1] This is noticed by Harnack (*History of Dogma*, chapter IV. § 2), who also says that Overbeck was the first to indicate convincingly this important characteristic.

obscurity; whether Simon of Gitta and Menander could in any sense be called Christians, is most doubtful. It is however not doubtful that in the latter half of the first century of our era a teaching became prevalent in Asia Minor and Syria (among Jewish Christians in the first instance, it would seem) which endeavoured to counteract that prejudice against Christianity which lay in the fact that Jesus had been crucified, by alleging that the true Christ had not suffered at all in the crucifixion; either because the body of Jesus (regarded as the Christ) was a phantasm and incapable of suffering, or because Christ, the true divine agent of redemption, was separable from Jesus the man, and departed from Jesus when the crucifixion took place. When the apostle John, in his epistles, gives as the mark of true faith the acknowledgment that "Jesus Christ has come in the flesh," it is the first of these two forms of error which he is combating; and Ignatius also, in his epistles, is vehement against it.

But the inspiring thought of Gnosticism, in its developed forms, was not so crude as either of the two forms of theory just referred to. What it rather sought to do was to surround the whole gospel history, that is to say the life of Jesus Christ, with so brilliant a light of imaginative conceptions and of intellectual theory, as to drown what appeared to be the commonplace parts of the actions and sufferings of Jesus, as these are narrated in the gospels. With whatever errors this effort was implicated, it was not in itself either unnatural or blamable. The Christian religion has its centre in the crucifixion; and every account of that event (superficially so tragic) which recognises its great spiritual value must give it an atmosphere quite different from that of an ordinary execution of a man convicted of an offence against his fellows. an atmosphere of heavenly light, illuminating the past and the future of humanity, breathing tender repentance and infinite hope. Every preacher of Christianity signalises this divine element in the crucifixion of Jesus Christ, and uses both the imagination and the intellect in the exposition of it; we must not find fault with the Gnostics because they did this. But we may say against them, that they were too ambitious to be successful, either in their use of the imagination, or in their exercises of intellect.

Let any one read the most complete Gnostic book which has come down to us, the *Pistis Sophia* ("Faith-Wisdom" is the literal translation of these words); he will feel that the writer of that work was in intention a true Christian; Jesus Christ

himself, and the leading characters in the gospels, are brought
before us, in some ways not unworthily. But the extraordinary
flood of groundless fancies with which the work is filled, the
Æons or divisions of the spirit world, the strangely named supernatural persons, the strange penalties and purifications, deprive
the book of all convincing power. Still, the general conception
of the *Pistis Sophia* is superior to the fantastic details of it. The
universe of living beings is regarded as a kind of hierarchy, with
the Divine Light and Power (faintly personified) at its head, and
from thence gradually sinking down by successive stages until
the familiar world, mingled of spirit and matter, is reached, with
its manifold errors and evils; and below this are still darker
regions. Great stress is laid on the necessity of redemption,
and on the principle that redemption is worked by Jesus as the
Saviour, with whom men are to co-operate through sacred ordinances and self-denying actions.

The *Pistis Sophia*, with all its abundant weaknesses, is not
devoid of merit. But it is a work hardly typical of Gnosticism
in its most characteristic forms. The two great intellectual
problems, the problem of the origin of evil and the problem of
the relation of the Old Testament to the New, problems to which
Gnosticism in general gave so startling an answer, are not recognised in it at all. The fanciful description of the Æons proves
it to be a Gnostic work; but in intellectual power it falls below
the main Gnostic teaching; and it is thought to be a late work,
dating perhaps from the first half of the third century of our era.

The main current of Gnostic religious doctrine is fairly intelligible, though doubt must lie on certain parts of it, owing to the
fact that the writings of its advocates have almost entirely
perished, and the real motive of any teaching is hardly to be
understood from the representations of its opponents. I have
already said that we have no real knowledge of what the Samaritans, Simon of Gitta and Menander, taught; nor do we know
much more of those two heretics who came in to Christianity
from the Jewish side, Cerinthus and Carpocrates. But of
Basilides and Valentinus, of Heracleon and Ptolemæus, and of
Marcion (rather different from the others) we are not entirely
ignorant. I must acknowledge some uncertainty in the view
that I shall proceed to give, for the questions involved are very
difficult, and I cannot pretend to a complete knowledge of the
manifold data on so wide a subject; but the following are the
conclusions to which I have arrived.

In the first place, all the five teachers whom I named last, and the Gnostics generally, must be considered as primarily Christians, secondarily heretics. They were not Greek philosophers with a tinge of Christianity; they were Christians bent and swayed away from the current Christian belief by certain influences, of which the Greek intellectual spirit was the strongest (though other influences entered in). They desired to remain in the Christian Church; they were ejected from it, but they did not voluntarily leave it. Moreover, it is much the simplest explanation of the course which their speculations took, to say that the Old Testament was the stumbling-block which overthrew them when they attempted to follow the ordinary Christian path. The Old Testament stood in those days in a contrast to the New Testament in a way in which it cannot stand now. We have ample experience of the fact that Christians can make war upon their enemies and use material compulsion against them even in times of peace, and it is hard to say that they are always wrong in doing so, though such unpeaceful action is to be deprecated. But in the second century Christians were unable to wage war and their principles appeared to be against their ever doing any such thing; and when a Christian read the Old Testament, the abundance of wars and slaughters committed by the chosen people of God, and often (according to the record) commanded by God himself, appeared a strange contradiction to the first elements of Christian teaching. Ought it very much to surprise us that some Christians looked on the Old Testament as the work of a Power not in the highest sense divine? Yet so closely had reverence for the Old Testament been inwrought into Christian belief, that absolutely to throw it aside was hardly possible for a Christian. There remained the inference, that the Old Testament was the work of a Deity, indeed, but not of the Supreme God; that the Supreme God had been revealed by Jesus Christ, and by him alone. But then let the next step in the process of reasoning be observed; it followed that the Deity who had created the world, as the first chapter of Genesis declared that he had created it, was not the Supreme God. Was not this then an explanation of the existence of evil in the world? The Christians of whom I have been speaking thought that it was an explanation; and thinking this, they thought that they knew the truth in a way in which others did not know it. This pretension to knowledge caused them to be called Gnostics, "persons who knew"; it is probable that they received this title first from others; but they did not always repudiate it themselves.

A conclusion so novel, and so startlingly opposed to the traditional belief of the Christian Church, could not be embraced without entailing some results which the authors of the new opinion had not foreseen; and one of these results was drawn from a word which is among the most common in the New Testament, the word Æon (in Greek αἰών). Æon, in its first signification, is "an age"; it is very often used in the plural, "the ages"; and sometimes, both in the singular and in the plural, it is used to mean "eternity," more particularly in the phrase "to the ages of the ages," which in our versions is translated "for ever and ever." But "eternity" is not the original meaning of Æon, and there are a great many passages in the New Testament where it plainly means "an age," that is a long period of time but still a finite period; and there are passages from which it would appear that there have been many such ages, separate and distinct in their characteristics. For instance, in the second verse in the epistle to the Hebrews, where our versions have, "through whom also he made the worlds," the literal translation is, "through whom also he made the ages." The peculiar force of the word is hidden from the English reader by this very fact that it is so often incorrectly translated "world"; but the fact that it can be so translated will explain to us the next step that the ancient Gnostics took. They interpreted "Æons" as meaning, not consecutive periods of time, but concurrent periods of time, in which beings of differing nature and unequal worth might live simultaneously, though not together. The more spiritual person lives in a higher Æon. The world or "Æon" in which we men live is plainly a very imperfect world; and the reason of this, according to the Gnostics, was that which I have indicated above, namely, because the Creator of it was imperfect. And since the Creator of this present world was the God of whom the first chapter of Genesis speaks, it followed that the "Creator" of whom the Old Testament tells us was a very imperfect being. But Jesus had come to enlighten and purify the minds of those who were willing to be enlightened and purified, and to lead them to the higher "Æons," where they would become perceptive of the highest Deity, whose essence was pure spirit, and who did not intermingle with matter at all.

Here, indeed, was Christianity without Judaism! and whatever we may think of the heretics who had devised this scheme of reasoning, it would be hard to deny them the title of Christians. They most certainly wished to continue in the Christian bond; and we need not be surprised that they were a little shy (as the ancient Fathers tell us that they were) in promulgating their own theories; and that they had an "esoteric" teaching, which not every one was permitted to hear. They had indeed not weighed and balanced either their own theories, or their own strength; and those of them who tried to develop the fundamental propositions which I have just explained were apt to run into ludicrous fancies, which the orthodox Fathers of the Church treat alternately with derision and with abhorrence. The Gnostics were in danger too on the practical side; some of them, through trains of thought that have been well known in modern times, ran into licentiousness; but on the whole a too severe asceticism was more common among them. The sanest and strongest of them was Marcion, who at any rate restrained undue imaginations, and whose followers continued in existence for many centuries; but his rejection of the Old Testament and of a great part of the New was an error, and though we may judge that he deserved personal esteem, we cannot regret that his opinions, or that the opinions of the Gnostics generally, disappeared from the world.

Yet if the account which I have given be correct, the Gnostics were not such purely wild and irrational thinkers as they have generally been held to be; there was a motive and a sequence in their reasoning; they may have been influenced by that suspicion of all things Jewish which was prevalent over the whole heathen world, but quite apart from any such suspicion the Old Testament presented to the thinking mind real difficulties in the region of morals, which have seldom been adequately estimated by Christians. The Gnostics were, in the history of Christendom, the first critical theologians, the first theologians who ventured to find any fault with those Scriptures which the generality of Christians regarded as infallible; this is their real distinction, and we owe them acknowledgment on this account. The religious elements which they absorbed from the East or from Egypt were generally (except some tinge from the Zoroastrian religion) a mere weakness in them, administering to imagination but not to truth; it was the Greek element in them, the portion of clear critical intellect which they really had, which constituted their value.

Perhaps, in the above account, I have not said enough of the tendency, which certainly existed among the Gnostics, to separate the man Jesus from the Divine Christ, and to represent the true Christ as free from suffering. But it is difficult, in view of the subtlety of the questions involved, and the narrow compass of the Gnostic literature that remains to us, to be sure how the different Gnostics severally regarded the point in question; and I do not feel certain that the distinction between the fleshly body of this life and the spiritual body of the resurrection, a distinction drawn by Paul himself in the fifteenth chapter of the first epistle to the Corinthians, was not, when drawn by the Gnostics, sometimes misunderstood as meaning a real substantial difference between the true Christ and the man Jesus. At any rate this should be considered. A very affecting and beautiful poem, generally (and I do not doubt justly) regarded as Gnostic, represents the human soul wandering amid the pollutions of earth far away from its Divine parents (the heavenly Father and Mother are both mentioned), having been sent to win a beautiful pearl which was under the guard of a dreadful serpent. This human soul is represented as forgetful of its mission, and sinking into a fatal sleep, until aroused by a message sent in love and sorrow by its heavenly Father. After the reception of the message, the human soul wakes up, and succeeds in casting the serpent into slumber; after which it seizes the pearl and returns to the heavenly mansion, clad in a heaven-sent garment, which was none else but its own native and original covering, temporarily resigned when it had been sent forth on its terrestrial wanderings. Now returning to heaven, the human soul is received with joyous acceptance by the Divine Father and by all spiritual beings, and with promises for the everlasting future[1]. Though it will be seen that Jesus does not enter into this poem, either as man or as the Divine Christ, the kind of representation offered may lead us to think that the Gnostics acknowledged a more essential unity of the human and divine in Jesus Christ than is sometimes supposed. The wanderer in the poem (who is of course not Jesus Christ) is the same person, whether he is among the pollutions of earth or amid the glories of heaven.

The Gnostics, with all their errors (which were by no means small), led the way to those two Fathers of the early Church in whom the approximation to the Greek spirit was greatest, Clement

---

[1] This poem will be found, both in its Syriac original and in an English translation, in vol. v. of *Texts and Studies*, edited by Dr J. Armitage Robinson. The translation and introduction and notes are by Mr A. A. Bevan; but the poem had been previously translated by Professor William Wright, in his *Apocryphal Acts of the Apostles* (London, 1871).

of Alexandria and Origen. But before coming to those two Fathers it will be well to cast a glance on the state of heathen thought at the close of the second century and early in the third century of our era. Stoicism has at that date passed its acme; the philosophy called Neoplatonism has begun to appear in Egypt. Neoplatonism was, as its name implies, an attempt to revive the Platonic philosophy, with all its spiritual exaltation and ideal government of mankind. The pious scepticism of Socrates was in the background in Neoplatonism; Platonic it is in very truth; but it is impossible not also to recognise that the success of Christianity had very much to do with the revival of a spiritual exaltation in heathenism. Ammonius Saccas, the founder of Neoplatonism, is said to have been a Christian, at any rate in his early years. It is true that Plotinus, who was far the greatest of the Neoplatonic philosophers, never mentions Christianity; but he has a book (the ninth of his second Ennead) directed plainly against the Gnostics (though he does not name them); and we can only suppose that he regarded them as the Christian theorists whom he was most concerned to meet. Yet in the most interesting of all the points of his attack upon them, the Gnostics were far from being typical Christians. The Gnostics held the Creation to be a work full of faults, produced by a Creator who himself was faulty: it is worth while to quote the reply of Plotinus to such a view:

He who complains of the nature of the world knows not what he does, nor how far his audacity goes. It is true that many men are ignorant of the narrow bond which unites things of the first, second, and third rank, and which descends even lower yet. Instead of blaming that which is inferior to the first principles, we ought to submit ourselves with meekness to the laws of the universe, to raise ourselves to first principles, and not to feel those tragic terrors with which some persons are inspired by those lofty spheres which only exercise on us a beneficent influence. What do these men, strangers to philosophy and to all sound instruction, fear in them? The spheres of heaven have bodies of fire; but they ought not to occasion to us any fear, since they are perfectly in harmony with the universe and with the earth. Besides, one has to reflect on the souls of the stars (and it is in the soul that these persons claim excellence); the stellar bodies, so much surpassing ours in grandeur and beauty, concur in producing things conformable to the order of nature, which things could not be born if first principles alone existed, and yet they complete the universe and are important members of it. If man has a great superiority over the animals, what must be the superiority of the stars, which are in the universe in order to make it beautiful and to make order reign in it, not in order to exercise in it a tyrannical influence? *Second Ennead*, book IX, chapter 13.

Hardly any passage could give a better idea of the real simplicity of the groundwork of the philosophy of Plotinus (in spite of the difficulty of many of his arguments) than the above ; he recognises the divinity manifested in the universe as a whole, notwithstanding the imperfection of many of the things most familiar to us. All things, he says, proceed from the One, who is God ; they are ordered by the Divine Intelligence ; they receive warmth and light from the Divine Soul. It is to be admitted that the practical evils of the world, the temptations which we have to meet, the sorrows above which we have to raise ourselves, the conflicts we have to wage, are too little dwelt on by him : on the practical side Neoplatonism is not the highest heathen philosophy. But yet such a passage as that which I have just quoted is well fitted to inspire us with trust in God ; and in saying this is not high praise implied ?

Though Plotinus quarrelled with the Gnostics, and especially disliked the tone of superiority which they assumed, he was yet not without kinship with them. In both Plotinus and the Gnostics the philosophic spirit is more dominant than in the generality of early Christian writers ; though not more than in Origen. When we read the *De Principiis* (περὶ ἀρχῶν) of Origen, we are sensible indeed of that reliance on sacred authorities, which was so deeply engrained in the Christian Church ; but all through we feel that Origen is trying to see things for himself, that he is not content with a barren acceptance of terms enforced on him by others It will be well to show this by a few instances. In the first book of the *De Principiis* he comes across the question, whether the heavenly bodies, sun and moon and stars, have life or not ; and he answers it in the affirmative, just as Plotinus does. No doubt in Origen, as in Plotinus, this belief rested on a sense of the paramount value and power of life, and especially of the Divine Life, in the universe. But Plotinus does not explicitly say this ; and Origen does explicitly assign other reasons, out of which I will quote the one in which (very characteristically) he bases himself on the Scriptures :

We think that they (i.e. the stars) may be designated as living beings, for this reason, that they are said to receive commandments from God, which is ordinarily the case only with rational beings. "I have given a commandment to all the stars," says the Lord. What, now, are these commandments ? Those, namely, that each star, in its order and course, should bestow upon the world the amount of splendour which has been entrusted to it. *De Principiis*, Book I. c. 7, § 3[1].

---

[1] I quote from the translation in the "Ante-Nicene Christian Library" (T. and T. Clark, Edinburgh). The Biblical quotation is from Isaiah xlv. 12.

The argument from Scripture is not Origen's sole ground for his belief; he also appeals to the regularity of the starry movements, as indicating implicit obedience to a command. But neither his argument from authority, nor his argument from external observation, can at the present day be considered to have any weight; and it is his instinct rather than his formal argument that appears to me valuable, as also is the case with Plotinus. That the power of life is deeper than material forces, and is capable of governing all such forces, was the instinct of both Origen and Plotinus, and also (at an earlier date than either) of Socrates[1]. This belief I have myself embraced and put forward in the first chapter of the present work; and though the instinct to which I have referred is the deepest source of my own conviction, I have also there tried to show that organisation, that principle to which all life bears witness, is the most rational ground on which we can explain the continuous splendour and manifold energy of the heavenly bodies. In saying this I have been obliged to draw a distinction between the sun and self-glowing stars on the one side, and the moon and the planets on the other side, which neither Socrates nor Origen nor Plotinus was able to draw; the former heavenly bodies being endowed with immense energy, the latter with comparatively little. But in the root of the matter I am in agreement with these ancient writers.

To return to Origen. In the transmigration of souls, according to the ordinary meaning of that phrase, Origen did not believe; that two men born in different ages could be in reality the same person, was not among the possibilities that he regarded as credible; and emphatically he did not believe that the soul of a man could so descend as to become the soul of a brute. But yet he did believe in the pre-existence of the human soul, and in this belief he found a reason for vindicating God's justice, as will be seen by the following passage:

As, therefore, when the Scriptures are carefully examined regarding Jacob and Esau, it is not found to be unrighteousness with God...that even in the womb Jacob supplanted his brother, if we feel that he was worthily beloved by God, *according to the deserts of his previous life,* so as to deserve to be preferred before his brother; so also is it with regard to heavenly creatures, if we notice that diversity was not the original condition of the creature, but that, owing to causes that have previously existed, a different office is prepared by the Creator for each one *in proportion to the degree of his merit....* And this, it appears to me, will be seen more clearly at last, if each one, whether of celestial or terrestrial

---

[1] See the 14th chapter of Plato's *Apology of Socrates.*

or infernal beings, be said to have the causes of his diversity in himself, *and antecedent to his bodily birth.* For all things were created by the Word of God, and were set in order by His Justice. *De Principiis*, Book II. c. 9, § 7.

A great sweep of intellectual imagination is shown us in this passage; and though the thought in it is beyond our power to verify while we are in this mortal state, there is nothing in it that we can fairly call irrational. We may hope that something like it is true.

So again, when Origen deals with the subject of the divine punishments, he keeps in view the infinity of time, and the eternal purpose of God for the reformation of souls. Let me quote from the third book of the *De Principiis* (c. 1, §§ 12–14) in illustration of this:

God leaves the greater part of men unpunished, both in order that the habits of each one may be examined, so far as it depends upon ourselves, and that the virtuous may be made manifest in consequence of the test applied; while the others, not escaping notice from God—for He knows all things before they exist—but from the rational creation and themselves, may afterwards obtain the means of cure, seeing they would not have known the benefit had they not condemned themselves. It is of advantage to each one, that he perceive his own peculiar nature and the grace of God....It is not without reason, then, that he who is abandoned, is abandoned to the divine judgment, and that God is longsuffering with certain sinners; but because it will be for their advantage, with respect to the immortality of the soul and the unending world, that they be not quickly brought into a state of salvation, but be conducted to it more slowly, after having experienced many evils....For God governs souls not with reference, let me say, to the fifty years of the present life, but with reference to an illimitable age: for He made the thinking principle immortal in its nature, and kindred to Himself; and the rational soul is not, as in this life, excluded from cure....Souls are, as one may say, innumerable; and their habits are innumerable, and their movements, and their purposes, and their assaults, and their efforts, of which there is only one admirable administrator, who knows both the seasons, and the fitting helps, and the avenues, and the ways, viz. the God and Father of all things, who knows how he conducts even Pharaoh by so great events, and by drowning in the sea, with which latter occurrence His superintendence of Pharaoh does not cease. For he was not annihilated when drowned: "For in the hand of God are both we and our words; all wisdom also, and knowledge of workmanship."

The quotation at the end of this passage is from the book of Wisdom (vii. 16).

The clemency of disposition shown in this last passage, and the intellectual breadth of it, are unequalled in any other Father of the early Church. Yet, in praising Origen, I must not forget to honour that other Father, antecedent to Origen, and though not equalling Origen in intellectual power, yet in tolerance, learning, and gentleness of disposition not inferior—Clement of Alexandria. These two men stood at the point when it was not quite inconceivable that Greek philosophy might have effected a lasting union with the Christian faith, have received into itself that living hope and assurance which Christianity alone had the power to give, and have softened the asperities into which the Christian Church was so rapidly tending. But so brief and happy a consummation was very difficult to achieve, and did not take place. Neoplatonism, which owed so much of its strength and beauty to the examples of spiritual life which Christianity had given to the world, was very unwilling to acknowledge the debt. Porphyry, the ablest successor of Plotinus in the Neoplatonic school, might possibly have done so; but his intellectual differences from Christianity hindered him. In saying this, it is impossible not to refer to one intellectual difference in which modern criticism holds him to have been correct—his attribution of the book of Daniel to an author living in the reign of Antiochus Epiphanes. In this judgment he showed a perspicacity rare in that age of the world; nor was he ever irrational or immoderate. Yet it is to be regretted that he did not feel that the Christians, with whatever errors they might be fairly chargeable, were bringing into human life a most extraordinary ardour of love and power of self-denial, such as the society of men had never known before. The great critic Longinus (that worthy statesman and martyr for political freedom) was perhaps the most cordially disposed towards Christianity of all philosophic heathens; at least if it be true that he wrote the words (found in a fragment in the Codex Vaticanus), "Paul of Tarsus, whom I even affirm to stand foremost in the teaching of such doctrine as does not admit of proof" (πρῶτόν φημι προϊστάμενον δόγματος ἀναποδείκτου). It was surely not a Christian who wrote those words; and if a heathen, why should not the attribution to Longinus be admitted, especially when we remember the commendation, by Longinus, of a verse in the first chapter of Genesis?

However, after the third century Neoplatonism sank into less worthy ways, into mysteries and wonder-working; in this also probably trying to imitate Christianity, though not as it had done in its earlier and purer days. After the third century, the time was over—or at any rate could not be renewed for many long centuries—when Greek philosophy, in any other but its most superficial aspects, could join in heartfelt alliance with Christian fervour. It might have been different, if Origen had been accepted as a dominating influence in the Christian Church. But the course of events was adverse to such a result; and though Origen had some deeply attached followers in the later history, his freedom of view fell gradually under the stigma of heresy, and three centuries after his death, under the emperor Justinian, his doctrines were disallowed, and his followers were scattered. It was a result deeply to be deplored; but it was the natural sequence of the inward difficulties and external troubles of the Christian Church; of the inward difficulties, because human impatience demanded a more absolute religious belief than was then rightly attainable; and of the external troubles, because the exercise of despotic authority had become natural to the rulers of the Church in their conflict with the heathen empire, and was not easily to be loosened when that conflict was over.

Except in regard of that impatience of which I have just spoken, the courage and piety of the Christian Church, in its conflict with the Roman empire, were truly admirable. We must not indeed think of the Christians of those times as mere innocent unwarlike victims. If the heathen authorities wielded the terrors of this world, the rack and the scourge and the fire, the Christian authorities wielded the terrors of the next world, the fear of the soul being lost, the fear of hell. Nor must we, when we consider the paucity of the weapons wielded by the early Christians, greatly blame them for wielding this weapon; the misfortune was, that they did not, when the conflict was over, know how to relax those spiritual terrors, and render them really consonant to the divine justice. But in the desperate battle which they were waging, they could not but call to their aid the world beyond death, with its fears as well as its hopes. It would be wrong not to add that the Christian martyrs did personally forgive their persecutors; and nothing can be more affecting than some of the accounts that we have received of their behaviour when summoned to the trial which was to end in their death. One may instance the condemnation and the death by fire of Polycarp, bishop of Smyrna (he was at last pierced with a dagger, if the account given be correct); the suffering and death of the martyrs of Lyons, in the year 177 A.D.; and the martyrdoms at Carthage at the beginning of the third century. Perhaps it may be desirable, as an example of these sad but soul-exalting tragedies, to quote part of the description which Neander gives of the last named events:

"Some few years afterwards," he writes, "three young men, Revocatus, Saturnius, and Secundulus, and two young women, Perpetua and Felicitas, were arrested at Carthage, all of them being still catechumens. The story of their imprisonment and of their sufferings presents us with many a fine trait of the power of Christian faith, combined with Christian tenderness of feeling. Perpetua, two and twenty years of age, who was a mother, with her child at the breast, had to struggle not alone with the natural feelings which shrunk from death, and with the weakness of her sex. The hardest conflict which she had before her was with those purely human feelings, grounded in the sacred ties of nature; feelings which Christianity recognises in all their rights, and makes even more profound and tender, but yet causes to be sacrificed to the One Thing for which all else must be yielded. The mother of Perpetua was a Christian, but her aged father was still a pagan. His daughter was dear to him, but he dreaded also the disgrace connected with her sufferings as a Christian. When she was first brought to the police-office, her aged father came and urged her to recant. Pointing to a vessel that lay on the ground, she said, 'Can I call this vessel anything else than what it is? No. Neither can I say to you anything else, than that I am a Christian.' In the meantime she was baptized; for the clergy usually found no difficulty in purchasing, at least from the overseers of the prisons, admission to the Christians in confinement, for the purpose of administering to them the offices of religion; although, in the present case, even this was perhaps unnecessary, as the prisoners were not as yet placed under a rigorous guard. Perpetua said, 'The Spirit bade me pray for nothing at my baptism but patience.' After a few days they were thrown into the dungeon. 'I was tempted,' said she, 'for I had never been in such darkness before. O what a dreadful day! The excessive heat occasioned by the multitude of prisoners, the rough treatment we experienced from the soldiers, and, finally, anxiety for my child, made me miserable.' The deacons, who administered to them the communion in the dungeon, purchased for the Christian prisoners a better apartment, where they were separated from other criminals. Perpetua now took the child to herself in the dungeon, and placed it at her breast; she recommended it to her mother; she comforted her friends; and felt cheered herself by the possession of her babe. 'The dungeon,' said she, 'became a palace to me.'

The report reached her aged father that they were about to be tried. He hastened to her and said, 'My daughter, pity my grey hairs, pity thy father, if I am still worthy to be called thy father.'..."

He renewed his entreaties when the trial took place; I quote what followed.

"Said the governor to Perpetua, 'Have pity on thy father's grey hairs, have pity on thy helpless child. Offer sacrifice for the welfare of the emperor.' She answered, 'That I cannot do.' 'Art thou a Christian?' 'Yes,' she replied, 'I am a Christian.' Her fate was now decided. They were all condemned together to serve, at the approaching festival, on the anniversary of the young Geta's nomination, as a cruel sport for the people

and soldiers in a fight of wild beasts. They returned back rejoicing to
the dungeon. But Perpetua did not suppress the tender feelings of the
mother. Her first act was to send a request to her aged father that she
might have the child, whom she wished to give the breast; but he refused
to part with it. As to Felicitas, on her return to the dungeon, she was
seized with the pains of labour. The jailer said to her, 'If thy present
sufferings are so great, what wilt thou do when thou art thrown to the
wild beasts? This thou didst not consider when thou refusedst to
sacrifice.' She answered, 'I *now* suffer *myself* all that I suffer; but then
there will be *another* who shall suffer for *me*, because I also will suffer
for him.'...

After they had been torn by the wild beasts, and were about to receive
the merciful stroke which was to end their sufferings, they took leave
of each other, for the last time, with the mutual kiss of Christian love."
Neander's *Church History* (translated by Torrey), vol. I. pp. 167–170.

More dreadful tortures were often inflicted on the Christians
than those described in the above narrative; but in hardly any
narrative of martyrdom is so much tender beauty on the part
of the Christian sufferers apparent.

As it is impossible for me to name all the brave and saintly
martyrs whose sufferings illustrated the meaning of Christian
faith, so it is impossible for me to name, much more adequately
to characterise, all the Christian writers who adorned those
ages when the Church was under persecution.

Two more martyrs let me name; one, Leonides, the father
of Origen, who was put to death at the beginning of the reign
of Septimius Severus; the other, Cyprian, bishop of Carthage,
put to death towards the close of the reign of Valerian, in the
year 258 A.D. Cyprian was one of the last of the martyrs slain
before that long truce between the empire and the Church
which was the result of Gallienus, the son and successor of Valerian,
declaring Christianity a lawful religion. This took place in the
year 261 A.D.; and for more than forty years after that date
the Church enjoyed toleration and peace. To such an extent
was the reconcilement between the Church and the heathen empire
carried, that when Paul of Samosata was accused of heresy, the
question whether he could lawfully hold the bishopric of Antioch
and the episcopal residence there was referred by the Church to
the emperor Aurelian; and Eusebius tells us that Aurelian
consulted the "Christian bishops of Italy and Rome," and on
their advice decided against the heretical bishop.

Before pursuing the history to the close of the dominance
of the heathen religion, it will be well to mention a few of the
distinguished writers of the early Church whom I have so far not

taken note of. Irenæus, a native of Asia Minor, but afterwards
bishop of Lyons; a writer against the Gnostic heretics, comprehensive though not altogether illuminating; a reconciler of
Victor, bishop of Rome, to the bishops of Asia in the question
of the proper celebration of Easter; a pious good man, possibly
though not certainly a martyr; he is the first to be noted. Next,
the aggressive Tertullian; the most passionate of the Fathers
of the Church; delighting in rhetoric, delighting in conflict;
especially keen against heretics, yet in the end becoming a heretic
himself, after his own fashion; we cannot by any means always
read him with pleasure, and yet he defends the Christian cause
against its persecutors with force and justice. His date (later
than Irenæus) is during the last forty years of the second century
and about the first thirty of the third century. Hippolytus of
Rome, early in the third century, was (like Irenæus and Tertullian)
a great chastiser of Gnostics, but also a writer on other interesting
subjects, among which his *Defence of the Gospel and Apocalypse
of St John* may be mentioned. Lastly, Cyprian, of whom as
a bishop and martyr I have already spoken; an earnest writer
and ruler of men, strong against too great readiness to receive
into renewed favour those who had denied their faith under
persecution; a strong asserter of ecclesiastical order, but in certain
respects an opponent of the then bishop of Rome, Stephen. In
naming these four writers, I mean to indicate their importance;
but I must say no more about them; and there are other Christian
writers of the first three centuries (especially the Apologists) who
must not be ignored. The heathen assailant of Christianity,
Celsus, known to us through Origen, though far from a just
critic, is not quite to be despised.

But I come now to the close of the historical drama with
which this chapter has been concerned. It was of course deeply
to be desired that that great conflict, in which the Christian
Church stood on the one side, and the heathen Roman empire
as the chief antagonist on the other side (with various foreign
religions, among which Mithraism was the most important,
joining in), should be settled on just grounds by the conscience
and intellect of mankind, and that action should only be taken
after judgment had been clearly formed. But such an achievement was quite beyond the powers of that age. The forty-two
years of peace and quiet which the Christians won from the
decree of Gallienus in their favour were far too short for the
decision of the momentous spiritual questions then before the

world; and there was a singular absence of Christian leaders of
high ability during the last forty years of the third century;
nor did heathenism supply the lack. Meanwhile the deep distrust
and suspicion with which the Christian Church was regarded was
not dispelled in the heathen mind; the passions which slumbered
were by no means brought to rest.

Then, at last, the timidity of the Roman emperors overpowered their prudence, overpowered all the dictates of mercy,
and impelled them to the conflict. It was in the year 303 A.D.,
in the reign of the emperor Diocletian, that the last and most
determined persecution of the Christian Church by the Roman
empire began. The real mover of it was Galerius, the colleague
(though a subordinate colleague) of Diocletian in the imperial
authority; Diocletian, though he might have been a persecutor
in any case, would not have carried persecution so far. For
eight years Christian bishops, clergy and laity, were tortured
and slain, and compelled (where compulsion availed through
terror) to surrender their sacred books; and indeed all men are
not heroes, and the surrender of books (a minor kind of lapse)
was not infrequent. Two years after the persecution began,
Diocletian abdicated; and Maximian, who had been appointed
by Diocletian as his colleague in the western parts of the empire,
abdicated also; and while Galerius took the place of Diocletian
in the east, Constantius succeeded to Maximian in the west.
Now Constantius was favourable to the Christians, and his son
Constantine, who in the year 306 A.D. succeeded to the imperial
authority in the west (his father having died), was still more
favourable to them; so that there was no more persecution of
the Christians in the territories governed by these monarchs.
But in the east, and in Africa, persecution still raged. Then,
towards the close of 310 A.D., Galerius fell ill. His administration
had been tyrannical and incompetent; and it would seem that
remorse and fear for what he had done agitated him. On the
last day of April, 311, he issued an edict, defending and yet
terminating the persecution; and within a week or a fortnight
he died. Tranquillity for the Christians immediately ensued;
and two years later, the joint emperors, Constantine and Licinius,
issued the edict of Milan, by which the principle of universal
toleration was laid down; and it was also enacted that restitu-
tion should be made to the Christians of all their sacred buildings
and of all the land and other possessions which had been forcibly
taken away from them. Nor did the Christian victory end here;

for when, in the year 324 A.D., Constantine became (after much warfare) sole ruler of the Roman empire, it became manifest that Christianity was now practically though not formally the religion of that empire.

The victory was well deserved ; but was it without drawbacks ? That could only be determined by the sequel.

CHAPTER XXI

VICTORIOUS CHRISTIANITY AND A FALLING EMPIRE

WITH the victory of Christianity over the heathen Roman empire, modern history begins. I am aware that the century and a half from the accession of Constantine down to the fall of the Western Empire is generally counted as the closing period of ancient history, and the centuries which follow, down to some quite uncertain date, are called mediæval history; but this kind of assortment of historical periods obscures the real truth of the matter.

Modern history is distinguished from ancient history in this, that in modern history the following problem for the first time becomes dominant; how such an organisation shall be introduced into human society, that not only shall every man abstain from wrong-doing and perform his natural duties, but also that every man shall be imbued in heart and soul with good and honourable feelings, right hopes and true knowledge. Those who believe that such an organisation has been made possible by the action and teaching, by the life and death, of Jesus Christ, are called Christians; and when I say "those who believe," I mean of course those who vitally believe this, and who make this belief the ground of their conduct. It is the ideal of Christians, the hope of Christians, the purpose of Christians, that they shall form one single society, not only in the thoughts and purposes of their hearts, but also in their organised action and in the aspect which they present to the world; but the weaknesses of mankind have hitherto prevented that ideal from being attained. That Christendom is divided, we see with our eyes, in this twentieth century after Christ. But this division of opinion among Christians as to what is right character and right belief does not preclude deep-lying sympathies; still less does it mean indifference as to right character and right belief; far from it. Even those in our modern society who look upon religion as a baseless imagination are interested in the intellectual and moral progress of the race;

more obviously in the intellectual than in the moral progress; but they recognise that, apart from material results, the character and mental capacity of men need guidance and improvement.

Now this persistent active interest, not in one man or one family or one set of men, but in all men, on the side of what we call character, the mental and spiritual part of their being, takes its rise from Christianity. I do not mean that men never took an interest in human character on a large scale before Christianity was thought of. This had by no means been unknown. For instance, when king Asoka, in the third century before Christ, caused the maxims of Buddhism to be carved upon the rocks throughout his wide Indian dominions, he was doing his best to foster human character on a large scale; and of course Gautama the Buddha himself had a profound interest in the character of mankind universally. But every one who compares the history of the two religions, Christianity and Buddhism, will see that there was an imperativeness in Christianity, in the Christian demand that all men shall be regenerated and led into the ways of truth and goodness, which is by no means equalled in Buddhism. When we look at the country in which Buddhism has the greatest number of adherents, that is China, we find Buddhism existing rather as a supplement to the really national religion of that country, which is not unfairly called Confucianism, than as the prime regulative force; and though we must commend the tolerance of Buddhism, we must also say that the fervour of it has been less than the fervour of Christianity. Nor did any other of the pre-Christian religions at all equal Christianity in this vital quality; Judaism came the nearest to it; but Judaism, even when most vigorous, was like a knight arrayed in armour too cumbrous to contend with the swiftly moving soldiers of the ordinary world.

This new purpose, which the Christian society engrafted in the world and still upholds and steadily pursues, is and must ever be central and cardinal in our thoughts, when we contemplate and try to promote the progress of the world. Not only does the material happiness of men need promoting, but their hearts and minds need educating, strengthening, and exalting. And before inquiring how this is to be done, the Christian society of those early days should receive our tribute of gratitude for having conceived and fostered such a purpose.

To conceive a purpose, however, is one thing, to carry it out is another thing. I remarked in the preceding chapter how great

were the disadvantages under which the Christian society laboured
during the early centuries of its career; persecuted, despised,
slandered; driven in upon itself, and precluded by the poverty
of its members from entering largely upon that inheritance of
knowledge which the heathen world had been accumulating;
could a society emerge from such a beginning as this into the
rule of a vast empire, and prove itself immediately adequate to
the charge?   For in very important respects indeed, the Christian
Church did govern the Roman empire, from the time when
Constantine became sole emperor.   Not, indeed, that the Christian
Church did of itself govern armies, impose taxes, or enact laws
on the administration of ordinary property.   But the Christian
Church did immediately assume an immense part in the regu-
lation of men's thoughts; it did enact what should be taught
and believed, and what teaching and belief should be forbidden
to men; it did direct the aspirations of men into new lines; it
destroyed temples, uprooted ancient priesthoods, and annihilated (as far as lay in its power) all new thoughts which did not
fit on to a certain model which it had prescribed.   In doing all
this, the Christian Church exercised government in the greatest
and most important particulars which belong to human life.
Moreover, the interval between the time when it was a suffering
and persecuted body and the time when it began to exercise
these imperial functions was the very briefest; was not more than
fifteen years at the largest computation!   So swift a trans-
mutation of fortune, on so large a scale, is not recorded elsewhere
in the history of mankind.

We cannot be surprised that the Christian society fell into
errors when it assumed to itself duties so novel and so vast as
those which came before it when the first quarter of the fourth
century of our era drew to its close.   The virtues which had
sustained, animated, and preserved it for nearly three hundred
years had not been lost; but new and quite different virtues were
needed for a new position.   Let us consider what these were.

So long as the Christian society had been exposed to persecution, so long had courage, endurance, and loyalty been the
qualities of which it stood in the highest need.   Not to disguise
the value which they set on the name of Jesus Christ; not to
diminish the honour which they paid to him, the obedience
which they rendered to his commands; these were the duties
which had been ingrained into the hearts of Christians; in the
practice of these duties they had stood side by side, holding

steadfastly what they had been taught; to inquire into first principles would have been dangerous when the foe was in front of them. But now the warfare was over; the Roman empire had not only ceased to persecute them, but was actually on their side; the emperor Constantine sat among Christian bishops and theologians, not as their master, but as their pupil. Now was the time when the Christian society might consider, with all humility, its past career; and especially might the Christian society have reconsidered the value of the chief authorities on which Christian belief rested, and have asked whether those authorities had in any respect determined wrongly; whether that long series of documents, which we call the Bible or the Scriptures, and which existed in that day very much as it exists to-day, was one into which error of any kind had entered; whether the conclusions, practical or theoretical, which had been based on this authority by Christians had been accurately drawn, and might be obeyed unswervingly.

The first error into which the Christian society fell, when it assumed that government of which I have spoken, was that it regarded loyalty as forbidding it to enter upon these most necessary questions. That this strain of opinion has lasted till our own day, does not make it less erroneous; but indeed the counteractive element of a much-needed criticism has entered into all Christian communities during the last two centuries, and the danger of mere indiscriminating trustfulness is not greatly to be feared in our modern world. But in the fourth century of our era the absence of a just caution in framing and enforcing a religious creed was more than a danger, it was a serious present evil. The case was briefly this: that whereas in dealing with our fellow-men a mingling of trust and distrust is always required, the Christian society in the times of which I am speaking placed the most absolute possible trust in the Scriptures and in certain conclusions which leading Christian authorities had drawn from this source, and the most absolute possible distrust in all other religions whatsoever.

If these other religions—the religion of Jupiter and Apollo, the religion of Mithra, and the religion of Isis—had been allowed to exist, an element of free thought would have been preserved in the Roman empire, and the Christian Church would have greatly benefited by it. But the second error into which the Christian Church fell was that it not only framed its own creeds without any real exercise of criticism, but that having done so,

it practically would not allow other creeds to exist at all.
Christians persecuted as sternly, though not as cruelly, as they
had been persecuted; and this second error was more serious
even than the error of framing a creed on grounds which had
not been subjected to criticism. But both errors worked together; and the good seed which Christianity had brought into
the world, the legitimate trust in God, the righteous and reasonable love which Christians bore to Jesus Christ, and the love
which they had been taught to exercise towards one another
and frequently did exercise, all these merits, though existing and
operative, were hidden from view and were greatly hindered by
the errors into which the Christian society fell, when the large
task of government was suddenly placed upon it. This result
was not unnatural; but it was greatly to be regretted.

It is natural to ask why these two errors lasted so long as
they did; for the first error, the refusal to exercise a sober
criticism on Christian beliefs, only began to give way, as regards
the most important points, about the beginning of the eighteenth
century; and the second error, the practice of persecuting
opponents, hardly gave way before the end of the same century.
A mere mistaken loyalty would hardly have borne its ill fruit
for fourteen or fifteen centuries, if special causes had not operated
to hinder all attempts at remedying it. There were special
causes. The whole belief in miracles, as miracles are related in
the Bible, involved the result that the region of divine powers
was regarded as essentially beyond human knowledge; anything,
however extraordinary, might be true in that region; it was
safest to take the doctrines given in the Scriptures (and especially
those reported to have been delivered by Jesus Christ himself)
literally, without attempting to discuss their probability or
justice. The reluctance and fear, springing from the source
just named, to submit Christian beliefs to real critical examination,
received strong reinforcement from another quarter. It was
thought that disbelief in the doctrines which God had vouchsafed
to bring to the knowledge of men was the most grievous of all
possible sins, and one which most distinctly excluded a man
from salvation, and (as a necessary consequence) involved him
in damnation—a terrible prospect—at least as damnation had
come to be regarded and believed in by Christians of the fourth
century. If any one asks why the Christian Church, which
ought to have been a deliverer, and had the capacity of being
a deliverer, acted for so long as an enslaver of men's minds, the

chief causes lay in the two erroneous convictions which I have just mentioned; the conviction that God has signified his will to men by methods quite separate from ordinary religious experience, and of a totally different type; and the conviction that a hopeless hell is the doom of unbelievers.

Thus was the Christian society, in the hour of its victory over paganism, animated by principles of opposite tendency and unlike fruitage; tender, heroic, and magnanimous on the one hand; timid, restrictive, and tyrannical on the other hand; and it was by no means uncommon for the same person to be an example of both tendencies; for both were deeply rooted in human nature. In the immediate consequence, the ill result was predominant; for in the wide field of government Christians were too ignorant to form accurate judgments, and wrong judgments in this field were followed by great disasters. But the tender, heroic element in Christianity had this advantage, that its results were not likely to be disturbed when once attained; they became a part of men's natural insight, and were generally seen to be really a sequence of true principles inculcated in the New Testament, principles which in the first hurry of action had often been overlooked; the spirit began to prevail over the letter in the interpretation of the New Testament, and the letter itself was more truly understood. The process of improvement was however a slow one; for the larger parts of the field of action were early occupied by dubious principles, in which error and truth commingled; and these soon acquired a prestige which made it difficult to replace them by views based on clear insight.

Among the more serious questions which had to be solved by the Christian society, was the question of internal discipline; for though every individual is prima facie the determiner of his own conduct, there are many questions in which individuals are obliged to seek guidance from others, and there are many acts in which individuals co-operate, and therefore have to accept external direction, if the co-operation is to have the desired end; and harmonious action is not to be attained without a willingness on the part of individuals to yield, in many cases, their own will and judgment to that of others. But to whom ought an individual to yield; and if an individual refuses to yield, what course ought the rest of the community to adopt towards him? Is there any final judge and authority to whom such questions ought, in the last resort, to be referred?

The problem indicated in the last paragraph is one that

concerns all men, Christians or not; but it had been the hope of
Christians that the wise charity and trustfulness which had been
infused into them by the precepts of Jesus Christ and by divine
communion and prayer would save them from any necessity for
external compulsion. This hope had been fairly well fulfilled
in regard to minor everyday questions, as long as the Christian
society was poor in earthly possessions and undistinguished in
worldly status; though even then there were times when questions
of principle arose, threatening to the unity of the whole society.
But when the Christian Church assumed the vast task of general
government (as, in the most important respects, it practically
did from the time of Constantine onwards); and when disasters
began to fall upon the world, and upon the Church itself, and
in no inconsiderable degree through faults of the Church; then
an organised government of more distinct kind than had before
existed began to be needful for the Church. Hence arose, in
the west, the Papacy: in the east, the patriarchate of Constantinople, not quite equal in authority to the Papacy, but still
on the same kind of level. Other patriarchates there were at
Antioch, Jerusalem, and Alexandria; but these did not in the
end maintain their position as at all equal to the two great
centres at Rome and at Constantinople. The rivalry between
Rome and Constantinople became in the end a serious evil and
a cause of disunion; but we cannot find fault with the Christian
Church, in this initial stage, for the forms of government which
it took. Only it ought to have been remembered that the form
of government which is best (and as we may believe, divinely
approved) at one stage of development, is not necessarily that
which is best at another stage.

This is the point at which a remark may be made respecting
the two phrases, "the Christian society" and "the Christian
Church," both of which I have used in the foregoing pages. "The
Christian Church," or more briefly "the Church," is a phrase
which has a tendency to imply unity of government, which as
a matter of fact does not exist, in any plainly visible manner,
among Christians at the present day; nor has it ever really
existed, though there was an approximation to it in the early
centuries. The western church, from the time when internal
heresy was crushed (which was not long after 600 A.D.) had a
very distinct and powerful unity of government, under the
Popes, up to the time of the Reformation; and in dealing with
western matters, it is often convenient to speak of the Western

Church as "the Church" simply; but it should always be remembered that the eastern Christians lay outside this rule, though often much influenced by the feelings and beliefs of western Christendom. At the present day, the phrase "the Church" is used by different persons with very different meanings; but the looser phrase, "the Christian society" may, I suppose, still be used as indicating the whole body of Christians under all their variety of governments. Possibly the day may come when the phrase "the Christian Church" will be understood at once as including all Christians, whatever their bias of opinion may be; but it cannot be intelligibly used in this sense at the present day.

But I must come to the detailed history, as this evolved itself after the accession of Constantine to sole imperial power; which took place, after much warfare, in the year 324 A.D. In the very next year after that date the great council of Nicæa assembled, in which the first formal attempt was made to lay down the fundamental elements of Christian belief for all future time.

The council of Nicæa was summoned by Constantine for the purpose of settling a bitter dispute which had arisen in the church at Alexandria between the archbishop Alexander and a presbyter, Arius; which dispute is generally called the Arian controversy. But even if there had been no Arian controversy, it would not have been unnatural for the Christian Church, when it had obtained peace from external persecution, to consider and determine for its own guidance the exact principles of Christian doctrine. It was indeed incumbent on the rulers of the Church, remembering the mystery in which the whole subject of God, of the divine nature and will, and of the relation of man to God, is involved, to provide for cases of possible disagreement on these points; whatever formula they agreed on, there might be some who dissented from it; and a dissentient was not necessarily to be adjudged out of the pale of Christianity, or even incapable of exercising the office of a minister in the Christian Church. At the same time each case of dissent would have to be judged on its own merits; there would be those whom the rulers of the Church would not consider entitled to teach with the sanction of the Church, but who yet ought not to be disallowed the title of Christians, or the position of laymen within the Church. Even if the rulers of the Church determined that a particular belief, or series of beliefs, deprived a man of any claim

to be a Christian in any sense at all, or to join in Christian ceremonies and associations, still even in that case a man was entitled
to his own individual liberty, and care ought to have been taken
that the Church did not in any way persecute outsiders. These
precautions having been taken, it would appear to have been a
reasonable and right measure for the rulers of the Church, not
regarding themselves as infallible but for the sake of practical
clearness, to assemble and determine what it was that they held
as essentials of Christian belief; and the peace which the Church
had obtained through the accession of Constantine to imperial
power gave an opportunity for the rulers of the Church to meet
and come to a decision on this important matter. How great
an influence they would have won over the minds of pagans, if
they had come to a decision which gave peace and freedom to
all mankind, need scarcely be pointed out.

But so happy a result was not likely, under the circumstances. When those followers of Jesus Christ who, successively,
for the best part of three centuries, had upheld the sacred name
of their Master against a world that denounced him as evil,
came suddenly, in the persons of their latest representatives,
into the possession of unlimited power—they were not likely
to be moderate either in the exaltation of him whom they
worshipped, or in the means which they took to keep that worship
at the height at which they themselves placed it. With the
fervour which filled their veins, had they added the virtue of
moderation, they would indeed have been transcendently great.
This they were not; but they had in some cases extraordinary
energy added to their fervour; and the leaders of the Church,
though we may regret their action, are not to be despised.

The history, or rather the main elements of it, must be told.
Perhaps I expressed myself too largely when I wrote that the
council of Nicæa attempted "to lay down the fundamental
elements of Christian belief for all future time." Something of that
feeling was in them, as it was much more explicitly in the second
great council of the Church, which met at Constantinople more
than half a century later; but the immediate cause of the meeting
of the council of Nicæa was accidental, and lay in the fierce controversy which had arisen at Alexandria between the archbishop
Alexander and the presbyter Arius. The fierceness of that local
controversy was imported into the proceedings of the Nicene
council, and it was a misfortune that it was so. But Arius was
regarded as betraying the Christian principle; and no toleration

was shown to any one against whom such an accusation was made, and was believed.

How was Arius regarded as betraying the Christian principle? Not through any avowed dissent from the New Testament; he professed acceptance of the whole of it. He had no objection to miracles, or to any miraculous narrative in all the pages of the Bible. He was not, like the Gnostics, an assailant of the Old Testament; prophecy and type were as sacred to him as they were to the archbishop of Alexandria, his opponent. Neither did he dissent from that doctrine which generally is called the Incarnation—the doctrine which represents Jesus Christ as having had, not merely a pre-existent life, but a pre-existent universal dominion, and as having been the actual agent in creating all things, in accordance with the will of the Divine Father; as being thus the exponent of the mind of the Divine Father, and therefore fitly called the Word, by which title he is named in the beginning of the fourth gospel. All this was accepted by Arius. The difference between him and the archbishop Alexander, between him and the bishops of the Nicene council, between him and Athanasius (I take his opponents in the order in which they appeared) lay in the interpretation of the Divine Sonship of Jesus Christ. Arius said that the Divine Son, who afterwards came into the world of men by being born as an infant and growing as a man, and who was then named Jesus, had originally been begotten by his Divine Father at a definite point of time, before which he had no existence at all; that point of time was indeed very remote, being before the creation of the world, but still it was a definite time. The Fathers of the Nicene council called this statement a blasphemy, but they did not themselves enunciate any phrase defining the precise contrary; afterwards however the Fathers of the council of Constantinople said that Jesus Christ was "begotten of his Father before all the ages[1]" (in our ordinary English version "before all worlds"). Arius also gave great offence by saying that the Son of God was capable of being turned from his purpose or changed, though he did not say that the Son of God ever had been actually turned or changed; and also by saying that the Divine Father had used the Divine Son "as an instrument" in creating the world.

---

[1] This phrase had been used by Eusebius of Cæsarea (the historian) at the time of the Nicene council (Socrates, I. 8) and was afterwards adopted by Arius himself (Socrates, I. 26).

The reader will see that Arius, while accepting the great body of Christian doctrine, was yet desirous of representing Jesus Christ as having a distinct inferiority, beyond that implied in the human nature assumed by him, to the Divine Father. How to express this inferiority, how to say in what it consisted, was a question answered by the Arians (and it would seem by Arius himself) differently at different times; Arius at any rate did not press, at a later period of his life, those opinions of his which I have just been describing. But some inferiority, over and above that implied in the human nature of Jesus Christ, the Arians did to the end maintain as belonging to him when compared with his Divine Father; this was their meaning when they refused to say that he was of the same substance (or essence) with the Divine Father. On the other hand, the greater number of Christians at that time, and almost the whole body of Christians in succeeding ages, maintained that Jesus Christ in his glorious ante-natal state, and always in his Divine being, was absolutely the equal of his Divine Father; and it is fair to refer not only to the so-called Athanasian creed as proving this, but also to the whole tenor of the writings of Athanasius, though one passage (his first Oration against the Arians, chapter 58) might possibly be thought to imply the contrary; but there is no real inferiority intended in the passage.

Now it is difficult for any one who has any belief in the Biblical criticism of recent times to judge adequately and thoroughly of the conflict between Arius and Athanasius, for this reason: that they both assumed, what a modern critic cannot assume, the absolute inerrancy of Scripture; and also they had much more clear-cut ideas about the nature of God and the nature and destiny of man than we can admit to be rightly held. As we are compelled to differ from both of them, it is not quite easy to say from which we differ most. But on the whole I think the kind of judgment we shall form is this: that while there were certain points in which Arius was wrong (and in particular we may say, against Arius, that the divine nature in Jesus Christ was and is essentially the same as the divine nature in the Almighty and Eternal Father), still Arius and the Arians were right in refusing to make that absolute separation which Athanasius made between the human and divine natures in Jesus Christ, which, in effect, made of him two persons (see the Appendix to this chapter); nor was it really altogether against them that they were changeable and vacillating in the creeds which they framed. It is no paradox to say this. Where clear truth is attainable, the clear and consistent expression of it is of course desirable; but in the mysterious subjects which were the theme of the Nicene council, clear truth is not attainable; we are not entirely ignorant, but we see imperfectly, and in such matters variation in the expression of what our mental vision indicates to us is natural and right. Now Athanasius set himself, with all his immense energy, to compel uniformity in the expression of belief; and this, which seems like strength, was a real weakness in him, and in the Christian Church for a long time afterwards. This is not offered as an adequate comment on the opinions which he was so zealous in enforcing; but detailed comment on those opinions would be improper in narrating the historical sequence of events. I will treat of them in the Appendix to this chapter, to which the reader who is interested in this subject may be referred; and as regards what we ought positively to think on these subjects, the sixteenth chapter of the present work has been an attempt to explain this, in so far as human thought is capable of attaining the truth and finding proper expression for it.

The council of Nicæa (the assembling of which is the point of history at which I have arrived) had as its result the absolute condemnation of those opinions of Arius which I first enunciated: the statements that the Son of God was begotten at a particular point of time, that he was capable of change, and that he was of a different substance or essence from the Divine Father, being in terms anathematised. A creed was drawn up, in which these condemnations were inserted; and two bishops alone, Theonas of Marmarica and Secundus of Ptolemais, refused to concur in it. Others indeed wavered for a time, but in the end came round to the decision of the council (a very slight further exception to this statement will be mentioned directly); and when more than three hundred bishops concurred, a minority of two might be considered insignificant. Also it must be said that the whole Christian community of that day coincided with the most important parts of this condemnation; and in the end Arius and his attached follower Euzoius largely though not entirely yielded to it—little as this fact is generally remembered or recognised.

Yet it did not follow that peace had been attained. To show in what manner it happened that the Arian controversy revived in new form, it is necessary to quote the creed drawn up by the

Nicene council. (It is given in the eighth chapter of the first book of the *Ecclesiastical History* of Socrates, and also, with very slight differences, in the first volume of the *Acta Conciliorum*, edited by Father Hardouin, of the Jesuits.) Here, then, translated into English, is the true creed of Nicæa (the creed commonly called such is of a later date):

We believe in one God, the Father Almighty, Maker of all things visible and invisible; and in one Lord Jesus Christ, the Son of God; only-begotten, begotten of the Father, that is from the substance of the Father; God from God, Light from Light, Very God from Very God; begotten, not made; of the same substance with the Father; through whom all things were made, both the things in heaven and the things in earth; who for us men and for our salvation came down and became flesh and was made man and suffered; who rose again on the third day, ascended into the heavens, and will come to judge the living and the dead. And we believe in the Holy Spirit. But as for those who say, There was a time when he was not, or, Before he was begotten he was not, or, He was made out of non-existent things, or who allege that he was of a different substance or essence, or that the Son of God was created or was capable of change or of alteration; these the holy catholic and apostolic church anathematises.

There were many Christians who, agreeing with the general purport of the above creed, yet thought that some difference, more than appears in the creed, ought to be shown between Jesus Christ the Son of God, and the Almighty Father. Now there is one word in the creed which is nowhere found in the New Testament; the word which is translated "of the same substance with," or "consubstantial with," the Father. The Greek word is Homo-ousios (ὁμοούσιος). The Christians of whom I am speaking alleged the danger of using, in a creed, a word which had not direct Scriptural authority, and they thought that it went too far in ascribing identity of substance (or essence) to Jesus Christ with the Divine Father. Many of them would have been willing that he should be called "of like substance" (or "essence")—Homoiousios (ὁμοιούσιος); but they refused to allow that Jesus Christ was of the *same* substance with the Divine Father. This refusal is the mark of the Arians generally after the council of Nicæa; and in respect of this particular and limited denial, they are sometimes called Semi-arians; it is plain, of course, when we compare their position with the original theses of Arius himself, that they had very much approximated to the creed of Nicæa. But there was by no means peace between them and the followers of that creed. The single word "Homo-ousios" was as efficacious in producing alienation between

Christians as the more complex denials of Arius had originally been.

Thus the Christian Church, immediately after its victory over paganism, got into troubled waters. The Catholics (it is convenient to use this term in speaking of the adherents of the Nicene creed, and it must not be taken as implying that the Arians were not Christians) had obtained a great victory at Nicæa, and it is clear that they thought at first that the controversy would occasion them no more trouble. As the civil power was now on their side, they used the civil power without scruple to bring their adversaries to silence, thinking this an easy matter. Let me quote from the ecclesiastical historian Socrates (I. 8):

> The council anathematised Arius and all those who held the opinions of Arius, and added the command that he was not to set foot in Alexandria; and a decree was issued by the emperor, banishing both Arius himself and also Eusebius and Theognis and their allies.

The Eusebius here mentioned was bishop of Nicomedia, and a person of great importance; he was one of the waverers whom I mentioned some way back, and (with Theognis) had consented to sign the Nicene creed; with the reservation, however, that he would not join in the anathema against Arius. For this reason, and perhaps for other reasons less known to us, he was banished by the emperor about three months after the termination of the council.

Whether the Nicene council thought themselves entitled by their own authority to forbid Arius to enter Alexandria, is not perhaps certain; but at any rate the command of the emperor, sending him into exile, was no doubt issued after consultation with the bishops who were present at the council. He was banished to Illyricum, where he remained for some years. I think we must also say that the following circular, which Constantine at this time sent to the whole body of Christian clergy and laity, was composed with the cognisance and approval of some (at any rate) of the bishops who were present at the council:

> Constantine the victorious, the most great and honourable, to the bishops and laity.
> Arius, having become an imitator of wicked and impious men, justly undergoes the same disgrace which belongs to them. Therefore, just as Porphyry, the enemy of divine worship, after composing lawless treatises against religion, met with his deserved reward, so that he is infamous for all future time and his name teems with dishonour and his impious writings have been destroyed; so now it is our decision that Arius and those of

like mind with Arius shall be called Porphyrians; so that they may have the title drawn from those whose habits they imitate. In addition, if any writing composed by Arius is found, it is to be committed to the flames; that not only may his miserable teaching be destroyed, but that not even the remembrance of it may be left. If however any one be detected as having concealed a writing composed by Arius, and not having immediately brought it forward and burnt it, for him I order that death shall be the penalty; and immediately he is convicted of this, he shall undergo capital punishment. Socrates, *Ecclesiastical History*, i. 9.

This letter, and the decree of the Nicene council forbidding Arius to enter Alexandria, as well as the decree of Constantine banishing Arius, are very notable as marking an epoch of time; for in this manner and at this time did the Christian Church become a persecuting church. It would be vain to say that the Christian Church of that day has no responsibility for Constantine's letter. Even if we were to suppose Constantine's letter written without the cognisance of any Christian bishop, which is very unlikely, it was issued to all the bishops, and no voice was raised against it: we should certainly have heard, if any bishop had remonstrated against it. But it was taken as a matter of course, that the emperor was well within his rights in commanding that any man who knowingly harboured heretical writings should be put to death. Yet is not that persecution? It would have mattered little, if Constantine alone had been responsible; a Roman emperor was not necessarily an authority on questions of moral conduct. But the Christian Church was the greatest authority then existing on these questions; and when the Christian Church began to sanction persecution, was not this a lamentable descent from divine purity?

At this point it will be well to take a review of the general position and conduct of the Church during the important period with which I am now dealing—the period during which the Church first obtained a partnership in the power of imperial Rome—in such power as lies in the sword and in armed legions. What I shall say of the Church will generally be true of the Arian Christians also; difference in religious belief did not imply difference of principle as to the important points of conduct which I now wish to mention.

I have said already that the Christian Church did right in consenting to the summoning of the Nicene council (it was the emperor Constantine who actually summoned that council). It was desirable that the Church should at that epoch consider its fundamental doctrines, and should state what they were.

The framing of the Nicene creed, in its doctrinal part, was not in itself an act of needless or irrational dogmatism; any mistake there may be in the articles of that creed does not prove that it was a wrong thing—the knowledge of men being what it was in that age—to frame these as they were framed. But the Nicene Fathers ought to have borne in mind that, though a council may have been needed for this practical purpose, that is for the direction of conduct, a council is not a body likely to attain absolute and perfect truth, where any difficulty exists in the inquiry. It ought to have been felt that the construction of a creed was a difficult matter. The Nicene Fathers thought they were quite safe if they kept to the actual words of Scripture; and this in point of fact they very nearly managed to do, except in regard to the word Homo-ousios—"Consubstantial"—which is not to be found in the Bible, nor anything very like it. The Arians took hold of what seemed to be a verbal aberration in the Nicene Fathers. But both sides were building on a wrong basis. Truth is not a matter of mere words; the spirit which animates those words is the real subject of consideration; and to get to the root of the real differences between Catholics and Arians, peaceable intercourse between the differing parties was necessary. Now when banishment is enacted as a penalty for wrong opinion, and death is prescribed as the penalty for making use of the writings of one of the two parties in the controversy, farewell to peaceable intercourse!

If the Arians had been weak, they might have been suppressed at once by the united forces of the Nicene council and of the civil power as represented by the emperor. But, though in the end weaker than the Catholics, they were much too strong to be suppressed at once by force; and the result of the decrees framed by the Nicene council and the emperor was to fill the whole Roman empire with tumult, confusion, and mutual suspicion; and this at a time when the growing power of the barbarians outside the empire made unity within it a matter of the highest importance! But there were pressing evils, not only outside but inside the empire, and such as it fell peculiarly within the province of Christian piety to mitigate and remove. These evils, amid the noise of doctrinal controversies, now received inadequate attention. Let me enumerate in order what they were.

The great cities of the Roman empire were full of the poor and needy; crowded also with slaves; and by slaves the whole, or nearly the whole, of agriculture was carried on. Torture was employed in courts of law; public shows, in which gladiators slew one another, were still common. Taxation was excessive; and under the despotism which had so long existed, the spirit and energy and even the physical strength of the inhabitants of the empire had suffered. War internal to the empire, through the rivalry of competitors for the imperial authority, had very recently been a cause of suffering.

When to these internal ills is added the danger of attacks from barbarians outside the empire, it will be seen that the Christian Church had plenty of matters before it, affecting the general well-being in the most intimate way, to which it was bound to give an intelligent care, and in regard to which it might have given counsel and often have instituted action.

Now it would be unjust to say that the Christian Church gave no attention to such duties as these. But it is not unjust to say that the Christian Church gave very little of its collective force, its collective energies of thought, towards remedying the evils which I have named. Even that evil which the Church really did put an end to, the gladiatorial exhibitions, did not receive its overthrow through mere deliberative decisions, but through the self-sacrifice of a single brave monk named Telemachus, who flung himself between the battling gladiators and was slain in doing so. The evil of slavery has no doubt all through the centuries been mitigated by Christian influences, and it is in the main through Christian influences that it has been abolished in modern times; but this is not the same as saying that the Church paid deliberate attention to its removal, such as the Church paid to the suppression of heresy. The thinking power of the Church was not employed in this direction; and still less was the thinking power of the Church employed in bringing poverty to an end. It is true that when the Benedictine order of monks arose, with precepts inculcating peaceful labour, a principle was engrafted in mankind of the highest value, and one which really tended to the amelioration of the lot of the poor; but this was two centuries after the council of Nicæa; and even when this salutary movement had taken place, the Church paid very inadequate attention towards curing what is the greatest cause of the poverty of the poor, namely the keen ambition on the part of the rich and powerful to make themselves richer and more powerful.

It cannot be said that the Christian Church did anything at all towards mitigating that most serious evil, judicial torture.

Augustine, in his famous treatise *De Civitate Dei* (book XIX. c. 6) shows himself perfectly alive to the unsatisfactory nature of the evidence procured by the torture of witnesses; he is sensible how odious the practice is; but for all that, he says that the judge ought not to resign his office on account of it; and it does not occur to him that it was the duty of the Church to reform the public sentiment on this point.

Lastly, with respect to war: there is doubtless something in the Christian religion which tends to mitigate the evils of war, and tends even in the end to abolish war; nor is it to be forgotten that the first Pope of the name of Leo more than a hundred years after the death of Constantine, did divert the fury of Attila from Rome, and softened the violence of the Vandal, Genseric. So too it is said that Lupus, bishop of Troyes, persuaded Attila to refrain from attacking that city. But single instances of this kind, though honourable to the bishops who did these services to their fellow-countrymen, prove little as to the general temper of the Christians of that age; and there are no signs at all that they thought of peace as a thing ardently to be desired and deliberately aimed at. Augustine, as a man of feeling, could lament the miseries of war (*De Civitate Dei*, XIX. c. 7); but this is not the same thing as trying to prevent war. The vehement quarrels between orthodox, heretic, and heathen within the bounds of the Roman state made it very difficult to form any scheme for preventing war or solving quarrels of any kind; and it also was very difficult, for the same reason, to form schemes for strengthening the internal fibre of the citizens of the Roman state. That fibre had been weakened by three centuries of heathen despotism; and though with the victory of Christianity new life of a kind had arisen in the world, perpetual religious quarrels prevented this life from bearing any such fruit as would make ordinary citizens, in the performance of their everyday duties, happy and secure. This is why the Roman empire lay so open to barbarian invasions.

It tended to increase the disasters of the state of things which I am describing, though also it gave an exaltation to the spirits of Christians which carried them through the disastrous period, that the common ideal which they held before their eyes, as Christians, lay beyond the grave and not in this present life. Nothing in the ideal which these Christians of the fourth century of our era hoped for, corresponded with that which the Hebrew prophet had entertained, of a time when "nation should not

lift up sword against nation, neither should they learn war any
more." The calamities of this life, the Christians thought,
would never be remedied in this life; the remedy was only to
come when our present being had passed away. It was a thought
not without nobility; but it should not have existed unbalanced;
for this present scene in which we live, this earth with the living
things that are upon it, alone gives us plain grounds of action at
the present day, and alone gives us visible tests of the rectitude
of our action, although it is true that we look for invisible things
in the future, beyond all which this life contains.

But I must return to the details of history. It is the first
scene of the first act of modern history at which my narrative
now stands, and it will be well to name and to describe the chief
actors in it.

First of these must be named Athanasius. He, though only
holding the office of archdeacon, had accompanied the archbishop
Alexander to the council of Nicæa, and had by the energy of his
mind and the clearness of his opinions been a great force there.
He himself became archbishop of Alexandria (upon the death
of Alexander) not long after the termination of the Nicene
council. Of all men in that day, Athanasius was the one who
knew his own mind best and who adhered most inflexibly to the
opinion which he had at first adopted. Moreover, he had great
courage, rapidity of action, and a power of dealing with men;
also a temperament neither morose nor despondent. In religion,
the sentiment of loyalty to Jesus Christ had extraordinary
strength in him. All these were qualities eminently conducing
to that victory which undoubtedly he did win, and the effects
of which remain in the Christian Church up to the present day.
Yet his character had a less favourable side. His opinions, so
confidently formed, were narrow and rigid; his temper, in
relation to his most famous opponent, Arius, was harsh in the
extreme. Gibbon, who does full justice to his eminent qualities,
says that he was "tainted with the contagion of fanaticism";
and this last word, implying as it does a fear of divine vengeance
overpowering the resolution to be just, was indeed the great
danger of that time. What Ezra was to the Jews, Athanasius
was to Christians; the man who defined religion, and narrowed
it in defining it, and cast out all those whose principles fell short
of his precisely worded rule. He was, it is true, himself the mark
of unjust attacks; and the skill and fortitude with which he met
them have justly enhanced his fame. We must not deny him

honour; yet the present age is bound to unloose the chains which he cast around the human spirit.

Arius, whose name stands as the symbol of the defeated party in the great religious conflict of the fourth century, claims our next consideration. Arius was a rationalist, however little he resembles those who have been called rationalists in modern times; the first foundation of his position (in so far as he differed from the opposite side) was a statement which in ordinary human affairs would be accepted by every one, that a father must be earlier in point of time than his son. But Arius did not sufficiently perceive that when a statement of this kind is taken out of the familiar surroundings of ordinary life into the transcendental region of divine relationships, it can no longer claim certainty. The inference which he drew from this premiss, that the Son of God had a beginning in time, was not a sure inference; and there were very obvious passages of the New Testament which, in their natural interpretation, were against him. It is impossible to be surprised that he failed in his first struggle against the archbishop of Alexandria, and against the energetic archdeacon Athanasius. But yet he and his adherents used arguments (as we may see from Athanasius himself, in his Orations against the Arians) which deserved much more attention than they received; and he might have claimed tolerance as a Christian, even if his belief did not receive approval. Still more must we think this, if we consider his later career. Never has Arius received a just acknowledgment of the amount of the surrender which he made, when he returned from his exile to which he was sentenced after the council of Nicæa. He has only been met with the taunt that his surrender was false and not sincere. But there is no reason to suspect his sincerity; he surrendered his own individual reasonings, which had found no support at all in the council; he did not surrender the point where he knew that a large number of the bishops attendant at the council felt with him, namely the disapproval of the word Homo-ousios, "Consubstantial." Yet even about this he was silent; he did not attack the word. I must touch upon these points in the later narrative; meanwhile I may say that few characters in history appear to me to have been more injuriously misrepresented than Arius. The reason is obvious; his enemies, in less than half a century after his death, obtained unquestioned dominance in Christendom; and wherever they had rule, it was unsafe to say a word in his favour.

Eusebius, bishop of Nicomedia, is the third of the important

actors in this great religious controversy. He was indeed, after
the close of the Nicene council, the greatest antagonist of
Athanasius. He had been in early life a friend of Arius; and to
that friendship he was faithful, and for this we must give him
praise. But it is the only praise we can give him; unless indeed
we add that in a kind of obscure way he did try after such a
solution of the controversy as should divide men least. But of
the great principle of mutual toleration of differences he does not
appear to have had any conception; and what was still worse,
he complicated the whole controversy by sanctioning and pressing
personal attacks on Athanasius, which had nothing to do with
the real question at issue, and which only served to embitter
feelings. He suffers, no doubt, in our estimation from the fact
that we have not his defence before us; but the broad facts
seem plain, and the above is the only judgment that we can form.
It was not indeed in the lifetime of Eusebius that that wonderful
moment occurred when Athanasius himself appeared ready to
accept the principle of tolerance, when (if we may trust the
historians Socrates and Sozomen) the emperor Constantius asked
him if he would allow the Arians to have a church in Alexandria,
and Athanasius replied that he would, if Constantius would
allow the supporters of the Nicene creed to have a church in the
cities where Arianism was dominant. If this proposal had been
accepted, a better prospect would have opened out to the world;
but the opponents of Athanasius declined it. Eusebius of Nicomedia was not personally responsible for this refusal, but his
followers only too faithfully followed the tone which he had
initiated. The truth is that Eusebius never extricated himself
from the difficulty in which his signature of the Nicene creed
involved him (though he did refuse to sign the anathemas of that
creed). He was at liberty, even after signing it, to say that he
preferred the absence of the word "Homo-ousios"; but he was
not at liberty to disallow that word, and yet practically his action
tended to disallow it.

The emperor Constantine, the fourth of the notable persons
of this age (and perhaps the most notable of them) was no
theologian, yet his influence on the course which the Arian
controversy took was not small, only the result of his action was
by no means what he intended it to be. He desired, above all
things, peace; but peace was not to be attained by favouring
first one side, and then the other, in the controversy. Where
he intended to produce a calm, he only heightened the fury of

the storm. Yet in spite of this, and in spite of some real and lamentable crimes which sullied his career, he was a great man; and when he raised the Christian Church from its low estate to dominance, he exercised a just judgment, and was a benefactor to mankind, though some of the immediate consequences of his action were very far from beneficial.

Eusebius, bishop of Cæsarea, is the fifth of the important persons of that epoch. To him we owe the sanest and most judicious of all the histories of early Christianity; and if any man could have reconciled the warring controversialists of that era, it was he. He was one of those numerous bishops who signed the creed of Nicæa (including the anathemas) and yet, as we must judge, would have preferred that the word Homo-ousios should have found no place in it. Even before the Nicene council, he had acted a friendly part towards Arius; and though he did not defend him against the anathemas of the Nicene creed, yet when Arius presented his revised creed (which constituted so great a surrender) to the emperor Constantine, Eusebius joined the great majority of the Eastern bishops in regarding Arius as having cleared himself of the charge of heresy, and he appears to have assented fully to the act of the synod held at Jerusalem, which readmitted Arius to communion. About the same time also Eusebius became more distinctly hostile to Athanasius than he had been before. (We learn this from the letter of the Egyptian bishops to the council of Tyre, quoted by Athanasius in his *Apology against the Arians*, c. 77.) The precise reason of this change of tone in Eusebius we do not know; but his action proves that he thought the conduct of Athanasius intolerant, as we have reason to say that it was. Eusebius of Cæsarea has no claim to be that great and picturesque combatant which Athanasius was; nor do I suppose that he ought to be regarded as an original teacher in religion; but our esteem he does at any rate deserve in no small degree.

One more person must not be passed over in any reckoning of the leading persons of this era, and that is Julius, bishop of Rome. To no man was Athanasius more indebted than to him; the staunch though not fanatical defender of Athanasius in his exile, we feel in his letters (quoted by Athanasius in his Apology against the Arians) a spirit of fairness which, though not exercised in the field of theology but in the vindication of ordinary justice, was in the circumstances of the case of great importance and deserves our recognition. A partisan we must account him, but not a wilful partisan; he writes as one who desired to hear that side of the case with which he was least acquainted; and the Eastern bishops were hardly well advised in not trusting him.

Such were the chief actors in the first great drama acted by the Christian Church, when it was relieved from persecution and raised to the duty and the honour of acknowledged rule in the world. And now to pursue the history.

It may justly excite our surprise, in view of the immense majority who subscribed the creed of Nicæa, and in view too of the great preponderance of Oriental bishops at the council, that so much resistance was made afterwards in the Oriental churches to the Nicene creed and its supporters. But I do not doubt that Neander is right when he says[1], "The voice of the emperor had, with many bishops, more weight than it ought to have had according to the principles of the gospel"; for Constantine was an ardent supporter of the creed in the form in which it was carried, and he was capable of banishing bishops who did not assent to the creed, and he did in fact banish them. The Nicene Fathers were thus influenced by motives inconsistent with entire impartiality; and, over and above their subservience to Constantine, they were too greatly desirous of peace, and they thought (as Constantine himself did) that a strong imperative was the best way of securing peace. There was, as a matter of fact, something peacemaking in a strong imperative; but the very slight change which took place in Constantine's own mind a few years after the council of Nicæa was sufficient to throw everything into disorder again. It is, I think, very doubtful if the candid opinion of the majority of the Nicene Fathers was in favour of the adoption of the word Homo-ousios as part of the creed; though this is quite different from saying that they disbelieved what the word implies; to say that they positively disbelieved it would be an attack on their honour which we are not justified in making.

The immediate practical result of the Nicene council was the banishment of Arius, and of two bishops (Theonas and Secundus) who maintained their dissent from the Nicene creed consistently to the end. Three months later, Eusebius of Nicomedia and Theognis were banished also, as I mentioned above.

Not long after the council, though how long we do not precisely know, Alexander, archbishop of Alexandria, died, and

[1] Neander's *General History of the Christian Religion and Church,* translated by Joseph Torrey, vol. IV. p. 44, note.

Athanasius was elected in his place.   We have no reason to doubt
the validity of his election; the Christians of Alexandria were
certainly on the whole in his favour.   Still Arius also had supporters there, and in view of the tension of men's minds, it is by
no means certain that peace reigned on the occasion.   We have
however not enough evidence to determine the point.

It was perhaps a couple of years after the conclusion of the
Nicene council (though again precise dates are unknown) that
the mind of Constantine underwent a change, by which the subsequent history was greatly complicated, and in a disastrous
manner.   A proverb of the poet William Blake may be recalled
here: "If the fool would persist in his folly, he would become
wise."   Constantine had been the fool when, in manifest contradiction to his own edict of Milan, which in the year 313 had
affirmed the principle of universal religious toleration, he banished
Arius and Eusebius of Nicomedia.   But having committed that
error, he had better have persisted in his folly; the ultimate
confusion would have been less.   He was, in fact, not sufficiently
in command of the just principles of universal toleration to be
able to determine what was or was not required by it; and there
were many pitfalls in his path.   He had a right to prevent the
Church from being tyrannous; but he had not a right to decide
who was and who was not a heretic; and in trying to effect the
former object, he forgot his incompetency to decide the latter
point.   Hence, while he desired to make matters better, he did
as a matter of fact make them worse.

The reason of his change of temperament, as it is told us, is
one of some pathos.   It was due to the dying request of his
sister Constantia, who earnestly pressed upon his esteem and
his care an Arian presbyter, by whom she herself had been much
influenced, and who thenceforth began to influence Constantine
also.   I incline to think that this was the real cause, for Constantine, despite his military vigour, was an impressionable
person; though if we were to take the historian Socrates literally,
we should have to suppose an earlier cause of the change; for
Socrates (I. 14 and 25) represents Eusebius of Nicomedia as
having returned from his banishment before Constantia had
exercised any influence on her brother, and Eusebius could not
have returned without the permission of Constantine.   But
supposing this to be true, we are left quite in the dark as to the
cause of the change in Constantine's mind; his sister's influence
is the only one we know of, and it is an adequate one.   The

probable order of events is then something of this kind: that Arius first, and Eusebius of Nicomedia afterwards, were permitted to leave their places of exile, having each of them successively purged themselves of the imputation of heresy in the opinion of important Asiatic bishops; for this we know that they did, and it is what Constantine would require as a condition of their being allowed to return. That Arius returned first, is plain from the letter of Eusebius given in Socrates (I. 14) and Sozomen (II. 16); a letter of which the genuineness has been suspected, but on no sufficient grounds. When they had both returned, Eusebius, having been restored to his bishopric of Nicomedia, would be in an important position, but Arius was still in the background, and did not even venture to ask to see Constantine. But Constantine, having been assured by the Arian presbyter above spoken of that the opinions of Arius did not really differ from those expressed in the creed of Nicæa, and knowing also the desire of Arius to return to his own city, Alexandria, where all the active part of his life had been spent (whether he had been born there is uncertain), now desired to see Arius. The interview took place; but before relating what happened at it, and what were the consequences of it, there is a point of the contemporary history, not connected with Arius, too important not to be noticed here.

When Eusebius returned to his bishopric of Nicomedia, he also returned to the neighbourhood of Byzantium; and it was at that very time that Constantine was devoting all his attention to adorning and enlarging Byzantium, to which he was about to give the new and more famous name Constantinople, naming it after himself. As he designed that it should henceforth be the capital of the empire, he also called it New Rome; but this appellation has not lasted. A wonderful act this was, and as often happens in important acts, there was a double reason for it, a political reason and a religious reason. The political reason lay in the fact that the enemies of the Roman empire were situated far more in the east than in the west; the Goths and other wild tribes pressing in from the northern shores of the Black Sea, and the more civilised Persian empire being in a condition of chronic war with imperial Rome from the south-east. Hence it was that Diocletian, the immediate predecessor of Constantine, had lived chiefly in the east, and had adorned Nicomedia till this city also seemed in a certain degree a capital city. But the situation of Byzantium excelled the situation of Nicomedia;

and it seemed well worthy to be the capital of an empire. But also we cannot doubt that the religious motive weighed with Constantine. Rome, at the beginning of the fourth century of our era, seemed to have paganism stamped upon it. Indeed it was more than mere seeming: it *had* paganism stamped upon it; and this condition did not alter till the fifth century, when floods of barbarians—all Christians and hostile to paganism, though heretics in the eyes of the Church—had swept through Rome again and again, and had in their fierceness assailed the pagan far more than the Christian elements in it. Thus at last Rome became wholly Christian; and from the very fact that an emperor no longer resided in it, the prestige of Rome became concentrated in the pope, and the immense authority of the pope through all western Europe began. But this could not be foreseen by Constantine; and to his mind the Christianisation of the empire was worthily marked by the institution of a new capital for the empire, a capital that should be eminently Christian from the first. Nor was his prevision quite wrong; though Constantinople never equalled Rome in religious authority, it had great sway in religion for more than a thousand years, and in the eyes of outsiders was often more impressive than Rome itself.

I return to Arius and Euzoius. They saw Constantine at Byzantium; and Constantine asked them if they agreed with "the faith." Arius and Euzoius replied in the affirmative; but Constantine was not content with this general answer, and required of them that they should put their belief precisely into words. After consideration, they replied in the following terms:

To our most pious master, most dear to God, the emperor Constantine, Arius and Euzoius write thus. As thy God-approved piety, lord Emperor, has bidden us, we lay before thee our own belief, and acknowledge before God in these written terms, that thus we believe, ourselves and our companions, as is declared herewith.

We believe in one God, the Almighty Father; and in the Lord Jesus Christ his Son, begotten of him before all the ages as the Word of God; through whom all things came into being, both the things in the heavens and the things on the earth; who came down and was incarnate and suffered and rose again and ascended into the heavens, who is coming again to judge the living and the dead. And we believe in the holy Spirit, and in the resurrection of the flesh, and in the life of the world to come, and in the kingdom of heaven, and in one catholic Church of God reaching from end to end of the earth. This belief we have received from the holy gospels, since the Lord bade his disciples, Go and make disciples of all the nations, baptizing them into the name of the Father and the Son and the holy Spirit. And if we do not believe thus and truly receive these articles of faith, as the whole catholic Church and the Scriptures teach, which we believe in all respects, God is our judge both now and in the future judgment-day. Wherefore we exhort thy piety, emperor, most dear to God, seeing that we belong to the Church and hold the faith and the spirit of the Church and of the holy Scriptures, that we may be united to our mother the Church through thy peacemaking and God-worshipping piety, all speculations and curious questionings being laid aside. In order that we and the Church having peace with one another may together make the customary prayers on behalf of thy peaceable reign and on behalf of all thy family. Socrates, *Ecclesiastical History*, I. 26.

In this letter lies the crucial point, upon which the whole of the after history turns. The letter does not, it will be seen, contain the word "Homo-ousios" ("Consubstantial") neither does it contain the anathemas with which the creed of Nicæa (see page 215) concludes. But it neither contains nor implies an attack on the word Homo-ousios; it neither contains nor implies an affirmation of the points against which the anathemas had been directed. It is a letter which in its tenor and in all its phrases breathes the desire for peace; and any ordinary reader would say that it was in practical agreement with the Nicene creed. Arius was an aged man, approaching his eightieth year. What danger was there in allowing his return to his place in the church at Alexandria? What was there, in the well-considered and final expression of his belief which he had given, in the smallest degree inconsistent with the Nicene creed?

So Constantine thought, and he at once accepted Arius as an orthodox Christian, and undertook to facilitate his return to Alexandria, and his reconciliation with the Church. But Athanasius was absolutely resolved that Arius should not be accepted by the Church; and though Arius did enter Alexandria, Athanasius, we are told, "turned away from him as from a pollution[1]." No wonder there were disorders in Alexandria; for the friends of Arius, though in a minority there, were not without influence. Further, Athanasius wrote to Constantine that "it was impossible for those who had once denied the faith and been anathematised, to be received anew as allies."

Now let it be granted, as seems to have been the case, that Constantine had expressed himself in too peremptory a tone, and had assumed as a matter of course that Athanasius would accept Arius, instead of appealing to his judgment in the matter. Allowing this, we must yet ask on what ground Athanasius repelled Arius so absolutely. Was it because he disbelieved in

---

[1] ὡς μύσος αὐτὸν ἐξετρέπετο. Socrates, I. 27.

his sincerity? The historian Socrates speaks of the "feigned repentance" of Arius, and of his "pretending to accept the faith ratified in Nicæa." But that was not what Arius had done. No doubt he was trying to minimise the difference between himself and the Nicene Fathers; and the manner in which he expressed himself was practically an engagement not to attack the Nicene creed. He desired, as he said, to have done with speculations and curious questionings. Was not that a very natural, very believable, and (finally) a right attitude for a man of his age to take? Even if he had been a young man, and therefore likely to resume "curious questionings" at some future time, the degree in which he had expressed agreement with the Nicene creed, though not absolute, deserved acknowledgment.

Athanasius ought candidly to have admitted that the new position taken up by Arius necessitated a reconsideration of the matter, as far as Arius himself was concerned. If he doubted the candour of Arius, he might have replied to Constantine that further inquiry should be made as to what Arius really held, and above all what Arius was prepared to teach in the future. But his rigid and unyielding attitude cannot be justified, and was the primary cause of the lamentable evils which from that moment began to fall upon the Church and the whole Roman empire; for Constantine naturally became angry with Athanasius, and many of the bishops became angry with Athanasius too, especially Eusebius of Nicomedia; and the quarrel became very acute.

Far am I from saying that the whole blame of the quarrel rests on Athanasius. The bishops who were opposed to him, with Eusebius of Nicomedia at their head, behaved as unwisely as was possible, timidly shirking the real question, which was whether the Church was to be tolerant or intolerant; they sought to fasten on Athanasius personal charges, and on the strength of these to deprive him of his archbishopric. The course of events was somewhat in this way. Though we do not know precise dates, the year in which Arius returned to Alexandria, and was debarred admission into the Church by Athanasius, is likely to have been 330 A.D., in which year, in the month of May, the building of Constantinople was completed, and the city was solemnly and religiously consecrated. It would then be in this year that Constantine (most probably urged thereto by Eusebius) wrote the angry letter[1] to Athanasius recorded by our authorities, threatening him with banishment if he continued to reject Arius

---

[1] Socrates, I. 27.

from the Church. At the same time Constantine did not follow up this letter by action; he wavered, in fact; and then it was that the personal charges which I mentioned above were started against Athanasius. One was no less a charge than that of murder; a priest named Arsenius was said to have been murdered by him; or at any rate to have been mutilated, one of his hands having been cut off. Another was that Athanasius had sent a priest named Macarius to a church where a person named Ischyras, claiming to be a priest, was officiating; and that Macarius had violently broken the chalice (the cup into which the consecrated wine was poured) while the service of the Eucharist was proceeding. This last story was circulated in various forms; the one at first propagated was that Athanasius himself had broken the sacred chalice; but this was not long believed; what Ischyras himself precisely said is to this day uncertain. I may say at once that I believe this particular story had some foundation; though not that part of it which said that the chalice was broken during divine service. Unworthily though Eusebius and his allies behaved, I do not believe them to have been deliberate deceivers and liars.

To take the story of Arsenius first; the accusation against Athanasius here was wholly unbelievable; and in fact Arsenius[1] was produced alive and whole before the council of bishops held at Tyre. But the countercharge made against Eusebius of Nicomedia was that he and his allies deliberately concealed Arsenius, in order to be able to accuse Athanasius of having murdered or mutilated that person. Of such wickedness there is no reason to accuse Eusebius, on the evidence that we now possess. Arsenius was plainly not a satisfactory person; he had reasons, which we do not now know, for concealing himself; and the Meletians (to whom he belonged) were thrown into a fever of suspicion by his disappearance. The Eusebians took up the case, not to their credit; and an amputated hand (how procured we know not) was supposed to be the hand of Arsenius. That appears to be a summary of the case. But in all these controversies we have to remember that the Athanasian party are the narrators; if we possessed the defence by the Eusebian party of their own actions, we should no doubt find that the narratives which we at present possess, which were almost entirely written by Athanasians, need some correction.

[1] The possibility might be suggested that there were two persons of the name of Arsenius; but all things considered, this is not a likely explanation of the facts.

As far as the case of Arsenius was concerned, the charge against Athanasius failed entirely. I have mentioned the council of bishops held at Tyre; by that council it was that Athanasius was tried (the emperor Constantine having so directed) on the two charges just mentioned, that relating to Arsenius, and that relating to Ischyras. The council, unable to convict him in regard to Arsenius, proceeded to make an extremely partisan inquiry, and convicted him in the case of Ischyras, and deposed him from his archbishopric. A miserable and unworthy decision! That a man of the eminence of Athanasius should be deposed from his archbishopric because one of his priests, with his sanction, had proceeded against a heretic with undue severity, and had broken a cup which that heretic regarded as a sacred chalice (the sacredness was of course not acknowledged by Athanasius) was a decision that could but aggravate the quarrels of the religious parties of that day. Those who attend carefully to the evidence as it is given in the account written by Athanasius himself (his Apology against the Arians) will, I think, come to the conclusion that violence was really used against Ischyras; the retractation which that person made of his accusation against Athanasius was plainly extorted from him[1], and was not voluntary; and insignificant though Ischyras was, he ought not to have been bullied. Still, we must note that it was not the rough usage from which Ischyras had suffered that the council of Tyre regard as an offence in Athanasius; that was too common in those times to excite much remark; it was because his emissary had broken a sacred chalice that they condemned the archbishop; for the council held Ischyras to be genuinely a priest, and the cup in which he administered the communion as sacred. It is plain however that the real reason of the condemnation of Athanasius was because the council of Tyre sympathised with Arius; a sympathy which was in itself to be respected, had it not been intruded into judicial proceedings with which it had no connexion whatever. Against the partisan judgment of the council Athanasius behaved with great spirit; he hastened to Constantinople, and made the emperor listen to his case; and though in the end Constantine banished him to Treves on the Moselle (rather for the sake of peace than as really condemning

---

[1] I say this, because (1) Ischyras retracted his retractation as soon as he was in the company of his friends, to whom he fled after making his retractation; and (2) because neither Athanasius at the council of Tyre, nor the Egyptian bishops in writing to the council of Tyre, brought forward this retractation, which if it had been voluntary, would have been so irrefutable an argument in their favour.

him) it was an honourable banishment, and no successor was appointed as archbishop of Alexandria; Athanasius was still regarded as holding the see. Meanwhile the bishops who formed the council of Tyre had gone to Jerusalem, and there had received Arius into the Church.

But the days of that most famous of heretics were rapidly drawing to a close. His presence at Alexandria (not through any fault of his own, as far as appears) was a cause of strife; and Constantine summoned him to Constantinople, to give an account of himself. Again he satisfied Constantine of the rectitude of his belief; and Constantine gave orders to the archbishop of Constantinople that Arius was to be admitted to the communion. But Alexander, the archbishop of Constantinople, was a fervent Athanasian; and he (we are told) lay down night and day in his church, prostrate on his face, close under the holy table, and prayed that either he or Arius might die. Then, on the day before he was to be received into communion, Arius suddenly died. It is not to be wondered at, though much to be regretted, that Athanasius said that this was the judgment of God. In reality, the death of Arius, though of course not to be expected beforehand, ought not greatly to surprise us. He was over eighty years of age; he had led a life in which much strife and hardship were involved; and now came a time of crowning excitement, in which, even yet, conflict was intermingled. It is not unlikely that the knowledge that fervent prayer was being directed to God against him had an effect upon him. Few persons are blameless; and that Arius was blameless I must not say. But as far as we can judge from the records before us, he deserves our sympathy more than any other of the actors in that era of vehement antagonisms. Let the reader look back at that letter which he wrote to Constantine, in which he set down the main points of his own faith (quoted by me on page 228) and say whether it does not breathe the true Christian spirit. Whether his theology was right or wrong is a question very proper in its own place, but it is not the main question; the main question is whether his spirit had a right tendency and a just balance. In view of the letter which I have quoted, I am sure we ought to give an affirmative answer to this question. What is there to be said against this? The historian Socrates, who is very bitter against him, accuses him of hypocrisy and wilful deception; but on what grounds? It is evident, in the first place, that Socrates distrusts the conciliatory character of the letter and

formal creed of Arius that I have quoted. But also Socrates
declares that Arius, in his last interview with Constantine, swore
untruly that he believed the Nicene creed in its entirety. In
answer to this it is enough to say that Athanasius, whose bitterness against Arius can hardly be equalled, gives a quite different
account of this matter, and says[1] that Arius then presented to
Constantine "a written declaration of his faith," which of course
was not the Nicene creed. It must not be understood that
Arius, in this declaration of his faith, was expressing all his
opinions; he was giving his *creed*, that which he thought important
for every man to believe. When this object is taken into account,
how was he hypocritical? I must say that I think Arius not
only blameless in the declaration of his faith, but also that the
creed which he submitted to Constantine, and which I quoted
above, was really the best solution of the controverted questions
that could then be devised. If it did not affirm the Homo-
ousios, neither did it deny it; and as it is quite plain that a very
large number of the Oriental bishops were not satisfied with
that word, was not that the best temporary solution of the
difficulty? The Christian Church had done without the word
Homo-ousios for three centuries, might it not have gone on
without it a little longer? Is it not plain that Athanasius tore the
Christian Church asunder in order to snatch a decision which
ought not to have been entered upon without the full concurrence
of all Christian authorities? The Nicene creed professed to give
such a concurrence; but we see that, in spite of the Nicene council,
doubts were largely entertained as to the disputed term.

As between Arius and Athanasius then, it appears to me that
Arius was right and Athanasius wrong; and I am not speaking,
be it well understood, of the actual belief of either, but of something much more important, of the method and the temper which
conduces to right belief.

But as between Athanasius and Eusebius of Nicomedia, the
case is quite different. Eusebius of Nicomedia followed the
disastrous course of endeavouring to thrust Athanasius out of
the way by a condemnation on side issues, which had nothing
whatever to do with the real question under dispute. In this
contest, all the superiority lay with Athanasius. In the end, he
and his friends were really persecuted; not by Constantine, but
by the son and successor of Constantine, Constantius. It took

---

[1] In his epistle to the bishops of Egypt and Libya. § 18, quoted by Neander in
his *Church History* (translated by Torrey vol. IV. p. 57).

a long time to bring Constantius up to the resolution of persecuting eminent Christian bishops; but at last he did so; and the result was that Athanasius had the opportunity of displaying his own remarkable powers in the highest degree. Often an exile, sometimes a fugitive for his life, but always accounted a hero by his own people at Alexandria, he died there at last in peace and honour, the acknowledged archbishop of that great see. It is impossible for us to commend him for his great mistake, his absolute determination to put down freedom of thought in religion; but in other respects, we too may regard him as a valiant and notable man.

Constantius was a persecutor; and it may be remarked that he persecuted the heathen religion more severely than he persecuted the Athanasian party; let him have due censure for both actions. So too let Valens, a subsequent emperor of the semi-Arian persuasion, be censured for similar conduct; though the worst act attributed to Valens, the burning of a ship with eighty ecclesiastics in it, is doubtless a partisan invention; the ship was burned, but we have no real reason to say that the burning was other than an accident. However, let Constantius and Valens receive due blame for their ill deeds. But what about the other side? What about Athanasius and Ambrose and Augustine? The actions of Constantius and Valens have no authority with men now; the actions, and still more the thoughts, of Athanasius and Ambrose and Augustine have great authority still. Did Athanasius and Ambrose and Augustine persecute? It is impossible to acquit Athanasius of the charge of having sanctioned that decree of the Emperor Constantine, which ordered that any one found in possession of the writings of Arius and not surrendering them to be burnt should be put to death. As to Ambrose, he was the chief author of those persecuting laws against pagans and heretics which are still to be read in the code of the emperor Theodosius[1]—the first Catholic emperor (unless Constantine is to be counted such) who had real power. Augustine was a very tenderhearted persecutor; one cannot but feel the amiability of his character; but he yielded to the current of opinion around him, and his defence of persecution as a Christian act may be read in his 93rd epistle. The main ground of his defence of it lies in the argument that by persecuting a heretic you may be

---

[1] A brief abstract of these laws will be found in the *Dictionary of Christian Biography*, art. "Theodosius the Great," in the 4th volume of the Dictionary, pp. 961 sqq. See also Gibbon ch. XXVII, and Hodgkin's *Italy and her Invaders*, vol. I. pp. 183 sqq.

able to save him from the much worse punishment which he will otherwise suffer after death—from hell in fact. In another interesting epistle, the 134th, Augustine intercedes for certain rebellious heretics among the Circumcelliones, who had confessed to having committed horrid deeds, and who were liable therefore to be put to death. It is very creditable to Augustine; but then it turns out that these Circumcelliones had been flogged in order to make them confess the truth. Augustine is evidently glad that they had suffered nothing worse than flogging. But is it not quite possible that a man who has been sufficiently flogged may confess ill deeds which he has never done in order to escape a repetition of the treatment which is intended to make him speak the truth?

Then again, in the last quarter of the fourth century, we find that the heretic Priscillian, with some of his followers, was put to death by the emperor Maximus, on the urgent pressure of some Spanish bishops. It is true that the celebrated bishop Ambrose, of whom I spoke above, joined with bishop Martin of Tours to protest against the deed. This was to their honour; but it must be added that Pope Leo I, writing in the fifth century, defended the execution of the Priscillianists.

Lastly, who can forget the terrible murder of the noble philosophic lady Hypatia by the fanatical monks of Egypt?

Any one who considers the instances just given will see that the Christian Church of the fourth and fifth centuries was not that innocent harmless body, afflicted by the ravages of cruel heretics, which so much of the language of Christian writers would lead us to think it was.

The reader will perceive from what has been said in the present chapter the nature of the problems imposed upon the Roman empire and upon the Christian Church after the victory of the Church through the conversion of Constantine to Christianity; the mistakes of the Church, not so much in the region of specific belief (though that some of the beliefs of the Church were erroneous, I have tried to show), but rather in the view which the rulers of the Church adopted as to the relative importance of the objects which in the then state of human affairs it was right to aim at; their underrating of temporal welfare, their overrating of minute precision in religious belief. In spite of the errors of the Church, a great deal that was truly divine remained in the consciences and emotions of Christians, and bore fruit that was to be revealed in after ages. But the

true virtues of Christian men and women, valuable though they
were, could not be so obvious in that age as the errors of the
Church; for a most immense task had suddenly been laid upon
the Church, the teaching and governing of men in matters of
high importance over the whole of the vast area of the Roman
empire; and errors on so wide a field could not but have most
striking results.   The virtues of Christians lay in the background,
and germinated slowly; the faults of Christians were manifested
on a great and conspicuous field of action, and the large results
of these shine clear in the pages of history.

It is history on a very large field that is my present theme;
and from what has been said in this chapter the causes of the
collapse of the Roman empire in its western portion in the fifth
century of our era will have been rendered plain.   There were two
main causes and one subordinate cause.

The first main cause was the weakening of fibre in the inhabitants of the territory governed by Rome; their physical
vigour was lowered by an inactive life, their mental vigour in
the affairs of civil life was lowered because no large resolve was
ever permitted to them; to exercise an independent judgment
on affairs of state was dangerous.   Every emperor wished to
confirm and consolidate his own power; he got his soldiers
how he could, often from the barbarian tribes which surrounded
the empire; the defence of the inhabitants of the empire,
though not wholly disregarded, was not the primary function of
the army[1].

The second main cause was that the Christian Church, when
it obtained power, not only did not set itself to retrieve the
internal weakness which the pagan empire had caused, but
actually made it worse by misdirecting the energies of the foremost
intellects throughout the empire, and exacting from men a
premature concurrence in religious belief; an exaction from which
discord and strife inevitably ensued.   No single individual was
so blamable in this way as the most vigorous character whom the
fourth and fifth centuries produced, Athanasius.

The subordinate cause of the fall of the western part of the
Roman empire was that Rome had ceased to be in any true sense
a capital city.   Constantinople had become the capital city of

---

[1] Coleridge in his *Table talk* says that the true key to the declension of the Roman
empire was "the imperial character overlaying, and finally destroying, the national
character."   There is force in the remark, and I have endeavoured in the above
paragraph to make it more precise; but Gibbon, whom Coleridge unduly disparages,
justly implies a larger field of causation.

the empire; against Constantinople the enemies of the empire, for more than eleven centuries, dashed themselves in vain. Rome and Italy were left comparatively defenceless.

But to narrate the fall of the western empire in detail is no part of the theme of the present work; and it will be long before Gibbon is superseded as the authority in that part of the world's history. One notable fact however deserves more prominence than Gibbon, or perhaps any historian, gives to it: with all the weakness of the western empire, no heathen assailant ever got near the heart of it, or in any sense whatever subdued it. Of the two heathen assailants of the empire, Radagaisus was overthrown and Attila defeated, though the damage they inflicted was immense; Radagaisus was overthrown by the great and faithful general Stilicho at the beginning of the fifth century, Attila was defeated in the battle of Chalons by Aetius in the middle of that century, and though still formidable after that battle, he was held off by the combined prestige of the Empire and the Church. The real conquerors of the western empire were two Christian nations, the Goths and the Vandals; Christians they were, though Arian Christians. Of these two nations, the Goths, though barbarians, were by far the nobler. They had been admitted peaceably within the bounds of the empire (having themselves suffered invasion from the aggressive Huns); and in the conflicts which afterwards ensued between them and the imperial authorities, the blame was very far from being wholly on their side. Alaric, their most famous leader, was not devoid of worth. Neither were they intolerant in their religion: Theodoric the Ostrogoth, who governed Italy and the countries north of Italy at the close of the fifth century and during the early part of the sixth century, was the most tolerant sovereign of those ages. Far more barbarous were the Vandals. Of their early progress through Gaul and Spain we know but little; but after they had crossed over into Africa, under their terrible leader Genseric, they began that long series of destructive wars and tyrannies by which north Africa, once distinguished in civilisation, full of well-ordered towns and fertile plains, capable of sending part of its corn produce for the sustenance of Europe, has been reduced to a chaotic barrenness—from which the efforts of European nations are only now endeavouring to raise it. Genseric was an intolerant Arian; he grew more of a persecutor as the years went on; and some of his successors exceeded even his intolerance. He, like Alaric before him, captured Rome;

the sacking of the city by the troops of Alaric lasted five days; but fourteen days was the duration of the plundering under Genseric, forty-five years later.

At the beginning of the last quarter of the fifth century, the western empire had disappeared; and though Italy still owed a nominal fealty to the emperor who reigned at Constantinople, no real protection was thereby afforded to this unhappy country, the most interesting, if we consider its whole history, of all the countries of the earth.

It was not then on the political side that the Christian Church could be considered a success, during its first two centuries of power. Under Christian emperors, full half of the empire had utterly collapsed; and what was there to show on the side of gain to mankind at large? Nothing certainly in the region of science or literature or general knowledge. Greek philosophy still showed a flickering flame; but it lay under the suspicion and disapproval of the Church; some of its representatives, such as Iamblichus, had lowered its dignity by an unavailing attempt to rival the miraculous side of Christianity; and though others, like Hierocles and Proclus, had a more genuine philosophical disposition, they were not creators in the region of thought. If we ask for eminent personalities outside the field of religion, we find two emperors, Constantine himself and Theodosius, who had a commanding character; and a very few warriors, of whom the father of Theodosius and Stilicho were the most distinguished; but otherwise, mediocrity of ability is almost universal.

Take even the region of religion itself; fidelity and courage had from the first been characteristics of the Christian society, and the fourth and fifth centuries contain many examples of both these virtues; but in the exercise of justice and sympathy towards theological opponents, in knowledge of the methods of attaining truth, there had been no progress. Misconception of the function and duty of a Church council was universal; it was held to be not merely a measure practically necessary for the provisional definition of truth, but also a divinely appointed means of enunciating truth that should never be alterable in any point. Hence it was that true unanimous consent never resulted from the decisions of councils; the ground had not been sufficiently prepared beforehand. The great heresies did not easily die out. Nestorianism, the heresy which was condemned in the council of Ephesus, in the year 431 A.D., was a heresy (like Arianism) which turned on the intrinsic nature of Jesus Christ;

I must not venture to enter on the actual question which was concerned in it. But Nestorius does not seem at first to have had any notion that his exercise of thought would be considered a heresy. He himself had not been free from the sin of persecuting; yet there was much that was noble in his character; he died from the ill-treatment which he suffered as an exiled man, just as the illustrious and noble saint, John Chrysostom, had died half a century earlier. Chrysostom had a narrow escape of being reckoned a heretic, through the animosity against him of that powerful person, the contemporary archbishop of Alexandria. Chrysostom however did escape the imputation; Nestorius did not escape it. Yet Nestorius had this distinction, that his form of Christianity, banished out of the Roman empire, took root in Asia, and spread for a long time over that vast continent, where some remains of it exist even at the present day, in spite of the tremendous assaults of Islam, which were continuous from the seventh century onwards. In the same quarter Eutychianism took refuge, a heresy very hostile to Nestorianism, and one which had the distinction of having Pope Leo—the first of that name—for its chief adversary. Of all heretics, none was so perfectly innocent of heretical intention as Eutyches was.

What can be said of Donatism, that schism which rent asunder the African church for a century and more, until the yet direr assault of the Arian Vandals brought still greater ruin? Neither the Donatists themselves, nor the churchmen who tried to suppress the Donatists, have left as a memorial of that strife any consolatory theme on which the after ages may repose with satisfaction. Donatism was not a heresy, however. Pelagianism was the single western heresy; and Pelagius, a monk, did kindle a spark of manly virtue, which unfortunately was not taken up into the system of the Church. Let me quote what Harnack says of him[1]:

> Roused to anger by an inert Christendom, that excused itself by pleading the frailty of the flesh and the impossibility of fulfilling the grievous commandments of God, he preached that God commanded nothing impossible, that man possessed the power of doing the good if only he willed, and that the weakness of the flesh was merely a pretext.

Harnack goes on to quote the words of Pelagius himself:

> In dealing with ethics and the principles of a holy life, I first demonstrate the power to decide and act inherent in human nature, and show what it can achieve, lest the mind be careless and sluggish in pursuit of virtue in proportion to its want of belief in its power, and in its ignorance of its attributes think that it does not possess them.

[1] *History of Dogma* (translated by James Millar, B.D., vol. v. p. 174).

Surely there was need of this vigorous exhortation to active virtue, in an age so full of despondency and fear as was the fifth century of the Christian era! There is much that man can do by his own power. It is true that man cannot do everything by his own power; and when we have our minds set on that great task, the bringing of harmony into the relations of men with each other, so that all men may peacefully cooperate, we must by fervent prayer win the divine help and strength for such an end; and it is true also that men find the root of their permanent union in the cross of Jesus Christ. But this does not mean that human virtue is nothing, or that human merit is nothing; both virtue and merit are in men, as we know by the admiration and gratitude which we so often feel for heroic characters and for tender acts of love. It was precisely because the age of Pelagius was so much in need of this teaching that it would not listen to it, rejected it, and counted it heretical.

Are we then, in view of the numerous instances of failure that I have recounted on the part of the Christian Church of the fourth and fifth centuries, to regard it as a pure failure; for besides the instances just given, a great deal of the life of the monks and hermits of those days must be reckoned a failure, and unprofitable?

This however is not the verdict that we must pronounce on the Christian society of those days, when we consider it in all its bearings. In whatever it was lacking, it was not lacking in fervour; and however strange or erroneous were the forms in which that fervour sometimes showed itself, there was life in it. If the manner of the intermingling of the divine and the human, as it has taken place and is taking place, was in some respects misconceived, yet it was never forgotten that love and self-denial were essential elements in forming this union; and the immense strain which countless individuals were willing to undergo, for the promotion of the heavenly ideal, had its value as a type and as an encouragement, even where there was no immediate fruit in the way of effective power or happiness. The inexperience of the Christian Church in the fourth and fifth centuries is a feature that has never been adequately considered. For nearly three centuries the Church had been in chains, with some alleviation, it is true, in the latter part of the third century (I mean for the forty years which preceded the persecution by Diocletian), but with no establishment of free and peaceful relations between Christians and heathen; then, suddenly, the heathen power revealed its underlying hostility, and Christians again became subject to torture and death, because they were Christians; then, with equal suddenness, the Christian Church became all dominant. Can we be surprised that, in so unexampled a change of fortune, it fell into extraordinary errors? It did so fall; but the lessons of its first teachers and the feeling that the true inheritance of men lay in a world greater than the visible world, and that faith and love would bring us to that inheritance, were never forgotten. The seeds of knowledge, of love, and of happiness were deep hidden, and were hardly discernible at the epoch of which I have been speaking, but they were not dead, and they slowly grew up. Their full maturity has not yet come, even now, in the twentieth century; but the promise of it has become brighter as time has gone on; amid sin and crime, the dominance of goodness has become more and more assured.

It would not be right to leave without notice some eminent persons of these early centuries, of whom I have so far made no mention, or only an inadequate one.

Let me begin by mentioning that Christian bishop and missionary—Christian though Arian—who had so great a share in the conversion of the Goths to Christianity, Ulfilas. It is probable that he never thought of himself as an Arian, though he knew of course that the Christian Church was divided, and that there was great dispute as to the word Homo-ousios; but in the middle of the fourth century those who accepted the word were not at any rate a clear majority. He lived among the Goths from his earliest years, being the son of a Christian whom they had captured (there were many of these captives, and Christianity grew among the Goths in this way). To Ulfilas the Goths owed, not only their Christianity, but also the first rudiments of civilisation. He taught them letters; he translated the Bible for them, with the curious and notable exception that he would not translate the books of Samuel and Kings, because he feared that those books would too much foster their warlike propensities. How much we must wish that they who were thus taught, and who reckoned themselves as Christians, had been acknowledged as such by the Christians of Italy! Then would the Ostrogoth king Theodoric have been able to give to the Italians something of those principles of settled government which he was intelligent enough to have conceived. But from an Arian they would not receive such a gift.

Were I writing only about the characters of individual men,

there are among the orthodox catholic Christians of the fourth and fifth centuries many in whom a strong interest might be felt. It may seem a small matter in comparison with conflicts that shake the world, but the lover of nature in modern times will feel a sympathy with Basil bishop of Cæsareia in Cappadocia, who in his youth (long before he was a bishop) settled in a romantic spot of glens and mountain torrents, and delighted in the beauty and the loneliness of it. In those days, such a preference had a near connexion with the preference for a monastic life; and the monastic community (as distinguished from the hermit life) is held to have taken its origin from Basil. Many such communities were founded by his influence in Pontus and Cappadocia; and like Benedict at a later date, he insisted that his monks should till the ground. We read too of hospitals for the poor, orphanages, and other institutions being founded through him; so that he well exemplified the beneficence of Christianity. As a stout opponent of Arianism he won perhaps even greater fame.

No mention of the eminent Christians of the fourth century ought to omit Ambrose bishop of Milan; whose peculiarly Roman character was shown unfortunately indeed in his approval of persecuting edicts, but more nobly in his reproof of the emperor Theodosius for ordering the massacre of thousands of men at Thessalonica in punishment for a serious riot in that city. The emperor acknowledged the justice of the bishop's censure, and did public penance for his fault; and no one can deny that the judgment of the Church was on this occasion worthily exercised.

The passionate and intolerant character of Jerome ought not to prevent our esteem being given to the man who translated the whole Bible into Latin, with an accuracy and dignity of style which had never before been reached.

I have left to the last the man who is perhaps the most famous of all the ancient Fathers of the Church—Augustine. May I be permitted, in speaking of a character so complex and so manifold, to refer to a work in which this subject is examined with a fullness and perspicacity which I could not rival, even had I the time necessary for such a work, and the space in which to set down the result? I refer to the fifth volume of Harnack's *History of Dogma* (it is the English translation that I have before me). The manifold religious tenderness of Augustine, and the way in which he thereby impressed himself on the generations that

came after him, are set forth by Harnack with extraordinary
clearness. Yet I confess I think the strength of native insight
in Augustine not equal to his sympathetic quality, or to his
capacity for receiving impressions; and herein I am perhaps
differing from Harnack. A single instance will show what I mean.
Harnack writes, on pages 82 and 83 of the volume before me, the
following sentence as expressive of the mind of Augustine (it is
not of course *quoted* from Augustine):

> Above all, the thought of God, the thought of the love of God, can
> never receive an irrefragable certainty, without being supported by an
> external authority.

I agree that that was the mind of Augustine; with all his
sensitiveness of perception, he was not at his ease unless he had
external authority with him; to him the external authority was
necessary. But I could not admit that such external authority
is, by the nature of the case, a necessity. To feel the support
of the strength of God in answer to prayer is an experience
which has a certainty of its own, whatever others may have said
on the matter. Augustine did feel that strength; but he had
not so much confidence in the genuineness of his own feeling, to
be able to dispense with the confirmation of it by others; being
possessed of that, he was satisfied. But then this reliance on
the authority of others had the disadvantage that it brought
with it the likelihood that you would rely on those others when
they were not so right as in the point where you had first accepted
their support. This did happen with Augustine; those who
read his *Confessions* or his work *De Civitate Dei* will see some
views expressed or implied of which the rectitude ought not to
have been lightly assumed, and the ground of which was plainly
authority and not personal insight. In saying this, I am far
from denying the lovableness of the man who could tell the secrets
of his own life, both in its external relations and in its internal
motives, with the candour which Augustine has shown in his
Confessions.

The fall of Rome—of the city of Rome as an imperial city,
and of the Roman empire in its western half—is a suitable
terminus for the present chapter. The next chapter will show,
by the side of a growing but perplexed and struggling Christendom,
the entrance of a new competitor on the religious field.

APPENDIX TO CHAPTER XXI

ON THE THEOLOGY OF ATHANASIUS

THERE were three stages in the development of the doctrine of the Incarnation, as held by Christians: the first stage was the presentation of it by the apostle Paul; the second stage was the presentation of it by the apostle John; and the third stage was the presentation of it by Athanasius, and this was the most clearly defined of the three.

According to the apostle Paul, the Son of God, in taking to himself a human form, "emptied himself." Paul does not explain this phrase; but it is natural to interpret it as meaning: "he emptied himself of those divine powers and that divine authority which he had before his human birth." Was Jesus Christ then, according to Paul, conscious while in the flesh that this divine power and divine authority had belonged to him before his human birth? To this question Paul does not anywhere give a direct answer; but the weakness of the flesh is so much insisted on by Paul that I think we must say that he regarded Jesus Christ while in the flesh as not wholly conscious of his pre-existent glory. But the fourth gospel does represent him as conscious of it in numerous passages; this clearly was the belief of the apostle John. There is however another point on which the belief of the apostle John is not clearly expressed: was Jesus Christ, while in the flesh, not only an agent on earth, doing and saying such things as a man would do and say, with infinitely larger powers than an ordinary man but still confining himself to action on earth; or was he also at the same time acting through the whole universe, preserving and sustaining and directing all things? I think we must hold, preferably, that John did not ascribe this universal action to Jesus Christ while in the flesh; for to be silent about it is naturally interpreted as not holding such action to have taken place. But Athanasius very distinctly holds that this universal action on the part of Jesus Christ did continue all the time that he was in the flesh; that the heavenly action and the earthly action went on side by side, not interfering with one another, but each operative in its own sphere. This is apparent all through the works of Athanasius; take, for instance, the following passage from the seventeenth chapter of his treatise *De Incarnatione Verbi Dei* (one of his early works):

For he (the Saviour) being in the body was not confined to the body; nor was he in such wise present in the body as not to be elsewhere. Neither can it be said that he moved his body but that the universe was left void of his energy and forethought; but what is most wonderful is that he, being the Word, was not comprehended by anything, but rather himself comprehended all things; and being present in all creation, he was in his essence outside the whole; and he inhabits the whole with all his powers, arranging everything, and in all things applying his own forethought to everything, and vivifying each thing and the whole sum of things, circumscribing the whole and not being circumscribed, but existing in his Father alone universally through all things. Thus while in his human body, and himself giving life to that body, he gave life also to the whole sum of things, and he existed in all things and was beyond all things. And while he was known from his body through his works, he was not invisible by reason of his energy over the whole universe.

Athanasius evidently thinks it open to us to hold this double conception of what Jesus Christ was and did during his earthly life—to regard him as hungering and thirsting in his human body, while at the same time with his spirit he was superintending all the courses of the universe; he thinks that our admiration and love, due to Jesus Christ as a patient sufferer in the cause of right, need no whit be diminished because this patient sufferer was also at the same time consciously living and working in a much mightier sphere, a sphere in which he did not suffer, but worked with full success, and was adored by the angels of heaven. But is it not plain that in any such combination of an earthly and a heavenly consciousness, the heavenly consciousness takes away all that terror, doubt, and anxiety which to an ordinary man is caused by scourging, crucifixion, and death? The heavenly consciousness may not take away the bodily pain; but it must take away that which is worse than bodily pain, the feeling that the end has come, that there is no remedy, no recompense for what the sufferer is enduring. It would not be difficult to endure crucifixion, if we were perfectly conscious that crucifixion only affected an infinitesimal portion of our living energies, that the pain of it would be over in a few hours, and that even while it lasted our spiritual being was engaged in tasks of vast and stupendous magnitude, and was conversant with other spiritual beings who were obedient to every expression of our will.

We have a right to object to the belief which Athanasius recommends to us; but it must be observed that the ground of our objection ought not to be the impossibility of it. I do indeed think it impossible, but a mistake in this region is pardonable, and the real mischief does not lie there. The mischief in the belief of Athanasius lies in the fact that it takes away that natural honour which belongs to Jesus Christ in virtue of his sufferings and death, the plain intelligible cause of our reverence and love towards him who suffered in order that we might know the secret of immortality, while it professes to substitute something greater, which yet is morally very inferior to the true cause of our reverence. The Arians (if we may judge by the quotations which Athanasius makes from them in the third of his orations entitled *Against the Arians*) dwelt too much on the intellectual difficulties of the position of Athanasius, so that he retorted on them that they were impious; but the moral difficulty of his position is more serious.

The treatise *De Incarnatione Verbi Dei* from which I have quoted above was a youthful work of Athanasius. But he never in the smallest degree altered his position; and it may be well to quote the following passage from his third oration against the Arians (chapter xxxiv); it is deserving of notice for another reason besides that for which I am primarily quoting it. He is answering the question, how he regarded the sufferings of Jesus Christ in the flesh; and this is what he says:

Let not then any one be scandalised by these human affections [being attributed to the Saviour] but rather recognise that the Word himself is in his own nature devoid of suffering, and yet these sufferings are spoken of in reference to him by reason of the flesh which he assumed, since these sufferings are proper to the flesh, and the [fleshly] body is properly the Saviour's own. And he himself remains, as he is, without suffering in his nature[1], not being injured by these affections, but rather causing them to vanish and destroying them; and men, seeing that their own sufferings have passed over into him who is without suffering, and have been taken away, become themselves also without suffering, and free for the future to all eternity, as John taught us, saying: "Ye know that he was manifested in order that he might take away our sins; and sin is not in him."...
For as the Lord, having clothed himself with the body, is become man, so are men made divine by the Word, being taken up to him through his flesh, and for the future inherit eternal life.

Let the reader, having this passage of Athanasius in his mind, reflect on the agony and the prayer of Jesus Christ in the garden of Gethsemane, as that is recorded in the gospels of Matthew, Mark, and Luke. If Athanasius is right, the proper expression of the mind of Jesus Christ on that occasion would

---

[1] αὐτὸς μὲν ἀπαθὴς τὴν φύσιν ὡς ἔστι διαμένει.

have been: "I cause this agony to vanish, I destroy it." How very far such an expression was from the mind of Jesus Christ in the garden of Gethsemane, no reader of our synoptic gospels can be ignorant. He overcame the agony; but it was through prayer that he overcame it, not through his own personal power.

It is true that Athanasius does, in a sense, represent Jesus Christ as receiving power from his Divine Father; but not at all in the way in which he is represented as receiving it in the accounts of the agony in the garden of Gethsemane. According to Athanasius, Jesus received from all eternity that which he received; whatever he received, there never was any moment when he had it not. This is carefully explained by Athanasius at the end of the thirty-fifth chapter of the oration on which I am commenting:

> If (he writes) what the Father has the Son has, and if the Father has these things eternally (ἀεί), it is evident that what things the Son has, seeing that they are the things of the Father, these exist eternally in the Son.

Did, then, Jesus Christ in the garden of Gethsemane receive from his Divine Father nothing but what he already had before he made his agonising prayer? The belief of Athanasius is destructive of all that is most genuine in Christian emotion.

Yet I am not saying that all the religious feeling in that passage which I have quoted from the thirty-fourth chapter of his third oration against the Arians, is false. Our sufferings do tend to pass away under those influences which respond to sincere prayer; if they do not wholly pass away, they are at all events lightened. And Jesus Christ has so well deserved the love and trust of men that prayer may be offered, as to the Divine Father, so also to him, and our sufferings may be lightened by the response which we receive and feel.

CHAPTER XXII

CHRISTIANITY FINDS A RIVAL IN ISLAM

THE crimes of conquerors are notorious, and are easily explained; for who is to restrain a conqueror from acting as he pleases towards those whom he has conquered, and even towards his own subordinates? He is the head, and others are his instruments; that is the principle by which his conquests have been won, and it is a principle which endures after they have been won. We must expect that a conqueror will commit errors; and if those errors have been prompted by ambition or selfish passion, we call them crimes.

Now the errors of victorious Christianity, of which I spoke in the foregoing chapter, were not as a rule prompted by ambition or selfish passion. Like the errors of Judaism, they had as their deepest cause a certain timorous distrust in the mercy of God; not indeed quite as the sole cause, for with it was combined a very great ignorance of the intellect and capacities of man, and especially of all which men had achieved in the way of knowledge and self-government before Christianity appeared in the world at all; but distrust in the mercy of God was the main source of Christian error. It was thought that God was so angry with Jews, heathen, and heretics, as to make it necessary for faithful men to separate from all intimate intercourse with these misguided people; and, little by little, heathen were compulsorily converted or driven out of the Roman empire, and heretics underwent very nearly the same fate; only Jews stubbornly remained, too faithful to their own creed to be converted, and not knowing where to turn for greater safety than they possessed in their condition as it then stood, unfavourable though this was. No wonder that turmoil and confusion, sorrow and distress, overspread all those great countries which had been subject to the dominion of Rome, and in which so high a civilisation, with whatever defects, had flourished.

Yet Christianity possessed in itself the seed of retrieval of its own errors, as these were exhibited by Christians; the good seed in it had the power of permanence, and not only of permanence but of growth, and it gradually did grow so that at this day we may recognise the root out of which it sprang, and the divine power with which it even now selects the good elements in all the world as its own, outgrowing and discarding its own mistakes. The good seed which Christianity bore was in its substantial quality ethical or moral, but it had also a historical attachment which was necessary for its exhibition as a fact of experience. In so far as it was ethical, this seed consisted, first, in the acceptance of beneficence as the primary duty of man, beneficence meaning the treatment of the desires and needs of others as if they were our own desires and needs; secondly, the acceptance of unlimited self-denial when this is required for the fulfilment of right and beneficent purposes; thirdly, the acceptance into our thoughts of eternal life as our own proper heritage, in spite of our ignorance of what that eternal life may be in its detailed character. These ethical precepts were and are vindicated by Christianity as not merely true in themselves, but as having animated Jesus Christ, from whom historically the acceptance of them has sprung, in his life and in his death; and hence it has followed that Christians have not looked upon eternal life as a mere abstract conception, but have believed themselves to hold communion and most intimate intercourse with Jesus Christ in that other state; the developments of which belief may not always be approved by us, but the belief itself is an opening into a new world, in a sense in which no other part of Christianity is so; a new world, animated by the presence of God.

The private lives of Christians did, from the very first, show the good fruit of these principles; and when the Roman empire became Christian, the desire to extend their operation on a large scale was natural and inevitable. The difficulties in the way of doing so were, however, great. For the civil government of the Roman empire, which might have seemed to have so great an opportunity for applying Christian principles to the welfare of man, and which in some degree did so try to apply them, was yet over the greater part of its field of action misled into the adoption of other and much cruder principles. It was not to be expected that all those maxims which had animated the heathen empire, maxims tending to despotism, which had received the sanction of so noble a spirit as Virgil, should all in a moment die out. That they should die out entirely was hardly to be wished; but they ought to have been gradually softened and mitigated; the

will of the subjects of the empire ought to have been recognised,
however informally, as having a just influence over the policy
of the imperial authorities.　But to admit this had been so
contrary to the policy of imperial Rome from the time of Cæsar
onwards, that Christian emperors never abandoned the theory
that the State must be essentially a despotism; and a kind of
improvement, which on Christian principles would have been very
natural, was deliberately shut out.　Moreover, though the Roman
empire had long ceased to make conquests, the Christian empire
did not any more than the heathen empire like losing what it
had once possessed, and in the sixth century we find the emperor
Justinian entering upon bloody wars to recover north Africa and
Italy as subject provinces of the power which ruled in Constantinople.　His able generals, Belisarius and Narses, procured for
him a temporary victory; but temporary it was; and these
wars of Justinian were but another affliction added to those
under which those unhappy countries laboured so long.　Hardly
can these be reckoned good deeds, or such as a true understanding
of the Christian faith would have inspired; and though we may
pardon Justinian for his bloody repression of the revolt of the
citizens of Constantinople, such an act can by no means be
regarded as of specially Christian character.　As to the religious
persecution of the Samaritans by Justinian, through which that
ancient nation was practically rooted out, we can but reckon
that act as one of those perversions of Christianity which became
so common in after times, and which stained the character even
of estimable princes.　Even when we look at the really good
deeds of Justinian, such as his codification (through eminent and
skilled lawyers) of the Roman law, or his introduction of the
silkworm into Europe, these can hardly be reckoned as genuine
fruits of Christianity.　Yet since the eggs of the silkworm were
brought from China by two brave and adventurous Persian
monks, one side of Christian character is honourably illustrated
by this performance, though the Christianity of Justinian himself
is not specially shown in it.　In fact, though Justinian, with all
his faults, does on the whole deserve our esteem, there is only
one side of his character which we can regard as testifying to real
Christian virtue, and that was his fidelity to his wife Theodora;
a lady whose conduct was confessedly pure all through her
married life, and whom (in spite of that double-faced slanderer
Procopius) I would fain believe to have been pure before her
marriage also; though Gibbon, I admit, holds the contrary

opinion. Needless it is to say that Justinian thought himself an eminent and exemplary Christian, and his zeal in detecting heresy was unsurpassed among the monarchs of those times; but it is not on this line that we can look for the fruits of true Christianity.

Except Constantine, Justinian is the most famous of all the monarchs who reigned at Constantinople (Theodosius is the only other emperor who can possibly be named as a rival); and when we note his aberrations from just and beneficent conduct, we can form some estimate of the difficulty that there was in bringing the true Christian spirit into the political sphere. Nor did the case alter at all speedily. We do indeed eventually come to kings and emperors who had the good of their peoples sincerely at heart, and such instances will be noted as they occur; but the growth of Christian beneficence did not take place primarily in the political line.

The first instance of Christian beneficence on a large scale, and such as really succeeded in propagating itself in the world in after times, was the establishment of the Benedictine order of monks in the south of Italy about the year 520 A.D., or somewhat earlier than the beginning of the reign of Justinian. Monks, indeed, there were in the Christian world long before the time of Benedict; but the earliest monks, those who retired to solitary places in the wilds of Egypt in the third and fourth centuries of our era, were too exclusively devoted to the single virtue of self-denial (without regard to the purpose for which self-denial may be needful) to be an element of progress in the world; and often they were fanatics in their religion. Much more on the true lines was Basil of Cæsareia, the founder, it seems, of monastic communities (for the monks before him had been solitary anchorites), and the promoter of active work as well as of religious exercises and asceticism. Much more on the true lines, also, was Patrick, the apostle of Ireland in the fifth century. But the order of Benedict, the rule of Benedict, had a development in after times far greater than the work of the other two eminent saints just mentioned ever had, though the result of Patrick's missionary work was not of small magnitude. Benedict it was who convinced the Christian world of the true character of labour, as a divinely sanctioned task; and learning, also, was honoured by him, and the pursuit of it enjoined. Let me quote Montalembert in illustration of this thesis; the passage will be found in his well-known work *The Monks of the West*, vol. II. pp. 45–6:

Benedict would not have his monks limit themselves to spiritual labour, to the action of the soul upon itself: he made external labour, manual or literary, a strict obligation of his rule. Doubtless the primitive cenobites had preached and practised the necessity of labour, but none had yet ordained and regulated it with so much severity and attentive solicitude. In order to banish indolence, which he called the enemy of the soul, he regulated minutely the employment of every hour of the day according to the seasons, and ordained that, after having celebrated the praises of God seven times a day, seven hours should be given to manual labour, and two hours to reading. He imposed severe corrections on the brother who lost in sleep and talking the hours intended for reading.

According to other authorities, the Benedictine rule allowed four hours to be given to reading and study; differences may well be imagined in different cases, but I am unable to give a certain solution of the discrepancy.

The rule just described was a severe one; severe in its demand of absolute obedience; severe in its implied demand (for this was understood but not expressed) of a celibate life; severe in its requirement of humility; and (I cannot but think) unduly severe in its requirement of "an almost continual silence during the whole day." We may criticise the author of this rule; but still, without severity he could have done nothing; and it is impossible not to acknowledge that his rule lay at the root of a great deal that was most typical, most valuable in our modern civilisation. The severe self-control which he enjoined, and which he succeeded in producing, had its fruit in most beautiful art and great accumulations of knowledge which grew up in the succeeding centuries; also in much valiant conduct, and much forming of new ties of spiritual relationship with new races, and among races already familiar with each other. It was not mere severity that produced such a result; it was the love that underlay the severity in the mind of the saintly Benedict; and I do not know how I can better illustrate this than by quoting the concluding paragraph of that exhortation which he prefixed to his rule; I will quote it from Montalembert (*The Monks of the West*, vol. II. pp. 44–5):

We must, then, form a school of divine servitude, in which, we trust, nothing too heavy or rigorous will be established. But if, in conformity with right and justice, we should exercise a little severity for the amendment of vices or the preservation of charity, beware of fleeing under the impulse of terror from the way of salvation, which cannot but have a hard beginning. When a man has walked for some time in obedience and faith, his heart will expand, and he will run with the unspeakable sweetness of love in the way of God's commandments. May he grant that, never straying from the instruction of the Master, and persevering in his doctrine in the monastery until death, we may share by patience in the sufferings of Christ, and be worthy to share together his kingdom.

It was a sober and reasonable mind that thus wrote; and religious minds responded to these words not fanatically, but reasonably. Montalembert tells us that the opening words of the exhortation, of which I have quoted the termination, the words "Ausculta, O fili!" ("Listen, O son!"), are depicted by mediæval painters on the book which, in their portraits of Benedict, they place in his hand; and these painters do in this way acknowledge the connexion of Benedict with literary labour, which was real and important. But it would be very erroneous to think that literary labour was the exclusive aim of the Benedictine rule. It was the design of Benedict that his monastery should be self-supporting, and not merely self-supporting, but that the products of monastic labour should overflow into the world outside the monastery, and be a benefit to all. If the monks sold any article, the price was to be below that charged by outside workers, and it need hardly be added that the purpose of Benedict in this command was not that his monks might undersell competitors and thereby win money for themselves, but for the very reverse reason—in order that his monks might not be avaricious, and might not try to gain an advantage over their neighbours. Concurrent with this was his command that they should be hospitable, that they should relieve the poor, and entertain strangers.

There is a great deal in the rule of which I have been detailing the characteristics that cannot help winning commendation; but the obligation to lead a celibate life which a monk under the Benedictine rule really (though not perhaps formally) took upon himself, does not in general receive approval in ordinary modern life. I will admit that permanent vows are dangerous, for a man's feelings may alter very much in the process of years; but a celibate institution, and particularly one having a religious basis, had in those days a power of self-preservation, and of organised work, and still more of missionary enterprise, which it would have been impossible to obtain in any other way; and it is hard to doubt the correctness of Benedict's judgment, in his own day, when he demanded celibacy of those who permanently adhered to his rule. Certainly this was, then, the universal judgment of Christians who were endeavouring to lead a life of special beneficence; though they over-valued asceticism, they were not mistaken in feeling that there was a power in it, and a power for good. Scarcely anything is more remarkable in the history of the whole Benedictine rule than the spontaneity with which the principle of it was caught up by men who might have seemed outside the influence of it, but whose minds were religiously inclined.   Justly does Montalembert say of Benedict:

What is most to be admired in his social and historical influence is that he seems never to have dreamt of it.   But is it not a sign of true greatness to achieve great things without any pompous commotion, without preconceived ideas, without premeditation, under the sole empire of a modest and pure design, which God exalts and multiplies a hundred-fold?   Strange to say, nothing even in his rule itself indicates that it was written with the idea of governing other monasteries besides his own. He might have supposed that it would be adopted by communities in the neighbourhood of those which he had collected round him; but nothing betrays any intention of establishing a common link of subordination between them, or of forming a bond between different religious houses, in order to originate an association of different and coordinate elements, like the great orders which have since arisen.   *The Monks of the West*, vol. II. pp. 65–6.

Looking at the results, we cannot but form the conclusion that the monastic system was the method by which, in that great and terrible upheaval through which the ancient world passed into our present order, the habit of faithful and trustworthy labour was engendered in the nations of western Europe, in a degree of which no previous country or age had given an example.   It would be hard to exaggerate the debt which we owe to Benedict on this account, and also by reason of the regard which he showed for learning, and which he inculcated on others; but yet it is not to Benedict that we owe the preservation of any part of that invaluable heritage, the literature of the ancient Greeks and Romans.   On that literature, we cannot but believe, Benedict looked with a careless eye; but there was a contemporary of his who did not do so.   This was Cassiodorus, who was born ten years before Benedict, and who for many years of his life was the able, honest, and tolerant minister of the famous Gothic king Theodoric, and in that capacity the colleague of Boethius, whose virtues he equalled without sharing his misfortunes.   In his old age Cassiodorus became a monk; and to show what his services to mankind were in this new station, I cannot do better than transcribe the interesting account given by the late Edward Mallet Young[1];

Upon the triumph of Belisarius and the downfall of the Ostrogoths, being now seventy years of age, he (Cassiodorus) withdrew to his native province, and founded the monastery of Viviers at the foot of Mount Moscius, which he describes.   Various reasons have been assigned for this

---

[1] In the *Dictionary of Christian Biography*, vol. I. p. 417.

retirement, but the true motive would seem to be indicated at the close of his treatise on the soul, where, addressing Christ in a strain of pious exaltation, he exclaims, "Tibi nobilius est servire quam regna mundi capessere[1]." For fifty years he had laboured to preserve authority from its own excesses, to soften the manners of the Goths, and to uphold the rights of the Romans; but he was weary of the superhuman task, and seems to have turned to the cloister for repose and freedom. His activity, however, was not to be satisfied with the ordinary occupations of monastic life. Hence while the summit of the mountain was set apart for the hermits of the community (Monasterium Castellense), there sprang up at its base, beneath his own immediate auspices, a society of cenobites, devoted to the pursuit of learning and science (Monasterium Vivariense). Foiled in his efforts to save the state of Italy from barbarism, he directed his remaining energies to elevating the standard of knowledge among ecclesiastics, and preparing the cloister to become the asylum of literature and the liberal arts. With this purpose he endowed the monastery of Viviers with his Roman library, containing the accumulations of half a century, which he continued to augment until his death. Not only were the monks incited by his example to the study of classical and sacred literature; he trained them likewise to the careful transcription of manuscripts, in the purchase of which large sums were continually disbursed. Bookbinding, gardening, and medicine were among the pursuits of the less intellectual members of the fraternity. Such time as he himself could spare from the composition of sacred or scientific treatises he employed in the construction of self-acting lamps, sundials, and waterclocks, for the use of the monastery. Nor was the influence of his example confined to his own age or institution. The system of which he was the founder took root and spread beyond the boundaries of Italy, so that the multiplication of manuscripts became gradually as much a recognised employment of monastic life as prayer or fasting; nor is it too much to say that on this account alone the statue of Cassiodorus deserves an honourable niche in every library.

The seminative power of Christian faith appears here no less than in the work founded by Benedict. It is true, that without the self-denying impulse of which Benedict was so great an example, and which he communicated to others, the literary industry which Cassiodorus fostered would not have had a field to work in; but from both these admirable men we see that the Christians of the sixth century, subject though they were in many respects to an erroneous bias, had a fervour which promised a future deliverance; where they failed, it was from erroneous conceptions, not from any lack of the warmth which nurtures the seeds of life. In those matters where they conceived any purpose truly, it prospered under their hands.

Further, the Christians of western Europe had a just instinct towards order and unity. Of eastern Christendom in the sixth

[1] "It is nobler to serve thee than to rule the world.'

century this cannot be said; but of eastern Christendom I must speak presently. All through western Europe, whatever might be the political convulsions, whatever the sufferings of peaceful men, there was in the religious sphere a consistent habit of mind, leading men to obey and trust the pope, the bishop of Rome, alike in creed and in religious practice. That this habit of mind was divinely sanctioned for ever, or that it is an essential and intrinsic part of Christianity in itself, the reader will have already perceived that I do not hold; and this is a point that will have to be dealt with when I come to the era of the Reformation. But in the sixth century and during some centuries afterwards (I think I should fix the year 1200 as the limiting time) it was a habit of mind that had real value, and, in the earlier part of this period, great value. This value did not lie in any special wisdom of the popes themselves (though some popes had eminent virtues), but rather in the means which the authority, thus centralised, afforded for preserving peaceful and affectionate sentiments and mutual understanding (without undue controversy) over many countries, different and distant from each other; and both that propagation of Christianity into heathen countries which ardent Christians keenly desired, and also the organisation of Christian work in nations that had already been converted, were thus facilitated.

The obedience to the popes of which I have just spoken, and the salutary and various labour of the monastic orders (who drew their primary inspiration from Benedict), were the most civilising elements in western Europe during many centuries of mediæval history; and though it was not possible that either popes or monks should be blameless, yet a great work was done by their means. This is illustrated at the close of the sixth century, by the career of one of the most famous of the popes, the first who bore the name of Gregory. Gregory had himself been a monk, under the Benedictine rule; he had shown extraordinary benevolence, and lived a life of singular austerity; this was the more notable in him, as he was of noble birth, and had held (before he became a monk) civil office of high distinction. From his monastery he was sent by pope Pelagius on an embassy to the emperor at Constantinople, where he remained six years, endeavouring to interest the successive emperors in the affairs of Italy, then suffering from the Lombard invasion. Returning, he was elected by the monks abbot of his monastery; then, in the year 590, Pelagius having died of the plague, he was made pope, against his own will (as we may truly believe). His reluctance to accept that high position was no indication of slackness of will; having once consented to be pope, his administrative energy was extraordinary. This was partly shown in his administration of the domains of the Church, in which he was sedulous in protecting the cultivators from over-exactions; partly in more general efforts against tyranny; in protection of the monks, and also in correction of ill-doers among the monastic fraternities; in similar efforts for purifying the character of the clergy; in gentle dealings with heretics; in correspondence with the Frankish monarchs; in care for music as employed in religious services, and even in religious painting and sculpture. If, in all this various activity, we sometimes detect the intolerance which so few escaped in that age, if he may justly be reproached with adulation of the wicked and usurping emperor Phocas—these were faults which were an exception to his ordinary character, not the rule of it.

So far I have not mentioned what is perhaps the most famous of all Gregory's acts, the sending of the monk Augustine for the conversion of the English. In our nation he had always taken an ardently benevolent interest, even before he became pope; he had wished to go as a missionary himself to Britain; and though this proved impossible he carried out his design at a later date, through the mission of Augustine, and successfully.

Something ought to be said about Gregory's writings, for he is reckoned one of the four chief doctors of the western church. It is a matter of course that we find in them piety and tenderness; but also, in such matters as lie within personal experience, we find good judgment and shrewdness; of which perhaps the two following passages will be considered instances, which I take from his *Pastoral* (part II. c. 8 and part III. c. 17 respectively):

It is very difficult for a man willingly to listen to the teacher whom he does not love. Therefore he who is to be above others must try to please in order that he may be heard, and yet he must not seek popularity for himself, lest he be convicted of being in his heart the enemy of him whose servant he is seen to be in his ministration.

From the translation by Henry Sweet of King Alfred's West Saxon Version of Gregory's *Pastoral*, pp. 146–7.

Again:

It must be borne in mind, that the proud can often be better rebuked if they are sustained during the reproof with a certain amount of praise. They are to be told of some of the good qualities that they have, or might have. We can best cut away that which we disapprove of in them by first making them hear from us something that pleases them, and thus inclining their hearts to us, that they may the more cheerfully hear whatever we wish either to blame or teach. *Ibid.* pp. 302–3.

It will be admitted that there is true humanity in these precepts. But we must not expect to find in Gregory any exercise of the intellect in matters unconnected with immediate practice. Like most of the early Fathers, he thought that the highest exercise of the abstract intellect lay in imaginative interpretations of Scripture; thus when he finds in the book of Job mention of "Arcturus, the Oriones, and the Hyades," he interprets Arcturus as meaning the Church, the Oriones as meaning the martyrs, and the Hyades the doctors of the Church. In such an interpretation we can recognise no value; but here he was out of his proper field. Neither can it be said that he had any regard at all for the ancient Greek or Roman civilisation or literature; though it is a calumny on him to say that he burned any of the ancient Greek or Roman writings; the story that he did so is too late to deserve attention.

We can in no respect praise the intellectual status of western Europe in the sixth and seventh centuries; it was indeed at the lowest ebb. How great were the cruelties and injustices, the crimes and the sufferings, which pervaded society from the highest members of it to the lowest, we may see if we dip into the pages of that other Gregory, the bishop of Tours, a contemporary of the illustrious pope of whom I have been speaking. Yet, amid all this darkness and misery, there were those living in whom the seed of true goodness germinated and grew. Such was our English Bede, the lovable and saintly; such, also from England, from the county of Devon, was that courageous and commanding monk Boniface, who played the chief part in converting Germany to the Christian faith. Can we, again, fail to admire the excellence of that organisation, whereby pope Vitalian, in the seventh century, could draw the monk Theodore from Tarsus in Asia Minor, and send him to bring order into the ecclesiastical system of England? And Theodore did what he had been commissioned to do. In spite of many errors, there was a power in the countries of western Europe, leading the way to a better state of things. Later than all those whom I have mentioned, can we forget the most dominating of all mediæval monarchs, Charlemagne, whom France and Germany may unite in honouring as their own? A faultless character he was not; it was difficult for a warrior in those days to be faultless; and Charlemagne sprang from a race of warriors. His grandfather, Charles Martel, had flung back the Saracens when they tried to conquer France; his father, Pepin, had defeated the Lombards and made an alliance with the pope. Into the story of Charlemagne's own wars and conquests I must not enter; but it is more appropriate to the theme of the present work to note his care for the arts of peace, the degree in which he fostered education, the way in which he united distant countries under one rule, and the honour which he paid the Church, and which was by the Church reciprocated. When, on Christmas Day in the year 800 A.D., pope Leo III crowned Charlemagne as emperor in the cathedral of St Peter at Rome, a new era began in European history, more full of vitality than any which had preceded it.

Thus, in western Europe, during those dark centuries of which I have been speaking, the sixth, seventh, and eighth of the Christian era, a new order began to arise amidst countless tumults, an order of which the greatest force lay in the popes and in the monastic orders, but in which the ordinary clergy also had no small power, and to which kings and secular authorities occasionally, though more rarely, contributed aid. Not only a new order, but a new vital power was beginning to arise.

What, during the same period, is to be said of eastern Europe? The Christian empire, which during the sixth, seventh and eighth centuries was in the west non-existent, having fallen before the crowd of barbaric invaders, was still powerful in the east during the same period, through the sovereigns who reigned in Constantinople. What am I to say about it? In the first place, let me note one element which can never be excluded when Christianity is spoken of, its theology. In western Christendom, theology had been merged in ecclesiastical obedience; inquiry had ceased; authority was the all-powerful agent in bringing unity alike into religious belief and into religious practice. But the eastern mind, and especially the Greek mind, was not so easily brought to resign inquiry; and hence, notwithstanding all the efforts of emperors and patriarchs, heresies did not die out in the east as they died out in the west. This was in the then state of the world a misfortune, because the disputed questions could not be traced to their root, and the discord only weakened the Church; but the cause of the weakness was not dishonourable; though the fact that difference of belief involved mutual anathematisation was of course deeply to be regretted. It should be observed that in the eighth century a quite new source of religious controversy was brought in by the emperor Leo the Isaurian, who tried to wean his subjects from the practice of image worship; we may sympathise with the spirituality of his intention, but in the end he failed in his object; and it was no doubt a mistake in him and his successor to use the imperial power for the benefit of their own side in a religious controversy.

Were we to ask whether the east or the west of Christendom had the advantage in respect of religious freedom during the centuries that I have named, it might seem that there was little to choose between them, or even that such advantage as there was lay with the east; but the greater natural energy of the races in the west implied a greater freedom of disposition, and this told in the end in favour of the west in all respects, and Latin rather than Greek Christianity, western rather than eastern, has been the source of regeneration for mankind at large. But still eastern Christendom had a superiority of its own in one respect, namely in the conservation of the philosophy and thought of the ancient world during the time when these treasures were most imperilled, and in the conservation also of a good deal in the way of artistic power. It is true that, as I mentioned in speaking of Cassiodorus, the monasteries of the west did much to preserve ancient literature by the transcription of manuscripts; but these manuscripts were for a long time almost exclusively Latin, and not Latin but Greek was the language in which ancient thought and philosophy were chiefly enshrined; and also the transcription of a manuscript did not necessarily imply the intelligent understanding of it. Nor was it only thought and philosophy, but even the ancient Roman law was preserved rather in the east than in the west. Let me quote, in illustration of this whole subject, two passages from the excellent essay of Mr Frederic Harrison on the Byzantine empire:

The most signal evidence of the superior civilisation of Byzantium down to the tenth century, is found in the fact that alone of all states it maintained a continuous, scientific, and even progressive system of law. Whilst the *Corpus Juris* died down in the West under the successive invasions of the Northern nations, at least so far as governments and official study was concerned, it continued under Emperors in the East to be the law of the State, to be expounded in translations, commentaries, and handbooks, to be regularly taught in schools of law, and still more to be developed in a Christian and modern sense. *Byzantine History in the Early Middle Ages*, p. 24.

Again:

The manufacture of silks and embroidered satins was almost a Greek monopoly all through the Middle Ages. Mediæval literature is full of the splendid silks of Constantinople, of the robes and exquisite brocades which kings and princes were eager to obtain. We hear of the robe of a Greek senator which had 600 figures picturing the entire life of Christ.

Costly stuffs and utensils bore Greek names and lettering down to the
middle of the fifteenth century.   *Samite* is Greek for six-threaded stuff....
The diadems, sceptres, thrones, robes, coins, and jewels of the early
Mediæval princes were all Greek in type, and usually Byzantine in origin.
So that Mr Frothingham, in the *American Journal of Archæology* (1894),
does not hesitate to write: "The debt to Byzantium is undoubtedly
immense; the difficulty consists in ascertaining what amount of originality
can properly be claimed for the Western arts, industries, and institutions
during the early Middle Ages."   *Ibid.* p. 33.

If, then, we are tracing the origins of our twentieth century
civilisation, we must not ignore that part of it which came from
the empire which had its centre at Constantinople. If the
feeling of the dignity of personal labour has been chiefly fostered
by western Christianity (and this indeed is the most momentous
step towards progress that has ever been made) the conservation
of the precious things of the past was more due to the east than
to the west. And now I must add that this conservation was
aided by the religion of Islam; and the religion of Islam must
be the main theme of the rest of this chapter.

It has been a too frequent habit of religious persons to consider
their own religion perfect, and other religions simply false. Thus
when eastern and western Christianity began to divide (a long
process, of which the beginning may perhaps be fixed in the
year 485 A.D., but which was not regarded as irremediable for
nearly a thousand years afterwards) the grounds of separation at
once came into prominence, and the many grounds of unity and
affection sank into comparative obscurity. I have tried, throughout this chapter, to bring into prominence the distinctive merits
of both western and eastern Christianity; not as ignoring the
subjects of difference between them, but as believing that the
collection of points of agreement is a very great help towards
solving the points of difference. That final and absolute truth
has lain neither with the eastern nor the western church, in
their accredited forms, is a conclusion maintained throughout
the present work; but while maintaining it, I have been anxious
to show the good effected in the world by Christianity both in
the east and in the west; and I have been desirous of showing,
too, that in the good thus effected, an element of profound truth
is implied, valuable for all ages.

It will perhaps seem to many impossible to treat Islam and
Christianity in the way in which I have treated eastern and
western Christianity, as joint workers in a common cause; but
yet I believe that that kind of view is the most profound that

we can take; that as in Europe, so in Arabia, the human race must be thought of as feeling its way towards truth in those topics by which our actions are most profoundly and most permanently regulated; and if the results of such a search differed in Europe and in Arabia, it does not follow that either result was valueless. In all human work, mistakes must be expected; but it is the worthy element in the work that we must seek to appreciate and retain in our minds. With this preface I come to consider the nature and history of Islam.

It was at the time when Christianity was beginning to settle down after the troubles that had attended its first victory, when the limits of the eastern empire appeared to be fairly settled, and the western church was extending itself under the papal rule, that in the wilds of Arabia, far beyond the confines of the Roman empire, a new religion came into being. Doubtless the religion of Mohammed was not purely and absolutely new; he would have himself disclaimed that character for it; there were prophets before himself, he said; and the prophets whom he named are to be found in the pages of the Bible, Jesus Christ himself being the last of the series previous to Mohammed. Hence we see that the religion of Mohammed—Islam, he himself called it, or the doctrine of resignation to God's will—owns the preaching of Jesus of Nazareth as a truly divine dispensation; and we, looking at the matter historically, may say that Christianity was one of the sources of Islam. Judaism was another source, as we may see from the fact that Mohammed, in the early part of his career, directed his followers, when they prayed, to turn their faces towards Jerusalem (afterwards this command was changed, and he bade them turn their faces towards Mecca); and indeed Mohammed had more to do with Jews than with Christians. Yet I must think that Mohammed derived his feeling, that the true religion was a world-religion, from Christianity, not from Judaism; and this was the most remarkable of all his clear obligations to his predecessors; for we cannot confidently say from what external sources the thought of monotheism was first suggested to him. It is an interesting question, but one not soluble by us at present, how far traditions reaching back to Abraham may have been preserved in the Arabian peninsula: Mohammed always refers to Ishmael as one of the true believers of ancient times, by the side of Isaac and Jacob. But the Arabian peninsula when Mohammed was born was full of idolatry; and we must not ignore or disparage the personal originality of

Mohammed in feeling that he was the messenger of God to men, and that he himself was a witness of that unity of God which he proclaimed.

Since I am not in the main writing for Mohammedans (though I should be honoured by any perusal of my work which Mohammedans may accord to me), it will be proper for me here to say something on that primary point, whether the career of Mohammed, and the religion proceeding from him, ought to be taken seriously at all, as a part of human development; whether it ought not to be considered a simple mistake, as far as its inner meaning and value are concerned; whether therefore it should not be treated simply externally, as a fact of human history, but not as a means of human education.

In answer to this doubt I do not think I can do better than quote a few sentences from the learned and temperate article on "Muhámmad" which the Rev. Dr Badger contributed to the *Dictionary of Christian Biography* (a dictionary not limited to Christian subjects, though limited of course to subjects which have a real relation to Christianity).   Dr Badger writes as follows:

> Up to the time of the Flight Muhámmad's life, both as a citizen and a teacher of religion, appears to have been blameless. He was uniformly grateful to those who reared him, true to his friends, faithful in his married life, upright in his moral character, frugal in his habits, tenderhearted, compassionate, and charitable. If exception is taken to his prophetic claims, it would be difficult to show that, up to the period specified, he was not in some guise inspired with a spirit not unlike that which moved the prophets of old; for, from whatever source derived, his doctrine, especially that respecting the unity of God and the duty of worshipping and praying to Him only, is in accordance with the Old Testament Scriptures. *Dictionary &c.* vol. III. p. 967.

The Flight (or Hegira, or Hejra) took place nearly at the close of the 52nd year of Mohammed's life, and he lived only ten years after that.   Dr Badger does not give equal praise to Mohammed after the Hejra; but the man who, for the first half century of his life, deserves to be described in the terms quoted above, ought to have a hearing as worth something in the development of religion, even if that something be not on the highest level of all.

Nothing, certainly, that I shall say about Mohammed will tend to dissolve the belief that in Jesus Christ is the true centre, the true origin, out of which the vital progress of mankind flows. But what Mohammed did, in inspiring the wild tribes of Arabia with a genuine and fervent belief in one God, and, further, in giving them so many precepts which lead to temperance, kindness, and justice, must not all be reckoned as of no account. Further, we must not treat him as if he had stood face to face with Jesus Christ himself, and had heard the gospel precepts in their entirety, and had then neglected and despised them, and had gone back to his own thoughts and his own beliefs. The case was very different. He knew but little of the gospels; the account of Jesus that had reached him was a travesty of the real narrative; and while he saw something to honour in Christians as he met them in the world, there was a great deal that could not but detract from that honour. Intolerance, and the bitterness of theological controversy, were too visible among the Christians of Syria and Egypt.

Let me come then at once to Mohammed, and take him, as it is just we should, on his own ground. He was born in the year 570 A.D. in Mecca, a city of Arabia regarded as sacred, because in it was the Kaaba, a famous temple connected by tradition with Abraham, but at the period of which I speak containing 360 idols. Before Mohammed was born, his father had died; and when he was six years old, his mother died also; his grandfather, who then took charge of him, died two or three years later; thenceforth he was under the care of his uncle Abû Tâlib, who proved a most efficient guardian and protector. With Abû Tâlib, Mohammed made journeys into Syria for mercantile purposes, and had some intercourse, as is believed and as is probable, with Christians.

But when he was in his twenty-fifth year, he took a more memorable journey to Syria; this time as the agent of a wealthy lady of the Koreish clan, to which Mohammed himself belonged; the Koreish being the leaders among the Meccans, and the guardians of the great temple. The lady was named Khadîja; and so well and faithfully did Mohammed discharge his duties, and so attractive was he personally, that Khadîja loved him, and they were married. She was many years older than he; but the marriage was one of true affection, and without Khadîja Mohammed would never have done the work he did. They had been married fifteen years, and three sons and four daughters had been born to them (but the sons all died in infancy), when the thoughts of Mohammed underwent a change, which can hardly but have been in preparation for a considerable time previously— a change in the way of dissatisfaction with the idolatrous religion in which he had been brought up. He did not stand alone in this dissatisfaction; scepticism had found a place in the intellects

of some of the inhabitants of Mecca; but in Mohammed, amid
the scepticism, lay the germ of a new belief. The collision of
scepticism with a dawning belief produced a terrible conflict in
his soul. He haunted the solitary mountains around Mecca,
and spent nights on them. One night—but here let me quote
the description given by Emanuel Deutsch[1]—

In the middle of the night, Mohammed woke from his sleep, and he
heard a voice. Twice it called, urging, and twice he struggled and waived
its call. But he was pressed sore, as if a fearful weight had been laid upon
him. He thought his last hour had come. And for the third time the
voice called:

"Cry!"

And he said, "What shall I cry?"

Came the answer: "Cry—in the name of thy Lord!"

And these, according to wellnigh unanimous tradition, are the first
words of the Koran. Our readers will find them in the ninety-sixth
chapter of that Book, to which they have been banished by the Redactors.

Deutsch goes on to say that there are differences of opinion
as to the meaning of the word here translated "Cry!" the more
usual translation being "Read!" But I agree with Deutsch
(and Syed Ameer Ali, no mean authority, also agrees) that the
translation "Cry!" can hardly but be legitimate for "Ikra," and
that it suits the passage far better. Let me give the context:

Cry, in the name of thy Lord, who did create—
Who did create man from congealed blood.
Cry! for thy Lord is the most generous,
Who has taught the use of the pen,
Has taught man what he did not know.......

Taken from the Introduction to the Koran, p. xxi, in vol. IV. of *Sacred
Books of the East*, written by that eminent scholar E. H. Palmer, slain
in the Sinaitic Peninsula in the year 1882, when in the service of the
British Government. I should say that Palmer translates "Read" where
I, following Deutsch, have written "Cry."

At these words, heard in his trance, Mohammed trembled all
over, and hastened home to his wife. "Oh, Khadîja!" he said,
"what has happened to me?" He feared that he was going
mad; but his wife comforted him, and watched by him, and
bade him have no fear, and assured him of her belief that he
would be the prophet of his people. But with all her devotion,
she could not quite bring calm to his soul. Let me quote the
sequel from the description of it by E. H. Palmer:

The thought that he might be, after all, mad or possessed was terrible
to Mohammed.

---

[1] *Literary Remains of Emanuel Deutsch*, p. 75. The article on "Islam," from
which this extract is taken, had appeared in the *Quarterly Review* for October 1869;

He struggled for a long time against the idea, and endeavoured to support himself by belief in the reality of the divine mission which he had received upon Mount 'Hirâ; but no more revelations came, nothing occurred to give him further confidence and hope, and Mohammed began to feel that such a life could be endured no longer. The Fatrah or "intermission," as this period without revelation was called, lasted for two and a half or three years.

Dark thoughts of suicide presented themselves to his mind; and on more than one occasion he climbed the steep sides of Mount 'Hirâ, or Mount Thabîr, with the desperate intention of putting an end to his unquiet life by hurling himself from one of the precipitous cliffs. But a mysterious power appeared to hold him back, and at length the long looked-for vision came, which was to confirm him in his prophetic mission.

At last the angel again appeared in all his glory, and Mohammed in terror ran to his wife Khadîja and cried daтнтнirûnî, "wrap me up!" and lay down entirely enwrapped in his cloak as was his custom when attacked by the hysterical fits (which were always accompanied, as we learn from the traditions, with violent hectic fever), partly for medical reasons and partly to screen himself from the gaze of evil spirits.

As he lay there the angel again spake to him: "O thou covered! Rise up and warn! and thy Lord magnify! and thy garments purify! and abomination shun! and grant not favours to gain increase; and for thy Lord await!"

And now the revelations came in rapid succession. He no longer doubted the reality of the inspiration, and his conviction of the unity of God and of his divine commission to preach it were indelibly impressed upon his mind.

His only convert was at first his faithful wife Khadîja; she was always at his side to comfort him when others mocked at him, to cheer him when dispirited, and to encourage him when he wavered. *Sacred Books of the East*, vol. VI. pp. xxii, xxiii.

It will be seen that Palmer in this passage refers to the "hysterical fits, accompanied with violent hectic fever," from which Mohammed suffered. They have sometimes been thought to have been epileptic; but, from the description, that hardly seems to have been their character; no doubt they produced some effect on the form of his visions and of his prophetic burthen, though we must not think that the substance of his prophecy came from this bodily ailment. Weakness may be a companion of strength, but does not give strength; and that there was a real true guiding strength in Mohammed no one who reads his history with impartial eyes can doubt. He could speak with penetrating force; and in his earliest deliverances, where the main gist of his teaching alone had to be put, without additions or explanations, this is done with striking brevity. Take for instance two of the Suras, the 97th and 99th, which, though placed very late in the series by the original editors of the Koran, are really among the earliest. The 97th Sura is called "The Chapter of Power," and runs thus:

> In the name of the merciful and compassionate God.
> Verily, we sent it down on the Night of Power!
> And what shall make thee know what the Night of Power is? the Night of Power is better than a thousand months!
> The angels and the Spirit descend therein, by the permission of their Lord with every bidding.
> Peace it is until rising of the dawn!

What was sent down on the Night of Power is not explicitly said; but we must understand it to have been a vision of truth, remarkable for a divine peace that breathed in it. Not very often, it must be admitted, does Mohammed lay stress on peace as an end to be accomplished and won here on earth; and the 99th Sura (called "The Chapter of the Earthquake") is more characteristic of his general mood:

> In the name of the merciful and compassionate God.
> When the earth shall quake with its quaking!
> And the earth shall bring forth her burdens, and men shall say, "What ails her?"
> On that day she shall tell her tidings, because thy Lord inspires her.
> On the day when men shall come up in separate bands to show their works: and he who does the weight of an atom of good shall see it! and he who does the weight of an atom of evil shall see it!

The prophecy, that men shall be judged for their works, was not indeed new in the mouth of Mohammed; it was a commonplace of Christian teaching; and it may be found in heathen writers (for instance in the sixth book of Virgil's *Æneid*) before Christianity began; and in the Old Testament also it is a frequent thought. Yet as Mohammed puts it, we feel that, though not new, it is original; of his own self he feels that this must be; his eyes have been opened to an eternal truth. It is not needless to have these renewals of well-worn truths, which always have a tendency to be disregarded unless there is some one to see them afresh in their native clearness and sharpness; and so it is that Mohammed sees this truth here—"Thou, O man, shalt be judged." His feet are on firm rock when he says this; for, while he sees it with native perspicacity, it is God on whom he relies to keep his vision clear. This is inspiration; it is the sustaining of the human soul by divine power to see what otherwise it could not see.

I am not saying that Mohammed's inspiration was perfect, but it was real; he did not see everything in the divine counsels, but he saw a great deal more than those who were about him saw. He began to preach in Mecca; he was derided, insulted. This indeed was natural; for he was opposing himself to the strongest sentiments of his tribe. He would have suffered much more seriously in his own person, if it had not been for the constant protection of his uncle Abû Tâlib, whom no one cared to offend; yet Abû Tâlib was not a convert to the teaching of his nephew. Presently the Koreish began to bribe Mohammed; but their bribes availed no more than their insults to change his resolution. Meanwhile he was winning converts one by one; Ali, the son of Abû Tâlib, who afterwards married Mohammed's daughter Fatima; Zaid, a captured slave whom Mohammed had set free; and more important than either, Abû Bakr, a wealthy and much respected merchant; these were his first converts; and in three years about forty had joined him as believers in one God and in the future judgment. Some of these were poor and defenceless (one, Billâl, was an African slave); these the Koreish now began to persecute with cruel tortures. By Mohammed's advice, many of them escaped and fled to Abyssinia; the Koreish in fury sent to the Abyssinian king to demand that he should give them up; the king sent for the fugitives and questioned them as to their belief. They answered thus (I quote the version given by Deutsch):

We lived in ignorance, in idolatry, and unchastity, the strong oppressed the weak, we spoke untruth, we violated the duties of hospitality. Then a prophet arose, one whom we knew from our youth, with whose descent, and conduct, and good faith, and morality we are all well acquainted. He told us to worship one God, to speak the truth, to keep good faith, to assist our relations, to fulfil the rights of hospitality, to abstain from all things impure, ungodly, unrighteous. And he ordered us to say prayers, give alms, and to fast. We believed in him, we followed him. But our countrymen persecuted us, tortured us, and tried to cause us to forsake our religion, and now we throw ourselves upon your protection with confidence.

They also explained some of the teaching of Mohammed about "Jesus the son of Mary"; which, though far from orthodox Christianity, was accepted by the Abyssinian king for the purpose which the fugitives desired. He refused to surrender them to the envoys of the Koreish.

I must not linger too long over the narrative, and must omit some particulars of great interest; but one incident I can hardly omit. A deputation of the Koreish, seeing that their previous efforts to stop the preaching of Mohammed had not succeeded, waited upon Abû Tâlib, and issued their ultimatum; either he must stop his nephew's invectives against their ancestral deities, or cease to protect him; otherwise they would be obliged to regard him, as well as his nephew, as their enemy. Abû Tâlib in consequence did make an appeal to Mohammed to cease inveighing against the idols; but Mohammed answered:

O my uncle, if they placed the sun on my right hand and the moon on my left, to force me to renounce my work, verily I would not desist therefrom until God made manifest His cause, or I perished in the attempt[1].

And the tears came into his eyes, and he turned to depart. But Abû Tâlib called him back. "Preach what thou wilt," he said; "I will never abandon thee."

It was about this time, perhaps a little before this time, that Mohammed won two of his most important converts; the brave Hamza, his uncle; and Omar, afterwards the second Caliph, whose sudden conversion by reading a few verses of the Koran at the very time when he was about to set out to slay Mohammed, was a most striking event.

The Koreish were now excited to the highest pitch of anger; and though they did not openly attack Abû Tâlib, they put the entire families of Hashim and Muttalib—Mohammed's nearest relatives, among whom were his chief supporters—under a ban; none were to buy or sell with them, or to enter into any intercourse with them whatever. Terrified at this procedure, which they feared might be a prelude to an actual attack, the Hashimites and Muttalibites gathered together round the quarter of Abû Tâlib, which was in a narrow defile east of Mecca; and there for three years they remained, subject to the greatest privations. Then at last, owing to the better feelings of some among the Koreish, the ban was removed; but shortly afterwards two most serious losses befel Mohammed. The first was the death of his faithful wife Khadîja; the second was the death of his uncle Abû Tâlib. As the former loss caused the greatest grief to Mohammed, so the latter placed him in the greatest danger; for the protection which Abû Tâlib accorded him had been his greatest security.

He began now to seek followers outside Mecca. He journeyed to Ta'if, a city sixty miles from Mecca, and preached; but the people of Ta'if would not hear him, and drove him away with stones; and he had to return. Just then a prospect of relief opened from an unexpected quarter. The inhabitants of a city called Yathrib (later called by the more famous name of Medina)

---

[1] I quote the version of these words given by Syed Ameer Ali, *Life and Teachings of Mohammed*, p. 111.

began to show an interest in the teaching of Mohammed; and
the fact that some of them were Jews lent a significance to the
movement, for it was natural for the Jews to feel a certain similarity between the doctrines of Mohammed and their own religion.
Interviews took place between inhabitants of Yathrib and
Mohammed at a hill near Mecca, called the hill of Akaba, and
solemn agreements were made between them. And now Mohammed, seeing the danger he was in at Mecca, determined upon
the removal of himself and his followers to the friendly city of
Yathrib. By his direction, his followers left Mecca; gradually
and not all at once, in order not to attract attention; until at
last but three of the whole Moslem community were left behind,
namely Ali, Abû Bakr, and Mohammed himself. But the Koreish
became aware of what was going on, and their wrath against
Mohammed could not be diminished by it, for Yathrib had been
for a long time a city unfriendly to Mecca. Accordingly they
took the resolution, probably to slay Mohammed, certainly to
capture him; and they set armed men round his house. But
he had been forewarned, and had taken refuge in the house
of Abû Bakr, while the valiant Ali, to delude the Koreish
liers-in-wait, put on Mohammed's mantle, and lay down on
the couch usually occupied by the latter. When night fell,
Mohammed and Abû Bakr escaped from the house by a back
window; and the Koreish, when in the morning they discovered
Ali in the place of Mohammed, allowed him to escape; con-
fiscating however, as a measure of punishment, all the property
of the fugitives.

But by no means were the Koreish minded that Mohammed
himself should escape. They scoured the country round; and
on one occasion drew so near to the mouth of a cave where
Mohammed and Abû Bakr were hiding as to cause great fear to
the latter; "We are but two," he said. "Nay, we are three,"
replied Mohammed, "for God is with us." They escaped, and
reached Medina (so let us call it now instead of Yathrib—"the
city" is the meaning of the new appellation). Here they rejoined
their old companions and were hailed by their new allies.

Such was the celebrated Hejra or "flight," which took place
in the year 622 A.D., thirteen years after the beginning of
Mohammed's preaching. Before this he had been a suffering and
persecuted man, after this he was a prince and a warrior; and
it has been a general opinion (and an opinion held by Dr Badger,
whose commendation of the earlier career of Mohammed I have

quoted) that the character of Mohammed from this time onwards shows deterioration. But in truth it was the circumstances that had changed, not the man; and this is the proper place for me to pass a certain criticism, not hitherto mentioned, on the teaching of Mohammed before the epoch of the Hejra. I trust the reader feels how great the courage and patience of Mohammed had been, and how clear in many respects his insight, up to that epoch; and these qualities had been the root causes of his success in attracting disciples. But any one who reads the Koran will see that as he strove to attract the nobler natures by awe and admiration, so he strove to move the baser natures by terror; he taught that a hopeless hell awaited the wicked, and awaited unbelievers; and his insistence on this teaching was more direct and emphatic, though not more distinct, than the teaching of the Christian Church to the same effect had been. No doubt he won disciples by these threatenings, just as the Christian Church moved the pagan populace to conversion by a similar doctrine; but in neither case was a victory won in this way honourable; and the deadening effect of these religious threatenings has been more permanent among the Moslem populations of the world than among the Christian populations. It will not be thought that I am deprecating all threatenings towards the careless and selfish, when their state after death is considered; such threatenings lie in the very nature of the loftiest conceptions of religion, and cannot be ignored; it is only when hopelessness is attached to the penalties which are threatened that the effect of the threatening becomes harmful.

I cannot then deny that there was a certain portion of the teaching of Mohammed which had harmful tendencies, no less in the earlier than in the later part of his prophetic career. When we come to his later career and to his life at Medina, when (as I have said) he was a prince and a warrior, we find him acting in a way which in his earlier years had been impossible, and we cannot help sometimes censuring his acts. But we shall remember the rudeness and barbarity of the age in which he lived; we shall see the naturalness of his acts, even though they were on a lower plane than those acts on which true religion ought to be founded; and we shall be ready to believe, what indeed is the case, that he was able to bequeath real virtues to those who in after times should believe in his message, though he had it not in his power to give permanent and ever-increasing life and prosperity to mankind.

When Mohammed arrived at Medina, he found himself face
to face with three distinct classes of persons: 1st, his own
devoted followers; 2ndly, the careless and indifferent people,
sometimes called the "hypocrites"; 3rdly, the Jews. Besides
these, who were his immediate neighbours, there were those
whom he had left behind him at Mecca, the Koreish, whose
enmity he had to dread. It was absolutely necessary for him
to have his eye on all these different classes of persons at once;
to treat those of them who were friendly in such a way as to
confirm their friendship, those of them who were indifferent in
such a way as to create loyalty in them, and those of them who
were hostile in such a way as to neutralise their hostility, or to
convert it into friendship; can it be denied that this was a most
difficult task? And it had to be done by a man who had had no
practice in government, as government is ordinarily understood.
Let any one consider the frequent quarrels which mar the political
schemes of monarchs and statesmen; and how rare are the
occasions when any statesman brings an absolutely successful
issue out of the conflicting elements with which he has to deal;
will he not admit that the chances were a hundred to one against
Mohammed being able to educe order out of the chaos which
confronted him? And now consider the results which he actually
obtained. Seven years after he had fled from Mecca, having
subdued the Jews (whom alone he had entirely failed to conciliate)
and having gained for himself the loyal support of all the other
inhabitants of Medina, he was in a position to make a peaceable
agreement with the Koreish to the following effect: that he
and two thousand of his followers should be permitted to make
a pilgrimage to Mecca, to the temple of the Kaaba; that they
should remain in the city three days, doing no damage whatever,
and then should retire again. It must be remembered, in
considering this surprising agreement, that Mohammed and his
followers looked upon the temple of the Kaaba with quite different
eyes from those with which they looked on the 360 idols which
the temple contained. The idols were abominations; but the
Kaaba itself was held to be the temple of Abraham and of Ishmael,
and sacred to the God of Abraham; hence to make a pilgrimage
to it was a sacred act. The agreement thus entered into with
the Koreish was faithfully performed on both sides; Mohammed
and his two thousand followers entered Mecca, remained there
three days, and then retired. While they were in the city,
the Koreish moved out of the city, and remained on the

surrounding hills, watching the Moslems below as they performed their pilgrimage, and returning to Mecca when the Moslems had left it. Could there be a more striking proof of the power of Mohammed, not only in making war, but also in making and carrying out peaceful contracts? But in the year which followed the event just named, certain allies of the Koreish violated the truce which had been agreed upon between them and the Moslems, invaded the territory of a tribe who were in alliance with the Moslems, and killed twenty of them. The Koreish would have offered reparation; but Mohammed determined that the only reparation should be the destruction of the 360 idols of the Kaaba; he accordingly marched ten thousand men to Mecca and accomplished this act; and at the same time destroyed three famous idols in the immediate neighbourhood. These acts were done not absolutely without fighting and bloodshed, but very nearly so; it had been the desire of Mohammed that blood, if possible, should not be shed. All this was followed by large submissions on the part of Arabian tribes to the creed of Islam.

Such a series of successes on the part of Mohammed could not have been accomplished without the conviction on the part of those whom he won over to his cause that he was a man worthy of trust and not self-seeking; and it is hard to think, in view of this, that any real deterioration of his character had taken place during the years when he was exercising sovereignty at Medina. It will however be proper to consider some of the details of his conduct more particularly; and first, as to the breaking out of war between himself and the Koreish, shortly after his escape to Medina, and before the events of which I have just been speaking.

After the flight to Medina, war between Mohammed and the Koreish was to be expected. If history permitted us truly to say that the aggressive impulse was confined to the Koreish, who had so long been the enemies of Mohammed, we could then affirm that the warlike spirit so eminently shown by Islam in the centuries which were to come originated in acts of legitimate self-defence. I do not think we can hold this; but a certain unwillingness on the part of Mohammed to enter into the conflict does, I think, appear. All authorities agree that, after his arrival at Medina, he sent out reconnoitring parties to watch the movements of the Koreish; and it appears that these parties conducted themselves peaceably till, on one occasion, a party of eight, happening to fall in with a Koreish caravan with only four attendants, attacked it, killed one or two of the attendants and took the others captive with the caravan. It is likely that a scarcity of provisions, which prevailed at Medina at the time, was an inducement to the followers of Mohammed to commit this act of violence. He himself was much displeased at it; but as to what he did, I find a certain discrepancy between the two modern English writers who relate the incident most fully. Dr Badger, writing in 1882[1], says that Mohammed, after some time, allowed the partition of the booty (but apparently not taking any share in it himself) and accepted a ransom for the two prisoners; for *two* are said to have been slain, according to this account. But Professor T. W. Arnold, writing in 1896[2], without denying the statement as to the partition of the booty (which therefore I suppose correct), adds that Mohammed "dismissed the prisoners, and from his own purse paid blood money for a Meccan who had lost his life in the fray." Between these two accounts I am unable to decide; but according to both the booty was kept (it is likely to have been a necessity to the Moslems); and we cannot suppose the Koreish to have been content. They complained, besides, that the attack had taken place during a month which was sacredly kept as peaceful by the Arabian tribes. Mohammed could only answer, "To war therein" (i.e. during the sacred month) "is grievous; but to obstruct the way of God, and infidelity towards him, and to keep men from the holy temple, and to drive out his people from thence, is more grievous in the sight of God" (Sura II. 213); which practically confesses the fault of his followers. Mohammed would not seem to have deliberately waged war against the Koreish; but the need in which he was, and the warlike habit of his followers, made it very difficult for him to avoid it. His immense energy led him to victory; and thus a stamp was put on his whole movement which turned out to be unalterable in the after times.

The relations of Mohammed with the Jews constituted one of his greatest difficulties. That he felt indebted to Jewish teaching may be inferred from the fact that in the early days of his preaching he directed his followers, when they prayed, to set their faces towards Jerusalem; and also, in that famous vision, which came to him shortly before the Hejra, he felt himself transported first to the temple at Jerusalem, and then to the heaven of heavens. He endeavoured also, after his arrival at Medina, to conciliate

---

[1] *Dictionary of Christian Biography*, vol. III. p. 968.
[2] *The Preaching of Islam*, p. 30.

them, adopting some of their fasts and their day of Atonement.
But, after all, he was compelled to say that he was the prophet
of God, and that the Jews owed him recognition of this fact;
and this recognition the Jews would by no means accord, at any
rate in the degree in which Mohammed claimed it. They showed
their hostile spirit very plainly; and two of the Jewish clans,
after fighting against Mohammed, were deprived of their possessions
and sent into exile. A third clan, the Banû-Kuraizha, who (like
the other two tribes) were under a compact of alliance with
Mohammed, deserted him at the moment when his military danger
was most serious, when a large army of the Koreish and their
allies had invested Medina, the sole material defence of which
city was a trench hastily dug. The Banû-Kuraizha gave material
help to the Koreish and the other besiegers; notwithstanding
which, the besieging camp was at last broken up, partly through
internal disunion, partly through the inclemency of the weather,
and through the courage of the Moslems; and then the Banû-
Kuraizha were left alone in their fortress six miles from Medina.
It is not surprising that Mohammed and his Moslem force marched
to besiege their fortress, and after fourteen days took it; and
it is not surprising either that the Banû-Kuraizha were deemed
worthy of punishment. They were in fact slain (to the number
it would seem, of six or seven hundred[1]) and their women and
children sold as slaves. Such a punishment was not, according
to the morality of those days, unwarranted; yet we must regret
that Mohammed did not reject this extreme severity; though the
adviser who counselled it had been selected by the Jews themselves
as the arbiter of the punishment to be inflicted on them. Similarly
when we find Mohammed sending messengers to kill certain
Jewish poets who had been stirring up the Koreish against him,
we must remember that these Jews (who belonged to a tribe
which had made a compact with Mohammed) were undoubtedly
committing a serious offence, and that there was no ordinary
means of punishing that offence, or of restraining them. Without
trying to exempt Mohammed from censure in these cases, we
must yet remember that the position in which he stood at that
time was one of continual danger, and more than usual guard
had to be maintained against enemies, open or secret.

When we consider the patience and firmness exhibited by
Mohammed up to the time of the Hejra (his flight from Mecca);

---

[1] Syed Ameer Ali says "200 or 250" (*Life and Teachings of Mohammed*, p. 174);
but the general estimate is certainly higher.

the large amount of truth contained in his religious message and
in his ethical precepts; the amount of trust placed in him by
those with whom he had to deal, and the amount of affection
which he inspired; and when again we consider how often the
career of great religious teachers and heroes has been marked by
blood-shedding, and how few have been altogether blameless; and,
again, how little instruction from without Mohammed had received
or could have received—I do not think we ought to deny him a
place among the religious heroes of the world, or refuse to extend
our sympathy to the Moslems of the present day. A fair reading
of the Koran will not lead to the conclusion that Mohammed
deliberately urged the use of the sword to produce conversion.
But the spirit of his time and country was warlike, and Mohammed
could not divest himself of this spirit. It cannot be said that he
sought ardently for peace; whereas true Christians, though not
always able to preserve peace, yet always ardently seek for it.
We do claim final truth for the Christian spirit; but as this must
not prevent our acknowledging the errors into which Christianity,
in the course of its long history, has fallen, so neither ought it
to prevent our acknowledging the virtues of Moslems.

It is proper to say something as to the relation of Mohammed
to women, and his conduct towards them. As long as Khadîja
lived, his relations with her were those of pure monogamy;
she elevated and comforted him; and he acknowledged how
great a thing this was. After her death, he adopted the polygamy which was natural to his fellow-countrymen. I will not
deny that this is to be regretted; in this part of human nature,
he did not carry out the highest ideal. Doubtless it is owing
to this that the ideal of womanhood has been lower in Moslem
than in Christian nations; though it must be added that Christian
nations have in some respects fallen lamentably short of that
ideal in their actual conduct.

The profoundest difference between Islam and Christianity
lies however in the relation which Mohammed on the one hand,
and Jesus Christ on the other hand, conceived to exist between
man and God. Who can read the narrative of the agony in the
garden of Gethsemane, and not feel that Jesus pleads with his
Divine Father, in one important respect, as equal with equal;
not equal in power, not equal in range of action or command of
view; but equal in essential nature? That position Jesus
vindicated for himself, and, I must add, for us also; though I am
aware that in this last clause I am going beyond what has been

held in ordinary Christian doctrine. But Mohammed taught that no one should approach the Most High, but as a servant. With any Mohammedan, whether in writing or by word of mouth, I would urge that in this most important point the author of the Christian faith touched the fountains of spiritual emotion more truly than did Mohammed.

Yet if I say that Islam is an imperfect religion, is that a reason for ignoring the degree in which it has exalted the thoughts and the courage of men? When Mohammed died, in the year 632 A.D., he had practically won all Arabia to adherence to his teaching; and that teaching included the belief in God, the inculcation of prayer to God, and the doctrine that men shall be judged for their actions, and shall receive the reward which their actions deserve. In one respect, Christians themselves may learn a lesson from him, namely, in recognising that prayer to God is natural to man in his needs, without any teaching of history. To say this, is not to despise religious history; but our judgment is required in historical conclusions, in a way in which it is not required in pure and simple prayer to a Being whom we know not, but whom we hope we may learn to know through that intercourse which we seek, and through that spiritual strength which we ask of him. Of all Christian teachers in ancient times, Augustine came the nearest to such a recognition of God; but he was frightened away from it by a misunderstood Christianity; we may read his account of the matter in the fourth chapter of the third book of his Confessions.

Mohammed did not realise the filial relation in which man stands to God; but he did feel how natural the belief in God is; it was enforced on him by experiences which we cannot entirely understand, but which I think we must say contained a portion of truth. His ethical system promoted courage, but not equally tenderness and love; yet much natural affection was in him, and has not been wanting in his followers.

I must touch on, though it is impossible for me to describe, the immense conquests which were achieved by Islam after the death of Mohammed. We must, indeed, stand amazed at the speed with which the new religion swept over Asia and Africa; tearing away from the Roman empire the fair provinces of Syria and Egypt, and presently all north Africa and Spain; winning to itself Persia, and lands beyond Persia, even to the confines of India; and all this in less than a hundred years. From France it was then thrown back by the valour of Charles Martel.

Though always a warlike, it was by no means a wholly barbarous movement; in my next chapter I will name some of its civilising tendencies. Nothing, in all this stirring history, equals in pathos the death of Hosain, the grandson of Mohammed, the son of Ali and Fatima; but space does not permit me to describe it.

Let me conclude this chapter by two brief quotations from the Koran; the first, on the duties of giving and of thrift:

Give thy kinsman his due and the poor and the son of the road: and waste not wastefully, for the wasteful were ever the devil's brothers; and the devil is ever ungrateful to his Lord....Make not thy hand fettered to thy neck, nor yet spread it out quite open, lest thou shouldst have to sit down blamed and straitened in means. Verily, thy Lord spreads out provision to whomsoever He will or He doles it out. Verily, he is ever well aware of and sees his servants. From the translation by E. H. Palmer, *Sacred Books of the East*, vol. ix. p. 4. Sura xvii.

And here is a passage concerning Christians (written after the Hejra):

Thou wilt surely find that the strongest in enmity against those who believe are the Jews and the idolaters; and thou wilt find the nearest in love to those who believe to be those who say, "We are Christians"; that is because there are amongst them priests and monks, and because they are not proud. *Ibid.* vol. vi. p. 109. Sura v.

With this note of acknowledgment from Islam to Christianity the present chapter may well terminate.

CHAPTER XXIII

THE WORLD-STRUGGLE IN EUROPE AND ASIA

IN the foregoing chapter I have described how, after the great crash produced by the fall of the Roman empire in the west, the first seeds of a new civilisation were sown through the monasteries planted in the desolated lands or in new countries inhabited by barbarous heathen tribes; for which monasteries the chief type and rule was given by Benedict of Nursia. I have described how the Roman empire still sustained itself in the east, with Constantinople as its centre, and with much of the ancient civilisation in literature and art preserved and even extended, though not in the way of political improvement or in the way of original thought. I have described how a new religion, Islam, rose up in Arabia, not without some affiliation to Judaism and Christianity, and even perhaps to Zoroastrianism, but still with a genuine originality of feeling and a character of its own. I have described how Islam, in the general crudity and darkness of men's thoughts, became a rival and a foe to Christianity, no meeting or common ground being then possible between Moslems and Christians; and how some of the fairest countries that had been under Christian rule were overwhelmed by the torrential force of the new religion and became Mohammedan. This I have described; and in the present chapter I must extend the theme, and tell of the relations between Christianity and Islam from the time of Charlemagne to the beginning of the sixteenth century, when the Reformation in western Europe produced a new way of viewing things and formed an epoch in history. Not that, in the present chapter, I can give even a slight sketch of that vast subject, the development of Christianity in mediæval times; there is a great deal that must be left for another chapter; but a general account of the relations of Christianity to Islam, and some comparison of the intrinsic character and force of the two religions, may be completed in the present chapter.

But I must give a certain warning to the reader before entering upon the history which is my present theme. It has not been possible for me to obtain a view of the origin and history of Islam on which I can rest with such confidence as I feel able to entertain in respect of the view of Christianity which I have given. It has not unfrequently been said that the life of Mohammed is much clearer in its details than the life of Jesus of Nazareth; and certainly it has not that special difficulty which is felt by an inquirer who seeks to determine what is true and what untrue in the miracles of the New Testament. But the character of Mohammed himself is far from an easy problem; I believe it to have been much less deliberately warlike, and more ethical and spiritual, than Christians generally have supposed; but there is a great deal in his reported deeds and sayings respecting which historians are not agreed, and which it would be proper to examine more minutely than I have done, had I had time and opportunity. Similarly, while the power of Islam in its actual development has rested far more on the warlike impulse than has been the case with the power of Christianity, there has been a great deal of thought and feeling, quite apart from the warlike impulse, exhibited by the adherents of Islam, which in a complete history would be fully recorded, and the value of it estimated. To do this adequately is a task beyond my powers; though I shall say something about that part of the thought of Islam which has distinctly helped modern civilisation, and has been a factor in the material progress of the world; but of the theology of Islam I can say hardly anything. Yet it may perhaps give the reader a new light on the Mohammedan temper if I quote an anecdote reported by Sale, the earliest translator of the Koran, in his Preliminary Discourse (§ VIII. p. 110) respecting the second great Mohammedan doctor, Mâlec Ebn Ans, who lived in the eighth century of the Christian era.

In his last illness, a friend going to visit him found him in tears, and asking him the reason of it, he answered, "How should I not weep? and who has more reason to weep than I? Would to God that for every question decided by me according to my own opinion I had received so many stripes! then would my accounts be easier. Would to God I had never given any decision of my own!"

Perhaps this was exaggerated humility; but genuine humility it does seem to have been.

Further, the great warriors and rulers of Islam do in themselves deserve a fuller account than can be given of them here; particularly the first four caliphs, Abû Bakr, Omar, Othmân, Ali, then among the caliphs of Damascus, Mu'âwiya and Walîd;

of the Abbassid dynasty, Harun Alraschid and Al Mamun; and two of the Moslem rulers of Spain, Abderrahman the Third and Almanzor. There are others of whom I must say more later on; but here I can only say that in almost all of these monarchs three qualities appear; first, a singular faithfulness to their religion; secondly, an indifference to shedding human blood; thirdly, a dignity of temperament, and frequently a pleasure in literature and art and even science (though in the earlier caliphs this is less conspicuous). Of those whom I have named, Al Mamun and Abderrahman the Third were perhaps the two who had the civilisation of mankind most at heart; but there has always been a tendency in the Moslem mind to follow religion as something superior to the civilising instinct and having but little relation to it. There was a great deal of this tendency in Christianity also, in those early centuries which are my present subject; and it was a tendency that made war between the adherents of the two religions almost inevitable. The present chapter is a sketch of the progress of Islam and of Christianity, involving a comparison between them, in their warlike as well as in their peaceful characteristics, during the seven centuries which elapsed from the death of Charlemagne down to the Reformation of the sixteenth century.

Were we to compare the external gains of Islam and of Christianity during the period that I have mentioned, they may not appear so very unequal. What Islam won from Christendom by war, namely Asia Minor, Constantinople, and the territories surrounding that great city, was indeed greater in extent than Spain, which Christendom won by war from Islam during the same period; but the whole north of Europe, won by Christianity from heathenism, would certainly seem not less than northern India and the adjacent parts, which were the gain of Islam from heathenism. Half of European Russia, it may be observed, was won from Christendom by the Mohammedan Tartars and then lost again in the course of the centuries from the thirteenth to the fifteenth.

But far more important than these external conquests is the question—Under which religion were the seeds of progress, spiritual and material, most effectively planted? The question is involved in some intricacies, owing to the presence of extraneous forces, over and above the religious element, influencing the result; and on the whole the extraneous forces acted for Christianity and against Islam. But when all allowance is made for this, it will be found that the true Christian religious feeling had a vigour, generative of spiritual and material progress, to which Islam had not attained.

It will be well to speak of the extraneous forces in the first instance. First, then, there was an extraneous force helping the development of Christian countries, to which Islam did not possess any parallel, in the Roman law and Roman municipal organisations surviving in Europe as a legacy from the Roman empire. Of course Roman law was often superseded by barbarian customs, and the municipalities had been greatly weakened; still enough of the old type remained to be a real help to Christian countries, though it did not spring out of Christianity; whereas Mohammedan countries had no equal inheritance from their own heathen past. Secondly, a blow from without fell upon Mohammedan countries in the thirteenth century, of the most extraordinary severity, from which Christendom did not at all equally suffer, though it did suffer; I mean the great Mongol invasion, begun by Jingis Khan[1], continued in the west by Batu and Khulagu, and having its last signal representative in Timur, who died in 1405 A.D. Timur traced his descent from the family of Jingis Khan; and, though he was a Moslem, it was the tradition of Jingis Khan that he continued, far more than any Moslem example.

How few in modern times have vividly before their minds that terrible era to which I have just referred! To how few does the name of Tartar come now with any association of immense power! The Mongols were not identical with the Tartars, but they were leaders of the races who collectively were called Tartars, and who in the thirteenth century burst upon the whole of Asia and upon the eastern part of Europe with a fury to which history supplies no equal. In Europe, they conquered the east of Russia, and remained masters of it for two and a half centuries; they overran Hungary and Poland, Serbia and Bulgaria, making great devastations, but receded from those countries. Western Europe was untouched by them, yet heard of them with terror. Under Khubilai Khan (who, like Batu and Khulagu, was grandson of Jingis Khan) they conquered China. But it was Islam that suffered most from them; and though in the end the Tartars of the west were converted to the religion of Islam, yet before that happened, the destruction of Mohammedan civilisation that

---

[1] I do not know that I can do better than follow the spelling of this name sanctioned by the English historian of the Mongols. Gibbon however writes it Zingis; and there are variations beyond number.

took place was beyond anything which Christendom ever suffered from the outer barbarians, even from such fierce warriors as Genseric and Attila.

Were one, in all history, to select a period in which all the nations of the world might seem to be contending together for supremacy, and waiting for the divine judgment (a war to which Christian usage attaches the mystical name of Armageddon), the thirteenth century of our era might best seem to be such a time[1]. Yet, though great controversies lead to war, the decision of great controversies, whether national or religious, does not as a rule come through war; and certainly the thirteenth century of the Christian era, though a period of immense conflicts, was not a period when any great conflict received decision in any memorable manner. The Mongol outburst sank down, having in the end reinforced the ranks of Islam as far as numbers are concerned, but having in the meantime destroyed elements of science and learning that could ill be spared.

Undoubtedly this great calamity does in part, though not entirely, excuse the religion of Islam for its subsequent barrenness in the realms of philosophy and science; perhaps even for the absence of civic development in its cities; and before proceeding further, it will be well to make some quotations to show the true nature of the history to which I refer. My first quotation shall be from Professor T. W. Arnold's *Preaching of Islam*, pp. 185, 186: it will be seen that he quotes contemporary evidence:

There is no event in the history of Islam that for terror and desolation can be compared to the Mongol conquest. Like an avalanche, the hosts of Jingis Khan swept over the centres of Muslim culture and civilisation, leaving behind them bare deserts and shapeless ruins where before had stood the palaces of stately cities, girt about with gardens and fruitful cornland. When the Mongol army had marched out of the city of Herat, a miserable remnant of forty persons crept out of their hidingplaces and gazed horror-stricken on the ruins of their beautiful city—all that were left out of a population of over 100,000. In Bokhara, so famed for its men of piety and learning, the Mongols stabled their horses in the sacred precincts of the mosques and tore up the Qur'ans to serve as litter; those of the inhabitants who were not butchered were carried away into captivity and their city reduced to ashes. Such too was the fate of Samarcand, Balkh, and many another city of Central Asia, which had been the glories of Islamic civilisation and the dwellingplaces of holy men and the seats of sound learning—such too the fate of Baghdad that for centuries had been the capital of the Abbasid dynasty.

Well might the Muhammadan historian shudder to relate such horrors;

---

[1] These words were written early in the year 1913. I write this note in September 1915; Armageddon might seem to be now going on.

when Ibnu-l Athir comes to describe the inroads of the Mongols into the countries of Islam, "for many years," he tells us, "I shrank from giving a recital of these events on account of their magnitude and my abhorrence. Even now I come reluctant to the task, for who would deem it a light thing to sing the death-song of Islam and of the Musalmans, or find it easy to tell this tale? O that my mother had not given me birth! Oh, would that I had died ere this, and been a thing forgotten, forgotten quite[1]! Many friends had urged me and still I stood irresolute; but I saw that it was of no profit to forego the task and so I thus resume. I shall have to describe events so terrible and calamities so stupendous that neither day nor night have ever brought forth the like; they fell on all nations, but on the Muslims more than all; and were one to say that since God created Adam the world has not seen the like, he would but tell the truth, for history has nothing to relate that at all approaches it. Among the greatest calamities in history is the slaughter that Nebuchadnezzar wrought among the children of Israel and his destruction of the Temple; but what is Jerusalem in comparison to the countries that these accursed ones laid waste, every town of which was far greater than Jerusalem, and what were the children of Israel in comparison to those they slew, since the inhabitants of one of the cities they destroyed were greater in numbers than all the children of Israel? Let us hope that the world may never see the like again."

This dirge, which Professor Arnold quotes from the Mohammedan historian, does worthily convey an idea of events from which the world still suffers; for Central Asia has not yet recovered from the desolations of that terrible time. The Mongol invasions were the last outburst of pure heathenism in the world; the last, and the fiercest; for Attila, fierce as he was, is not to be held as equally terrible with Jingis Khan. The destruction of Nineveh (which modern research has shown to have been accomplished by wild hordes similar to the Mongols) is the nearest parallel to the destruction of Baghdad; the two cities were not very unlike in magnitude and splendour; but the Arabs in Baghdad had attained a higher degree both of morality and of civilisation than the Assyrians in Nineveh, who lived nearly nineteen centuries before them. It is not without some real reason, some well-founded confidence, that we may echo the words of Ibnu-l Athir, and say that destruction by the hand of man reached its culmination at that epoch, and that the world will never see the like again.

But now let me quote Syed Ameer Ali's[2] brief summary of what the Mongols did, and the final effect of their invasion:

The eruption of the Mongols upon the Saracenic world was not like the invasion of the Roman empire by the northern barbarians. These

[1] These two sentences are quoted from the Koran, XIX. 23.
[2] *Life and Teachings of Mohammed*, pp. 562-3.

had proceeded slowly; and in their comparatively gradual progress towards the heart of the empire they had become partially softened, and had to some extent cast off their pristine ferocity. The case was otherwise with the hordes of the devastator Chengiz. They swept like overwhelming torrents over Western Asia. Wherever they went they left misery and desolation. Their barbarous campaigns and their savage slaughters put an end for a time to the intellectual development of Asia. But the moment the wild savages adopted the religion of the Prophet of Arabia a change came over them. From the destroyers of the seats of learning and arts they became the founders of academies and the protectors of the learned. Sultan Khoda-Bendah (Uljaitû-Khan), the sixth in descent from Chengiz, was distinguished for his attainments and his patronage of the sciences. But the fearful massacres which the barbarians had committed among the settled and cultured population of the towns destroyed most of the gifted classes, with the result that, though the great cities like Bokhara and Samarcand rose again into splendour, they became, nevertheless, the seats of a narrower culture, more casuistical and theological than before.

It is to the credit of Islam, as Syed Ameer Ali truly says, to have converted the barbarous Mongols to a disposition of greater mercy and enlightenment; but a full remedy for the past calamity was not won, and has not been won up to this day.

It must not then be denied that the Mohammedans had a harder task in promoting the well-being of the world than Christians had, and that from causes quite irrespective of the intrinsic character of the two religions. Yet when full allowance has been made for this, it will be found none the less that Christianity, not Islam, supplied the seed out of which modern civilisation has sprung. This I must endeavour to show; but it would be a very false and delusive way of showing it, were I to conceal the real virtues, the real attainments, which were nourished in the bosom of Islam, and which have left their mark permanently on the world. In truth, the blossoming of Islam preceded the blossoming of Christianity; and to show what Islam did for the benefit of the world is the step which lies next before me. A great deal of it is written in the impartial pages of Humboldt, from whom I will now quote. The following sentences, not strictly consecutive, but yet in the order in which they appear in the chapter from which they are quoted, will be found in the translation of Humboldt's *Cosmos* by E. C. Otté, vol. II. pp. 571–600[1]:

The Arabs, a people of Semitic origin, partially dispelled the barbarism which had shrouded Europe for upwards of two hundred years after the storms by which it had been shaken, from the aggressions of hostile nations.

[1] It is rather singular that Humboldt, in the passage from which I quote, commends the Arab race but not their religion. Yet the "Arabs" were of course the early Mohammedans, and Islam was the stimulus that had awakened them.

The Arabs lead us back to the imperishable sources of Greek philosophy; and besides the influence thus exercised on scientific cultivation, they have also extended and opened new paths in the domain of natural investigation....This people, after having continued for thousands of years almost without contact with the rest of the world, and advancing chiefly in Nomadic hordes, suddenly burst forth from their former mode of life, and acquiring cultivation from the mental contact of the inhabitants of more ancient seats of civilisation, converted and subjected to their dominion the nations dwelling between the Pillars of Hercules and the Indus to the point where the Bolor chain intersects the Hindoo Coosh. They maintained relations of commerce, as early as the middle of the ninth century, simultaneously with the northern countries of Europe, with Madagascar, Eastern Africa, India, and China; diffused languages, money, and Indian numerals, and founded a powerful and long-enduring communion of lands united together by one common religion....The Arabs possessed remarkable qualifications, alike for appropriating to themselves, and again diffusing abroad, the seeds of knowledge and general intercourse from the Euphrates to the Guadalquiver, and to the south of Central Africa....No other race presents us with more striking examples of extensive land journeys, undertaken by private individuals, not only for purposes of trade but also with the view of collecting information, surpassing in these respects the travels of the Buddhist priests of Thibet and China, Marco Polo, and the Christian missionaries, who were sent on an embassy to the Mongolian princes. Important elements of Asiatic knowledge reached Europe, through the intimate relations existing between the Arabs and the natives of India and China....

Of the long series of remarkable geographers presented to us in the literature of the Arabs, it will be sufficient to name the first and last, El Istâchri and Alhassan (Johannes Leo Africanus). Geography never acquired a greater acquisition of facts, even from the discoveries of the Portuguese and Spaniards. Within fifty years after the death of the Prophet, the Arabs had already reached the extremest western coasts of Africa and the port of Asfi....Geography was no longer limited to a representation of the relations of space, and the determinations of latitude and longitude, which had been multiplied by Abul-Hassan, or to a description of river districts and mountain chains; but it rather led the people, already familiar with nature, to an acquaintance with the organic products of the soil, especially those of the vegetable world....As a botanist we must name Ibn-Baithar of Malaga, whose travels in Greece, Persia, India, and Egypt, entitle him to be regarded with admiration for the tendency he evinced to compare together, by independent observations, the productions of different zones in the east and west. The point from whence all these efforts emanated was the study of medicine, by which the Arabs long ruled the Christian schools, and for the more perfect development of which Ibn-Sina (Avicenna), a native of Aschena near Bochara, Ibn-Roschd (Averroes) of Cordova, the younger Serapion of Syria, and Mesue of Maridin on the Euphrates, availed themselves of all the means yielded by the Arabian caravan and sea trade. I have purposely enumerated the widely removed birthplaces of celebrated Arabian literati, since they are calculated to remind us of the great area over which the peculiar mental direction, and the simultaneous activity of the Arabian race, extended the sphere of ideas....The most powerful influence exercised by

the Arabs on general natural physics was that directed to the advances
of chemistry; a science for which this race created a new era. The
labours of Geber[1], and the much more recent ones of Razes[1], have been
attended by the most important results. This period is characterised
by the preparation of sulphuric and nitric acids, aqua regia, preparations
of mercury and of the oxides of other metals, and by the knowledge of
the alcoholic process of fermentation. The first scientific foundation, and
the subsequent advances of chemistry, are so much the more important
as they imparted a knowledge of the heterogeneous character of matter,
and the nature of forces not made manifest by motion, but which now
led to the recognition of the importance of *composition*....

Among the advances which science owes to the Arabs, it will be sufficient
to mention Alhazen's work on refraction, partly borrowed, perhaps, from
Ptolemy's Optics, and the knowledge and first application of the pendulum
as a means of measuring time, due to the great astronomer, Ebn-Junis.

The Arabs were in possession of planetary tables as early as the close
of the eighth century. We have already observed that the *Susruta*, the
ancient incorporation of all the medical knowledge of the Indians, was
translated by learned men belonging to the court of the Caliph Harun
Al-Raschid—a proof of the early introduction of Sanscrit literature. The
Arabian mathematician Albiruni even went to India for the purpose of
studying astronomy. His writings, which have only recently been made
accessible to us, prove how intimately he had made himself acquainted
with the country, traditions, and comprehensive knowledge of the Indians.

However much the Arabian astronomers may have owed to the earlier
civilised nations, and especially to the Indian and Alexandrian schools,
they have, nevertheless, considerably extended the domain of astronomy
by their own practical endowments of mind; by the number and direction
of their observations; the improvement of their instruments for angular
measurement; and their zealous efforts to rectify the older tables by
a comparison with the heavens....

Besides making laudatory mention of that which we owe to the natural
science of the Arabs in both the terrestrial and celestial spheres, we must
likewise allude to their contributions in separate paths of intellectual
development to the general mass of mathematical science.

I need not quote more; but the reader will sufficiently perceive
from these observations of Humboldt, that the earlier half of
Mohammedan history, reckoning from the Hejra (622 A.D.) to the
present time, was a period of great and useful mental activity
among the races that had embraced Islam, of whom the Arabs
were then the chief. Moreover there were parts of the Arab
nature which lay outside the scope of Humboldt's treatise, and
which therefore he did not mention; the courage and chivalry
of many of the Mohammedan warriors; the merit of their historians
and philosophers; the great excellence, sometimes, of their
architecture. Sculpture and painting (as far as living forms are

---

[1] Humboldt adds in the text the correct Arabic forms of the names of these two
chemists, viz. Abu-Mussah-Dschafar-al-Kufi and Abu Bekr Arrasi.

concerned) were forbidden to Mohammedans on religious grounds; but Firdousi and others were renowned in poetry, during the ages of which I am here speaking.

Thus, in the early centuries, did Islam preserve the memory of the genius of the ancient Greco-Roman world, and added achievements of its own to that which it had received. For this performance the gratitude of posterity is due; but the weakness of Islam lay in another quarter, which must now be mentioned. Nowhere in the Mohammedan world were the relations of man to man worked out with such a careful apportionment of rights and duties as should ensure permanence to the society so constructed. The structure of society, in so far as it had any structure, was military; this was not because Mohammedans cherished any definite determination to propagate religion by warfare, but because they held that the true religion must be supreme, and warfare was in those days (and often in our own days) thought to be the natural way of vindicating supremacy. Then, when warfare once began, the religion of Islam inspired its adherents with extraordinary force in carrying it to a successful issue. As a matter of fact Islam did progress through the sword; it was therefore natural that the head of the religion, and its chief propagators, should in all the early times be warriors. But there came a time when Islam had reached the limit of the progress which then was possible for it; Christendom was no longer easily to be overcome, either in the east, or in the west; and though the Turks, north of the Persian dominion, were gradually being converted, this was not a speedy process, and warfare does not appear to have taken place in the course of it. Thus in the' ninth century, in the most flourishing period of the Abbassid dynasty, it seems that there might have been an opportunity for organising society on principles of equal right for all; or at any rate for beginning such an organisation; Mohammedan society might have learned to censure the wrong-doings of its rulers, or to defend itself against them, when needful. But no tendency of this kind showed itself. It was possible to rebel against a caliph; it was possible to assassinate him; but peaceable censure or contracts between a sovereign and those whom he ruled, out of which permanent rights of subjects might grow as against the despotism of their ruler, were impossible. Let me not be supposed to say that Mohammedan rulers were always arbitrary in their conduct; there were great instances to the contrary. It is worth while to refer to the *Treatise on the Principles of Government*, drawn up in the eleventh century of our era at the instance of the Seljuk emperor Melik Shah, by his prime minister Nizam-el-Mulk; the intention of the treatise is to secure perfect justice in a Moslem ruler towards his subjects. Let me quote a few sentences from Mr Stanley Lane-Poole[1], descriptive of this work.

"The most striking feature," he writes, " in the system of government outlined by Nizam-el-Mulk is his constant insistence on the duties of the sovereign towards his subjects, and the elaborate checks suggested for the detection and punishment of official corruption and oppression. Twice a week the Sultan was obliged to hold public audience, when anybody, however humble and unknown, might come to present his grievances and demand justice. The Sultan must hear these petitions himself, without any go-between, listen patiently, and decide each case in accordance with equity. Various precautions are recommended to ensure the free access of the subject to the king....Extraordinary pains were to be taken lest the maladministration of local governors should escape detection....Constant inspection of the taxgatherers and other officials is recommended, and severe punishment is to be meted out to the unjust. 'Spies,' he says, 'must perpetually traverse the roads of the various provinces, disguised as merchants, dervishes &c. and send in reports of what they hear, so that nothing that passes shall remain unknown.'...These provisions for just administration and frequent inspection were all the more necessary in an empire which was founded upon a military organisation, wherein the government was vested in the hands of foreigners."

It would seem that Melik Shah did conscientiously carry out the system thus sketched for him, and that roads were safe under his sovereignty, commerce was fostered, and the prosperity of his subjects was at a high level. But the weakness of such a system of government lies on the face of it. It is a government assumed to be despotic; if the ruler fulfils his duties, things may go fairly well; but if the ruler does not fulfil his duties, or gives way to sudden passion in the execution of them, all manner of injustices are sure to ensue; and in default of any strong instinct in the community at large, that such injustices must be corrected, they will not be corrected. Now it was this instinct, this brotherly instinct, to see that in the affairs of ordinary life injustices shall either not be committed, or if committed shall be remedied, or if remedy be impossible, then that security shall be taken that the like shall not occur again—this instinct it was which was feeble among Mohammedans. Take a couple of instances. The Ommeyad dynasty, in the day of their power as caliphs at Damascus, may have been guilty of many crimes; but the bloodthirsty determination to root them out which

---

[1] From his work on *Saladin*, pp. 13–15

actuated the first of the Abbassid caliphs, showed none of that care which ought to accompany a just condemnation; yet none protested against it. The only Ommeyad who escaped in the general slaughter of his kindred did so by flying to Spain at the other end of the Mohammedan world, where he found followers, and in the end established a durable rule. But no feeling of moderation or justice availed to protect the Ommeyads, wherever the sword of the Abbassid could reach them. Nor, when Harun Alraschid destroyed the Barmecide clan, who had been the most devoted of his adherents, was there anyone to require of him a reason for the bloody deed; it was accepted as a legitimate act of the ruler to whom all submitted. The real motive for this massacre is to this day matter of conjecture merely. Thus, though there might be prosperity, piety, and increase of knowledge throughout the Mohammedan world, and though there were Mohammedan rulers who deserve our respect and even admiration (none more so than the famous Saladin), yet regard for individual rights was feeble; alliances of citizens against the sword of the monarch were unknown; the principles of justice were crudely held and easily overstepped, without stirring up any public resolution to guard against future tyranny by permanent defences.

There may be some who explain this characteristic of Moslem peoples, their inability (at any rate as far as past ages are concerned) to build up any government which is not simply despotic, as a result of their being Orientals. It is by Europeans, it is thought, that freedom is valued; Asiatics can hardly conceive it; they may get rid of a despot, but from despotism they can never emancipate themselves; it is supposed that there is some sluggishness in their blood which is adverse to the energies by which freedom must be maintained. I do not deny that there is some truth in this explanation. In so far as it is true, it is the great histories of Greece and Rome that have sunk into the blood of European nations, and have imparted to them the capacity of building up constitutions; the barbarian Goths or Franks may have valued freedom, but they had no practice in building it up on a large scale. There has been nothing in Asiatic nations precisely parallel to the influence of ancient Greece and Rome on Europe. Yet I cannot but think that it is from the east, even more than from Greece and Rome, that Christian nations have derived their power of building up free constitutions, which has been wanting to Moslem nations. They have derived it from the race of Israel more than from any other quarter. True, the Bible does not record among the Israelites anything like the popular constitutions of modern nations. But what the Bible does continually record, is the free speech of heroic men, who were not kings, in censure (when that was needed) of the kings to whom they were subject; a censure quite distinct from hostility, and very rarely accompanied by active hostility[1], but exceedingly plain in impressing upon the public mind the wrong which the kings had done. These heroic men were the prophets. Nothing more stimulative of a free spirit can be conceived than the prophetic utterances as recorded in the Old Testament; and the rôle of the prophets was taken up by the Christian Church, and was an abiding counteractive of despotism in the west at all events; to some extent in the east also, though the eastern mind was so much bent on theology that freedom in civil affairs was not attained in that quarter. But without disparaging the east, it was in western Europe that Christian activity found its main channel; and here it was that the modern civilised world began to be formed. The Koran was unable to frame a civilisation in Moslem countries as durable as that which we see in western Europe to-day, because the Koran, though not incognisant of the ordinary duties of men, lays far less stress on them than on religious belief, and in particular almost ignores the great temptations which monarchs, more than other men, are liable to, where ordinary moral action is concerned.

I have tried to show the merits, I have tried also to show the failings, of the religion of Islam as it has been displayed in history, as educative of the human soul, and as a guide to human conduct. Let us not disparage it; but yet I think we must see that something greater than Islam is needed, in order to set mankind in a condition of stable progress. And now I come to the much more complex subject of the Christian Church; and I am at present treating of it, be it remembered, as it existed in the centuries between the time of Charlemagne and the beginning of the Reformation in the sixteenth century.

I have extolled the Christian Church as one of the chief causes, indeed in connexion with the Bible as the chiefest cause, of modern freedom. But strange to say, in one particular direction, namely in the exercise of the intellect, the Christian Church was

---

[1] There are, I think, only two instances of actual rebellion, by Israelites of very high character, against the monarchs to whom they were subject; one is the rebellion which Elisha promoted, through Jehu, against Jehoram the son of Ahab; the other is the rebellion of the Maccabees against Antiochus Epiphanes.

the most powerful adversary to freedom that the world has ever
known. In its direct action the Christian Church was such an
adversary; that is to say, free inquiry was by the Church absolutely
prohibited whenever the tendency of such inquiry appeared in
the least likely to oppose the doctrinal decisions of the Church;
and Christian authorities had the eye of a lynx for detecting
tendencies which were likely to oppose them. Thus the direct
action of the Church was as adverse to intellectual progress as
could be conceived; and if we ask why the Church was so adverse,
it must be answered that it was partly from a motive which
merits our respect, namely anxiety lest the honour of Jesus
Christ should suffer detriment through novel processes of thought;
but even more from a motive which we can only lament, namely
the fear lest God should send to hell those who think erroneously
of Jesus Christ. To save such persons from hell, the Church
resolved to frighten them into belief; and except in the case of
very brave persons, the Church had very effective means of
frightening them. But curiously enough, while the direct action
of the Church was thus repressive in the extreme, the indirect
action of the Church did in some ways foster the intellect, and
that in no slight degree. For first, except in some special instances
(of which the Crusades were the most remarkable) the Church
was very much against warlike excitements; peace was really
valued; and among the pleasures of peace, the exercise of the
intellect is in itself one of the most useful and blameless. Next,
the quiet of the monasteries, and even of ecclesiastical life outside
the monasteries, was very favourable to intellectual research in
the case of persons who had by nature inquiring intellects. Then
too the art of writing was specially cultivated by ecclesiastics;
and the copying of manuscripts (and their adornment too by
illustrative pictures) was a favourite employment of the monks;
and though the manuscripts transcribed were generally of a
religious nature, yet Latin and even Greek manuscripts of classical
authors were not wanting, and the transcription of these involved
their perusal, and this brought about a good deal of enlargement
of mind. Translations of Arabian philosophers were presently
available also, and served to assist the improvement of the
European intellect. Slow as this process of intellectual revival
was, it nevertheless did take place during the centuries of which
I am speaking, and through the action of that very Church
which was so determined an adversary of free thought. I do
not think I can better illustrate this more genial and salutary

side of the Church's action than by quoting some sentences from
the French historian of mathematics, Montucla (as he is given
in Whewell's *History of the Inductive Sciences*, vol. I. pp. 274–5):

"And here," writes the eminent Frenchman, "it is impossible not to
reflect that all those men who, if they did not augment the treasure of
the sciences, at least served to transmit it, were monks, or had been such
originally. Convents were, during these stormy ages, the asylum of
sciences and letters. Without these religious men, who, in the silence
of their monasteries, occupied themselves in transcribing, in studying,
and in imitating the works of the ancients, well or ill, those works would
have perished; perhaps not one of them would have come down to us.
The thread which connects us with the Greeks and Romans would have
been snapt asunder; the precious productions of ancient literature would
no more exist for us, than the works, if any there were, published before
the catastrophe that annihilated that highly scientific nation, which,
according to Bailly, existed in remote ages in the center of Tartary, or at
the roots of Caucasus. In the sciences we should have had all to create;
and at the moment when the human mind should have emerged from its
stupor and shaken off its slumbers, we should have been no more advanced
than the Greeks were after the taking of Troy."

Strange it is that the same institution should have been the
nurse of the intellect, and yet the persecutor of the intellect !
An internal conflict was going on, all unconsciously to those who
were waging it, within the Church herself; a living energy was
coming to birth; but the pangs were as the pangs of childbirth.

However, I must for the present recede from the subject on
which I have just touched, the intellectual development of
mediæval Europe, and revert to the more ordinary courses of
life as they showed themselves in Christian countries. I have
said that Islam, while anticipating Christianity in intellectual
progress, was defective as regards making any efforts towards
determining the relations of men with each other. Now the
Christian nations of the west did make such efforts, and these
efforts were fruitful. The task was an arduous one, and if we look
at the Christian countries of this twentieth century after Christ,
it is impossible to say that the relations of men to each other
have even yet been determined in a satisfactory manner; far
from it. But there has been progress towards such determination;
the Christian nations of Europe have accomplished something
towards it since the days of Charlemagne. Indeed the beginnings
of such progress were before the days of Charlemagne. From the
time when the Benedictine monks, often men of noble birth,
began to plough the land and do duties accounted servile with
their own hands, from that time it became apparent that the
social relations of men were undergoing a change of a very radical

sort, the end of which none could know. Nor was it a less noticeable fact that the authorities of the Church stood as the counsellors
and reprovers of emperors; I do not say that such counsel,
such reproof, was always just, but it was very important that it
should be exercised.

Yet it was also important that the imperial authority and
the Church authority should on the whole be friendly to each
other. It was inevitable that their friendship should be subject
to strains; and as long as the ancient Roman empire was represented only by the emperor at Constantinople, the strain
between the emperor and the western church, represented by the
bishop of Rome, had been too great for real friendship. Hence
it was very welcome to the western church, and a real gain for
mankind, when the surpassing power of Charlemagne made it
natural for pope Leo III to crown him at Rome, as Roman
emperor, in the year 800 A.D.; it was an act that made no formal
breach between the eastern and the western church, but still
it came to pass in consequence of it that the two branches of the
Church went their own ways. In the end there was that
regrettable disruption and separation between them which still
exists; but that did not come at once.

Both in the eastern and in the western church, the general
tone of the civil to the ecclesiastical authority was one of respect;
there were quarrels indeed, and sometimes bitter ones; but
neither civil nor ecclesiastical power wished to uproot its rival
and to reign alone. And as I must necessarily say less of the
eastern than of the western church in the present chapter, it
may be well to illustrate this point from the annals of the eastern
church. In the latter part of the tenth century, the great country
of Russia had been converted to Christianity, and had by
preference taken the form professed at Constantinople as its
model, and adhered to the doctrines and rule of the church of
that city. A century and a quarter later, in the year 1113 A.D.
Vladimir the Second came to the Russian throne, and received
(Dean Stanley tells us) from the Russian primate a copy of the
101st Psalm, as a description of what a ruler should be. How
he interpreted and carried out the instruction thus supplied will
be seen from his will, in which he left his dying counsels to his
sons: I quote it from the work to which I have just alluded
(Stanley's *Eastern Church*, pp. 372–374):

O my children, praise God and love men. For it is not fasting, nor
solitude, nor monastic life, that will procure you eternal life, but only

doing good. Forget not the poor, nourish them; remember that riches come from God, and are given you only for a short time. Do not bury your wealth in the ground; this is against the precepts of Christianity. Be fathers to orphans. Be judges in the cause of widows, and do not let the powerful oppress the weak. Put to death neither innocent nor guilty, for nothing is so sacred as the life and soul of a Christian. Never take the name of God in vain; and never break the oath you have made in kissing the crucifix. My brethren said to me, "Help us to drive out the sons of Rostislof, or else give up our alliance." But I said, "I cannot forget that I have kissed the cross." I opened then the book of Psalms, and read there with deep emotion: "Why art thou so vexed, O my soul, and why art thou so disquieted within me? Put thy trust in God. I will confess my faults, and he is gracious."

Be not envious at the triumph of the wicked and the success of treachery. Fear the lot of the impious. Do not desert the sick: do not let the sight of dead corpses terrify you, for we must all die. Receive with joy the blessing of the clergy: do not keep yourself aloof from them: do them good, that they may pray to God for you. Drive out of your heart all suggestions of pride, and remember that we are all perishable— to-day full of hope, to-morrow in the coffin. Abhor lying, drunkenness, and debauchery. Love your wives, but do not suffer them to have any power over you. Endeavour constantly to obtain knowledge. Without having quitted his palace, my father spoke five languages; a thing which wins for us the admiration of foreigners.

In war be vigilant; be an example to your boyards. Never retire to rest until you have posted your guards. Never take off your arms while you are within reach of the enemy. And, to avoid being surprised, be always early on horseback. When you are on horseback say your prayers, or at least the shortest and best of all, "Lord, have mercy upon us."

When you travel through your provinces, do not allow your attendants to do the least injury to the inhabitants. Entertain always at your own expense the master of the house in which you take up your abode.

If you find yourself affected by any ailment, make three prostrations to the ground before the Lord; and never let the sun find you in bed. At the dawn of day, my father, and the virtuous men by whom he was surrounded, did thus: they glorified the Lord, and cried, in the joy of their hearts, "Vouchsafe, O my God, to enlighten me with thy divine light." They then seated themselves to deliberate, or to administer justice to the people, or they went to the chase; and in the middle of the day they slept; which God permits to man as well as to beasts and birds.

For my own part, I accustomed myself to do everything that I might have ordered my servants to do. Night and day, summer and winter, I was perpetually moving about. I wished to see everything with my own eyes. Never did I abandon the poor or the widow to the oppressions of the powerful. I made it my duty to inspect the churches and the sacred ceremonies of religion, as well as the management of my property, my stables, and the vultures and hawks of my hunting establishment.

I have made eighty-three campaigns and many expeditions. I concluded nineteen treaties with the Poloctzy. I took captive one hundred of their princes, whom I set free again; and I put two hundred of them to death, by throwing them into rivers.

No one has ever travelled more rapidly than I have done. Setting out in the morning from Tchernigof, I have arrived at Kieff before the hour of vespers.

In my youth, what falls from my horse did I not experience! wounding my feet and my hands, and breaking my head against trees. But the Lord watched over me.

In hunting amidst the thickest forests, how many times have I caught wild horses and bound them together! How many times have I been thrown down by buffaloes, wounded by the antlers of stags, and trodden under the feet of elks! A furious wild boar rent my sword from my baldrick: my saddle was torn to pieces by a bear; this terrible beast rushed upon my courser, whom he threw down upon me. But the Lord protected me.

O my children, fear neither death nor wild beasts. Trust in Providence: it far surpasses all human precautions.

That is a production distinguished by the simple natural trust which it shows in the excellence of Christian teaching, and by the respect which it breathes for Christian teachers. The writer, indeed, is one with whom it would not have been safe to take liberties! But summarily as he might deal with individuals, Vladimir the Second has plainly an esteem for the clergy that would not be affected by any unfavourable judgments which he might chance to form respecting individuals among them; they are in his view performing a necessary and divine office. Further, his character, even if there be some remaining elements of barbarism in it, is generous, brave, and Christian; he is a man who has his work in the world, and who does it without fear. Even if we should say that in the after history of Russia the religious authority became too subservient in presence of the power of the monarch, there is not, as far as Vladimir is concerned, any sign of arrogance in the temporal ruler; he treats the Divine Power as something to which he himself has to render an account; his religion is interwoven with all his actions.

What Vladimir was to the eastern church, that Charlemagne was to the western church; the honoured protector; fortified by spiritual aids which the Church supplied; not an immaculate person by any means; but an organiser, and sustaining the fabric of government by his organising power. And though after the death of Charlemagne in 814 A.D. the great dominion which he had built up broke gradually into separate portions under his successors, yet did the effect of his work not wholly pass away; there was strength enough in those separate portions to repel the wild marauding bands who kept streaming from Asia westwards; or if not wholly repelled, they were absorbed and Christianised, as were the Magyars early in the tenth century. Sea robbers there still were; the Northmen committed their plunders and ravages round the coasts of Europe; and yet these too gradually became softened and civilised; and it was the spiritual power, with the Pope for its centre, to which they rendered their homage.

We must bear in mind that throughout all these ages, weak though they were on the side of literary culture, the gospel precepts of humility, compassion, and forgiveness kept filtering through to the laity by way of the clergy, and were not without fruit in those parts of society where there was the budding of native force, prefiguring future developments[1]. What is called the feudal system was one of these formative movements; peculiarly personal in its primary character, being the attempt to bind the whole of society together through links of reciprocal duties, descending from the highest to the lowest. The feudal system was slowly coming into existence during the ninth and tenth centuries; in the three centuries which followed we find it more stable and more definitely connected with land tenure than it had been before; then it slowly lost its strength, through the increased power of monarchs, the growth of towns, the progress of legislation (which tended to supersede personal claims), and more or less through all those numerous ties which developing knowledge brings with it, especially in the regions of commerce and of art. The bias of the feudal system towards embodying duty in personal relations was very favourable to many tender emotions and to the romantic poetry in which those emotions have a natural outlet; but when taken as a substitute for formal law, it was capable of being harsh and tyrannous; and in many parts of Europe this inferior character was the impression which it left behind it in the after history. Still it is true that the feudal system was a genuine attempt at organisation, and in many respects it did organise the races of Europe in those ruder times of which I am speaking, though it needed the supplement and correcting force of other principles afterwards.

Side by side with the feudal system, and in many respects antagonistic to it, yet cooperating in the same work of inter-penetrating society with institutions and forces which made it easier to live peaceably and happily, was the municipal government

---

[1] The remarks on the imperfection and yet the merit of feudalism, in Sidgwick's *Development of European Polity*, p. 208, will illustrate what I say in the following sentences.

in the cities of western Europe. This, as I have said, was partly an inheritance from the Roman empire; and partly also the strong individualism of the feudal system kindled a retaliatory passion in the inhabitants of the cities; arrogance was answered by defiance. But we must not leave out, as completing the list of influential forces, that equitable temper which Christian teaching inspired, and which enabled citizens to stand together against despotism and military aggression, and to recover from most serious losses. Nowhere, perhaps, was this temper so markedly shown as in the great republic of Venice; which, brought into life originally by the fugitives from the exterminating sword of Attila, and sheltered behind the lagoons of the Adriatic, was able in the year 810 to repel the son of Charlemagne, and in the after centuries wielded supreme maritime power. But I need not say that Venice did not stand alone, nor need I enumerate the famous Italian cities that were her rivals, some of which have not maintained their importance with the progress of time; for instance, the seaport Amalfi, which in the tenth century had fifty thousand inhabitants, in the twentieth century is reduced to the tenth part of that number. The tokens of an improving morality are discerned fitfully and accidentally, a golden thread among a confusion of glaring or dingy circumstance; here is an example from the history of Venice:

An extant edict of the year A.D. 960, in the reign of Peter Candiano IV... forbids the slave trade under temporal and spiritual penalties, and it mentions Pola in Istria as a principal seat of the trade[1].

In Germany and France the ninth and tenth centuries were a period of slow growth for the municipalities, which were continually assailed by the feudal lords; but in the eleventh century, after arduous struggles, they won their independence, and extorted charters from their feudal superiors; a movement which was completed in the eleventh century. The kings on the whole helped the municipalities in their struggle, though not invariably[2].

In England the ninth and tenth centuries were notable for the tremendous inroads of the heathen Danes, and for their gradual conversion to Christianity. Neither the feudal system, nor the growth of municipalities, marked this period in England:

[1] From that valuable work, the *Early History of Venice* by F. C. Hodgson, p. 150. Mr Hodgson adds that even in the eighth century pope Zacharias had censured this trade.
[2] See, in respect of this whole subject, Guizot's *History of Civilisation in Europe*, Lecture VII. I have been greatly indebted to Guizot, than whom there is no more sympathetic, no more discerning, critic of the Middle Ages.

the struggles were more simple, more elemental; everything is
gathered up into the one great issue, whether Saxon or Dane,
whether Christian or heathen, shall be the ruler. But in truth
the issue denoted by the phrase Christian versus heathen was
far more profound than that denoted by the phrase Saxon versus
Dane. We should find it difficult to say whether Saxon or Dane
really won in that conflict of two centuries long; there can be
no question at all that Christianity won, and that heathenism
disappeared, as the result of it. Moreover, the evidences of the
Christian spirit, in its most loveable form, are singularly strong
here. We may look far among the records of the monarchs of
the earth before we find one so attractive, so excellent in all
relations of life, as Alfred; whether we regard him as soldier,
as statesman, or as literary author and translator of classical
works. If the narrowness of the kingdom allotted to him prevented
his attaining the greatness of Charlemagne, he was yet purer in
his actions than Charlemagne; and it was his intrinsic worth,
even more than his success in battle, that made permanent the
conversion of his Danish foes to the Christian faith. Nor were
the descendants of Alfred unworthy of him, at any rate for three
quarters of a century after his death. But towards the close of
the tenth century there does appear some degeneration among
the Saxon race in England. Conjectural causes may be assigned
for this, but the history is too little known by us to trace them
with certainty; we can only be certain that seeds of virtue
remained in the land, which had a blossoming at a later time.
But before that happened, England was subdued first by Danish
kings (of whom Canute was far the greatest), and then, after an
interval, by the Normans. The Normans had themselves been
of the race of the sea-robbers; but a province of France had been
assigned to them as their possession by the king of France (to
whom they were thenceforth in feudal subordination), and there
they had dwelt for a century and a half before they invaded
England. During that sojourn they had acquired certain
refinements, certain powers, in which the English were lacking,
and their rule proved in the end (though not immediately) of
real service to England.

Let me return to the main European history; first remarking
that the fall of Ireland into disorder, after much pristine virtue
and learning, happened very nearly at the same time as the
decadence of Saxon England.

There can be no doubt that the three centuries after

Charlemagne, with all their tumults and wars, and disorders of
Church and State, did result in a greater fixity of governments,
and a more exact determination of the duties by which every man
was bound. The year 1000 A.D. (or shortly after the accession of
the dynasty of Hugh Capet to the French throne—one of the most
enduring of all lines of monarchs known to history) is spoken
of by Guizot as the date after which real national feeling begins
in Europe. Especially were Germany and France then finally
separated; and demarcation of countries began to be roughly
fixed by demarcation of languages. I must not dwell on details;
but perhaps the year 1100, more than the year 1000, is the epoch
of history which marks the basis of the Europe which is now. Let
us see what by that time had been effected in Christendom, as
steps on the way to that perfect union which, it is to be hoped,
mankind may attain. Three forms of union have been mentioned
above, and may be briefly repeated here:

Firstly, the union implied by feudal duties and privileges—
secondly, the union implied by belonging to a city with municipal
regulations—thirdly, the union implied by that much larger
conception, a common country or nationality—all these were
existent and had true force in Europe, especially in western
Europe, in the year 1100 A.D. Besides all these, and underlying
them, was the union implied by a common religion; but this
must not be said without some qualification, and some explanation.
The qualification is this: that before the year 1100, in fact in
the year 1054 A.D., a complete separation must be regarded as
having taken place between the eastern and western churches.
In that year, after centuries of discord, the two churches reci-
procally excommunicated one another; and though there were
efforts for reunion afterwards, it never came about. It was a
calamity, and was felt as such on certain very important occasions;
but in everyday life it was not noticed at all, so great was the
natural separation, enforced by mere distance and difficulty of
travelling, between Rome and the east. In speaking of western
Europe, we may generally leave this bar to unity out of
consideration.

Then, even in western Christendom, the unity which existed
must not be thought of as meaning entire internal agreement in
the Church. It is true that of heresy, or independent thought,
there was very little. In the ninth century, an unfortunate
monk of the name of Gottschalk was cruelly scourged and
imprisoned, by order of the archbishop of Rheims, for advocating

the doctrine of predestination; and when in these centuries the doctrine of transubstantiation was first enunciated, it created some controversy, and Berengar got into trouble by denying it, and was forced to recant his denial. It must be added that in the year 1017, certain heretics, who (when manifest falsehoods are discarded) appear to have been men of much worth, but heretics beyond a doubt, were burned near Orleans by order of king Robert (son of Hugh Capet), after they had been condemned by a council of bishops[1]. I believe there are other similar instances; but, on the whole, dissensions within the Church at this period related to a quite different class of subjects—whether the clergy must necessarily be celibates; whether their appointment by lay persons (and especially by princes), and their subordination to princes, should be allowed; these were the questions which aroused strife in the tenth and eleventh centuries; and for an understanding of the way in which Christendom has developed, it is absolutely necessary to trace the course of these controversies. But before following out this sequence let me make some remarks illustrative of what I have said respecting the unity of the Church.

When we read of such an act as the burning of heretics, of which I have been giving an instance, or when we think of the minuteness and number of the restrictions which were imposed by the Church on Christians in those days, we are tempted to think that the bonds which knit the Church together must have been very formal and slavish, and that true inspiration must have been quite wanting to them. Formality and slavishness there were in the Church no doubt; but true inspiration was not wanting also. There was a just sense of the deep mystery, full of self-denial and love, surrounding the name of Jesus Christ; of the sustenance that our own life derived from that self-denial and that love, and its capacity to engender similar qualities in ourselves; and a feeling of greatness surrounded the whole subject, elevating the mind above the petty sorrows, the petty conflicts, of this life. The beauty and interest of life as we see it was indeed held of little value in those days; there was no union of men for purposes of literature or philosophy, of. art or science; we must content ourselves with very few indications of interest in these directions. There had been the intellectual John Erigena in the ninth century, and Gerbert, who studied in the schools of the Spanish Moors (and who afterwards became pope Sylvester II)

---

[1] See *Acta Conciliorum* (Paris, 1714), vol. VI. pp. 821–6.

at the end of the tenth; Charlemagne also and Alfred did their best to increase the knowledge of their respective subjects, and learned men, such as Alcuin and Asser, were in their courts. In the eleventh century, Anselm was an original, and yet an orthodox, theologian. Still no one can possibly say that intellectual merits were typically the merits for which the three centuries which ended in the year 1100 were notable. It is quite otherwise. But human affection, and a serious regard for duty (which are the seed-ground out of which the flowers and fruits of science and art have their nurture) did exist in those centuries, and were ingrained in the life of the Church; and it may be well for me to illustrate this in some degree.

Let me take my first instance from the life of a Saxon bishop, who survived the Norman conquest, dying in 1095 A.D., in the 87th year of his age—Wulstan, bishop of Worcester. Wulstan had submitted to the conqueror, feeling that his true work in the world could be carried on under a Norman, as it had been carried on under a Saxon, king; but he was no flatterer, and when he was called on to speak against Norman nobles and bishops, could do so with dignity and force. Here, then, is the narrative of one of his deeds; I quote it from *Lives of the English Saints,* vol. v. p. 41 (the writer of this particular life was the late Dean Church):

In the Norman court, however, Wulstan's voice was now become of weight. The king listened to him with respect, and his cooperation was used and valued by Lanfranc. A slave trade chiefly with Ireland had long been carried on at Bristol. The slaves were English peasants and domestic servants, the born thralls of the lords of the land, whom their owners found it convenient to get rid of. Among them were many women servants who had been debauched by their masters, and sold when pregnant. The trade was a profitable one both for the dealers and for King William's revenue. Lanfranc however and Wulstan resolved to attack it. With great difficulty, their united influence induced the king to relinquish his duties and declare against it. But King William's opposition was not the greatest obstacle they had to meet; it was easier to bring over the iron-hearted conqueror than the wild savage race of slave merchants who had been established at Bristol from time out of mind, and were not men to submit easily to any interference with their authorised and gainful traffic. "The love of God had little power with them," as little had the love or fear of King William. Wulstan however undertook the task of persuading them. He knew their fierce obstinacy; but he was a Saxon like themselves, and they might listen in time to their countrymen, and their own language. Accordingly he used to go down and stay among them for two or three months at a time, and every Sunday he preached to them in English. And he did destroy the slave trade at Bristol. He completely won the hearts and enthusiastic reverence of these wild people;

the trade was given up and proscribed; and when they found one of their
own number still determined to carry it on in spite of the Bishop, they
rose in fury upon him, and having turned him out of the city, they tore
out his eyes.

This last sentence will remind us that the society with which
Wulstan had to deal was barbarous, even in its best moods;
but Wulstan was not responsible for an act which, by whatever
sense of justice inspired, was certainly savage. On the main
question, could anyone have behaved more heroically, more
considerately, than he? Nor must we suppose that he was a
single or exceptional example; though it is necessarily rather by
chance that we meet with specific instances of evil overcome, it
is plain that a loving temperament was a natural and very common
accompaniment of the monastic career, and that it did overflow
into the world outside the monastery. Let anyone look at the
account which Guizot gives of chivalry, and of the oaths which were
exacted from knights at different periods from the eleventh to
the fourteenth century; let him bear in mind that the style and
purport of the engagements entered into must have been due to
the clergy; and he will be convinced that Christian teachers
had in all that time a lofty feeling as to the duties of man. The
first article to which the knights swore had reference to religion
and to Christianity; then follow the moral duties, of which I will
quote a few:

To serve their sovereign prince faithfully, and to fight for him and their
country most valorously;

To maintain the just right of the weak, such as of widows, orphans,
and maidens in a good quarrel, to expose themselves for them according
as necessity required, provided that it was not against their own honour,
or against their king or natural prince;

That they would never offend anyone maliciously, nor usurp the
possession of another, but rather that they would fight against those who
did so;

That avarice, recompense, gain or profit, should never oblige them
to do any action, but only glory and virtue;

That they would fight for the good and profit of the state;

That they would keep and obey the orders of their generals and captains
who had a right to command them;

That they would observe the honour, rank, and order of their companions, and that they would not encroach by pride or force upon any
of them;

* * * *

That they would be faithful observers of their word and pledged faith,
and that being taken prisoners in fair war, they would pay exactly the
promised ransom, or return to prison at the day and time agreed upon,

according to their promise, on pain of being declared infamous and
perjured;

That, returned to the court of their sovereign, they would give a true
account of their adventures, although it should be sometimes to their
disadvantage, to the king and to the master of their order, under pain of
being deprived of the order of chivalry;

That, above all things, they would be faithful, courteous, humble, and
would never fail in their word, for any ill or loss that might thence happen
to them. Guizot's *History of Civilisation*, translated by William Hazlitt,
vol. III. pp. 109–111.

A knight who observed all those promises faithfully and
unswervingly would be a singularly perfect specimen of humanity;
and perfection is rare. But to have the ideal of conduct such as
this before one is no slight gain to the character, and the Christian
Church must receive just honour for having inspired such rules;
they formed part of the increasing store of spiritual strength for
mankind.

But it is a theme yet more mingled good and ill on which
I must now enter. If the development of the Christian Church
was accompanied by increasing powers, as certainly was the
case, there were none the less sins committed, and mistakes
incurred, in the course of that development; and we have to
survey these, and trace their consequences, even as we trace the
progress of the good. I am not speaking chiefly now of the sins
of individual bad men; there were many such in the middle ages,
in consequence of the lawlessness of the times; but it was out
of apparent virtue, not out of manifest crimes, that the greatest
dangers and the most tragic issues had their rise. Faith and
self-denial, capable as they are of being the seed of infinite virtue,
are capable also, when their nature is misunderstood, of becoming
sources of very profound evil. How the first great error of the
Church, after the time of Charlemagne, arose, is not difficult to
understand.

The government of the western church by the popes had on
the whole been salutary. Some of the popes had been personally
distinguished; and even where this was not the case, the tacit
agreement of Christians (as far as the west of Europe is concerned)
to acknowledge the pope as the judge in disputed matters, which
lesser authorities had not availed to decide, was an agreement
which facilitated peaceable settlements of disputed points. In
wild and rough times, a speedy decision in controverted matters
may be more valuable than a decision more technically correct
but tardily arrived at; and for this reason, and also on account

of the value of a visible type of spiritual unity, we must recognise
the papal government of those early ages as having been really
beneficial to mankind.   But it must always be remembered
that a visible type of spiritual unity may be too dearly purchased;
and, in the same way, a speedy decision will be too dearly purchased
if the decision be very wrong.   The tendency of all governments,
if they be not subject to constant criticism, is to overrate their
own value.   Now this was precisely the error into which the
governing power of the Christian Church in western Europe had
fallen, in the ninth century of our era; and this error found very
precise and concrete expression, not long after the death of
Charlemagne.

   Just as the pious Jews, in the reign of king Josiah, in their
dismay at the idolatry and polytheism which they saw rampant
among their fellow-countrymen, wrote the document which formed
the first sketch of our present book of Deuteronomy to counteract
those false tendencies, so certain pious Christians, at the time
I have mentioned, seeing the growing disorder of the world,
thought to correct that disorder by a precise delineation of the
constitution of the Christian Church, with the pope at its head;
such a delineation as should compel submission by the authority
on which it was professedly based.   With this purpose in view
one of these pious Christians wrote or compiled a series of letters,
professedly the composition of very early bishops of Rome, from
Clement downwards.   I say, "wrote or compiled," for there
are large quotations from older writers in these documents.
But the concentrated purpose of these spurious Decretals, namely
to commend Church order, to commend the papal supremacy,
to protect ecclesiastics from accusations on the part of the laity,
is a purpose that does not in at all equal degree belong to the older
writers out of whom the borrowings are made.   It will be well
to give an instance of the way in which the ninth century
compiler (Isidorus Mercator he calls himself, and though this is
generally supposed to have been a nom de plume, I do not know
why it should not have been his real name) improves upon the
author whom he quotes.   The series of the spurious Decretals
begins with five letters alleged to have been written by the
famous Clement of Rome, in the first century of the Christian
era.   These five letters altogether are at least as long as the gospel
of Matthew; and about half their contents are a transcription,
slightly altered, of passages from those old Jewish-Christian
writings, called the *Clementine Homilies* and *Recognitions*, of

which the date is approximately 200 A.D. Take then the *Clementine Recognitions*, book VIII. chapter 4; these words are there found (I copy them from the translation by the Rev. Thomas Smith, D.D., contained in the " Ante-Nicene Christian Library," published by T. and T. Clark of Edinburgh):

Then Peter began to say: Those who speak the word of truth, and who enlighten the souls of men, seem to me to be like the rays of the sun, which, when once they have come forth and appeared to the world, can no longer be concealed or hidden, while they are not so much seen by men, as they afford sight to all. Therefore it was well said by One to the heralds of the truth, "Ye are the light of the world, and a city set upon a hill cannot be hid; neither do men light a candle and put it under a bushel, but upon a candlestick, that it may enlighten all who are in the house."

It will be seen that this passage is not in the least concerned with the Christian ministry, or with bishops; nor is the context in the Clementine Recognitions in the least concerned with ecclesiastical authority; the question being discussed is the very fundamental one, whether the world is governed by Divine Providence or by *genesis* (which is pretty much what we in these modern days call evolution). But now let me repeat my quotation of the passage just quoted, with its context as that appears in the spurious *Decretals* (in the *third* epistle attributed to Clement):

Moreover they who, walking in the paths of righteousness and of the divine precepts, willingly obey their teachers, who are rightly understood to be the bishops, obtain a gift from God of the highest value (summi muneris). Concerning whom the blessed Peter, our teacher and organiser, the chief of the apostles, plainly instructed all who heard him, saying: "*Those who speak the word of truth, and who enlighten the souls of men, seem to me to be like the rays of the sun, which, when once they have come forth and appeared to the world, can no longer be concealed or hidden, while they are not so much seen by men, as they afford sight to all. Therefore it was well said by* the Truth himself *to the heralds of the truth, Ye are the light of the world, and a city set upon a hill cannot be hid ; neither do men light a candle and put it under a bushel, but upon a candlestick, that it may enlighten all who are in the house.*" If therefore anyone shall be obedient to these, he offers (as has been said) a great gift to God. But he who shall oppose these, or shall be disobedient to them, opposes not them but our Lord and Saviour, whose ministry they discharge.

I have italicised the passage which is a real quotation from the Clementine Recognitions; and it will be seen how Isidorus Mercator gives it a turn which was by no means in the mind of the author of the Recognitions, so that it shall give support to the authority of *bishops*. Without denying that these two treatises, the Homilies and the Recognitions, give their sanction to episcopal authority (they do so when relating the ordination of Zacchæus as bishop, and also in the description of the ordination of Clement, now found in the Homilies alone), this is very far from being one of their principal themes. But Isidorus Mercator was no doubt tempted to make use of these treatises by the extreme predominance of the apostle Peter which appears in them; and though their author regarded the apostle Paul as an enemy, as a careful perusal of them shows, Isidorus Mercator was not likely to notice this, and did not notice it.

The supremacy of the pope is not directly affirmed in the five epistles that I have just been speaking of[1], but it is repeatedly mentioned in the spurious Decretals which follow, and it is generally assumed even where not explicitly mentioned. It may be well to quote one passage where it is affirmed, from the third letter attributed to Anacletus:

> But this sacrosanct Roman and Apostolic church has obtained its primacy not at the hands of apostles, but from our Lord himself, our Saviour, and has thus acquired the chief power over all churches and over the whole flock of Christian people, as he himself said to the blessed apostle Peter: "Thou art Peter, and on this rock I will build my church etc."

We must not think of Isidorus Mercator (if that be his real name) as a deliberate forger. He tells us (in the preface to his work) that no fewer than eighty bishops and other Christians had urged him to make a collection of canons (under which term he evidently included the Decretals or papal letters); and with the loose notions of history then prevalent, he gathered materials from all quarters available to him, connecting them together by explanatory matter of his own. His object was really the organisation of the Church; and while we cannot approve of his methods, we must not think too severely of him personally. In some things we may even sympathise with him where many of his contemporaries would not have done so; for instance, in his collection of Apostolical canons (the genuineness of which he admits to be not absolutely certain) he includes one which directs that bishops, priests, and deacons, if married, should not under pretext of religion send their wives away[2]. So again, he quotes from the Clementine Recognitions a passage which lays great stress on the duty of keeping the body clean;

---

[1] It is rather curious that it might appear to be *denied* in the heading to the first Clementine epistle (literally translated from the Homilies) where James the Lord's brother is affirmed to be bishop of bishops, and ruler not only of Jerusalem but of the churches everywhere.

[2] Dionysius Exiguus, at a much earlier date, had inserted what is practically the same direction in his collection of the Apostolical canons.

and declares that, where the flesh is not cleansed, the mind and heart cannot be pure[1].

It will be gathered that while these spurious Decretals do really affirm the papal supremacy over the whole Church in a very marked way, this was rather the interpretation which their author gave to the feeling of his own time (and as far as the western church was concerned, not a very wrong interpretation) than any conscious object on his part. It was a more conscious object of his to protect the clergy, and especially the bishops, from accusations on the part of the laity; and this did act in favour of the papal supremacy, in the days when popes and emperors came into conflict.

To advance the doctrine of papal supremacy had been the more deliberate object of another spurious production, which had preceded the Decretals by some three quarters of a century, the famous *Donation of Constantine*, a document professing to record the gift to the pope by the first Christian emperor, not only of supremacy over the Christian Church (which it was beyond the right of Constantine to give) but also of large territorial sovereignty, especially over Italy. This is the document to which Dante, in the 19th canto of the *Inferno*, refers with deep regret indeed, regarding the gift as noxious, but still not questioning its genuineness. It has long been known to be spurious; and there seems no doubt that it was forged at Rome, in the third quarter of the eighth century. Though in itself absolutely without historical ground, it was the reason of real donations to the pope (the exact limits of which, in the uncertainty of history, it is hard to know) made by both Pepin and Charlemagne[2]; and the temporal power of the popes had thus its origin.

Yet neither the imagined Donation of Constantine, nor the spurious Decretals, availed to save the papacy from a period of great weakness, in the latter part of the ninth and in the tenth centuries. I must not, in this brief sketch, give details of the history to which I am referring; it will be sufficient to say that after one eminently strong pope in the middle of the ninth century, Nicolas I (he intervened in the disputes at Constantinople about the patriarchate with rectitude and sound judgment), the personal character of the popes gradually declined; and simultaneously the restless character of the Roman nobles, and attacks on Italy

---

[1] See the fourth of the epistles attributed to Clement, towards the end. Mediæval Christians were not addicted to cleanliness.

[2] On this point the *Cambridge Mediæval History*, vol. II. pp. 587–8 and 597–600 may be consulted.

by the Saracens, produced the highest degree of confusion in Rome and in Italy. One of the greatest of German emperors, Otto the First, came down into Italy in the middle of the tenth century, and produced quiet for a time; but no real amendment came till the Normans, who early in the eleventh century had invaded Italy as foes, began, about the middle of that century, to show themselves real, cordial, and reverential supporters of the Papacy. And now, indeed, a change was at hand; we are approaching the era of Hildebrand.

Before entering upon the history with which that great name is associated, let me bring to mind some of the characteristics of the period which immediately preceded him.

The extraordinary wildness of the middle ages, especially before the year 1000 A.D., was caused not only by the natural propensity of strong men, but lately emerged from barbarism, to despise law and morality when opposed to their own inclinations; it also arose from there being real and serious doubt as to what the precepts of morality were. The doubt existed in many parts of practical conduct, but in none so much as in that which concerned the relations of the sexes. That relation is the subtlest part of human nature; nor is there any part of human nature which, in the complexities of life, brings the need of self-denial into such prominence. This indeed is far from being the sole thought which the relation of the sexes calls up into pure minds and warm hearts; faith and hope are deeply concerned with this relation; but the frequency with which the desires of mankind go wrong in this respect is plain, and that means that self-denial is here of great importance. Now the tendency of the Christian community, from very early times, had been to exalt the value of self-denial in this respect beyond the right bounds. If there are cases where self-denial is a necessary element of a man's future welfare and of the welfare of those around him, there are also times when self-denial is unnatural and harmful; and very often a minute knowledge of the particular case is necessary before we can decide a man's real duty in matters of this kind. Speaking generally however, the roughness of the work which an earnest Christian missionary had to undertake during the centuries from the fifth to the tenth inclusive, was such as to enhance the value and power of a celibate life very considerably; and though even so we may doubt whether *vows* of perpetual celibacy were desirable, we may honour in their degree the celibate monks and nuns, especially those who were

missionaries in heathen countries. It is much more doubtful
whether the parochial clergy ought to have been in any degree
expected to remain unmarried; and this was one of the points
on which the churches of the east and west quarrelled in the
year 867, when a council held at Constantinople denounced the
stringent requirement made in the western church. Yet that
the western church was itself not united on the question will
have been plain from the fact that Isidorus Mercator published
Apostolical canons in which bishops, priests, and deacons are
forbidden to send away their wives under the pretext of religion
(religionis prætextu). In truth, up to the time of Hildebrand,
the practice of the western church was ambiguous and uncertain;
the clergy had wives of whom they were ashamed, and whom
they more or less strove to conceal. Such a confusion in the
minds and habits of those who ought to have been the leaders
was not likely to encourage moral conduct in the Christian
community at large; and some reform was certainly needed.
Even in the monasteries there was laxity; and the reforms made
at Cluny in the tenth century, and by the institution of the
Cistercian order in the eleventh century, were efforts to make
the strict rule imposed by the founder of the Benedictine order
again operative.

Again, from another point of view there was a singular severity
as to the degree and kind of relationship which was held to make
marriage unlawful between the parties so related. That very
pious king Robert, son of Hugh Capet, whom I have already
mentioned as notable for being one of the first monarchs to preside
at the burning of heretics, had married his fourth cousin; and
he had also been godfather to one of her children by a former
marriage. On these grounds[1] the marriage was declared by pope
Gregory V to be incestuous, and king Robert was condemned to
seven years' penance, being of course obliged to dismiss his wife;
after which he married another wife, much more imperious and
less to his mind. His first marriage had been sanctioned by the
archbishop of Tours and other bishops; the difference of their
judgment from that of the pope proves the extraordinary chaos
in which the laws concerning marriage were at that date (998 A.D.).

Those who consider the points just mentioned will not doubt
that in one very important province of human conduct the
Christian Church at the beginning of the eleventh century did

[1] I must admit that I do not find the precise degree of consanguinity stated in
the *Acta Conciliorum*; I am relying for this on Milman's *History of Latin Christianity*,
vol. v. p. 24.

need a reforming hand; and this was also true in another matter of great consequence. It must be borne in mind that all through the centuries of which I am now speaking (I know not when precisely they ought to be considered to terminate) the clergy were almost the only literary persons; laymen were seldom fitted to act as secretaries. But secretaries and literary persons were needed by monarchs; and hence it was habitual for the clergy to be employed in civil offices, and especially were the higher clergy so employed. It followed as a natural consequence that the higher clergy were habitually appointed to their ecclesiastical offices by the monarchs who wished to employ them for civil purposes; and this happened the more because archbishops and bishops were persons of great consequence in a realm, and a monarch would gladly be sure that they were likely to be friendly to himself. Another consequence followed; the great offices of state were naturally much coveted, and those who sought them were not unwilling to pay money for the privilege of being appointed to them; which money the monarchs were in no wise unwilling to receive. But then the money so paid was paid not only for the appointment to a civil office, but also for the appointment to some bishopric or ecclesiastical office with which the civil duties were connected. Hence the transaction became liable to the formidable imputation of *simony*, or attempting to win the Spirit of God by the payment of money; and though the whole subject was viewed in those days in far too technical a manner (and often is so still), it may readily be admitted that an ecclesiastic who was also an official of the civil power would be in some danger of disregarding those religious duties which ought to have come first with him. Moreover, money was often paid for the office of bishop even where no secular duties were attached to the office. It was a symbol of the subordination in which the clergy, and especially the most distinguished among the clergy, stood towards the civil power, that laymen, and above all the monarchs of each realm, invested Church dignitaries with the ring and crosier which were symbols of their office[1]. The controversy which presently flamed up on this subject centred, as was perhaps natural, in this symbolic rite; but the real issues were of course much wider.

The two questions to which I have just been referring, the question of the right conditions of a true marriage, and especially

---

[1] I have drawn something of this historical statement from the clear account in A. J. Grant's *History of Europe*, pp. 264–5.

whether the clergy could rightly marry, and the question how
far the clergy could rightly pledge themselves to obedience to
the civil power, and do the work commanded them by the civil
power, were real questions which needed a solution, and so long
as a solution was not attained there was danger of a gradual
disintegration of society. This was discerned by the man who,
of all those between Charlemagne and Luther, possessed the most
dominant energy, Hildebrand—in his later years known as pope
Gregory the Seventh.

There is no man in all history—not even Ezra or Athanasius—
in relation to whom we have so much to remember the maxim
Humanum est errare—the interpretation of which is that the
cause of the errors of mankind is much more to be found in the
great complexity of human affairs than in individual selfishness
or blindness. And here it may be well to recall a saying of a
distinguished Scotch philosopher, Ferrier (whom I have mentioned
before in this present work). Ferrier is speaking of theoretical
rather than practical questions, but what he says is true of both.
The first result of contemplating a new topic of inquiry is a
confusion of mind, in which nothing is clear to the inquirer;
the next result, when the inquirer begins to determine his bearings
and arrange his outlines, is an erroneous and not a true determination, an arrangement that will not ultimately stand; and
it is only when the error is made plain by further experience
that those further determinations can be made, which slowly
bring out the perfect truth. This sequence is true in matters
of practice as well as in matters of theory, and Hildebrand is
a conspicuous instance of the second stage in the process—the
strong resolve which begins the work of bringing organisation
out of chaos, but which, as cannot be helped, makes many wrong
determinations; and yet which, none the less, has its value, and
prevents the worst of evils, the laxity of soul which drifts along
and surrenders itself as a prey to any external power that may
chance to seize upon it.

Hildebrand was born and educated in Rome, and trained in
the monastic life by an uncle who was an abbot; afterwards he
left Rome as the companion of that pope, Gregory VI, who by
a simoniacal transaction (not devoid of some excuse) had bought
the papacy, and then, confessing his guilt, had resigned it (not
without some compulsion) and retired to a monastery in Germany.
It must be taken for granted that Hildebrand approved of his
friend's resignation of his great office; yet, possibly from the

loyalty of friendship, he would not admit that Gregory VI had not been truly pope, and he made this plain in after years, when, being himself chosen pope, he took the title of the *seventh* Gregory, thereby making it impossible for any who came after him to destroy the title of the *sixth* Gregory as a true pope. Whether, after the death of Gregory VI, Hildebrand remained in Germany, or retired to the monastery of Cluny, where he had been in earlier days, is uncertain. However this may be, he returned to Rome in the year 1048 as the companion of pope Leo IX; and from that day onwards he was the trusted adviser of each succeeding pope, until he himself in the year 1073 was elected to that supreme station. He had not hastened his own advent to power; he had been content to serve under others; but now that he was in possession of a spiritual autocracy, he was the last man in the world not to use his power. Those great subjects, the marriage of the clergy, and the lay authority exercised over the clergy, came now necessarily under his direct notice; and it was impossible for him not to try to bring about their settlement.

But in both subjects he was in danger, without any insincerity or partiality on his own part, of going wrong. So long had it been the habit of the Christian Church to regard self-denial as a virtue in itself, quite apart from the reasons which in our experience render it so frequent a duty; so long, also, had it been the habit of the Christian Church to regard virginity (whether in man or woman) as a state of especial holiness, which the married state could not equal; so anxious had Gregory the Seventh been in all his early life to follow every call of duty, which in his mind was closely allied to obedience—that, when he sought for a corrective of the disorderly condition of the clergy as he saw them, such large numbers of them being connected with women by a tie that should have been marriage but was scarcely re-garded as such, he at once took the line which to him seemed obviously right, of putting an end, in so far as his power lay, to all those relations between the clergy and women which so few dared openly to defend. He would allow no married clergy at all; the rule, to him, was without exception. I must not say that even on his own showing he was altogether right. He had great authority, no doubt, on his side (that of pope Siricius was perhaps the most important that he could have alleged); but ought he not to have remembered that the famous council of Nicæa, while apparently disapproving of marriage on the part of one already in ecclesiastical orders, had refused to enforce the separation of one in orders from a wife whom he had already married? I do not think we can quite acquit Gregory VII of over-severity, even on those grounds of ecclesiastical discipline on which he himself relied.

But indeed we read of one bishop among his contemporaries, who openly adopted a more liberal, and (to our thinking) a juster line. This was Cunibert, bishop of Turin; concerning whom let me quote Neander (Torrey's translation, vol. VI. p. 150):

He gave all his clergy permission to marry, without doubt, on the principle, that by so doing he should preserve his own see from the immorality which prevailed in other portions of the church; for he himself led a strictly unmarried life; and Peter Damiani, the zealous advocate of the celibacy of the clergy, was forced to acknowledge, that the clergy of this church were markedly distinguished by the purity of their lives, and by their knowledge, from the clergy of other churches.

We may think, and certainly I do, that Cunibert was a wiser man than Hildebrand in this particular matter. Still we ought to remember that some change was really needed from the amorphous state of half-licence half-prohibition in which the clergy were placed before Hildebrand's time; and great as was the suffering occasioned by his imperious action (for the separation of the clergy from their wives, or half-wives, was amid great resistance actually though slowly carried out) the result was no doubt better than a continuance in a disapproved licence, which certainly was the worst possible example.

The other controversy which lay before Gregory VII was yet more famous, and also more complex. Perhaps I have not given quite a sufficient idea in the above remarks of the very great degree in which simony, or the purchase of bishoprics and other spiritual offices, now prevailed in the western church. For this nothing could be said; and Gregory set himself with all his power to correct the evil. But even more was he bent on delivering the clergy from the rule of the laity, and especially from the rule of those in royal station, above all from the rule of the emperor. There was truth in the feeling that the spiritual direction of men was a higher thing than the command over their material actions; and the clergy above all men were bound to remember that the authority to which they were ultimately responsible was heavenly and not earthly. Hence it was a matter of real importance from whom a bishop received his investiture, which consisted in the giving of a ring and a crosier. Moreover there was real danger that a bishop, when too much under the command of a monarch, might follow material and not spiritual ends; and lastly, when a monarch appointed a bishop, the insidious danger entered in, that the monarch might leave bishoprics long vacant, while he himself drew the payments which the bishop should have received; and this actually happened.

Great reform then was needed here too, as well as in the marriage relations of the clergy; but it was a reform that distinctly ought not to have been hurried. The questions at issue were complex and difficult; nor ought it to have been forgotten that the Church really owed a great deal of the reverence paid her, and many material advantages, to the intervention of the State in her favour. Whether a monarch were the proper person to appoint bishops might not unfairly be doubted; probably he was not so; but still the case in his favour might reasonably be argued and, from the intimate relations between Church and State, he might justly claim some voice in such an appointment. Even simony, or the direct purchase of bishoprics, though it could not be defended at all, yet from the very prevalence of the evil ought to have been treated with a cautious hand, and rather prevented in the future, than punished in the past.

But by Gregory the Seventh all considerations of caution were swept away; he treated simony as if it had been murder, and the investiture of bishops by temporal authorities as a crime of the deepest dye. Of persuasion and argument in such cases he would have nothing; excommunication of offenders was his weapon, and he used it on every occasion. Excommunication, it must be remembered, was a measure that struck real terror in those days, when it was believed that a person who died excommunicate went straight to hell.

Need I tell in detail that famous history, the quarrel of Gregory the Seventh with the emperor Henry IV? It is a history in which the leading features lie on the surface, and are indubitable, the absolute demand of Gregory that the emperor shall refrain from holding intercourse with excommunicated persons (some of these being among the emperor's most trusted counsellors); that he shall refrain from appointing bishops, and (as is implied) undo what he has done in this way; that was the beginning of the strife. It is generally believed (though Neander doubts it) that Gregory almost at the same time that he sent the letter conveying these requirements, sent also an embassy to Henry, summoning him to Rome the next Lent, there to give an account of himself, on penalty of excommunication. Whatever precisely happened, the wrath of Henry IV was aroused in the highest degree; summoning a council of his own, he declared Gregory deposed from his high office of pope. Yet he was not strong enough, in the disturbed state of affairs in Germany, to maintain his opposition to Gregory; and his own excommunication having as a matter of course followed upon his defiance, he crossed the Alps in midwinter, and made the most humble submission to Gregory at the castle of Canossa, where the pope was staying under the powerful protection of the countess Matilda of Tuscany. It is, I think, probable that, if Gregory had really, cordially, and fully trusted Henry at that moment, the quarrel would have ended. But it was perfectly evident that Gregory did not trust him; and that being so, it became almost impossible for Henry to fulfil what he had promised in the hour of his humiliation; his followers in the north of Italy (who were many) would not permit him to obey the pope. The quarrel broke out afresh; and though the German enemies of Henry appointed another emperor in the person of Rudolph of Swabia, yet when Rudolph was slain, the cause of Henry began to obtain the superiority; he descended into Italy not now as a suppliant, but as a conqueror; and though Gregory was defended, and successfully defended, by the Normans under Robert Guiscard, he found his defenders worse enemies to his cause than his nominal foes. For such extraordinary destruction, such conflagrations, were caused by the Normans in Rome, as neither Goth nor Vandal nor any enemy had caused before that time; and in this great disaster Gregory suffered his crowning calamity—he lost the affections of the Romans themselves. He had to retire to Salerno, and there died in the year 1085, having been twelve years pope.

Such was the end of Hildebrand's mortal career. I must say that, in spite of my profound sense that he was in error (and even more in error in his methods than in his specific aims) I find it impossible not to have regard and affection for him. His faith, his courage, were so very high, it is so clear that he never was animated in the least by selfish desires, his survey was so large, his general purpose so clear. Nor did he ever spare himself, or shrink from danger.

There can be no doubt that his greatest error, in his whole career, was—not the enforcing of humiliation on Henry IV at Canossa, but—the distrust in Henry which he continued to show after Canossa. He ought to have known that what Henry had done at Canossa to show his penitence—standing three days outside

the castle in the snow, waiting with tears for permission to enter—
was a trial of the keenest kind, altogether unexampled in history
at that time.   Had Hildebrand acknowledged it for what it was,
had he shown that he felt how true an example of humility the
emperor was exhibiting, had he embraced him, comforted him,
shown his trust in him, it is impossible to believe that the
tragedies of the years which followed would have occurred.
Hildebrand was not unfriendly to the emperor, but he would not
fully pardon him; Henry was to stand another trial, another
set of accusations, even after Canossa; and that was the last
straw of insult, which Henry and his friends found it impossible
to bear.   I do not call Hildebrand arrogant; but his sense of
duty was extravagant, and blinded him to those generous
considerations which ought always to accompany our sense of
human infirmity.   It is not necessary to maintain that Henry IV
would have been a perfect ruler if he had been fully forgiven at
Canossa; he might have broken his promises again, no doubt;
but the pope would have had a hold on his gratitude, and Henry,
with all his faults, was not a man who would have failed to
recognise that[1].

Let me mention a more pleasing side of Hildebrand's character,
and one which will serve to carry on the history in its natural
course.   If I say that Gregory VII was the first person who
appears to have had any such war as the crusades in his mind
as a future possibility, it may not, considering the disastrous
issue of the crusades and the great instances of wrong-doing
with which they were sullied, appear much in his favour; but
yet it is impossible to read without some emotion the letter
which, in the year 1074, in the days when he was yet friendly
with the emperor Henry IV, he wrote to that emperor, setting
forth the sufferings of the eastern church at Constantinople and
in Armenia, and asking for his counsel and help that assistance
may be rendered to them against the aggressive Mohammedans.
He knows that the people of Constantinople and of Armenia
differ from himself respecting the Holy Spirit; he thinks they
will listen to him as holding the place of the apostle Peter; but
his immediate request is that they shall be helped.   More than
fifty thousand soldiers, he writes, are ready to go on such an
expedition; they ask him, the pope, to go with them and be

---

[1] At this point it may be well to say that I regard the charges made against Henry
at a later date, at the two councils of Constance and Piacenza, as, under all the circumstances, unworthy of belief.

their leader (alike in warfare and in religion, it would seem—
"duce et pontifice" are his words); he expresses his willingness
to go, and hopes to reach the Lord's sepulchre. After enunciating
this project (somewhat amazing as far as his personal share in
it is concerned—and yet who knows that Hildebrand would not
have made an excellent general?) he continues with a sentence
which, in view of the after history, is pathetic:

But because a great affair needs great counsel and the help of great
men, if God permits me to begin the work, I ask counsel of thee, and,
if it seems good to thee, help; because if by the favour of God I shall go
thither, it is to thee, after God, that I leave the Roman church, that thou
mayest guard it as being thy holy mother, and defend its honour. Let
me know as speedily as possible what is thy mind on these matters, and
what thy prudence, through divine inspiration, shall decide.

The pope leading the armies of Christendom! The emperor,
in the pope's absence, faithfully guarding the Church! It was
a great conception. Alas, that the result should so ill have
answered to it.

What was the result of Hildebrand's reforming action? It
may appear that he was completely victorious in the matter of
the celibacy of the clergy; for that was more and more successfully
enforced after his day, and is now the unchallenged rule of the
Roman church. Yet can we doubt that a secret resistance to
this rule was one of the causes that promoted the Reformation
of the sixteenth century; and if so, Hildebrand's victory was
not altogether a victory? In the question of the investitures,
a reasonable compromise was arrived at (after the death of both
Hildebrand and Henry IV) at the Concordat of Worms, in the
year 1122. That was a happy event; but the dominating spirit
of Hildebrand produced greater consequences in after times than
any special result of his action, and consequences that we must
regret. One thing only remains to be said before I leave this
great man; the excess of despotism in him, not due (as I have
said) to personal arrogance, must be largely ascribed to his un-
questioning acceptance of the spurious Donation of Constantine
and the spurious Decretals. We are sure that Hildebrand
accepted the former document, because pope Leo IX relied on
it and quoted largely from it in his long letter to the patriarch
of Constantinople, and Hildebrand was at that time the pope's
most trusted adviser; and of the Decretals Hildebrand himself
makes use. It is true that, even apart from these untrustworthy
incitements, Hildebrand would have exalted the Roman church;
but not, it is probable, with the same degree of absolutism.

Ten years after the death of Hildebrand, the first crusade began, to be followed by other crusades in due course. This whole series of wars occupied the period of a century and three quarters, from the year 1095, when pope Urban II gave his official sanction to the ardent preaching of Peter the Hermit, and called upon the faithful to take arms for the recovery of the holy places from the infidels, down to the year 1270, when the saintly king Louis IX of France died in Tunis, in the course of a last effort to defeat and convert the Mohammedans in that quarter.

How, in brief space, am I to give an idea of the causes, the character, and the results of this long and stupendous conflict? The crusades were by no means the first, and by no means the last, of the warlike conflicts between Christendom and Islam; rather must we date the first beginning of such conflicts from the year 634, when Syria was lost by the emperor Heraclius to the invading Moslems; and the close of these conflicts was reached in the memorable year 1683, when the Turks were defeated before Vienna by the Polish king John Sobieski. But the crusades, which occupy the very centre of the long military conflicts between Christendom and Islam, are also the only portion of those conflicts when Christian religious zeal was at the height of its fervour; the Christian religion, as understood in mediæval times, was the inspiring spirit of the crusades, in a degree in which it was not the inspiring spirit either of Heraclius in the seventh century, or of John Sobieski in the seventeenth. The passion of religion which was in the preachers and warriors of the crusades deserves very special notice; but before entering on this point, there is another point of view from which they must be regarded, which is not without importance.

The crusades mark, not only the acme of a certain kind of religious zeal in Christendom, but also the consciousness in Christendom of a certain rising power, which had never been felt before, and never in the same way since. Never, except during the crusades, has Christendom been able to unite for external military achievements. It is true that the union was not perfect even during the crusades; the eastern church generally stood outside the movement (though far from being unaffected by it); but in western Christendom there was hardly an exception to the identity of sentiment, and to the consciousness of a new spring of internal force, at that time. We must not omit to take notice of this feeling of strength; and though the crusading armies were not so strong as Christians hoped they would be, the feeling was not quite unfounded.

But still more must we note the kind of religious sentiment in which the crusading armies had their unity. The exaltation of the person of Jesus Christ had long been held to be the central point of the Christian religion; and in the thoughts of the multitude it seemed a natural consequence that every place where the feet of Jesus Christ had trodden during his earthly life, especially Jerusalem, the city where he was crucified for our salvation, and the rockhewn tomb where his sacred body had once been laid, should be endowed with a supernatural sanctity. Pilgrims from Christian lands continually visited these places, and believed that their doing so was an act of true religious merit. Nor, till the eleventh century, had the Moslem rulers of Syria offered any hindrance to these pilgrimages. But in the eleventh century there were two periods during which Christians at Jerusalem were subject to violent ill-treatment—in the first quarter at the hands of Hakem, the fanatic Fatimite caliph, whose centre of government was in Egypt; during the last quarter through the Seljukian Turks, who had driven the Fatimites out of Syria. All Christendom thrilled with indignation at the dishonour done to its tenderest religious sentiments; and though at the beginning of the eleventh century it did not feel powerful enough to vindicate the natural rights of pilgrims in Syria, at the end of the eleventh century (mainly, we must think, through the strenuous character of Hildebrand) Christendom believed itself to have such power. Hence came the crusades; and it was believed that the Turks could be driven out of Syria.

That belief was erroneous; and the crusades, in so far as the military ends which it was intended that they should accomplish are concerned, were an entire failure. But did they deserve to succeed? I think not; and the point is one of too much import- ance not to be discussed here. It is true that the Christian Church had just ground of complaint against the Moslems of Syria in the eleventh century. It is true also that the defence of the Christian empire seated at Constantinople against the ever- encroaching Turks was a worthy aim. If the remedying of the evils implied in these two points had been steadily kept in view, and the proper means applied (including, in the last resort, warfare), we could have had nothing but sympathy with the crusaders. But such rational ends as these would have been thought by the actual crusaders a very small thing; nothing

less than the ejection of the infidel from the Holy Land (or at
any rate from all authority there) would satisfy them at all;
and for the Christian empire seated at Constantinople they had
no sympathy whatever, as their conduct showed. Further, the
cruelty of the Christians, in these wild attempts, exceeded that
of their enemies, the Turks.

Take the first crusade, the only one in which the Christian
armies had any real success, though after tremendous losses.
Jerusalem was really captured in this crusade, in the year 1099,
and was not only captured, but remained under Christian rule
for the greater part of a century. But of what nature was this
capture? Let me quote the brief description of the campaign
as given in Hallam's *Middle Ages*[1]:

> The Christian lances bore all before them in their shock from Nice
> to Antioch, Edessa, and Jerusalem. It was here, where their triumph
> was consummated, that it was stained with the most atrocious massacre;
> not limited to the hour of resistance, but renewed deliberately even after
> that famous penitential procession to the holy sepulchre, which might
> have calmed their ferocious dispositions, if, through the misguided
> enthusiasm of the enterprise, it had not been rather calculated to excite
> them.

Supposing it to be urged, as mitigating the censure implied
in such a passage, that all the wars of that time were barbarous
and bloody, that indeed is true; but in no ordinary war was
there any tendency to represent the barbarous and bloody acts
of warriors as a direct fulfilment of the will of God. There was
this tendency in the crusades.

Take the second crusade, the immediate motive for which lay
in the fact that Edessa and the parts around it, won by the
Christians in the first crusade, had been captured anew by the
Mohammedans. To recover these, Bernard of Clairvaux, a name
deeply to be respected for true piety and excellence, though
not without a share in the errors of his age, preached the second
crusade with ardour equal to that of Peter the Hermit in the
first crusade. The immediate consequence was a great massacre
of the Jews in Germany! It is true that Bernard, by great
efforts and true humanity, repressed the murderous assailants of
the Jews; but how deeply ingrained the persecuting impulse
was in the mind of Christians, may be seen by the fact that another
eminent Christian (really admirable, too, in his own way), Peter
of Cluny, while disapproving of the massacre of the Jews, yet
urges that they should be deprived of their property, which, he

[1] Vol. I. p. 36.

says, they had acquired unrighteously. The second crusade accomplished absolutely nothing in Palestine.

The third crusade, made picturesque and memorable by the valiant deeds of Richard I of England, yet failed in its object, which was the recovery of Jerusalem; for Saladin had captured Jerusalem for the Moslems in 1186. It must be added that this crusade was sullied by the massacre of 2700 Mohammedan prisoners after the capture of Acre.

The fourth crusade accomplished nothing but the capture of Constantinople, and the conflagration of a great part of that renowned city! More damage, it is said, was done on this occasion than on the capture of it by the Turks two centuries and a half later; nor did the Greek empire ever recover from this grievous blow. I am not indeed bringing forward this event as an instance of cruelty; but is it not clear that there must have been something wrong in the religion of the Christians of the west, when a war deliberately undertaken on their part for the advancement of their religion had its sole issue in their attacking, and permanently crippling, the Christians of the east?

The crusades that took place after that of which I have just spoken were too entirely unsuccessful to deserve notice (though everything connected with Louis IX of France must be interesting —but not necessarily in itself meritorious).

Let me try, after this brief survey, to put into a few words the moral lesson which the crusades teach us. It is this: that though the name of Jesus Christ will ever be dear to Christians; though he will ever be recognised as the founder of the divine order upon earth, the establisher of a firm basis upon which the hearts of men may rest, the institutor of eternal purposes, and our present ruler and guide; still it is useless and harmful to act as his partisans simply and solely; that the natural instincts of justice and mercy lie deeper in us than any details of the Christian history can possibly lie, though, when Christian history is rightly understood, the details of it do greatly illustrate the supreme value of justice and mercy.

To this may be added that, full of error though the crusades were, it was yet very difficult for the Christian Church in that age to escape some such error; and there were certain gains from them, in spite of their general ill success; not only the memory of brave deeds (which can never be valueless) but also the acquisition of much experience both in the external world and in human character, that had fruit in the generations afterwards. Whatever we may think of them, they were in the fullest sense the act of the Christian Church (the eastern church gave the first stimulus to them, though the realisation of them took place through the western church); the popular mind embraced them with enthusiasm, some of the most powerful popes and famous monarchs incited to them or took part in them; and a saint of the highest devotion, Bernard of Clairvaux, was by his preaching the main cause of the second crusade.

I have dated the close of the crusades at 1270 A.D.; but the period might be prolonged to 1291 A.D. when the fortress of Acre, the last Christian possession in western Asia, fell before the Mamelukes of Egypt; or indeed the period might be still further extended, if we take into account the Christian monarchs before whose mind such an enterprise flitted, of which an example is commemorated at the beginning of Shakespeare's play of *Henry IV*; but 1270 is the real end of the crusading period. Nearly two centuries and a half still separate us from the Reformation, which is the close of the present chapter; and much happened within the bounds of Christendom during that time. But the great movements inside Christendom which took place between 1100 and 1520 must receive attention in another chapter; I must briefly close the present chapter with an account of the great world movements during the thirteenth, fourteenth, and fifteenth centuries.

It was the Seljukian Turks who had repelled the third crusade towards the end of the twelfth century (the time when the most stubborn fighting between Christian and Moslem took place); before doing this, they had won Asia Minor from the Christians, and Egypt from the Fatimite caliphs. The Seljukian Turks had had some great warriors; the period of their power was during the eleventh and twelfth centuries; they had taken the place of the Arabs as the great Moslem power of the east, though an Arab caliph still nominally reigned at Baghdad. Under Saladin they had attained their greatest power; he was the most religious, the most civilised, and the bravest of them; he had died in the year 1193. But after Saladin the Seljukian Turks decayed; and early in the thirteenth century came down upon western Asia that tremendous onslaught of Jingis Khan and the Mongols of which I spoke at the beginning of this chapter. I say western Asia; but indeed the Mongol armies went eastwards as well as westwards; if Persia fell before them, so also did China. But western Asia concerns me here; as the Mongol flood slowly retreated, the Ottoman Turks came to the front. All through the fourteenth century the Ottoman Turks held Asia Minor; in the middle of that century they crossed over into Europe; before the end of that century they possessed Thrace, and the countries up to the river Danube. Then, at the beginning of the fifteenth century, there came a check upon them; but not through any Christian power. It was Timur, himself descended from a Mongol family, but a Moslem (as indeed all the western Mongols by this time were) who measured swords with the Turkish sultan Bajazet II, surnamed the "Lightning," and utterly overthrew him at Ancyra in Asia Minor. But Timur died not long after (need I enumerate his immense conquests, of which scarce a trace remained after him?) and the Ottoman Turks again recovered power; and in the year 1453 Constantinople fell before the arms of the sultan Mohammed II. Thus was Islam planted in the "New Rome," the city which Constantine had built eleven centuries before as the special home of that Christianity which he had made victorious over all the foes that he knew.

Islam triumphed in the east of Europe; but if this was in itself a great blow to Christendom, a compensation came not altogether unequal to the loss. For the Greek learning which had had its home in Constantinople now flowed westwards; and all through Christian Europe the thrill of a new knowledge, of a new intellectual power, flowed. But this must be part of the theme of my next chapter; it remains for me now to review some other parts of the great world (as it was then known) and to trace into whose hands they had fallen.

In the first place, then, though I have said that Islam triumphed in the east of Europe, this statement is subject to one important exception. I mentioned, at the beginning of this chapter, how the Mongols, early in the thirteenth century, conquered the east of Russia, and remained masters of this territory for two and a half centuries. The conquest took place under Batu, one of the grandsons of Jingis Khan; the recovery by the Christian inhabitants of Muscovy took place in the fifteenth century. The "Golden Horde" (as the Tartars in this part of the world were called) had at an early period become Moslems, like the Mongols generally after their great conquests; Christian priests and monks had no slight share in causing their expulsion. One of these monks was named Sergius; he lived towards the close of the fourteenth century, when the beginning of the Christian recovery took place in the victory of the Don. Of Sergius Dean Stanley writes thus:

When the heart of the Grand-Prince Demetrius failed in his advance against the Tartars, it was the remonstrance, the blessing, the prayers of Sergius that supported him to the field of battle on the Don, which gave him the cherished name of Demetrius of the Don. No historical picture or sculpture in Russia is more frequent than that which represents the youthful warrior receiving the benediction of the aged hermit. Two of his monks, Peresvet and Osliab, accompanied the Prince to the field, and fought in coats of mail drawn over their monastic habit; and the battle was begun by the single combat of Peresvet with a gigantic Tartar, champion of the Mussulman host. Stanley's *Eastern Church*, p. 402.

The battle of the Don was fought in 1380 A.D.; and the Sergius who animated the hearts of the Russians for that victory was not forgotten a century later. Let me continue my quotation from Dean Stanley:

The two chief convents in the suburbs of Moscow still preserve the recollection of that day. One is the vast fortress of the Donskoi monastery, under the Sparrow Hills. The other is the Simonoff monastery, founded by the nephew of Sergius on the banks of the Mosqua, on a beautiful spot chosen by the saint himself, and its earliest site was consecrated by the tomb which covers the bodies of his two warlike monks. From that day forth he stood out in the national recollections as the champion of Russia. It was still from his convent that the noblest patriotic inspirations were drawn, and, as he had led the way in giving the first great repulse to the Tartar power, so the final blow in like manner came from a successor in his place. When Ivan III wavered, as Demetrius had wavered before him, it was by the remonstrance of Archbishop Bassian, formerly Prior of the Trinity Convent, that Ivan too was driven, almost against his will, to the field. "Dost thou fear death?" so he was addressed by the aged prelate. "Thou too must die as well as others; death is the lot of all, man, beast, and bird alike; none can avoid it. Give these warriors into my hand, and, old as I am, I will not spare myself, nor turn my back upon the Tartars." The Metropolitan, we are told, added his exhortations to those of Bassian. Ivan returned to the camp, the Khan of the Golden Horde fled without a blow, and Russia was set free for ever.

This final victory took place in the year 1477. It is an event which must always be a matter of rejoicing to us; the Tartars, in that part of the world at any rate, were devoid of the seed of progress; the Christians, however imperfectly, had it. Not with such unalloyed pleasure can we look upon the Christian victory over the Moslems of Spain. There had been much true civilisation among the Moors; cultivation of the land had been carried by them to a high point of excellence; their cities were beautiful and stately. Their tolerance of other religions much

surpassed the tolerance of contemporary Christians. They had
their full share in that scientific and philosophical culture which
distinguished the early Mohammedans, concerning which, at the
beginning of this chapter, I quoted the testimony of Humboldt.
One of the monarchs of the Ommeyad line, Hakam, is said to
have accumulated 400,000 volumes in his library at Cordova;
he sought for rare manuscripts from every quarter of the
Mohammedan world. It is to be granted that these tokens of
human welfare were marred by that ingrained weakness of the
religion of Islam, the inability of its adherents to organise a stable
civil community; thus in the end they fell before the reviving
strength of Christian Spain. The battle of Las Navas, in the
year 1212, brought about the first downfall of the Moors; in the
next half century after that date they lost all Spain except
Granada. Then, in the year 1491, Granada fell before the arms
of Ferdinand and Isabella; and little by little the Moors, except
such as consented to accept baptism, were banished from Spain.
But when the desolations and slaughters which accompanied
this Christian victory are considered; when we remember that
the Spanish government which followed upon this victory was
the most intolerant, the most persecuting, that has ever been
seen in the world; is it pure joy that we can feel at such a victory?
Let me give one small instance of the contrast between the religion
which was defeated, and the religion which was victorious, as
these were displayed in Spain, by quoting two sentences from
Mr Stanley Lane-Poole's book, *The Moors in Spain*, pp. 135–6;
he is speaking of the magnificent city of Cordova:

> The whole city was full of noble buildings, among which were counted
> more than fifty thousand houses of the aristocracy and official classes,
> more than a hundred thousand dwellings for the common people, seven
> hundred mosques, and nine hundred public baths....When Spain had at
> last been restored to Christian rulers, Philip II, the husband of our English
> queen Mary, ordered the destruction of all public baths, on the ground
> that they were relics of infidelity.

It is a pity that king Philip did not pay more attention to
the spurious Decretals on the point in question! But the Spanish
Inquisition did worse things than hinder men from washing.
Christian Spain, however we may account for the fact, was the
country which plunged deepest into the errors that were common
to all Christendom; and while in the time of Ferdinand and
Isabella there was no small store of valour among the Spaniards,
it was a destructive and even suicidal valour, as was shown in

the generations that came afterwards. From that abyss Spain is recovering to-day; for which let us thank God fervently.

One more country let me name, as concerned in that great world conflict which is the theme of this chapter—India. From the eleventh century onwards, when Mahmud of Ghazni came down upon Afghanistan, the religion of Islam made its way into India slowly from the north-west. The great conqueror Timur penetrated as far as Delhi; but it was the descendant of Timur in the fifth degree, Baber, who first planted at Delhi a Mohammedan dynasty, that reigned over the whole north of India. Who shall describe Baber, that child of nature, delighting in battle, and it must be admitted shedding blood without stint, yet far from unenlightened in intellect and emotions, and tender-hearted towards those he loved? His religion at least saved him from superstition; and if his actions prove the inadequacy of Islam to be the world's religion (for indeed he had no thought of that divine peace in which the divine life is centred) yet there is much in his life which proves Islam to be not without a divine touch. Above all his death proves this; let me quote the account of it from *The Life of Baber, Emperor of Hindostan*, written by R. M. Caldecott in the year 1844 (the *Life* is in the main Baber's autobiography, but this passage of course is not so):

After he [Humaioon, son of Baber] had resided at Sambal for six months he fell into a dangerous illness, and in that state he was conveyed on the water by order of his father to Agra. All hope of his life was given up, when Abul Baka, a man venerated for his knowledge and piety, remarked to Baber that in such a case the Almighty had sometimes deigned to receive the most valuable possession of a man as a ransom for the life of his friend. Baber exclaimed that next to the life of Humaioon his own life was what he most valued, and that he would devote it as a sacrifice for his son. The noblemen around him entreated him to revoke the vow, and give the diamond obtained at Agra, reputed to be the most valuable on the earth, since ancient sages had said that it was the dearest of our earthly possessions that was to be dedicated to Heaven. But he declared that no jewel was equal in value to his life. He walked thrice round the body of the dying prince, a solemnity similar to that used in sacrifices and heave-offerings; then retiring he prayed earnestly to God, and after some time was heard to say, "I have borne it away, I have borne it away." The Moslem historians affirm that Humaioon immediately began to recover, and Baber proportionally to decline. Humaioon was young, and the expectation of death would accelerate the progress of disease in his father[1]. The last instructions of the Emperor were communicated to Khalifeh, Kamber Ali, and other Begs, commending Humaioon to their protection. He earnestly besought the Prince to be

[1] Baber had been in poor health for fifteen months before this.

kind to his brothers.　Humaioon promised to act as he desired, and kept his promise faithfully.　Baber expired at the Charbagh near Agra in the forty-eighth year of his age, on the 26th of December, 1530.　His body was conveyed in compliance with his desire to Cabul, where it was buried in the hill that bears his name.　The grave is marked by two upright pieces of white marble, and in front of it there is a small mosque in a simple and chaste style of architecture.　Near it are interred the remains of his wife and children.　All around there is a profusion of anemones and other flowers.

Such was the pathetic death of the first of the line of Mogul emperors of India.　Twenty years previously, the first Christian colony in India had been planted by the Portuguese at Goa.

CHAPTER XXIV

THE INWARD GROWTH OF MEDIÆVAL CHRISTENDOM

In the preceding chapter I have given a brief account of those immense struggles which took place over the whole of Asia and Europe, and over the north of Africa, during the seven centuries which followed the death of Charlemagne—struggles in which religious rivalry was the predominant feature. I have also touched upon some of the internal relations of Christian communities during the same period; but this last-named subject is very complex, and demands some further treatment, especially from the beginning of the twelfth century onwards.

The reader will perhaps have discerned from what has been already said that the most important difference between Christianity and Islam has lain in the far greater universality of the sense of duty[1], as governing all actions whatsoever, entertained by Christians, when compared with the sense of duty entertained by Mohammedans. If we say that Christianity is a true religion, this is the central point of its truth, but the truth of the universality of duty was liable to be turned to the disadvantage of mankind through a danger which is very obvious, and very difficult to avoid, namely that men may have wrong ideas as to where their duty lies. Such wrong ideas were in fact entertained by mediæval Christians, and for some centuries apparently placed the religion of Christ in an inferior position, as regards civilising power, to the religion of Mohammed. The real superiority, however, in the possession of the seeds of progress, always lay with Christianity; and this became manifest as time went on.

The first point, in the ordinary affairs of life, in which the merit of Christianity came out, was the serious way in which it encouraged legislation, with a view to just dealings between man and man. This was in great part an inheritance from the Roman empire, and thus had a non-Christian origin; but Christianity, in adopting the pagan legislation, did very much to expand it,

---

[1] I cannot doubt that duty, rather than love, was the most practical impulse in mediæval Christianity. Duty ought to be animated by love, but is not always consciously so animated.

soften it, and appropriate the spirit of it while ignoring the
letter.   In nothing is this more manifest than in the slow and
gradual way in which the Church discouraged slavery; not
definitely abolishing it, but humanising it, until at last slavery
disappeared of itself, as a spontaneous result of the better feelings
that had become natural in European countries.   That other
deleterious practice, the torture of witnesses in law-courts, was
not indeed lessened; but it may be noted that that excellent
pope of the ninth century, Nicolas I, in writing to the Bulgarians,
protested against it[1].   Moreover when we regard that notable
fact, the splitting up of the area of Christendom into different
countries, we shall see that the law-abiding instinct had much to
do with this.   Europe was too large for the same detailed system
of laws to be accepted in every part of it; yet detailed systems
were needed; and this could only be effected by the whole being
broken up into smaller portions, each having its own legislation
and its own characteristics.   On the other hand, the cruder
legislation of Islam was capable of being accepted over a very
large area, from its simplicity; and hence Islam, though always
under many rulers, has never been divided into countries as
definite as those into which Christendom has been divided; and
the loss to Islam has been considerable thereby.   Not that
division is in itself a source of power; but precision in conceptions
of justice is a source of power; and this is what Christendom
gained, and Islam did not gain.   Moreover wars were quite as
numerous and as serious between the different rulers in Islam as
between the different nations of Christendom.

Here, however, it will be well for me to sum up briefly what
has to be said about Islam as a whole, before coming to the main
subject of this chapter.   The chief flowering time of Islam came
to an end (though there were some later periods of distinction)
about the end of the twelfth century.   It was then that the
Arab race lost its predominance in Islam; a loss which it took
a long time to consummate, and which was not completed until
Baghdad was captured and ruined by the Mongols in 1258 A.D.
But in the region of thought we may say that the death of the
Arabian follower of Aristotle, Averroes, which took place in Spain
in 1198 A.D., marks the close of an era.   After the Arabs, over
nearly the whole of the east, the Turks became the great Mussulman power; the Seljukian Turks came before the fall of Baghdad,
the Ottoman Turks after that event.   Not very civilised, nor

---

[1] See Neander (Torrey's translation), vol. VI. pp. 56–7.

very civilising, have the Ottoman Turks been at any period of their history; but brave and simple-minded they have been, during many centuries a very formidable warlike power, and prone to deeds of blood. They have a poetical literature[1], but not such as implies great intellectual power.

Half Turk, half Mongol, was that dynasty of Moslem rulers in India, of whom Baber was the first, but Akbar the most famous; and Akbar had no small independence of mind. Literature was not neglected under these monarchs; and the buildings erected by them are among the glories of architecture.

It is singular, indeed, with all the ignorances, all the crimes of the Turks, what dignity they have been capable of showing. Among the most memorable sayings of men condemned to death was that of al-Kundurí ("generally known," Professor E. G. Browne tells us, "as the Amídu'l Mulk") the Prime Minister of the sultan Tughril; who, when Tughril died, unluckily supported the claims of Suleymán as his successor; Alp Arslán, brother of Suleymán and nephew of Tughril, won the crown and imprisoned al-Kundurí. After a year's captivity al-Kundurí learned that he was to be put to death; whereupon he sent this message to Alp Arslán:

Lo, a fortunate service hath your service been to me, for thy uncle gave me this world to rule over, whilst thou, giving me the martyr's portion, hast given me the other world; so by your service I have gained this world and that!

Could a man die more bravely? Alp Arslán and his victim were both Seljukian Turks.

Professor E. G. Browne, from whom I have culled the above anecdote, is also the writer[2] whom I must call as witness to the great compass and worth of the Mohammedan Persian literature. I have no right to speak on that subject; but Firdousi and Hafiz are famous names. Nor ought any notice of Islam, as it has existed in Persia, to omit mention of that saintly reformer surnamed the Bâb (that is, "the gate of Heaven") who in the middle of the nineteenth century died a martyr to his belief.

Lastly, amid all the disorders of the religion of Islam as it exists in Africa to-day, I believe it is true that it has a power of elevating the native races; and if so, Christian missionaries ought not to ignore so important a fact; and though they may claim

---

[1] For information as to this, the two learned volumes entitled *History of Ottoman Poetry*, by E. J. W. Gibbs, should be consulted.

[2] In his two volumes on *The Literary History of Persia*.

to transcend Islam, they ought not to look upon it as altogether a foe.

An impartial historian, who knew the history of the Mohammedan religion thoroughly, would be able to add instances of true worth in that history beyond those just noted, which I contribute out of a scanty knowledge; but an impartial historian will assuredly not find that Islam has been able to start mankind on the lines of permanent progress; and to Christianity, which has had that power, I now return.

It is western Christianity that is my main theme; but let me glance one moment at eastern Christianity, in the second quarter of the thirteenth century, when the Greek emperor, John Ducas Vatatzes, was reigning at Nicæa in Asia Minor, in rivalry with the Latin emperor whom the crusaders had established at Constantinople. Vatatzes was a ruler of no small ability, but he had a mistress for whose sake he neglected his true wife; and this mistress (a very powerful person) on one occasion paid a visit to a monastery, and proposed to partake of the communion there. But the abbot, whose name was Nicephorus Blemmydes, would not receive her, and shut the door in her face. The lady, in great anger, demanded of the emperor that he should punish the daring abbot; but Nicephorus, who could not but expect this result, anticipated her by issuing a circular explaining the reasons of his conduct, from which one sentence may be quoted:

"Though by this sudden and unexpected appearance," he wrote, "we were taken by surprise, yet we did not for a moment hesitate to drive away from the common prayer and song of the faithful, the adulteress, who, in an unheard-of manner, insults the laws of Christ and makes the insult a public one, and to banish with all our power the unholy from holy places; not without fear, indeed, owing to the weakness of the flesh, but overcoming the fear of man by the fear of the Lord, so that we would rather die than act contrary to his laws."

Plainer speaking cannot be conceived; and Vatatzes had sufficient rectitude to leave Nicephorus unharmed. It is evident from this that the eastern church, though naturally more under the sway of the civil power than the western church, was by no means altogether servile. The same is apparent from other incidents which took place about this time, and which may be read in Neander, from whom I have gathered the above anecdote[1]; and it is illustrated further by the steady resistance which the laity and lower clergy of the eastern church always made to any compromise of their conscience in the way of consenting to add

[1] In vol. VIII. p. 337 (Torrey's translation).

to their creed for the sake of obtaining support from the west against Islam. Some of the eastern emperors were willing to do this, but the great body of the laity and clergy steadily refused to do so. We may wish that the Christian commonalty in the east had shown more public spirit in the ordinary affairs of life than they did; circumstances were adverse to them here; yet even in this respect the instances which I gave in my last chapter of ecclesiastics in Russia taking the lead in expelling the Mongol invaders will show that the Christian Church in this quarter was not wholly lacking in firmness and manliness of spirit.

I come to the western church.

When I said that the first point of ordinary life in which the merit of the Christian religion was plainly disclosed, was its encouragement of laws such as bind communities together, I was not forgetful of those instances of general courage which had so often occurred in Christian history, or of the patient work of monks in tilling the ground and labouring for their own maintenance. But these were rather the seeds than the fruits of good; whereas a community that is strong through its enjoyment of good laws is pre-eminently entitled to be reckoned as evidence of the truth of the principles which have animated it. It is true that the phrase "good laws" is one of flexible import; the spirit in which laws are accepted and administered is as important as the laws themselves; and also laws which are good for a people in one stage of progress will cease to be good for a people in a more advanced stage. But while admitting these qualifications, we may still make the affirmation that the temper of the Christian nations of western Europe was growing stronger, and was finding more support in stable institutions, continually during the whole period between Charlemagne and the Reformation. Amid all the wars and disorders of these centuries, something was growing which elevated the spirit of men, and which had part at any rate of its expression in laws.

No country affords clearer evidence of growth, alike in public spirit and in legislative ability, than England in the thirteenth century. The ever-memorable Great Charter, signed reluctantly by king John in the year 1215, was the culmination of legislative attempts that had long been in process of formulation. Let me quote, as illustrative of this important subject, some sentences from Green's *History of the English People*. After remarking how the defeat of king John in France encouraged his subjects in England to resist his arbitrary conduct, Green adds:

The author of this great change was the new Archbishop whom Innocent had set on the throne of Canterbury. From the moment of his landing in England, Stephen Langton had assumed the constitutional position of the Primate as champion of the old English customs and law against the personal despotism of the kings. As Anselm had withstood William the Red, as Theobald had rescued England from the lawlessness of Stephen, so Langton prepared to withstand and rescue his country from the tyranny of John. At his first meeting with the King he called on him to swear to the observance of the laws of the Confessor, a phrase in which the whole of the national liberties were summed up. Churchman as he was, he protested against the royal homage to the Pope; and when John threatened vengeance on the barons for their refusal to sail with him to Poitou, Langton menaced him with excommunication if he assailed his subjects with any but due process of law. Far, however, from being satisfied with resistance such as this to isolated acts of tyranny, it was the Archbishop's aim to restore on a formal basis the older freedom of the realm. In a private meeting of the barons at S. Paul's he produced the Charter of Henry the First, and the enthusiasm with which it was welcomed showed the sagacity with which the Primate had chosen his ground for the coming struggle.

That is an important passage for it expresses clearly the fact that the spirit of law and of freedom—of freedom under the sanction of law—was no new thing in England in king John's time; that this had long been the aim of the leading persons in the country, and of the clergy as much as the laity; that in certain respects the clergy had even taken the lead in withstanding despotism. Emphatically does Magna Charta lay down the principle that a man's person and property, while amenable to lawful judgment, are not subject to any arbitrary power.

"No freeman," so runs this memorable vindication of liberty, "shall be seized, or imprisoned, or dispossessed, or outlawed, or in any way brought to ruin: we will not go against any man nor send against him, save by legal judgment of his peers or by law of the land. To no man will we sell, or deny, or delay, right or justice. No scutage or aid shall be imposed in our realm save by the common council of the realm[1]."

These principles, held as sovereign in practical affairs, are incompatible with absolute and irresponsible power in the monarch, and have been the fruitful germ of liberty in our country, and through our country have had an influence on the entire world. We may admit that Magna Charta is not perfect; it does not, for instance, take up the cause of the villeins at all; but the spirit which breathes in it goes further than its precise enactments, and is applicable to cases which it does not positively name. Something ought to be said about its first article, which guarantees the

---

[1] Some specified exceptions to this rule ought to be noted, but they do not alter its real and main tenor.

liberty of the English Church, and which must have been peculiarly due to archbishop Langton; we see that this liberty meant specially liberty of election, so that a chapter should elect its own bishop, and a monastery its own abbot. This had indeed been promised by king John in a charter issued seven months before Magna Charta[1], in which probably we may see Langton's influence; though Langton was not induced thereby (as probably the king hoped he would be) to dissociate himself from the barons. It is hard to deny that this first clause of Magna Charta is favourable to liberty; nor ought we to impute to Langton the secret meaning that bishops and abbots were to be appointed by the pope; though in the reign succeeding to that of John, this certainly often happened.

The age of king John in England has nothing to show in the region of the intellect which can bear the remotest comparison with the productions of Athens in the time of Pericles or of Rome in the time of Augustus. But where shall we find, in any era of ancient Greece or Rome, a document so full of practical political wisdom as Magna Charta; a document going so straight to the needs of ordinary men and women in their daily life, so free from partisanship, so permanent in the principles vindicated by it? Surely it is a document testifying to a new spirit in the world; a spirit not of knowledge, not of scientific curiosity, not of emotional expansiveness, but in the highest degree of justice and equanimity; and whether we look at the general tenor of Christian ethics, or at the names of the great ecclesiastics who stand first in the list of the king's advisers (given just before the actual Charter commences), or at the great part which Stephen Langton played in bringing about the ultimate result of the acceptance of the Charter by the king, can we doubt that in so great an achievement the Christian spirit was dominant?

I think it must be admitted that Magna Charta is in its main substance a Christian work; that the mere desire for liberty could not have created it, if that desire had not been supplemented by a feeling of discipline and duty, the obligatory nature of which had been inspired into men by Christian teaching. And we may even do honour in the matter to the powerful pope Innocent III (a tyrant in some respects but intellectually and practically great) whose action did so much to bring Magna Charta about, though with his imperfect knowledge he did in the end disapprove of it.

[1] See Stubbs, *Documents Illustrative of English History*, pp. 279–280.

Nearly half a century after Magna Charta, the first real parliament assembled in England; the first parliament which included members of the burgher class. This was a natural sequence of Magna Charta; and the statesman to whom it was chiefly due, Simon de Montfort, though he has been called ambitious, had no lack of Christian principle. He was the son of a terrible father, the destroyer of the Albigenses; but to himself no fanaticism is imputable.

Not for the best part of three centuries after the assembling of the first English Parliament did any fresh advance obviously and formally take place in the structure of English society; not, in fact, till the Reformation of the sixteenth century; which mighty event is beyond the bounds of the present chapter. During the greater part of the long period which I have named, the period between the year 1265 and the year 1530, war is unusually prominent in English history; war in Scotland first, in France afterwards, and lastly, both of these wars having been unsuccessful, the terrible civil wars of the Roses, by which the noble families of England were so largely destroyed. It must be said that during this period the errors rather than the virtues of Christian people were most prominent in England; we cannot refer to it as plainly showing the advantage of the Christian faith; and yet, so natural is it for the Christian spirit to progress in virtue and happiness, that I do not believe English people, for all the calamities that had befallen them, to have been less virtuous, less happy, in the year 1530 than they had been in the year 1265. These centuries must not be counted as among the decadent periods of history.

Some persons, indeed (if I may be allowed a little digression), may ask whether there have ever been any decadent periods in history? For an opinion is not unknown that progress is the invariable law of human society. But this will not be the opinion of those who consider ancient history, and even some parts of modern history. Did not Persia decline between the era of the first wars with Greece and the era of Alexander of Macedon? Did not Athens and Sparta decline between the fourth century and the first century before Christ, for though the Greek spirit was still throwing out blossoms in the first century, it was not with the old exuberance? Did not the Roman empire, taken as a whole, decline between the death of Marcus Aurelius and the fall of the western empire? And I believe that the Saxon kingdom in England, three quarters of a century after the death of Alfred, also showed symptoms of true decline. But real decline there

has not been in England at any time since the Norman conquest;
many calamities there have been, and now and then there have
been threatening symptoms; but there has always been sufficient
virtue in the nation to preserve it from decay. Thomas à Becket
was a tremendous reactionary; but his valour atoned for his
mistake. And coming to the time of which I am especially
now speaking, during the years between 1265 and 1530, we
find that Edward I, with all his warlike spirit, and occasional
cruelty (of which his expulsion of the Jews from England is not
the least notable instance) had yet in many respects a just and
fair mind, and the advantages which the nation had won in the
previous reigns were by him consolidated. Even those two
kings whose reigns were so largely occupied with the French war,
Edward III and Henry V, despite their injustice in waging war
against a nation that abhorred their rule, did yet keep in the
veins of their countrymen the salt of vital energy; and vital
energy the English nation had in no small degree through all these
centuries. But it was an energy which, in outward visible success,
had singularly little to show in comparison with the labour,
thought, and courage that were continually at work. It is true
that the towns became stronger as against the feudal lords, and
villeinage and serfdom died out during this period. But these
gains, important though they were, hardly strike the ordinary
reader of history at all; on the other hand the disastrous conflicts
which filled England after the terrible pestilence of the Black
Death in the year 1349 were, and are, unescapable to the eye of
the most casual inquirer.

It was the Black Death which, in its sequel, gave rise to those
premature but courageous efforts after civil and religious freedom
which we associate with the names of John Ball and Wat Tyler
in civil affairs, and with the Lollards in religion; the illustrious
Reformer, Wycliffe, having been an inspirer of the religious
movement especially, but also in part of the uprising in civil
matters. A few words must be given to that pestilence which I
have twice named, and which was so important an agency.
Can we be mistaken in saying that the Black Death was the
demonstration, on the most imposing scale and of the most
terrific sort, of the falsehood of that theory which was prevalent
in mediæval times, which associated dirt and sanctity? For
many centuries had cleanliness been ignored and despised in
Christendom; now, just when order was beginning to reign and
population to increase, came the angel of destruction from the

east, and swept away half the inhabitants of Europe in vindication of the duties which had not been performed, in reprobation of that vice which had posed as a virtue.   In England the result was shown in the sudden upstarting of social problems which in the ordinary course of events might have received a gradual and peaceful solution.   Where were the labourers to come from who should till the fields?   Thousands of them everywhere had departed to that bourne from whence no traveller returns; and those who remained, being for the most part free men, found their services more valuable than before, and demanded higher wages.   But Parliament, though in its birth the offspring of the spirit of freedom, was astonished and dismayed by so wide an extension of freedom as was now claimed, and joined with the king in the endeavour to suppress it, and to force labourers to work in the fields, and to work at the old wages. Then burst out the native spirit of Christianity, the Christianity of the poor, against the Christianity of long custom, which the rich had accepted, enduring its chains since it allowed them their riches.   Wycliffe, who up till then had been supported by the nobles (and especially by John of Gaunt), since his main task had appeared to be the liberation of the English nation from the papal power in temporal matters and from ultra-ecclesiasticism generally, was now repudiated by these same nobles when he was known as approving the spirit which animated the peasants, and still more when his doctrinal dissent from the Church became known; for in matters of doctrine the English laity had then little interest.   The immediate result was tragical.   Wycliffe himself died unharmed; but the two movements which owed so much to his teaching, the movement of the peasants and the movement of the Lollards, were quenched in fire and blood. Not yet could any general sympathy be given to the rhyme of John Ball (to which Hume himself is constrained to give some approval),

> When Adam delved and Eve span,
> Who was then the gentleman?

The age was not ripe for deep reform of any kind.   Yet, after all, these movements were not altogether futile.   Wycliffe's translation of the Bible remained, and helped reform at a later time; the Lollards were never quite trampled out; and even the rebel peasantry left their memorial behind them, and the twentieth century acknowledges some truth in the maxims which the fourteenth century enunciated.   It was at this time, too, that

English literature begins with the genial Chaucer and the mournful William Longland (author of *The Complaint of Piers the Plough-man*)[1].

The man who was almost capable, and yet not capable, of bringing those difficult times of which I have been treating to a happy issue, was that king little noted save for his misfortunes by the ordinary reader of history, Richard II. He was a king who had a truly generous feeling for his people; but towards his personal opponents he had not equal generosity; hence he failed, was dethroned, and murdered. Then came the last French war, with its brilliant beginning at Agincourt and its disastrous ending after the death of Henry V; and then the nobles of England annihilated one another in the wars of the Roses. Christianity had been very vital in England during the whole period from the twelfth century to the fifteenth, but it had become divided against itself in the way that I have described; and after the reign of Edward I the fruits of it do not appear obviously on the surface of things. The works of architecture however produced during this period should be mentioned as singularly beautiful; and amid all the injustices of statesmen, and the wickednesses of warriors, it is hardly possible not to recognise the cessation of villeinage as a result of the Christian spirit. The evil was remediable; the good remained as a permanent possession.

Not equally with England, but still in certain ways very remarkably, was France being organised in a way to produce greater efficiency and general power, during the centuries from the twelfth to the fifteenth inclusive; and it is impossible not to recognise Christianity at work in producing this change, though the exact method of its operation is not always easy to trace. The great country which we now call France, and of which the boundaries northward, westward, southward, appear fixed by nature (not equally towards the east), was then broken up into many parts under different governments; and the instinct of the inhabitants of the whole was towards union, towards unity. Liberty, in a certain sense, might be desired by the French of this period; both the municipality of Paris and the country peasants after the battle of Poitiers, rebelled against the taxation which weighed so heavily upon them; and a similar rebellion occurred after the death of Charles V in 1380. But these were isolated outbreaks; no help came to them from the nobility; no

---

[1] The reader of Green's *Short History of the English People* will perceive how much, in these remarks, I have been indebted to that work.

tradition of the past, adverse to despotism, supported them; the Church gave them no recognition. Hence it was that liberty, slowly but surely, was suppressed in France, all through mediæval times. The desire for it was not strong enough to be effective. On the other hand, the desire for union, among provinces speaking the French language, was natural and spontaneous, and realised itself in spite of many obstacles. Thus when the saintly king Louis IX, having but an imperfect perception of the rights of ordinary men, and an over-keen anxiety to establish friendship with king Henry III of England, surrendered Limousin, Perigord, and other provinces to that monarch, his act in so doing excited much displeasure among the people surrendered; and Guizot tells us[1]:

We read in a manuscript chronicle of the time of Charles VI with regard to this treaty of 1259 between Louis IX and Henry III:

"At which peace the Perigordians and their neighbours were so indignant, that they never liked the king afterwards, and for that reason, even to the present day in the borders of Perigord, Quercy, and other places, although Saint Louis is canonized by the church, they regard him not as a saint, and do not keep his festival as is done in other parts of France."

Is it not plain that the Perigordians felt that they were French and not English? As to Louis IX, we must honour his spirit of equity and conciliation, while at the same time we regret that he lacked that granum salis, that circumspect caution, by which the spirit of self-sacrifice ought always to be tempered. But as to the Perigordians: it is true that if they had lived in ancient, pre-Christian times, they might have objected to having a foreign king put over them, just as they did in the reign of Louis IX, in the thirteenth century of our era; but any one who considers the animus of the passage just quoted will see that there underlies it the feeling, not only that the Perigordians were not English, but that they were positively French; that a link joined them with other Frenchmen, which they could not suffer to be broken without great reluctance. It may be said perhaps that the Greeks, the Hellenes, of the time of Socrates felt the link of a common nationality. In certain respects they did so; but neither Athens, nor Sparta, nor Thebes, nor any famous Greek city, was willing to consider its own honour and reputation as of lesser importance than the honour and reputation of Greece, of Hellas, as a whole. Now the French generally, in the thirteenth century of our era, and still more in the fourteenth and fifteenth

[1] *History of Civilisation* (translated by William Hazlitt), vol. IV. p. 245.

centuries did subordinate themselves to France; I do not mean of course that there were not many and serious exceptions to this; but the sentiment of a common nationality was effective in them, and was the main cause why they did not succumb to the English invasions which pressed so very hardly on them. Indeed the strength of this sentiment is the chief reason why they were so little solicitous about defending their liberty; in their determination not to be subdued by English kings, they were obliged to run the risk of being despotically governed by their own king. Their subservience in this latter direction was not due to want of manhood.

Thus it was that loyalty and patriotism were intimately combined in the French of the fourteenth and fifteenth centuries; and in no person was this more signally displayed, and in none more manifestly connected with the Christian spirit, than in that inspired deliverer by whom France was finally rescued from formidable perils—Jeanne d'Arc. For who shall doubt that Jeanne d'Arc was inspired? Whatever precisely we may think of her visions, the simplicity and goodness of her purpose is the guarantee to us of the divine impulse which actuated her. That the true king of France should be crowned king at Rheims; that the English armies should go out of France back to their own country; these were the great and simple purposes which possessed her soul, and she accomplished them. For though she did not in this life see their full accomplishment, they were accomplished, and through her. Why should we not accept what is so legibly written on the pages of history? It is not to be supposed that the French soldiers were saints; but they had the capacity of catching the fire which the Maid, who was a saint, communicated to them; and thus was the victory won. Her last words, when burned at the stake, were to call on God, on the saints (and she named the saints who, in her belief at all events, had been her companions), and on Jesus; and such exclamations are not to be forgotten, when we ask ourselves what is the true force of Christianity. Nor have we any reason whatever to say that Jeanne d'Arc hated those against whom she fought; her patriotism was pure.

England and France were the two countries of the middle ages in which patriotism was most unmistakably shown, whatever deductions we may make by reason of the frequent selfishness of individuals and of parties. In Germany and Italy there were hindrances to the patriotic spirit, and through similar causes:

the emperor neglected Germany; the pope set himself against the unity of Italy.

Why did the emperor neglect Germany? Because he thought that he had a greater sphere than Germany to rule over. That was the tradition of the old Roman empire; it had been revived by Charlemagne; and though it might have been laid aside when Charlemagne's empire was broken up, so great a tradition was not easily abandoned. We must not greatly blame Otto, the emperor who had conquered the Magyars, because in the tenth century he persevered with the traditional task of ruling Italy as well as Germany. That he would have done better to confine himself to Germany, we must on the whole think; though the question, under all the circumstances of that turbulent time, is debatable.

Why did the pope set himself against the unity of Italy? Because the pope claimed for himself the civil rule over a certain district of Italy; but he was aware of his own inability to rule in civil matters over the whole of Italy; and the consequence was that in civil rule Italy must be divided.

Thus, though patriotism of a kind was possible both in Germany and Italy in mediæval times, it was an imperfect patriotism, like the Hellenism of old among the Greeks; it did not attain to the full scope of the patriotism of England or of France. The great cities, separately speaking, were the subject of patriotic feeling to their respective inhabitants; and a larger patriotism was sometimes evoked, though fitfully and uncertainly. Even, however, in that narrower patriotism which has a city rather than a country for its theme and motive, there is value; and the German bishops had a great share in nourishing the early city life in Germany, and making it expansive through the influences of trade and commerce. Let me quote, as illustrative of this point, a paragraph from Henry Sidgwick's *Development of European Polity* (p. 246):

Partly through the policy of the Frankish monarchs (i.e. the successors of Charlemagne in Germany), partly through the influence of religion on their minds and those of other wealthy landowners, remarkably large tracts of land came—through royal grant, through gift or bequest, sometimes through the surrender of small landowners seeking the protection of the Church in troubled times—to be held by bishops and abbots, who thus entered into the feudal system, and became co-ordinate with the great lay-feudatories; their military tenants being bound to obey the king's summons to military service, as much as any vassals of lay lords. But though thus semi-feudalised, the Church did not strip off its distinctive character; and through the special effectiveness of the protection that its

religious influence enabled it to give, it took the lead in fostering the growth
of cities.   This was a part of its general civilising work in the regions
beyond the Rhine and the Alps.

It must be remembered that trade and commerce, on a large
scale, were fostered by cities in a degree in which they could not
be fostered by the scattered inhabitants of rural districts; so
that the work of the Church in rendering city life possible and
energetic was one of the cardinal points in the development of
modern civilisation.   It is true that this alliance between the
religious spirit and the commercial spirit was exposed to those
dangers to which every human alliance must be subject, and did
not always maintain itself; but the beginnings of commerce,
as of every kind of fruitful energy, are more in need of help
than any of its subsequent developments; and we must
not think lightly of the aid which the Church gave in this
critical time.   Moreover in Germany, as elsewhere, the influence of the Church was always directed to the diminution of
serfdom.   The powerful Hanseatic league, consisting of the chief
cities of north Germany, which attained its culmination early in
the fifteenth century, must not be left unnoticed; but it did not
as a league owe anything to the Church (as far as I am aware).

In Germany, as in France and England, the civilising effect of
Christianity as regards the ordinary relations of men with each
other cannot be doubted through all the period with which this
chapter is concerned.   In Italy this is not so obvious; but here
indeed there meets us a singular and wonderful spectacle.   On
the one hand, throughout the twelfth, thirteenth, fourteenth, and
fifteenth centuries, we find in all Italy north of Rome (and partly
even south of Rome) such varied life, intellectual energy, and in
the case of one famous city even political wisdom, as has seldom
been seen in any country; and moreover religious affections were
strong in the people, as is shown us by many evidences.   Yet that
which is the natural fruit of true religion—unity of sentiment,
purpose, resolve—was never more absent from any country than
it was from Italy during this period.   How are we to explain this
contrast?

I think we must say that the moral instinct, in its application
to politics, was less pronounced among the Italians of that day
than it was among Englishmen, Frenchmen, or Germans.   The
time when it was most nearly being evoked on a large scale was
when the Lombard cities united against the despotic emperor
Frederic Barbarossa, and defeated him in the battle of Legnano,

1176 A.D.   Had the value of the principle of union been recognised
by the cities which won that victory, had they found a permanent
defence in the spirit which gave them victory, then they would
have discerned a value in religion as aiding and strengthening
their union, and Italy would have had a far happier history than
she had in the ages which followed.   The internal dissensions of
the Italian cities prevented this; and it is impossible to deny the
tragedy of the result[1].   Moreover, even the merits of the Italians,
their artistic and intellectual powers, were probably a difficulty
in the way of their attaining political unity, for these merits
allured the Italian mind away from duties which we cannot but
consider more urgent.   Still, having allowed all this, having
allowed, that is, a certain deflection from rectitude in the Italian
mind as known to us in mediæval times, let us not fail to recognise
how much there was of value in the outcome, all deductions
having been made, and how much that could not have been
produced without the inspiration of religion.

I have already observed that there was one city in which even
political wisdom was memorably shown; that city was, I need
not say, Venice.   It is a matter of course that not all the acts of
the Venetian republic were wise or good; the frailty of man does
not permit this in a career so long as that of Venice.   To-day
Venice is a part of the Italian kingdom, and shares in the prosperity
of that kingdom.   But I am speaking of the days when Venice
stood by herself, a single imperial city.   The true Venice, the
Venice of the Rialto, began in the days of Charlemagne, early in
the ninth century; and in the hour of her birth she was too
strong for the assaults of Pepin, the masterful son of Charlemagne.
Then, after long stability of government, towards the end of the
sixteenth century, Venice took a chief part in defeating the
Turkish navy at Lepanto; and at the beginning of the seventeenth
century, that man of genius, Fra Paolo Sarpi, beneath her
sheltering guard, defied the despotic pope.   If Venice declined
after that, as she did in the seventeenth and eighteenth centuries,
yet eight centuries of signal power, broken by no overwhelming
calamity, constitute a splendour which few cities have rivalled;
and surely it must be confessed that her rulers were wise.

> Once did she hold the gorgeous East in fee;
> And was the safeguard of the west; the worth
> Of Venice did not fall below her birth,
> Venice, the eldest child of liberty.

So sang Wordsworth, and truly.

[1] See, on this subject, Hallam's *Middle Ages*, vol. I. pp. 373–377.

To have wise rulers was not the lot of Italian cities in general; but the tokens of genius are everywhere. "The love of equal liberty and just laws in the Italian cities," writes Hallam[1], "rendered the profession of jurisprudence exceedingly honourable"; and Italians were the first in modern times to comment on and explain the laws of Justinian. To Italians, more than to any other nation, we owe the revival of classical learning in the fifteenth century; and who shall say if, without this, the intellect of modern Europe would have had the brilliant success which it has attained? It may be thought that, in saying this, I am wandering away from the subject of religion; but if there had been no religion in the Italian soul, should we have had all these fruits of the intellect? I think not; for intellect receives its stimulus from the overflowings of the spirit; and the spirit, as it means freedom, so also means divine love. If other countries won political unity in those days, Italy won a unity of aspiration, of which we must not underrate the value.

Spain, it is not to be denied, is the disappointing country, when the value of mediæval religion is under consideration (I am speaking, of course, of Christian countries). Strength there was in Spain, and piety, and genius too; but the fatal canker of intolerant cruelty here, and here alone, was stronger for corruption than the vital forces were for creation. At least, so it was for two or three centuries. Some of the smaller countries such as Switzerland and the Netherlands, deserve, though for different reasons, singular respect.

So far in this chapter I have chiefly been dealing with the way in which civil government progressed in Europe in mediæval times, and I have tried to show that the general operation of Christian faith was towards stability and freedom in civil affairs, in a degree in which no other religion has been so. But human affairs comprise a great deal besides formal government, and something must be said of the operation of the Christian faith in these less formal ways. I have already remarked on the double operation of the Christian Church in regard to intellectual pursuits; how, on the one hand, any exercise of the intellect that had the smallest sign of differing from decisions of the Church was sternly and cruelly suppressed; and yet how, on the other hand, the natural bias of Christianity towards peace and freedom did manage to penetrate through all obstructions, and gradually laid foundations out of which genuine science might spring. Popes

[1] *Literature of Europe*, vol. I. p. 62.

were sometimes enlightened students and patrons of knowledge; as for instance Gerbert (Sylvester II) about 1000 A.D. and in the fifteenth century the singularly humane, learned, and munificent Nicolas V. The beauties and delights of this earthly abode of ours were sometimes valued. We are acquainted with the fruit-trees, herbs, and flowers, grown in the garden of Charlemagne[1]; so that Charlemagne must have taken an interest in such matters; and certainly he was a man who valued learning and knowledge. So did king Alfred value them. These were men who, by natural strength of soul, anticipated the era that was to dawn some three centuries later. Not that the Christians of the ninth century were asleep, but their eyes were dim; their hearts had been touched by truth, but were still struggling with ancient error; so that some of the faculties which had enlightened men in heathen days were actually quenched now. Happily the records of heathen times had been in part preserved, and the flame of knowledge latent in them was capable of being rekindled; the more so as Islam had preserved some knowledge of their true meaning and force, before Christendom had learnt to value them.

Even in the darkest times, the region of art was not wholly barren; buildings of some architectural dignity were built, and frescoes were painted on the walls of Roman churches; and histories were written, in which the abundant presence of legend was co-existent with some real truth. Religious poetry also was not quite dead. In intellectual regions, John Erigena had done something to pierce the darkness of the ninth century, and Anselm of the eleventh.

But in the twelfth century, a more daring strain of thought originated with Abelard; and this was an event of real note. Bernard of Clairvaux was said to have refuted Abelard; I suspect that what he really did, was to frighten him; for Abelard appealed to the judgment of the pope. Such an appeal would have been out of place had mere intellectual argument alone been concerned; but Abelard wished to be sure that he was not incurring the danger of imputed heresy. Abelard had some indirect knowledge of the Socratic school of philosophy, and even quoted[2] from Aristotle to show the value of doubt as a step towards exact knowledge; perhaps the earliest instance, in mediæval writers, of direct reference to this philosopher; and a noteworthy piece of philosophy for a mediæval theologian to have accepted! In all that I have

---

[1] See Miall's *Early Naturalists, their lives and work*, p. 8.
[2] See Neander's *Church History* (Torrey's translation), vol. VIII. p. 135.

read about Abelard, I have felt the presence of a vigorous inquiring
spirit; but he did not step beyond the bounds of theology.

That enthusiasm of the intellect, which Abelard had kindled
in the first half of the twelfth century, advanced to higher power
in the thirteenth; and from that time onwards we see Christendom
recovering from the darkness into which it had sunk after the
barbarian invasions, and slowly overcoming a worse foe than
barbarism, the scrutinising suspicion drawn from religious fear.
Not that the thirteenth century was irreligious; far from it.
Consider Albertus Magnus, that earliest of German philosophers,
born in the year 1193, and living till November 1280; what can
be more religious, and yet more truly original, than the following
passage, in which the idea of creation is brought into close
connexion with that phenomenon of growth which we see
daily[1]?

As in nature, it is the same power which brings forth a formative
principle in the seed, produces from the seed, and guides that which is
produced, in its development, by extending its influence to each member
in particular, and at the same time communicates to the entire product
a quality and character, by virtue of which each individual member is
conducted onward to its proper destination, and each finds its right place
in the order of the whole; so in the Creator of the whole world, the power
is the same by which he created the world, and by which he continues
to work in each individual thing, and in the organism of the whole—
appointing to each its proper place and guiding the development of all
the individuals in the connected system, so that every individual maintains
its proper position in the order of the whole.

Is not that precisely the position which religious persons in
recent times have felt themselves obliged to accept through the
discoveries of physical science—the position that creation is no
single act, or limited series of acts, but a perpetual divine process;
the treasures of life and of reality being brought out one by one
from their secret sources, through an operation which we can
feel and apprehend, but not understand in its entirety? Is it
not something to know that this kind of view was held by a
mediæval philosopher, in an age when physical science was quite in
the background; so that we may know that this kind of view
is not now forced on religious persons by the exigencies of the
present time, but has always been natural to them?

I come to Roger Bacon, born in 1214, dying in 1294, the
first propounder, in modern times, of the philosophy of experience.
Let me quote from Hallam's *Middle Ages*[2] the following lucid

---

[1] I quote this passage from Neander, vol. VIII. p. 250.
[2] Vol. III. p. 431.

passage in the *Opus Majus*; Hallam gives the original Latin,
but I take the liberty of translating it into English:

There are two modes of getting knowledge (cognoscendi); by argument
namely and by experiment.   Argument decides, and makes us decide, a
question; but it does not certify the answer or remove doubt, so that the
mind may rest in the intuition of truth, unless it finds truth by way of
experience; because many men have arguments directed to knowable
things, but neglect them because they have not experience, and so neither
avoid what is hurtful nor pursue what is good.   For if any man who had
never seen fire, proved by argument that fire burns and injures and destroys,
yet would the mind of his hearer never acquiesce in what he alleged, or
avoid fire, until he applied his hand or some combustible thing to the
fire, so as to prove by experience what his argument taught; but when
he has gained experience of burning, his mind is assured of it and rests in
the light of truth, to which end argument is not sufficient, but experience
alone.

My own knowledge of Roger Bacon, as of Albertus Magnus, is
entirely second-hand; yet I trust that even at second-hand one
may have true admiration for noble thoughts.   The following
passage from Hallam, on the same page with the quotation just
made, is worth quoting:

The knowledge displayed by Roger Bacon and by Albertus Magnus,
even in the mixed mathematics, under every disadvantage from the
imperfection of instruments, and the want of recorded experience, are
sufficient to inspire us with regret that their contemporaries were more
inclined to astonishment than to emulation.

And in Whewell's *History of the Inductive Sciences*, vol. II.
p. 377, I find the following:

The principle that a ray refracted in glass is turned towards the
perpendicular, without knowing the exact law of refraction, enabled
mathematicians to trace the effects of transparent bodies in various
cases.   Thus in Roger Bacon's works we find a tolerably distinct explanation of the effect of a convex glass; and in the work of Vitello the effect
of refraction at the two surfaces of a glass globe is clearly traced.

Vitello was a Pole, living in the same century as Roger
Bacon; let his name not be forgotten, as one in whom the spark
of incipient knowledge is found; but it is of Roger Bacon that I
am now mainly speaking.   He has been accused by some of
superstition; but from superstitious fear he was, it is clear,
singularly free; he may perhaps be chargeable with an excess of
imagination.   No one was more emphatic than he in denouncing
too great dependence on authority, and in advocating free inquiry;
he desired that the laity should read the Scriptures for themselves;
he desired also that students should study them in the original
languages, and not rest satisfied with the Vulgate version.   So

bold a spirit frightened the Franciscan friars (for into the Franciscan order Roger Bacon had entered by the advice of his learned patron, Robert Grostête, bishop of Lincoln) and they imprisoned him for many years in a cell; the influence of powerful friends at last set him free.   Thus he was a confessor for truth, although not actually a martyr; but it shows what discordant elements permeated the Church in that day, that he composed his Opus Majus actually on the invitation of pope Clement the Fourth.

Just as Roger Bacon preferred experience to argument, so did he prefer practice to speculative philosophy; and practice is in his conception intimately associated with religious truth.   He represents religion as having an element transcending speculative philosophy, but not at discord with it.   Can we say differently nowadays?   But Roger Bacon is so often thought of as a physical philosopher pure and simple that it will be well to show that religion was sincerely and truly in his thoughts, and that he embraced religion with the same simple naturalness with which he investigated physical science.   Three memorable passages[1] does Neander give from his works; I will quote them all.   The first is on the nature of religious knowledge; it will be seen that Roger Bacon does in effect identify this with inspiration, and he represents it as realisable through practice.   Here are his words:

All truth springs from the same source, from the divine light which, according to the gospel of St John, enlightens every man that cometh into the world.   Human reason is only a capacity to be filled, and knowledge can be imparted to it only by *that* reason which alone is reason *in actu.*

Or in other words, the Divine Mind has its being in action, and is known by us in proportion as it acts upon us: a profound truth; and the correlative truth is no less profound, that the divine touch stimulates our reason to the learning and appropriating of all knowledge.

The second of the three passages refers to that imaginative apprehension which we call faith, and declares that it is in the first instance good in itself, and in the second instance that if truly apprehended, it receives confirmation from the philosophic reason.   The passage runs thus:

A great joy we may gain for our faith, when philosophers, who follow only the decisions of reason, agree with us, and so confirm the confession of the Christian faith; not that we are to seek for rational grounds before faith, but only after it; so that, made sure by a double confirmation, we praise God for our salvation, which we can hold fast without wavering.

[1] Neander's *Church History* (Torrey's translation), vol. VIII. pp. 191, 193, 245.

There is nothing in the above passage to bind us to follow in all details the religious belief of Roger Bacon personally; it merely declares the general principle that faith, whether right or wrong, is not the offspring of theory; though if right, philosophic theory will be seen to confirm it. In details, the faith of the twentieth century is likely to differ from the faith of the thirteenth century; but this will not preclude a general resemblance in character. The third passage that I will quote is subject to a similar qualification:

Every action of man is stronger and mightier when he bends his mind thereto with firmness of purpose, and confidently expects to compass what he aims at. And because the word is formed out of the thought and longing of man's heart, and man has his joy in it, and it is the most connatural instrument of the rational soul, therefore has it the power of producing the greatest effects of all that is done by man; especially when it proceeds from a sure intention, a great desire, and a strong confidence. A proof of this is, that all the miracles wrought by holy men were, from the first, performed by the power of words.

There is practically no doubt that Roger Bacon must have accepted as true many miracles which the present generation will not accept; but his general statement stands on stronger ground than any particular application of it; the word of man, instinct with thought and desire, reaches to the inmost being of other men, and there performs wonders. But what wonders, we can only know by experience.

To think that the writer of the above passages should have been imprisoned for fourteen years as a dangerous person, and that by the followers of Francis of Assisi! But I come to another of the children of the thirteenth century; and again I rely on Neander.

Raymund Lull might be instanced as a most fervent Christian, in which respect he was not excelled by Francis of Assisi himself; but that which makes him so remarkable a person is not so much the fervour of his Christian belief in itself, as the enlightenment of the methods by which he sought to propagate Christianity. He was born at Majorca in the year 1236; up to the age of thirty, he lived a worldly life, and would seem to have been a man of passionate feelings from the first; he married, and had children; but he was assailed by temptations to love a woman other than his wife. One day, while writing a poem under the stress of this feeling, a reaction fell on him; and he saw before his eyes a vision of the crucified Christ. No longer could he write poetry; the vision recurred again and again, and kept him awake at nights; and a strain of piety, familiar to him in childish days,

rose up within him. He resolved at last to consecrate himself
to the service of Christ; and the thought of converting the
Saracens became prominent to his fancy. The crusades were then
nearing their unsuccessful end; and now it seemed to Raymund
Lull that if he could write such a book as should exhibit the whole
relations of Christianity to science and philosophy, the truth of
Christianity would shine out so clearly that the Saracens would
spontaneously embrace it as preferable to the creed of Islam.
To write then became his determination, and with tears and
prayers he besought God to help in his work. Nor did he confine
himself to the thought of writing such a book; he felt that it
must be translated into Arabic, if the Saracens were to understand
it; and he framed the project of calling on the pope and the
monarchs of Christendom to establish schools in connexion with
certain monasteries, in which the Arabic language and other
eastern languages might be taught. Meanwhile he would himself
be writing the great work on which his thoughts were bent.

It was a matter of course that one who thought in such a
way as this should endeavour to see what relation his own project
bore to the great war of the crusades, which even then was being
waged for the recovery of the holy sepulchre and for the conversion
of the Saracens. It was long before Raymund Lull ventured to
say that the method of the crusades was erroneous; for a long
time he thought that the two methods, of warfare and of missions,
might be carried on side by side; yet he never doubted that the
method of missions (and of martyrdom if necessary) was the
method to which he himself was called. At last he appears to
have come to the conviction that the method of warfare was
altogether wrong; and it may be well to quote the words he used,
though it must be borne in mind that the date of this expression
was not early in his life, but late:

" I see," he writes, " many knights going to the Holy Land, in the expectation of conquering it by force of arms; but instead of accomplishing their
object, they are in the end all swept off themselves....Therefore," says he,
addressing Christ, " it is my belief that the conquest of the Holy Land
should be attempted in no other way than as thou and thy apostles
undertook to accomplish it,—by love, by prayer, by tears, and the offering
up of our own lives."

I do not think I am wrong in saying that this was the true
principle of Raymund Lull always; at any rate, he never acted
on any other. I related how he determined to write an exposition
of the Christian faith in its relation to philosophy, and how he

determined to petition the pope and the monarchs of Europe to establish schools in which Arabic and other eastern languages might be taught, for the better communication of Christian truth to the eastern nations. After making these great determinations, he had a period of lassitude; but he was roused from it by a Franciscan sermon, in which the entire renunciation of the world by Francis of Assisi was held up as an example; and Raymund Lull resolved to follow that example. He sold his property, left his wife and children enough for their sustenance, and then departed from his home, intending never to return. We may shrink from giving our approval to his leaving wife and children; but it is impossible to read of the course of his life afterwards without sympathy and emotion. His efforts to procure the establishment of schools in which Arabic should be taught continued all his life (and he learned Arabic on his own account); but in the year 1287, finding his large plans met with no response, he began to entertain the idea of going out as a missionary himself. Partly through fears of his own, partly through illness, he did not accomplish this resolution till the end of the year 1291. Then he took ship and landed in Tunis, and immediately sought for the most learned Mohammedans, and endeavoured to convince them of the truth of the doctrine of the Trinity. As he anticipated, he ran into real danger; he was thrown into prison, and some among the Mohammedans would have put him to death; but others honoured his boldness and zeal, although not converted by him; at last they put him on board the Genoese ship in which he had come to Tunis, just as it was about to depart, and sent him back to Italy. Here he lectured, and wrote his great work, and endeavoured to obtain help for his missionary enterprises, but in vain; till at last he went himself, with but one companion, to his native island of Majorca, and endeavoured to convert the Jews and Saracens there. Then, with the same companion, he travelled to Cyprus and Armenia, and endeavoured to bring the eastern church over to the western faith. At last, in the years 1306 and 1307, he visited North Africa once more, and again preached Christianity publicly, and made, it would seem, some converts. For this he was thrown into a painful imprisonment, which lasted six months; like the apostle Paul, he was scourged; but at last he was put on board a ship and sent out of the country. The ship was wrecked in a violent storm on the coast of Italy, near Pisa; many were drowned, but Raymund and his companion were among those saved. He was received with great honour at

Pisa; and not being yet fully convinced of the error of the crusades, he sought to gather together an order of spiritual knights who should be ready to go to war for the recovery of the holy sepulchre from the Saracens. Had he any knowledge of the fact that the great Order of the Knights Templars was even then being caught in the treacherous snare laid for them by the king of France? Whether he knew it or not then, he must have known it by the year 1310; and it is with regret we hear that Raymund Lull dedicated one of his works, composed in that year in Paris, to this king, Philip the Fair. It may be that he believed the incredible charges brought against the Templars. Much more pleasant is it to record that at the general council of Vienne, 1311 A.D., the scheme for which he had so long laboured, the establishment of professorial chairs for teaching the eastern languages, received at any rate nominal acceptance: the pope ordered that this should be carried out[1] "in all the cities where the papal court resided, and also at the universities of Paris, Oxford, and Salamanca." Yet it cannot be believed that the order was actually carried out. But Raymund Lull now felt that his work was done, and that it only remained for him to die as a martyr to his faith, the end which he had long desired for himself. For the third and last time he crossed over into North Africa, and in that city, Bugia, where he had last preached, he taught again, in the latter part of the year 1314. At first he taught only the few converts he had made on his previous visit, and secretly; but afterwards (ten months after his first landing) he preached the gospel in public; telling all men that he was the same person whom they had banished before; and bidding them, under penalty of the divine judgment, abjure Mohammedanism. The result of so bold a defiance could not be doubtful; he was dragged out of the city, and by order of the king, stoned to death. Merchants from Majorca were permitted to carry back his body to his native island, and there it was buried.

Surely, whatever fault we may find with him, a very brave and faithful man! Neither, even though his arguments may have been mistaken, was he in any way an obscurantist; his whole desire was to meet his opponents in sheer downright argument; his zeal for the teaching of eastern languages was simply meant to facilitate the way to such argument. Let me quote a passage from the termination of his great work, the *Ars Generalis*:

[1] Neander's *Church History* (Torrey's translation), vol. VII. p. 95.

"Let Christians," he writes, "consumed with a burning love for the cause of faith, but consider that, since nothing has power to withstand the truth, which by the strength of arguments is mighty over all things, they can, with God's help and by his might, bring back the infidels to the way of faith; so that the precious name of our Lord Jesus, which is in most regions of the world still unknown to the majority of men, may be proclaimed and adored; and this way of converting infidels is easier than all others. For, to the infidels, it seems a difficult and dangerous thing, to abandon their own belief, for the sake of another; but it will be impossible for them not to abandon the faith which is proved to them to be false and self-contradictory, for the sake of that which is true and necessary[1]."

There is no timidity in that challenge. I must not refuse to believe, as they who have really read this great work of Raymund Lull affirm, that there are absurdities in it; with his temperament, this was perhaps to be expected. But Neander quotes from him passages of true sanity and worth; which I have not space to reproduce here.

In speaking of these mediæval reasoners (the "Schoolmen" as they are often called) we have to remember that the prohibition of all criticism of the great Christian authorities, and especially of all criticism of the Bible, which lay as a weight upon their intellects, could not but make their theories more or less artificial; formal argument was required, if formal statements were to be upheld; and when they became acquainted with the Greek reasonings, and especially those of Aristotle, an additional bias was imparted to them to attempt a perfection of argument, which was not really suited to their subject-matter. Of none of the schoolmen is this more true than of the most famous of them all, Thomas Aquinas. I do not think, either from what I have read in him, or from what I have read of him, that Thomas Aquinas was equal in natural genius to the three men of whom I have just been speaking, Albertus Magnus, Roger Bacon, and Raymund Lull. But he had a singularly well-balanced intellect, and his temper, as far as we can judge, was never ruffled; he deals with innumerable questions, and always in the same careful measured way, never leaving anything out of sight which could occur to any inquirer. Some of his questions are interesting to us at the present day, others are too subtle to be generally interesting, or even perhaps intelligible. Let me give some examples of the former class.

Whether all men are bound to love their enemies.
Whether knowledge is loftier than love.

[1] Neander, Torrey's translation, vol. VII. p. 91.

Whether it is necessary for a man to believe something of which he has not knowledge.

Whether it was suitable for Christ to pray.

Whether it is suitable for God to adopt anyone into sonship.

Whether the active life is more noble than the contemplative life.

These questions are from among his comments on the third book of the *Sentences* of Peter Lombard; and I could conceive them all being discussed at the present day, though no doubt they belong to a style of question which is not often discussed. Let me give just one example (from the same volume) of a question which would *never* be discussed at the present day; it is this: "Whether the book of life is something created." That, I am sure, is quite out of the field of twentieth century thought.

My general criticism on Thomas Aquinas is, that in reading him one cannot see the wood for the trees; argument is heaped on argument, and one is at a loss to know where the real centre of the reasoning lies. But there can be no doubt that in his own day he was felt to be a power, more than any of the three whom I mentioned just before him; he was felt really to comprehend, to understand, the things of which he spoke. His lecture room, we are told, was crowded; and he was honoured by kings and by popes. We must feel real esteem for him; and I may in conclusion quote one of his decisions which will commend him to the present generation; in treating of the relation of master to slave, he declared it not to be within the competence of the master to prevent his slave from marrying. That saying is an instance of the tendency of Christian feeling which in the end abolished slavery.

I have been endeavouring in the above pages to show that the thirteenth century was, in the countries of western Christendom, an era of awakening energy; and those who remember how very largely at that date Christianity was the formative power of men's minds in western Europe, will not doubt that Christianity stimulated and nourished this awakening. What I have said will be confirmed to those who remember the splendid specimens of Christian architecture built at that time; and painting in that century took a fresh start through Cimabue and Giotto. In that century, it is probable, the mariner's compass was first brought to Europe; and in that century one of the greatest travellers whom the world ever saw, Marco Polo, made his famous journey to China. Was not the breath of a new life in western Europe when these things were being done?

Then, at the turning of the thirteenth and fourteenth centuries, we find the great poet Dante engaged on his *Divina Commedia*; a poem, of which it is scarcely possible to exaggerate either the intellectual or the imaginative power. One thing must be said against Dante; though in his day the belief in hell was unavoidable, yet to emphasise it, to exemplify it, as he did, does somewhat diminish the love in which we hold him. But we owe him much, and our posterity will do so for ever; he begins the conscious modern world in which we live.

Perhaps I ought to have mentioned before now the Arthurian legends and the *Nibelungen Lied*, which in their present form date from the twelfth century, but yet are reminiscences of much earlier legends. These, and the *Poem of the Cid* in Spain, the lyrics of Walther von der Vogelweide in Germany, and the songs of the troubadours in southern France, testify to a warmth and vigour of soul that we may honour. They are a forecast of advancing civilisation; and the care taken to preserve them is further evidence of this. Another evidence of the same, though in a different line, is the first manufacture of linen paper, which Hallam dates at about 1100 A.D. among Christian nations, though the Saracens would seem to have used it earlier.

The gathering signs of intellectual progress are not absent from the fourteenth century (to this belong the memorable names of Petrarch and Boccaccio, Chaucer and Froissart) but shine more clearly in the fifteenth. What power lay in the discovery of printing, whether we attribute the first germ of it to Gutenberg and Fust in Germany, or to Koster in Holland! How far beyond the achievements of any former sailors are those of Columbus, the discoverer of America, of Bartholomew de Diaz, who discovered the Cape of Good Hope, and of Vasco di Gama, who sailed round that cape and reached India! These were not mere casual winnings of adventurers; they indicated a strength in the human spirit which had not been reached in former ages; and what the first discoverers won, others were ready to follow up. This it is which differentiates the Christian voyagers of the end of the fifteenth century from any that had ever been seen in the world before; it was no mere isolated flash of courage that was shown in them, but a steady enduring determination to lay bare to the knowledge of man whatever the surface of the earth had to show. A power lay in the resolutions of Christian nations, more than there had been in the age of Constantine, more than there had been in the age of Charlemagne, more than there had been in the age of

Hildebrand. Nations which were not Christian had no such power; the mere lapse of time had not created it in Chinese, or Hindus, or Saracens. I do not depreciate what those races had won; but their power was not equal to the power of the Christian races. It was not merely that knowledge had increased; apart from all knowledge, the spirit of man was more powerful, more dominant over external things, wherever it had been fostered by Christianity.

We shall come to the same conclusion as to the force of the Christian spirit if we consider another fact, slightly posterior in time to those which I have just named. It was shortly after the end of the fifteenth century that Copernicus (an ecclesiastic, be it remarked) first conceived that theory which revolutionised astronomy, and brought into being a multitude of new thoughts respecting the position of man in the universe. One ancient astronomer, Aristarchus of Samos, had conceived the theory that the earth, together with all the planets, revolved around the sun. But mankind were not ripe for the reception of such a theory then; they were ripe for it in the days of Copernicus. This did not come through any improvement in astronomical instruments; the telescope was not yet invented. But the thoughts of men were more mature; and the reason of this was that character had been built up.

A similar conclusion is to be drawn from the growth of the art of painting, which attained so great a splendour in the fifteenth and sixteenth centuries. This art of painting is a very subtle thing, and the power to bring it to high perfection may easily be lost; but when we find it used with consummate imagination and illustrative of some deep truth, we cannot but honour the age in which it so appears. Beauty of form and colouring must indeed accompany the other excellences just named; and these actually are found at the period of which I am speaking, and it would be hard to deny that Christian faith prompted the genius displayed in the pictures which were then created and which we see to-day. The most profound truth, as far as I can judge, which any existent picture illustrates, is that which we discern in the fresco by Perugino of the crucified Christ, which is in the large chamber (formerly the chapterhouse of a monastery) adjoining the Via della Colonna at Florence. It is a well-known picture, often reproduced, but hardly to be quite appreciated save in the original; every line of it breathes peace. That the cross, which is a symbol of pain, should also be the symbol of eternal peace and love, is a thought which might be deemed a paradox if experience did not prove it to be a truth. What nobler truth could any art give to the world?

More beautiful as a mere work of painting than the Perugino, and also worthy of note in its inner meaning, is the famous Madonna di San Sisto by Raphael, in the gallery at Dresden. The mother of Jesus, with the holy child in her arms, has been caught up to heaven, where she has seen the image of the suffering which is to be; the child also has seen it; now they are descending, as is shown by the mantle which has been caught and swells upwards with the wind; the resolution depicted on the child's mouth is of a rare strength; the wide-open eyes of the mother show that she has seen a sight not to be forgotten[1]. This is of course imagination; but how tender and touching an imagination! The reader must not think that, because I disbelieve in the virgin birth, I therefore think the mother of Jesus a person to be neglected in history; if he will look to what I have said[2] about the narrative of the empty tomb, he will conclude differently.

Next, let me mention the picture of the creation of Adam, by Michael Angelo, on the ceiling of the Sistine Chapel at Rome; the face of Adam shows the purest expression of trust in God that ever was delineated by man. This again is an imaginative picture; it is symbolic, not literal truth, that we find in it.

Next, let me name another picture of the crucifixion, a great contrast to that of Perugino; that by Tintoretto, in the Scuola di San Rocco at Venice. Here all is vehement action, or else the pathos of piercing grief. It shows us something not so far from the literal reality but that we can conceive it to be the representation of what actually happened, save that the divine and ideal truth, which could not be represented to the senses, is typified by the glory round the head of the crucified Jesus.

Add the "Last Supper" of Leonardo da Vinci; these five, if I might express my own feelings, might be selected out of all which the world contains, as having most to say to the heart of man.

I have given the evidences which show that the true power of Christianity (notwithstanding the collapse of the Christian Roman empire in the days of Christian inexperience and error)

---

[1] This explanation of the picture here named was given me by a lady whom not all of my contemporaries, I think, will have forgotten, Fraülein Kretzschmer of Dresden. She told me, but I cannot recall, from whom she derived it; I have always found it convincing. I may observe that Crowe and Cavalcaselle, in their life of Raphael, recognise that the Madonna is descending; but why she should be descending, they do not say.

[2] See chapter XIX above.

did really renovate the society of which the Christian Church was the acting centre, and renovated it more and more as time went on. One more evidence let me produce; that religious book, so profound in its inculcation of patience, so full of consolations which reach into the heart of suffering, which is called *On the Imitation of Christ*. I would gladly think that Thomas à Kempis was the real, as he is the reputed, writer of it; I know very little against this; but the question is not absolutely decided.

It is very necessary to vindicate the reality of spiritual causes, on a large scale, in the formation of the world of men as it lies before us; so that we may be sure that the enlargement of the intellect of men and the softening of their passions and the humanising of their character does not come by accident. That Christianity, in its true meaning and substance, was the cause of that civilisation of which I have been endeavouring to trace the growth in mediæval times, I feel sure; though in so subtle a region it is not easy to connect causes with effects in a way that shall be convincing to everyone. But that Christianity in its accepted form has been entirely good cannot be truly said; the good and evil that are in man are not so sharply separated as to enable us to say that the Christian Church, in its organised form, has been entirely the cause of good, not at all of evil. The case is by no means so; and if I have shown the good, I must also show the evil.

In the tenth and eleventh centuries, we hear complaints by pious Christians of the decadence of monastic institutions; they had become, it was said, less spiritual and more worldly. The true cause no doubt was that that extraordinary degree of self-sacrifice, which had been of service in the first breaking up of the Roman empire under the barbarian inroads, was less required now; some mitigation of the severe "rule" of Benedict of Nursia might reasonably have been made, and if made with judgment, would have carried on the monastic principle towards a safe development. But no one, in the ninth and tenth centuries, drew this inference; distinguished churchmen saw that the growing laxity in monasteries and convents was in itself wrong; it never occurred to them to ask whether some just instinct of human nature was not at the bottom of it. Hence all efforts at reforming the monasteries took the form of bringing back the severe old Benedictine rule; this is what was done in the estab-lishment of the Cluniac order in the tenth century, and of the Cistercian order at the end of the eleventh; and when the

celebrated Bernard, at the beginning of the twelfth century, joined
the latter order, and became abbot of the monastery of Clairvaux,
a very powerful force was added to the party which strove to
bring about reform of the monasteries not on new lines but on
old ones. It was an error, and the violent uprooting of monasteries in after times was the result of it; but we must not think
badly of the authors of the error; the reactionaries, as has so
often happened in history, were in all their ordinary actions not
only religious, but good and merciful persons. Still, they did their
share of evil; and the first evil done was the undue restriction of
normal human impulses.

If there was frailty in the monasteries, there was sure to be
frailty in the lives of ordinary persons outside the monasteries;
and by far the greatest of the reformers who strove to counteract
this was Francis of Assisi. He was born nearly a century after
Bernard, in the year 1182; and the progress of time has done little
to take away the charm which belongs to his mild and yet daring
character. Where so much elicits our sympathy, we may be
permitted to regret one thing, namely, that amid all his ardent
and most just efforts to diminish the luxury and licentiousness
of mankind, he made so little direct effort to diminish their
cruelty[1]. The reason no doubt was that cruelty was in those days
no small part of the weapons used by ministers of justice, whether
in Church or State; and it was difficult for Francis to attack it,
without attacking the great authorities under whom he desired
to work, and whose support was so important to him. This is
in part, but only in part, a sound defence of his conduct in this
respect; we cannot but wish that he had done something to correct
the vice of cruelty, but we must acknowledge that the task, had
he attempted it, would have been one of exceeding difficulty.
Personally, he was blameless in this respect; and that, in those
days, was a merit.

When we think of Francis of Assisi, we have to dismiss all
idea of his having been a monk, or in any way attached to
monasteries. It is true that in the after times the Franciscan
houses differed little from monasteries; but the whole idea of
Francis himself was that his followers were to travel and preach
to the common people; their work was not to lie in the house of
their order. The case was the same with the Dominican friars;

---

[1] I read in Milman's *History of Latin Christianity* (IV. 183) that Antony of Padua,
a Franciscan, reproved Ecelino the tyrant of Verona for his cruelties; but they were
cruelties indefensible even according to the moral code of that time.

they were called "the order of preachers"; that, and not staying
at home, was their proper function. We may infer, I think,
from this new beginning in the Christian Church, that European
society at the beginning of the thirteenth century, though far
from tranquil, was yet not in quite so lawless a state as in previous
centuries. At the same time the *women* attaching themselves
either to the Dominican or to the Franciscan order appear to have
been no more free than those in a Benedictine convent, or in any
way distinguished from these; but it is to be remembered that
what was called the Second Order among the Franciscans, or in
other words the order of female adherents, had its origin not in
the mind of Francis himself, but in the enthusiasm of a girl who
had been attracted by his fame, and probably had heard his
preaching—the famous Clara of Assisi.

Francis of Assisi, the evangelist who sought to reform the
wickednesses of the world by gentleness and patience, has been
spoken of here as evidence that there were such wickednesses in
Christian society; and we behold in him the purest possible type
of reformer on mediæval Christian lines; and had I space, I
might enlarge on his wisdom in forming his Third Order, the
order of men and women who did not desire to quit the ordinary
life of men and women, but who yet did desire to bind themselves
to lead a self-denying and honest life. Or I might quote sayings
of his that show his moderation; but I must content myself with
one:

"Blessed," he said, "is that servant, who no more values himself on
that which God speaks or works through him, than he does on that which
God speaks or works through another."

In that saying lies the true corrective of personal ambition.

Why, it is natural to ask, had Francis of Assisi such crowds
of followers, while Raymund Lull, so like him in all moral qualities,
had so few? The answer is not doubtful: Francis of Assisi did
not confront any intellectual question; Raymund Lull added to
his moral ardour the task of intellectual inquiry. The intellectual
inquirer is apt to be solitary; and if Raymund Lull was, as is
said, eccentric in his conclusions, so much more was he bound to
be solitary. I have not denied the honour due to Francis of
Assisi; but I confess that, eccentric though Raymund Lull may
have been, I feel myself bound to him by an additional link of
spiritual kinship. His conversion, be it observed, was sixty
years later than the conversion of Francis.

I come, after speaking of the sins of Christians, to the sin of the Church; and therewith I come to the saintly persecutor, Dominic de Guzman.   It is impossible not to regret that a man so fervent in feeling, so self-denying and devoted, should have applied his energies to the task of quenching and annulling that precious heritage of man, intellectual insight—a heritage which belongs to each individual as much as his eyesight does, and which cannot be replaced, or the loss of it compensated for, by any knowledge obtained from others.   To show more precisely what Dominic did, I will quote a passage from what I believe to be the last authoritative account of him that has appeared—the *Cartulaire ou Histoire Diplomatique de Saint Dominique*—a work in two volumes, published at Paris, by ardent Dominicans, in the year 1893.   The passage that I will quote occurs in volume I. pp. 488–490; I will give it, as usual, translated into English :

In regard to heretical doings (pour des faits d'hérésie) Saint Dominic at the same period brought to an issue a judicial act of much graver importance at Toulouse.   In that town, in spite of the extreme tolerance shown by Raymond VI to catharist errors, it was many years since there had been an entire abstention from the repression of these false doctrines and from the punishment (according to the laws interpreted and sanctioned by custom) of obstinate sectaries; if at least one believes the consuls and council of the fortress and city, who wrote in the year 1211 to Peter of Aragon, complaining to him of the reproaches directed against them by the legate Arnald Amalric, for leaving certain suspected persons unpunished. "This reproach," they tell him, "has greatly surprised us, for it is known that in past time Raymond V, father of the reigning count, received the mandate (through authentic procedure of the people of Toulouse), that if a heretic be discovered in city or fortress, he and his shelterer should be given up to punishment and their property put up to auction.   In fact," add the Toulouse consuls, "we have burnt a good number of them, and when we discover any of them, we do not cease doing so.   We have besides answered the letters and the messengers of the legate, saying that he should point out those whom he regards as suspect, and we will bring them to trial before the episcopal court of our town, with the knowledge of the legates of our lord the Pope, or of our lord bishop, according to the precepts of the canon law and the practice of the holy Roman church." Notwithstanding this plea, the council held at Montpellier had thought it necessary to urge the rigorous application of the ancient canons relative to the Albigensian heresy, which the council of Avignon, held in 1209, had already renewed.   Now at this very time there had been arrested in the town of Toulouse men suspected of catharism.   The saint, who had received the powers of cardinal legate, was called upon to judge of their faultiness, and without any innovation on custom or arbitrary action of his own, but according to the ordinary procedure, he examined and questioned them.   After a serious inquiry, he convicted them of error, and in consequence declared them formally heretical.   They were then exhorted to return to the catholic faith; they obstinately refused, and as

impenitent and hardened men, they were handed over to the secular
court, which condemned them to the punishment of fire.

But at the very moment when the officers of the court laid hold of the
condemned men, to conduct them to the place of their punishment, the
saint fixed his regards on one of them, and as if he perceived on his face
a ray of divine predestination, cried out: "Take that man aside, and do
not let him be burnt with the rest." Then turning to him with kindness,
he added: "I know, my son, yes, I know, that in the end, however late,
thou wilt become a good and holy man."

And we are told that twenty years later this man, who all the
intervening time had remained a heretic, became reconciled to
the Church.

Now I must not assume absolutely the truth of the above
narrative; but there is nothing to hinder its being true, and something like it will at all events probably have happened. Before
saying anything about the part which Dominic plays in it,
something must be said about those persons whose part in it was
quite as essential as that of Dominic, namely the heretics. For
what, precisely, were they condemned?

For heresy, of course; the heresy of the Cathari, or Albigenses
(to use the ordinary appellation). But what did their heresy
imply? I have looked through all the long pages of Harduin's
Acta Conciliorum which bear on this point, beginning with the
first slight mention of the heresy in the canons of the council held
at Toulouse in 1119; through the records of other councils, and
Papal letters, before and during the great cataclysm when the
whole of Languedoc was devastated by fire and sword, after
pope Innocent III had called for a crusade against the heretics;
and ending with the reconciliation of the count of Toulouse to the
Church, in the year 1233, and with the severe statutes passed by
the count against the heresy of which he had been lately the supporter. In all this period I find that the main heresies of which
they are specifically accused are three: Contempt of the Lord's
Supper and of infant baptism; contempt of the Christian ministry
as then organised; and condemnation of lawful marriage as if
it were an unlawful act. But from the records of the council of
Lombers, held either in 1165 or in 1176 (both dates are assigned),
we find that they were also accused of contempt of the Old Testament, and of the refusal to take an oath. Also it is not to be
denied that in many cases (though not, I think, universally)
these particular points of heresy were accompanied by a strong
strain of Manichæism or Gnosticism, involving a tendency to
think of the existing world as evil and created by an evil power:

this does not appear from any of the official documents to which I referred above, but there is adequate evidence for it, and it would be naturally allied with their reprobation of the Old Testament and of marriage. With respect to their reprobation of marriage, it is natural to think that this would be held by them with some reserve, and not absolutely; and so one would infer from the line which they took at the council of Lombers. The record of that council is by far the fullest official account that we have of them; it is plain that the bishops of the council and the accused heretics regarded one another as enemies; and the heretics, after a certain amount of fencing with their questioners, turned to the bystanders, who were numerous, and said that for love of them they would render to them an account of their faith, and they proceeded to render it; and it was more orthodox than one would have anticipated. Some have thought that they were insincerely concealing their real opinions; but it is hardly possible to reconcile such a supposition with the courageous demeanour which they showed, according to the account of their trial which we possess, drawn up (be it remembered) by their enemies. There was no doubt considerable variety of opinion among the heretics of that age.

So far I have been speaking of the definite charges brought against the Albigenses, or Cathari (whichever name we prefer); but there were indefinite charges, the consideration of which must not be omitted. The council of Lavaur, held in 1213, the year in which they were finally crushed in a military sense, wrote a letter to pope Innocent III in which they speak of the "abominable enormities and other wickednesses" committed by the Albigenses; some of which, they say, their messengers will relate to the pope by word of mouth. The council of Toulouse, held in 1229[1], has a clause in which they forbid the approach of a heretic to any sick person, because, they say, they understand that "enormous wickednesses" have often taken place through this means. In these two passages there is clearly an attribution of immoral conduct to the Albigenses; are we to believe it as affecting the whole body? Those who attend to the evidence will, I am sure, answer this question in the negative. The council of Lavaur was held at a time when feeling was at a white heat; the council of Toulouse, in 1229, was held at a time of scarcely less

---

[1] By a curious mistake, a part of the decrees of this council are duplicated in Harduin's *Acta Conciliorum*, and are made to appear as if they were issued in 1129 as well as in 1229; it is evident that 1229 alone is the real date.

excitement, the excitement of victory after a most bloody war, when the Inquisition, by virtue of the third section of the decrees of the Lateran council (held in 1215) had long been at work, though not so formally as was afterwards the case. Those were not favourable conditions for framing true accusations against the Albigenses. Why, if these accusations of immorality were true, was nothing said about them in the council of Lombers; or in the third Lateran council, held in 1179; or in the letter of pope Lucius III, so denunciatory of the doctrines of the Albigenses, written in 1183; or in the fourth Lateran council, held in 1215? And Raynier Sacchoni, that inquisitor who once had belonged to the sect which he persecuted, charges them with heresy but not with immorality, as I understand him.

Or again take this fact: the dean of Nevers in the year 1198 was accused both of heresy in his own person, and also of having intimate association with heretics. He pleaded his cause before Innocent III, just elected pope; who, without absolutely acquitting him, yet directed the archbishop of Sens to acquit him, provided he would publicly break off all connexion with the heretics; provided also, on further examination, his own innocence of heresy was completely established. These points being made clear, the pope is urgent that the archbishop shall make no delay in restoring the dean of Nevers to his office, from which he had been suspended. The dean of Nevers, therefore, was a person worthy in a general way of our respect; and he had been in intimate association with the heretical Albigenses. Is it not clear that he, at all events, knew nothing of any general immorality practised by these heretics; and if Innocent III at that date had heard of such immorality, would not that have appeared in his letter to the archbishop of Sens, which is our authority for the facts just narrated? Moreover the prelates of Languedoc were accused by the papal legates of general neglect in rooting out heretics. Would these prelates have been so neglectful if to heresy had been added general immorality? Add to all this that the Albigenses (or Cathari, if the more correct term be preferred) showed unflinching courage in submitting to be burnt for their creed; is that a characteristic likely to be combined with general immorality? Let me in fine quote a sentence from Neander, which from my own reading I should have held probable, but Neander speaks with more assured knowledge:

According to the testimony of the first opponents themselves, it was their blameless and strict mode of life that distinguished the Catharists generally; that they abstained from cursing and swearing, and simple yea or nay was a substitute with them for the strongest attestations[1].

Neander goes on to remark on the differences that may have existed between them in this respect; but he is emphatic in rejecting any idea of their having been guilty of gross immorality[2].

The reader will not think that I have perused all the evidence which exists on this subject; but the evidence which I have given is of no slight value in their favour; and it is hardly necessary to remark that the same sort of accusation was commonly brought against the early Christians by pagans of the time of Nero and Domitian.

If the Albigenses were free of blame on the score of general morality, were their doctrines so perverse as to deprive them of any title to our sympathy? I certainly think not, though some of them, perhaps most of them, fell into blamable errors; but the special point in which they deserve our sympathy is one that I must mention later.

I return to Dominic. What are we to think of him, as he is described to us in the passage from the *Cartulaire* quoted above, in which his judicial dealings with the heretics are described?

Let me remind my reader of what I wrote at the beginning of my twenty-first chapter, that with the advent of Christianity to temporal power, which happened in the reign of Constantine, the following problem became for the first time of supreme importance—how so to organise society, that not only shall men's actions be good in their purport and effect, but that their thoughts and feelings shall be good as well. That is a result which we aim at in this twentieth century; but our methods of accomplishing it are very, very different from the methods employed in the twelfth or thirteenth century. Dominic was trying to make men good in heart and soul; but unfortunately he thought, as people did in his day, that the burning of heretics was necessary, as a remedial measure, before the happy end, the purification of the Church and of mankind, could be attained. Let us lament that he should have been so mistaken. He was a man of wonderful energy, and as has been seen, not inaccessible to pity, and great men in the ages that followed owned him for their master. But it was more than a mistake, it was a sin in him, to think that

---

[1] Neander (Torrey's translation), vol. VIII. p. 389. The whole dissertation of Neander on the Catharists is valuable.

[2] I have had in my mind, all through, the attack on the Albigenses in the *Cartulaire de Saint Dominique*, vol. I. pp. 90–92. Dominic himself does not appear to have condemned them for anything beyond heresy (see page 363 above).

errors of belief could rightly be repressed by burning those who erred. In truth, he distrusted the power of the spirit of God; which certainly is not exercised by sword and fire[1].

A sin is lightened by the difficulty of escaping it; and it was difficult, in that age, to escape (if you had the power and the will) the sin of burning heretics. The responsibility lies on the whole Church, and to the whole Church too belongs this cardinal error, the idea that neither the Bible nor the leading doctrines of the Church must ever be criticised or dissented from in the smallest degree. A most irrational metaphor was adopted to commend this error; it was said that the doctrines of the Church were the "deposit of faith"; so that, just as a man, having been entrusted by a friend with some precious work of art, is bound to hand it over undamaged when his friend asks for it again, so, it was thought, was a Christian bound to preserve undamaged the belief which he had been taught, and to hold it without alteration to the end of time. But the metaphor does not hold. A person who instructs you in some new and valuable truth may have made you a gift; he certainly has not made you a loan. If it is really true, you never hand it him back again.

By the middle of the twelfth century, the suspicion had arisen in the minds of some Christians that the Church, which they saw exercising such active power in the world, might go wrong, had gone wrong. When this suspicion had become a conviction, the question, "Where then is the truth?" could not be evaded. Now a large number of these Albigensians had answered this question by embracing opinions of Manichæan or Gnostic type, in which there was much serious error (not unmingled however with truth). But not all of them erred in this way; and still less did the Waldenses of Switzerland, who likewise held the existing Church to be in error. All of them, Albigenses and Waldenses alike, held that the true Church must be characterised by goodness; and the Church which was before their eyes, with the powerful pope at its head, and archbishops and bishops and abbots beneath him, all delighting in worldly power and worldly display, did not appear to them good. This was the great disturbing conviction which possessed them and made them adversaries to the ecclesiastical authorities of their own day. They might differ in the degree in which they held actually heretical

---

[1] Our estimate of Dominic would be very unfavourably affected if we thought of him as the founder of the Inquisition in its final form. The Inquisition, however, in its extreme form, was a gradual growth.

beliefs; the one thing which united them all was disbelief in the inerrancy of the Church as it stood. Were they wrong in this?

Assuredly they were not wrong. There were indeed true spiritual Christians in the Church which they saw before their eyes; I have devoted a great part of the present and the foregoing chapter to the description of what these true spiritual Christians had done and were doing; there was a slow building up of society going on, a slow maturing of character, in which popes and bishops and monks and kings and nobles and ordinary persons had joined hands and worked together. But there was a great deal also of very opposite type; a great deal of self-seeking, of quarrelling, of greed; the clergy accumulating earthly possessions, indulging in ambitious show; and there was no kind of tendency for higher ecclesiastical rule to imply greater holiness. Then, over and above all the rest, came this madness of persecuting heretics; a very plain surrender of belief in the power of God's spirit to reform the hearts of men, and a seizure of material weapons against spiritual belief. It is impossible to give all the evidences of this madness; but it may be desirable to give one out of many, in order to show that it was not Languedoc alone which suffered in this way. Under the date 1233[1] in the *Acta Conciliorum*, mention is made of heretics called the Stadingi in North Germany, who are said to have had a demon for their teacher; an "innumerable multitude" of them, says the historian (who is anonymous, but trusted), were burnt through the whole of Germany. This was done under the direct authority of the pope of that time. It is hard to conceive clearer evidence of error, in a most important matter, attaching to the formal head of the Christian Church of the west, at that date.

We must then distinguish the excellence of the spirit in Christians, which sometimes was very great all through the middle ages, from excellence in the formal structure of the Church, and in the formally accredited ministers of the Church, which was by no means equally great. Hence the inference was inevitable that the Church as formally constituted, though it might rightly claim obedience in ordinary matters, could yet not claim unlimited obedience; there were very great exceptions to its holiness and justice. Whatever errors, then, the Albigenses and their allies may have committed, we owe them gratitude for this, that they looked for the true assembly of redeemed souls, the Church of God, in another quarter from that which usurped the name as

[1] It is under the heading "Conventus Moguntinus."

its exclusive property. It is probable, no doubt, that some of these heretics were too much disposed to concentre the Church of God in themselves; frailties they had, and this may have been among them.

The heretics of the thirteenth century were put down, and in the main destroyed, in the manner that I have indicated; but in destroying them the popes had reached the summit of their power, and the reverence which men had entertained for the papal authority had begun, by the end of the century, to decline. Hence when Boniface VIII, at the beginning of the fourteenth century, tried to surpass the thunders of Innocent III, he fell into irretrievable ruin; and though there are incidents in the conflict that must attract our pity for him, the weakness of the papacy was shown in the fact that for more than a century afterwards the Church suffered from ever-increasing disorder. It was no discredit to the papacy to have been for a moment brought low by that subtle tyrant, Philip the Fair of France; it was the inability of the papacy to recover from that blow which pointed the doubts which so many were disposed to entertain, whether the papacy were a divine institution.

For, first, what more serious dishonour to the papacy can be conceived than that Clement V, the Frenchman who was made pope two years after the death of Boniface VIII, should have allowed himself to be the submissive tool of Philip the Fair, and should have consented to the judicial murder of the Templars? A greater crime is not to be found in history than the sudden and treacherous seizure of that company of warriors, their subjection to extreme tortures in order to force from them confessions of secret infidelity and gross superstition, and their final extermination. Scarcely is such a crime lightened, when all the circumstances are considered, were we to suppose the Templars guilty; but it seems to me preposterous, and against all the weight of the real evidence, to regard them as guilty. If the reader thinks this too confident an assurance, let me quote one sentence concerning the behaviour of the Templars in the Holy Land:

The Templar fortress of Safed surrendered with its garrison of 600 knights, all of whom preferred death to apostasy (June, 1266)[1].

Were these Templars secret unbelievers? Or again, let it be considered how exactly the charges made against the Templars were such as base enemies in that age were sure to invent; how

[1] *Encyclopædia Britannica* (eleventh edition), vol. XXVI. p. 595.

very unlikely to be true of men engaged in serious warfare for the honour of Christ! Mistaken heroes the Templars may have been, but they were true to their mission.

If the papacy stained itself in the betrayal of the Templars, there was no recovery of its dignity during the century which succeeded that event. For before the affair of the Templars had begun, those seventy years had commenced, during which the pope had his seat at Avignon, not in Rome, to the surprise and dismay of Christendom; only once did the bishop of Rome visit his own city during those seventy years. But a still greater scandal followed; for then, during forty years, there were two popes, one at Rome, one at Avignon; and either pope was supported by men of ability and worth. But which was the real pope? That question, in view of the general assumption of Christendom that there could be but one pope, was perplexing.

Such a condition of things could not but shake the credit of the papacy in the eyes of men; and, over and above all this, there was the feeling that the hierarchy of the Church, as it actually existed, was worldly—was not according to the pattern which Jesus Christ had laid down as a guide for those who should follow him. This was the condition of things which, in the latter part of the fourteenth century, impelled two men to ask that question which Albigenses and Waldenses had asked before them: Where is the true Christian Church? Wycliffe, in England, was the first of these; I have already spoken of him in this chapter; then came, about a quarter of a century later, Huss, in Bohemia. But it must not be supposed that during the whole interval between the suppression of the Albigenses and the rise of Wycliffe there had been no movement of reform within the Church. Such movements there were; for instance, a body of men called "Apostolicals," in the north of Italy, had a considerable number of adherents in the latter part of the thirteenth century, and preached rather an extreme form of self-denial. But they were adverse to Rome, and though expecting a new and worthier pope to assume power, regarded the existing government of the Church as antichristian. The Inquisition, which had a most formidable power in all the Latin countries, burnt many of these "Apostolicals" at the stake, and frightened the rest into silence.

More sober, more learned, more influential than the Apostolicals, Wycliffe and Huss enjoyed considerable freedom in England and Bohemia respectively; in neither of which countries had the Inquisition any great sway. But even where the Inquisition existed not, the power of the Church to uproot all that was called heresy was still terrible. I must be brief in describing the movements of divine freedom, which bore their fruit afterwards, in spite of the determination of the nominal authorities of the Church that they should be trampled out.

The heartfelt desire, both of Wycliffe and Huss, was that the Christian Church should be truly saintly, and that the rulers of the Church should be the most saintly members of it. When they saw that this was not the case, and that among the nominal rulers of the Church, whether popes or bishops, there were men whose private lives were bad, and whose conduct was tyrannous, they said, "That is the work, not of Christ, but of antichrist." Wycliffe said this in more daring terms, but not more bravely, than Huss. Perhaps both Wycliffe and Huss pressed it unduly on the clergy as an absolute duty, that they should be poor. More justly might they have said that a Christian minister, if wealthy, ought to use his wealth primarily for the benefit of others, and to regard his own right to it as of less account. The most important positive work done by Wycliffe was his translation of the Bible into English; this must be reckoned more valuable, because more seminative of future good, than his attacks on special religious errors of his day. But still more valuable than any nameable piece of work done by Wycliffe or Huss, was their constant assertion that Christ and not the pope was the head of the Christian Church. Of these two heroes, when all is considered, Huss ought to take the precedence. Of all saints that have been from the time of the apostles to our own day, I know none who is more saintly than Huss; who, having to bear the burden of resistance to his own order and to his own intimate companions, in accordance with the dictates of his conscience, did so with such deep humility and such entire absence of rancour against his assailants; who never forgot that he himself might err; who, when imprisoned by his enemies in filthy dungeons (before he had ever been tried at all) and made ill by cruel usage, yet never lost the sanity and uprightness of his mind, or the resolution of his heart; who never, in the last extremity, forgot to love those who were dear to him, and to forgive those who ill-treated him; and who, always comforted by the thought of the sufferings of Jesus, sent out his last words, when burned at the stake, to Jesus in heaven. This took place in July 1415; just sixteen years before Jeanne d'Arc was slain, she too a saint and a martyr, in a similar way, and by a similar unjust judgment.

Let me sketch the career of Huss, that had so tragic and yet so glorious an end. Born about 1373 in a village of Bohemia, near the borders of Bavaria, he suffered much from poverty in his childhood; but when about sixteen years old he went to study at the university of Prague, founded some forty years previously. There he obtained distinction and made friends, of whom the most famous was Jerome of Prague, intimately associated with Huss afterwards. He had to practise strict economy; but when he became a lecturer at the university (in 1398), he was relieved from real straits. From the year 1391 onwards he was familiar with the writings of Wycliffe, which were much read at Prague, and was much drawn to the views therein expressed (not, however, agreeing with all of them). In 1401 he was appointed preacher at a chapel called the Bethlehem chapel, recently built at Prague; in 1402 he was made rector of the university. Already, for some forty years, there had been in Prague preachers who had felt the Church to be in a state that needed great reform, and not least in regard of the mendicant orders of friars, who had by no means kept up their original habits of energy and self-denial. Of these reforming preachers the most powerful had been Militz, who on one occasion suffered imprisonment for his attacks on the friars; but Matthew (or Matthias) of Janow was a more learned writer than Militz, and had had a more direct influence on Huss. The idea that antichrist as well as Christ was in the world, and that the two were working against each other, was common to both Militz and Matthew of Janow (as it had belonged to Wycliffe also).

But Huss far surpassed any of his predecessors in Bohemia in general influence over the nation. There must indeed have been something singularly lovable about him, for he held for a long time the affections of those who stood in positions of constituted authority, as well as of the ardent youth of the nation. But it was plain that he never held the papal authority to be absolute; for nothing is clearer, all through, than his determination to acknowledge Christ, and not the pope, as head of the Church; hence this doctrine, with its consequences, made the clergy continually more hostile to him. Perhaps this might not have been the case if he had merely enunciated the doctrine in an abstract manner; but he assailed with the greatest vigour the practical faults of the clergy, especially the buying of ecclesiastical offices, which (in spite of all the efforts that Hildebrand had made) still went on; and other clerical faults did not pass unblamed. Lastly, when pope John XXIII proclaimed a crusade against his enemy, king Ladislaus of Naples, and issued a bull granting a full indulgence to all who took part in this crusade, Huss was unable to avoid indicating his disapproval of such a procedure. This was the critical act by which he lost the support of some who had so far gone with him, but who now, terrified at the possible consequences to themselves, shrank into an unworthy submission to him who, for the moment, bore the title of the vicar of Christ.

It will easily be understood how the real opposition of Huss to the ecclesiastical authorities of his own day came to be misrepresented; how it could be falsely said of him at the council of Constance that he called the Church the synagogue of Satan, or again that he urged his followers to take up the sword; how all the opinions of Wycliffe were fastened on to him, whereas he drew distinctions between those opinions, and (for instance) did not agree with Wycliffe's rejection of the doctrine of transubstantiation. Yet it must not be thought that Huss spoke or wrote without ardour or vehemence; he felt that great evils were dominant in the Church, and in the highest places in the Church; how could he be mild in attacking these? The following is one of his severer denunciations; it was written after he had been exiled from Prague, but before his journey to Constance; it is contained in a letter to a friend. For the explanation of one phrase in it, we have to remember that the word "Huss" in the Bohemian language means "goose," and Huss continually refers to himself as the "goose":

"As to my body," he writes[1], "that I hope, by the Lord Jesus Christ, if mercy bestow the strength on me, to offer up, since I desire not to live longer in this miserable world, if I cannot stir up myself and others, according to the will of God, to repentance. This I wish for you also; and I exhort you, in the Lord Jesus Christ, with all the companions of your board, that you be ready for the trial; for the prelude of antichrist must begin first, and then the contest will go on in right good earnest. And the goose must flap her wings against the wings of behemoth, and against the tail which always conceals the abominations of antichrist. The Lord will reduce the tail and his prophets to nothing, i.e. the pope and his prophets, the masters, teachers, and jurists, who, under the hypocritical name of holiness, conceal the abominations of the beast."

Did Huss speak too strongly when he characterised the pope in this way? The reader may consider, when I quote the parallel language of the council of Constance respecting pope John XXIII.

---

[1] See Neander (Torrey's translation), vol. IX. p. 423.

It had not been at all the first object of the council of Constance to deal with the heresies of Wycliffe or of Huss; the first object of that council had been to settle the question, who should be pope. The pope whom the council in the first instance acknowledged was pope John XXIII, by whose authority, nominally, the council had been convened; but there were two other popes, calling themselves respectively Gregory XII and Benedict XIII, who had long been rival popes, and were still held as such by their respective adherents. Had there, however, been no special objection to John XXIII, it would have been natural for the council of Constance to confirm him in his tenure of the papacy; for Gregory XII and Benedict XIII had both been deposed by the council of Pisa, held six years before the council of Constance, and Alexander V had been then elected pope; and John XXIII was the successor of Alexander V. Why then should not the council of Constance have adhered to John XXIII as the true pope, and simply discarded Gregory XII and Benedict XIII? (Alexander V, who was and is regarded as a true pope, had styled Gregory XII "a child of perdition" and Benedict XIII "a "nursling of iniquity.") Why was not the recognised title of John XXIII to be pope continued in its validity by the council of Constance? Let me give the reasons as stated by the cardinals and bishops who were the authorities in the council of Constance; premising that John XXIII, from fear of some such decision, had fled from Constance some time before. Here then is the decree of the council:

In the name of the holy and undivided Trinity, Father and Son and Holy Spirit. Amen.

The sacred general council of Constance, lawfully gathered together in the Holy Spirit, representing the Church universal, having called on the name of Christ, having God alone in view, has seen the articles drawn up and put forward in this case against the Lord Pope John XXIII, and has tested their truth; and after his voluntary submission, accompanied by the whole process of the case, and after mature deliberation, pronounces, decrees, and declares, by this definite written sentence, that the withdrawal from this city of Constance and from this sacred council of Constance, effected by the aforesaid Lord Pope John XXIII, secretly and by night, at a suspicious hour, in indecent disguise, was and is unlawful, of notorious scandal to the church of God and to the aforenamed council, disturbing and hindering to the peace and unity of the church itself, giving nutriment to an inveterate schism, and being an abandonment of the promise and oath rendered to God and to the church and to this sacred council by the Lord Pope himself; and that the Lord Pope himself has been and is notorious for simony, a notorious plunderer of the property and rights of the Roman church and of many other churches and of other

places of piety, a bad administrator and dispenser of the spiritual and
temporal possessions of the church; by his detestable and dishonourable
life and habits scandalising notoriously the church of God and the people
of Christ, both before his rise to the papacy and afterwards up to the present
time; that he himself in the aforesaid ways has scandalised and does
scandalise notoriously the community of Christian men; and that after
due and affectionate warnings repeatedly made to him, he has pertin-
aciously continued in the aforesaid evil ways and in his arrogance, and has
thus rendered himself notoriously incorrigible; and that he himself on
account of the aforesaid and other wrongdoings brought out in the process
of the case, must be removed, deprived, and deposed, as an unworthy,
useless, and harmful person, from the papacy and from all spiritual and
temporal government.   And therewith this sacred synod does remove,
deprive, and depose him, by declaring all worshippers of Christ, collectively
and individually, of every rank, dignity, and condition, free from their
obedience, fidelity, and oath in his regard.

Perhaps I need not quote more; the sentiments of the council
of Constance towards pope John XXIII will not be doubtful.
Huss, in the quotation which I made from him above, is much
briefer and more picturesque than the council; but do not the
council and Huss exactly coincide in their estimate of pope John
XXIII; and if the pope was so bad a man, is it not clear that other
members of the Church must have been greatly blamable also?
What then was the remedy which Huss would have applied?
Free speech concerning these things; the general recognition of
evil as evil; the inculcation of faith in Christ, as superior to the
visible government of the Church, and as sure to provide a
remedy, if the voices that reproved evil were not forcibly silenced.
Through this kind of spiritual censure and arraignment of evil,
it dawned on the mind of Huss that a Church under the direct
government of Christ would come into being, purified of the taints
with which the Church as he saw it was sullied.   He had no direct
intention of overthrowing the ecclesiastical organisation as he
saw it; the purification of it, not the overthrow of it, was what he
aimed at.   But it was not in the visible organisation of the Church
that he saw divinity; the divinity, he thought, lay elsewhere.
Now the council of Constance, though they felt the necessity of
removing an unworthy pope, yet did entertain the opinion, that
the visible organisation of the Christian Church, with the pope at
the head of it, was in itself divine.   Therefore, feeling that Huss
did not hold this, they regarded him as a heretic; and they
welcomed, and readily believed, all sorts of assertions about him,
attributing to him a crudeness in denying accredited beliefs,
which was very far from being a characteristic of his.   All through

his trial at Constance, there was nothing of which Huss so much complained as of the misrepresentation to which his beliefs had been subjected; and considering the technical habit of mind which mediæval theologians cultivated, this was probably unavoidable. When he appealed from the pope to Jesus Christ, he met with derision; and yet in that appeal lay the genuine belief in an invisible world beyond the world of sense; which the theologians of the day professed to recognise, but in effect denied.

Of the shameful treatment which Huss met with at Constance I need say no more than I have said already. The council were unworthy enough to sanction the breach of faith committed by the emperor Sigismund, who had given Huss a safe conduct, guaranteeing that he should not only go safely to Constance, but also that he should return safely from Constance; the heresy of Huss was held to be a valid reason for this breach of a solemn pledge.

The name of Jerome of Prague, not so brave as Huss and yet brave, and a martyr in the same cause, must not be left unmentioned. Of the wars that followed the death of Huss no account can be given here; they belong to a less memorable order of things than his own deeds and sufferings. The latter half of the fifteenth century, memorable in many ways, was almost a blank in the way of religious reform; the great name of Savonarola shines out however as a light in the darkness.

A few sentences from the touching address which Huss, nearly a month before he died, wrote from his prison to "the whole Bohemian Nation" may fitly close the present chapter:

Faithful in God, men and women, rich and poor! I beg and entreat you to love the Lord God, praise His word, gladly hear it and live according to it. ...I beg you to love, praise, and honour those priests who lead a moral life, those in particular who work for the word of God. I beg you to beware of crafty people, particularly of unworthy priests of whom our Saviour has said that they are clothed like sheep, but are inwardly greedy wolves. ...How God has acted towards me, how he has been with me during all my troubles—that you will only know when by the grace of God we shall meet again in heaven[1].

[1] Quoted from Count Lützow's *Life and Times of Master John Hus*, pp. 264–5.

CHAPTER XXV

THE REFORMATION ERA

It would be affectation to style the great religious upheaval of the sixteenth century otherwise than by that name which is universally accorded to it, the Reformation; but it must be said at the outset that the name is, strictly speaking, an incorrect one. The movement in which Luther was the leader was a just rebellion; but if by a reformation we mean, as I think we should mean, a reconstruction on fairly permanent lines, the title is too large a one to be properly claimed for it. The time was not ripe for so great an achievement as that. None of the Reformers knew, or could know, the precise extent and kind of the erring elements in the Christian society. They sought to counteract the evils which came most prominently before their eyes; the despotism on the one hand, the subservience on the other hand, through which religious doctrines had been made the instruments of pecuniary greed; the gross misplacement of reverence, through which popes, notoriously immoral in their lives and intriguers for temporal power, were officially regarded as holy; the deterioration of character in the community which they saw taking place through an artificial scheme of making satisfaction for sins. In all this the direction of their efforts was generally right; but when they tried to replace the discarded errors by sound positive teaching, they continually mistook the real limits of truth and error, sometimes rejecting aspirations that had a heavenly origin, and sometimes exalting too highly the authorities to whom they gave their allegiance. Such mistakes could scarcely have been avoided; but in one way they even entered upon new error (although error of which the seeds lay in well-known Biblical passages), I mean in their doctrine of the divine predestination of all the actions of men, and of the destinies of each individual man. With all the faults and imperfections of the Reformers, we owe them great gratitude for the freedom they won for us; though naturally not to all in the same degree, and it is a necessary though difficult task to mark the differences between them.

Since, however, the whole survey of the case presented in the foregoing paragraph will be traversed at once by the church of Rome as an erroneous statement of the case—and the church of Rome is too important a part of the Christian society to be disregarded—the next step in this chapter must be the consideration of this bar which is drawn across my path, and the removal of it if it may be removed.

There are two distinct grounds on which the Reformers may be regarded as wrong in that which I have called their just rebellion against the Roman see; first, the ground of the intrinsic divine authority of that see, guaranteed (it is alleged) by Jesus Christ himself; secondly, the ground which any government may claim, not to be disturbed without sufficient reason—the sufficient reason being, it is alleged, non-existent in this case. The second of these grounds can only be treated by a narration of the history of the Reformation era, which is the entire theme of the present chapter; the first ground requires an explicit argument; but before entering on that argument, it should be observed that the prestige of the Roman church at the present day (and I mean by prestige the apparent authority) is not so much derived from historical arguments, as from the unity and discipline of that church, and (some would add) from the notable instances of piety within it. Piety and discipline are excellent things, and their presence in the Roman church may freely be acknowledged and commended; but to produce their right effect in vivifying the hearts of men and bringing the whole world in which we live into harmonious order and fruitful happiness, there is need besides of personal individual energy; and the Roman church has no superiority here. Taking the whole synthesis of goodness, it cannot be said that the Roman church obviously makes men better and happier than the Reformed churches do at the present day; but I concede the imperfection of the Reformed churches as cheerfully as I claim, also, that the Roman church is imperfect. The Reformed churches make no such claim as the Roman church makes, to be intrinsically devoid of error; it is the claim of infallibility which the Roman church regards as its divine prerogative which is the bar in the way of the history which I am recording, and which has now to be surmounted.

In the interior of the cathedral of St Peter at Rome, round the dome of it, are written in very large letters, so that all who see may know and perpend them, these words: *Tu es Petrus, et super hanc petram ædificabo ecclesiam meam*: "Thou art Peter, and upon this rock I will build my church." Why are these words put there? Because it is affirmed by the whole Roman church that "Peter" does not mean Peter alone, but that it means the bishop of Rome, whoever he may be, at any time. Simon Peter was of course not bishop of Rome at the time when these words were spoken to him, nor for long afterwards, if indeed he ever was so; it was not as bishop of Rome that he was thus addressed. The Roman church considers that the words have an official implication, over and above their primary personal application. I am unable to think that this official implication is a part of their meaning. I have endeavoured to show, in an earlier chapter of this work, how well and faithfully Simon Peter performed the part which Jesus assigned to him; how, in that moment of apparently desperate failure, when Jesus himself had been crucified, he by faith discerned, and was truly and absolutely convinced, that Jesus, though dead in the flesh, was alive in the spirit; how he led all the disciples to the same belief, and to the inward experience of its truth; how, through this faith and this experience, he made them a well-ordered community, animated by the Spirit of God, capable of withstanding the assaults of the world around them. Was not the Christian Church then, in a very true sense, built upon Simon Peter? It does not matter whether he were bishop of Rome or not, afterwards; it was not as bishop of Rome that the Church was built upon him.

Moreover, let us consider the way in which Simon Peter's work was extended. The great converter of the heathen world to the gospel was Paul; who, though he had not the special distinction of Peter, that of having rescued the work of Jesus Christ from its apparent downfall and its lowest state, had yet a wider genius than Peter; surely the Church was in some measure founded on him too. And so the Christian Church, in its earliest days, always held: Peter and Paul were the two great apostles; both preached at Rome; and it was from the fact that both preached at Rome, combined with the central and unique position of Rome, as capital of the then known world, that the church of Rome first derived its great authority. But no one pretends that Paul was bishop of Rome; and I find it very difficult to think that Peter was bishop of Rome either; though that both these apostles preached in Rome I do not doubt at all. It will be observed that the text written round the dome of St Peter's, if it means what the church of Rome says it means, deprives Paul of any title to equality with Peter, as ruler of the Church. But it is certain that Clement, and Ignatius, and Irenæus, all considered Peter and Paul as equals in instructing the Romans, and in laying down precepts for the entire Church; the idea that Peter was the single ruler of the Church did not enter the imagination of those holy men.

Again, I cannot but remark how very far from the thoughts of Jesus Christ was any idea of the unconditional superiority of any disciple of his, as ruling the other disciples. That Simon Peter, by virtue of his own native qualities, did for a certain time rule the other disciples, and in the most important way, I maintain; but this is quite a different thing from a ruling office guaranteed to him during all his earthly life and converse with his fellows, which the church of Rome affirms that he had. Consider how the evidence stands in this respect. In the nineteenth chapter of the gospel of Matthew it is recorded how, after the rich young man had sadly given up the idea of discipleship and had gone away, Peter said to Jesus: "Behold, we have left all and followed thee; what shall we have therefore?" How does Jesus answer him?

Verily I say unto you, that ye which have followed me, in the regeneration when the Son of man shall sit on the throne of his glory, ye also shall sit upon twelve thrones, judging the twelve tribes of Israel. And every one that hath left houses, or brethren, or sisters, or father, or mother, or children, or lands, for my name's sake, shall receive a hundredfold, and shall inherit eternal life. But many shall be last that are first; and first that are last.

Now observe, that had Peter's authority over the other disciples been a clear immutable commission, a clear office assigned to him, this is a passage in which one would expect mention of it; whereas it not only is not mentioned, but the words used preclude the supposition that Peter was to hold any such office; for the passage ends with the warning, "Many shall be last that are first, and first that are last." That is to say, the present superiority of any apostle does not imply his permanent superiority. What can be more adverse to the idea of an office of pre-eminent authority given once for all to Simon Peter, and never to be reversed? It was the very object of Jesus to render such a supposition untenable; and he enforces his statement by a parable, and at the end of the parable, repeats the statement, rather more briefly: "So the last shall be first, and the first last." That Simon Peter was the most commanding, the most energetic, the most worthy to be a leader, of all the twelve apostles, was true; it was on this personal quality of his that Jesus relied when he said, "On this rock I will build my church"; but Jesus emphatically warned him against considering this leadership an immutable prerogative. Indeed all through the Bible the same tone is preserved; take those remarkable words in which God is said to have addressed the pious but erring high priest and judge, Eli:

> Therefore Jehovah, the God of Israel, saith; I said indeed that thy house, and the house of thy father, should walk before me for ever; but now Jehovah saith, Be it far from me; for them that honour me I will honour, and they that despise me shall be lightly esteemed. 1 Samuel ii. 30.

That is to say: All the promises of God must be regarded as given with the understanding that those who receive them shall act in a manner worthy of the promise received. The promise is, in every case, to be understood in the spirit, not in the letter; no man, no body of men, is privileged to say, "We have received this promise from God, our personal unworthiness cannot prevent our claiming its fulfilment." Does not every Christian hold that it was the personal unworthiness of the Jewish priests, and of the Pharisees, Sadducees and scribes and other leaders of the nation, which caused the promises of God to his people to flow in another line from that indicated by the literal meaning of the Old Testament writings? This most fundamental law of the divine method is no whit altered by Christianity; it is implied in the words which I have quoted, addressed by Jesus himself to his most valiant, most trusted disciple, after the promise of rule which he had given to all the disciples, "But"—observe the qualification of the promise which this particle implies—"But many shall be last that are first, and first that are last." Neither Peter nor any other apostle must presume on the promise given them, as if their right of judging the twelve tribes of Israel was indefeasibly assured to them, irrespectively of all that they might afterwards do or feel or say.

Thus the words on which the church of Rome relies, "Thou art Peter, and upon this rock I will build my church," do not, even in their application to Simon Peter himself, imply an unconditional pre-eminence over all other Christians. Yet they were not vain words; they had their fulfilment, and an adequate fulfilment. Simon Peter was the apostle who carried the society of believers in Jesus through the first and most desperate danger to which they were ever exposed; the danger of dissolution when the Master had been taken away from them. The Church was built on him; but we must not press this metaphor so stringently as to say that he was the sole foundation of the Church. The Church was built on Jesus Christ himself (as Paul tells us), and even in a more absolute sense than that in which it was built on Simon Peter; and I think we must say that, as far as the first building of the Church is concerned, Paul was the equal of Peter. This it is which Paul claims for himself; he claims no more than this, but he does claim this:

"When they saw," he tells the Galatians (i.e. when the chief apostles saw), "that I had been intrusted with the gospel of the uncircumcision, even as Peter with the gospel of the circumcision (for he that wrought for Peter unto the apostleship of the circumcision wrought for me also unto the Gentiles)"

—perhaps I need not finish the passage; it is plain from it that Paul acknowledges no duty of looking up to Peter as the divinely appointed head of the visible Church. Yet if the interpretation of the words "Thou art Peter, and upon this rock I will build my church" given by the church of Rome be correct, Paul ought to have acknowledged Peter as the head of the visible Church. It is perfectly plain that Paul did not acknowledge him as such.

If then Simon Peter himself was not the head of the visible Church in his own day, how can any of his successors be so, or have been so?

I will not argue the further point, whether the bishops of Rome are the successors of Peter; if Peter was not head of the Church, neither can the popes be so. But it is worth while to remind my reader again that the great authority of the Roman church in the early centuries, which in mediæval times was enlarged to a supremacy over the whole western church, had its origin in the two circumstances—first, that Rome was the metropolis of nearly all the world then known, and secondly, that the two greatest apostles, Peter and Paul, had preached there, and had received the crown of martyrdom there; Rome was sacred as the place which had witnessed their holy sufferings and which still held their mortal remains. Greatness and holiness thus met in Rome in a degree in which they met in no other place on earth; for though the sufferings and death of Jesus Christ would render Jerusalem still holier, Jerusalem had no title to greatness, and besides was mixed up with a Jewish Christianity which had been decadent even before the close of the first century. There can be nothing to surprise us in the authority which the church of

Rome exercised over the other Christian churches; but it was an authority which, as I think I have shown, ought never to have been regarded as absolute.

Still, an authority it was; and now the question arises, whether the Reformers of the sixteenth century were justified in disobeying it; whether, in disobeying it, they did not break through Christian law, a law sacred even if not absolute. For there are many ties and obligations and mutual agreements between men, to which no one would ascribe an absolute character, but which still ought not to be broken without just cause. Was there just cause in this case? There was; and I must now say why.

I have not, in the foregoing chapters, minimised the services which the Christian Church rendered to mankind from the very first, in spreading abroad the maxims of love, forgiveness, self-denial; in proclaiming the doctrine that all the deeds of men shall be judged by the righteous judgment of God; in holding out to men the promise of eternal life; in pointing to the death of Jesus Christ as the efficient cause whereby eternal life might be realised as a truth in our own experience, even while we are still in the flesh; in preserving the sacred ceremony by which the present love of Jesus Christ towards us, his support of us, is symbolised. In all this the Christian Church had done well; and amid many crimes and wrong-doings, a real purification and strengthening of human nature had been taking place during the twelve centuries which had elapsed since the conversion of Constantine.

But I need hardly remind my reader, after all that has been said in the previous chapters of this work, of the other side of the picture—of the oppression exercised by the Church over the free intellect of man; of the innumerable burnings of heretics that had taken place during the five centuries from 1000 A.D. to 1500 A.D.; and lastly, of this ultimate stretch of tyranny, that it had been reckoned a heresy to appeal from the judgment of the visible society of pope and cardinals and prelates to the judgment of Jesus Christ in the heavens; whereby it ensued that the complaints of all subordinate Christians were quenched in fire and blood.

It was a terrible evil; and we must not be surprised that, in the gradual uprooting and expulsion of it, which took place very slowly in the sixteenth century, more rapidly in the seventeenth, and at last with a great rush of popular feeling at the end of the eighteenth, a loss should have been incurred of things very valuable to human welfare; although the loss was not, as we must hope and believe, final. The Christian Church in the west was shattered; that was one loss; and a very extensive disbelief in the whole value of Christianity, and of religion altogether, grew up in the most civilised parts of the world; that was another loss. We must not underrate our misfortunes; but the gain is greater; and for the reparation of our ills, for the construction of the true eternal society, in which every member shall feel the wrongs of another as his own wrongs and leap forward spontaneously to the remedying of them, we must look, as Huss did, to Jesus Christ in the heavens; and even beyond, to that Almighty Divine Love in which all life is rooted; and thus shall the spiritual Church, which never can fail, grow gradually about us. For, as Luther said—

We tell our Lord God plainly that if he will have his Church, he must maintain it himself; for if we could maintain it, we should be the proudest asses under heaven.

As one step in the way to this final result, the great religious outburst of the sixteenth century, though in itself imperfect, is justified.

The beginning of it is well known; how pope Leo X, being in need of money for many purposes, and more especially for the building of his new cathedral of St Peter in Rome, determined to obtain it by a liberal granting of "indulgences" to penitent sinners. What were, or rather what are, indulgences (for the Roman church, as is well known, still grants them)? To explain this, it is necessary to refer to some of the elements of morality and religion.

To every Christian, and to many who have belonged to religions outside Christianity, this question is all-important; How may man be at peace with God, in harmony with God? or to use a word which is still more familiar in this kind of question, How may man be reconciled to God? There may be readers of mine who do not believe in God, and for their sakes I will put this question in a form which will be more intelligible to them: How may man obtain or at any rate approach rectitude and purity of action? To a believer in God, the possession of rectitude and purity does of itself imply having peace, harmony, reconciliation with God; and indeed a man may be said, in a very true sense, to be reconciled to God if he be set in the right way, even though still subject to many faults; provided, of course, he be in the way to amend his faults. There may be true reconciliation, without the full attainment of that end which reconciliation has in view; but the right tendency must be there.

Now the method of attaining reconciliation with God which the whole western or Roman church had in Luther's time come to accept was this: First, it was assumed that a man must be baptized, confirmed, and receive the sacred bread which was held to be the body of Christ (the sacred wine was not given to laymen); Secondly, in respect of particular sins which he might commit, he must feel contrition for them, he must confess them to a priest, and he must render satisfaction to God for having committed such sins. This last clause was the one on which the dispute between Luther and the pope arose. For from it the question immediately followed, What satisfaction did God require from a man who, having committed sins, was sorry for them and had confessed them? The Roman church answered: The penalty to be paid may be prescribed by the priest to whom the sinner confesses; or, if not so paid, it will consist in purgatorial pains after death.

(It is worth observing here, parenthetically, how entirely the thought of making satisfaction to a fellow-man whom one has injured is ignored in the whole of this discussion. It ought not to have been ignored; but the discussion even without it is not a meaningless one.)

I have not come to the indulgences yet; and therefore I have not got to the point which occasioned Luther's actual quarrel with the Roman church, but it is important to say here that, even in what has been stated, the Roman theory did not meet with Luther's approval. For Luther thought: The Christian faith brings us in direct contact with God, and with the Son of God, Jesus Christ, who died for us; is not trust in God, trust in Jesus Christ, and the vivid sense of what Jesus Christ did and of his sacred death upon the cross, the real touch of reunion between ourselves and God? If a man has this, will he not by the natural truth of the feelings so entertained be put in the right way, be reconciled to God? Is it not putting the thoughts of men in an altogether wrong direction to tell them that God needs special acts of satisfaction before he takes us into his love and favour? Far otherwise is the case; God wants us to trust him; and above all, God wants us to feel what Jesus Christ has done, the worth of that divine self-surrender which first brought the human race into perfect communion with God. Feel this, and rectitude of action will follow naturally, as a stream from its source.

I have not been quoting Luther; and the dialect of Luther cannot be the dialect of the twentieth century after Christ; were I to quote him, the interpretation would still be needed. But I have tried to express, in the English language of the twentieth century, the thought and the feeling which animated Luther four hundred years ago. Was it not a most worthy thought and feeling, even though we may not assent to all the ideas which Luther attached to it? But to these I have not come yet.

This belief of Luther was in him before ever the question of indulgences met him at all. It will be understood of course that baptism and the reception of the Lord's Supper were as sacred to Luther as to the Roman church; nor did he deny that Christians ought to be sorry for their sins, and confess them; it was the idea that God needed a satisfaction to be paid him, before he could be reconciled with an offender, to which Luther raised his demurrer. No, he said; God needs that we should trust in him; that will set us right.

It is a question which cannot now be answered, whether the dissent of Luther from the doctrine of the Roman church in the point named would ever have been expressed openly, if a practical reason had not entered in, which moved him in a way in which mere difference of theory could not have moved him. I incline to say that he would have expressed it; but with what consequences, who shall say? However, I come to what actually happened.

In explaining the theory of the Roman church, I had got so far as this, that the sinner, in order to be received into God's favour, is held bound to make satisfaction to God for his sin. Perhaps he may not be able to make entire satisfaction in this life; in that case he will pay what is due by suffering, after death, the pains of purgatory. But then it is also held that the pope has command of a treasure which will relieve the sinner from a part of this payment; indeed (if the pope wills) even from the whole of it (except only from that sacramental penance which his confessor may impose for immediate performance); this treasure has been won by the merits of Jesus Christ himself, of the Virgin Mary, and of the saints; and by applying this treasure in any particular case, the pope can relieve the penitent sinner from the need of any further suffering, here or hereafter, which the Divine Justice would otherwise require. This relief, if given by the pope, is called an "indulgence[1]."

---

[1] The reader will not expect from me that intimate personal acquaintance with the theories of the Roman church which a Roman Catholic would have; but I believe that the statement above given is correct.

Now at the present day the Roman church does not sell indulgences; but it is impossible to deny that the Roman church sold them in the days of Luther. As I said, pope Leo X was greatly in need of money for the building of his new cathedral of St Peter's at Rome; and the sale of indulgences was a way in which it was possible to get money, and he resorted to this method accordingly. In buying an indulgence, a man thus paid, not indeed for the pardon of his sins, but for the remission of certain pains which (it was held) he must otherwise endure, here or hereafter. Further, it was held that, by buying an indulgence, a man might buy off some one dear to him, who had died, from suffering the full measure of purgatorial pains now being inflicted. The thought that a man's father or mother, by a little expenditure of money on his own part, might be relieved from severe present pain, was a very powerful motive towards buying an indulgence.

Luther, then, was led to dissent from the church of Rome on two distinct grounds, though pertaining to the same subject: First, he disapproved of the idea, which lay at the root of the indulgences, that God, in pardoning a sinner, required of him a formal satisfaction by way of penalty; Secondly, he still more disapproved of the idea that a man, by purchasing an indulgence from the pope, could obtain an exemption from the whole or a part of this penalty. In any just consideration of the origin of the Reformation, these two grounds of complaint must be kept separate, and must be treated separately; but they were so much allied that at the time it was very difficult to separate them. I think, however, it will plainly appear from the quotations which I shall now give that in regard to the second of these complaints made by Luther, he was not only right, but is now acknowledged to be right by everyone, the Roman church included. And though Luther did not formally separate his two grounds of complaint, yet it was the second on which he mainly insisted when he began to attack the indulgences; he did not at first attack indulgences considered as the remission of external penalties.

This, then, is what happened. When Luther found, in his office of a priest of the Church, that the penitents who came to confess their sins to him regarded those sins as easily remitted, by virtue of the indulgences which could be purchased (and practically the indulgences were regarded as conveying pardon for sin, though this was not the precise theory of them, as I have said), he felt deeply opposed to the light and easy temper thus indicated. But he considered that the whole question needed sifting; and being a university professor at Wittenberg, he posted on the doors of the Castle church in that town, on the 31st October, 1517, ninety-five theses (as was the custom with learned men in those days) inviting disputation on the whole subject. A copy of these theses he sent to Albert, archbishop of Mayence and of Magdeburg, his own ecclesiastical superior, and with them a letter, an extract from which will be the best way of showing what was Luther's mind at this time[1]:

Under thy most illustrious sanction (titulo) there are being carried about papal indulgences for the building of St Peter's; in regard of which I do not so much accuse the utterances (exclamationes) of the preachers, which I have not heard; but I lament that the most serious misunderstandings (falsissimas intelligentias) on the part of the common people have been drawn from them, misunderstandings which are a common theme of their boasting everywhere; namely, because these unhappy souls believe that, if they have bought letters of indulgences, they are secure of their salvation; also, that souls forthwith fly out of purgatory, when they have thrown their contribution into the box: moreover, that these divine favours are so great, that no sin is so huge as not to be atoned for by them; also, that a man through these indulgences is free from all punishment and all guilt. O most good God! It is under thy care, most excellent Father [Archbishop] that souls are instructed thus, handed over to death, and most hard is the account that has to be rendered by thee, gathering and growing, on all these matters. Therefore was I not able to keep silence longer about them. For it is not by any gift of a bishop that a man becomes secure of his salvation, since he does not even become secure through the grace of God poured into him, but the apostle bids us work out our salvation always in fear and trembling; and it is with difficulty that the righteous man shall be saved; and so narrow is the way that leads to life, that the Lord through the prophets Amos and Zechariah calls those who are to be saved "brands plucked from the burning"; and everywhere the Lord proclaims the difficulty of salvation. How then do they by these false fables of pardons, by these promises of theirs, make the people secure and free from fear? Since indulgences convey no profit at all to souls for their salvation or holiness, but only take away the outward penalty, which formerly was wont to be imposed by canonical rule. Lastly, works of piety and charity are infinitely better than indulgences, and yet they do not preach these with so much pomp; nay, they rather keep silence about them in order that they may preach pardons.

That is Luther's own evidence as to the effect of the indulgences on the characters of those with whom he was concerned. Before considering other evidence, let us ask whether there are matters which ought to have been mentioned, passed over by him. It may seem that he ought, in justice to the Church, to

---

[1] I translate from the original Latin, which I find in *Documents Illustrative of the Continental Reformation* by the Rev. B. J. Kidd, D.D., page 27.

have mentioned that "contrition" of heart which, in the theory
of salvation then held, was the first obligation of a penitent, and
which was to be succeeded by confession of the sin committed.
No doubt, if such contrition had been urged upon the penitent
with seriousness, as the thing of first importance, and as necessary
for the future reformation of his character, the complaint of
Luther would have been partly met; though the intrinsic value
of the indulgences would still have been open to question. But
in fact the obligation of contrition of heart was expressed in so
bare and technical a manner that the penitent might easily
hold it a slight and perfunctory obligation, whereas all the stress
was laid on the "satisfaction," which was to be duly made by
purchase of the indulgences. Thus in the long letter of instructions which the archbishop of Mayence wrote to the sub-com-
missaries who were to sell the indulgences, contrition is mentioned
in the following manner[1]:

In the first place let everyone who is contrite in heart, and who has
confessed with his mouth, visit at least seven churches assigned for this
purpose, those namely on which the Papal arms are affixed, and in each
church let him devoutly say five Paternosters and five Ave Marias, for
the honour of the five wounds of our Lord Jesus Christ by whom our
redemption was accomplished.

Slight though the mention of contrition of heart here is,
and little though the commands here imposed have to do with
contrition, they may yet be accompanied by contrition; they
do not belong to a totally different order of thought and feeling.
But the payment of money (which is enjoined in addition) is
not naturally combined with contrition; it belongs to an entirely
different sphere of thought; it is mercantile, and not spiritual.
The man who, by paying for an indulgence, has escaped the
penalty which his sin would otherwise have brought on him, is
not likely to be keenly affected by a guilty conscience. His
contrition, he would think, is over.

This is the probability of the case, and therefore we have
ground, even if we had only this probability to go on, for believing
Luther, when in the passage above quoted he tells the archbishop
of Mayence that the penitents who came to him took their sins
very lightly. But there is other evidence which goes to support
Luther's assertion.

Let me first quote part of the letter[2] of Erasmus to the archbishop of Mayence, written in 1519, before Luther had been

[1] See page 14 of Dr Kidd's *Documents* above-mentioned.
[2] From Dr Kidd's *Documents*, p. 55.

excommunicated, and when the excitement caused by Luther's ninety-five theses was at its height:

" First of all," he writes, " we must look to the sources of this mischief. The world has been burdened by human arrangements, has been burdened by the opinions and dogmas of the schools, by the tyranny of the mendicant friars, who, though merely subordinate ministers of the Roman See, have yet arrived at such a pitch of power and numbers, as to be formidable to the Pope himself and even to the monarchs. When the Pope is on their side, he is more than God; in what is done contrary to their advantage, he has no more power than a dream. I am not condemning all of them, but there are very many of this kind, who for the sake of gain and power sedulously ensnare the consciences of men. And with unabashed forehead they had already begun, leaving Christ unmentioned, to preach their own new and often too impudent dogmas. About indulgences they spoke in such a manner that even idiots could not endure it. By this means, and by others of this kind, the vigour of evangelical teaching was gradually vanishing; and the prospect was that as things grew ever worse, that spark of Christian piety which might have rekindled the lost love would be extinguished; the whole of religion was tending to a more than Jewish ceremonialism."

It will be conceded that, if that description be true—and Erasmus was never a rebel against the church of Rome—a warning voice was urgently needed for the remedy of such a disastrous state of things; and it will be observed that Erasmus explicitly speaks of the indulgences as being preached in an intolerable manner.

Let me next quote a few sentences from the long and elaborate recommendations, with a view to reform, which nine great Church dignitaries (selected for this purpose) addressed to the recently appointed pope Paul III in the year 1538. So candid a document is this, so plain-spoken and yet so respectful, that the names of those who drew it up ought not to be forgotten; here they are:

> Gaspar card. Contarenus.
> Joannes Petrus card. Theatinus.
> Jacobus card. Sadoletus.
> Reginaldus card. Anglicus.
> Fredericus arch. Salernitanus.
> Hieronymus arch. Brundusinus.
> Joannes Matthæus episcopus Veronensis.
> Gregorius abbas S. Georgii Venet.
> Frater Thomas magister sacri palatii.

Such are their names and offices; and now for some of their words:

Most blessed father, we are so far from being able to express in words the thanks which the Christian republic must pay to God the Greatest and Best, for having set thee in these times as high priest (pontificem) and shepherd over his flock, and for having given thee the mind which thou hast; how great thanks, we cannot in our hopeful thoughts give measure to. For that Spirit of God on which the high goodness of the heavens is based (as the prophet says) has determined to restore by thy hand the tottering church of Christ now almost fallen headlong, to give support to this ruin, to raise it up and to restore it to its original sublimity and to its first beauty....Now since thy Holiness, taught by the Spirit of God, which (as Augustine says) speaks in the heart with no sound of words, has well discerned that the beginning of these evils has come from hence, namely that some Popes (pontifices) thy predecessors, having itching ears (prurientes auribus), as says the apostle Paul, have heaped up to themselves masters according to their desires, not in order to learn from them what they ought to do, but in order that by their cleverness and zeal a method might be discovered of making licence lawful; hence it ensued (besides that all princedom is followed by flattery as a body by its shadow, and truth is always slow to reach the ears of princes) that straightway there came forward teachers who taught that the Pope was the lord of all clerical benefices; and therefore since a lord sells that which is his own, it follows necessarily that no charge of simony can attach to the Pope....This above all things, most blessed father, we wish to be ordained, as Aristotle says in his *Politics*; that as in every republic, so in this ecclesiastical government of the church of Christ, one law is to be supremely kept, namely that as far as possible laws should not be broken; nor should we think it allowable for us to make dispensations in the matter of keeping the laws, unless for some urgent and necessary cause. No more pernicious custom can be implanted in any republic than this disregard of the laws which our ancestors have deemed sacred, and have called venerable and divine. All these things thou, most excellent Pope, knowest and hast long ago read in the works of philosophers and theologians; but there is one thing which we do not merely regard as coming next to the above, but as coming before it and preferable to it, namely that it is not allowable for the Pope, the vicar of Christ, in the exercise of his power conferred on him by Christ (we mean the power of the keys), to make any gain. For this is Christ's command; Freely ye have received, freely give....This command has relation not only to thy own holiness but to all who are partakers of this power, we would therefore wish it to be observed by thy legates and ambassadors. For as the practice which has now become customary dishonours this See, and distresses the people, so if things were done in contrary fashion, the greatest honour would be obtained for this See, and the people would be wonderfully edified....Nor should indulgences be granted save once in the year in each one of the cities that have an illustrious name. Dr Kidd's *Documents*, pp. 307–318.

I have not had space to give the long list of abuses enumerated in this document as points in which reform is required; the point of the indulgences is that which here needs notice.

After Erasmus and the cardinals, let us see what the council of Trent says on the subject of indulgences. It emphatically

sanctions them, as a privilege committed by Christ to the Church,
to be administered for the benefit of the Christian community;
but to the sanction it appends the following caution[1] (the date
of this deliverance is the 4th December, 1563):

But as to the abuses which have crept into these matters, by reason
of which (quorum occasione) this noble name of indulgences is blasphemed
by heretics, this sacred synod, desiring that such abuses shall be amended
and corrected, decides in general terms by this present decree, that all
base gains (pravos quæstus) received as payment for indulgences (out of
which great cause of abuses has flowed into the Christian community)
are to be entirely abolished.

At a previous meeting, held on the 16th June, 1562, the
council had decreed[2] that if any money was paid by persons
receiving indulgences, it was to be devoted to purposes of charity,
and was not to be treated as if it were a price paid for the
indulgences, which is absolutely forbidden. Similarly in the
decree[3] about purgatory, enacted by the council on the 3rd
and 4th December, 1563, it is ordered by the council that things
which "savour of base gain" (quæ turpe lucrum sapiunt) are
not to have any entrance where the prayers of the faithful for
souls detained in purgatory are concerned.

Now consider the passages that I have quoted, first from
Erasmus; secondly from the committee of cardinals, writing
in the year 1538; thirdly, from the council of Trent, issuing its
decrees in the years 1562 and 1563; is it not clear that all these
authorities regard it as a fact that the issuing of indulgences
had been accompanied by grave abuses; and that finally the
sale of indulgences was absolutely forbidden by the council of
Trent? Can there be stronger evidence that Luther, when he
preached against the sale of indulgences, was acting according
to the dictates of his conscience; that he really had found, as
he said he found, that the souls of men were being damaged
by such a sale, and were imbued with the persuasion that the
payment of money was the important matter for removing the
consequences of sin?

But, says the Roman church, even supposing this to be true,
Luther was a heretic. Was it not, then, the very thing to confirm
him in his heresy if his just representations were ignored? If
Luther had consented to be silent, when a practice was being
carried on which he knew to be detrimental to those under his

---

[1] From Harduin's *Acta Conciliorum*, vol. x. p. 190.
[2] *Acta Conciliorum*, vol. x. p. 125.
[3] *Acta Conciliorum*, vol. x. p. 167.

charge, it would not have been faithful obedience, but cowardly betrayal. There was a time when he would have given up everything except this; namely, when he wrote his[1] letter to cardinal Thomas Cajetan on the 17th October, 1518, and again when he wrote to pope Leo X[2] on the 3rd March, 1519. In each of these letters he offers to keep silence about the indulgences, if his opponents will keep silence also, that is, not preach the indulgences in the manner in which they had done so. He would have kept silence about his personal opinions; but not about an evil which he saw practically at work.

There was in the early conduct of Luther when he preached and wrote against the indulgences a persistent unwillingness to believe that the pope would really silence him, while leaving the practice of the sale of the indulgences as it then stood. He distinguishes between the pope himself and the flatterers of the pope; he asks Leo X to look into the matter himself, and not to be misled by those about him. He was sensible that in the pope the knot of the whole difficulty lay; that if he could gain over the pope, the contentions of inferior ecclesiastics against him would not stand; here it was that the visible structure of the Church must be saved, if it was to be saved at all. It is very unjust to forget, in judging of Luther, that the visible integrity of the Church was a thing naturally dear to him; he did not wish to violate it; even when the evidences kept crowding on him of the obduracy of his opponents, he still hoped that the pope would not wholly condemn him. But it resulted from this conflict of motives in his mind that his expressions appear not always consistent with one another; his lingering faith, that the Church in its established form would justify its divine vocation, was at times expressed by him, even after the reverse conviction had made great progress in his thoughts. The most remarkable instance of this contrariety in the expression of his sentiments is well known. On the 3rd March, 1519, writing to Leo X, he called God and the whole creation to witness that he neither had wished nor did wish any harm to the Roman church, which he acknowledged to be above all things in heaven and earth, save only Jesus Christ the Lord of all. There spoke his lingering faith; and indeed the importance of the external form of the visible Church was so great that we must not be surprised at Luther testifying to it in this manner. But nine days after this

---

[1] *Lutheri Opera*, vol. I. p. 216 a;
[2] *Lutheri Opera*, vol. I. p. 236.

he wrote to Spalatin (one of the most important of his friends—
the secretary and court preacher of the elector Frederick of
Saxony)[1]: "I know not whether the pope is antichrist in person
or his apostle." There spoke the conviction to which experience
was bringing him, even against his own wishes. It is no doubt
true that a man who measured his words carefully would have
modified his expression, certainly in the latter of these utterances,
perhaps in both. But Luther was inapt at measuring his words;
and according as he looked to one side or the other, so did he
express himself; in both cases naturally, though inconsistently
no doubt.

Of these two mighty waves, contrary in their direction and
bias, which swept through Luther at this time, the wave of
reverence for the papal church and the wave of opposition to it,
the latter, as everyone knows, won the day in his breast; and
through the whole year 1519 the force of it in him was increasing.
Nor was this without cause, even independently of the question
of indulgences; many things combined to give it strength.

For first, it is not to be forgotten that in the year 1511, six
years before the dispute about indulgences broke out, Luther
himself had been at Rome, sent thither on a mission from his
convent; and he had been witness of a fact very momentous
both in itself and in its consequences, the decay of Christian
faith which had set in, even amongst the clergy, through the
influence of that movement which is known as the Renaissance.
By the Renaissance is meant the revival of the classical spirit in
Italy and other countries of western Europe, resulting from the
great spread of Greek learning; the progress of the Turks and
their conquest of Constantinople in the middle of the fifteenth
century having been the means of diffusing many Greek manuscripts (and Greek interpreters of those manuscripts also) through
Italy and other Christian countries. The spirit of ancient Greece,
with its beauty and its variety of intellectual energies, now
began first to be appreciated by Christians; and since the proper
balance and true coherence between the natural intellect and
religious reverence had never been reached in Christendom, it
followed that the free intellect, once admitted, began to expel
religious reverence. Even the popes themselves were subject to
this tendency; and not only religion but morality was undermined,
in a serious degree. The evidence of this Luther had had in the
language which he heard and in the things which he knew were

[1] See Köstlin's *Life of Luther* (English translation), p. 134.

taking place during his sojourn at Rome; and he felt the presence there of an antichristian power. Not that the Renaissance was not productive of much good; but there were parts of it that were capable of being used for evil, and the popes of that time, Alexander VI and Julius II and Leo X, fell largely into the evil vein. It was impossible that Luther should not feel this as a weight against the papacy.

This adverse feeling was reinforced, again, by the indignation so abundantly felt in Germany at the way in which that great country was impoverished by papal demands, and ruled in matters in which Germany could better have ruled herself; there was a national criticism of the papacy as a power unworthily grasping and arrogant. Luther could not but sympathise with his fellow-countrymen in these complaints of theirs, and they told with him against the supposed divine station and prerogative of the pope.

Thirdly, it must never be forgotten that, from the first preaching of Luther against indulgences down to the time of his excommunication (and very likely afterwards—but the early years were the dangerous time), the pope and the chief Roman authorities did their utmost to capture him, with the view of forcible repression (if he did not recant). At a very early period of the controversy James van Hoogstraten, a Dominican prior of much note at Cologne, had published the opinion that Luther should be sent to the stake as a dangerous heretic. On August 7th, 1518, Luther received an order to present himself at Rome within sixty days; on the 23rd of the same month, the pope wrote to cardinal Cajetan, whom Luther was about to meet at Augsburg, instructing him to arrest Luther and his adherents. I must not enumerate all the efforts which the pope and the Roman Curia made with the view of getting Luther brought before them at Rome. Why did these efforts not succeed? Primarily and chiefly because the elector Frederick of Saxony, the political ruler under whom Luther lived, was determined to see fair play; and to all the demands of the pope that he should give up Luther he consistently replied that he must himself be convinced of Luther's wrong-doing before he would surrender him. Again, when Luther went to meet Cajetan at Augsburg (the step most perilous to himself that he ever took) it was the elector Frederick who smoothed the way for him, and personally requested Cajetan to treat him with kindness, and to allow him to depart in safety. This Cajetan promised to do—no doubt sincerely; but it is very doubtful if he would have kept his promise; for it was after making it that he received the pope's order to arrest Luther; and had he been able to act upon this, he would probably have considered that this order was the dominating feature of the situation. But Luther's prudence had forestalled him. For thirteen days Luther had remained at Augsburg, and had had several interviews with the cardinal; then, feeling that there was danger in the air, he escaped, and returned to the dominions of the elector, where he was in safety. For his great services in this respect, the elector Frederick ought always to be held in honour. But the difficulty which any man must find in reverencing a person, or a group of persons, who are seeking to burn him, may well be understood; and when we ask the reason of Luther's vehemence against the pope and the papal authorities, reconciliation with them having proved impossible, this is a part of the reason which must not be omitted.

For all the reasons mentioned above, Luther did continually become more vehement against the papacy. As early as the 28th November, 1518, he had appealed from the judgment of the pope to a General Council (though even a General Council he did not regard as infallible); in July, 1519, came his long and formal disputation with Eck at Leipzig, when (to the scandal of duke George of Saxony) he defended Huss for having said that the papal primacy was not a divine institution; and in the year 1520 he issued three treatises more deliberately argumentative against the whole Roman system than anything which he had before written; one, *An Address to the Christian Nobility of the German Nation*, treating especially of the political side of the question; another, *On the Babylonian Captivity of the Church*, treating of the religious side; the third, *On the Liberty of a Christian Man*, which he sent, with a letter, to the pope. But long before this letter reached the pope, indeed even before it was written, the pope's answer had been drawn up; the bull of excommunication against Luther was published in Rome on the 16th June, 1520; not in Germany (to which country it was brought by Eck) till September. The bull allowed Luther 120 days to retract; a permission of which, it is needless to say, advantage was not taken. On the 3rd January, 1521, "Leo X finally pronounced the ban against Luther and his followers, and an interdict on the places where they were harboured[1]."

---

[1] Köstlin's *Life of Luther* (English translation), p. 221.

Thus was the breach completed; and this appears to be a proper occasion for reviewing what Luther so far had done; and though the work of his life was not over, the most important part of it was already done. Here, then, is a summary of his work up to the end of the year 1520.

He had given a deathblow, not indeed to indulgences, but to the selling of indulgences. How long the traffic in them continued I am unable to say; but it would seem that those nine great Roman Catholic theologians whom I quoted above, who in the year 1538 condemned base gains made on behalf of the pope, must have found that the sale of indulgences no more existed.

He had given his strong protest against the burning of heretics; the thirty-third of his affirmations condemned by the pope runs thus: "For heretics to be burned is against the will of the Spirit"; and he had enforced this maxim by scriptural passages, such as the rebuke of the two sons of Zebedee by Jesus Christ, when they wished to call down fire from heaven on the inhospitable Samaritans. He wrote this in 1520; and in 1528 he told the people of Nuremburg that he never could approve of the execution of teachers of error; it was sufficient to expel them[1].

I see no reason why even Roman Catholics of the present day should not agree with me as to those two merits of Luther which I have just stated. In what follows, they will naturally not agree with me; but I rely on the reasons already given.

It must be reckoned a great merit in Luther that he regarded the constitution of the Christian Church, on its formal material side, as human and not divine. This must not be taken as meaning that he ignored a certain divine instinct as having intermingled in the formation of the Church as it then was; but the human element had been there too, and had remained while the divine instinct was decaying, and the human element was now claiming for itself an intrinsic divinity to which it had no title. Most especially was this the case with the papacy, which in Luther's time had sunk deeply in respect of moral worth, and was showing itself unworthy to be the ruler of men. The time had come when the spirit of man must be renewed by

---

[1] I do not believe that Luther ever changed his opinion against inflicting capital punishment on preachers of heresy. He held, I suppose, that Anabaptists were punishable with death (the evidence lies in the library of the University of Heidelberg, not accessible to Englishmen at present); but the Anabaptists were active rebels. P. E. Henry's *Life of Calvin* (vol. II. p. 236 of the English translation) gives the case *against* Luther in the matter; I concede that he might have imprisoned preachers of heresy, though I do not believe he ever did so.

God through channels which were not those of the old ecclesiastical order; and for preaching this Luther deserved, and deserves from us, honour and reverence.

Of the subordinate reforms which Luther advocated while remaining in the Roman church, the most important was the removal of the obligation of celibacy from the clergy; this enters into his Address to the Christian Nobility of the German Nation, and was eminently a timely and salutary proposal. But this, as likewise the other points that have been just mentioned, belongs to the class of liberation from evil, not to the class of positive building up in good; to the building up in good, as described by Luther, I now come, and thereby to that doctrine which has become so barren, so hard, so little-meaning, in the mouths of many who have proclaimed it, but which still has the seed of life in it, not incapable of being recovered even now— the doctrine of "Justification by Faith." Let me try to set it forth in its natural original meaning.

Our vital progress is individual, and yet not simply individual; we are constantly forming ties with others, and these ties are so important to our individual life that without them we should be poor creatures indeed. Yet if the present life were all, such ties would be very transitory; it would be beyond our power to give ardent energy and sedulous thought to their cultivation. But Jesus Christ assumed that this life is not all; that we have the seed of eternal life in us; and if so, the ties which connect us with our fellows in true affection are like the nerves in our present perishable bodies, but yet distinguished from those nerves by their capacity of surviving our physical death. They are the messengers of a living energy, more penetrating than any merely physical energy, expanding continually and flowing into new regions and gathering new fruits, uniting life with life by ever new methods. Such is the nature of eternal life. But in that gathering together of energies which I have described we need an orderly sequence; the raising of the human spirit from the temporal to the eternal sphere, from the visible to the invisible, from the measured and numbered array of things revealed by our present senses to the tentative apprehension of things possibly to be revealed beyond our present senses—this is a task not to be entered on at random, or without carefully weighing the true character, the true value, of the objects and purposes which lie before us. Most men who have reached mature age, everyone who with a feeling heart has arrived at old age, must be aware that the eternal life, if it be truly attainable by us, contains things more precious than any which the realm of sensuous perception could give us, though we had instruments a thousand times more powerful than our present telescopes, microscopes, or any other apparatus of the scientific sort. If the eternal life possesses these treasures, how shall we put ourselves in the way of winning them? To win them is salvation; or in other words, it is the saving of life beyond that which appears to destroy life, namely physical death; the saving of it, the extension of it, in ever worthier and more fruitful capacities. If such a preservation, such an enlargement of our being is a thing that mankind may look forward to, how shall we attain it?

Human sympathies are not absent from our present life, and even in our present life we find that the power of God, responsive to our prayer, helps to confirm and increase them; but our present life is too brief and fleeting to be able to give us a permanent hold upon purposes that shall endure for ever. If we wish to organise the temporal, we must take the eternal to our aid. This was the very thought in the mind of Jesus Christ when he laid down his life in the flesh; this was his central purpose. It is his purpose which we appropriate to ourselves when we seek for salvation beyond death; shall we not seek help from him who has given us our basis on which we may build for ever? When we read the details of the earthly life of Jesus Christ, we feel, despite all the doubts that may hang over particular parts of it, that there was no swerving in his mental grasp of the object at which he aimed; and he has handed down to us the outline of all human efforts in the future. Whatever may be our own shortcomings, the deed is done which gives eternal hope to men; a prospect of action is before us, to which we can affix no limitation in time.

Supposing then we have committed sins for which penitence may rightly be required of us, yet there is a consideration even more important than that need of penitence; the consideration that no sin of ours can preclude the fact that a beginning of right-doing in the supreme sense has already been made; that a hope is present to all mankind, which no unworthiness, no sinfulness of our own can prevent our having a share in; the thought of our sins is as nothing compared with the thought of that which will rescue us. This thought, which may and should be ever present to mankind, is what Luther meant by Justification by Faith. Yet, even after the explanation which I have given,

I use that phrase with some hesitation; so much has it been narrowed in the use of it; and even Luther himself, ardently though he embraced it, fell short of seeing the universality of the consolation that it offers. Nor, in saying this, is there any detraction from the duty of repentance when sins have been committed, or when a sinful temper exists. Repentance is needed too frequently; but faith is needed always.

Thus, when we ask how we may rightly order our minds with a view to eternity, we see the beginning of such ordering; and it is particularly to be noticed that to embrace faith demands some passion, some struggle on our own part; it is not easy to grasp a thing so shadowy as eternal life is apt to appear, when visible objects, much desired by us, are present and obvious. Yet the transition must be made, the greater life of which we have dim foreshadowings must be taken into our souls; and Jesus Christ, who has gone through the struggle before us, will help us in surmounting it; such is the experience of Christians. In reference to this contact of the heavenly Christ with our souls, there is a memorable sentence of Luther's in a letter to Melanchthon, which it will be well to quote here: "Listen not," he says, "even to Jesus in his glory, unless thou hast first seen him crucified." That experience of suffering, which in Jesus was completed on the cross, becomes a revealing power to ourselves in our own sufferings and efforts; by this he helps us, and in remembrance of this we raise our prayers to him, and from him our salvation begins.

In giving this sketch of Luther's most characteristic positive doctrine, I must not conceal from the reader that I have omitted some elements which Luther, in his own day, would have regarded as essential, or (at least) of which he would not have endured the denial; for he adhered with great simplicity to the general scheme of Scriptural doctrine. It is indeed to be noted that in his treatise *On Christian Liberty* he calls Christ "our firstborn brother" (frater primogenitus) which is an appellation that unites Christ with ourselves in one common nature; but he fully accepted that account of the matter which separates Jesus, in his original nature, from ourselves. It is possible that Luther, in his own day, would have banished or even imprisoned me (that he would have burnt anybody I totally disbelieve); but our debt to him remains, and we must remember that he was taking the first tentative steps in a new order of things, and he could not venture upon untried novelties of opinion.

It was no fault of Luther to adhere to the old Christian doctrine,

even where we may think it in error; but there were some errors
in his doctrine, even in the early time of which I have been
speaking, which were more peculiarly his own, and which we cannot
but regret. It is of course a very old charge against him that he
denied any merit in good deeds, and encouraged men to disregard
sinfulness in practice, since faith was all that was necessary. Put
in this form, the charge is an unjust one; he takes great pains in
his treatise On Christian Liberty to show that men are not to be
idle in good works; that the Christian spirit cannot help producing
good works, and that anyone who does not produce good works
cannot have the Christian spirit. But he denies (as I understand
him) all value to the good deeds of those imperfect persons who
have not got the Christian spirit. He says (in his *Disputatio de
Homine*) that the light of God's countenance does not rest at all
upon the natural man. This is against all right instinct; many
heathen and unbelievers have sacrificed themselves for the good
of others, have devoted themselves to the good of others, and
it is impossible not to say that such persons have had something
of the divine light in them, and have deserved well of mankind.
But there was a natural exaggeration in Luther's temperament
which misled him. He might reasonably have said that the good
deeds of heathen and unbelievers did not give them salvation,
in the proper sense of salvation, that is to say the entrance into
eternal life and happiness. But to say that they had no tendency
in the way of salvation is quite another thing. All good self-
denying actions, by whomsoever performed, have such a tendency;
they make the world better; they are part of the fire of life,
though they may not be able to overcome the calamitous passions
among men which are so often deadly. Luther ignored this;
and again he was apt to look upon deeds merely externally as
senseless things ("res insensatæ" he calls them), in contrast with
the vital spirit. But deeds are not senseless things; they are
animated by a spirit, sometimes by a bad spirit, sometimes by
a good one; and if they have been animated by a good spirit,
they are not without merit. Lastly, it is difficult not to think
that Luther's disparagement of good deeds was partly occasioned
(as was the case with the apostle Paul also) by his sense of
the futility of formal religious acts, when despotically pressed on
men; but truly good deeds stand on a quite different basis.

I must not and cannot defend all which Luther said and wrote
on this subject; but his great conceptions remain, when the
exaggerations with which he accompanied them have been laid

aside, and form a worthy ground of human conduct. And now, before continuing the history, let me pause and ask a question. What, in all the controversy of Luther with the pope, was the deepest point—the most important issue? Was it the question whether the granting of indulgences was a rightful act? Was it the question whether the selling of indulgences was a rightful act? Was it the question whether the pope held a divine authority over all Christians and (ultimately) over all men? These were important questions, and questions that had been abundantly argued between Luther and the papal authorities; but they were not the most important. The most important question was, whether Luther should be permitted to discuss at all any of these points. Shall free speech on religious questions be allowed? The pope, in the bull which excommunicated Luther, emphatically said, No. Luther, when he publicly burnt the pope's bull, emphatically said, "Free speech, in the points which I have brought forward, is an obligation not to be laid aside." When it is denied, as it is denied by some, that Luther was an advocate of freedom, it is merely meant that he was not an advocate of freedom under all circumstances, for every man, in every cause. But it would have been truly unpractical for Luther to have aimed at any such wide assertion of freedom as this; what he did for freedom was immense, in counteracting the most formidable adversary of freedom that has ever existed on earth, while preserving, as far as action went (I cannot say the same of his language) a modera-tion of a very remarkable kind. He was the beginner of our modern religious freedom; if his conception of religious freedom did not reach to ours, it was at all events far in advance of any which had been seen in Europe up to that time.

Again let me ask another question: who was Luther's adver-sary? The pope; or the Roman church; most people would say. That is truth, but not the whole truth. It was the Christian Church of the west that was Luther's adversary; the Christian Church, which had very early drawn into itself the seeds of intolerance, out of which intolerant acts had grown and multi-plied as the centuries went on. This was the spirit of antichrist, the spirit most adverse to the teaching of Jesus Christ, and it certainly did reside in Rome (as Luther said), and it was in Rome that it most threatened Luther, but it resided in other places too, and even in the Reformed churches it was not absent when these began to be established. It was the power of the flesh contending against the power of the spirit.

The pope's bull outlawed Luther, and bade every temporal prince or ecclesiastical authority seize Luther and his adherents and hand him over to the agents of the pope, or at the very least expel him from their territories. Now came to the front, not obtrusively or with ostentation, but with quiet firmness, that admirable prince, the elector Frederick of Saxony, Luther's sovereign. It was he who procured that Luther should plead his cause before the recently elected emperor Charles V in a Diet to be held at Worms; and it was he who provided, as far as he could, for Luther's safety in attending that Diet. It was impossible, indeed, that Luther should not run some risk, in adventuring into an assembly so largely composed of his enemies. But his courage never failed him, either in the journey to Worms, or while pleading his cause before the Diet at Worms; he conducted himself at once with modesty and with resolution; nor was he treated otherwise than well during his sojourn at Worms. But the Diet was an assembly before which he could not in any case hope actually to win his cause; and the emperor Charles V, with his Spanish traditions inherited in his blood and fostered by his education, was very unlikely to be favourable to him. The emperor respected Luther's safe-conduct, and allowed him to return to the place he came from; but issued, after he had gone, the ban of the Empire against him, following the pope's bull strictly. Luther was thus in great danger; and even his own sovereign might not be able to protect him against the ban proclaimed by the emperor, if it were known where Luther was. But the elector Frederick had provided against this contingency also (the elector had been at Worms, but had left before the ban was issued); he caused Luther, while returning on his way towards Wittenberg, to be secretly seized, and to be carried to the Wartburg near Eisenach; of this design Luther had been cognisant beforehand.

For ten months, from the beginning of May, 1521, to the beginning of March, 1522, did Luther remain in this retreat, few men knowing where he was; and during this time he began one of his greatest works, the translation of the Bible into German. At last, finding his presence needed at Wittenberg, he returned there, disregarding the advice of the elector Frederick, who still feared for his safety.

But now, indeed, things were changed; in Luther's absence, the new movement had taken root and spread. The emperor Charles V had left Germany and a Council of Regency had taken his place; and on that Council were some warm friends of Luther.

I am not writing a history of the Reformation, but am merely endeavouring to characterise it in its start and in its development; to show what kind of a movement it was and is (for I need not say that the Reformed churches are a great factor in the world of to-day). So far I have been vindicating its origin, which was in Luther; but is it to be expected that the whole course of its development can be equally vindicated? The faults of human nature are always at work in the world, and the reformers were not and could not be exempt from them. The very cause that summoned Luther back to Wittenberg was the tumultuous agitation raised by certain persons who styled themselves prophets, who came from a village or small town called Zwickau; they preached open warfare against the Roman church and its officials, and advocated universal equality. One of Luther's own companions, Carlstadt, had gone some way towards joining them, being especially zealous for breaking up the images of saints in churches. Luther quieted the disturbance for the time, but it broke out again in the next year (1523) under a leader called Münzer, and swelled at last into a rebellion of the peasantry against the nobles. Luther, in such a case, stood for law and order; of anarchy he would have nothing; and though not devoid of sympathy with the peasants, he urged the nobles to suppress them—too truculently, it is to be admitted. But the danger of the insurrection, the insane fury of the peasants, did call for prompt measures; and Luther never minced his words. But I must not waste much time either upon this subject, or upon the insurrection of the Anabaptists, ten years later. These were the wild and stormy fringes of the Reformation movement, in which the agents had no proper consideration of their own fallibility, and committed crimes and suffered punishments which no man can read of without censure and without pity. This notice of them must be sufficient here.

But those great movements which we associate with the names of Zwingli in Switzerland, and Calvin in France and Geneva; and again the valorous resistance of the Protestants in the Netherlands to the crushing despotism of Spain; and again our Reformation in Great Britain, so much more varied in its texture than any of the continental movements; these belong to the very heart of the Reformation conflict, and I must presently characterise them, but not quite yet. So likewise the great counter-movement of the Jesuits, which won so much back for the Roman church, must not be passed over. They who are our foes in one sense, are not our foes in every sense; and if we refuse to regard the church of Rome as infallible, we must none the less do honour to those real instances of heroism and devotion which appear in the annals of that church, and not least among the Jesuits.

I return to the German reformation, which was the heart and the centre of the whole Protestant movement, and to Luther, who was the heart and the centre of the German reformation. Two qualities combined in Luther, which seldom are combined; a singular prudence in action, a singular rashness in speech. With respect to the first, it will be well to quote what Ranke says of him: "Of all the men who ever placed themselves at the head of a great movement, Luther was perhaps the most averse to violence and war." It was the result of this, that in Germany, and in Germany alone, were serious efforts made to repair the breach which the Reformation had caused. These efforts reached their highest point in the Diet of Augsburg, held in June, 1530; and the Confession of Faith which Melanchthon drew up and Luther approved, which was submitted to the members of that Diet, is clear and moderate. Luther, writing to the Elector of Saxony, said of it that he "had read Master Philip's (Melanchthon's) Apology....It pleases me well, and I know not how to better it...for I cannot tread so softly and gently[1]." In view of this praise given by Luther, it will be well to quote two sentences from the Confession relating respectively to freewill and to good works. Of freewill it is said:

Our churches teach concerning freewill, that the human will has some freedom in promoting civil justice and in the selection of things that are subject to reason. But it has not, without the Holy Spirit, the power of producing the righteousness of God or spiritual righteousness, because the carnal man does not perceive the things which belong to the Spirit of God; but this righteousness is caused in our hearts, when it is conceived by the word of the Holy Spirit. *Documents*, etc. p. 266.

What a contrast between this careful statement and the vehement fulminations of Luther against the doctrine of human freewill which he indited in his controversy with Erasmus! His wild assertions in his treatise, *De servo arbitrio*, are greatly responsible for the hardness of that theory which we generally name Calvinism, and which Calvin elaborated fully. I think it must be doubted whether Luther in his true mind went so far

[1] Dr Kidd's *Documents*, etc. pp. 255–6.

as his expressions seem to imply; but he wrote very rashly, following a careless phrase of the apostle Paul. The passage about good works in the Confession of Augsburg runs as follows:

Falsely are our preachers accused of forbidding good works; their writings concerning the ten commandments, and others in a similar strain, bear witness that they have taught profitably about all kinds of life, and life's duties; what kinds and what works, in every vocation, are pleasing to God. *Documents*, etc. p. 267.

If Luther had always had a restraining friend near him, to correct his unbalanced utterances, how much better it would have been for the world! Yet the power of conception and of feeling was in him, as it was in no one else of that age. Some of his errors arose from a too literal acceptance of the Bible; thus antichrist was thought of by him as a definite person, and not as a spirit; and in his controversy with Zwingli about the bodily presence of Christ in the sacrament we must account him wrong from the same cause; it was an error that had a noble side. When we have enumerated all his faults—and these include coarseness, superstition, and that well-known lapse of integrity in allowing Philip of Hesse to commit bigamy—it yet must be acknowledged that he was the person above all in that period who penetrated into the centre of true religion; who had the most ardent feelings of affection for his friends and the greatest unwillingness to be cruel to those who were in error; who met dangers most cheerfully and with the most conscious reliance on the Divine strength. His translation of the Bible has been a possession for ever to his nation; and so have his hymns been; and we may well think that his delight in music has been one cause of the great and continuous excellence of the German nation in that art. With the German painters too he was in friendship; though painting never flourished in Germany as it did in Italy.

Luther's correspondence is in many respects deeply interesting; yet I must refrain from giving any specimen of it; only I may refer to the letter in which he tells his friend Nicolas Specht, who was on the eve of marriage, that he sends him as a wedding present a portrait of "the saintly John Huss." I must not pass without mention his pure and beautiful wedded life (so much assailed by his enemies as a breach of his monastic vow); and it will be well to quote from Köstlin's life of him (pp. 544–6 of the English translation) one pathetic incident of it; his behaviour when his daughter Magdalene (or Lena) died at the age of 13:

His favourite child was little Lena, a pious, gentle, affectionate little girl, and devoted to him with her whole heart. A charming picture of her remains, by Cranach, a friend of the family. But she died in the bloom of early youth, on September 20, 1542, after a long and severe illness. The grief he had felt at the loss of his daughter Elizabeth was now renewed and intensified. When she was lying on her sickbed, he said, "I love her very much indeed; but, dear God, if it is Thy will to take her hence, I would gladly she were with Thee." To Magdalene herself he said, "Lena, dear, my little daughter, thou wouldst love to remain here with thy father; art thou willing to go to that other Father?" "Yes, dear father," she answered; "just as God wills." And when she was dying, he fell on his knees beside her bed, wept bitterly, and prayed for her redemption, and she fell asleep in his arms. As she lay in her coffin, he looked at her and exclaimed, "Ah, my darling Lena, thou wilt rise again, shine like a star—yea, as the sun"; and added, "I am happy in the spirit, but in the flesh I am very sorrowful. The flesh will not be subdued: parting troubles one above measure; it is a wonderful thing to think that she is assuredly in peace, and that all is well with her, and yet to be so sad." To the mourners he said, "I have sent a saint to Heaven: could mine be such a death as hers, I would welcome such a death this moment." He expressed the same sorrow, and the same exultation in his letters to his friends. To Jonas he wrote: "You will have heard that my dearest daughter Magdalene is born again in the everlasting kingdom of Christ. Although I and my wife ought only to thank God with joy for her happy departure, whereby she has escaped the power of the world, the flesh, the Turks, and the devil, yet so strong is natural love that we cannot bear it without sobs and sighs from the heart, without a bitter sense of death in ourselves. So deeply printed on our hearts are her ways, her words, her gestures, whether alive or dying, that even Christ's death cannot drive away this agony." His little Hans, whom his sick sister longed to see once more, he had sent for from Torgau a fortnight before she died: he wrote for that purpose to Crodel, saying, "I would not have my conscience reproach me afterwards for having neglected anything."

Does not such a picture of family union give us reason to believe that Luther's marriage was a right act? He was responsible to God for what was technically a breach of his vow; but in that responsibility it is not necessarily involved that this technical breach was real disobedience to God's will; all the signs are that it was not so. This opinion will receive yet more reinforcement if we look at the terms in which his wife wrote of him, in a letter to her sister, six weeks after his death. I quote it from the latest English biography of Luther, by Dr Preserved Smith (p. 424):

Catherine Luther to Christina von Bora.

Wittenberg, *April* 2, 1546.

Grace and peace in God the Father of our Lord Jesus Christ. Kind, dear sister! I can easily believe that you have hearty sympathy with me and my poor children. Who would not be sorrowful and mourn for so noble a man as was my dear lord, who much served not only one city or a single land but the whole world? Truly I am so distressed that I cannot tell my great heart sorrow to anyone, and hardly know what to think or how I feel. I cannot eat nor drink, neither can I sleep. If I had had a principality and an empire, it would never have cost me so much pain to lose them as I have now that our Lord God has taken from me, and not from me only, but from the whole world, this dear and precious man. When I think of it, God knows that for sorrow and weeping I can neither speak nor dictate this letter; you yourself, dear sister, have experienced a similar sorrow.

Was the death of a hero ever more worthily celebrated; and since it was his wife who so celebrated him, was it not an evidence from the spontaneous depths of the human heart that their marriage was true and righteous, and not deformed by such wrong as, had it existed, must have left a stain on the conscience?

But I must revert from the personality of Luther to the general course of the German reformation. In spite of the excommunication of Luther and his having been made subject to the ban of the empire at the Diet of Worms, it was long before hope was entirely given up of the restoration of the old religious unity. The Diet of Augsburg in 1530, as I have mentioned, had this for its object; but it did not succeed; and the only gain was, that two years later, on the 23rd July, 1532, an agreement was arrived at at Nuremberg for the practical toleration of the Reformed religion in those states which had embraced it, until such time as a free Christian council could be held for the settlement of the disputed points. It was the imminent danger from the Turkish armies, now pressing on Austria from the direction of Hungary, which moved the emperor to show this conciliatory spirit; and by the union of Catholic and Reformed, the Turks were defeated and driven back. Then, nine years later (the interval having been filled with various controversies), in April, 1541, a Diet was held at Ratisbon (Regensburg), which endeavoured to bring unity to the divided Church. But the severance was too deep; and the Reformation had already had many martyrs, whose memory forbade surrender of the cause for which they had died. Reunion proved impossible; and the only gain of the Diet of Ratisbon was that the Reformers retained for the present that toleration which had been gained for them at Nuremberg.

But the church of Rome in its Italian centre had now for twenty years been girding itself up for a conflict that was evidently to prove arduous; and the Reformed churches outside Germany had been seeking for a leader who should take up the conflict in a more directly warlike sense than that in which Luther had carried it on (for Luther aimed at toleration, not at conquest), and also who could take it up with younger and fresher strength; for Luther was now subject to illness and verging on old age. Both sides found their champion; for, on the one hand, Ignatius Loyola had arrived at Rome, and the Society of Jesus received the sanction of pope Paul III on the 27th September, 1540; and Ignatius Loyola was one of those who assented to the establishment of the Roman Inquisition in the year 1542. On the opposite side, it was in 1541 that Calvin obtained practically despotic power in Geneva; and to Calvin, rather than to Luther, continental reformers (and even many in Great Britain) looked for practical and detailed direction. But in saying this, some observations must be made, which will partly qualify the last assertion.

Zwingli had been the earliest of the Reformers outside Germany; a clear-headed thinker, though less powerful in character than Luther; but his place knew him no more; he had been slain, fighting bravely (yet hardly with adequate justification) against the Swiss Roman Catholics in the year 1531. The English Reformation had had its beginning with Henry VIII, a truculent tyrant, and with no just cause, but not quite so unconscientious as some have thought; the English Reformers, under all the circumstances, and with the memories of Wycliffe and the Lollards in the past, had a fair cause in following him.

Whether we look at Paul III and Ignatius Loyola on the one hand, or at Calvin and Henry VIII on the other hand, we are sensible that war was in the air. Let us consider the antagonists.

Though in practice the Jesuits were the enthusiastic maintainers of the pope, it was a still more fundamental characteristic of theirs to exemplify the ancient Christian Church on its hard military side, with literal acceptance of the maxims that had been laid down, and none of that softening and none of that concession to new needs which the development of the Christian society really required. Thus when Ignatius Loyola considered that saying of Jesus Christ, "If anyone will come after me, let him deny himself, and take up his cross, and follow me," he interpreted it as meaning that a true disciple of Jesus Christ must subject himself voluntarily to all imaginable pains, quite apart from any special purpose other than the mere ascetic principle; and he did subject himself to the severest pains. Then, again, he regarded obedience as the greatest and most necessary of virtues;

obedience in thought, in word, and in deed; he was prepared himself to render this obedience to the pope, and when he was himself established in authority, he expected his followers to render it to him. Lastly, while repudiating the individual intellect as a wholly untrustworthy guide in divine things, he relied absolutely on that visionary and imaginative faculty which is in many ways so great a help to our souls, but which does need intellectual caution as its correlative and its corrective; the only guide which Ignatius permitted in the use of it was that it should be in concurrence with the doctrines of the Church. He himself had numerous visions; but I must not dwell upon these, nor upon his interesting personal history; those who (not being Roman Catholics) desire to know more of this will find it sympathetically given by Sir James Stephen, in the *Essays on Ecclesiastical Biography*. But I must now mention two advantages which Ignatius Loyola and the Jesuits had in their warfare, which gave them great gains though not absolute victory in the result.

First, though I have said that Ignatius Loyola made no concessions to human needs in his interpretation of Christianity, this must only be held to apply to his manner of dealing with first principles, or what he regarded as such; after these were accepted, he did consider the intellect as a most useful servant in promoting the welfare of a Christian as well as the interests of the Church; he had himself an acute judgment, and in those purposes which he took for his own he had preserved it unharmed; and his followers in succeeding generations have never wanted the ability to adapt themselves to the affairs of the world, and to appropriate to themselves knowledge of all kinds. Next, he and the whole Roman church had the great advantage, as against the Reformed churches, of having their case predetermined for them; there was comparatively little for them to decide on the theoretical or doctrinal ground; whereas that use of personal judgment, which it was the great merit of the Reformed churches to bring into religious questions, had the inevitable disadvantage of producing differences of judgment, from which not unfrequently alienation ensued, and weakness in the conduct of affairs.

These advantages the Jesuits had naturally in the position which they took up; and yet these advantages would have availed nothing if they had not had the qualities adequate to their use. But they had these qualities. We must stand amazed at their unremitting energy, their undaunted courage; at the persistency with which they pressed into the most remote corners of the world, and into countries where they were likely to be apprehended and slain; it would be base not to give them their due honour, though we must disapprove of much in the first principles which they took for their own. Some of them also, like Xavier, were truly lovable.

And now I come to Calvin.

The general scheme of Christian doctrine laid down by Luther was accepted by Calvin with some modifications and some hardening of the lines; and Calvin, like Luther, was strong in urging every Christian to read the Bible, as the word of Divine truth. But Calvin was distinguished from Luther by his disciplinary power. He had not Luther's originality or deep tenderness or agonising internal struggles in the search after truth; but there was a precision in his conceptions and acts, a power of systematisation in all that he undertook, which made him in the conflict with adverse forces a better leader than Luther. The present generation has quite outgrown his peculiar doctrines, and he can hardly be considered a leader of men's thoughts at the present day; but his services in his own day and long after his own day, in animating men against a religious despotism far more dangerous than that which he himself wielded, were great. The following passage from J. A. Froude's *Address to Scotch Students* is designed to commend Calvinism rather than Calvin, but the effect of it is to raise the credit of Calvin personally, and it is a just consequence that is thus drawn:

I am going to ask you to consider how it came to pass that if Calvinism is indeed the hard and unreasonable creed which modern enlightenment declares it to be, it has possessed such singular attractions in past times for some of the greatest men that ever lived. And how—being, as we are told, fatal to morality, because it denies freewill—the first symptom of its operation, wherever it established itself, was to obliterate the distinction between sins and crimes, and to make the moral law the rule of life for States as well as persons. I shall ask you, again, why, if it be a creed of intellectual servitude, it was able to inspire and sustain the bravest efforts ever made by man to break the yoke of unjust authority. When all else has failed—when patriotism has covered its face and human courage has broken down—when intellect has yielded, as Gibbon says, "with a smile or a sigh," content to philosophise in the closet, and abroad worship with the vulgar—when emotion and sentiment and tender imaginative piety have become the handmaids of superstition, and have dreamt themselves into forgetfulness that there is any difference between lies and truth —the slavish form of belief called Calvinism, in one or other of its many

---

[1] *Calvinism: an address delivered at St Andrews*, pp. 8, 9

forms, has borne ever an inflexible front to illusion and mendacity, and
has preferred rather to be ground to powder like flint than to bend before
violence or melt under enervating temptation.

It is enough to mention the name of William the Silent, of Luther—
for on the points of which I am speaking Luther was one with Calvin
—of your own Knox and Andrew Melville and the Regent Murray, of
Coligny, of our English Cromwell, of Milton, of John Bunyan. These
were men possessed of all the qualities which give nobility and grandeur
to human nature—men whose life was as upright as their intellect was
commanding and their public aims untainted with selfishness; unalterably
just where duty required them to be stern, but with the tenderness of a
woman in their hearts; frank, true, cheerful, humorous, as unlike sour
fanatics as it is possible to imagine anyone, and able in some way to
sound the keynote to which every brave and faithful heart in Europe
instinctively vibrated.

I could not countersign every word of that panegyric; and
the evil done by the followers of Calvin (in which they deserted
the teaching of Luther) in the great destruction of beauty in
architecture and sculpture and painting, which accompanied
their chief triumphs, must be reckoned against them. But
Froude's words have a measure of truth, which, considering
the past importance of Calvinism and the present discredit
under which it lies, deserves to be weighed.

Both Calvin and the English Reformers deserted Luther's
moderation when they put heretics to death; the name of
Servetus, burnt for heresy by Calvin (though the dreadful form
of death was not Calvin's personal wish) and of Joan Boucher,
burnt for heresy by Cranmer, remind us of a regrettable intolerance. But the reformed English church has the honour of having
preserved a reverence for antiquity, which as a sentiment is
truly valuable, though we must not allow it to dominate our
actions where clear reason is on the other side; a tenderness
from this source animates the writings of Richard Hooker in a
peculiar degree, and unites with his philosophic breadth. Without
denying the courage of Latimer and Ridley and other martyrs
(the names of Nonconformists are not to be forgotten in this
connexion), it remains true that Hooker was the most eminent
and most characteristic of religious teachers in England in the
sixteenth century.

The church of Rome with the religious orders (and above all
the Jesuits) on the one hand; Lutherans, Calvinists, Anglicans
on the other hand; these were the two sides in that tremendous
struggle between Ancient Christianity and Reformed Christianity
which had its first beginning in Luther, but which did not manifest

its plain tendency to issue in absolute bloody warfare till about the year 1542.

Perhaps the council of Trent—held between the years 1545 and 1563, or at the beginning of that period when events were turning distinctly towards war—ought to receive from me a few words in this place. The reader will not doubt my being on the side of the reformers in their struggle for freedom; but I confess that I feel a respect for the council of Trent which no sense of my difference from that council in point of doctrine can hinder. The great ecclesiastics who met there took as a matter of course the conservative side in the great question of the day; we may differ from them, but we must not quarrel with them on that score; on the other hand, the confession of personal fault on the part of the rulers of the Church goes beyond what we might have expected, and is expressed in terms that must move an opponent. Here are a few sentences from the solemn address of the papal legates, given before the assembled prelates, at the first meeting of the council:

"As to what we say," the legates urge[1], "that we the shepherds have given cause for the ills of the Church; if anyone thinks this too harshly said, and with more exaggeration than truth, experience, which cannot lie, will prove it to be true. Let us look for a little while at the evils, and at the same time at our own sins....There are three evils, which we have already mentioned; heresies, the decay of moral discipline, and war civil or foreign. Let us see and consider, since for so many years the church has been harassed by these calamities, whence they took their origin; whether we have not originated and fostered them....Let those examine themselves, who are husbandmen in the Lord's field, let them ask their conscience, how they have borne themselves in the cultivating and in the sowing. Those who ask thus, will have little doubt as to whether the fault of heresies budding in the Church belongs to themselves. But this we say merely for warning's sake....As to the second evil, the decay of moral discipline, and abuses (as they are called), there is no need of long search, since there is no one whom we can even name as their author besides ourselves."

It was not to be expected that the ecclesiastics of that day should recognise what really was the chief fault of the Church, the cruel repression of what was deemed error; but the sincerity with which they acknowledged the faults that they knew deserves our esteem. That the conflict which then was beginning should have taken the terrible form which it did must be a matter of deep regret; but it can hardly surprise us, when we remember the unmerciful character of men in that day, and the greatness of the issues involved.

[1] Harduin's *Acta Conciliorum*, vol. x. p. 12.

How is it possible for me to tell in detail the mighty series of events indicated in the foregoing paragraph? The brave and successful struggle of the Netherlanders, unsurpassed in any age of the world, for their freedom from the tyranny of Spain; the brave resistance of England to the same power, and the defeat of the arrogant Armada; the wars of the French Huguenots, which came to a pause with the accession of Henry IV; the Thirty Years' War which devastated Germany in the seventeenth century; the civil war in England, partly of political partly of religious import, in which Cromwell was the most commanding genius. Politics and religion were intertwined in the most singular manner all through this struggle, and sometimes acted in opposite directions; for instance, no one, not even the hero Gustavus Adolphus, was so much a cause of the deliverance of Protestantism in north Germany from the papal power, as the Roman Catholic cardinal Richelieu.

We cannot but be sensible that the first animating cause of these religious wars was the resolution of the church of Rome to preserve, if possible, its own dominion over western Europe, a resolution which the states that had received the Reformation naturally resisted to the utmost of their power. This is not of course equivalent to saying that the adherents of the Reformation were blameless; and in England and Ireland the case was in great measure reversed, and the difficulty there was for Roman Catholics to obtain their natural rights; though it must be added (not that this mends matters) that Protestant Nonconformists in Great Britain were for a long time subject to as severe a persecution as were the Roman Catholics. But the greatest discredit to the English Government came from its bitter and long continued intolerance towards the Roman Catholic Irish.

If we condemn the church of Rome for its intolerance, we must also condemn the Reformed churches for their intolerance. We are only entitled to urge that the intolerance of the Roman church was much severer, much more thorough-going, than the intolerance of the Reformed churches. The Reformed religion was absolutely destroyed in Italy and Spain; the Roman Catholic religion in Ireland, though treated always with injustice and frequently with cruelty, still survived. That is, I think, a fair measure of the degree in which the Roman church, and the Reformed churches, respectively, had incurred the guilt of religious persecution. The Reformation did not escape that guilt, did not take away that bad practice; but I think we may say, that it did a little lighten it.

It would, however, be a very mistaken method of arguing, to judge either the Christian religion, or the Reformation, only by the worst results that may seem to have come from either. In speaking of the mediæval Church, I endeavoured to show that the balance of its effects was for good; and if we consider the whole spirit of the Reformation era, we may say that the temper of men, which certainly was religious all through the sixteenth and seventeenth centuries, shows an advance on anything which had been seen in the world before; the achievements of men were greater. It may be asked, whether the countries in which the Reformation had obtained a predominance showed a distinct superiority, during those centuries, over the countries which had adhered to the ancient form of Christianity? The question is an intricate one; but the following observations will at any rate be a guide to us in considering it. The greatest development of external power made during the sixteenth and seventeenth centuries was made by Great Britain, Holland, and France; those were the countries whose fleets roamed over the world most, whose colonists settled most in foreign lands. It is true, that at the beginning of the period which I have named this was by no means the case. At the beginning of the sixteenth century Spain and Portugal were the two great colonising countries. But by the end of the seventeenth century this had entirely changed. Spain and Portugal still retained vast colonies on the other side of the Atlantic; but the lifeblood beat low in Mexico and Peru and Brazil, because it beat low in Spain and Portugal; progress there was none. On the other hand, the colonial possessions of Great Britain and Holland and France were progressing; there was lifeblood in these. France was still Roman Catholic, Great Britain and Holland had embraced the Reformed creed; knowing all that we know of the after history, we must say that Great Britain and Holland were outstripping France in colonising power; but this was not perfectly clear during the two centuries which I have named.

In internal politics, Great Britain had made a start in self-government which has been the seed of liberty in many countries; and the Netherlands were also free countries; and the two parts of the Netherlands used their freedom in different directions, religiously speaking: Holland had received the Reformation, the southern part of the country, which we now call Belgium, adhered to the church of Rome. Germany was too unfortunately divided to make any progress in politics, external or internal.

But the French spirit was high, and made itself felt in the internal politics of Europe more than either Great Britain or Holland; we may remember that though France did in the end, by the revocation of the Edict of Nantes in the year 1685, cast out the adherents of the Reformed religion, they had been in France till then, and had contributed to the well-being and force of the country. Italy and Spain were sinking, politically, all through this period.

In science, the great name of Galileo shines out as an Italian and a Roman Catholic; nor was there a want of other distinguished names in Italy in the scientific line; let me mention Torricelli in hydrostatics and Malpighi in biology. It may be my own ignorance, but I know of no name from Spain or Portugal during these centuries, distinguished in science. In France, the most famous names in science are Descartes and Pascal; and Descartes, besides, is famous as a philosopher, Pascal as a theologian. In Germany, we have Kepler in astronomy, Leibnitz in mathematics and philosophy; both belonging to the Reformed church, and great names. Need I mention, in England, the enthusiastic forecasts of Bacon as to the noble fruits obtainable by careful observation of the physical universe; or the supreme intellect of Newton, busy in detecting the secrets of that universe; or the strong sense of Locke? I have not space to mention the distinguished naturalists of this period, whether in Germany, Holland, France or Great Britain.

In literature, the transcendent imagination of Shakespeare has enriched the whole world; and the majestic harmonies of Milton are not to be forgotten. But it is to be admitted, that in the mere number of famous literary names during the sixteenth and seventeenth centuries the Roman church has the advantage over the Reformed churches; for in Germany the literary impulse was in the background; and two English writers have to stand against seven of universal fame on the other side, Tasso and Ariosto in Italy, Cervantes in Spain, and Rabelais, Corneille, Molière and Racine in France. It would be possible to add to both lists, but the comparison as I have put it may stand. How many of the other writers would go to make up Shakespeare, is a question which I need not discuss.

Do the Reformed churches, in this entire comparison, stand at a disadvantage when compared with the church of Rome? I think not; but this is not the most important question. What we are most interested in asking is, whether the great religious movement of the sixteenth century, adverse to the church of

Rome and to the whole mediæval conception of Christianity, but still undoubtedly Christian, was a movement that advanced mankind in the way of strength and happiness or not? Against it might be alleged the quarrels, hatreds, and wars which it occasioned. But in favour of it we may point out the extraordinary degree in which it elevated and strengthened the human spirit, the powerful seizure of all reality which attended it, the increased share which it gave to the commonalty at large in fashioning the course which the central government should take in all the affairs of men. I feel sure, myself, that the gain outweighed the loss.

APPENDIX TO CHAPTER XXV

ATONEMENT AND JUSTIFICATION

Since in the foregoing chapter I have spoken with some severity of the manner in which the doctrine of Justification by Faith is popularly held, it may be well for me to show precisely what I mean by so speaking. It may be that I shall reflect in some degree on Luther himself; however it is one thing to fall into an error in the first enthusiasm of exposition, another thing to persist in it for three or four centuries.

Before however speaking of the doctrine of Justification by Faith, it will be well to say something about the doctrine of the Atonement, which in natural sequence precedes it, and concerning which I have said but little hitherto directly, though I have implied a good deal.

Certainly I hold, as all Christians do, that Jesus of Nazareth reconciled God and man; and that, as I understand, is the doctrine of the Atonement. How did he effect this reconciliation? By preserving the Divine Spirit intact, uninjured, amid all those assaults to which it was exposed through the terrors which preceded his death, and through his actual sufferings and death.

What is the Divine Spirit? What it is in God we cannot fathom; that is beyond us; but in man it is the spirit which may be expressed in those three well-known words—faith, hope, love. How these were preserved by Jesus is described by the apostle Peter:

Who, being reviled, reviled not again;
When he suffered, threatened not;
But submitted himself to him that judgeth righteously.

That is the essence of right feeling and right doing in such a case; and now let me add that, whereas I have said in my seventeenth chapter that Jesus, in submitting to baptism, meant to confess his own sinfulness, now, in speaking of the sufferings attendant on his death, I may say that, as far as we can judge, he was sinless during those hours of suffering. That was the impression he made on his disciples, and that is the impression he makes on us, whatever doubt may be felt as to parts of the gospel narratives of the crucifixion. He never despaired (those who quote the exclamation "Eloi, Eloi, lama sabachthani," as proof that he did, forget that it is a quotation from the Psalms); he never expressed any desire for the punishment of his enemies; he submitted his own will, so that it should be made one with the Divine will. Moreover, we have reason to believe that he carried this spirit through death, and administers help through it to us. The Divine Spirit, as I have described it, is our own proper birthright; but it has been blurred and lost in mankind generally; Jesus has laid the way open for its new birth in us.

That is the Atonement seen from the human side; but what corresponds to it on the divine side? It is justly said that God was and is displeased with the sins of men; though we must also say that he is pleased with those who struggle upwards towards the light; and there have been saintly men who did so, even before Jesus. But before Jesus, their success was but partial; their aims were imperfect; they did not become one with the Divine will in its inmost essence. Those who read the first fifteen chapters of the present work will see what I mean more precisely than I can express it here. Hence it came that the acceptance of Jesus by the Divine Father was perfect in a degree in which the acceptance of others had not been; restoration began on this earthly scene in a way in which it had not begun before; man was redeemed.

That is the simple, and as I hold adequate, account of the matter; the attempts to explain the matter by saying that a debt was due from man to God and that Jesus paid the debt, are the application of a very imperfect simile. Similes are not forbidden, but must not be insisted upon as if they were exact statements. Again, it is true that Jesus suffered vicariously for us; vicarious suffering is a very common thing; every mother who suffers from grief at a son's wrong-doing suffers vicariously; if she undergoes trouble and pain in rescuing him, she suffers voluntarily as well as vicariously. Jesus suffered for us, voluntarily as well as vicariously. But to say that the Almighty

Father deliberately punished Jesus instead of punishing ourselves is to introduce an altogether wrong idea into the death of Jesus, an idea drawn from very imperfect human conduct. That it was the will of God that Jesus should suffer is no doubt true; it is a fact paralleled by many human experiences on a lower level, but it is not paralleled by anything which, in human affairs, we ordinarily call punishment.

I trust that I have spoken of a solemn subject not otherwise than in a solemn manner; but it does not seem to me a complex or mysterious subject at all—given, of course, that there is a world beyond sense, and a life beyond the present life.

And now I come to the doctrine of Justification by Faith. The meaning of it is, that a foundation for human action, for human harmony, for human progress, has already been laid; or to put the matter otherwise, that a root has been planted, from which harmonious action and steady progress of mankind will naturally grow; that this foundation, this root, was the death of Jesus Christ in this visible scene, followed by his rising again in the eternal invisible world. That is a doctrine which, if it be true, is surely a happy one. If it be true, then all our actions must have regard to that which has been already done; to the work of Jesus Christ; to his penetration, through death, into eternal life. Our own works are not thereby rendered worthless; but if we would be perfect, we must in the first instance look to what has been already done. This looking to what has been already done, to what Jesus Christ accomplished, is faith or trust; we take that into account before we take into account any of our own works; this it is which reconciles us to God, reconciles us to each other, and builds us up into a permanent never-failing society.

Such is the doctrine of Justification by Faith; but it is a corruption of the doctrine to say that our own good works are of no value at all. They have a value, even though we are quite devoid of faith; but there is one value that they do not possess, namely the power of building up mankind into a permanent society filled with mutual sympathies. It is a very great task to do that; and we shall not do it unless we begin with faith. Yet those who miss faith while in this earthly life may obtain it hereafter; and we must not be too ready with our condemnations.

CHAPTER XXVI

THE GATHERING FORCES OF SCEPTICISM

THE reader will remember that charming story by Hans Andersen, in which it is told how twelve brothers have been magically changed into swans, and can only be brought back to their human form by the patient endurance and industry of their sister, to whom has been allotted the task of making for each brother a garment that shall clothe him from head to feet. The time in which this has to be done is limited; the work with the needle must be assiduous; and the condition is imposed, that during the whole process of working she must keep absolute silence. She accomplishes the task; but so great is the hurry towards the end, that the twelfth garment lacks a sleeve, and when flung over the person of her youngest brother, it fails to cover the left wing; whence it results that the youngest brother all through his life bears, instead of his left arm, a swan's wing.

I am in the habit of regarding this fairy story as a parable. The twelve brothers are the mighty spirits who, in former generations of men, left the impress of their thoughts and deeds for mankind to profit by eternally; and they themselves indeed are always truly human, but to us they are changed; the impurities of our earthly atmosphere have blurred their outline, and they look strange and alien from the men whom we know. It is the historian who has to clear the vision of his contemporaries; he has to find, amid multiform shadows, the clues which indicate the true realities; and this can only be done by unremitting care and love, such as animated the silent sister in the story. If, in this restoration of the past, something is wanting to the historian's full success, we may reflect that imperfection in so difficult a region is scarcely avoidable, and that the confession of this is one of the truths taught in the fable itself. But I must revert to my delineation of our modern world, and take it up at the point where I left it.

It is the sequel of the Reformation era to which I come. The Christian Church in its western branch had been broken asunder; two-thirds of the Papal or Roman church continued in that obedience, but one-third of its former adherents had abandoned it; and a deep hostility reigned between these divided portions of the former society.   Such was the religious condition of western Europe at the beginning of the eighteenth century.   Religious discord was no longer directly provocative of civil warfare; but it was in itself most embittered, and graver consequences were pending.

The Roman church still continued one, with even an extra insistence on its unity, seeing that the condition of warfare was now incumbent on it still more than in past generations, and for warfare unity of purpose is essential. But the Reformed churches had not attained unity. The question had arisen, as it could not but arise, How far, and in what particulars, were they to diverge from the beliefs of the elder church? That the elder church had gone wrong, they all agreed; but when had it been right? For to say that the Christian Church always had been wrong was a thesis hard to be distinguished from infidelity. Practically the Reformed churches were agreed in accepting that important creed which we (with some inaccuracy) call the creed of Nicæa; and it might have been thought that in this there was a fair basis for unity. It was not so, however; for differences of belief respecting the sacraments, and respecting church government, came to the front, and made unity impossible. This was neither surprising nor altogether to be regretted; for the knowledge on which a permanent unity could be based was not possessed by anyone at the beginning of the eighteenth century, and the divided condition of Christendom made men conscious of imperfection in theory, and stimulated inquiry.

It is the progress, and the immediate consequences, of that inquiry, which must be the theme of the present chapter; in the next chapter I shall try to gather up the final results. But there is a remark which I must make initially respecting the substratum of those historical events which are the material foundation of my narrative. Whether peace or war were reigning in the world, under every phase of belief or scepticism, the Christian society, in all its various divisions, kept on working. Though not perfectly enlightened, though divided into sections imbued with mutual hostilities, it yet was not unfaithful. Jesuit and Jansenist, Lutheran and Calvinist, Anglican and Independent, all appealed to Jesus Christ as their head, and all taught a doctrine of patience, beneficence, and hope, strengthening to the heart and regulative of action, whatever exceptions and drawbacks

have to be admitted as coexistent with their fruitful work. There
was unpretending goodness in many quarters, of a kind which
cannot here be explicitly named, but which I should be sorry
to be thought to ignore; and while the Roman church preserved
more perfectly the old traditional Christian virtues, discipline
and obedience, the Reformed churches had a more diffused and
expanding energy in many various directions. To both divisions
of western Christendom belonged one particular form of emotional
utterance, religious music; but more deeply and more amply
to the Reformed churches, and especially to that church which
had the nearest connexion with Luther. The two most deeply
religious composers, of all that have been up to the present day,
are Bach and Handel; and it will be well to show how the case
stands as to this, because I suppose it must be said that the
nineteenth century excelled the eighteenth in the art of music
(though the inequality between the two centuries is extremely
small), but in religious music the superiority is the other way.
The French Revolution was the catastrophe which separated the
two centuries; and while the revolutionary impulse of that era
gave an extraordinary vigour to the natural emotions of man
as shown in this visible scene (attaining their most various musical
expression in the great soul of Beethoven), it did on the other
hand rather blur religious faith. Hence in the religious music
of the nineteenth century, the religion is fitted on to the music;
the music comes first, the religion afterwards, in the mind of the
composer; but in the religious music of the eighteenth century,
and above all in Bach and Handel, the religion breathes itself
out in music, inspires the musical utterance. In the Passion
music of Bach (I speak of the *St Matthew* Passion music)
the deep suffering and yet the deep restfulness of the crucifixion
of Jesus Christ (the first twilight of hope gleaming through the
suffering) is felt precisely as it is felt in the picture of the crucifixion by Perugino, of which I spoke in my twenty-fourth chapter.
The deepest of all truths, the emergence of a new world of perennial
living activity out of the dying forms of earthly life, is felt and
expressed by Bach, as it was felt and expressed by Perugino;
and what more memorable thing could be expressed in either
art? On the other hand, the *Messiah* of Handel is distinguished
from all other Christian compositions of any kind by the fact,
that it represents Christianity as a religion that gives happiness
to every individual soul. There are many masses and oratorios,
there are many poems and pictures, which render powerfully

the grandeur and the pathos of the Christian faith; but the personal happiness of the individual is apt to be little regarded in them; and too often it is rendered impossible by the dreadful conception of hell, which, to those who believe in it, destroys happiness. But in the Messiah of Handel, with all its immense breadth of imagery, you will not find hell at all. Sin, indeed, which is a true earthly fact, you will find depicted, and in that satiric vein which is allowable to those who perceive that sin is being overcome in the world. "All we like sheep have gone astray" is, in the music of the Messiah, sometimes thought too light-minded in its satire; but those who think this have not attended to that most solemn counterbalance of it which immediately succeeds, "The Lord hath laid upon him the iniquity of us all." The personal consolation and happiness, which is so marked an element all through the Messiah, from the "Comfort ye" at the beginning to "I know that my Redeemer liveth" near the end, is never light-minded, but always true and deep. Again, the earthly warfare against which Christianity has so often to contend is given with rare emphasis in that melody, "Why do the nations so furiously rage together"; and lastly, in those great themes which have so often and so worthily engaged the Christian imagination, the pathos of Gethsemane and Calvary, the triumph of the kingdom of God, the Messiah is at the very highest level. I have dwelt at some length on this noble piece of music, because of late years there has been a tendency to disparage it—from motives not, I think, altogether legitimate; but it will survive as one of the truest expositions of the Christian faith, in its essential character, that has ever been given in any age.

To the history of the eighteenth and nineteenth centuries I now revert. In external history, the countries which had embraced the Reformed religion obtained, all through the eighteenth century, great extensions of dominion, alike in North America, South Africa, India, and the eastern archipelago; Great Britain came first in this enlarged sway, and Holland second. In the latter part of the century, the great country of the United States, till then a British colony, separated from the mother country, but by no means from the Reformed religion. The church of Rome, however, retained within its obedience the French colonists of Lower Canada; and South America remained and remains, wherever civilisation reaches, Roman Catholic.

No great changes have taken place since the eighteenth century in the territorial limits of the different branches of Christendom; but the great change which the eighteenth and nineteenth centuries have witnessed in the sphere of religion has been the immense increase of religious scepticism all over the Christian world, and extending even to non-Christian countries. The Shintoism and Buddhism of Japan, the Brahminism of India, have to a certain extent yielded of late years to a general scepticism; but much more extensive has been the anti-religious movement in Europe. Scepticism, agnosticism, atheism; these are the three phases, in order of increasing stringency, of the movement which tends to cast aside all religion from human life, which we behold to-day. The reader will not need to be told that I do not belong to any of these three phases of irreligion; but the causes which have produced them are plain, and their adherents have sometimes been men of singular worth. Women have far more rarely belonged to the sceptical movement than men; this has partly come from their want of learning, but partly also from their just sense that Christianity has raised women, especially in that most delicate relation, marriage, in a way in which no other moral or religious principle has ever raised them.

Let me then give the history of this sceptical movement, and endeavour to weigh its force; first observing that it must be distinguished from the movement which has for its aim a just criticism of the Bible and of the Christian Church, which has also had a strong development in the last two centuries. Criticism may lead to scepticism, but does not necessarily do so. When Christianity in its entirety is held to be untrustworthy, we may justly say that we are in the presence of scepticism; and this degree of doubt is an important factor in the world to-day.

Even in the sixteenth century, and much more in the seventeenth, the inquiries which had been necessitated by the Reformation movement, and which had the whole of the Christian religion for their subject, could not but produce doubt as to the truth of some parts of that religion; and in England, by the end of the seventeenth century, doubt had begun to attach itself especially to the Biblical miracles. I hardly think this could be said of the sceptical movement in France or Germany at so early a date; but it was not many years before the movement seized upon France with a fury and thoroughness compared to which the English scepticism was mild indeed. Of the agents of this great outburst of revolutionary denial, Voltaire was by far the foremost, and it is of him that I must now speak; but before doing so, let me note the year 1736 as an epoch when scepticism had attained great strength; the evidence of which lies in the following words, written by bishop Joseph Butler in the Advertisement which he prefixed to his famous *Analogy*:

It is come, I know not how, to be taken for granted, by many persons, that Christianity is not so much as a subject of inquiry; but that it is, now at length, discovered to be fictitious. And accordingly they treat it, as if, in the present age, this were an agreed point among all people of discernment; and nothing remained, but to set it up as a principal subject of mirth and ridicule, as it were by way of reprisals, for its having so long interrupted the pleasures of the world.

It is quite evident that when those words were written, scepticism was a formidable power; yet of the two most famous sceptics whom the eighteenth century produced in Great Britain, Hume and Gibbon, Hume had as yet published nothing, and Gibbon was not born till a year later; and I am quite at a loss to know what name Butler could have mentioned, to justify his words; yet the truth of the words is unquestionable. Voltaire had visited England during the years 1726 to 1729; and what he had seen and heard in England contributed not a little to the force of that which he was about to say and to do in France. The prescient bishop was a worthy defender of Christianity; but even he did not know the strength (not in every respect an unjust strength) of his adversary.

The difference of the results which scepticism produced in Great Britain and in France is most remarkable, and is readily to be understood. The lay element both in England and Scotland had obtained the mastery over the clerical element from the very beginning of the eighteenth century; not indeed quite to the extent to which it has done so in this twentieth century, but still in such a manner as to leave it quite beyond doubt on which side the superiority lay. Hence on this side the Channel, though sceptics were subject to disapproval, they were not subject to penalties; and the British Government, though still censurable for intolerance towards the Irish Roman Catholics, was otherwise free from any imputation of tyranny.

Far different was the case in France. The wise tolerance which marked the rulers of France in the first half of the seventeenth century was gradually undermined and at last overthrown by Louis XIV; and the revocation of the Edict of Nantes in 1685, with the banishment of the French Protestants as the result of it, was the beginning of a long decay in the worth of the French upper classes. Louis XIV died in 1715; the latter years of his reign provided a scene of hypocritical piety for the satire of the world; after his death a licentious orgy followed, base in itself, and powerless to restrain the insolent tyranny either of nobles or of ecclesiastics.   Never was government, never was religion, seen under a worse aspect.   What happened is so vividly depicted by Buckle, in his *History of Civilisation* (vol. I. pp. 670 sqq.), that I cannot do better than quote part of his description:

The great Frenchmen of the eighteenth century being stimulated by the example of England into a love of progress, naturally came into collision with the governing classes, among whom the old stationary spirit still prevailed....Unfortunately, the nobles and clergy had been so long accustomed to power, that they could not brook the slightest contradiction from those great writers, whom they ignorantly despised as their inferiors. Hence it was, that when the most illustrious Frenchmen of the eighteenth century attempted to infuse into the literature of their country a spirit of inquiry similar to that which existed in England, the ruling classes became roused into a hatred and jealousy which broke all bounds, and gave rise to that crusade against knowledge which forms the second principal precursor of the French Revolution.

The extent of that cruel persecution to which literature was now exposed, can only be fully appreciated by those who have minutely studied the history of France in the eighteenth century.   For it was not a stray case of oppression, which occurred here and there; but it was a prolonged and systematic attempt to stifle all inquiry and punish all inquirers. If a list were drawn up of all the literary men who wrote during the seventy years succeeding the death of Louis XIV, it would be found that at least nine out of every ten had suffered from the government some grievous injury; and that a majority of them had been actually thrown into prison.   Indeed, in saying thus much, I am understating the real facts of the case; for I question if one literary man out of fifty escaped with entire impunity.   Certainly, my own knowledge of those times, though carefully collected, is not so complete as I could have wished; but among those authors who were punished, I find the name of nearly every Frenchman whose writings have survived the age in which they were produced.   Among those who suffered either confiscation, or imprisonment, or exile, or fines, or the suppression of their works, or the ignominy of being forced to recant what they had written, I find, besides a host of inferior writers, the names of Beaumarchais, Berruyer, Bougeant, Buffon, D'Alembert, Diderot, Duclos, Freret, Helvétius, La Harpe, Linguet, Mably, Marmontel, Montesquieu, Mercier, Morellet, Raynal, Rousseau, Suard, Thomas, and Voltaire.

Buckle proceeds to give details of the persecution which he has described in general terms.   I need not quote the well-known sufferings of Voltaire; but here is a noteworthy list:

Rousseau was threatened with imprisonment, was driven from France, and his works were publicly burned.   The celebrated treatise of Helvétius on the Mind was suppressed by an order from the royal council; it was burned by the common hangman, and the author was compelled to write

two letters, retracting his opinions. Some of the geological views of
Buffon having offended the clergy, that illustrious naturalist was obliged
to publish a formal recantation of doctrines which are now known to be
perfectly accurate. The learned Observations on the History of France,
by Mably, were suppressed as soon as they appeared; for what reason it
would be hard to say, since M. Guizot, certainly no friend either to anarchy
or to irreligion, has thought it worth while to republish them, and thus
stamp them with the authority of his own great name. The History of
the Indies, by Raynal, was condemned to the flames, and the author
ordered to be arrested. Lanjuinais, in his well-known work on Joseph II,
advocated not only religious toleration, but even the abolition of slavery;
his book, therefore, was declared to be "seditious"; it was pronounced
"destructive of all subordination," and was sentenced to be burned. The
Analysis of Bayle, by Marsy, was suppressed, and the author was imprisoned.
The History of the Jesuits, by Linguet, was delivered to the flames; eight
years later, his *Journal* was suppressed; and, three years after that, as
he still persisted in writing, his Political Annals were suppressed, and he
himself was thrown into the Bastille.

I need not perhaps quote more instances of the persecution
of literary men, though Buckle quotes nearly forty more of the
kind; but it may be well to quote an instance of tyranny of
another kind, even more odious. Here it is, with the reflections
of Buckle upon it:

In the middle of the eighteenth century, there was an actress on the
French stage of the name of Chantilly. She, though beloved by Maurice
de Saxe, preferred a more honourable attachment, and married Favart,
the well-known writer of songs and of comic operas. Maurice, amazed
at her boldness, applied for aid to the French crown. That he should
have made such an application is sufficiently strange; but the result of
it is hardly to be paralleled except in some eastern despotism. The
government of France, on hearing the circumstance, had the inconceivable
baseness to issue an order directing Favart to abandon his wife, and intrust
her to the charge of Maurice, to whose embraces she was compelled to submit.

These are among the insufferable provocations, by which the blood of
men is made to boil in their veins. Who can wonder that the greatest
and noblest minds in France were filled with loathing at the government
by whom such things were done?

To this question of Buckle's we may fairly add another:
Can we be surprised that the religion which caused some of these
instances of oppression, and even where it did not cause them,
refrained from censuring them, was rejected by the sufferers?
I am not doubting that there were in the lower orders of the
Christian ministry, as it existed in France at that era, worthy
and even saintly persons; as also, no doubt, among the laity.
But the higher ecclesiastics were corrupt; and their religion
shared in their discredit. Hence it was that the liberal movement in France, all through the eighteenth century (and of course

especially during the revolutionary era), showed a bitterness against Christianity which had no parallel in England.

I am not saying that this was to the honour of Voltaire, who was the most conspicuous (though by no means the most thorough-going) of the assailants of Christianity; he was not a profound thinker, and he did not weigh the testimony of history in impartial balances. But though Voltaire was not a profound thinker, he had merits of an extraordinary kind, which, in spite of his real faults, render him a man to whom mankind will always be grateful, and in no slight measure. To begin with his intellectual merits; he inherited that clear persuasion, that the intellect must not be forced, but must be trained to see things naturally, carefully, and penetratingly, which had characterised Montaigne and Descartes and Bayle; and he delighted in the great triumphs of the intellect, notably in the discoveries of Newton. Further, to come more nearly to the moral region; there is a great deal of morality which is not very deep nor very commanding over the whole range of human feeling, but which nevertheless has constantly to be remembered and is in many respects a true guide to us; the necessity of industry, the power that lies in an active life, the worth of those faculties which bring nature into the service of man. All this belongs to Voltaire, both in his practice and in his teaching. The moral of *Candide* is never to be forgotten; when, after all the extraordinary troubles which had befallen Candide and his friends, they had settled peacefully in Constantinople, and Dr Pangloss urges this as an indication that we are living in the best of all possible worlds; the sceptic Martin answers, "Very possibly; but let us cultivate our garden." When all our theories are exhausted, the simple duties of life remain; that is a truth which never admits of denial. Allied to this truth is the value of good humour and cheerfulness, which did pre-eminently characterise Voltaire.

All these qualities are valuable; and yet it is not in any of them that the greatest service done by Voltaire to mankind lies. His greatest honour lies in this, that he was the first person in the world's history who expressed with a full heart that abhorrence of cruelty which we all feel to-day, but to which the consciences of men were so long dulled by the fact that cruelty was held to be one of the legitimate weapons of government. Voltaire was not likely to think better of cruelty, because it was a weapon employed by governments; still less, because the authorities of the Christian Church chose to make use of it; and these two causes of cruelty were so conspicuous in his day (and had been so conspicuous for many centuries) that the suspicion would be not unnatural, that his zeal against cruelty had something of the aspect of partisanship in it.   I do not think however that those who consider his entire character, his actual expressions, and above all his actions, will hold the suspicion to be well founded. Voltaire would have abhorred cruelty, by whomsoever committed. No doubt the cruelty which came before him in his own experience was that committed by governments, and especially in the way of religious persecution; and many eminent English writers have spoken of his benevolent ardour against judicial wrong-doings. Macaulay is one of these; but perhaps I had better quote from Lecky and from Lord Morley.   Here is what Lecky says (*History of Rationalism*, vol. II. pp. 72, 73):

Voltaire was at all times the unflinching opponent of persecution. No matter how powerful was the persecutor, no matter how insignificant was the victim, the same scathing eloquence was launched against the crime, and the indignation of Europe was soon concentrated upon the oppressor.   The fearful storm of sarcasm and invective that avenged the murder of Calas, the magnificent dream in the *Philosophical Dictionary* reviewing the history of persecution from the slaughtered Canaanites to the latest victims who had perished at the stake, the indelible stigma branded upon the persecutors of every age and of every creed, all attested the intense and passionate earnestness with which Voltaire addressed himself to his task.   On other subjects a jest or a caprice could often turn him aside.   When attacking intolerance, he employed, indeed, every weapon, but he employed them all with the concentrated energy of a profound conviction.   His success was equal to his zeal.   The spirit of intolerance sank blasted beneath his genius....He died, leaving a reputation that is indeed far from spotless, but having done more to destroy the greatest of human curses than any other of the sons of men.

So writes Lecky; and now let me quote from Morley's *Life of Voltaire* (p. 217) the brief but adequate account of the two cases of Calas and Sirven:

The Protestant Calas was broken on the wheel (1762), because his son had been found dead, and some one chose to say that the father had killed him to prevent him from turning Catholic.   There was not the smallest fragment of evidence, direct or indirect, for a single link in the chain of circumstances on which the unfortunate man's guilt depended; while there were many facts which made the theory of his guilt the most improbable that could have been brought forward.   The widow and the children of Calas were put to the torture, and eventually fled to Geneva to take refuge with Voltaire.   During the same year the same tribunal, the parliament of Toulouse, did its best to repeat this atrocity in the case of Sirven.   Sirven was a Protestant, and his daughter had been with perfect legality snatched away from him, and shut up in a convent, there to be better instructed in the faith.   She ran away, and was found at the bottom of a well. Sirven was accused of murdering his daughter, and he only escaped the wheel by prompt flight. His wife perished of misery amid the snows of the Cevennes, and he joined the wretched family of Calas at Geneva, where the same generous man furnished shelter and protection.

From the same work (pp. 221–2) let me quote Voltaire's own words on the doings of the merciless French judges. He is writing to his friend D'Alembert:

This is no longer a time for jesting: witty things do not go well with massacres. What! these Busirises in wigs destroy in the midst of horrible tortures children of sixteen! And that in face of the verdict of ten upright and humane judges! And the victim suffers it! People talk about it for a moment, and the next they are hastening to the comic opera, and barbarity, become the more insolent for our silence, will tomorrow cut throats juridically at pleasure. Here Calas broken on the wheel, there Sirven condemned to be hung, further off a gag thrust into the mouth of a lieutenant-general, a fortnight after that five youths condemned to the flames for extravagances that deserved nothing worse than Saint Lazare. Is this the country of philosophy and pleasure? It is the country rather of the Saint Bartholomew massacre. Why, the inquisition would not have ventured to do what these Jansenist judges have done....What, you would be content to laugh? We ought rather to resolve to seek vengeance, or at any rate to leave a country where day after day such horrors are committed....No, once more, I cannot bear that you should finish your letter by saying, I mean to laugh. Ah, my friend, is it a time for laughing? Did men laugh when they saw Phalaris's bull being made red hot?

I cannot but think that this extract is proof of the real seriousness of the writer, in matters where seriousness was needed. Till someone is found who acted and wrote with equal energy against judicial and religious cruelty, I must continue to believe that Voltaire is the man to whom the cessation of this kind of iniquity and its present absence through the greater part of the civilised world is mainly due.

Yet, in saying this, I must not leave out of sight the greatest real fault of Voltaire, by which he inflicted a damage on the world not indeed capable of obliterating his merits, but still serious; I mean the light-minded way in which he looked on the relations of men and women to each other. The most tender, the most life-supporting and life-giving, of all the relations in which human beings commonly stand towards each other; the relation capable of giving birth to the greatest developments of sympathy and consequent happiness, though also singularly liable to be corrupted by temptations; the relation called marriage—this formed no part of his programme of an ideal life; but instead, random sexual pleasures. The depth of the relation of husband and wife was hidden from him; and in this respect, though not in every respect, he must be called light-minded and shallow. He had no lack of companions in his light-mindedness, which is a disposition that many men are quite contented with; with what sad effect, the dishonoured lives of many women show. The worst of it was that Voltaire misled worthy and eminent men in this respect. His error can be amended in future generations; for his merits we may always be grateful.

As Voltaire was the adversary of deliberate cruelty, Rousseau was the great agent in stirring men's minds towards the recognition, and towards attempting the remedy, of the other greatest evil which the artificial texture of society has largely increased—the extreme inequality between the lot of the rich and the lot of the poor, an inequality in which great misery of the poor is sometimes involved. Christian teaching had indeed been directed towards relieving this misery, and in one respect with success, namely in the gradual abolition of slavery; but this amendment of social relations was neither perfectly accomplished nor, even where accomplished, did it dispel the evil altogether. To this day it has not been dispelled altogether; but, little by little, in all the great Christian countries, the poor have been receiving self-confidence, and weapons of self-defence, which, if they learn to use them, will in the end reform the structure of society in this most important respect. That this will not be done without the help of the Christian spirit is my conviction; but the Christian spirit had in the eighteenth century been so overladen with controversies and jealousies of various kinds, as to make men oblivious of this profoundly vital portion of the teaching of Jesus Christ, the duty of raising the condition of the poor; and the remedy had to be sought outside Christianity, and it was from Rousseau that it took its source. Though, in saying this, I must not be understood to deny that some strain of vital Christianity, forgotten by the Christian hierarchy, may have found its way into the heart of Rousseau, as a similar strain of Christianity may have found its way into the heart of Voltaire. It is probable, indeed, that this was the case; but we cannot say for certain; and Rousseau, like Voltaire, was so spontaneous in the expression of his feelings, that while it is certain that they were genuine in him, it is far from easy to trace their origination. In much of his conduct, Rousseau, like Voltaire, was very faulty, and in a manner peculiarly adverse to those Christian precepts and habits which had obtained most recognition among Christians;

it is not necessary to dwell in detail on this point (of which all
readers of modern history or of modern literature are well aware),
but the merits of Rousseau do need some explanation. I do not
know any maxim of his which expresses the heart of his belief
so clearly and in so short a compass as a sentence which is found
in a note to the eleventh chapter of the second book of his *Contrat
Social*; it runs thus:

Do you wish to give stability (*consistance*) to the State? bring the
extremes of society, as much as possible, to approximate to each other;
let there be neither millionaires (*gens opulens*) nor beggars.

It would be difficult to overrate the importance of this maxim;
and though when the words are taken literally, it should be added
that it is much more important that there should not be beggars
than that there should not be millionaires, it is literally true that
a millionaire who does not consider it his primary duty to
administer his property for the benefit of mankind is a curse and
not a blessing to those among whom he lives. Nor can I doubt
that the legislature in any country ought to endeavour to produce
that approximation of rich and poor which was advised by
Rousseau; not forgetting indeed the dangers which must accompany such an attempt, and guarding against the excitement of
social jealousies, but still bearing in mind that main object which
I have just stated. It must be a matter of continual experiment
how much the State, through its legislature, can do towards raising
the condition of the poor, and disposing the administration of
wealth so that it shall be beneficial to the whole community;
but that the State should be animated by these motives I do not
doubt at all[1].

That the natural rights of man were vindicated by Rousseau,
is a fact much better known than the cautious phrase which I
have quoted from the Contrat Social; but it would be hard to
prove that this wider expression of the claims of the poor contains
anything of substantial value which is wanting to the narrower
phrase; though it is more calculated to move men, and had more
revolutionary force. Similarly when Rousseau spoke of goodness
as being natural to man, he uttered a deep truth, and one of which
the utterance was much needed; but to make the truth complete,
he ought to have added that vice and sin are also natural to man,
and that human progress, in its essential character, means the

---

[1] I am not quite sure whether that able writer, Sir R. K. Wilson, who in his work,
The Province of the State, has discussed the proper limits of legislative action, would
agree with this sentence. His theory appears to be against it; in practice he might
not be altogether adverse to it.

eliciting of the good natural disposition from the midst of its erring surroundings, and enthroning it for ever.   This point not having been observed, vice and sin played a notable part in the results of Rousseau's teachings (as it must be confessed that they did in his personal conduct); yet the good seed which he sowed was ultimately far more influential for the progress of mankind than the ill seed was for their detriment.

Voltaire and Rousseau were the two greatest motive powers of the eighteenth century; and the sequel of their action was momentous in all countries of the earth.   It is impossible to deny that their teaching gave a stimulus to the North American colonies in the revolution which separated them from Great Britain; a just revolution, and conducive to the future harmony of mankind.   Moreover, that feeling respecting human nature, that it claims and merits our sympathy in all its forms, a feeling which amid many difficulties was preserved in the United States in a degree exceeding the general acceptance of it in Europe, came largely from this French teaching.   Scepticism as regards Christianity has been less powerful in the United States than in western Europe on the whole, though of course it has not been absent.

Only a few years later than the accomplished independence of the United States of America came that French Revolution, which of all the results of the teaching of Voltaire, Rousseau, and their compeers, was the most startling, the most terrific. With what hopes was it ushered in; with what tragic massacres and wars did it run its course; with what a new modelling of the internal structure of the nations of western Europe did it terminate; what seeds of future change did it leave behind it, which have been developing until our own day! Now, at the close of this year 1915, when I write these words, we perceive France republican indeed with an immutable resolve, but as to religion, still divided between the ancient church which accepts the pope as its religious head, and a scepticism of various shades, generally defiant of Christianity.   That is the present internal state of France as to religion; but on which side does the intellect of France lie, and the prophetic power that shall sway future generations?   As in the seventeenth century the most famous Frenchmen who were held as instructors were undeniably Christian and Roman Catholic—Pascal and Bossuet and Fénelon, and even Descartes not adverse—so in the eighteenth century the intellectual and moral teachers of France were wholly on the sceptical side. Who, then, in France are they that have ruled the temper of men in the nineteenth century; can there be said to be any who rule it in the twentieth century? In the first half of the nineteenth century De Maistre and Lacordaire and Montalembert were famous writers on religion, on the Christian side—Roman Catholic, of course; but Lamennais found himself compelled to desert their company, and is counted among the sceptics. On the side of the sceptics must be counted that great imaginative writer Victor Hugo; a sceptic, yet very far from scornful of Christianity, and a believer in God. Again, early in the nineteenth century appeared in France that famous philosopher, Auguste Comte, who sought to confine the thoughts of men to that which was positively known or clearly knowable, and who constructed a religion in which every item should be clearly knowable, among which he did not count the nature of God or the life of Jesus Christ. His effort to unite the scientific with the ethical instinct was valuable, and he still has followers, but he does not govern even the sceptics of Europe to-day.

Looking at the whole state of France to-day, we cannot attribute to it any overpowering weight either on the Christian or on the sceptical side. In politics the sceptical side has made itself strongly felt; my impression is that it is also more represented in ordinary literature, though not vehemently urged; there have been eminent religious writers, such as the historian Duchesne in the Roman church, and the two Sabatiers among Protestants (but Protestants are of course in a very small minority in France). Italy, apart from the pope and his immediate surroundings, is in the same state of balance as France. The admirable Roman Catholic novelist Manzoni, in the early part of the nineteenth century, deserves notice as presenting the church of Rome in the most attractive light; and a very different person, the famous political leader Mazzini, had deep natural religious belief and sentiment, but was not a Christian.

In political and social change all the countries of Europe have had a share, and the revolutionary impulse of the eighteenth century has borne fruit in all of them, and on the whole for good; but I do not think it can be doubted that the sceptical element in the revolutionary impulse was met and examined more directly and with a fuller candour in Germany than in any other country. That the Germans have solved the problem I do not think; but they have made noble efforts towards solving it; and of those efforts I must now give an account. It will be understood, of course, that I am assuming the sceptical movement to have some real justice in it; those who think it mere cavilling will naturally not agree with the praise I have given to Germany; but all through this work I have endeavoured to show that the Bible and the Church have been implicated in errors, and these errors if real cannot be ignored; it was a duty to estimate their effect, and a merit in those who did so.

It must be borne in mind that the sceptical movement reached Germany with far more direct force than that with which it reached England and Scotland; the most natural reason for this is that intercourse took place between Germans and Frenchmen more easily and more freely than between Englishmen or Scotsmen and Frenchmen; and this probably was the main reason, though other causes may have contributed. At any rate the fact was so; and the feeling of a common human nature belonging to all men, of a present constraint and a possible, eagerly desired liberation, began to seize upon Germans about the middle of the eighteenth century, in a way in which it did not seize upon Englishmen or Scotsmen. No abstruse scholarship was required to produce this feeling; Christianity, as known and experienced in daily life, seemed narrow; and various parts of the Bible, especially in the Old Testament, appeared ethically unworthy, and superstitious. Yet Germans never rejected Christianity in the stormy manner in which Frenchmen did so; they meditated upon it, in many respects sympathetically; they gave much labour and gathered together much learning with a view to elucidating its true nature, in the light of that expansion of thought which they were sensible had taken place in their souls. There were of course among them many Christians who retained the ancient stamp; but a fruitful activity lay rather in those who did not; and some of these were sceptics with friendly sentiments towards Christianity, others were Christians with elements of scepticism taken into their souls, and transforming their ancient belief. Of the sceptics Lessing is one of the most noteworthy examples, and his famous fable of the three rings is the very type of a scepticism which has some wisdom at its root. It is the best known passage in his drama *Nathan der Weise*, and it runs thus:

An opal ring of priceless value has been handed down in one family from generation to generation; it has the power of making him who possesses it universally beloved; and therefore each possessor of it in turn leaves it to his best beloved son, to whom the power of ruling the entire family belongs in consequence. But at last one of the possessors of it has three sons equally dear to him; he cannot bring himself to leave it to any one of the three, to the exclusion of the other two; what must he do? He summons an expert jeweller, and bids him make two other rings, exact copies of the ring that has this wonderful power. The jeweller does so, and with such skill that the original ring and the two copies are absolutely alike; no eye can see any difference between them; and the father now summons each of his three sons separately and gives to each of them one of the rings, not knowing to which of the sons the original ring has fallen as his inheritance. Hence, after the father's death, each son claims to be ruler of the family; but each is astounded to find that his two brothers have severally received from their father a ring precisely similar to his own. Anxious to decide the question of headship, the three brothers go before a judge and request him to say which is the original ring. The judge replies: Am I here to answer riddles? Your father very likely lost the original ring and the three rings before me may probably all be copies. Yet stay! your father was a worthy man; it may be that he did not wish any of his three sons to rule over the other two, and used an obvious device to prevent it. I cannot decide between you, I can only give you my advice: Practise, each of you, the habitudes which will make you well beloved, and instruct your children to do the same; then, in a thousand thousand years, let each possessor of one of these three rings come before the judge who shall sit in the seat in which I sit now; he will know, better than I do, who is the possessor of the true original ring; for the results will speak for themselves.

It is scarcely necessary to add, the fable being told by Nathan the Jew to Saladin the Mussulman, at the time of the crusades, that the three rings represent the three religions, Christianity, Judaism, Islam, or rather the prime essence of each of these religions, and not their present outward appearance; and the moral is: The true religion is that which makes those who embrace it most genuinely lovable; therefore let Christian, Jew, Mussulman, alike endeavour to show that his religion makes him worthy of being loved. The fable authorises, and yet tends to dispel, scepticism.

But now let me take those two poets who still, I suppose, count as the greatest names in German literature, Goethe and Schiller, both of them examples of the sceptical tendency of their

age, but very differently. Schiller affects us, both in his life and
in his writings, by his purity and candour; in his great drama
of *Wallenstein*, the true hero, Max Piccolomini, moves with
heavenly unselfishness among the treacherous plotters who
scheme for their own gain; and if I read Schiller's life rightly,
he was unselfish. He believes in human freedom, in human
virtue, and in God—"a holy will that abides, though the human
will wavers." He unites loyalty to the powers that be with
the sense that human nature is excellent beyond all artificial
appendages; he addresses Germany thus:

> Great monarchs didst thou beget, and thou art worthy of them; he
> that commands is made great only by him who obeys. Yet endeavour,
> O Germany, and make it harder for thy rulers to be great as kings, easier
> to be, in simplicity, men.

Surely a counsel that deserved attention, and not alien from
Christian humility; and in many ways one would say that
Schiller was Christian. Yet he will not stamp himself as such,
definitely; take this distich (a hexameter and pentameter in
the original):

> What religion do I acknowledge? None of all that thou namest to
> me. And why none? From religion.

That is to say, Schiller acknowledges the religious impulse,
but cannot accept any creed. I must not dwell on his touching
personal history, or on the extraordinary variety and beauty
of his ballads and minor poems; or on his dramas generally;,
what I have said will be enough to mark the character of his
mind, and his honourable place in the world's history.

I come to the great name of Goethe. He has not the purity
of Schiller, either in his life or in his writings; but an energy of
purpose is in him, which has seldom been exceeded, the purpose
of understanding the world in which we live. A passionate
temperament is natural to him, but he will not allow it to obtain
the mastery over him; he resolutely puts it down, he studies it
scientifically. What he studies in himself he studies in others
too; he learns their characters, he expresses the rarest moments
of passion in unsurpassed lyrics; that he sympathises with passion
cannot be denied; but beyond all his sympathy, above all his
sympathy, is his constant remembrance that he is on a quest;
he desires to understand what man is meant for, what man should
aim at, what is the secret which gives power, knowledge, and
happiness. Now this is not exactly the Christian character,
nor is it altogether the right method; for we have to act before

we can fully understand; and the sympathetic impulses in Goethe did suffer some restraint in their practical effect through this keen desire to understand. Moreover, there was another thing which Goethe put aside as unpractical, which is very far from being unpractical, namely repentance for wrongs done by oneself. Repentance is the first step towards making amends; if you do not repent, you will not make amends, and then you will forget that you have done any wrong at all; and then you will do the wrong thing again. Goethe was far too prone to look upon life as a series of scientific experiments, in which you may simply disregard your failures, and start afresh on a new course. Most remarkably is this shown in the second part of *Faust*; the extraordinary tragedy in which the first part of that drama has ended, a tragedy of which Faust himself has been the principal cause, is simply forgotten by him in the second part; the tragedy is to him a sorrow to be put away, not a fount of inward meditation which may guide him towards better courses, and perhaps have fruit in a higher world than this world of sense. Thus, in seeking to understand, Goethe misunderstands; and yet this saying must not be pressed too far; it applies to a particular vein in Goethe's mind and life, but the sincerity of his quest is beyond doubt, and if he did not see everything, he saw some things very important for human welfare. Thus in that drama of Faust of which I have been speaking, and which is the greatest and most arduous production of his mind, the keynote of which is the demand, "Give me such a moment of happiness, that I may say, Would that this may last for ever!" the answer, discovered at the end, is that in doing good, happiness is found. Faust discovers this, and exclaims, "How lovely is this! would that this may last!" Upon this comes the knot of the whole difficulty, which the drama has to solve; for Faust has made a compact with the Devil (Mephistopheles) that to obtain a moment when he shall experience this supreme happiness, he will sell his soul; and the Devil now claims his soul. But the compact, though of technical validity, yields before the inward spirit of Faust's action, which has not been due to the Devil, but to Faust's own better spirit; the heavenly powers intervene, saying, "He who ever strives onwards, him can we deliver"; and by their help Faust is delivered from the diabolic conclave who are waiting to seize him, and reaches heaven. In heaven Margaret, the maiden whom he has loved, whom also he has betrayed, who loves him after he has betrayed her, a ransomed sinner, even as he is a ransomed sinner, meets and embraces him. The saintly choirs stand around; and all through this close of the drama of Faust Goethe shows his preference (which has not been uncommon among sceptics) for the church of Rome over the Reformed churches. In the first part of Faust Goethe had spoken of Luther in not very respectful terms; yet he was not always incognisant of the debt which men owe to that great cleaver asunder of ecclesiastical chains.

When all things are considered, we must acknowledge great though not perfect truth in Goethe's presentation of the duties of man. It is worth observing that in his story entitled *Wahlverwandtschaften* he lays great stress on the need of natural affinity of spirit in the man and woman who unite in the marriage bond; and this in itself indeed is a truth; but Goethe falls short of true Christianity in failing to recognise how such affinities may exist below the surface, and may be drawn out by heavenly aid, and grow into living energy. It is really by prayer that, in this relation of marriage as in all other relations, human beings attain harmony with each other.

It is, I believe, through their failure to realise the power of prayer, and the manner in which instinctive prayer acts, that the candid and laborious German thinkers of the last century and a half have failed to solve the problem which the Christian religion presents to us. Now I have necessarily but an imperfect acquaintance with German literature, and perhaps some one may come forward who, with a wider knowledge, will convict me of error in this point; but the assertion which I have made is one to which all the evidence which I know points. I cannot believe that either Lessing or Schiller or Goethe had the instinct of prayer in its true and formative power; Schiller came the nearest to it, but fell short of it. The illustrious founder of German philosophy, Kant, who saw clearly that our moral nature demands assumptions which can only be verified by practical action, and not by any argument or observation antecedent to practical action, was not, to the best of my belief, cognisant of the way in which direct intercourse between man and God affects our well-being and our capacities; and though Fichte thought in a sublime manner about God, I hardly think that this intimate laying open of the heart before God, this submission before God, belonged to him: still less to Schelling and Hegel, in whom, successively, the intellectual element became more and more prominent. I am not denying the force or the importance of these four eminent men, but am merely saying that they did not penetrate clearly to the point from which spiritual growth proceeds. In all four there is no passage so famous as Kant's saying about the starry firmament and the moral law; it is given by Dr Merz (*History of European Thought*, vol. III. p. 29) with more fullness than as generally quoted, and it will be well to write it down here:

Two things fill my mind with ever new and ever growing wonder and reverence, the more often and continuously my thoughts are occupied with them: the starry heavens above me, and the moral law within me. Neither of these ought I to seek for or merely to assume, as if they lay outside my horizon, clothed in darkness and the unreachable. I see them both before me and connect them directly with the consciousness of my existence. The first begins with the place which I occupy in the outer world of the senses and expands the connections in which I stand into the invisibly great, with worlds upon worlds and systems upon systems, moreover, into limitless ages of their periodic motion, its origin and duration. The second begins with my invisible Self, my personality, and represents me as standing in a world which has true infinity, but is accessible only to Reason, and with which I stand not only—as is the case with the outer world—in accidental, but in a general and necessary relation.

A true and memorable passage; but it does not dwell (and as far as I know Kant never did dwell) on the difficulty which we all at times experience both in perceiving and in following the dictates of the moral law. Some clear perception there must be if Kant's "categorical imperative" or in other words the command of duty is to have effect; and it may have effect even where our perception is not clear in the full sense, but still clear enough for a practical resolve; there are however many most important cases where we have to act, if at all, in great obscurity, and where, if possible, we ought to wait before acting. Now it is in this twilight of our discernment that religion, of which prayer is the first beginning in act, has its chief field of action; the power of God, which we call to our aid in prayer[1], strengthens our vision to a more accurate discrimination, and sustains us after conscientious action, even though it may turn out in the end that that action was not altogether right (and there are very few of our actions that do not admit of improvement in one way or another). The command which we call duty is strictly speaking independent of religion; but religion nourishes it, interprets it, multiplies it both in the direction and in the amount of its results;

[1] A friend of mine once said to me that he could not help feeling that prayer was rather mean; but is it mean for an infant to suck its mother's breast? To acknowledge our dependence, where that dependence is real and unavoidable, is very far from being a mean act.

and this is because religion, explained as I have explained it, strengthens both the vision and the action of men.

Now I do not believe that any of the four philosophers whom I have named, valuable though their thoughts have been in interpreting many parts of moral and spiritual truth, ever took into account the way in which that intercourse between man and God, which we call prayer, strengthens a man's inner being, and how from this cause an improvement has taken place in general morality, especially among Christians, during the nineteen centuries which have witnessed the growth of Christianity. The improvement of morality has not always begun with Christians (though generally it has done so) but Christians have been ready to accept each improvement in the long run, even against great prepossessions the other way, and that is because Christians have always prayed, and have been conscious of their own imperfection.

Now the German thinkers in the early part of the nineteenth century did not realise this; but it is right that I should refer to that one among them who came nearest to realising it, a theologian who was also a philosopher, and a very lovable person too—Schleiermacher. I have no right to say that the German philosophers and poets whom I have named above had never anything of the disposition to pray, but this is a point of which I am ignorant; Schleiermacher certainly had it, as we may see from what he wrote to his friend Charlotte von Kathen on the occasion of the birth of his son:

You may conceive with what joy and thankfulness I received him, and that my first prayer to God was, to be inspired with wisdom and power from above to educate the child to His glory.   Join with me in this prayer, I beg you, all you dear ones!   *Life of Schleiermacher*, translated by Frederica Rowan, vol. II. p. 285.

This passage however does not show us whether Schleiermacher opened the inmost recesses of his soul to the Divine power. The passage which comes nearest to telling us whether he did so is one, I think, in the first of his speeches *On Religion*, addressed, he tells us, to its "cultured despisers"; perhaps I ought to call it *two* passages, but they unite very naturally:

Why do you not regard the religious life itself, and first those pious exaltations of the mind in which all other known activities are set aside or almost suppressed, and the whole soul is dissolved in the immediate feeling of the Infinite and Eternal? In such moments the disposition you pretend to despise reveals itself in primordial and visible form. He only who has studied and truly known men in these emotions can rediscover religion in those outward manifestations. ....You must transport yourselves into the interior of a pious soul and seek to understand its inspiration. In the very act, you must understand the production of light and heat in a soul surrendered to the Universe. *On Religion*, by Friedrich Schleiermacher. Translated by John Oman, B.D. pp. 15, 16, 18.

In a note written some years later, Schleiermacher explains that the "surrender to the Universe" of which he speaks involves the surrender to God, from whom the soul receives a creative warmth. Far must I be from undervaluing such a passage; it does represent to us God, and the infinite heart-stirrings of the Universe going on for ever, as a refuge from the trials of life, and as kindling warmth and light in the soul; but it does not represent to us how the trials of life are in themselves transformed and the difficulties solved by the Divine power entering the soul. It is this last process, the solution of difficulties, and not merely the taking refuge from difficulties, which constitutes the ultimate test of Christian faith; this it is in which prayer takes such a leading part; and I do not think that any of the German philosophers or theologians of the nineteenth century has fully apprehended this. Yet Germany, in the latter part of the nineteenth century as well as in the earlier part, produced many religious minds whom we may honour; what I miss is the profound seizure of the habit of prayer as that which shall gradually dissolve differences and bring harmony into all the relations of men.

At this point, however, it will be expedient for me to break off from the history of religious development in its deepest sense, and come to one of its minor adjuncts, though an important one, namely the examination of the Bible. If there is any truth in Biblical criticism, it cannot but produce an effect on Christian faith in its broader aspects. Let me then set down what appear to me the chief results of this criticism as obtained up to the present day with the names of their discoverers; I must not include criticisms of doubtful validity or lesser importance; nor of course can I include criticisms which are specially my own and at present unshared by others. But the following results appear to me certain:

First, the composite nature of the Pentateuch, and the diversity of its sources. This was first observed in the year 1753 by a French physician in Languedoc, Jean Astruc; who distinguished between those parts of Genesis where the Hebrew for God is Elohim, and those parts where the Hebrew is Jehovah[1], or Jehovah Elohim. Astruc did not discard the Mosaic authorship,

---

[1] Yahweh, according to modern scholars.

but he thought that Moses had two sets of documents before him, and that he used both.   This general view has been greatly expanded by later critics, who have for the most part denied the Mosaic authorship of the Pentateuch, and justly, as is held in the present work.

Secondly, about 1780, J. B. Koppe, in the German edition of Lowth's *Isaiah*, was the first to point out that the book of Isaiah could not all have been written by one and the same author.   In 1789, Eichhorn and Döderlein followed in the same sense.   The separation of the last twenty-seven chapters of the book from the rest is of course the clearest point in this critical decision, and is the only one that need be mentioned here.

Thirdly, in 1783, Corrodi declared the book of Daniel to have been written in the time of Antiochus Epiphanes, or about 170 B.C., nearly four hundred years later than the date at which it professes to have been written.   This opinion had already been advanced by the Neoplatonist philosopher Porphyry, in the third century of the Christian era.

In the beginning of the nineteenth century De Wette startled the religious world by declaring that Deuteronomy, so far from being Mosaic, was not known at all till the time of Josiah; he founded this statement on the narrative told in 2 Kings xxii.

About seventy years after De Wette had published his view about Deuteronomy, Wellhausen announced, on the strength of the 44th chapter of Ezekiel, that that prophet did not know the book of Leviticus, which must therefore have been written after the Babylonian captivity.   In recording this criticism, with which on the whole I agree, I ought to add that it does not appear to me to apply to every part of Leviticus, e.g. it does not apply to the last chapter[1].

The comparatively late origin of most of the Psalms has been, I believe, a gradual discovery; very few of the Psalms being now reckoned to belong to David, at any rate in their present form.

Now take these results as I have given them; omit the more subtle points of Old Testament criticism, which are innumerable, and which are necessarily more subject to doubt than the broader conclusions which I have mentioned; omit too the criticism of the New Testament, as to which more vacillation has been shown by critics, both as to the date of composition of each book and

---

[1] The above statements as to the first authors of the criticisms mentioned have been drawn partly from Hastings' *Dictionary of the Bible*, partly from the last edition of the *Encyclopædia Britannica*.

its authorship; can anyone fail to see what a weakening of the evidence for the miraculous history is implied in these generally accepted conclusions? I am not speaking now of my own opinions, which have been given in earlier chapters of this work; but I think that critics, in regard to the Old Testament, deserve to be considered as holding a certain authority. Moreover this authority is reinforced from the side of physical science, which has contributed evidence, hard to be challenged, as to the non-historical character of the creation and the flood, as those narratives are recounted in the early chapters of Genesis. It is in Germany that these results have been most largely accepted; and hence the recent German defenders of Christian faith, such as Ritschl and Harnack and Herrmann and Kaftan, have concentred themselves on the New Testament, on the life and work of Jesus Christ, as the origin from which all religion springs. I think that they ought to have begun with prayer to the invisible God, which is an act, and implies a relation, not dependent on history at all, and then they might have gone on to the life and work of Jesus Christ, as the first full exemplification in history of the divine power; but to begin with history appears to me an error in method. Hence I do not regard them as perfectly successful; but I must not deny the value of their writings.

One more remark I may make, before I leave the subject of the development of religion in Germany. The revolutionary impulse of the eighteenth century, as it let loose the spontaneous desires and passions of man in no ordinary degree, so let loose the desire for military conquest. Two famous monarchs are the evidence of this, Frederick the Second of Prussia, and the emperor Napoleon. The emperor Napoleon was overthrown, and more than half a century later his nephew, heir to his name, was overthrown too, and France no longer thinks of him very greatly. But the spirit of Frederick survives in Germany, as a part of the national genius. If any German historian of the future, looking back upon the war which is now tearing Europe to pieces, inquires whence it came, he can hardly avoid saying that the aggressive disposition which Frederick initiated was one of the causes leading to it. Would it have been possible to prevent the working of that spirit in Germany? Had that movement[1] prospered, which grew up in the first half of the nineteenth century, to bring the religious spirit of Great Britain into fruitful contact

---

[1] Dr Arnold of Rugby, in England, and Bunsen in Germany, are the best known names connected with this movement.

with the religious spirit of Germany, the Reformed religion in both countries being recognised as inheriting the Christian promise, I cannot but think that the Christian spirit would have replaced the military spirit in Germany, and our own country would have profited also. But "the nations were walking in darkness."

I come, at the close of this chapter, to the part which Great Britain has taken in the religious movements of the last two centuries, and of the effect which religious scepticism has had in this country. It was not till the middle of the nineteenth century that scepticism really invaded Great Britain, although two of the world's most famous sceptics, Hume and Gibbon, adorned our literature in the eighteenth century, and it would be easy to name others. But scepticism, and even criticism of any decided character, as applied to the Biblical books, were for a long time held at bay, partly by certain strong religious revivals, of which in the eighteenth century Wesleyanism was the most powerful, and partly by the influence of laymen of strong character, of whom Dr Johnson is the most famous in the eighteenth century. The English poets of both centuries have often been purely orthodox Christians; as for instance the much-suffering William Cowper; also Wordsworth, the ardent lover of nature and imaginative interpreter of man, distinguished in his early years for his strong sympathy with the French Revolution; and Robert Browning, curious in his originality, with deep flashes of insight into the frailties of man. But indeed almost through the whole of the nineteenth century there were in this country laymen, of great distinction and power in various modes of life, who adhered to and advocated the Christian faith in its traditional form, according to the creeds. It is a matter of course that there should have been clerical supporters of the creeds, often of great ability too; and what is known as the Oxford movement, of which Keble, Newman, and Pusey were the best known leaders, had almost its *raison d'être* in the support of the creeds. Of one of these, John Henry Newman, known in his later years as a cardinal of the Roman church, I may say something more, mainly on account of his eminence; but partly also because he was my uncle, and I hold him in great esteem and affection. The criticism I make on him is (and this applies to the whole of his life) that while himself personally most humble and self-sacrificing, he yet expected and demanded of the Christian society an open and obvious imperial character, which it was not possible for that society to have.   I do not think I need say more than this; but I should like to set by the side of his name that of his brother (also my uncle) Francis William Newman, a sceptic as to Christianity but deeply interested in it, valued by me not less than his brother, who however was more famous. Of Francis William Newman I would say this, that while the style of his writing was sometimes rash and to be regretted, his religious sentiment was sincere and his criticism often perspicacious; nor did he ever forget that religion demands fearlessness, and that practical good must be our aim as well as theoretical truth.   I have always lamented that these two uncles of mine could not have interwoven, and by interweaving have modified, their respective first principles.

I have begun, it will be seen, to mention British sceptics; and it will be proper for me now to mention those two unwilling sceptics, Thomas Carlyle and John Ruskin.   No one who reads Carlyle's earlier writings can doubt that he would gladly have been a Christian, if it had been possible for him conscientiously to be so.   He drew his scepticism from Germany; and he drew also from Germany great breadth of sympathy, although it cannot be denied that in his later years this was narrowed; his picturesque, singular, and forcible style was his own.   Ruskin was a far more unwilling sceptic than Carlyle; his sympathies were deeply bound up with Christian art and Christian feeling; and the pathetic weakness of his later years was doubtless due to this clash of reason and feeling in him; he is, after all, an interpreter of Christianity in some of its most characteristic manifestations, and no reader of his ordinary writings would suspect that he was a sceptic at all.

James Martineau (a philosopher as well as a theologian) would have disclaimed the character of a sceptic, and hardly ought to be reckoned as such; but he is so very critical that he does appear to be on the borders of it, as far as Christianity is concerned.   This disposition is shared by many of the Germans, though not, I think, by the Ritschlian school; and it is really difficult to know where criticism attacks so many points as to pass over into scepticism.   That Martineau had a strongly religious mind there is no doubt whatever, and in this sense neither he, nor Carlyle, nor Ruskin, nor F. W. Newman, was a sceptic; but the crucial difference which separates a Christian from a non-Christian appears to me to be this, that a Christian believes Jesus of Nazareth to have a real government over us, a real direction of us, now; the non-Christian does not believe this.

My own knowledge of Martineau's works is not so thorough as
to enable me to say confidently how he would have placed himself
in regard to the difference of which I have spoken.

If I have referred to British poets who were orthodox Christians,
I ought to notice the fact that others have been sceptics. Byron
and Shelley were such, though with a regard, and I think I may
say reverence, for the name and character of Jesus Christ. Such
a reverence undoubtedly was felt by Matthew Arnold; by
Swinburne not so clearly; though it should be remembered that
one of Swinburne's most beautiful poems was in praise of a female
saint of the Roman church, Catherine of Siena. Students of
physical science have naturally some disposition to religious
scepticism, for the faculties which they especially cultivate are
quite different from religious faith; yet I do not think that in
Great Britain, on the whole, physical science has given its
authority to scepticism. Darwin partly did so; but humility
and candour are never wanting in his utterances on this subject.

No mention of British sceptics ought to leave James Mill
unmentioned, or his more famous son, John Stuart Mill, who
followed in his steps, but with much reserve; the approximations
of the younger Mill to Christianity, though limited in degree,
were very touching, and very noteworthy. Of Herbert Spencer
I have spoken in the first chapter of the present work.

I must be slow to speak about religious tendencies in Great
Britain during the last twenty-five years, beyond saying that
Biblical criticism has been greatly extended in this country during
that time. That Great Britain has taken a worthy part, though
with some deficiencies, in the development of the modern mind
on this most important of all subjects, I would maintain; and
perhaps I may fitly end this chapter with a few quotations from
British writers which appear to me worthy of being remembered.
First I will give that noble passage from Richard Hooker's
Ecclesiastical Polity, at the close of his first book, concerning
the function and importance of law in the universe:

Wherefore that here we may briefly end: of Law there can no less be
acknowledged, than that her seat is the bosom of God, her voice the
harmony of the world: all things in heaven and earth do her homage,
the very least as feeling her care, and the greatest as not exempted from
her power: both Angels and men and creatures of what condition soever,
though each in different sort and manner, yet all with uniform consent,
admiring her as the mother of their peace and joy.

Next let me refer to bishop Butler, who in the first chapter
of his *Analogy* expressed the opinion (which neither philosophy

nor religion will scorn) that in some sense the lower animals may possibly be immortal. But quite as original, and more moving, is the following passage from his sermon on the Love of God:

Consider wherein that presence of a friend consists, which has often so strong an effect, as wholly to possess the mind, and entirely suspend all other affections and regards; and which itself affords the highest satisfaction and enjoyment. He is within reach of the senses. Now, as our capacities of perception improve, we shall have, perhaps by some faculty entirely new, a perception of God's presence with us in a nearer and stricter way; since it is certain he is more intimately present with us than anything else can be. Proof of the existence and presence of any being is quite different from the immediate perception, the consciousness of it. What then will be the joy of heart, which his presence, and the light of his countenance, who is the life of the universe, will inspire good men with, when they shall have a sensation, that he is the sustainer of their being, that they exist in him; when they shall feel his influence to cheer and enliven and support their frame, in a manner of which we have now no conception? He will be in a literal sense their strength and their portion for ever.

I conceive that the above passage expresses a truth which even now is dawning on mankind.

It is, of course, easy to make affirmations concerning the value of Christian faith, and such avowals will be readily accepted by Christians. It is not Christians, but sceptics, whom I would ask, not indeed to accept as truth, but to consider whether some truth may not belong to the words which Samuel Taylor Coleridge, twelve days before his death, wrote for the future perusal of his godson, then an infant:

I now, on the eve of my departure, declare to you...that health is a great blessing—competence obtained by honourable industry a great blessing—and a great blessing it is to have kind, faithful, and loving friends and relatives; but that the greatest of all blessings, as it is the most ennobling of all privileges, is to be indeed a Christian.

From the close of the *Tabletalk*.

My interpretation of what it is to be a Christian has not been altogether the interpretation of Coleridge; but I do not think it so alien from his, but that I may quote the above passage with commendation.

Both sceptics and Christians might consider the words of Byron—a sinner, but not a fool—when he contrasts Christians with the Master of Christians. He has been speaking of the injustice of mankind to their teachers, and has appealed to Locke, Bacon, and Socrates; and then he adds:

> and thou, Diviner still,
> Whose lot it is by man to be mistaken,
> And thy pure creed made sanction of all ill
> *   *   *   *   *   *
> How was thy toil rewarded?
>
> From Don Juan, canto xv.

I am taking, it will be seen, passages that have struck me, and have remained in my memory.

That profound poem, Tennyson's *In Memoriam* (which unintelligent persons misunderstand as an attempt to prove immortality—it is really an attempt to conceive what immortality may be, especially in relation to our visible experience) contains a few stanzas, well known indeed, but so important as a new development of Christian faith, that they must not be omitted here:

> Oh yet we trust that somehow good
> Will be the final goal of ill,
> To pangs of nature, sins of will,
> Defects of doubt, and taints of blood;
>
> That nothing walks with aimless feet;
> That not one life shall be destroyed
> Or cast as rubbish to the void
> When God hath made the pile complete;
>
> That not a worm is cloven in vain;
> That not a moth with vain desire
> Is shrivel'd in a fruitless fire,
> Or but subserves another's gain.

The poet goes on with words of humility; but the humility does not debar the hope.

Lastly, let me quote the poet, from whom the verses are taken, which appear on the title-page of this work—Arthur Hugh Clough. No tenderer, no wiser spirit breathed in the nineteenth century. He is generally counted as a sceptic, and a sceptic as to miracles he certainly was; he discarded, with pain and anguish, the belief in the physical resurrection of Jesus Christ; but his conclusion is affirmation and not denial, and appeals to the higher life beyond sense:

> Though dead, not dead;
> Not gone, though fled;
> Not lost, though vanished.
> In the great gospel and true creed,
> He is yet risen indeed;
> Christ is yet risen.

CHAPTER XXVII

THE HOPE OF THE FUTURE

In the work of which I am now entering on the concluding chapter I have endeavoured to trace through all history, and even in those ages which on earth preceded human history, the tokens which show that life is both attracted and nourished by powers which are not manifest to our bodily senses; which attraction and nourishment is the theme expressed by the word religion. I have endeavoured to show that the experiences of religion have culminated in Christianity, which has strengthened the energies and faculties of men in no common degree, and has thrown light on the nature of those invisible powers which surround our visible life; and yet I have been obliged to argue that Christianity, no less than other forms of religion, has been subject to drawbacks, owing to the natural tendency of men to mingle error with truth, and especially their tendency to assimilate the divine government of the world to the government which has been exercised by earthly kings and rulers. I have tried to separate the true from the false by the evidence of history; and now I must try to show what the result should be when we regard the conduct of mankind in the future.

Mankind ought to be taught first of all to aim at right conduct; and by right conduct is to be understood conduct which increases living energy and happiness. I put living energy before happiness, because living energy is the cause and happiness the effect; if we disregard living energy, we may obtain happiness by chance, but we shall not be secure in it.

We must begin with trying to determine right conduct and to practise it; the details of right conduct will differ with every different person, but the general principle always is, to bestow our labour on that which will increase living energy in ourselves and others to the greatest degree; we cannot help giving some preference to ourselves by reason of the fact that we know our own circumstances and active possibilities so much

29—2

better than we know those of anyone else, but any preference given to ourselves on other grounds than this is an error in conduct.

Right conduct must engage our attention before we come to religion, and this is practically affirmed by the most theological of all the writers in the New Testament when he says:

He that loveth not his brother whom he hath seen, cannot love God whom he hath not seen.

We begin with human affections and with acts which have mankind in view, before we come to divine affections and acts which have God in view. No recent writer has expressed this sequence so clearly and tersely as the poet Arthur Hugh Clough, whom I have already twice quoted, and will now quote again; the following lines, addressed to God, are entitled *Qui laborat, orat*:

O only Source of all our light and life,
　Whom as our truth, our strength, we see and feel,
But whom the hours of mortal moral strife
　Alone aright reveal!

Mine inmost soul, before Thee inly brought,
　Thy presence owns ineffable, divine;
Chastised each rebel self-encentered thought,
　My will adoreth Thine.

With eye downdropt, if then this earthly mind
　Speechless remain, or speechless e'en depart,
Nor seek to see—for what of earthly kind
　Can see Thee as Thou art?—

If well-assured 'tis but profanely bold
　In thought's abstractest forms to seem to see,
It dare not dare the dread communion hold
　In ways unworthy Thee.

O not unowned, thou shalt unnamed forgive,
　In worldly walks the prayerless heart prepare;
And if in work its life it seem to live,
　Shalt make that work be prayer.

Nor times shall lack, when while the work it plies,
　Unsummoned powers the blinding film shall part,
And scarce by happy tears made dim, the eyes
　In recognition start.

But, as thou willest, give or e'en forbear
　The beatific supersensual sight,
So, with Thy blessing blest, that humbler prayer
　Approach Thee morn and night.

It will be seen that Clough acknowledges a certain awe before the Unknown Supreme Power as befitting mankind at all times, and concurrent with the very first efforts after practical action; and this may be conceded; but for nearer approach to the Deity he regards the performance of our duty towards men as the essential precedent. In this he appears to me to lay the way open for a teaching which shall be truly Christian, and which yet shall acknowledge the natural rights of sceptics; for in the complexities of circumstance many men are quite blamelessly agnostics, or even atheists. How to conduct an argument with agnostics or atheists cannot be determined in the general, for every man differs in his preconceptions, and agnostics and atheists differ among themselves just as other men do; but it is a necessary question how a child shall be taught his or her moral and religious duties. I think it would be somewhat in the following way that I would teach them, or rather that a mother might teach her child:

You should always try to be nice to other people, and kind to them. If you find that you do not get what you want, or if somebody hurts you, do not be in too great a hurry to cry out or to quarrel with the person who has hurt you, but say in your own mind, O God, help me. Now I must tell you who God is. He has never been seen by anyone, but we know that he lives and helps those who ask him for help; and the person who has told us most about him is Jesus Christ, of whom I will tell you more presently, but just now you may only remember that he was the wisest and best man who ever lived. He taught us to speak to God as our Father. Now you know that you have a father whom you can see, just as you can see me, your mother; and your father helps you, just as I help you; but God helps you in a different way, and a way which I cannot describe to you, but you will find it out for yourself. He helps you not to be greedy and not to be quarrelsome; and if you say to him in your own mind, O God, help me, he will make you so strong that you will be happy even if you do not get your own way, and even if you are hurt you will feel it less and will presently not feel it at all.

When you say, O God, help me, that is called praying. It is not always easy to pray, and perhaps at first you may think it no use praying; but it is of use, and we all may get help in this way, and the world has become a happier place to live in because men have prayed to God.

You must not think that I know all about God. There is a great deal which I do not know, and there is a great deal which no one knows, not even the wisest people that have ever lived; but we are not quite ignorant of what he is. When there is something which we partly know, but which nobody knows entirely, we call that thing a mystery, or mysterious; and most things are mysterious, but nothing is so mysterious as God. We are however sure of this, that in a certain sense we have come from him; he is the parent of all of us, not in the same sense as that in which your father and mother are your parents, but quite as truly; and though it is a very mysterious thing, yet we believe that if he had not willed it, you would not have been born; and no one is born without God's will that he or she should be born.

Now I must tell you about Jesus Christ, who has helped us to know what God is more than anyone else who ever lived. His first name was Jesus, but his disciples felt truly that he, and he alone, could lead men into eternal life, which is the greatest thing any man has ever done, or can possibly do; and hence they were sure he was the king whom God desired all men to obey; and that is the meaning of Christ. So they called him, and we call him, Jesus Christ. When I say that he was a king, or rather that he is a king, you must not think that he is a king like those who reign here on earth in great outward splendour and with armies to defend them. There is some outward splendour belonging to him, for all the cathedrals and churches in Christian lands were built in his honour; but he would still be a king even if there were no church or cathedral in the world. He is a king because many men love him and trust him, and do what he has told them to do; and when all men understand him, he will be still more obeyed than he is now.

He is loved and trusted because he was so good, and because he has made it clear to men that there is another life beyond this life. He did not despise this life; he liked to be happy in this life just as we all like to be happy in this life; but he would not make other people unhappy in order that he himself might be happy. On the contrary, he went without things himself in order to make other people strong and happy. But he could not help offending his fellow-countrymen, because they were wrong in some things, and he could not help telling them so; and they were angry with him, and caused him to be crucified and slain. He knew that they would do this, and of course it was great pain to him to be crucified and slain; but he felt sure that God would recompense him for all his pain. He trusted in God; and you may ask if God really did recompense him. Yes, that is what we believe; and we believe it because we find that by believing it, by praying to Jesus in heaven as well as to God in heaven, we obtain a strength which we cannot obtain otherwise, and a power of uniting among ourselves for all good works.

Remember, my child, to pray to God first, for this is what Jesus Christ has told us to do, and this is what will show you that there is something which is a help to you beyond all the things which we see and know in this world; but when you ask yourself what is most pleasing to God, remember that what is most pleasing to him is that you should attach yourself to Jesus Christ, praying to Jesus Christ also as to one who hears you, since Jesus Christ has restored among men that divine spirit which mankind had lost, and which gives us assurance that we shall live again after dying in this world.

I must tell you, now, what I mean by speaking of that divine spirit which mankind had lost. The men and women who live in the world now, and the men and women of whom you read in past times, have all been imperfect; they have not been altogether kind to one another, nor have they always prayed to God, or trusted in God; but there is in every man and every woman and every boy and every girl something which tells him or her to be kind to others and to trust in God; and there is reason[1] to think that this love and trust was our first original state, when long before our birth in this world we lived in the bosom of God our

---

[1] See pages 462 and 463; and compare (as a similar though not identical view). the passage on the Fall in Coleridge's *Table Talk*, p. 61.

heavenly parent. This is a very mysterious subject, and religious people express it by saying that mankind are a fallen race. But those who regain this spirit of love and trustfulness will after their death, as we believe, live with God and Jesus Christ in heaven, and will help those who come after them to be good and trustful, even as they themselves have learnt to be good and trustful. Love and trust are what bind all good men and women together, whether in this life or in the next life; and you may always pray to anyone whom you love and trust who has died and whom you believe to be with God and with Jesus Christ, though this is another great mystery, for you cannot see or distinguish them, and strictly speaking you do not know that they answer you; but when men become better and more religious, we hope to have clearer knowledge as to this.

Remember that sympathy with others, that is to say feeling what they feel and helping them, is one of the most important things in the world; and to trust others is no less important, though we cannot always trust everyone, and even good people sometimes say and do things in which they are not to be believed or followed; but we may always trust God and pray to God, and if we bear in mind our own ignorance and our own liability to go wrong, we shall learn more and more where we are right in trusting others and where we cannot trust them or follow them. We have good hope that in this way all men will become stronger and more united; and then they will form what is called a society, that is a number of people acting together and helping one another. A society of men and women who unite because they believe in God and in Jesus Christ is called a church, for a church does not properly mean a building, though some buildings are called churches, because Christian men and women meet in them to pray. But the proper meaning of a church is a society of men and women who unite together because they believe in God and in Jesus Christ. Churches may go wrong, just as men and women may go wrong; but the power and the spirit of God which makes men and women better will make churches better too as time goes on; this is what has happened in the past and this is what we believe will happen in the future.

I think that that would be an intelligible account, even to a child, of what we mean by duty and religion, though I do not say it could all be given to a child at once, and everyone must speak as he or she individually believes, and I am not prescribing any form of words. This however is the kind of foundation of instruction that I would lay; and if the reader feels that his own belief is not wholly alien from what I have just said, I may go on to say what appear to me the most important subjects among men to-day, and how religion may help in the treatment of them.

Bodily health is one of the most important subjects of human interest, and all men ought to pray for it, and not merely for health in the abstract, but for strength when their health is endangered in any particular way. The first threatenings of illness can often be successfully met, whereas if it be allowed to gather head, it will become serious; and it is in the perception of these first threatenings and in the instantaneous lifting up of the heart to God for strength to meet them that the value of religion in this particular respect mainly consists; though of course in serious illness we ought to pray also, but without expecting immediate deliverance from it; for there are many cases in which the bodily functions have been put so awry that it takes time to straighten them out, even with all proper restfulness and the greatest care. Prayer does help in these cases, though as a rule gradually; and in mortal illnesses it helps in quieting and elevating the soul.

The poverty of the necessitous poor is to societies what ill-health is to individual persons; the remedies for it are neither easy nor simple; but a right temper is the condition without which all remedies will fail, a temper which can take advantage either of individual self-denial or social agencies or legislative action according to the possibilities and requirements of the situation, but which never ceases to have for its aim the removal of those evils which come from the inequalities of fortune among mankind. The faults which produce these inequalities lie partly with the poor, though on the whole more with the rich; the remembrance of the divine judgments, by which the patient worker is rewarded even in this life if we have regard to broad issues, but in any case in his eternal welfare, is the substratum of reasonable hope for the future on which we have to build.

Nothing that I have said above, either as regards bodily illness or as regards poverty, ought to be interpreted as under-valuing purely human agencies for the removal of these evils; medicine, surgery, education, sanitation, and many other arts and fields of working might be instanced as distinguishing the present age in a peculiar manner, and as causes of great improvement in the welfare of human beings. But religion occupies a central position among them all, setting right the tone of the mind, and thereby enabling a due proportion to be preserved in the various forms of action, and enabling men to wait for those critical moments when the time is ripe for improvement to be achieved successfully.

It is now proper to say something about the relation of Christian churches towards each other. Of Christian churches, I say; but it may be asked me, Is the Christian Church, as a single society, to be ignored? No, I do not ignore it; but the Christian Church, spoken of thus absolutely, transcends our knowledge; the elect, who are all around us, are not easily discernible as the elect. The elect are the true Christian Church, to be revealed

in due time. What we see plainly with our present senses are
Christian churches; each church an imperfect semblance of the
true Church of the elect, each church aiming at perfection, but
at present falling short of it in one way or another. Between
churches which differ in doctrine, friendship may be aimed at;
the likenesses should as a rule be brought into prominence more
than the differences; but of course discussion of differences is
unavoidable, and may take place in a perfectly friendly manner.
The greatest practical difficulty which attends such discussions
is that they have generally no effect whatever in changing the
belief or the practices of any religious body taken as a whole;
individuals change their beliefs and their practices, but changes
on a large scale do not take place, and hence religious discussion
appears to have a paltry and artificial character, and is discredited
before it is started. But those who feel the Christian religion,
and Christian theology, to be of real and great importance, may
revive its credit among ordinary people who have no liking for
theology by following the two following principles: First, by
promoting the co-operation of differing religious bodies in all
matters which lie outside religious differences. There is, for
instance, a great deal of knowledge of the poor possessed by the
clergy and religious ministers of all denominations, which is
ineffective because it is confined to so few, intercourse being
comparatively rare between Roman Catholic priests and Anglican
clergy, between Roman Catholic priests and Nonconformist
ministers, between Anglican clergy and Nonconformist ministers.
Such intercourse ought not to be enforced in any way, but if the
ministers of religion felt how greatly their own authority would
be extended by a larger and freer intercourse among themselves
on ordinary social matters, I think they would somehow manage
to procure such intercourse, and that the whole community
would profit by it. But secondly, those laymen in any religious
body who feel that religion, and in particular the Christian
religion, has real value, ought to study the principles of religion
more than they do. I must add that they ought to study
sceptical writers as well as religious writers; they ought to see
what can be said against Christianity, or any form of Christianity,
as well as what can be said in its favour. This is an essential
condition of real and genuine interest being taken in religion,
such as is taken at the present day in physical science. I doubt
however if discussion between the ministers of differing religious
bodies is very much to be recommended; they are too much

bound to support their respective beliefs for it to be easy to be perfectly fair in such a discussion. Laymen are not exposed to this difficulty in anything like the same degree, and if laymen would study the subject of religion, discussion might take place with really valuable results. I am not, be it observed, saying anything against the clergy writing on theology; that is to be expected as a matter of course; it is only when such writing has a partisan character that it is necessarily difficult for them to preserve fairness.

I do not believe reunion between separated religious bodies to be at all possible at the present day; friendliness between them is possible, and should be aimed at. I think, too, that friendliness between Christians on the one hand, and the followers of the other great religions of the world on the other hand, should be aimed at; those religions, in spite of their defects, have real value; and this may be acknowledged without impairing the superior claims of Christianity.

By candour, patience, and industry it may be hoped that mankind will in time approximate to each other on this profound and difficult subject of religion; and (I may add) it is to be hoped that there will be a real revelation of a spiritual world, imperfectly apprehended by us now, a world in which death does not occur. But mutual good feeling must precede the attainment of any such sublime vision.

It will be seen that I am trying to show what should be the practical direction of the efforts of mankind in the future; and I am therefore noting the difficulties which have to be removed before harmonious co-operation can be arrived at; and the next great difficulty on which I must touch is that which arises from the simultaneous existence of different powerful nations, neighbours to each other, each keenly desirous of surpassing the others in power. The rivalry thence ensuing is the chief cause of wars; and at the moment when I write, one of the greatest wars of all history is going on. One remark, and one only, will I make about that war. Among the many painful discords which it has evoked, none concerns us in England so intimately as the charge brought against us by the Germans, that we, the English, planned the war secretly beforehand. The evidence which they bring forward for that assertion lies in certain documents which they found in the state archives in Brussels after their armies had captured that city; and this evidence is put forward in a pamphlet (clearly semi-official, and published in Berlin, I believe in December,

1914) entitled "Die Belgische Neutralität." I have read that pamphlet very carefully, and am certain that no fair-minded inquirer will say that it shows any design on the part of the British Government to make or promote war against Germany. It does show that the British Government were afraid lest Germany should invade Belgium (was their fear unwarranted?) and tried to guard against such invasion. But of intended aggression by England there is no trace in it; and if anyone wishes to see absolute disproof of the idea that Great Britain contemplated such aggression, he will find it in the despatch[1] written by Sir Edward Grey in April, 1912, in which that statesman describes his interview at that time with the Belgian Minister in London. Be it remembered that the charge made by the German semi-official pamphlet was not made against England alone; it was made against Belgium also; it was to the effect that Great Britain and Belgium, together, were conspiring to attack Germany. Now this interview of Sir Edward Grey with the Belgian Minister shows Great Britain and Belgium, not as fellow-conspirators, but as divided by a very real suspicion. The Belgian Minister has heard that Great Britain may possibly invade Belgium in order to forestall an invasion of Belgium by Germany; Sir Edward Grey assures him that no British Minister could possibly think of such a course, or could be the first to violate the neutrality of Belgium. As a matter of fact, Great Britain only sent troops into Belgium, in August, 1914, at the request of the Belgian Government, and after Germany, with overpowering forces, had invaded that country.

I trust that it has not been out of place for me to defend the good faith of my own country here; it is not an abstruse matter, and the case is perfectly plain; yet it is the kind of accusation that is capable of sowing hatred in the minds of many generations, and it is very desirable that the means of refuting it should be clearly known. Of the general causes of this great war, and its possible issues, I must say nothing; it is too great a subject to be treated as a detail in a work like the present. But respecting the peace which must at some time or other follow this war it is desirable to say something. How soon that peace will come, or what will be the terms of it, we know not; but whenever it comes, and whoever may have been victorious, then will be the opportunity for the Christian spirit to show itself. That there

---

[1] This despatch will be found on pp. 368–9 of Mr J. W. Headlam's work, *The History of Twelve Days*.

are true Christians in every country of Europe cannot be doubted; men who can be patriotic without being unjust; men who can value their own form of Christianity without despising other forms. What can these true Christians do, to heal the wounds of the nations, and to make future wars impossible?

Let them remind all men, not obtrusively but firmly, that our first aim should be the welfare of all; that in the intercourse between men, forgiveness is one of the things most needed; forgiveness implying that hope takes precedence in our minds over distressful memories. Let them remind all men, again, that in order to secure victory over nature, the united efforts of all are needed; for the blind agencies of nature will assuredly overpower human life and bring it to nought, if our union as men is corrupted and lost. The mechanical forces which mankind utilise for their own benefit are for the most part expended as they are used; coal, for instance, is almost sure to come to an end some day, though how soon we do not know. To say that it does not matter what happens when we are dead and gone, is to throw scorn on the generations of the future. We cannot help some losses in the future; but we can at any rate do our best to make the forces of life mutually co-operative, not mutually destructive. Life reproduces life; the living energies of our globe will not necessarily die out. But they will die out, if they are arrayed against each other for their mutual destruction; and then all the labours of past ages on earth will be brought to nought. We cannot look upon such an end with equanimity; and therefore we cannot but ask whether the influences which promote friendship and unity may not be made to prevail over the influences which promote discord and death; thus, and thus only, can we quench for ever selfish indolence, greedy ambition, revengeful hate. Let us pray to God with all our heart and soul that none of these evil passions may survive in us. If love can overpower hatred in the minds of men, then is there hope for the future of mankind. That is what all religious men should strive and pray for; men who are not religious may strive for it (and we must not scorn their aid), but the Divine help cannot, I feel sure, be dispensed with.

Many, many other difficulties are there which must be met by mankind in the future, many labours that must be undertaken, many traditional errors and faults that must be mitigated and abolished, many new perceptions that must be cultivated; and this must be done with moderation, not in undue haste, but with a careful survey of what is possible, and steady application and energy.

Of the physical problems before us, the reclaiming of deserts is probably the most important; of human problems, I have not mentioned in this chapter, though I have in previous chapters, the relation between the sexes. No one who candidly considers the state of the world can doubt that women need more protection than they have at the present day. If love could be made a permanent element in family life, that would be the most efficient protection for them; but selfishness will not very soon be annihilated on earth; and the ways in which women suffer need very serious and deep attention.

The different colours of different races of men is a fact not strange in itself, but it engenders contempt and dislike in a notable degree. It should be our endeavour to overcome these feelings; but this cannot be done all at once; and it is not desirable that, at present, marriages should be frequent between men and women differing in hue. But everything should be done to promote a general unity of sentiment between different races; that is to say, a willingness to admire virtue and courage by whomsoever displayed, whether the doer of good deeds be white or black yellow or copper-coloured, and every effort also should be made to raise the inferior races in the scale of intelligence and civilisation. In this way true and perfect unity of mankind may at last be achieved, with all the outward signs of such unity; and if we must not be too hasty in our efforts to realise this unity, we must never lose sight of it as our ideal aim.

The government of the inferior animals, and their utilisation for human needs as well as the care of them for their own happiness, is a subject that does attract much attention at this moment, and deserves even more attention than it obtains. It cannot be denied that their happiness has generally been postponed, in those who have to deal with them, to their utilisation for human needs; and I am afraid that this will continue to be the case for a considerable time; but it should be the effort of all right-feeling persons to raise in our estimation the value of the happiness of the whole animal world. It is a difficult question whether there is any animal so deleterious as to deserve absolute extinction; I am not able to deny that there are such, but a more clear-seeing person might convict me of error. What however is really to be lamented is that some of the noblest animals are in danger of extinction, owing to the sporting propensities of man, as for instance elephants; care should be taken to prevent this, and to preserve them. But it may be impossible to preserve lions and tigers, bears and wolves; all that can be said is that it is not right to prejudge the question too absolutely against them. As to insects, it is difficult not to desire the extinction of mosquitoes; though it is said (with what truth I know not) that they are necessary for the production of beautiful flowers in Siberia. Whether they have any value of this kind elsewhere, I have not heard.

To what end do these great and difficult problems, which I have just been enumerating, point? What is the final goal of humanity? We cannot imagine it; but if it be true, as in my first chapter I have argued that it is true, that the earth is capable of an eternal development, then the organising power of man, aided by God, may transform the whole human race, and indeed all terrestrial life, in a manner and to an extent far surpassing any development known to have taken place in past ages. Further, I would connect this future development with a change which has taken place in the past, which is usually thought of as simply material, but in which there may be a spiritual significance as well. I have spoken of it as probable that the heat, light, and energy of the sun result from organising power, which we cannot but connect with life. If so, then there was organising power at work in the earth in those remote days when the earth was a part of the solar orb; and we must suppose that the whole earth, and not merely its surface, was then the recipient of this organising power, and was being modelled by it throughout the whole of its texture. But now, at the present day, we have no reason to suppose that there is any organising power in the interior of the earth, though we know that the living creatures on the surface of the earth are organised, and that man in particular is not only an organised being, but wields no small organising power on his own account. Is it not clear, if this account be true, that the separation of the earth from the sun was not merely a material separation, but that it involved a separation of a spiritual kind? By that separation life must have been almost entirely extinguished, though not quite entirely; for we know that life still exists on the earth's surface. In every age the earth's surface has been in contact with the solar rays, has been receiving influences from the sun; and it is therefore probable that the seeds of life have never been wholly absent from the earth, though the manner in which they may have been preserved is wholly outside our

present experience. We are in presence of a mystery; but it is
not an irrational mystery; it simply means that we are ignorânt
of certain primæval forms of life, and of the environment in which
those primæval forms were situated. We must suppose that
environment to have been aerial, but full of moisture; as to its
temperature, we have little means of judging; but we may
remember that, just as at the present day the earth's centre is
probably at a temperature which would at once destroy all terrestrial life known to us, so in those remote ages the molten or
gaseous state of the earth may have been quite compatible
with a moderate temperature on the exterior of its gaseous
envelope.

If the hypothesis I have just ventured to frame be true (and
I think it is, all things considered, the most reasonable hypothesis
respecting the origin of terrestrial life), then there has been, in
the inhabitants of the earth, a spiritual Fall, or in other words
a disorganisation not wholly destructive of life, but rendering
life difficult and imperilling it. The history of life on the earth,
as far as we know it, exactly coincides with this description.
Life, even at the present day, is difficult, is subject to perils;
but it was more difficult, more subject to perils, in the ages that
are past. There never was an age in which it might not have
been said, in the words of Hamlet, "The time is out of
joint."

Reflecting on this, we shall see that the doctrine of the Fall
of man, though not literally true according to any of the forms
in which it has hitherto been conceived, has yet a truth in it;
spiritual life, as we know it, has been subject to an ancient
degeneracy—a degeneracy more ancient than anyone has yet
conceived. But though that degeneracy in certain of its aspects
is still with us, yet the human race, in the person of Jesus of
Nazareth, has touched the bottom of it, and has arrived at contact with that Divine power which can sustain us and deliver us,
not from physical death, but through physical death. The
warmth of spiritual love connects us with those who have passed
away; and this spiritual love accumulates as the years roll on;
gallant deeds are performed anew in one generation after another,
and propagate a fire in the hearts of men. There is variety in
the acts done, in the words spoken, but the passion and the
stimulus which prompts them is always of the same quality, and
that quality is divine. That there will be errors and sins in the
future we must still expect; but there is more and more power

in our regenerate race to overcome the corrupting influence which impaired human nature in the ages that are past.   Thus, with more definite meaning and with a more definite hope than the apostle Paul himself could have entertained, we may repeat his words:

We all, with unveiled face reflecting as a mirror the glory of the Lord, are transformed into the same image from glory to glory.

POSTSCRIPT

I HAVE written in this book of great teachers and of great kings, of the rise and fall of empires, of the conflict of religions. I have drawn my inferences, and have explained my religious belief.

But are the historical narratives which I have pursued in their course from the beginning of the earth's existence down to the present hour the sole premisses of the conclusion that I have drawn? Have my affirmations never been taken from some other quarter, scarcely named as yet? It cannot but be that my personal experience has been a part, and an important part, of the ground of the reasonings which I have propounded. So it must be with every one; every one must have his own life, his own actions and sufferings, before his mind, when he asks himself the question, "What shall I believe as to the true nature of that world in which I have my being?"

But my own premisses of this kind cannot be the premisses of my reader. Had that been possible, my own experience would have been rightly placed in the forefront of this book; for my own experience is certainly the premiss that I know the best. But it cannot be the premiss which my reader knows best; he will, if he reasons at all on the subject of religion, have his own experience before him, in that place where I put my experience. I cannot take his experience as equivalent to my own; nor can he take mine as equivalent to his.

I respect my neighbour's experience, if I know it; I respect, for instance, the experience of John Bunyan, who in that picturesque and imaginative work, *The Pilgrim's Progress*, has narrated what he calls a dream, but what really is a parable or simile, expressive of the things which he himself had known, felt, or believed as to religion in the course of his earthly life. Perhaps, therefore, I may without blame give my own experience. Only I cannot tell the whole of it, for there are many things which I have done and suffered which in their details would naturally raise discussion as to who had done right and who wrong; and such discussion would not be profitable. The broad outlines of my experience are much more certain in their effect than the details of it.

I must begin by distinguishing between a religious atmosphere, religious inquiry, a religious act, and religious experience. There never was a day in my life when I did not live in a religious atmosphere; I began to inquire into religious beliefs somewhere about my sixteenth birthday (rather before that date, I believe); the earliest religious act done by me, that is to say the earliest act with a religious motive of my own inspiring it, was when I was twenty-six years of age; and it was years after that before I had any religious experience of my own.

I was brought up in the religious atmosphere of the High Church party of the Church of England; and that that atmosphere had its imperfections may be inferred from the fact that till I was fifteen years of age, or thereabouts, I had scarcely a will of my own at all; in the ordinary affairs of life I was very helpless; I was like a leaf blown about by the wind. But I must do the High Church party the justice to say, that if on the one hand they threw me into inactivity, on the other hand they roused me from it. I must ever be grateful to Samuel Wilberforce, who when bishop of Oxford confirmed me according to the rites of the Church of England, for the vivid and forcible address in which he urged those who heard him to lead an active and good life; this it was which first stimulated me to exert myself in independent action; it was perhaps not unnatural, considering the number of the religious books which I had read, that this independent action first showed itself in religious inquiry. However, apart from this, I had the greatest love of natural scenery, and used to desire ardently to walk over mountains and in remote glens; I did so a little, though not so much as in later years. It was some years after I left school (I was a colleger at Eton) that my godfather, Samuel Rickards, a well-known High Church clergyman of the Church of England in that day, asked me suddenly whether I had ever thought what would make me a strong man? Now, I had never thought of that; I had sought for knowledge, I had sought for intellectual power; but how to be a strong man, in the full sense of that word, I had not inquired. This again was something added, and beneficially added, to the religious atmosphere in which I lived.

My religious inquiries, which began (as I have said) when I was not far from my sixteenth birthday, were very various.

I read, while I was at Eton, the first three or four chapters of Butler's *Analogy*, and nearly the whole of Paley's *Horæ Paulinæ*; also, I remember, an article in Kitto's *Biblical Cyclopædia* on David, by my uncle Francis William Newman (the article was sufficiently unorthodox to be expelled from the next edition of the Cyclopædia); also the early *Tracts for the Times*, not knowing that they were by my uncle John Henry Newman; I was filled with enthusiasm by them, but on reading some old *Edinburgh Reviews* which I found in the school library at Eton, I perceived that there was something to be said against the Tracts. When I was seventeen years old, I was filled with new and painful thoughts by a case of suicide; the person who committed the unfortunate act had been justly esteemed, and was dear to myself; yet the religion which I had been taught was stern enough to make me draw the inference that, if nothing could be said on the other side, he must have gone to hell. Never do I remember weeping such floods of tears as when I was told the truth about his end (I had been previously told of his death, and had felt simple but not overwhelming sorrow, regarding it as an accident); and immediately I began reading religious works in order to find out whether there was any hope for the lost. I was not fortunate enough to fall in with the works of Frederick Denison Maurice; but gradually, and more and more, I felt that the divine mercy must penetrate everywhere.

I am not writing an autobiography, and must leave many things unmentioned. At Cambridge I met with the scepticism which then was beginning to appear in the English Universities; I was slow in forming judgments about it; but from my twenty-first year onwards the question of the Biblical miracles was continually before my mind. I was glad to find that Samuel Taylor Coleridge (a touching and tender religious writer, even as he was a touching and tender poet) did not think the miracles the real basis of Christian belief; he comforted me much. It was perhaps when I was twenty-four years of age (but possibly older) that I said to Henry Bradshaw, the well-known librarian of Cambridge University, "There are many miracles with which I could dispense without any demur; but if the miracles of the Exodus are untrue, I do not know where I am." He answered me, "That is exactly my position." When, some years after that, I came definitely to the conclusion that the miracles of the Exodus, and most others in the Old and New Testaments, were untrue, I certainly did not know where I was; but yet the definite conclusion freed me from entanglements which had impeded action; and the first religious experience which I had was not long after that.

However, to return. To obtain clearer insight into spiritual things, I read philosophy, and not altogether without advantage; but Hegel's *Phänomenologie des Geistes* proved too much for me; and at last, in the summer of 1866, I spent a month at Bangor on the Menai Straits, trying to solve the mystery of the universe. I did not solve it. I have often thought of those lines of Heine, inimitable in their mixture of pathos and mockery, in which he describes a young man such as I was—

> By the sea, by the wild sea, dark in the night,
> Stands a youth,
> His breast full of sadness, his head full of doubt,
> And with mournful lips he questions the waves;
> "O solve for me the riddle of life,
> The tormenting primæval riddle,
> Over which so many heads have puzzled,
> Heads in hieroglyphic caps,
> Heads clad in turban and black biretta,
> Bewigged heads,
> And a thousand other poor, perspiring human heads;
> Tell me, what is the meaning of Man?
> Whence has he come? whither does he go?
> Who lives there aloft on the golden stars?"
> The waves murmur their eternal murmuring,
> The wind blows, the clouds are borne along,
> The stars glitter, indifferent and cold,
> And a fool waits for the answer.

I confess my method had been wrong; for action must be added to thought, if the depths are to be fathomed.

It was not long after that, that I did what I call the first religious act which I ever did in my life. But I perceive that in saying this I am speaking in a dialect of my own; for most people call saying prayers and going to church religious acts. Going to church may be a right act, but if done from custom or from a sense of duty, or from a mere feeling of the beauty of the service, I do not call it a religious act. It is only a religious act if done with the feeling that we need God's help (or perhaps with the feeling that God has helped us); for this help rendered by God is the essential relation between God and man. After the acceptance by my future wife of my offer of marriage, I went to chapel at my college in Cambridge. I had done the same thing hundreds of times before, but now first I did it with a motive properly my own. For I felt, "I am a man full of infirmities; I have not been very successful in my practical life hitherto; I am entering on a life wholly unknown to me, and I know well that it is possible to make shipwreck of married life; surely I need protection." It was divine protection that I sought; I doubt if I expressed this in words; but I did seek it, and this was a true religious act. We were married rather more than two years afterwards; but it was not till some years after our marriage that I felt how great were the problems involved in it.

Of these problems, the only one which I can mention was the religious difference between us. My wife had never been in the sceptical atmosphere at all; she had embraced religion, as so many have done, and as I myself had done originally, in the High Church form; but the many years of thought and reading through which I had emerged out of those opinions had had no parallel in her life. On the other hand, she had more practical ability in the ordinary affairs of life than I had; and it was with amusement and pleasure that I heard a countryman whom we met once in our walks express bluntly his opinion of her superiority to me.

However I could not, in those matters of ordinary life in which we differed, readily admit that I was wrong, any more than in the religious question. But both in the religious question, and in the questions of ordinary life which divided us, there was needed a mediator between us; yet who shall mediate between husband and wife? It was the power which I hold to be divine which regulated, harmonised, and strengthened our relations to one another; and this result is the sole decisive proof within my own experience of the reality of religion. No doubt the mutual love between myself and my wife was an indispensable condition, without which this harmony could not have been attained; but the difficulties which tended to separate us were very great, and I do not believe that of ourselves we could have surmounted them.

Well do I remember my first experience of the strength which comes through prayer, when these difficulties first began to assume a dangerous form. I had done all in my power; but had I remained quiescent, all manner of doubts and temptations were ready to assail me; it was only by prayer that these were averted. At the same time a change took place in myself, transforming me in certain ways; and the thought came across me that perhaps in death one would experience a similar transformation; that this is the first essential characteristic of immortal life. Did Jesus Christ, I thought, experience a spiritual transformation in his death, and was he able after his death to make his disciples acquainted with it? If so, the resurrection may have a new meaning.

My wife, I know, prayed too, and there was hope in us both. It must not be thought that the ordinary course of our life was otherwise than tranquil; and our love for each other increased, though the strain to which it was subjected became at times almost unendurable. I must pass over many things, but one thing I must not pass over. I had a sense of frustrated effort, of not making way towards the ends which I desired; and this at last made me ill, and I suffered acute pain. Then it occurred to me that it might be the will of God that I should pray to Jesus Christ. I did so pray, and the pain gradually left me; the result was certainly not accidental, though I must not urge it as in itself proof of the heavenly supervision by Jesus Christ over his followers on earth. However, I think I should fix upon that as the moment when our difficulties first began to show signs of yielding.

On the thirtieth anniversary of our wedding day, my wife remarked to me, in reference to some poems I had written, that I had never written a poem to her. She was mistaken, as I speedily convinced her; however I thought her remark equivalent to a request that I should write a poem to her, and I wrote the following stanzas:

What was it linked us, Edith, of old?
    Was it the spoken
Word of the lips, and a ring of gold?
    Or with the token
Flashed there something of mystical might,
Kindling our wedding's clouded light
    In rain and snow
    Thirty years ago?

We gave the promise, Till death us part,
    Edith mine;
Is not that enough for the heart,
    Mine or thine?
No, you cry, for love is eternal,
Reaching up to the realm supernal,
    And binds us twain
    After death again.

May it be ours to win that lot,
    My love, my wife!
But vow and ring will avail us not
    In that new life;

Only the mystical might can blend
Our lives in the life that hath no end,
    And through us pour
    Love for evermore.

Dearest, if we would frame and fashion
    In our two hearts
One strain that shall divinely impassion
    Their varying parts,
We must watch and listen well
For the key and the beat and the sounding swell
    That shall create
    Songs of happy fate;

Listen, listen, in hope and prayer!
    God inspires
The searching spirit, and things most fair
    Aid our desires;
The flush on the hills we have trod together,
Alpine snows and the purple heather,
    Our inner eye
    Sweetly doth descry.

Surely earth conspires with heaven,
    Read we but right;
Surely all things at last are given
    For our delight!
Labour and listen, listen and pray,
My love, till out of the dim to-day
    Riseth to-morrow
    Ending all our sorrow.

A few years after I had written this, our elder daughter fell ill; she died after four or five years' illness. I did not mention that our eldest boy had died through an accident when we had been married rather over eleven years. In both these deaths lay an influence which forced us to put the present life in the background; it appeared less worthy to cause estrangements; and in both cases, this feeling had considerable force in making our unity predominant over our differences. I never forgot those words which the early Fathers attribute to Jesus Christ, how the kingdom of God should appear—

When the two shall be one,
And that which is without be as that which is within,
And the male with the female be neither male nor female.

I interpreted this text (which I have explained in the body of this work) as meaning the perfection of the married state; and the mutual affection of the family seemed no longer restricted to the present life alone, but to stretch beyond it. The death of my wife took place four years and nearly nine months after the death of our daughter. Some months previously (perhaps through some prescience on my wife's part) we went together over the points on which we had differed, and gave them full consideration. In religious doctrine I had not moved my wife from that central belief which the Nicene creed expresses; in some other parts of religion she had changed, partly (I do not doubt) through my influence, but these were not equal in importance to the creed. I must not boast of what might have been my power of convincing her under other circumstances, but the fact of there being other points, not relating to religion, on which it was very desirable that we should reach agreement but on which we had not reached it, was a hindrance to our attaining full concurrence on the religious question. Of all our points of difference there was nothing on which I was so anxious to attain agreement as in respect of something known to us both, but to no one else, to which I attributed a vital significance and value, which she did not accord to it. It will be understood that this was not a matter relating to religion; and we did arrive at a perfect understanding of each other's position in respect of it, and an allowance of each other's position, though not to absolute agreement.

Here perhaps I had better stop. The degree of intimate concordance which my wife and I had reached, after many difficulties, is certainly attributed by me, and would I am sure have been attributed by her, to the religious belief and practice which, though we differed in some important parts of it, was still strong in us both.

For some reasons, indeed, I should have wished to add in this place a more detailed account of that dream to which I referred on page 22 of this volume; for it was a dream into which my wife entered, and it had real results. It happened about two years after her death. But it may be better for me to avoid a kind of premiss which, at present at all events, cannot be held to be certainly valid. As it is, I am asking my reader to take something on trust, but that is unavoidable. The proof of what I believe, that my wife is still present with me, can only be obtained by the experience that real force lies in this belief in the way of organising the things known to me; and to win this experience is necessarily a matter of time.

INDEX

rom him, 126, 127; his religious character, 128; his death, 129; mourned by his disciples, 129; his literary works ran great danger of being destroyed, two or three centuries after his death, but were in the end rescued, 130, 131; an anecdote showing his humility, 132. (*See also* II. 57, 204)

Constantia (sister of the emperor Constantine), II. 226

Constantine, succeeded his father as emperor in the west, 306 A.D., II. 201; favourable, like his father, to the Christians, and in the year 313 joined with the eastern emperor, Licinius, in issuing the edict of Milan, proclaiming universal toleration, 201; became in 324 A.D. sole emperor, 202; he sat among Christian bishops as their pupil, 206; summoned the council of Nicæa, 210; after that council banished Arius, 216, and issued a persecuting edict, 216, 217; a general characterisation of his action, 223; in spite of all his errors, a great man, 224; but his vacillation on the religious question was not good for the end which he proposed to himself, i.e. the peace of the empire, 226; was moved by the appeal of his sister to see Arius (just about the time when he was founding Constantinople), 227, 228; received with approval the revised creed of Arius, 229, and was angry with Athanasius for rejecting Arius still, 230; yet was reluctant to quarrel with Athanasius, and though banishing him to Treves on the Moselle, regarded him as still archbishop of Alexandria, and no successor was appointed there, 233. The meaning and force of his act in founding Constantinople noted, 227, 228; the most famous of all the emperors who reigned in that city, 252; his *Donation* to the pope a spurious document, 309

Constantinople, founded with the intention that it should be the Christian capital of the Roman empire, II. 227, 228; religiously consecrated, 230; the scene of the death of Arius, 233; for more than eleven centuries held out as the centre of the empire against all enemies, 238; the splendour of Constantinople in the middle ages, 261, 262; there was a certain purpose of helping it in the crusades, but in the end it was fatally injured by the crusades, 318, 321, 323; captured by the Turks under Mohammed II, 325; the result of this was a great diffusion of Greek manuscripts, and Greek interpreters of those manuscripts, in Christian countries, 395. (*See also* 282, 333, 429)

Constantius (father of Constantine), II. 201

Constantius (son of Constantine), II. 223, 234, 235

Consuls, I. 194, 201

Contrat Social, II. 433

Copernicus, I. 189, II. 358

Cordova, II. 327

Corinth, II. 180, 181

Corinthians, I. 157, II. 182

Corneille (poet), II. 417

Cornelius, II. 160

Corrodi (Biblical critic), II. 444

Councils of the Church. More important are: Nicæa, 325 A.D., II. 9, 23, 210-219, 221-226, 230, 234; Constantinople, 381 A.D., 211, 212; Ephesus, 431 A.D., II. 239; Chalcedon, 451 A.D., not named, but Eutyches referred to, II. 240; Third Lateran, 1179 A.D., II. 366; Fourth Lateran, 1215 A.D., II. 366; Vienne, 1311 A.D., II. 354; Constance, 1414-1418 A.D., II. 374-377; Trent, 1545-1563 A.D., II. 392, 393, 414. Of lesser importance are: Tyre, 335 A.D. II. 224, 231-233; Constantinople, 867 A.D., II. 311; Orleans, 1017 A.D., II. 302; Constance, 1094 A.D., II. 318; Piacenza, 1095 A.D., II. 318; Lombers, 1176 A.D., II. 364, 365; Avignon, 1209 A.D., II. 363; Lavaur, 1213 A.D., II. 365; Montpellier, 1215 A.D., II. 363; Toulouse, 1119 A.D., II. 364, 1229 A.D., II. 365

Cowell, professor, I. 60

Cowper (poet), II. 446

Cranmer, II. 413

Crete, I. 142, 143

Crito, friend of Socrates, giving his name to a dialogue of Plato, I. 163, 177, 179, 182

Critobulus, friend of Socrates, I. 165

Cromwell, II. 413, 415

Crowe and Cavalcaselle, II. 359

Crusades, an exception to the peaceable ways of the Church, II. 293; their first conception, 318; their history, and the lesson to be drawn from them, 320-324; Raymund Lull gradually convinced of their error, 352, 354; a crusade against heretics, 364; against a temporal king, 374

Cumæ, I. 195

Cumont, M., I. 91

Cuneiform inscriptions, I. 31, 78, 103, 278

Cunibert, bishop of Turin, II. 315

Cunningham (*Archaeological Reports*), I, 64

Cyprian, Christian Father and martyr, II. 199, 200

Cyprus, II. 161, 353

Cyrene, II. 161

Cyrus, the conqueror of the Medes, not a Zoroastrian, I. 86, 100; the imaginative life of him written by Xenophon (*Cyropædia*), 181, 182; hailed by the prophet of the exile as the deliverer of Israel, 316, 318, 319; he gave permission to the Jews to return from

by Isaiah, 291. Israel an ideal conception, not limited in any precise manner, in Ezekiel, 311; in the prophet of the exile, 319, 320, 323, 331; in the Psalms, 340; in the general Jewish conception, 404; but in Zechariah "Israel" is equivalent to the ten tribes, 358; in the New Testament sometimes used as equivalent to the Jews (and in this sense the exaltation of Israel is ardently desired by the Jews), but generally with something ideal in the acceptation of the term, II. 19, 58, 60, 90, 114, 143, 145, 151, 162, 163, 168, 169, 285, 381. (For the tribe of Judah, see Judah)

Italy, under the ancient Romans, I. 210, 212; in mediæval times, II. 238, 252, 256, 299, 317, 343–346; in modern times, 435

Ivan III, Tsar of Russia, II. 326

Jacob, ignorant of writing, I. 224; the picturesqueness of the stories relating to him, 229; a great and venerable person, 230; the first of the patriarchs to repress idolatry among his followers, 230; his migration, with his sons and his clan, down into Egypt, 229; his taking the name of Israel, 231; his death, 232; his name a synonym for the people of Israel, 320, 323

Jacobus card. Sadoletus II. 391

Jaddua, Jewish high priest, I. 382, 383, 385; referred to though not named, 363

Jainism, I. 57

Jairus, II. 30

James, apostle, son of Alphæus, II. 79, 136

James, apostle, son of Zebedee, his call to be a disciple, II. 73; his call to be an apostle, 79; his presence at the transfiguration, 99; his presence at the discourse of Jesus on the Mount of Olives, 115; his presence in the garden of Gethsemane, 123; his probable sentiment towards the Jewish ceremonial law, 151; his martyrdom, 154; rebuked by Jesus Christ when he wished to call down fire from heaven on the inhospitable Samaritans, 398. The incident Mark x. 35–45 is not mentioned in this treatise

James, "the Lord's brother," not one of the twelve, II. 136; accompanied Jesus on his last journey to Jerusalem, 102; a son of Mary, 134–138; a distinguished Christian leader, 153; author of the epistle contained in the New Testament, 27, 156; peculiarly hopeful of the conversion of his own nation, but possibly somewhat narrow in his conduct towards the Gentiles, 156; even the Jews considered his martyrdom a sin in those who slew him, 157; when he died, the cause of Jewish Christi-

anity was greatly weakened, 164; his permanent residence had been in Jerusalem, 163; in the Clementine Homilies affirmed to be bishop of bishops, and ruler of the churches everywhere, 308

Jansenists, II. 422, 431

Janus (Roman deity), I. 193

Japan, I. 111, 135, II. 425

Javan (Greece) I. 355

Jeanne d'Arc, the inspired deliverer of France, II. 342, 372

Jedidiah, a name conferred on Solomon, I. 284

Jebusites, I. 258

Jehoiachin (king of Judah), I. 309, 311

Jehoiakim (king of Judah), I. 309

Jehoshaphat (king of Judah), I. 221, 270

Jehovah, reason for adopting this spelling (though an incorrect one) of the divine name found in Hebrew, I. 245. (See also 225, 247, and frequently afterwards in vol. I.)

Jehu (king of Israel), I. 268, 269, 274–278, II. 292

Jephthah, I. 228, 249

Jeremiah, probably believed in the miracles of the Exodus, but his trust in God is independent of them, I. 296; praises king Josiah, 303; but nowhere speaks of Josiah's religious reform, 307; this silence accounted for, 307, 308; predicts the captivity, 306, and also the return from the captivity, 310; not the author of the "Lamentations," 313; his regard for others outside Israel, 315; his friends, 315; his prophecy of a "righteous Branch" ruling in Judah, known to Zechariah, 352, II. 95

Jericho, II. 107, 108

Jeroboam, son of Nebat, rebel against the line of David, and first king of the ten tribes, I. 267; probably did not intend idolatry in setting up the gold calves at Dan and Bethel, 268, 269; yet lightminded and arbitrary in his religious measures, 269, 270

Jeroboam II (king), I. 267

Jerome quotes the gospel of the Hebrews, II. 3; translator of the Bible into Latin, 243

Jerome of Prague, II. 373, 377

Jerusalem, I. 157, 221; said by Manetho to have been founded by the Shepherd kings after they left Egypt, 237; a stronghold of the Jebusites, captured by David and Joab, 258; the temple built there, 259, 265 (see also 268, 274, 282); saved from the army of Sennacherib, 289, 290; idolatrous in reign of Manasseh, 293; purified by Josiah, 298, 299; idolatrous again after Josiah's death, 305; besieged by Nebuchadnezzar, 309; the extraordinary variety of hopes, fears, and prophecies, attending

the physical resurrection of Jesus, 11, 12; the resurrection is shown, both by the inconsistency of the gospel narratives relating to it, by the account of the conversion of Paul in the Acts, and by various expressions in the epistles of Paul and Peter, to have been an event occurring in the spiritual supersensuous sphere, not in the visible world, 14–18; some further elucidation of this topic, continued through the rest of chapter XVI; the question as to the cause of the disappearance of the body of Jesus from the tomb touched on, 134; the unfavourable and misleading effect which the belief in miracles has had on our estimate of Simon Peter, 154; the reason why the Jewish authorities rejected Jesus lay in their belief in miracles, 153, 157; the belief in miracles hindered critical inquiry in the early Church, because it tended to make the whole subject of religion appear outside human knowledge, 207; doubt in miracles began in England, but extended with far greater vehemence to France, 425; and, with more careful criticism, to Germany, 445

Miriam, I. 244

Mithra, Mithraism, I. 90–93, II. 200, 206

Mitra (Hindu deity), I. 38

Moabites, I. 227, 244, 247, 255, 258, 259, 264, 309, 339, 341, 359, 361

Mohammed, general remarks on his religion and on his personality, II. 263, 264; born in the year 570 A.D. at Mecca, and in his twenty-fifth year married a wealthy lady of the Koreish clan, Khadîja, whose agent he had been, 265; in his fortieth year, at a time when he was greatly dissatisfied with the idolatrous religion of his countrymen, a conflict arose in his soul, and he heard a voice bidding him "cry in the name of the Lord!" 266; he feared that he was possessed, but his wife encouraged him, 266, 267; he began to preach in Mecca, and made some converts, but was met with much derision, 269; his uncle, Abû Tâlib, though not a convert of his, yet supported him, 270; he and his followers were subjected to great privations, 270, till at last he escaped with them to Medina, 271, an event called the Hejra (see Hejra); both his wife and his uncle had died before this took place, 270; a certain fault in his preaching is noted, 272, yet his extraordinary ability and success in governing is noted as well, 273; he destroys the idols in and around Mecca, and wins the submission of many Arabian tribes, 274; some of his acts cannot be approved of, yet his character must be accounted lofty and heroic, 275–277; after the death of Khadîja, he adopted the polygamy which was customary in his nation, 277; the most signal difference between the teaching of Mohammed and the teaching of Jesus Christ is noted, 277, 278; his religion warlike, yet warlike rather through circumstances than on principle, 277, 278; the military successes of his followers after his death, 278; he acknowledges the humility of Christians, 279

Mohammedans, see Islam

Mohammed II (sultan), conqueror of Constantinople, II. 325

Molière, II. 417

Mommsen, I. 207–209

Monastic orders, see Monks

Mongols, II. 283–287, 324, 325, 331, 334

Monier Williams, Sir M., I. 38, 42, 47, 55

Monks, in the Buddhist religion, I. 64, 65, 70–72; in the Christian religion, II. 219, 236, 240; the first monastic community (as distinguished from hermits) originated with Basil bishop of Cæsareia, 243; Persian monks, 251; the Benedictine order of monks was the first instance of Christian beneficence on a large scale, 252–260; the quiet of monasteries tended in some ways to foster the intellect, 293, 294; the celibacy of monks did increase their missionary power in the rough times after the fifth century, 310; yet in the later centuries it would have been better if the severity of the Benedictine rule had been mitigated, 360, 361; valiant monks of the Eastern church, 325, 326, 333

Montalembert, II. 252–255, 435

Montesquieu, II. 427

Montucla, II. 294

Morley, Lord, II. 430

Moscow, II. 326

Moses, indebted, in some respects, to Egypt, I. 34; not the author of the book of Deuteronomy, 221–223; did not originally circumcise his own children, 233; his part in the deliverance of the Israelites insignificant if we believe the miraculous history, worthy and noble if we discard the miracles, 234, 235; a warrior, 235; a religious patriot, 236; great in organisation, a military leader, lawgiver, and ethical instructor, 239; his leadership of the Israelites during the Exodus and desert wanderings, 239–242; the author of the main substance of the ten commandments, 243; he made the ideals of Abraham a great practical force in the world, 243; his death, 244. (See also 263,

Cambridge:
PRINTED BY J. B. PEACE, M.A.
AT THE UNIVERSITY PRESS

SELECTION FROM THE GENERAL CATALOGUE
OF BOOKS PUBLISHED BY
THE CAMBRIDGE UNIVERSITY PRESS

The Religion of Israel. A Historical Sketch. By R. L. OTTLEY, Canon of Christ Church and Hon. Fellow of Pembroke College, Oxford. Crown 8vo. 4s.

A Short History of the Hebrews to the Roman Period. By Canon R. L. OTTLEY. With 7 maps. Crown 8vo. 5s.

The Historic Church. An Essay on the Conception of the Christian Church and its Ministry in the Sub-Apostolic Age. By J. C. V. DURELL, B.D. Crown 8vo. 5s net.

The Reformation. Cambridge Modern History, Vol. II. Edited by Sir A. W. WARD, Litt.D., G. W. PROTHERO, Litt.D., and STANLEY LEATHES, M.A. Royal 8vo. 16s net.

Forerunners and Rivals of Christianity. Being Studies in Religious History from 330 B.C. to 330 A.D. By F. LEGGE, F.S.A. In 2 volumes. Demy 8vo. 25s net.

Paganism and Christianity in Egypt. By PHILIP DAVID SCOTT-MONCRIEFF, M.A. With a frontispiece. Crown 8vo. 6s net.

The Realm of Ends, Or Pluralism and Theism. The Gifford Lectures delivered in the University of St Andrews in the years 1907—10. By JAMES WARD, Sc.D., Professor of Mental Philosophy, Cambridge. Second edition, with Some Replies to Criticisms. Demy 8vo. 12s 6d net.

Roman Stoicism. Being lectures on the history of the Stoic Philosophy with special reference to its development within the Roman Empire. By E. V. ARNOLD, Litt.D., Professor of Latin in the University College of North Wales. Demy 8vo. 10s 6d net.

Zeus. A Study in Ancient Religion. By A. B. COOK, M.A., Fellow and Lecturer of Queens' College, and Reader in Classical Archaeology, Cambridge. Vol. I, Zeus God of the Bright Sky. With coloured frontispiece, 42 plates (3 of which are coloured), and 569 text-figures. Royal 8vo. 45s net.

Themis. A Study of the Social Origins of Greek Religion. By JANE ELLEN HARRISON. With an Excursus on the Ritual Forms preserved in Greek Tragedy, by Professor GILBERT MURRAY; and a chapter on the origin of the Olympic Games, by Mr F. M. CORNFORD. With 152 illustrations. Demy 8vo. 15s net.

Euripides the Rationalist. A Study in the History of Art and Religion. By A. W. VERRALL, Litt.D. Reprinted 1913. Demy 8vo. 7s 6d net.

Outlines of Jainism. By JAGMANDERLAL JAINI, M.A., Barrister-at-Law, President of the All India Jaina Association. Edited, with preliminary note, by F. W. THOMAS. Crown 8vo. 4s net.

Comparative Religion. By F. B. JEVONS, Litt.D. Royal 16mo. Cloth, 1s 3d net; Leather, 2s 6d net. Cambridge Manuals Series.

The Idea of God in Early Religions. By F. B. JEVONS, Litt.D. Royal 16mo. Cloth, 1s 3d net; Leather, 2s 6d net. Cambridge Manuals Series.

The Coming of Evolution. By JOHN W. JUDD, C.B., LL.D., F.R.S. With 4 plates. Royal 16mo. Cloth, 1s 3d net; Leather, 2s 6d net. Cambridge Manuals Series.

A Companion to Biblical Studies. Being a Revised and Rewritten Edition of *The Cambridge Companion to the Bible.* Edited by W. EMERY BARNES, D.D., Fellow of Peterhouse, Hulsean Professor of Divinity. With 8 illustrations and 10 maps. Royal 8vo. 15s net.

The Gospels as Historical Documents. By VINCENT HENRY STANTON, D.D., Fellow of Trinity College, Ely Professor of Divinity. Part I. The early use of the Gospels. 7s 6d net. Part II. The Synoptic Gospels. 10s net. Demy 8vo. To be completed in four parts.

Modern Study of the Old Testament and Inspiration. By the Rt Rev. T. H. SPROTT, M.A. Crown 8vo. 3s net.

The Parables of the Gospels in the Light of Modern Criticism. Hulsean Prize Essay, 1912. By L. E. BROWNE, M.A., Lecturer at St Augustine's College, Canterbury. Crown 8vo. 2s 6d net.

The History of the English Bible. By JOHN BROWN, D.D. With 10 plates. Royal 16mo. Cloth, 1s 3d net; Leather, 2s 6d net. Cambridge Manuals Series.

The Bible of To-day. By the Rev. ALBAN BLAKISTON, M.A. Large crown 8vo. 3s net.

Forgiveness and Suffering. A Study of Christian Belief. By DOUGLAS WHITE, M.D., Trinity College, Cambridge. Crown 8vo. 3s net.

The Interregnum. Twelve Essays on Religious Doubt. By R. A. P. HILL, B.A., M.D. Crown 8vo. 4s 6d net.

Evolution and the Need of Atonement. By STEWART A. McDOWALL, M.A., B.D., Trinity College, Cambridge. Second edition, revised and enlarged. Crown 8vo. 4s 6d net.

Evolution and Spiritual Life. By STEWART A. McDOWALL, M.A., B.D., Trinity College, Cambridge. Crown 8vo. 6s net.

The Origin and Propagation of Sin. Being the Hulsean Lectures delivered before the University of Cambridge in 1901–2. By F. R. TENNANT, D.D., B.Sc. Second edition. Crown 8vo. 3s 6d net.

The Sources of the Doctrines of the Fall and Original Sin. By F. R. TENNANT, D.D., B.Sc. Demy 8vo. 9s net.

The Concept of Sin. By F. R. TENNANT, D.D., B.Sc. Crown 8vo. 4s 6d net.

The Moral Life and Moral Worth. By W. R. SORLEY, Litt.D. Royal 16mo. Cloth, 1s 3d net; Leather, 2s 6d net. Cambridge Manuals Series.

Cambridge University Press
Fetter Lane, London: C. F. Clay, Manager